LABOUR LAW IN AN ERA OF GLOBALIZATION

Transformative practices and possibilities

Edited by
JOANNE CONAGHAN
RICHARD MICHAEL FISCHL
KARL KLARE

OXFORD
UNIVERSITY PRESS

*This book has been printed digitally and produced in a standard specification
in order to ensure its continuing availability*

OXFORD
UNIVERSITY PRESS

Great Clarendon Street, Oxford OX2 6DP

Oxford University Press is a department of the University of Oxford.
It furthers the University's objective of excellence in research, scholarship,
and education by publishing worldwide in

Oxford New York

Auckland Cape Town Dar es Salaam Hong Kong Karachi
Kuala Lumpur Madrid Melbourne Mexico City Nairobi
New Delhi Shanghai Taipei Toronto
With offices in
Argentina Austria Brazil Chile Czech Republic France Greece
Guatemala Hungary Italy Japan South Korea Poland Portugal
Singapore Switzerland Thailand Turkey Ukraine Vietnam

Oxford is a registered trade mark of Oxford University Press
in the UK and in certain other countries

Published in the United States
by Inc., New York

ISBN 0-19-927181-X

Antony Rowe Ltd., Eastbourne

For
Paddy, Pam, and Hallie,
and
to the memory of
Massimo D'Antona and Gary Bellow—
friends, comrades, mentors,
lawyers for social justice

Contents

Part IV. Same as the Old Boss? The Firm, the Employment Contract, and the 'New' Economy

Part V. Border/States: Immigration, Citizenship, and Community

Part VI. Labour Solidarity in an Era of Globalization: Opportunities and Challenges

Notes on Contributors

Harry Arthurs is University Professor at Osgoode Hall Law School, York University, Toronto. He is President Emeritus of York University and Dean Emeritus of Osgoode Hall. He has published extensively on labour law theory and doctrine, and his recent research addresses the effects of the new economy on democratic institutions, especially labour markets.

James Atleson is Professor of Law at the State University of New York at Buffalo. He has also taught at the Georgetown University Law Center and at the law schools of the Universities of Minnesota, Pennsylvania, and Texas. He has written and lectured widely on labour law, and his books include *Values and Assumptions in American Labor Law* (Amherst, Mass., University of Massachusetts Press, 1982) and *Labor and the Wartime State: Labor Relations and Law During World War II* (Champaign, Ill., University of Illinois Press, 1998).

Paul Benjamin practises labour law in Cape Town, South Africa. He has worked closely with the South African trade union movement for the last two decades. He is the co-author of a leading textbook on South African labour law and has been involved in drafting South Africa's post-apartheid labour dispensation.

Linda Bosniak is Professor of Law at Rutgers University Law School, Camden, New Jersey. Her research and writing have concentrated on problems of immigration, citizenship, and nationalism in law and political theory.

Bruno Caruso is Professor of Labour Law and Comparative Labour Law at the Faculty of Law, the University of Catania, Sicily. He has written extensively on labour and employment law and related fields (such as immigration policy) in the Italian and European Union contexts.

Hugh Collins studied law at Oxford and Harvard Universities. He is currently Professor of English Law at the London School of Economics, and was formerly a Fellow of Brasenose College Oxford. His publications include *Justice in Dismissal: The Law of Termination of Employment* (Oxford, Oxford University Press, 1992).

Joanne Conaghan is Professor of Law at the University of Kent at Canterbury and Managing Editor of *Feminist Legal Studies*. Her areas of research include labour law, tort, and feminist legal theory, and she has published widely in all three fields. Together with Richard Michael Fischl and Karl Klare, she is Co-Secretary of the International Network on Transformative Employment and Labour Law (INTELL).

Massimo D'Antona was, at the time of his assassination on 20 May 1999, Professor of Labour Law at the University of Rome 'La Sapienza' and advisor to the Ministry of Labour. He had previously taught at the Universities of Catania and Naples and served as under-secretary in the Ministry of Transport. He was one of Italy's most important scholars of labour and European community law.

Dennis M. Davis has been a judge of the High Court of South Africa, sitting in Cape Town, since 1998. His appointment to the bench followed a distinguished academic and research career: at the University of the Witwatersrand where he was Director of the Centre for Applied Legal Studies; at the University of Cape Town, where he continues to teach in an adjunct capacity; and as a guest professor at major universities outside South Africa. A prolific author, lecturer, and public commentator, Davis's work ranges across legal and constitutional theory, human rights, labour, insurance, tax law, and other fields.

Carlos de Buen Unna is a labour lawyer in Mexico City. He recently left private practice to work for the Secretarìa de Desarrolo Social (Ministry of Social Development). He also devotes time to writing and lecturing on labour topics, and he teaches labour law at Universidad Panamericana.

Simon Deakin is Robert Monks Professor of Corporate Governance at the University of Cambridge, where he is also Assistant Director of the ESRC Centre for Business Research and a Fellow of Peterhouse. He specializes in labour law, corporate governance, and the economics of law, and he is co-author (with Gillian Morris) of *Labour Law* (3rd edn., London, Butterworths, 2001).

Richard Michael Fischl is Professor of Law and Master of Pearson Residential College at the University of Miami, Coral Gables, Florida. A former appellate lawyer with the National Labor Relations Board, he teaches various courses on labour and employment law. His articles have appeared in *Columbia Law Review* and *Law & Social Inquiry*, and most recently he is co-author (with Jeremy Paul) of a book on legal reasoning and law examinations. Together with Joanne Conaghan and Karl Klare, he is Co-Secretary of INTELL.

Alan Hyde is Professor of Law and Sidney Reitman Scholar at Rutgers University Law School, Newark, New Jersey. He has written numerous scholarly articles on American labour law, and his most recent work has focused on the high-velocity labour market in Silicon Valley. He is also the author of *Bodies of Law* (Princeton, NJ, Princeton University Press, 1997).

Paddy Ireland is Senior Lecturer in Law and Head of the Law School at the University of Kent at Canterbury. His teaching and research interests focus on company law, and he has published widely in this field. He is also co-editor of the *Critical Lawyers' Handbook* (London, Pluto Press, 1992) (with Ian Grigg-Spall) and the *Critical Lawyers' Handbook 2* (London, Pluto Press, 1997) (with Per Laleng).

Makoto Ishida is Professor of Law at Waseda University, Tokyo, Japan. He has written extensively on labour and employment law from a socio-legal perspective, and his publications include 'Japanese Companies and Employment Contracts—Preliminary Study for International Comparison' in the *Nagoya University Journal of Law and Politics*.

Claire Kilpatrick is Senior Lecturer in Law at Queen Mary and Westfield College, University of London. Her research interests are exploring the processes and outcomes of Europeanization of labour law, policy, and industrial relations. She carried out research on integration through courts in Europe in the field of gender equality at work as part of a four-year cross-national research project directed by Professor Silvana Sciarra at the European University Institute in Florence, now published in S. Sciarra (ed.) *Labour Law in the Courts: National Courts and the ECJ* (2001). She was a Jean Monnet Fellow at the European University Institute, Florence in 2000 and is co-editor of *The Future of Remedies in Europe* (2000).

Karl Klare is George J. and Kathleen Waters Matthews Distinguished University Professor at Northeastern University, Boston, Massachusetts. He has been a visiting professor at the Universities of British Columbia, Michigan, and Toronto, and at the European University Institute. A former labour union lawyer, he has published extensively on labour and employment topics. He was a founding member of the critical legal studies movement in the USA, and also the original and principal organizer of INTELL. Together with Joanne Conaghan and Richard Michael Fischl, he is currently INTELL Co-Secretary.

Margriet Kraamwinkel works as a lawyer and policy analyst for the largest construction trade union in the Netherlands. She obtained a doctorate at Utrecht University with a book on pensions and equality. She has continued to write on those topics as well as on feminist legal theory and labour law.

Brian A. Langille is Professor of Law and Dean of the Graduate Programme at the Faculty of Law, University of Toronto, where he teaches labour law and legal theory. His writing and research now concentrates upon labour policy in the context of the global economy, and he has advised the Canadian Government on ILO matters.

Patrick Macklem is Professor of Law at the Faculty of Law, University of Toronto. He is the author of *Indigenous Difference and the Constitution of Canada* (Toronto, University of Toronto Press, 2001), and he teaches and has written extensively on labour law, constitutional law, and international human rights law.

Molly S. McUsic is a senior fellow at the Wyss Foundation. She was previously Professor of Law at the University of North Carolina, Chapel Hill, and Counselor to the Secretary of the Interior in the Clinton Administration.

Guy Mundlak is Senior Lecturer at the Faculty of Law and the Department of Labor Studies, Tel Aviv University. He teaches and studies the role of law in the design of social policy and its effects on labour market institutions.

Maria L. Ontiveros is Professor of Law at the University of San Francisco. She is past Chair of the Labor and Employment Law Section of the American Association of Law Schools and currently a member of the National Advisory Committee for the North American Agreement on Labor Cooperation (the NAFTA Labor Side Agreement). Her research and publications focus on issues at the intersection of race, class, and gender, with a particular emphasis on organizing immigrant workers and workplace issues affecting women of colour.

Frances Raday is the Elias Lieberman Professor of Labour Law at the Hebrew University of Jerusalem. She is author of *Adjudicating Interest Disputes: The Compulsory Arbitration Model* (Jerusalem, Harry Sacher Institute for Legislative Research and Comparative Law, 1983) and co-author and chief editor of *Women in Law and Society in Israel* (Jerusalem and Tel Aviv, Shoken, 1995). Her articles on comparative labour law have appeared in *International Review of Law and Economics, Comparative Labour Law and Policy Journal, Industrial Law Journal,* and the Hebrew University's

Israel Law Review, where she currently serves as chief editor. She was founding chair of the Israel Women's Network Legal Centre, and she continues to engage in appellate work on labour and discrimination issues. She has recently been appointed an independent expert to the United Nations (UN) on the Convention for the Elimination of All Forms of Discrimination against Women (CEDAW).

Kerry Rittich is Assistant Professor in the Faculty of Law and the Women's Studies Programme at the University of Toronto. She researches and teaches in the areas of international law and institutions, labour law, human rights, feminist theory, and critical legal theories. She has written on the distributional effects of economic restructuring for women, and her current work examines the legal reform projects promoted through international institutions.

Michael Selmi is Professor of Law at George Washington University Law School, Washington, DC. He teaches employment law and civil rights. Prior to entering academia, he was a civil rights attorney with a concentration on employment discrimination.

Lucy A. Williams is Professor of Law at Northeastern University, Boston, Massachusetts, where she was the School of Law's 1994–5 Public Interest Distinguished Professor. She has written and lectured widely in the area of welfare and poverty law. Before entering academic life, Williams practised poverty law at the Legal Assistance Foundation of Chicago and later at the Massachusetts Law Reform Institute.

Acknowledgements

The editors wish to express our immense gratitude to the many people without whose support this project could not have come to fruition. We are indebted not only to those who assisted with the book itself, but also to those who helped create and sustain the warm, engaging, and challenging intellectual community of INTELL (the International Network of Transformative Employment and Labour Law) that gave birth to the project and nurtured editors and contributors alike.

Our contributors' work forms the core of the book, and we are enormously grateful for their insight, imagination, perseverance, and commitment to a vision of law in the service of social justice. Alan Hyde and Lucy Williams served well beyond the call of duty, contributing translations and editorial work, and a special debt is owed to Paddy Ireland for his generous efforts and expert editorial assistance throughout the project. We are grateful as well to our editors at Oxford University Press and in particular to John Louth for his confidence in and support for the project; to Geraldine Mangley and Michael Watson for the conscientious efforts that turned our sprawling manuscript into a gorgeous book; and to all concerned for their good-humoured patience with our many shortcomings. In Kent, we could not have done without Erika Rackley's research assistance, Mark Dean's consummate IT skills, and the office support of Hilary Joce and Yasemin Akokan; in Miami, Erna Stoddart laboured diligently and cheerfully, keeping track of multiple drafts, editors, and contributors scattered across the globe, and Susan Mohorcic expertly assembled the index and table of abbreviations on very short notice; at Northeastern, Jan McNew and Abby Melia provided invaluable support.

INTELL meetings are the foundations of the intellectual community that made this book possible. We are deeply grateful to the many individuals who have worked so hard to organize these meetings, to the institutions that hosted us and/or provided other forms of vital support and subsidy, and of course to all of our INTELL colleagues for nurturing and sustaining that intellectual community. Invaluable advice, logistical help, and diligent performance of tedious organizational work were provided by: Enrique Alonso, Tom Archibald, Harry Arthurs, Dan Badulescu, Paul Benjamin, Helen Booher, Allyn Chudy, Carole Cooper, Ronald Daniels, Guy Davidov, Dennis Davis, Carlos de Buen Unna, Ockert Dupper, Darcy Du Toit, Jorge Esquirol, Catherine Fisk, Gail Hupper, Makoto Ishida, Jonathan Joffe, Evance Kalula, David Kennedy, Brian Langille, Gavin Leeb, Patrick Macklem, Bárbara Martínez, Kerry Rittich, Barbara Steyn, Jennifer Tam, Arizbeth Ugalde, Marley Weiss, and Lucy Williams. We proudly acknowledge the institutions whose generous assistance helped us to launch INTELL and sustain its trajectory: the Centre for Applied Legal Studies of the University of the Witwatersrand, the European Law Research Center and the Graduate Program at Harvard Law School, Northeastern University's George J. & Kathleen Waters Matthews Distinguished University Professor Program, the Institute for Juridical Research of the National Autonomous University of Mexico, the Real Colegio Complutense, both in Madrid and at its Harvard extension programme, and the law faculties of Northeastern University and of the Universities of Cape Town, Kent, Miami, Stellenbosch, Toronto, and the Western Cape. In addition, Cathi Albertyn, Fred Block, Duncan Kennedy, Clare McGlynn, Jeremy Paul, Silvana Sciarra, Bill Simon, Bo Stråth, and David Trubek contributed to our project by engaging with and challenging our ideas.

Last, but by no means least, we thank our partners and families for 'nigh limitless patience and moral support, and for their abundance of love.

List of Abbreviations

AFL–CIO	American Federation of Labour–Congress of Industrial Organizations
AIP	Apparel Industry Partnership (US)
ANC	African National Congress
ARD	Acquired Rights Directive (European Community)
BC	British Columbia, Canada
BCEA	Basic Conditions of Employment Act (South Africa)
BJIR	*British Journal of Industrial Relations*
CAC	Central Arbitration Committee (UK)
CCMA	Commission for Conciliation, Mediation and Arbitration (South Africa)
CGIL	Confederazione Generale Italiana del Lavoro
CGOCM	General Confederation of Workers and Peasants of Mexico
COFESA	Confederation of South African Employers
CROC	Revolutionary Confederation of Workers and Peasants (Mexico)
CROM	Mexican Regional Confederation of Workers
CTM	Confederation of Workers of Mexico
CVWP	Countervailing workers' power
DEE	Department of Education and Employment (UK)
DES	Department of Education and Skills (UK)
DTI	Department of Trade and Industry (UK)
EC	European Community
ECJ	European Court of Justice
EEA	Employment Equity Act (South Africa)
EEC	European Economic Community
EMU	European Monetary Union
EU	European Union
FAT	Workers Authentic Front (Mexico)
FDN	National Democratic Front (Mexico)
FIFA	Fédération Internationale de Football Association
GATT	General Agreement on Tariffs and Trade
GDP	Gross domestic product
GDR	German Democratic Republic
GFR	German Federal Republic
HRM	Human resources management
ICFTU	International Confederation of Free Trade Unions
ILA	International Longshoremen's Association
ILJ	*Industrial Law Journal* (United Kingdom)
ILJ (SA)	*Industrial Law Journal* (South Africa)

ILO	International Labour Organization
ILWU	International Longshore and Warehouse Union
IMF	International Monetary Fund
INTELL	International Network on Transformative Employment and Labour Law
ITF	International Transport Workers' Federation
JIT	Just-in-time (inventory-purchasing system)
LQR	*Law Quarterly Review*
LRA	Labour Relations Act (South Africa)
MFN	Most-favoured-nation status
MLR	*Modern Law Review*
MNC	Multinational corporation
MNE	Multinational enterprise
NAACP	National Association for the Advancement of Colored People
NAALC	North American Agreement on Labour Cooperation (NAFTA Labor Side Agreement)
NAFTA	North American Free Trade Agreement
NAO	National Administrative Office (NAFTA)
NGO	Non-governmental organization
NIP	Net internal product
NLRA	National Labor Relations Act (US)
NLRB	National Labor Relations Board (US)
NMWA	National Minimum Wage Act (UK)
OECD	Organization for Economic Cooperation and Development
PAN	National Action Party (Mexico)
PGFTU	Palestinian Federation of Trade Unions
PNR	National Revolutionary Party (Mexico)
PRD	Party of Democratic Revolution (Mexico)
PRI	Institutional Revolutionary Party (Mexico)
PRM	Party of the Mexican Revolution
PRONASOL	National Solidarity Programme (Mexico)
PRWORA	Personal Responsibility and Work Opportunity Reconciliation Act of 1996 (US)
SEIU	Service Employees International Union
TNC	Transnational corporation
TQM	Total quality management
TUC	Trades Union Congress (UK)
TULR(C)A	Trade Union and Labour Relations (Consolidation) Act (UK)
UDHR	Universal Declaration of Human Rights
UEFA	Union des Associations Européennes de Football
UI	Unemployment Insurance (US)

UK	United Kingdom
UN	United Nations
UNCTAD	United Nations Conference on Trade and Development
UNT	National Union of Workers (Mexico)
UPS	United Parcel Service (US)
US/USA	United States/United States of America
WFTC	Working Families' Tax Credit (UK)
WHO	World Health Organization
WTO	World Trade Organization

Introduction

It is now virtually *de rigueur* to locate academic and political debates within the discursive framework of the idea of globalization. But while many scholars genuflect at the altar of globalization, very few other than specialists have actually worked at specifying and interrogating the concept itself, and few debates have radically changed in content. In particular, the parameters of legal thought outside international law have remained remarkably resilient in the face of what are, arguably, fundamental challenges to our conventional understandings. This is nowhere more evident than in labour law, where global economic, cultural, and political developments render uncertain and unstable the strategies and institutional arrangements familiar to labour lawyers, and, along with them, the egalitarian values and political aspirations many of us hold dear. In the wake of the collapse of 'classical' labour law models—British collective *laissez-faire* and US industrial pluralism in particular—not to mention the difficulties faced by protectionist and/or paternalist labour regimes of Continental Europe and Japan—scholars within the discipline seem faced with an unhappy choice of either proceeding as though the traditional theoretical frameworks still had purchase or of working in a theoretical vacuum. As a result, contemporary academic engagement with labour law is too often technical and particularist in approach, self-consciously eschewing theoretical engagement.

There is, of course, a way out of the current theoretical impasse, and that is actively to seek out new understandings of labour law and the regulation of work amidst the debris of our discarded visions. Many labour and employment scholars world-wide are engaged in this project. This book represents the efforts of some of those scholars who, under the auspices of INTELL—the International Network on Transformative Employment and Labour Law—have come together for a number of years to engage in transnational dialogue that seeks to identify, analyse, and respond to the conceptual and policy challenges posed by globalization.

The origins of INTELL—and this international collection of essays—lie in a fine old Edwardian house, set in delightful grounds in Andover, Massachussets, where, in the fall of 1994, over seventy legal scholars specializing in labour law and related subject areas assembled, at the invitation of Karl Klare, to discuss the challenges facing the discipline. The Andover meeting generated a network of progressive labour law scholars who have continued to meet over the years at what have now become regular INTELL conferences, taking place in wide-ranging locations, from Toronto to Cape Town, from Miami to Canterbury, from Mexico City to Catania.

INTELL has involved leading labour and social law scholars from all over the world, many of whom are represented directly as authors in this volume. Participants have journeyed to our conferences from Australia, Austria, Belgium, Canada, Finland, France, Germany, Hungary, Israel, Italy, Japan, Mexico, the Netherlands, Peru, South Africa, Spain, the UK, and the USA, and it is from these conferences and the discussions to which they led that this collection is drawn—a set of essays which are at once individual and even idiosyncratic, while at the same time the product of fruitful dialogue and exchange among INTELL participants.

While an informal, loosely organized group with no dominant ideological viewpoint, INTELL is nevertheless self-consciously political: we recognize that law and legal discourse have an inescapably political dimension and seek openly to engage with that dimension. In this sense INTELL bears some of the hallmarks of the US critical legal studies movement, an intellectual tradition of which INTELL is, to some extent, an offspring. INTELL participants generally support legal, social, and political transformation to construct more just, equal, non-hierarchical, culturally and sexually pluralistic, and democratic societies, and they believe that law, legal practices, legal work, and legal scholarship can and should contribute to social justice and egalitarian social change. Within that broad orientation, INTELL is a non-sectarian and inclusive network, welcoming a variety of philosophical and scholarly outlooks, approaches, and methodologies.

The ensuing collection seeks to capture both the substantive aspirations of INTELL and its commitment to dialogue and conversation as one means among many by which such aspirations may be realized. In a sense, it is a record of a set of interconnected discussions which began at Andover and have continued, collectively in conference fora and individually by e-mail, telephone, and post, over the years since.

At first, many of us who came together through INTELL were much in the position of the blindfolded child groping part of an elephant—vaguely and uncertainly aware that the domestic legal, social, and economic institutions with which we were individually familiar constituted only a segment of the creature we were exploring, and struggling to get a better grip of its wider contours. Gradually, however, those contours have begun to come into focus as exposure to a multiplicity of national, cultural, and disciplinary perspectives offered new insights while also checking the academic habit of viewing legal developments solely through the lens of the familiar and the local. In addition, INTELL has sensitized us to the constricting force of boundaries we have all taken for granted—whether legal, disciplinary, theoretical, political, or geographical—and much of the work in this volume seeks to highlight and destablize the boundaries within which traditional labour law discourse is located.

A consequence of adopting and applying critical, interdisciplinary, and international perspectives to labour law is that the resulting work does not fit neatly into traditional or clearly defined categories. This has presented a great challenge to the editors in organizing this collection. Although individual works range from detailed studies of intensely local issues (such as Mundlak's vivid description of the plight of Palestinian workers in Israel and Ishida's account of death and suicide as a result of overwork in Japan) to critical overviews of broad international developments (such as Rittich's exploration of the gender issues emerging with the increase in contingent work relations and Arthurs's analysis of the increasing regulatory role of corporate codes of conduct), they all are informed by and participate in a common conversation. Thus, while we have decided to structure the book around the principal themes emerging in the course of that conversation, many of the essays also speak to other themes—and to essays in other parts of the collection—and the editors have attempted to flag those conversations and connections in individual pieces. At all events, here is a brief guide to the book that we have produced.

I LABOUR LAW IN TRANSITION

The collection begins with Karl Klare setting the scene in which the principal 'dramas' of the book are played out, immediately followed by Massimo D'Antona's effort to rethink fundamentals, what he calls 'the pillars of identity of labour law'. D'Antona was one of the most innovative voices in contemporary labour law. His untimely death in 1999 was a tragic loss to Massimo's family, friends, and colleagues, and to the working people to whose service he committed his intellectual and political gifts. For labour lawyers, his passing was an incalculable setback to efforts to re-envision our field. Massimo honoured the INTELL project by journeying from Italy to our first meeting at Andover. The editors take special pride in publishing here Alan Hyde's posthumous translation of one of Massimo's essays, by which we pay tribute to his commitment to social justice and his intellectual courage.

Both initial overviews recount the erosion or collapse of the old certainties in labour law and trace the emergence of new issues, themes, and dilemmas. Klare (Chapter 1) points to the accelerating gap between labour law's seminal ideas and institutional achievements, on the one hand, and unfolding political, legal, social, and economic developments on the other. Focusing on labour law's capacity, in these new circumstances, to accomplish projects of egalitarian redistribution, he calls for a reinvention of the discipline so that it can contribute effectively to social

transformation in the twenty-first century. D'Antona (Chapter 2) assesses
the extent to which traditional labour law assumptions and reference
points, embodied in what he identifies as the twentieth century 'constitutionalization' of labour law, still have purchase in very different social,
political, and economic conditions. His is an anatomical study of traditional labour law, raising pertinent questions about its adaptability
outside the environment in which it evolved. Both scholars present in
uncompromising terms the scale of the problem with which progressive
labour lawyers are currently faced.

II CONTESTED CATEGORIES: WORK, WORKER, AND EMPLOYMENT

A central difficulty within the discipline in recent years is the destabilization of its most fundamental concepts, in particular, its notions of
'work', 'worker', and 'employment'. The essays by Conaghan, Benjamin,
and Williams all observe that these key concepts have become 'contested
categories' as radical changes in the organization of labour and production, as well as in our understanding of work, cast doubt on regulatory
provisions premised on sharp distinctions between paid and unpaid
work, between 'employed' and 'self-employed' workers, between
employment and unemployment, and between 'work' and other life-
activities. Addressing the efforts of the Blair government in the UK to
develop and implement so-called 'family-friendly' policies, Conaghan
(Chapter 3) shows how such policies both undermine and, at the same
time, reinforce the work/family dichotomy upon which traditional
labour law is based. She questions the extent to which policies ascribing
economic value to paid work for the market while denying it to unpaid
family/caring work are likely to benefit women. Drawing on the experience of South Africa's ambitious efforts to reform labour law so as to
serve a people left impoverished and under-skilled by apartheid,
Benjamin (Chapter 4) explores the folly of deploying a binary and
centuries-old legal distinction to sort out the gradations of dependency
and subordination found in contemporary work relationships. Finally,
Williams (Chapter 5) considers how the received wisdom within and
disciplinary boundaries between labour law, welfare law, and immigration law, as well as most progressive critiques of those doctrines and
disciplines, unwittingly reflect and reinforce discourses which legitimate
the economic *status quo*, including the legal and institutional structures
that create and sustain poverty. All three essays reveal both the fragility
and the tendentiousness of precepts upon which labour law has traditionally rested.

III GLOBALIZATION AND ITS DISCONTENTS

These essays examine the pressures on domestic labour markets produced or intensified by an increasingly integrated global economy, and the potential role of labour law in resisting and even reversing some of the more pernicious consequences. Rittich (Chapter 6) explores the connection between the steep rise in the participation of women in paid work and the emergence of an economy in which temporary, self-employed, and other forms of 'contingent' work play an increasingly important role. She argues that these developments not only cast further doubt on the validity and coherence of the distinction between 'market' and 'non-market' work, but also belie the emerging conventional wisdom that workers can safely jettison traditional strategies of labour market regulation and collective action, and rely instead on individual human capital in bout after bout with the invisible hand.

In similar vein, Langille and Davis consider and ultimately reject the argument that regulatory strategies and collective action are doomed to failure because of constraints imposed on nation-state capacity by global economic imperatives. Langille (Chapter 7) defends what he sees as the considerable virtues of free trade—resulting from comparative advantage and specialized production—while at the same time arguing forcefully that markets ought to serve democracy rather than vice versa and that, accordingly, some things must not be for sale. Indeed, if the central insight of traditional progressive labour law was that 'labour is not a commodity' for exchange within a domestic economy, then, Langille contends, the point to be pressed now is that 'labour *law* is not a commodity' up for sale in the globally integrated economy. Labour law must not be seen as one more means by which to secure competitive advantage, but rather as a site for democratic dialogue and multilateral negotiation about the appropriate scope and structures of market ordering.

Davis (Chapter 8) echoes this argument in warning developing nations against 'racing to the bottom', as well as in responding to broader claims about the 'death of labour law' in an era of globalization. Davis makes the case that even an impoverished nation experiencing extraordinarily high unemployment, like the new South Africa, should resist the temptation to lower labour standards, citing evidence that other factors have a greater impact on export performance and foreign direct investment than protective labour legislation. Davis concludes that the nation-state can still play an important role, both in developing new forms of regulation suited to new economic circumstances (for example, a 'right to training') and in enabling new forms of resistance to and struggle against work-based forms of inequality and exploitation.

IV SAME AS THE OLD BOSS? THE FIRM, THE EMPLOYMENT CONTRACT,
AND THE 'NEW' ECONOMY

In this section, the focus shifts to the employment relationship and its place in the corporation, but what comes into view is very much in controversy. On the one hand, recent developments—associated with new forms of production and industrial organization and with a dramatic increase in global economic integration and competition—have undeniably had an impact on the firm, the employment relationship, and the nature of work itself. On the other, there are also signs that the 'new' boss is still very much like the 'old' boss, and that the era of flattened work hierarchies, co-operative employment relations, and fluid labour markets is not yet upon us. Against this backdrop, it is no surprise that the role of law in shaping and regulating employment is likewise in dispute. In particular: to what extent are the 'old' legal forms anachronistic? how far do 'new' work forms replicate the same old legal problems? and what would a 'new' labour law for a 'new' economy look like? The chapters in this part suggest starkly contrasting approaches to these challenges.

Deakin (Chapter 9) focuses on the historical development in the UK of the contract of employment, exploring its role in bridging the gap between the 'Master and Servant' era and that of the welfare state. Emphasizing the mutability and adaptability of the contract of employment in the face of radical changes in labour market structures and workplace organization, he is optimistic about contemporary efforts to re-mould contract to fit new and diverging forms of work relations. Ireland (Chapter 10) addresses company (corporate) law, challenging the disciplinary demarcations between corporate and workplace organization. Examining recent proposals to accord employees status as corporate 'stakeholders' and similar initiatives, he questions whether such strategies are truly 'transformative' or merely 'ameliorative'. Concluding that the very legitimacy of the corporate share as a form of property must be challenged, he calls for a reconceptualization of the corporation as a *social* institution.

Ishida (Chapter 11) discusses the death and suicide resulting from the stress of overwork, offering a stark picture of the 'dark side' of the once highly touted 'Japanese miracle'. He shows how laws designed to prevent overwork and compensate for industrial injuries were undermined in Japan by judicial decisions and cultural practices, but concludes that the pressures of the 'new' economy may soon bring similar problems to workplaces everywhere. On a more optimistic note, Hyde (Chapter 12) visits the world of professional work in Silicon Valley as a model for the 'high-velocity labour markets' of the future, and in which post-war assumptions of long-term job attachment and guarantees of 'career' employment have little purchase. Hyde asks whether these novel employment arrangements have any positive potential and explores strategies to protect employees who find themselves in such labour markets. Finally Fischl (Chapter 13) reflects upon the impact of the background employment-at-will rule in the USA on employment equity, labour law, and other regimes of protective labour legislation. He urges caution about jettisoning traditional legal strategies, arguing forcefully that there can be no workplace equity without workplace justice, and that there can be no workplace justice 'in the shadow of employment at will'.

V BORDER/STATES: IMMIGRATION, CITIZENSHIP, AND COMMUNITY

Post-war labour law was very much a creature of the nation-state, and the labour markets it sought to regulate were almost entirely domestically based. The ability of internationally mobile capital to 'exit' or threaten to exit in order to shop for cheaper labour, as well as rising regional labour migration, present serious challenges to traditional strategies for regulating domestic labour markets. To what extent can 'the region' assume the regulatory role formerly played by the nation-state? Whatever the unit of government, will the transnational regimes we can envisage protect only some labourers and leave others to fend for themselves in underground or shadow economies? What happens to the concept of 'citizenship' in a world where borders and states matter less and where markets are increasingly erasing and replacing other institutional forms of human association? The first three chapters in this section address these questions in the context of current efforts to develop and deploy regional regulatory strategies. Mundlak (Chapter 14) considers the problem of cross-border capital flight from countries with relatively more developed economies and protective labour law to their relatively less developed and protected neighbours. Focusing on the Middle East but offering an analysis with implications for other contexts of intraregional inequality, he concludes that there may be brighter prospects for successful labour regulation in local efforts (co-operation between neighbouring towns, cross-border interest group coalitions) than in supra-national approaches. Caruso (Chapter 15) examines a different dimension of regionalism, focusing on a highly developed regional community (the EU) and explores Member State treatment of non-EU immigrants. He rejects both the *status quo* and an overly rigid application of non-discrimination principles that might eliminate rather than equalize employment prospects for immigrants, locating a middle ground in trade union representation and advocacy to achieve a nuanced and flexible application of the 'right to work'.

Kraamwinkel (Chapter 16) addresses a different challenge facing the EU: how citizenship is and should be defined in a 'community' which is primarily a market and in which non-market ties (political, cultural, social, national) are relatively less articulated. Kraamwinkel argues that, notwithstanding broad phrases in the Treaty, access to 'EU citizenship' is in practice conditioned upon performance of *paid* work (housewives need not apply). She nevertheless contends that progressive possibilities remain in a 'notion of a citizen imagined not only as a man but also as a woman'. Bosniak (Chapter 17) concludes this part of the book with a critical exploration of the concept of citizenship. She, too, finds progressive possibilities in the inclusionary dimension of citizenship and its implicit rejection of structured inequalities. On the other hand, she criticizes the exclusionary and nation-centred assumptions of much contemporary citizenship discourse. Although sceptical that we can develop a 'post-national' conception of citizenship, she concludes that the effort may well be worth the candle given the term's 'tremendous rhetorical power and sometimes progressive history'.

VI LABOUR SOLIDARITY IN AN ERA OF GLOBALIZATION: OPPORTUNITIES AND CHALLENGES

In progressive legal discourse, the idea of labour solidarity has lost a good deal of critical purchase, as the contemporary focus on group identity and cultural difference have replaced an earlier preoccupation with class conflict. Economic globalization exacerbates the fragmentation of labour in many ways, but at the same time it generates commonalities in the experience and aspiration of workers world-wide and gives the concept of transnational labour solidarity a new urgency. The essays in this section explore the possibilities and challenges posed by collective labour strategies in this wider economic and political context.

The authors show considerable divergence in approach and focus. Raday (Chapter 18) concentrates on the extent to which the decline in trade union power can be considered a 'natural' consequence of current economic developments. She concludes that the political and legal policies of individual nation-states have had a considerably greater impact on union power than is generally recognized, thus suggesting that collective labour strategies can be significantly enhanced or inhibited by particular legal regimes. Atleson (Chapter 19) recounts the troubled voyage of the *Neptune Jade*, a cargo ship caught in the midst of a dock-workers' dispute that began in Britain but attracted expressions of solidarity from dockworkers all over the world. Atleson deploys the image of the endlessly voyaging *Neptune Jade* as a metaphor for the relentless search for solidarity in the midst of changing and highly unpredictable economic and political seas.

De Buen Unna (Chapter 20) traces the history of corporatist unionism in Mexico since the Revolution. He reflects particularly on union fortunes since the opening of the Mexican economy in the 1980s, vividly illuminating the defects of a model of union action premised upon dependence on and incorporation into a one-party political structure. Finally, both Ontiveros (Chapter 21) and Selmi and McUsic (Chapter 22) directly address the problems posed for and the opportunities offered to union organizing by identity politics. Ontiveros makes the case for 'identity-based' organizing, shifting the focus away from the 'workplace' and 'workers' (as traditionally understood) and taking union organizing efforts into the home and the local community. Selmi and McUsic negotiate a path between the apparently conflicting pulls of difference and solidarity. Their concept of 'cosmopolitan unionism' locates unity in the recognition of difference and in mutual respect for and empathy with those who are different but with whom one shares a common bond as workers.

VII LAYING DOWN THE LAW: STRATEGIES AND FRONTIERS

To what extent does globalization challenge the authority and utility of legal activism as a strategy for social transformation? What political purchase does it have if the capacity of the nation-state to bring about political and economic change is—or is perceived to be—seriously eroded? And how adaptable is law in the face of radical and unpredictable changes in the political and economic environment in which it operates? In different ways, the final set of essays in this collection consider these issues. Collins (Chapter 23) charts the efforts of the New Labour government in the UK to carve out a 'third way' in labour law that avoids the polarized politics and sectionalism of the past. He analyses the limits of a high-profile example of labour law reform while demonstrating how the rejection of old principles can bring forth new opportunities. Arthurs (Chapter 24) assesses the value of corporate codes of conduct as a mechanism for ensuring fair labour standards. He extends the frontiers of labour regulation to embrace what are essentially private international mechanisms, although he is candid in his assessment of the difficulties thereby posed. Kilpatrick (Chapter 25) considers the potential role of transnational legal institutions in countering the diminished capacity of the nation-state to advance progressive legal reform. Focusing on the development of sex equality jurisprudence in European law, she considers the costs and benefits of legal strategies which entail transnational dialogue and 'transplantation' into alien legal and political cultures. Finally, Davis, Macklem, and Mundlak (Chapter 26) consider constitutionalism and rights discourse as emancipatory and egalitarian political strategies. Drawing from the diverse experiences of South Africa, Israel, and Canada, they examine the arguments for and against social rights, testing them concretely by tracking the development of a right to health-care in the three legal regimes. The authors plead for the continuing relevance of rights discourse and the promise of transformative constitutionalism despite (indeed perhaps because of) the apparent incapacitation of the nation-state in an era of global economic and political integration.

JOANNE CONAGHAN
MICHAEL FISCHL
KARL KLARE
July 2001

Part I
Labour Law in Transition

1

The Horizons of Transformative Labour and Employment Law

KARL KLARE

I BRINGING REDISTRIBUTION OUT OF THE CLOSET

Legal discourses have no inherent political tilt; a legal discourse is a medium or location of ideological encounter and conflict.[1] However, the dominant discourse in most legal fields is conservative and apologetic. Labour law[2] is a rare exception, a legal discipline whose mainstream tradition is progressive. To be sure, labour law provides fertile ground for centrist and conservative projects designed to legitimate inequality, justify entrepreneurial prerogative, shore up the public–private distinction, and induce employees to consent to their own domination.[3] The watchwords today are 'growth', 'flexibility', and 'efficiency'; 'redistribution' and 'empowerment' are considered anachronisms. Some scholars argue that labour law no longer serves a legitimate mission and should be dissolved back into contract.

But the field is also a promising site for transformative projects—practices and discourses that challenge hierarchy and domination and seek to transform, or at least to nudge, existing institutions and power relationships in a more democratic, participatory, and egalitarian direction. Labour law evolved in response to (although it also channelled and contained) worker resistance to injuries and injustices visited upon them by industrial capitalism. Influential scholars and jurists believed that labour law has a vocation 'to address and seek to relieve a fundamental social and economic problem in modern society: the subordination of labour to capital, or of employee to employer'.[4] A premise is that law can

---

[1] See Kennedy, D., *A Critique of Adjudication: {fin de siècle}* (Cambridge, Mass.: Harvard University Press, 1997).

[2] In the USA, 'labour law' refers to the field of collective bargaining and union representation, whereas 'employment law' connotes other regulation of the employment relationship. For ease of presentation in this chapter, 'labour law' encompasses both facets of the discipline.

[3] See Klare, K., 'Critical Theory and Labor Relations Law' in Kairys, D. (ed.), *The Politics of Law: A Progressive Critique* (3rd edn., New York: Basic Books, 1998); 'Labor Law As Ideology' (1981) 4 *Ind. Rel. L. Journal* 450; and 'Judicial Deradicalization of the Wagner Act and the Origins of Modern Legal Consciousness, 1937–1941' (1978) 62 *Minnesota L. Review* 265.

[4] Collins, H., 'Labour Law as a Vocation' (1989) 105 *LQR* 468.

and should be deployed to redistribute wealth and power. Worker-solidarity and collective action are values respected by the discipline.[5] Labour law introduces democratic and participatory norms into the so-called 'private' realms of firm and market. It facilitates the representation and empowerment of subordinated groups. It challenges entrenched power and, on occasion, helps dislodge it. Its venerable progressive tradition and perceived *raison d'être* to ameliorate capitalist domination frequently give labour law a critical edge and egalitarian thrust that draw many of us to it.

This book's point of departure is that a commitment to egalitarian redistribution and the empowerment of subordinated groups should inform legal work, in practice and in scholarship. The contributors arrive at diverse observations, some inchoate, some inconsistent with others. The common thread is the conclusion that—to be true to its egalitarian and liberating potential under twenty-first century conditions—labour law must be reinvented. The work collected here and the larger project from which it draws illustrate efforts to modernize and recharge the discipline. Borrowing freely from the chapters to follow, this overview elaborates on the dimensions of the crisis in labour law and the challenges ahead.[6]

II THE DISCIPLINE AND ITS DISCONTENTS

Labour law examines the employment relationship, not in the abstract, but in light of certain images of and understandings about the organization and sociology of economic activity and the *dramatis personae* 'employer' and 'employee'. This conception of employment is the object of study, but labour law also plays a significant role in constructing the institutions and identities it describes.[7] However, the social and political world classically imagined by labour law is disappearing, gradually in some places and quite abruptly in others. Realities on the ground increasingly diverge from dated assumptions and discursive conventions.

The unfolding changes may be grouped in three broad, converging streams. Technological advances and managerial innovation have transfigured the *organization of production and employment* in ways that at least potentially conflict with presuppositions of the established labour law model. Even labour law's basic conceptual building block—the employment relationship—is losing its analytical purchase as more and more

---

[5] See Fischl, R. M., 'Self, Others, and Section 7: Mutualism and Protected Protest Activities under the National Labor Relations Act' (1989) 89 *Columbia L. Review* 789.

[6] It also draws upon ideas developed collectively by the authors and other INTELL participants. However, I am solely responsible for any errors or misinterpretation.

[7] See Klare, above, n. 3 and 'Law-Making As Praxis', *Telos*, #40 (Summer 1979) 123.

paid work is performed outside conventional employment. Union density and long-term employment in large organizations are declining in many developed nations, and insecure employment and informal sectors are growing. At the same time, labour movements have taken on entirely new challenges, particularly in the developing world where worker militancy has been a crucial force behind transitions from authoritarian to democratic regimes. Third-world industrialization follows paths and gives rise to practices and identities that could not have been imagined by labour law's formative thinkers.

Secondly, the *cultural context and meaning of work* are in flux. Social practices and identities long taken for granted are fragmenting or transmuting. New social movements that politicize gender, race, and other social identities have destabilized the binary capital-labour frame within which labour law developed. The world of work has been irrevocably altered by the massive entry of women into paid employment; by women's struggles to achieve economic equality, fashion new social roles, and renegotiate the relationship between paid and unpaid work; and, in many parts of the world, by the weakening of the male breadwinner model, the rise of dual career and single-parent households, and the loosening of the linear life-course (one marriage, one family, one career-at-work) in favour of a wider range of life paths (alternative family structures, break-up and reconstitution of marriages and families, career changes, new, mutable combinations of paid work and other major life-activities).[8]

Thirdly, a range of developments, often grouped under the rubric 'globalization', have resulted in an *intensification of international economic and political integration* ('deep integration'). The component trends include trade liberalization and a rising volume of international trade; currency market liberalization and an enormous increase in international currency transactions; liberalization of the rules governing foreign investment and cross-border capital flows; the emergence and dominance of multinational enterprises (MNEs); increased manufacturing in developing nations; heightened international wage competition; and steady increases in cross-border labour migration. These trends are facilitated by dramatic advances in communications, information, and transportation technology allowing greater co-ordination and dispersion of international economic activity; exponentially heightened transaction speed; and greater portability of advanced, highly productive technology to low-wage regions. This enumerates the major economic and trade-related trends, but deep

---

[8] See Block, F., *Postindustrial Possibilities: A Critique of Economic Discourse* (Berkeley, Cal.: University of California Press, 1990), and 'The New Left Grows Up', *Working Papers for a New Society* (Sept.–Oct. 1978) 41.

integration is not simply a product of the maturation of these economic forces. There is also an institutional or governance dimension. A key, politically driven feature of the contemporary form of integration is the expansion and reconfiguration of the system of international institutions, with the effect of curtailing the autonomy of nation-states. These new institutional arrangements are inspired by the triumph of neoliberal politics and beliefs, which favour limitations on the exercise of political power for egalitarian purposes (either at nation-state or international level) and call for deregulation, privatization, supply-side rather than demand-side macroeconomic measures, and a withering away of the welfare state.

Apart from neoliberal hegemony, these three streams of change hold great emancipatory potential. But they also pose grave dangers. Reorganizing economic activity and employment relationships can make work more fulfilling and democratic and, by increasing the efficiency and reducing the intensity of labour, can assist people to combine paid employment with other major activities and thereby to lead more rewarding lives. The danger is that, without significant change in the political arena leading, *inter alia*, to the implementation of new strategies for job creation, small high-performance sectors will be surrounded by oceans of insecure, low-wage work and unemployment. The promise of cultural transformation is to undermine racial, patriarchal, and sexual domination and loosen the clutch of gendered and racialized roles that so powerfully constrain human self-determination. 'Flexibilization' should be a progressive rallying cry, not a neoliberal shibboleth. The danger, however, is that loosened social constraints without appropriate changes in law and policy to support alternative life-paths may impoverish or victimize already subordinated groups. The liberating promise of international economic and legal integration is to encourage peaceful resolution of international disputes and, by increasing efficiencies and diffusing advanced production methods to the developing world, to raise living standards and reduce poverty. The all too apparent danger is that the world economic order will continue to be constructed on its current basis, which does little or nothing to alleviate poverty or rectify the grotesque maldistribution of global income and wealth, and which generates new dynamics of conflict that threaten world peace and security.[9] The protestors at economic summits and World Trade Organization (WTO) conclaves do not 'oppose globalization', as is ludicrously claimed by the mass media. No one disputes the promise of greater global interconnection. The protests concern what *type* of globalization we will construct, what its goals, motivating values, and institutional architecture should be.

---

[9] See Klare, M., *Resource Wars: The New Landscape of Global Conflict* (New York: Henry Holt & Co., 2001).

The question is whether labour law can and will lend force to the liberating potential, and help to neutralize the dangers, of postindustrial transition.[10] Formerly excluded and newly emerging groups and employment structures must be brought under its umbrella, so that old strategies can go to work for new constituencies (the 'inclusion problem'). But labour law's crisis runs much deeper than this. Even assuming a revitalization of unions and expansion of the protective ambit of labour law, serious questions arise whether its vintage strategies—fostering independent, countervailing workers' power (CVWP) and entrenching minimum labour standards and entitlements—can still deliver on their promise to enhance human well-being and equality.

An ancient argument against protective labour legislation is that it can succeed only at the expense of its intended beneficiaries or other deserving groups. As an *a priori* proposition, it has been refuted many times. It is not necessarily true even in the imaginary world of perfect, self-clearing labour markets. The costs associated with improved wages and working conditions can be offset by gains in productivity achieved due to improved working conditions and heightened employee loyalty and/or from reduced profit-rates rationally taken by employers who enjoy price-setting power in the product market. Admittedly, however, the effectiveness of labour-law strategies is undermined where capital has ways to escape regulated and/or unionized labour markets by shifting business or costs to low-wage, uncovered, and non-union labour markets at home or overseas (the 'displacement problem').

Conceding that in some contexts incomplete labour law coverage may generate horizontal inequities, these effects can be neutralized or greatly mitigated through political and institutional innovation.[11] In many developed nations in the post-war era, a dense web of equality-seeking political and labour-relations institutions counteracted the cartel and

---

[10] Following the work of Fred Block and Larry Hirschhorn, 'postindustrial' refers here to an array of economic, social, and technological developments, discontinuities, and possibilities, of indeterminate direction. The term embeds the methodological premise that social realities cannot be divorced from our constructions and representations of them; thus, 'postindustrial transition' comprehends not only the evolving trends but also our efforts to identify and understand them. 'Postindustrial' is not meant to bear the *marxisant* connotation of a distinct, objectively determined phase of economic history or the postmodernist connotation that we have arrived at a new stage or condition of consciousness. The globalization phenomenon, advances in communications technology, and the portability of industrial production methods make the concept of 'postindustrial transition' relevant to developing nations just now undergoing industrialization. See Block, above, n. 8; Block, F., and Hirschhorn, L., 'New Productive Forces and the Contradictions of Contemporary Capitalism: A Postindustrial Perspective' (1979) 7 *Theory and Society* 363; Hirschhorn., L., *Beyond Mechanization: Work and Technology in a Postindustrial Age* (Cambridge, Mass.: MIT Press, 1984).

[11] Polanyi, K., *The Great Transformation: The Political and Economic Origins of Our Time*, orig. pub. 1944 (Boston, Mass.: Beacon Press, 2001).

disemployment dangers of CVWP and protective legislation. The principal strategies employed were to keep labour markets tight through demand-side macroeconomic measures; to eliminate incentives and legal options for businesses to compete by depressing wages ('closing off the low road'); and to provide transfer payments to poor and outsider groups. Extension laws, which spread collectively bargained wage rates to an entire economic sector (including non-union enterprises), are a classic example of a labour market institution designed to suppress inter-firm wage competition. Other institutions and practices conducive to positive and egalitarian labour law outcomes include centralized collective bargaining, some labour-market adjustment policies, generous welfare spending or, in the USA, military spending, full employment policies (albeit full employment based on a male breadwinner model), and controls on currency trading and capital flight. An additional, critical piece—equality legislation and the diffusion of norms of equal treatment in employment—followed later as a result of human rights struggles. In some combination, these conditions generated strong pressure for economic equality and vast improvements in living standards in much of the post-war, developed world.

The problem is that the political and institutional supports for egalitarian labour law existed in weakened forms or not at all in many countries, and they are now unravelling in developed nations where they were once strong.[12] Mobile capital, liberalized currency markets, portable technology, and regulatory competition have superseded the Bretton Woods arrangements. Supply-side economics, fiscal discipline, and monetarism have replaced post-war Keynesianism. Both developed nations ('welfare reform', 'family-friendly policies') and developing nations ('structural adjustment', 'market liberalization') are offloading onto the household economy care-giving costs and income-interruption burdens formerly met by government.

Thus, contemporary political, economic, social, and legal developments, largely unforeseen by the traditional labour law model, have reinstated the displacement problem in a new and treacherous context. Neoliberals and conservatives vigorously argue that labour law's strategies to promote equality and empowerment are obsolete or perverse. Specifically they claim that, whatever may have been the case in the past, labour law *cannot* produce downward redistribution under present conditions. The costs of gains by workers within labour law's traditional frame of reference (successful collective bargaining, elevated legislative entitlements and protections) will not be absorbed by capital. In the

---

[12] Stråth, B. (ed.), *After Full Employment: European Discourses on Work & Flexibility* (Brussels: P.I.E.-Peter Lang, 2000).

evolving social and institutional context, workers' gains either will be dissipated by 'market forces',[13] or the costs they generate will be passed on to consumers (including workers themselves) and to 'outsider' social groups such as secondary sector workers, the unemployed poor, and the masses in the Third World. The criticism has four strands: first, that strong unions and generous social protections in the developed nations mostly benefit primary-sector employees at the expense of uncovered groups; secondly, that they inhibit job-creation at enormous cost to women, immigrants, and young adults ('eurosclerosis'); thirdly, that they exacerbate global inequality (especially when combined with protective trade and immigration measures); and finally, that even well-intentioned efforts to insert social clauses in trade agreements and to impose generous labour protections on the developing nations will, if successful, condemn Third World nations to perpetual poverty by preventing them from taking comparative advantage of cheap labour.

These charges are in many respects unproven or mistaken. There is remarkably little evidence for the cliché that strong unions and/or generous social welfare policies are responsible for recent, high rates of unemployment in Western Europe.[14] Rather more likely, conservative fiscal and monetary policies are to blame.[15] Indeed, income equality and generous social welfare provision seem to correlate with *lower* unemployment rates in Europe.[16] Similarly, countries that observe core labour standards

---

[13] Quotation marks are used to indicate that those who launch this line of criticism typically assume that 'free markets' have a fixed or natural structure. As will be argued, this premise is false.

[14] See, e.g., Baker, D., and Schmitt, J., 'The Macroeconomic Roots of High European Unemployment: The Impact of Foreign Growth', unpublished paper presented to conference on Creating Competitive Capacity: Reassessing the Role of the US and German Labour Market Institutions in the New Economy, Washington, DC, 1998 ('[a]lthough the microeconomic explanation for high European unemployment is widely accepted among economists and in policy circles, it actually rests on very little evidence'); Gregg, P., and Manning, A., 'Labour Market Regulation and Unemployment' in Snower, D., and de la Dehesa, G. (eds.), *Unemployment Policy: Government Options for the Labour Market* (Cambridge: Cambridge University Press, 1997) 395 (evidence for the ability of labour market deregulation to reduce unemployment 'is much less persuasive than is commonly believed'); Krueger, A., and Pischke, J.-S., 'Observations and Conjectures on the US Employment Miracle', Working Paper No. 6146 (National Bureau of Economic Research, 1997) 8 ('the evidence that labour market rigidities are the main source of Europe and Canada's employment problems is not as strong as is conveyed by the widespread consensus in support of this view, and the stridency with which some people argue it'). See also Campbell, D., 'Labour Standards, Flexibility, and Economic Performance' in Wilthagen, T. (ed.), *Advancing Theory in Labour Law and Industrial Relations in a Global Context* (Amsterdam: Royal Netherlands Academy of Arts & Sciences, 1998) 229 (evidence provides weak support for the general thesis that labour-market rigidity causes high unemployment).

[15] See Martin, A., 'Social Pacts, Unemployment, and EMU Macroeconomic Policy', Working Paper RSC 2000/32 (Florence: European University Institute, 2000).

[16] Galbraith, J., Conceição, P., and Ferreira, P., 'Inequality and Unemployment: The American Cure', *New Left Review*, #237 (Sept.–Oct. 1999) 28.

grudgingly do not enjoy better export performance or foreign direct investment experience.[17]

Nonetheless, labour law is in crisis today, and not only because it must devise ways to cast a wider and more inclusive net. The deeper predicament is that downwardly redistributive implementation of protective labour strategies under twenty-first century conditions, without undesirable side effects on outsider groups, probably will require the invention and political success of a new matrix of equality-seeking political and legal supports, replacing or refining those that fostered collective bargaining during its post-war golden age, that address both 'domestic' and global inequalities.

III WORK VERSUS EMPLOYMENT: THE JOB-BASED PARADIGM

Labour law is grounded in a *job-based* and *workplace-focused* conception of work, workers, and employers. It does not treat work in general, but only the subset performed within dependent employment relationships. For labour law purposes, 'work' means paid work typically occurring outside the home and done by someone holding a job. In a labour law perspective, people obtain the means to secure social and economic welfare primarily through job-related income.[18] To gain anything from labour law, a worker must either be or be the dependent of someone who is an incumbent of, retiree from, or applicant for a job. Labour law achieves its goals by assisting employees to improve their position in distributive conflict with employers. Trite as these observations may be, they point to fundamental limitations and biases of the discipline.

A memorable account of the start of a 1936 strike in a US automobile-tyre plant provides a window on the forms of industrial organization and worker resistance that shaped modern labour law:

The tirebuilders worked in smooth frenzy, sweat around their necks, under their arms. The belt clattered, the insufferable racket and din and monotonous clash and uproar went on in steady rhythm. . . .

. . . [T]he tirebuilder at the end of the line walked three steps to the master safety switch and, drawing a deep breath, he pulled up the heavy wooden handle. With

---

[17] *Trade, Employment and Labour Standards: A Study of Core Workers' Rights and International Trade* (Paris: OECD, 1996); *International Trade and Core Labour Standards* (Paris: OECD, 2000). Cf. Deakin, S., and Wilkinson, F., 'Rights vs Efficiency? The Economic Case for Transnational Labour Standards' (1994) 23 *ILJ* 289.

[18] It is understood, of course, that the distribution of income through breadwinner wages is supplemented by public provision (if not to all, at least to citizens). However, in practice, social welfare law reinforces the breadwinner-wage model. The most generous and least stigmatized social protection programmes are typically conditioned upon, and their payouts calibrated to, labour market status and earnings history. See Williams, in this volume.

this signal, in perfect synchronization, with the rhythm they had learned in a great mass-production industry, the tirebuilders stepped back from their machines. Instantly, the noise stopped. The whole room lay in perfect silence. The tirebuilders stood in long lines, touching each other, perfectly motionless, deafened by the silence. A moment ago there had been the weaving hands, the revolving wheels, the clanking belt, the moving hooks, the flashing tire tools. Now there was absolute stillness, no motion, no sound.

Out of the terrifying quiet came the wondering voice of a big tirebuilder near the windows: 'Jesus Christ, it's like the end of the world.'

He broke the spell, the magic moment of stillness. For now his awed words said the same thing to every man, 'We done it! We stopped the belt! By God, we done it!' And men began to cheer hysterically, to shout and howl in the fresh silence. Men wrapped long sinewy arms around their neighbors' shoulders, screaming, 'We done it! We done it!'[19]

The employer is a large organization engaged in mass manufacturing of uniform products with dedicated machinery. It is heavily invested in fixed capital. The employees' experience at work is a crucial fount of their consciousness, identity, and solidarity. Work organization is Taylorist. The worker is a command-follower, a pair of hands performing repetitive tasks paced by the assembly line. Workers' brainpower and learning capacity are scarcely tapped as productive assets, although surely they gave birth to considerable disruptive ingenuity, as employers of the period learned to their chagrin. Workers are men (elsewhere the book discloses that these particular workers were almost all white and migrants from a poor farming region), working full-time shifts on-site (when work was available). Women are offstage and, aside from the author, inaudible.

Public law plays an ambiguous role in the drama. The incident occurred after the enactment of the National Labor Relations Act (NLRA), but well before it was declared constitutional and effectively enforced. Private law plays a critical role, although it is so far in the background as to be virtually invisible. Stopping the belt was such a momentous step only because everyone took for granted that the employer owned the plant, machinery, and finished products, and that ownership entails the right to control access to the property and determine its uses. Similarly, everyone assumed that domestic care-giving costs are chargeable to the household, not to the employer's production budget, an accounting treatment derived from and

---

[19] McKenney, R., *Industrial Valley* (New York: Harcourt, Brace & Co., 1939) 261–2. McKenney's book apparently combines journalism, second-hand accounts, and imaginative reconstruction. It brilliantly captures general industrial and social themes, although as a history of particular events it must be read with caution. This anecdote and one to follow concerning home-care workers no doubt reflect peculiarities of their US setting but nonetheless illustrate general features of work-structure and labour law in the industrialized nations.

Karl Klare

reflected in a bundle of property, domestic relations, and taxation law rules.

The excerpt vividly captures the almost apocalyptic sense of empowerment generated by collective action, but also how precisely the workers' instincts and actions mirrored the discipline imposed by industrial organization. The skilfully executed strike was most effective in halting the system, as distinct from continuing production under an alternative institutional design. As everyone assumed, when the strike was over, the switch would be thrown, and the belt would start moving again. Labour law accepts the permanence of managerial domination.

Some economists imagine that a labour market resembles a daily bazaar bringing together sellers and purchasers (technically, lessors and lessees) of commodified labour power. This may be a passable description of what happens in a few labour markets, but most labour economists, students of industrial relations, and labour lawyers take a more institutional view that sees employment as an on-going relationship. In performing their joint activity, employer and employee not only make widgets but also construct or enact the employment relationship itself and its principals, the identities of 'employer' and 'employee'. These identities are not entirely exogenous to productive activity or labour markets. They are partially constituted by the legal rules and discourses.[20]

There are well-known exceptions, but labour law predominantly focuses on continuing employment. Typical employees are breadwinners who work full-time and indefinitely, often for long periods. They have 'careers at work'.[21] Paid employment is their principal life activity; at any rate, labour law is not much concerned with their other life activities. Typically, they are attached to a particular work site, often for long periods of time. They hold a job with an identifiable employer, which usually appears to them as a bureaucratic organization with well-defined structures and boundaries. Workers leave strategic decision-making and risk to the employer in return for a modicum of security, fair play, and (theoretically) a family wage. The image of the worker is demographically specific. Continuous, site-attached employees in twentieth century industrial economies were predominantly men. Better, more secure jobs are disproportionately filled by whites and non-immigrants.[22]

---

[20] On the role of law in constructing identities of class, see sources cited above, n. 3. See also Frug, M. J., 'A Postmodern Feminist Legal Manifesto (An Unfinished Draft)' (1992) 105 *Harvard L. Review* 1045 (legal construction of gender identities); Haney López, I., *White by Law: The Legal Construction of Race* (New York: New York University Press, 1996).

[21] See Sabel, C., *Work and Politics: The Division of Labor in Industry* (Cambridge: Cambridge University Press, 1982).

[22] See Cobble, D. S., 'Making Postindustrial Unions Possible', in Friedman, S., Hurd, R. W., Oswald, R. A., and Seeber, R. L. (eds.), *Restoring the Promise of American Labor Law* (Ithaca, NY: ILR Press, 1994) 285.

In traditional labour law thinking, employment is presumed to be a power-relation of domination and subordination. Labour law came into its own as a modern discipline by decisively rejecting the liberal assumption that the contract of employment is a product of the parties' autonomous choices. Of course, labour law similarly rejected the view (descending from Marx) that the contract of employment is always a product of coercion. The position is that the labour contract reflects elements of both freedom and coercion (otherwise, collective bargaining would lack principled justification).

Having said this, mainstream labour law makes the bedrock assumption that employers ordinarily possess superior bargaining power to employees.[23] And almost all labour lawyers accept that *during the course of employment*, employees are and should be command-followers who take direction from the employer. All the industrial nations have a complex body of law classifying workers as either 'dependent employees' or 'independent contractors' ('self-employed'), or some variation on this terminology. Invariably, whether the purchaser of labour power has a right of direction and control is a key (if often circular) distinguishing factor. From an institutional perspective, free contract merges easily into dominant and subordinate statuses.

The job-based conception of employment links to well-known theories about social conflict and reform developed by nineteenth- and twentieth-century political and social thinkers. While not necessarily explicitly embraced by labour law, these sentiments diffusely and indirectly influenced the development and spirit of the discipline. The central themes are that the employment relationship is an, if not *the*, essential substrate of social organization, and that capital/labour conflict is a defining feature of modern politics. Workers' identification as such and their conflicts in that capacity with employers give rise to unique aspirations, experiences of solidarity, and modes of consciousness. When respected by modern legislation, the worker identity can support ideals of social citizenship and experiences of political inclusion by hitherto exploited and marginalized groups.

Few influential figures in labour law believe that the domination of labour by capital can ever be totally eliminated, but it is common ground in the disciplinary mainstream that ameliorating and constraining capital/labour domination is a necessary condition of establishing a democratic and tolerably egalitarian society. Indeed, much social democratic writing suggests that free collective bargaining, combined with labour or

[23] Even Adam Smith believed this. See Kaufman, B., 'The Evolution of Thought on the Competitive Nature of Labor Markets' in Kerr, C., and Staudohar, P. (eds.), *Labor Economics and Industrial Relations: Markets and Institutions* (Cambridge, Mass.: Harvard University Press, 1994) 145.

socialist representation in parliamentary politics and generous social provision, is a *sufficient* condition.[24]

IV JOBS AND THE LOGIC OF LABOUR LAW

A logic to labour law's fundamental approaches and characteristic silences can be discerned in the light of the job-based conception of work. First, labour law remains within the hold of the purported distinction between 'public' and 'private law'. Missing from its vision are the background rules that structure the fields upon which distributive conflict plays out between capital and labour, between subgroups of workers, and between workers and other subordinated groups. These are largely 'private law' rules of property, contract, tort, crime, juridical capacity, business organization, and domestic relations, but also include the market-structuring ground rules of international trade and investment. Most writing in labour law either ignores these background rules or treats them as answering to an inflexible logic embedded in capitalism. Both approaches view labour law as a contingent, political artefact superimposed on an immutable private law background. The purpose of labour law 'intervention' is to ameliorate the harsh results that would occur in the absence of 'regulation'.

An accomplishment of critical legal theory has been to show that the content of private law and the distributive consequences flowing from its rules are neither 'natural' nor systemically pre-ordained. They are chosen by responsible human agents. The ensemble of private-law rules in place at a given historical juncture constitutes a form of political intervention ('regulation') that may have dramatic impacts on capital/labour, gender, racial, and international outcomes. As an historical matter, these rules buttress systems of domination and inequality.

In its seminal formulations, labour law largely leaves existing property and private law regimes undisturbed. For example, most labour law systems do not challenge the assumption that, because the employer 'owns' the company's assets, it may use this wealth to rebuff or defeat workers' aspirations for collective representation and economic betterment. In fact, whether and to what extent ownership includes this right

---

[24] Some founding fathers were very optimistic about the capacity of collective bargaining to promote political self-determination. For example, Senator Robert Wagner, a chief architect of US labour law, once effusively said that union organization 'convert[s] the relation of master and servant into an equal and co-operative partnership [and] plants in the heart of every worker a sense of power and individuality, a feeling of freedom and security, which are the characteristics of the kind of men Divine Providence intended us to be', 75 Cong. Rec. 4918, 72nd Cong., 1st Sess. (1932), quoted in Wellington, H., *Labor and the Legal Process* (New Haven, Conn.: Yale University Press, 1968) 88.

are not logical entailments of the concept of 'private property', nor are the legal definitions and meanings of ownership systemically given by the 'inherent logic of capitalism' (or, for that matter, an inherent logic of the 'social' in regimes with some progressive tilt). These are contingent and contested political judgements about how the bundle of property rights and entitlements should be defined and applied. A weakness of the great, post-war schools of labour law—'voluntarism', 'collective laissez faire', and 'industrial pluralism'—is their failure to theorize so-called private law as an aspect of society's regulatory regime for work, employment, and labour markets. The project of renovating labour law must bring all these background rules into the foreground, thereby making them available for criticism and reconsideration from an egalitarian perspective.[25]

Secondly, the institutional understanding of employment makes sense of the foundational legal strategy of promoting CVWP by facilitating collective bargaining. CVWP does not *require* full-time, continuous, site-attached employment. In craft unionism, short-term and itinerant workers exercised countervailing power by capturing the supply of scarce, indispensable skills and production knowledge, and this is still the case in certain occupations. However, under modern industrial conditions, skill is largely endogenous to the firm and frequently in over-supply. Thus, the modern labour law approach to CVWP is to foster workers' *institutional* power. The union is supposed to be a permanent feature of the organization of employment, rooted in the workplace but independent of the managerial hierarchy, taking a continuing interest in events and conditions on-site, and nurturing employee solidarity as a source of labour-market strength. The union does not simply enforce a schedule of prices for discrete units of labour. It negotiates, monitors the performance of, and enforces compliance with standards and entitlements that amount to rules of industrial governance. Thus, labour law's core conception of democracy and representation is functionally linked to the long-term, site-attached model for organizing production.

Thirdly, the CVWP approach primarily aims to increase employee *bargaining* strength, that is, to enhance employees' position in negotiating the contract of employment. This is consistent with hinging household well-being to job-related income. Once the contract has been settled for a time, CVWP falls into a 'reactive' mode: unions monitor to ensure that the employer abides by its promises. In this sense, industrial unionism and

[25] See Kennedy, D., 'The Stakes of Law, or Hale and Foucault!' in his *Sexy Dressing Etc.* (Cambridge, Mass.: Harvard University Press, 1993) 83; Klare, K., 'Legal Theory and Democratic Reconstruction: Reflections on 1989' (1991) 25 *University of British Columbia L. Review* 69, revised version in Alexander, G., and Skąpska, G. (eds.), *A Fourth Way? Privatization, Property, and the Emergence of New Market Economies* (New York: Routledge, 1994) 310; and Stone, K., 'The Post-War Paradigm in American Labor Law' (1981) 90 *Yale L. Journal* 1509.

collective bargaining mirror the rule-based, high-monitoring framework of Taylorism. This model has little to say about pro-active participation in the firm's strategic decisions or in organizing day-to-day operations. Works councils, labour membership on corporate boards, and other 'second channels' of representation open doors to more robust forms of worker participation; however, except perhaps for the most advanced forms of co-determination found in a few systems, they do not supplant management's prerogative to manage. For the most part, labour law does not challenge or even question the bureaucratic and authoritarian structure of the employment relationship itself.

Finally, the job-based conception of employment synchronizes well with premises about democracy and representation that inform labour law, notably, that workers clustered within the firm ought to have some voice with respect to decisions that affect their working lives, and that the employing unit or sector is the logical district or constituency for representation in economic matters.

V TRANSFORMATION OF THE EMPLOYMENT RELATIONSHIP

Recent trends in business organization and strategy, labour market structure, workforce composition, and the design of work, in both the developed and developing nations, are knitting together to establish new frameworks for economic activity and employment. Observers disagree sharply about the extent to which these changes have occurred. There is widespread agreement that they are occurring and gaining momentum, and that together these developments have or may soon produce significant departures from, if not the complete erosion of, the employment model presupposed by labour law. Enduring changes in the structure and organization of employment 'challenge . . . the viability of labor-law and social-insurance regimes rooted historically in bureaucratic, mass-production enterprises . . .'.[26]

Particularly in the developed nations, many observers detect a weakening of internal labour markets, a decline in high-attachment, long-term employment relationships founded on implicit promises of job security, and a growth in market-mediated employment relationships. Increasingly, employment relationships disavow promises about future tenure. Risk is being shifted from employers to employees, who are being asked to become more 'entrepreneurial'. Employers are devoting fewer resources to training and expecting employees themselves to make

---

[26] Barenberg, M., 'Law and Labor in the New, Global Economy: Through the Lens of United States Federalism' (1995) 33 *Columbia Journal of Transnational Law* 445.

greater investments in human capital. Variable, performance-based pay schemes are replacing fixed wage rates, as 'flexible', open-ended responsibilities displace rigid job descriptions. Large, primary-sector employers are departing from norms they had observed for decades against shedding workers or reducing pay rates in response to competitive pressures. Insecure jobs and involuntary part-time employment are growing, and therefore the protective ambit of labour law is shrinking (because these types of jobs frequently fall outside the applicability of employment legislation). Many employers now combine a highly attached core workforce with a large number of peripheral, low-attachment employees. Millions of workers who are dependent in all meaningful senses (they own no assets and are not entitled to share residual profits) are legally classified as self-employed.[27]

The trend in business organization is away from huge, centralized, and vertically integrated entities toward decentralized networks of smaller, more flexible, specialist units. A parallel to this development in some countries is a break up of sectoral collective bargaining relationships and a devolution of bargaining downward to plant level. Geographic as well as organizational dispersion is occurring through outsourcing, off-siting, increasing homework, and telecommuting. Assignments and signals go out by internet and beeper, and employees are paid through electronic direct deposit without collecting their pay cheques at the office or plant. Vertical devolution, decentralization, and business networking blur the boundaries of the employer–employee relationship. Sometimes it is difficult to discern who the employer is. In other cases the nominal employer, say, an employee-leasing agency, is in no financial position to bargain about wages and conditions, whereas the real party-in-interest, say, the lessor of employees, is not an employer in contemplation of law.

Work itself is being redesigned in some sectors. Ironically, this often occurs at the behest of management, not labour. Many employers have discovered that hierarchy and command are suboptimal from the point of view of output, product quality, and employee loyalty, whereas flatter, more participatory arrangements that treat employee intelligence, team work, learning capacity, and problem-solving ability as valuable productive assets are more efficient. Genuine participation schemes (some are superficial or, worse, crude anti-union devices) pose two risks. They may erode traditional solidarities and identification with unions, upon which

---

[27] On these themes, see Cappelli, P., Bassi, L., Katz, H., Knoke, D., Osterman, P., and Useem, M., *Change at Work* (Oxford: Oxford University Press, 1997); Hertzenberg, S., Alic, J., and Wial, H., *New Rules for a New Economy: Employment Opportunity in Postindustrial America* (Ithaca, NY: ILR Press, 1998); Osterman, P., *Securing Prosperity—The American Labor Market: How It Has Changed and What to Do about It* (Princeton, NJ: Princeton University Press, 1999); Cappelli, P., 'Rethinking Employment' (1995) 33 *BJIR* 563.

CVWP depends; and they may accentuate the stratification of the work-force between elite, high-performance sectors and low-wage, low-tech sectors.

These trends destabilize the traditional labour law model. Compared to most forms of grassroots mobilization, a unique feature of unionization is that it creates a permanent, organizational presence speaking for subordinated groups within institutions that are central to their lives. CVWP may be undermined where site-attached, full-time, continuing employment of the type that generated the modes of worker identification and consciousness characteristic of the industrial era gives way to mobile, contingent employment, in which the real employer's identity may be obscure, and in which traditional class-based appeals to solidarity compete with a complex web of gender, race, cultural, and national identifications.

The erosion of the industrial model in the developed nations and the tendency of industrialization in developing nations to bypass classical forms and stages cast doubt on age-old assumptions about economic democracy that inform labour law, particularly the principle of providing employees with a voice in decisions that affect them. Of course, there is nothing wrong with employee voice in the abstract.[28] The question is whether economic democracy should be limited to employees but not also encompass participation by and representation of, for example, spouses, consumers, and/or local residents affected by capital flight or environmental hazards. Traditional notions of economic democracy carried forward in labour law are problematical and perhaps anachronistic, in that they are so strongly site-focused. Opportunities for participation and representation are implicitly conditioned upon an intense, lasting connection to an employing unit or sector.

At a minimum, economic democracy activists and labour lawyers must imagine new forms of worker representation and collective action addressed to the needs of mobile, temporary, part-time, and other employees with reduced physical and psychological attachment to a work site. Moreover, the conventional image of industrial democracy as being about and for workers congregated in an enterprise assumes an experience of time available to people with minimal care-giving or home-making responsibilities, an obvious gender bias. This vision of economic democracy is also complacent about the philosophical undesirability and the serious public-health dangers of overwork.

---

[28] Employee-voice mechanisms can enhance productive and allocative efficiency. See Freeman, R., and Medoff, J., *What Do Unions Do?* (New York: Basic Books, Inc., 1984); Hirschman, A., *Exit, Voice, and Loyalty: Responses to Decline in Firms, Organizations, and States* (Cambridge, Mass.: Harvard University Press, 1970).

Labour law has been more effective in challenging the subordination of labour on the job and in the terms of exchange, less so with respect to the domination of labour *by jobs*. As applied political theorists, labour lawyers should consider whether democracy and human self-determination may be better served by taking advantage of technological progress gradually to release people from paid work and to reduce its centrality as a life-activity (while maintaining living standards), rather than by intensifying people's commitments to paid employment (as seems to be implied in the traditional view). Conceivably, arranging flexible entry to and exit from well-compensated, flexibly scheduled jobs and between jobs and other life-contexts such as family, community, and education may contribute more to ending the subordination of workers than, say, a right to vote on enterprise financial planning.

VI FROM THE WORKPLACE TO WORK'S PLACE

The question of the relationship *between* paid employment (jobs) and unpaid work, principally women's domestic labour and reproductive contribution, raises analogous issues of displacement and stratification to those posed by ongoing changes *within* employment relationships.

As several contributors to this volume discuss, the law treats women's reproductive labour and home-making and care-giving undertaken by a family member for the benefit of the household as contributions or gifts to the household.[29] Such work is not exchanged or purchased in the manner of an ordinary commodity, and its value is not usually taxed as imputed income. Undoubtedly this type of work has value. It attracts compensation when performed in someone else's household.

Production for profit requires socialized, fed, clothed, and cared-for employees. While care-giving can be an end in itself, some part of household work is performed only as an adjunct to paid employment (for example, laundering uniforms). This portion is a cost of and, unless paid for, a subsidy to business production. It can be argued that wages reflect these costs as well as the value added to the product by the employee. But far too many market failures intervene to make this anything but a wildly implausible hypothesis. To cite a few examples, wage earners may systematically under-appreciate, and therefore fail to bargain for, the

---

[29] See particularly the essays by Conaghan, Kraamwinkel, Rittich, and Williams, in this volume. See also Conaghan, J., 'The Invisibility of Women in Labour Law: Gender-neutrality in Model-building' (1986) 14 *Int'l. Journal of the Sociology of Law* 377; ead, 'Feminism and Labour Law: Contesting the Terrain', in Morris, A., and O'Donnel, T. (eds.), *Feminist Perspectives on Employment Law* (London: Cavendish, 1999) 13; and Williams, L., 'Welfare and Legal Entitlements: The Social Roots of Poverty' in Kairys, above n. 3, 569.

interests of those who perform household labour (a negative externality or third-party effect). Or those performing domestic labour may have internalized the patriarchal norm that they are not entitled to and cannot expect compensation for such effort (a problem of endogenous or adaptive preferences). Or wage earners may regularly fail to return some portion of wages to the household (an agency and monitoring problem). Or a household may contribute to production but not receive wages (such as the case of a disabled head of household who is not a labour market participant but who raises and socializes children who are future labour market participants). These and many other market failures permit employers to displace some portion of labour costs onto subordinated groups.

A transformative project in labour law must unearth and challenge practices and beliefs underlying illegitimate economic hierarchy and domination *and* the legal rules that construct and legitimate such practices and beliefs. This, in turn, will require a conceptual revolution. Labour law must get beyond its fixation on paid employment and reconstitute itself as a discipline concerned with all legal rules and policies bearing on work. The object of study must be not just the workplace, but every facet of *work's place* in personal, social, and economic life, in social reproduction, and in offering possibilities for and imposing constraints upon human self-realization.[30]

VII SOLIDARITY ALONG A CALIFORNIA FAULT LINE

Postindustrial trends in employment structures, the organization of work, and socio-cultural patterns play out in widely different ways in different contexts. An illuminating view of how these developments affect traditional models of labour representation in one setting is provided by a second anecdote, this one about workers in Los Angeles County, California, who provide in-home personal care to elderly and disabled people ('home-care aides').[31]

Recently, about 74,000 home-care aides in Los Angeles County became unionized, by far the largest accession of an employee group to organized

---

[30] In a similar vein, see European Commission (A. Supiot, *rapporteur*), *Transformation of Labour and Future of Labour Law in Europe: Final Report* (Luxembourg: European Communities, 1999), which proposes the concept of 'social drawing rights' based not on 'the restrictive criterion of employment, but on the broader notion of work'.

[31] This account draws primarily on a lecture by a union official, David Rolf (Northeastern University School of Law, 31 Jan. 2000), and Greenhouse, S., 'In Biggest Drive Since 1937, Union Gains A Victory', *NY Times*, 26 Feb. 1999. Compare the low-wage, low-tech example of home-care with Hyde's discussion in this volume of high-tech workers in the Silicon Valley region of California. See also Zlolniski, C., 'The Informal Economy in an Advanced Industrialized Society: Mexican Immigrant Labor in Silicon Valley' (1994) 103 *Yale L. Journal* 2305.

labour in the USA in over sixty years. The vast majority of aides are women of colour. They interface with people, not machines. Instead of producing commodities, they solve problems and construct healing relationships. No doubt most perform an unpaid 'second shift' of care-giving at home. They come from diverse ethnic and national backgrounds and language groups (Latina, Asian, African-American, and European-American). Many maintain deep ties to their cultures and communities of origin. Immigrants from Mexico, for example, send home about US $ 6.3 billion each year, which represents Mexico's second or third largest foreign-income source.[32] In 1995, remittances 'were equivalent to fifty seven per cent of the foreign exchange available through foreign direct investment . . . and five per cent of the total income supplied by exports'.[33] Complex forms of cross-border politics and overlapping nationality are emerging. Mexican politicians now make campaign appearances in Los Angeles and other US localities with residential concentrations of eligible Mexican voters. The Mexican government and US labour leaders are cultivating ties in support of their common position that undocumented Mexican immigrants in the USA should be granted legal status. Mexico's Foreign Minister Jorge Castañeda recently urged this view at a union convention in Los Angeles. A journalist suggested that Castañeda took this unorthodox step 'because he recognizes that organized labor [in the USA] is one of the strongest voices to advance [Mexican] President Vicente Fox's goal of winning legal status for Mexican illegal immigrants in the United States'.[34] Both major political parties in the USA actively court the 'new citizens' vote'. Politicians of immigrant backgrounds are gaining ground in US politics. Antonio Villaraigoso, a Mexican-American politician and former labour organizer (who once worked for the home-care aides' parent union) recently mounted a formidable race to become the first Latino mayor of Los Angeles in nearly 130 years.

The union drive faced staggering logistical and legal problems, took well over a decade to complete, and cost about US $ 20 million. Annual turnover among aides was estimated to be about 40 per cent. The employees are not concentrated at central work-sites and have little on-the-job contact with each other. Aides usually report directly to clients' residences in response to telephoned instructions (periodically they visit an

[32] Thompson, G., 'Migrant Exodus Bleeding Mexico's Heartland', *NY Times*, 17 June 2001. Studies identify oil, tourism, and remittances from migrants as the top three foreign income sources, but disagree about the rank ordering.
[33] Report of the Binational Study on Migration, *Migration between Mexico and The United States* (report of independent study team convened and funded by the governments of Mexico and the USA, 1997).
[34] Greenhouse, S., 'In U.S. Unions, Mexico Finds Unlikely Ally on Immigration', *NY Times*, 19 July 2001.

administrative office briefly to drop off paperwork). The clients' homes are spread out all over Los Angeles County, which occupies 4,000 square miles and has a population of over nine million (meaning that LA County has about one third the land area of Belgium and a larger population than Sweden). The tried and true tactic of leafleting at plant gates was out of the question; the only practical way for union activists to reach the employees with their message was to visit them personally in their homes, which are also widely dispersed. The union made home visits to approximately 33,000 employees. Eventually the union held neighbour- hood meetings and rallies and communicated with and served its prospective constituency through a toll-free '800' telephone number and an internet job-referral registry. Mobilization techniques included street demonstrations, appeals to politicians and public figures, ballot initiatives on such matters as the minimum wage, in sum, everything except tradi- tional strikes, which were completely impractical in this context.

Strikingly, when the union campaign began there was no identifiable employer. By virtue of a classic jurisprudential circularity,[35] the absence of a recognizable employer rendered uncertain which body of law (federal or state) should be consulted to determine who the employer was. A California court eventually ruled that there was no employer of record, at least for purposes of California labour law. To fit their aspira- tions into the classical labour law model, the workers literally had to bring an employer into existence.

Much of home care is provided to subsidized consumers, whose expenses are defrayed by a complex, multilevel funding scheme financed by federal, state, and local governments. (Some care is financed privately or by private insurance schemes.) Clients have considerable power to select or reject individual aides and to supervise their work, but no involvement in wage-setting or in determining qualifications or working conditions. County social workers set the number of hours aides work. The patchwork of referral agencies regarded the aides as self-employed. Although a governmental reimbursement scheme effectively controlled wage rates, the governmental payors played no part in hiring or directing aides or determining their working conditions (apart from a general, licensing function). Yet the residual category of 'independent contractors' hardly fit this group of low-wage employees who contribute no fixed or financial assets and have no claim to profits (in fact, the entire enterprise is not-for-profit).

After some false starts, the union concluded that it would have to create an employer, an objective that could be accomplished only through

---

[35] See Cohen, F., 'Transcendental Nonsense and the Functional Approach' (1935) 35 *Columbia L. Review* 809.

the political process. After years of lobbying, California enacted legislation authorizing its county governments to establish 'home-care authorities' which would receive and dispense the funding and act as employers. To achieve this, the union had to sustain the energy and enthusiasm of its ever-changing grassroots base. And it needed to forge alliances with and persuade sceptical non-worker groups (such as those speaking for elders, the disabled, and patients' family members) that unionization could lead to better client service and higher funding levels. To build solidarity in this postindustrial context, the union restyled its efforts to look more like a civil rights crusade or political advocacy group than a traditional organization of workers. Notwithstanding the union's skill and success, one must wonder about the adequacy of a model of redistribution classically wedded to the employer–employee dyad, when traditional workers and traditional employers are replaced by a complex variety of social actors in paid employment.

VIII LABOUR LAW AND GLOBAL INTEGRATION

The intensification of international economic and political integration generates two major dilemmas for traditional labour law thinking. Deep integration, at least as currently constructed, imposes significant restraints on the ability of unions and social movements to fight for economic redistribution and on the capacity of nation-states and supranational institutions to pursue egalitarian social policies. And deep integration fragments national legal orders, whereas the seminal work implicitly sees labour law as growing out of a relatively unified, coherent, and nationally based legal regime.[36] Both problems are illustrated by the home-care aides' story.

There is no such thing as 'free trade'

The term 'free trade' often refers simply to the reduction or elimination of tariff and similar barriers to the importation of goods across international frontiers. Frequently, however, the phrase is meant to carry the more robust connotation of an ideologically favoured end-state, namely, an 'unregulated' world economy. Markets and economies are never unregulated. The

---

[36] The significance of this is illuminated in Trubek, D., Mosher, J., and Rothstein, J., 'Transnationalism in the Regulation of Labor Relations: International Regimes and Transnational Advocacy Networks' (2000) 25 *Law and Social Inquiry* 1187. See also Trubek, D., 'Social Justice "After" Globalization: The Case of Social Europe', Working Paper no. 9, MacArthur Consortium Research Series on International Peace and Cooperation (Madison, Wis.: University of Wisconsin Global Studies Program, 1996).

point was made earlier that product and labour markets are and must be structured by ground rules of property, contract, tort, crime, domestic relations, and other legal fields; that these background rules have distributive consequences; and that therefore the ensemble of 'private law' rules in place at any given time comprises a form of regulation of economic activity.

A similar analysis applies to the international economic arena. Even if customs duties were reduced to zero, the exchange of goods across borders would still be regulated by a myriad of rules and policies addressing an endless set of diverse issues such as agricultural subsidies, shipping, domicile, foreign aid, currency exchange, letters of credit, conflicts of laws, and so on. Some such rules are highly visible and understood to regulate international economic activity (such as the rules embodied in the GATT or the criteria for entry into the European Monetary Union). Others are in the background (for example, laws against piracy on the high seas). The ensemble of ground rules governing international economic activity comprises a system of regulation. In this sense, there is no such thing as free trade.[37]

Consequently, international economic integration or 'globalization' cannot be discussed in the abstract. Rather, we must examine the goals and effects of the rules and institutions currently in place that structure international economic activity. Although one can easily cite important exceptions, the overall direction of these rules today is hostile to the egalitarian ambitions of labour law.

Constraints on redistributive leeway and state capacity

One effect of deep integration as currently constructed is a variation on the theme of the public/private distinction. The emerging architecture or 'constitution'[38] of the world economic order affords private power (as represented by capital investment and disinvestment decisions) dramatically increased capacity to influence public policy, to escape the reach of protective laws and egalitarian policies enacted by democratic political majorities, and to withstand workers' and other social movements' efforts to improve their lot. Conversely, nation-states and, for that matter, supranational institutions face tighter constraints on policy-making, often

---

[37] See Paul, J., 'Free Trade, Regulatory Competition and the Autonomous Market Fallacy' (1994–5) 1 *Columbia Journal Eur. L* 29.

[38] See Schneiderman, D., 'Investment Rules and the New Constitutionalism' (2000) 25 *Law and Social Inquiry* 757, and 'The Constitutional Strictures of the Multilateral Agreement on Investment' (2000) 9/2 *The Good Society*, 90. See also Buchanan, R., *Making Women's Work: Global Restructuring and Local Development in the Call Center Industry*, S.J.D. thesis (Madison, Wis.: 2000).

self-imposed, and subordinated groups have less room for manœuvre in their quest for economic justice.[39]

There are several reasons for the augmentation of private economic power. One is the increasing mobility of capital, which allows owners more easily to depart and relocate elsewhere, or credibly to threaten to do so, if displeased with a particular nation's social policy and labour laws. The impact of the credible exit option is strikingly apparent in the obeisance governments must pay to currency markets, avoiding like the plague social programmes that may even be suspected of inflationary potential. Workers do not have equivalent legal entitlements or practical possibilities to exit the polity.

Capital has become more mobile primarily due to the liberalization of financial markets and currency trading, investor-friendly policies adopted by capital-poor countries and regions, and strong protections for property and investments entrenched in bilateral and international agreements. In addition, machinery, production facilities, and information systems are becoming more portable. Businesses employing advanced, computer-driven technologies are less vulnerable to strikes and other traditional labour self-help weapons. Together these developments create opportunities and incentives for regulatory competition between nations and regions.

A second source of constraints on nation-state capacity to pursue progressive social policies is the emergence and expansion of the system of international institutions whose decisions bind nation-states *de jure* and/or *de facto*. As a result, decision-making processes become more opaque and seemingly inaccessible, and the efficacy of popular political participation is diluted. Some international institutions and governance processes, such as the European Parliament, do provide for limited and attenuated citizen participation, but the most important international economic institutions do not, nor are their workings notable for transparency.

Third is a series of self-imposed legal obligations entrenched by treaty. In this respect, the 'hollowing out' of the nation-state is the product of, and could not be accomplished without, the active participation of nation-states.[40] At least this means that, in principle, democratic politics can someday undo these fetters. The emerging regime of international economic law effectively obliges nations to refrain from egalitarian social measures and redistributive projects that impair opportunities for or the value of private investment.[41] Investment protections are widely

---

[39] On these themes see the essays by Arthurs, Davis, Langille, and Mundlak, in this volume.
[40] See Schneiderman, above, n. 38.
[41] See ibid., and Trubek, *et al.*, above, n. 36.

Karl Klare

entrenched in trade and investment treaties that guarantee free cross-border movement of capital, 'national treatment', and most-favoured-nation status (MFN). National treatment and MFN provisions make it difficult for poorer nations to screen investment plans or favour local companies with an eye toward encouraging sustainable growth and job creation. Standard treaty provisions also bar subsidies and uncompensated takings, and takings are now interpreted so broadly as to inhibit governments from undertaking garden variety social and environmental programmes, for fear that a restriction on dangerous chemicals or a proposal for public investment will be challenged as an expropriation of inchoate investment interests. Other widely adopted mechanisms of constraint are treaty provisions obliging signatory nations to enforce a specified intellectual property regime, to recognize private investor standing to enforce treaty provisions against the sovereign, or to submit trade and investment disputes to a specified conflict-resolution procedure (often private arbitration conducted in camera). Supranational constraints on nation-state politics reach a pinnacle in the provisions of the European Community Treaty that place a ceiling on deficit spending by Member States.

At first glance, the home-care aides' story appears to suggest that claims of the anti-democratic or anti-progressive impact of deep integration are exaggerated. Unskilled, low-wage workers with no visible economic clout managed to enlist the help of local governments and succeeded in establishing a beachhead of countervailing workers' power. But there is a more pessimistic reading of this experience which ironically confirms that deep integration poses a serious threat to worker empowerment. Most obviously, the home-care enterprise is not-for-profit and its key financial decisions are ultimately driven by governmental processes rather than ostensibly unregulated market forces. In today's environment of fiscal austerity and down-sized social protection, this factor may be less important than a truly unusual feature of the aides' case: they perform a kind of work that, by definition, cannot be sent offshore. Home-care of Los Angeles patients cannot be transferred to a lower-wage zone. This opens room for redistributive manœuvre (in technical terms, imperfection in the market for home-care labour generates a rent). A half-century ago, workers who made automobile tyres had a comparable strategic advantage. Few workers in today's world economic order do. Moreover, the precise distributive consequences of home-care collective bargaining will turn on highly contextualized particulars concerning the demographics of the catchment area, tax base, and consumer group, the share of public financing, and the incidence and degree of progressivity of the underlying tax programmes.

However, that the aides' case may have unique qualities should not be taken to mean that deep integration removes redistributive organizing and labour law projects from the agenda or that the twenty-first century is going to be a steady race to the bottom for poorer nations. The burden of my argument is that the power of capital to escape the ambit of labour law or to displace the costs of social reform onto already victimized groups can be countered if progressive political and institutional innovations supplement progressive labour law initiatives. Particularly in the international economic arena, we need to invent new political forms—including effective, multilateral labour rights and standards guarantees, transnational collective bargaining systems, and cross-border networks and coalitions—to solve collective action problems and to deter capital from evading efforts by progressive governments and international institutions to carve out space for social justice.

Multivalent legal orders

Another consequence of deep global integration is that the unitary legal regime is becoming an antique. Phrases like 'Italian' or 'Mexican' or 'South African labour law' now must be used with some caution. Increasingly, legal regimes are comprised of multiple, overlapping layers of sovereignty and norm-creation. This results from the growing number, types, and importance of federal and quasi-federal systems and supranational institutions, the expanded reach of international law, and the proliferation of bilateral and multilateral treaty obligations and entitlements. Overlapping sovereignties exist both within and across national frontiers. Sovereigns can be supranational and subnational as well as national. Quasi-sovereign power is routinely exercised by MNEs and other nominally private entities, while grass roots movements, NGOs, and transnational political networks seek a law-making role by defining and advocating for 'best practice' standards in economic activity and human rights compliance. New, variegated forms of nationality and citizenship complicate the picture.

These complex, multivalent legal regimes have two features long familiar to lawyers working in federal regimes (such as the USA). First, the boundaries between various sovereignties and sources of law—for example, whether a particular matter falls within European Community or Member State competence—are indistinct, porous, and constantly shifting. Secondly, the order of hierarchy between layers is often indeterminate. A hornbook precept of US law is that, in the event of conflict, federal norms trump state and local norms. Yet ambiguities, exceptions, and historic twists have generated uncertainty and heated controversy about the application of this principle for over 200 years.

Deep global integration is making lack of clarity about norm-hierarchy a universal characteristic of contemporary legal work. This is alarming for egalitarian labour law, in so far as investment protections, fiscal discipline, and exit ramps for capital are setting the substantive agenda, rather than, say, establishment of a transnational floor of social and economic rights or democratization of intellectual property. Ambiguity about the applicable legal regime stalled the home-care aides' unionization drive for years.

But the home-care case equally demonstrates that multivalent legal regimes can also present opportunities for egalitarian projects. The transfer of legal problems from inhospitable to friendlier legal terrain is an age-old technique of American lawyers in such contexts as labour, welfare, and civil rights cases. The home-aides' union succeeded in part by creating and then invoking a novel legal framework for collective bargaining (if not an entirely new jurisdiction). A striking contemporary example in Europe is the advances for gender equality made possible by creative invocation of Community law.[42] However, it is important to note that the political implications of either increased federal/European Community competence or an increased role for localities/Member States are indeterminate. US history is replete with instances in which conservative and progressive political movements switched long-settled views on federalism, and even cases in which a given ideological slant gave rise to conflicting federalism positions depending on the non-federalism issues at stake. Thus, one cannot say, *a priori*, whether local, centralized, or supranational competencies are more or less democratic or more or less progressive. Too much turns on the particularities of history and political context.

IX CONCLUSION

A transformative project in labour law must tackle a lengthy agenda. New instruments of egalitarian redistribution and new models of collective action and representation must be envisioned, attuned to new forms of organization of production and to differences as well as commonalities among workers (only some of whom are employees) in identification, consciousness, and life path. Transformative labour law has a vital contribution to make in fashioning an alternative international economic constitution, one that works toward rather than against equality between and within nations and regions. To be transformative, labour law must take a global perspective and be immersed in transnational dialogue; de-centre

---

[42] As discussed by Kilpatrick, in this volume; and see *ead*, 'Gender Equality: A Fundamental Dialogue' in Sciarra, S. (ed.), *Labour Law in the Courts: National Judges and the European Court of Justice* (Oxford: Hart Publishing, 2001) 31.

paid employment and switch focus to work and social contribution; escape the continuing grasp of the purported distinction between 'public' and 'private law'; reinterpret class in light of other social identities; conceive institutions and work relationships that combine flexibility with security; and assist in devising egalitarian development strategies. It should work to undo gender and racial domination. Undoubtedly labour law must pursue many different approaches, rather than imagining that twenty-first century complexity can be squeezed into a single, over-arching paradigm.[43] Some labour lawyers lament the crisis of the discipline. Interrogating and rethinking tradition may involve disorientation and loss, but opportunity and hope also await down this path. And, to borrow the moral of an old Jewish fable, at least the work is steady.

---

[43] Cf. Collins, H., 'The Productive Disintegration of Labour Law' (1997) 26 *ILJ* 295.

2

Labour Law at the Century's End: An Identity Crisis?

MASSIMO D'ANTONA*

I THE CONSTITUTIONALIZATION OF LABOUR LAW

The constitutionalization of labour law took place in the historic context of the post-war. The new constitutions and constitutional practices that took shape in Western Europe after the Second World War set out, as juridical values for the entire society, the details of a compromise among social classes. Moreover, these shared constitutional values have until now stood in stark opposition to the unequal distribution of power and income associated with different positions in the spheres of production. The social constitutions of the post-war period may thus be seen as acts of political pacification, supported by ruling classes who feared the looming menace of internal civil war, in a world divided into ideological and power blocs. The guarantees of organizational rights and legitimate union opposition; the protection of labour standards, both by contract and through such specific conditions as fair wages and the protection of women and minors; and, more generally, the principles of the welfare state, labour law, and social security, though originating in this political compromise, took on, for the first time as constitutional principles, a kind of axiological existence and normative substance from which the European countries drew, from then until now, a decisive measure of legitimation. (The extraordinary post-war economic development then confirmed this political compromise through an effective transformation of the social structure, integrating increasing numbers of citizens into the labour market and the welfare state.)

Now, at the end of the twentieth century, may one pose the question:

* Late of the Università di Roma La Sapienza. This essay originally appeared as 'Diritto del Lavoro di Fine Secolo: Una Crisi di Identità?' (1998) 48 *Rivista Giuridica del Lavoro e della Previdenza Sociale* 311. This translation was prepared for this volume by Alan Hyde, with the assistance of Bruno Caruso, Karl Klare, and Silvana Sciarra, and appears through the kind permission of the original publisher. As originally published, the essay did not have citations in the English language manner, but was followed by a four-page bibliographic note containing citations to many works, mostly in Italian but also in English and French. There seemed little point in translating this bibliographic note; readers who speak Italian are encouraged to consult the original. The footnotes in this translation were inserted in order to identify specific legal events and were provided by Bruno Caruso.

how many of these axiological reference points and normative principles collected in the Constitution remain current, and which belong to the climate and context of the short twentieth century that, to invoke the brilliant synthesis, began with the First World War and ended definitively with the fall of the Berlin Wall?

II THE PILLARS OF IDENTITY OF LABOUR LAW AS WE KNOW IT

The identity crisis of labour law, in the historic period coinciding with the end of the twentieth century, is under discussion in Italy as in other industrial countries. On all sides the accents are both stressed and distressing. For example, in Britain, where one sees the effects of severe deregulation shrinking the protected area immune from the normal acquisitive model, one now asks whether there has not been a 'death of labour law' and a return to contract as the exclusive regulatory instrument for labour relations. In France, the manuals have abandoned the traditional title 'labour law [*droit du travail*]', and prefer 'the law of employment [*droit de l'emploi*]', in order to underline that the epicentre has moved from labour relations inside the firm to the labour market generally, with its new problems of market access, job creation, sharing of labour time, 'employability', and connections between working conditions and social citizenship.

The diagnoses are diverse, but share one point. Labour law's identity crisis is tied to a transformation of its object, that is, labour, or at least the labour with which labour law was traditionally concerned: the status of 'employee' ('*il lavoro subordinato*') which, as everyone knows, does not now include, and never has included, all the labour that moves the mechanisms of the economy and gives form and life to the institutions of society. So, the labour with which labour law has until now been concerned seems to be found less and less, at least in European postindustrial societies and, where it is found, exhibits characteristics not readily reconciled with the traditional model. The debate over job security starts here, as does the eventual revision of the normative criteria to identify 'employment'. We do not lack for those who maintain that such relations of 'employment' (understood almost ontologically) are found less and less in Europe, precisely because labour law intervenes to prevent free contracting between those who offer their own labour and those who have the means and resources to employ it profitably. By contrast, free contract is said to prevail (with not a few corrections, in truth) in the vast field of self-employment. Labour law would represent, they say, an infantile phase of the juridification of the labour market, to be superseded in the name of a maturity already attained, that will restore the reign of liberty of contract of the parties over the diverse forms of labour, whether of 'employees' or 'self-employed'.

Although pertinent in certain respects, this diagnosis is nevertheless incomplete. One must keep in mind, when speaking of labour law's crisis of identity, that labour law as we know it is an historic construction, not a matter of ontology. Labour regulation in European countries took shape following industrialization, and thus, at different times, following the different starting points of that process (in Italy, the final two decades of the nineteenth century). The actual configuration that took place everywhere following the Second World War was, as mentioned, within the framework of a process of constitutionalization (with forms and materials varying in each national context) of certain values and principles, tied strictly to a larger political compromise.

In attempting to generalize, one might say that the identity of labour law as we know it rested on four pillars, each architectonically pertinent during this historic period, each now in the midst of profound restructuring, if not demolition.

III FIRST PILLAR: THE NATION-STATE

The construction of labour law's identity has been tied to the historic turns of the nation-state, a form that is today undergoing evident transformation. The nation-state is that state that, within its territory, regulates both political and economic phenomena. It achieves a sort of Aristotelian unity among political, civic, and market institutions. The concrete developing history of labour law manifests the aspiration of the nation-state to contain social conflicts within their proper boundaries, using diverse modalities of intervention: first the corporative state, and then, successively, the welfare state, the distributive state of Keynesian faith, and the entrepreneurial state, as necessary to preserve the mechanisms of capitalist accumulation and, at the same time, maintain social order and the bases of democratic legitimization of the state itself. A nexus of reciprocal implication thus arises between the nation-state and labour law as we know it, a nexus that becomes evident in the moment in which the nation-state gives up increasing shares of sovereignty over the economy, monetary policy, and the market to supranational institutions of political administration such as the European Union, which lack the same democratic legitimacy of national states. (The so-called 'democratic deficit' of the supranational European government—the Council–Commission–Parliament triad—may be seen to have little to do with the division of power in European constitutions. In each case, with the possible exception of the agricultural sector, the decisional processes of the Union are

conditioned far less by those of the national states than by constitutionalized social values and the political force of organized labour.)

The nation-state's loss of control over economic factors changes, not
merely its regulatory competence, but also the material conditions from
which labour law as we know it has been made. One size must fit all: the
extreme mobility of investments and, indeed, of production facilities
restricts the space available to the nation-state to govern firms that operate within its territory through labour legislation, the restrictions and
costs of labour protection. One might say that, in an open, supranational
market, and in a global economy, firms 'vote with their feet', meaning that
disagreement with a particular social policy of the nation-state (that
might, for example, emphasize particular restrictive guarantees for
labour, or impose particularly costly taxes or contributions) may be
expressed simply by moving elsewhere, to Southeast Asia or Poland or
Hungary, but equally to Wales, if different national or local policies make
that convenient.

IV SECOND PILLAR: LARGE FACTORIES

The second pillar of labour law is the organization of industrial labour,
symbolized by the great factories of the post-war period: places in which
the factors of production are concentrated, so that labour is regulated by
rigid procedures and employer power exercised in hierarchical form,
necessarily influencing the form of labour regulation. One need only
recall the legislation on workplace democracy, for example, the Italian
Statuto dei lavoratori, to cite one of the most significant laws. That statute
codified the chief rights of the worker against the domination created in
the first place by the law of business organization: the rigidity and hierarchy of large industrial factories. By now we have at our disposal entire
libraries on how to overcome this concentrated, rigid, and hierarchical
organization of industrial labour, the literature on what some call 'post-
fordism'. The phenomena of outsourcing production, network organization, telecommuting, even more importantly, the dematerialization of the
organization of production into relations of information and automation
have changed profoundly, along with the form of the direction and
control of labour, the very risks inherent in being a worker. Certainly if
one were to re-examine today a law on democratizing the 'workplace',
one would above all have to take note of the fact that production is everywhere and the 'workplace' equally so. The *Statuto dei lavoratori* is still relevant for an important sphere of the actual world of labour. At the same
time, however, it has become inadequate, whether through overprecision
or undercoverage, where the personal dignity of the worker is threatened,

not by the terroristic practices of security guards or searches on exiting
the plant, but by the punctual and continuous control, immanent in digital systems of communication, through which the worker produces access
to private information on the state of his or her health. Today's new
assaults on the 'dignity and security' of the worker probably arise from
the illusory autonomy, and actual solipsistic isolation, of those 'independent' and nominally self-employed workers, the so-called 'Iva party'
(after the tax paid by the self-employed). Thanks to the new models of
work organization and to the great freedom of recourse to flexible
contractual forms, they are controlled by post-fordist firms, even better
than before, with the clever simplicity of the 'long leash'. Their autonomy
is liberation: from the burdens of synchronizing the rhythms of life with
many other workers, of working together each day in the same place, and
of sharing, even physically, the same working conditions. Yet, such
autonomy remains hard, insurmountable personal dependence on the
fate and profitability of somebody else's company that remains in control
of one's individual destiny and life plan—a dependence in certain
respects even more burdensome than that of the traditional factory, inas-
much as it is experienced outside any experience either collective or solidaristic.

There are probably no longer any solid reasons to restrict a statute of
labour's fundamental rights, such as the *Statuto dei lavoratori* as currently
interpreted, only to those legally classed as 'employees', employed in
productive units with more than fifteen employees. The *Statuto dei lavoratori* was intended, as everybody knows, to bring the Constitution inside
the factory gates. Some time ago, labour walked right through those
factory gates and dispersed among the network of subcontractors, franchisees, and small service contractors. The Constitution too should be able
to take a few steps in the same direction.

V THIRD PILLAR: FULL-TIME EMPLOYMENT

The 'right to work' (in the European sense of right to a job) in many
contemporary constitutions, beginning with Italy's own, implied that
each citizen might legitimately aspire to a job as an employee, through
which might be satisfied a person's fundamental needs: an income
adequate to a standard of social dignity, a certain equilibrium in the
distribution of social power, prospects of a life stable enough to permit
the creation and growth of a family, security against unforeseen events
that might impede the ability to work, and maintenance during old age of
an income not too different from that formerly earned through labour.
The 'right to work' was conceptualized in contemporary constitutions

essentially as a concrete means to a larger end. All citizens might live in
dignity and sheltered from need through stable employment. The latter
socio-economic condition seemed possible, and even necessary during
the exceptional economic development of the post-war period when the
expanded productive industrial base appeared correspondingly at our
disposal. A significant part of labour law and virtually the whole of the
law of social security until recent years were founded, not necessarily
explicitly, on full-time employment of wage labour, seen both as a
promise and a concrete opportunity.

For all that contemporary constitutions continue to maintain the
promise, few believe it possible today either that younger generations can
rely on stable employment in a fully-employed workforce or that they can
be guaranteed a standard of living and level of protection against social
risk that, if not superior, is at least not inferior to that of the generation
now retiring. Programmes based, conceptually and financially, on the
centrality of stable employment from school to pension, cannot support
the aging population and 'jobless growth' to which European society
appears condemned. Thus emerges the problem of 'jobs' that puts into
crisis the criteria marking the realm of employment, what is now referred
to as the law of 'occupation' or, as they say in France, employability.

For present purposes it is unnecessary to choose between two models
usually counterposed. On the one hand, the USA, which accepts low,
even poverty level wages and does not oppose an explosion of 'bad jobs',
wields the scissors of social inequality to cut society into unprecedented
maldistribution, but lower unemployment, and effectively increases the
likelihood of work for everyone who wants it. On the other, continental
Europe, which wants to preserve the dignity and security of labour and
will not officially acknowledge salaries under the social minimum, maintains tight restrictions on entrance to or exit from work, preserves union
control over labour standards, but pays for all this with a lethal combination of high unemployment, illegal labour, and immigration that diminishes the chance of employment for entire social groups, such as young
people generally, or those who have been unemployed for a long period,
or women with medium-high qualifications.

Whichever model is preferred, one must admit that, since full-time
employment in paid labour is not a sustainable promise, labour law will
not be able to be identified solely with legislation on the relations of
'employees' in stable jobs. Labour market conditions for someone who
hopes to work, no matter in what contractual form or on whom dependent, cannot be distinct from, or even opposed to, the conditions of who
actually works. Labour, the designated subject of all legal relations,
underneath the concrete modality of its presentation in particular actions,
must be transformed into labourers, understood as people who construct

life plans that pass through labour, whether employed or self-employed, and who need both a reasonable package for everyone who works, and also, and perhaps even more, a labour market governed so as to make available adequate chances of work, and instruments, institutions, and contractual forms to sustain over time the employability of all labour (without adjectives).

VI FOURTH PILLAR: GENERAL REPRESENTATION OF LABOUR THROUGH THE UNION

One cannot characterize as distinctly Italian the idea of the general representation of labour through the union, or rather the idea that the great union confederations, historically well-dispersed among firms and in society, might aspire to unitary representation, whether in the economic or political arena, of the interests of diverse components of the world of labour. From this idea of the general representation of labour through the union were born the practices that signify labour law as we know it: the neo-corporative practices of northern Europe; the practices of social contracting, more or less institutionalized, of Mediterranean Europe. Beyond these national differences, labour law as we know it draws two features from the historic monopoly of the representation of labour by the great centralized unions: limitation of interests and access. First, political practice is marked by simplification of the plurality of interests of the world of labour. Secondly, privileged access to the processes of legislative decision (which basically are, or at least normally were, between those concerns of big business and those of qualified intermediaries of the labour force) is borne by hegemonic organizations.

The contradiction between the voluntary and plural nature of labour's interests and the political institutional role granted to certain large organizations has become deeper, with the changing composition of the world of labour and with the decline in the unifying role of the national state. One need only recall the Italian experience with the referendum, that ended the phase of legal monopoly of the 'major representative confederations on the national level', an extraordinary success of the politics of social contracting, and, at the same time, a latent erosion of the capacity of its principal actors to represent effectively the interests in the name of which this designation was awarded.[1]

The large union confederations, and the employers' association

---

[1] The Italian referendum of June 1995 repealed the provision of Art. 19 of the *Statuto dei Lavoratori* that had restricted the right to appoint shop stewards to unions affiliated with national confederations. The effect is to permit all unions, even those unaffiliated with national confederations, to appoint shop stewards.

Confindustria, each in its own way, draw an exceptional legitimation at the national level from their political recognition by the government. But the interests in the name of which they are so designated are, in reality, increasingly articulated either at the material base (workers in sectors protected from competition and workers in sectors of the global economy; small, medium-sized, and large firms; the service or public sector etc.), or at a territorial base (north, northeast, prosperous centre, centre in crisis, south, declining areas, exporting areas etc.). Synthesis is certainly not favoured by the informality that characterizes union law in Italy (with the exception, however, of the public sector, which under law 396 of 1997 has completely institutionalized the 'recognition' of the union parties to the 'final contract' of collective bargaining, on the basis of their representativeness, objectively measured). Meanwhile, the decline of the national state as the level of political and administrative unification, due to the ceding of portions of power towards both the supranational level of the European Union and the infranational level of local government, refashions the role of the large national organizations, union and employer, that monopolize representation at that level and with that negotiating partner. Material modification, supranational and infranational localization of the interests of the world of labour, and redistribution toward the top or bottom of the political and administrative functions formerly unified in the national state, shake the fourth pillar of labour law as we know it, even if it is by no means clear whether this implies resettling or imminent collapse.

VII UNSTABLE PILLARS AND POSSIBLE SCENARIOS: LABOUR LAW THAT IS
DIFFERENT, BUT STILL LABOUR LAW

Watching the wavering pillars of labour law's identity is truly to ask oneself whether, with the fall of the Berlin Wall, an historic phase has definitely closed, and with it the conditions that pushed labour law from the periphery of liberal codes to the heart of contemporary constitutions. At the end of the day, to the question 'towards what new and different identity is labour law headed', one might respond with the most extreme formula advanced in the debate in Britain: no identity at all, or rather no labour law; the state would step back from any pretense of regulating labour relations, and the contractual autonomy of the parties would be restored.

The diminution of labour legislation to a few isolated regulations (above all, anti-discrimination law, pension funds, the rights of representatives in the workplace, health and safety provision), leaving to the free play of contractual negotiations all that remains (hours, wages, duration of a non-exclusive contract), is precisely the experience of the United States, where, besides the federal legislation, not much else was ever put forward and an organic labour law in the European sense has never existed. However, in Europe, not even the entrepreneurial and liberal political forces seem to cultivate the prospect of a deregulation driven by the labour market and company relations. It seems clearly understood that to eradicate from the collective consciousness of European societies the complex of values and security included in labour law, from which have evolved a political tradition and practice quite different from that of the United States, would be to ask again for political conflicts that are costly and ultimately destructive.

By contrast, the European experience teaches that a system of shared rules, and a public framework for ensuring the socialization of certain risks, are stabilizing elements for the economic system. They work to favour the negotiated control of conflict, normalize the state of agreement, and, when social contracting works, can involve large union organizations in income policies and thus contribute to growth without inflation. Naturally, employers and liberal political forces prefer more flexible rules, less uniformity in salaries, larger margins of discretion in the direction of labour, the elimination of protective legislation that creates barriers to entry into jobs and exit from them. In short, they want a different labour law, perhaps quite different, but, for all that, labour law.

A different labour law, perhaps very different, yet labour law still: towards what new identity?

The response, if any response is possible, depends on quite complex political variables. In this rapid finale of the twentieth century, labour finds itself at the epicentre of seismic events that shake the constitutional order. But it is also held upright by forces that surpass the binary conflict between capital and labour that lay at the origin of the compromise inscribed in the base of the social constitution of the post-war period. These forces spring forth from new conflicts of interest, add other dimensions to collective life, and place into play values formerly outside the sphere of production.

We shall see, at the conclusion of this essay, how one might re-propose today, in new and even more complicated terms, the genetic constitutional problematic of labour law. For now, we need only note some new and unforeseen questions that have placed themselves on its agenda. Some conceptual formulas can assist in fixing the boundaries: a labour law that is no longer identified with the nation-state (as political actor, normative power, or national community) and that therefore realizes a complex 'denationalization'; that no longer has as its exclusive centre of gravity the labour relations of stable, full-time workers, and might, therefore, be defined as 'postoccupational'; and that does not merely look after the material needs of a standardized worker, conceived abstractly as the weaker party to the contract who is subject to risks in the face of the employer's hierarchical organization, but increasingly stresses the worker in flesh and bone, as a person bearing his or her own identity, comprised not only of equality, but also of differences that call for respect, and that for this reason might be termed 'postmaterial'.

VIII DENATIONALIZATION: VALUES, POLITICS, ECONOMY IN SUPRANATIONAL AND INFRANATIONAL LABOUR LAW

The growing importance of centres and institutions of supranational regulation of the market and the economy (World Trade Organization, NAFTA, etc.) creates a new type of value question tied to the 'denationalization' of labour law. The debate over the 'social clauses' to be inserted in the international trade agreements promoted by the WTO, for example, poses in new terms the question at which level one should set minimum conditions of labour protection (questions until now left to the work, meritorious but rather harmless, of the International Labour Organization). On this question there is an open conflict within the WTO between advanced and emerging countries. The latter accuse the advanced countries, with high levels of protection and high costs of living, of using social clauses as a form of indirect protection. Excluding developing countries from reciprocal trade access due to their failure to meet minimal labour standards might be a powerful incentive to their governments. It is also true however that, in a global trading system, to raise all labour costs to the level of the rich countries would be the equivalent, for developing countries, of taking out of competition just their competitive advantage in entering the markets of the rich countries. Imposition of social clauses thus implies protection in favour of the rich. However, this makes it no easier for the consciences of the rich countries to deal with a comparative advantage of poor countries founded on the exploitation of child labour. (To call this a 'comparative advantage of poor countries' is to set aside the fact that, even in the global market, profits have a nationality. Although the elusive organization of the large multinationals makes it difficult to establish, Robert Reich maintains and the Nike example teaches, which nationality it is).

The international public order of labour law in the age of globalization is a site of values in conflict. Globalization, competition, growth, fundamental rights of labour, are the terms of a great question that transcends the boundaries of states, but which at the same time calls on the responsibility of each one in the international community.

The other face of the denationalization of labour law arises from the integration of Italy into the European Union. At the point at which integration becomes normative, it is not so important to measure the influence of Community sources on labour law (the area of labour law under

Community authority is notoriously large, even if incoherent) so much as to reflect on the fact that, here as elsewhere, the sovereignty of the state is now limited by having conferred dominant legislative power to a supranational authority that is devoid of real democratic legitimation (the Council, the Commission, and the Court of Justice), let alone the strict financial limitations deriving from the unified currency system, in turn governed by a technocratic supranational authority (the European Central Bank).

A striking disparity thus appears in the evolution of labour law between politics (which develop at the national level through democratic parliamentary channels, but not at the Community level, where the Parliament is limited to non-deliberative functions) and the economy (which becomes regulated, in crucial respects, by intergovernmental or technocratic institutions at the level of the European Union), constituting the contradiction immanent in the process of European unification. The judgment of the Court of Justice rebuking Italy over its failure to eliminate the public monopoly on job placement, apart from the specific aspects of the event, shows that the presence of a Community judicial system that coexists with domestic law and prevails where they intersect produces effects in labour law that are not linear.[2] Anyone who had imagined that 'harmonization' would consist of a continuous race to the top, or rather towards the best standard among all European labour regulation, would have misrepresented the meaning of a rather more complicated event. Harmonization is 'cohesive' (in Community jargon) when it forces national regulation to adapt itself to the substantive principles of labour protection gathered into Community law (principles that may, or may not, be compatible with the substantive principles of national legislation). Harmonization is functionalist when it protects, not labour, but free competition, and only in an instrumental manner requires national regulation to adapt itself to certain normative parameters in labour matters (and the imposition may be seen both in the *imposition* of a level of labour protection to avoid social dumping, and in the *elimination* of labour protection found to be a protectionist barrier). In either case, the consequences of harmonization on labour law are neither one-sided nor predictable. European Community jurisprudence on equality of treatment between women and men shows that cohesive harmonization can reinforce a principle of protection found in national regulation, but the case of prohibition on night work shows that sources and actors of the Community juridical system can, in pursuing this principle, shed basic principles so as to create enormous dissonance with the references presented in national regulation.[3] As for functionalist harmonization, it is

---

[2] Case C–55/96, *Job Centre Coop. Arl.* [1997] ECR I–7119.
[3] Case C–345/89, *Alfred Stoeckel* [1991] ECR I–4047.

ever more evident that Community legislation over the next few years
will be aimed, not at the risk of social dumping, but rather at overcoming
public and private monopolies, and liberalizing protected markets. The
effect will not be the generalization of minimum protection, but the elimination of labour provisions that limit access to markets.

IX POST-OCCUPATIONAL QUESTIONS AND POSTMATERIAL INTERESTS: A NEW AGENDA

Once one notices that the promise of full employment in stable jobs has
become ever less redeemable, new themes necessarily appear on the
agenda of labour law. One concerns the displacement of the epicentre of
the subject—'employment law', and not the traditional 'labour law', to
signify that it concerns, not particular 'employee relations', but rather the
worker's position in the whole labour market, with its institutions,
dynamics, and limits. Until now, the labour market meant, for its most
thoughtful and learned observers, the complex of relations that precede
hiring or follow dismissal, and thus functioned as a site of public intervention, with the worker in the capacity of 'consumer' of services and
collateral benefits associated with stable employment. But the labour
market, like any market, works if the level of demand (for labour) is
constant, but also if the quality of the supply (of labour) is such as to
attract all the opportunity that the market offers. How to sustain the
supply of professionalism or, to use the term prevalent today, the
'employability' of labour, through professional training and continuing
education, detailed and rapidly changing information, and also through
the construction of new contractual forms, to regulate, not a predetermined labour service, but the employment of the same worker in more
activities and more forms of work over a temporal arc within a negotiated
and shared framework, made for times both of certainty and of change,
will become the crucial question of the next few years.

A second theme, much debated, is summarized in the formula of the
'crisis of subordination', and permits the thought, in light of the tradition
of Italian labour law, that we may be returning to its origins. At the beginning of this century, in the classic *Il contratto di lavoro* by Ludovico Barassi,
both employed labour and the contractual forms of self-employment
formed the object, as yet undivided, of the nascent labour law. Later,
labour law became identified with the typical figure of the employed
worker, and took that reflected image even at the level of its normative
contents, detaching itself entirely from self-employment and its contracts.
Today, this total identification with the stereotype is in decline, and
labour law seems on the way to retracing the path that went from 'labour'

(as an employee) to 'workers' (employed or self-employed), that is to return to the entire gamut of contracts through the mediation of which is realized, in the multiple forms allowed by a productive organization today less rigid than formerly, the integration of predominantly personal labour into the economic activity of others.

The new orientation is confirmed in the divisions and concerns of legal scholarship. In the treatise *CicuMessineo*, today directed by Luigi Mengoni, the commentary to the chapter of the Civil Code regarding self-employment is edited by a young labour law scholar, denoting a new sensitivity and suggesting that, at least in the world of scholarship, an historic separation could be overcome. Self-employment, in addition to summarizing some types of contract that revolve around the contract of work, reappears as a type of the same genre to which the contract for wage employment belongs, the genre of 'labour without adjectives'. This genre could include the diverse contractual modalities of including labour into productive organization, maintaining the distinction among the various contractual schemes and protective statutes, but also drawing out the element common to each: that, independent of the contractual scheme utilized, human labour is integrated as a normal and constant element in the cycle of firm production. The decisions and luck of the employer affect, beyond the occasion of the contract, the destiny and life plan of an individual. Yet the traditional boundaries of the contract of employment are limited to wages. Contract thus does not include all the matters dealt with in labour law or represent an adequate replacement for labour law. In such a case, it may be necessary to apply additional protection to the self-employed—not necessarily the same in all cases, but in each case a minimum common denominator. However, today only employed wage labour can claim such protection, internally ever more differentiated according to obscure and arbitrary criteria, while self-employment is practically devoid of protection except for the right to some compensation. For, when all is said and done, whenever personal labour is a constitutive factor in the activity of others, implying economic dependence and a chosen life condition, then, despite the historic separation that divides the world of labour into sectors based on the type of contract, it is the same political compromise standing at the base of the social constitution that is put in play.

In short, new and unforeseen demands advanced by workers will complicate the basic scheme of labour relations which identifies redistribution as the typical and characteristic interest of the worker, understood as the means of liberating the worker and his family from need.

For example, the theme of health and safety assumes an ever-increasing importance. Beyond the general obligation of protection under Article 2087, of the Civil Code, a new paradigm of the humanization of production through law is arising, partly under the influence of Community law. The objective of improving the workplace environment, to improve the protection of health and safety according to the interpretation of the European Court of Justice (rejecting the opposing British argument), includes all measures that affect the psychological well-being of the worker, and offers a legal basis for partial harmonization of legislation dealing with hours of work. (The European Community directive on hours of work was thus able legitimately to claim a legal basis in Article 118(a) of the Treaty, dealing with the work environment).[4] A vision of the human condition in the production process, not subaltern, is made clear by this particular normative current—a fragile condition, affected by the material environment and ergonomic conditions, stress and effort, light and noise, day and night, rhythms and pauses, and so on—that treats human psycho-physical benefit as an absolute value for labour, opposed to the stern processes of production.

It is necessary, moreover, to consider the new aspect assumed by the problem of work time, seen from the point of view of the interests of working people, and not merely the classic aspiration to work fewer hours for the same wage. New organization of time is under discussion, to overcome rigid synchrony between production time and the time for life. Working people show increasing interest in enjoying more time for care of others, education, and other non-economic activities, particularly during certain stages of life or on the occurrence of particular personal conditions, even if this means a proportional reduction in income, and using for this purpose diverse formulae that combine flexible work and time for living (part-time work, job sharing, sabbaticals, and leaves of absence).

The final post-material interest worth mentioning, beyond the obvious, is the new interest in worker participation as owners of enterprise (really, of anything on which one depends). In this new phenomenon, the contribution of ownership to redistribution is not particularly important, since share ownership inserts into compensation an element of chance, tied to the success of the company. What is more important is the alteration of the classic scheme of subordinate wage labour (which as we know presupposes insulation from risk and alienation from the outcome produced), at the moment in which the employee shareholders, particularly if quantitatively significant, organized in stock ownership trusts, and capable of assembling to vote their shares in common, or even to designate the corporate officers, assume a measure of control and risk in the enterprise.

---

[4] Case C–84/94, *United Kingdom of Great Britain and Northern Ireland* v. *Council of the European Union* [1996] ECR I–5755, upholding Directive 93/104/EEC of 23 Nov. 1993 [1993] OJ L307/18.

In this sense, participation as a shareholder in the firm for which one works implies a post-material interest beyond its economic connotation. Shareholding matters, not merely as a right to profits, but also for the different position that the employee-shareholders will assume in the firm, the possibility of mattering more in company decisions, as a group that contributes to the success of the company, and by using the same social devices that the capitalist partners use in order to participate in decisions, profits, and risks. In the Anglo-Saxon countries the term 'stakeholder' has entered the discussions on the democratization of the economy, meaning that, without necessarily owning shares or assets, one is still involved in the activities of the company, whether one suffers its externalities or shares its fate as a dependant. Worker ownership of shares is a factor in the spread of economic power through the socialization of property in favour of the non-capitalist components of the firm. In this sense, it inserts into labour relations a previously unknown element.

X THE CONSTITUTIONAL PROBLEMATICITY OF LABOUR LAW AT THE END
OF THE CENTURY: FEDERALISM INTERNAL AND EXTERNAL;
INTERGENERATIONAL JUSTICE; IMMIGRATION AND SOCIAL CITIZENSHIP

Behind the new questions on labour law's agenda remains the crucial matter of the continuing force of the ethical-political references that led to its becoming constitutionalized in the post-war period. The contemporary constitutions, more than sets of superordinate values immanent in the legal order, have become instruments of the dynamic composition of conflict between sets of values that are implicit, but must be adapted in practice, if that order wants to maintain coherence and legitimization.

In this sense, the constitutional problematicity of labour law, in the onrushing end of the century, consists in the complication of conflicts of interest and emerging values within its domain, and in the urgent need to adapt equivalent values, deserving of legal protection, that derive from it. This need may be seen at the moment of political decision that generates law, in the moment of judicial decision that applies the law, and in the interpretation that relates the significance of the law for the system. On top of the binary conflict between capital and labour—to which the social constitutions of the post-war period provided a basis for compromise, successively developed through the edifice of the welfare state—are placed ever new conflicts of interests that, as mentioned, add new dimensions to collective life and place into play values that until now lay outside the sphere of production.

Worth mentioning are at least three sites on which the binary conflict between capital and labour is complicated through the interference of other, directly connected, conflicts of interests and values. The first site includes the growing, and frequently noted, disparity among state, market, and community, a site on which one may note a double opposition between interests and values: national/supranational, and national/infranational: large markets open to the competition that increases productivity, but escaping the sovereignty of national states and subject to regulation by technocratic supranational authority; regional or municipal communities that exercise within their areas a certain kind of sovereignty, following centrifugal trajectories, claiming, for example, the principle of subsidiarity against the state. Within the directives and among the respective diverse combinations, conflicts of constitutional ordering emerge that transcend, but also affect directly, the evolution of labour law.

The national/supranational opposition produces what we may call 'external bond syndrome', and a virtual conflict between the social values found in the national constitutions and the concrete modalities of exercising sovereignty, granted by the centres of supranational regulation that takes place in a different constitutional framework, shaped by treaties and agreements. In the experience of the European Union, constitutional courts—at different times, the German federal, Italian, and Spanish— have all claimed, with different arguments but with harmonious results, the power to identify the moments when, in the process of European integration, the fundamental rights of their respective constitutions are at risk. The German court has added the condition that Community powers should prevail before the process of democratization. Yet this reservation of fundamental rights is still at best a warning, an extreme resource of constitutional law. It is not a procedure for combining, at the level of the European Union, multiple sets of values, comprised in a legal system becoming ever more complex, even in the rate of interference between a supranational order and many diverse national systems, each interrelated through its respective constitution. (Not even the European Court of Justice, based on a treaty that is not a federal constitution, can fill this gap.) In the political realm, the danger of a reactionary nationalism emerges from the historic source of organized labour. Increasingly, labour politics and the level of social protection must surmount the 'external bond' that derives from agreements and regional institutions (of which the European Union represents the most advanced form). The strong resistance of labour unions to European integration that has emerged in many countries (not in Italy, due to the conscious decision of the union confederations), the even more significant resistance that has occurred in the United States to the creation of the NAFTA free trade zone between the United States, Mexico, and Canada, are united in an evident fact, but one that destabilizes consolidated institutions that regulate the binary conflict between capital and labour: the evolution of labour law. The resulting levels of protection do not depend on the state and are not influenced by its political processes or within the ambit of its traditional parties, including labour organizations. They depend, in the first place, on competition among states; secondly, on the formation of a functioning global market; thirdly (if one must believe that the multinationals have no homeland), on the decisions and outcome of giant transnationals, with centres of decision at unknown locations; and, finally, to mention a different implication, on the decisions of supranational institutions that regulate regional markets or, in the European case, even the economy and the money supply, and that do not respond democratically to citizens, but speak only with intergovernmental entities.

The national/infranational opposition produces, by contrast, the decomposition of Community references created in the shadow of the nation-state. The national community constitutes the natural frame of reference for the social solidarity set out in European constitutions. The Republic of Italy recognizes labour law and labour protection in all their forms, in Articles 4 and 35 of the Constitution. The Republic here includes the state, other public authorities, and the national community. The decomposition of the national community, the valorization instead of local communities, autonomous regions, *Länder*, municipalities, disarticulates a consciously constructed solidarity, particularly when associated with ethnic diversity, historic regions, or socioeconomic particularism. Traditionally, unions, social security, and collective bargaining have been the responsibility of national communities, even if not everywhere nor in the same manner. Some countries that have long had federal constitutions or strong traditions of local autonomy have already experimented with balancing national community and internal federalism in diverse aspects of social organization and solidarity. For others, particularly Italy, the process of infranational redistribution of power includes an administrative federalism, of which no one can yet predict how much will be regional and how much municipal, how much governmental competition and how much co-operation. This will undoubtedly have consequences for the great solidaristic institutions of the world of labour, beginning with the union and collective bargaining, let alone the social security system.

The second site, even more important, of values and interests in conflict concerns the generations: those fully in working life, those who have left or are leaving, and the younger generation that is preparing, at times with great pain and sacrifice, to enter the world of work. There is no doubt that, in Europe and in Italy in particular, the evolution of labour law is a site of conflict among generations, that is, more precisely, a site at which is posed, in dramatic fashion, a constitutional problem of intergenerational justice (that in essence may be summarized in the apt headline: less to the parents, more to the children). This is evident when the reform of the welfare state is discussed in Italy, given that the Italian pension system is still almost entirely devoted to intergenerational solidarity (in which a demographically preponderant generation, today on the road to its pensions, expects that the active generations, and even those who would like to be but have not yet had the opportunity, both demographically shrinking, will foot the bill for an expensive system of old-age payments). However, it is becoming evident as well in discussions of jobs and how to expand the economic base.

Analysis of the Italian job structure, for example, reveals a paradox without equivalent in other countries: the rate of unemployment for male heads of households between the ages of thirty and fifty is much lower than the European average, while the unemployment rate among those not heads of families and younger than thirty is much greater than the European average. In Italy, unlike the rest of Europe, employment and unemployment do not unite the generations; they divide them. The younger generation disproportionately bears the weight of this dramatic condition. Naturally, the family (where it exists) assures the necessary exchange of income and of support, but normally does so one way, so that the fathers and mothers live in the sphere of production, while children are confined to the sphere of consumption.

The deregulation advocated by many removes this type of generational conflict by creating a different one. The risk that emerges in countries that have severely deregulated the labour market, placing parents and children into competition (the first with more experience, but often overworked or with obsolete skills, the latter less expert but more open to innovation and responsive to incentives), is a shortened working life, in which one enters earlier but also leaves earlier, because one is worn down more quickly (both professionally and in terms of output). Generational replacement is always possible, making appropriate the French saying, 'Papa, I found a job—yours'.

The third and last site of conflict between interests and values that intersects the binary conflict between capital and labour grows out of the phenomenon of immigration and places workers in mutual opposition on the basis of different birth (in so far as this influences citizenship). In the European countries, a growing portion of work, indeed the hardest, most dangerous, and unpleasant portion, devolves on those who are not part of the national community because they are not citizens, perhaps have no interest in becoming citizens, and quite often lack even valid documents for remaining in the country. This too is a theme that links up with a fundamental constitutional question, that of citizenship and its significance in a world in which migratory movement intensifies, society becomes multi-ethnic, and, at the same time, ethnic states rise again, and with them the cruel barriers of differences of birth. The political compromise, on which the social constitution rests, showed labour to be a force for integration into the community, not just for social equality. Article 3 of the Italian Constitution sums this up in the justly celebrated formula of the inclusive value of labour, requiring the Republic to remove obstacles that impede the full participation of labour in the economic, political, and social life of the nation. But the labour thus protected is, according to the Constitution, that of members of the community, citizens, who are the subjects of that Constitution. Under the European Union, citizenship is vast, and as regards labour, Europeans enjoy the same rights, irrespective of different nationality. But what statute of rights and duties gives the title of labour to those who, without being part of the national community, not even the embryonic European homeland, increase the wealth of a country?

Part II

Contested Categories:
Work, Worker, and Employment

3

Women, Work, and Family: A British Revolution?

JOANNE CONAGHAN

I INTRODUCTION

Currently, the UK is in the midst of a huge social and legal experiment, the object of which is to promote a better balance between work and family life. Foremost among those calling for change is the 'New Labour' Government which has self-consciously promulgated and pursued 'family-friendly' working policies since election to its first term of office in 1997. Now in its second term, the government continues to deploy a range of approaches—information, education, exhortation, and legislation—the overall thrust of which is to 'change the culture of relations in and at work . . . to reflect a new relationship between work and family life'.[1]

A cautious concern with helping parents to balance work and family commitments was evident in the Labour Party election manifesto in 1997.[2] By May 1998, with the publication of the White Paper, *Fairness at Work*, providing the legal and rhetorical framework for an extensive programme of labour law reform (most of which has since been implemented), that concern had become much more explicit and, viewed in conjunction with other policy objectives, has since emerged as a central feature of government policy on employment, social security, tax, and the family.[3]

This pursuit of family-friendly working policies is driven by a dual concern to combat poverty and 'social exclusion', on the one hand, and to

---

[1] Tony Blair, Prime Minister, 'Foreword', Department of Trade and Industry (DTI), *Fairness at Work*, Cm 3968 (London: the Stationery Office, 1998).

[2] See especially paras. 83 and 84. In the 2001 election manifesto, family-friendly policies were an integral part of New Labour's strategies to promote employment, combat child poverty, and modernize the welfare state. See *Ambitions for Britain: Labour's Manifesto 2001*, especially chs. 1 and 3, available from the Labour Party website (www.labour.org.uk).

[3] See, in particular, *Fairness at Work*, above, n. 1, ch. 5; Home Office, *Supporting Families: A Consultative Document* (London: the Stationery Office, 1998); Department of Social Security (DSS) Green Paper, *New Ambitions for Our Country: A New Contract for Welfare*, Cm 3805 (London: the Stationery Office, 1998); DTI Green Paper, *Work and Parents: Competitiveness and Choice*, Cm 5005 (London: the Stationery Office, 2000), hereinafter cited as 'Work and Parents'.

enhance productivity and economic competitiveness, on the other.[4] In this context, access to and participation in paid work are viewed as crucial, not only because they reduce unemployment and, correspondingly, state dependency and expenditure, but also because they provide business with the skilled but flexible human resources it needs to compete in a global economy. As commodity markets become increasingly unstable and subject to the risks and consequences of capital flight and plant relocation, and as production processes and techniques race to keep pace ˒ with technological change, the old post-war social settlement, with its full-time, lifetime male employment, family wage, comprehensive welfare system, and a gendered allocation of labour, is no longer viable. Changing labour market demographics and more flexible employment practices have compelled its demise, thrusting British workers and their families into an uncertain future where inequality and poverty beckon those who fail successfully to negotiate the risks associated with the 'New Economy'.

Family-friendly working policies are a large part of New Labour's solution to the social exigencies of rapid economic, technological, and social change. They form part of a strategy of eliminating, as far as possible, obstacles to labour market participation so that everyone has an *opportunity* to flourish and secure economic *independence*. As no one able to work is to be excluded from this *community*[5] of citizen-earners, the workplace must adapt to the needs of parents and other carers, bringing economic advantages, it is argued, not just to workers and the state purse but also to employers, who can then enjoy the benefits of a wider, more skilled, and more flexible pool of workers with lifestyles and employment expectations that better correspond with the modern working environment. Productivity will be improved; investment in training and the development of skills will not be wasted; demand for goods will increase. Family-friendly policies, it seems, are good for everyone.[6]

---

[4] See the documents cited above, n. 3, especially the DSS Green Paper.

[5] On the influence of Communitarian ideas on New Labour policy see, e.g., Smith, J., 'The Ideology of "Family and Community": New Labour Abandons the Welfare State' in Panitch, L. (ed.), *Socialist Register 1997: Ruthless Criticism of all that Exists* (London: Merlin Press, 1997) 176; Driver, S., and Martell, L., 'New Labour's Communitarianisms' (1997) 17 *Critical Social Policy* 27.

[6] For a clear statement of the perceived business advantages of family-friendly policies see the Department of Education and Employment (DfEE), discussion document, *WorkLife Balance: Changing Pattern in a Changing World* (London: DfEE, Mar. 2000), ch. 2.

II THE FAMILY-FRIENDLY WORKPLACE AS A PROGRESSIVE LABOUR LAW
STRATEGY

The UK government's efforts to ease the difficulties workers face in seeking to balance work and family obligations are worthy of close attention
by labour lawyers for a number of reasons. Most obviously, of course,
they raise the question of gender (in)equality in the workplace, as well as
in society at large. On the one hand, strategies to accommodate work and
family life seem to fit squarely within an equal opportunities agenda
aimed at eliminating obstacles to women's participation in paid work.
On the other hand, it cannot be *assumed* that such strategies will necessarily operate to women's benefit. They may conceivably harm women's
employment prospects by fostering a reluctance to hire women because
of the perceived costs;[7] they may increase the 'double burden' of paid
and unpaid work which many women carry, particularly if they fail
significantly to affect the gender division of labour in the home.
Moreover, some women—and some families—may benefit from family-
friendly policies more than others, depending on the extent to which
such policies are sensitive to the broader factors—ethnic, social, and
cultural—affecting women's employment participation.[8] In any case,
experience elsewhere (most notably in the former planned economies of
Eastern Europe as well as, to a lesser extent, the Nordic countries) does
not bear out the assumption that women's participation in paid work
necessarily guarantees their social, economic, or political equality.[9] The
gender equality implications, therefore, of a family-friendly political
stance are by no means clear-cut.

New Labour's family-friendly strategy is also of interest because it
troubles the boundary between work and family as traditionally understood, revealing it to be contingent and unstable. In so doing, it makes
possible a new and better understanding of labour law, one which
acknowledges that workplace and family concerns are inextricably linked
rather than distinct and only occasionally overlapping. Indeed, the whole
notion of *family-friendly* working policies challenges a conception of the

---

[7] See Reeves, R., *Mothers Versus Men: Why Women Lose at Work* (London: Industrial
Society, 2000).

[8] On the potentially uneven impact of family-friendly policies see Conaghan, J., 'The
Family-Friendly Workplace in Labour Law Discourse: Some Reflections on *London
Underground Ltd* v. *Edwards*' in Collins, H., Davies, P., and Rideout, R. (eds.), *Legal Regulation
of the Employment Relation* (The Hague: Kluwer International, 2000) 161, 174.

[9] On women in Eastern Europe see, e.g., Einhorn, B., *Cinderella Goes to Market: Gender and
Women's Movements in East Central Europe* (London: Verso, 1993). On the persistence of
unequal pay, sexually segregated labour markets, and gendered care responsibilities in the
Nordic countries see Kalliomaa-Puha, L. (ed.), *Perspectives of Equality—Work, Women and
Family in the Nordic Countries and in the EU* (Copenhagen: Nordic Council of Ministers, 2000).

workplace as a discrete and bounded sphere of social and economic activity in which its participants are fully and exclusively engaged—a typical, if not fundamental, feature of labour law discourse.

Such perceptions no doubt derive from a social division of labour in which men occupied the 'productive' sphere of paid work while women assumed primary responsibility for 'reproductive' work in the family and local community. Unsurprisingly, as women engaged in unpaid caring work have entered the labour market in ever increasing numbers,[10] it has become more difficult for employers to assume that workers have no family responsibilities beyond providing financial support. In so far as the demands of the market and/or the policies of legislators *require* such workers to be economically active, the workplace must yield to some extent to their concerns. But it would be wrong to conclude from this that the family has only recently impinged on workplace organization and practice. Indeed, what a focus on family-friendly working policies underlines is the *dependence* of workplace organization to date on the traditional family form and the extent to which workplace practices are formed and informed by particular assumptions about the allocation of labour in the productive and reproductive spheres. It also raises questions about how we determine what *counts* as work and how the costs and benefits of work should be distributed. Once the interdependence of work and family responsibilities is acknowledged, it becomes harder to attribute value only to paid work. Thus, the pursuit of family-friendly working policies goes beyond the problematization of traditional labour law assumptions about the boundaries of 'work' and 'workplace'. It compels the integration of unpaid care work into economic, political, and legal discourse.[11]

A final reason for focusing on this state-driven renegotiation of the work–family boundary is that it raises directly the question how far the nation-state *can* engage in progressive social change in a globalized economy. It is has been widely argued that as regional economies become subordinated to the demands and fluctuations of global markets, the political role of the nation-state is diminished, and the possibilities for bringing about radical social reform at the national level reduced, if not eliminated.[12] This has led many progressive labour lawyers towards international strategies. In this context, the radical path New Labour has adopted in relation to work–family issues appears to challenge popular

---

[10] The biggest rise in UK women's employment participation in recent years has been amongst women with pre-school children. See generally *Work and Parents*, above, n. 3, ch. 2.

[11] See further Conaghan, above, n. 8, 168–71, and Rittich and Williams, in this volume.

[12] See Arthurs, H., 'Labour Law Without the State' (1996) 46 *University of Toronto L. Journal* (1996) 46, 1. For a sceptical approach to arguments about the reduced capacity of the nation-state see Davis and Raday, in this volume.

perceptions of the 'enfeebled nation-state'.[13] As part of a package of progressive political reforms marketed by politicians and commentators alike as the 'Third Way',[14] family-friendly policies exemplify an attempt to carve out a space for normative political discourse in a globalized economic context through a careful marriage of economic necessity and social need. They thus represent an attractive antidote to the dominant neo-liberal paradigm of the deregulated market, and suggest that a humane and socially democratic capitalism is within reach.[15]

Of course, such a perspective assumes that family-friendly policies are politically progressive or, more specifically, that the progressive dimensions of a family-friendly stance—promoting equal opportunities, and combating poverty and social exclusion by easing the path to work—retain some purchase when harnessed to economic requirements such as competitiveness and enhanced productivity. Certainly, the New Labour government sees these social and economic goals as compatible, indeed, complementary, and there is no doubt that a political strategy which integrates social and economic aspirations has widespread appeal within left and feminist political discourse. As leading feminist academic, Sylvia Walby, enthuses, 'One of the advantages of the new gender settlement is that improving justice for women can go hand in hand with increasing economic efficiency, instead of there being a trade-off between the two'.[16]

But, equally, there are those who question whether aspects, at least, of New Labour's family-friendly strategy can properly be described as progressive. Anne Barlow and Simon Duncan express concern about the extent to which single mothers may be compelled by government policies to take up paid work, against their own moral judgments about their children's welfare.[17] More generally, commentators have observed that UK government policies place parents in an invidious position, by binding them to the duties to be good citizen-earners *and* good parents in circumstances where the balance of economic and social rewards falls on the former rather than the latter.[18]

This suggests that the government has not yet got its incentives right, perhaps because, as Barlow and Duncan contend, it erroneously assumes that parents make choices about their moral economies based on

---

[13] Arthurs, above, n. 12, 45.

[14] On the 'third way' in labour law, see Collins, in this volume.

[15] On the possibility of a 'humane capitalism', see Ireland, in this volume.

[16] Walby, S., 'Introduction' to Walby, S. (ed.), *New Agendas for Women* (London: MacMillan, 1999) 1, 3. On the confluence of social and economic aspirations see also Langille, in this volume.

[17] Barlow, A., and Duncan, S., 'Supporting Families? New Labour's Communitarianism and the "Rationality" Mistake, Part 1' (2000) 22 *Journal of Social Welfare and Family Law* 23.

[18] See, e.g., Morris, L., 'Work, Gender and Unemployment: a Household Perspective' in Walby, above, n. 16, 32, 42–3.

economic self-interest.[19] But it also hints at the kinds of difficulties which may accompany any large-scale social engineering—from the preliminary adoption of false assumptions to the production of ineffective prescriptions and policy contradictions—resulting in unanticipated and often subversive consequences and illiberal political constraints on individual action (not to mention a distasteful degree of moralism and self-righteousness, perched uneasily amidst the progressive aspirations from which it originated).[20]

Can New Labour avoid these political risks in its pursuit of family-friendly policies? Can it negotiate the many difficulties which accompany the pursuit of national level social reform in the context of global level economic constraints? And where, in all of this, do women's interests lie?

III NEW LABOUR'S FAMILY-FRIENDLY WORKING POLICIES

Since the beginning of its first term of office in 1997, New Labour has introduced a range of new employment rights, made significant adjustments to tax and social security provision, and deployed a series of voluntary/exhortatory strategies to foster more family-friendly working attitudes in both employers and workers. For example, it has commissioned research and disseminated information about working parents' needs and experiences.[21] It has used policy documents, press releases, and political speeches to educate employers on the advantages of family-friendly employment, exhorting them to adopt working practices beyond the statutory minima.[22] In March 2000, it launched a nationwide campaign to promote family-friendly employment, including a £1.5 million Challenge Fund to help employers 'explore how work-life balance policies can help them deliver goods and services more efficiently and flexibly'.[23]

The government has also adopted a radically new approach to the provision of childcare, reconceiving it as a public policy issue requiring a nationally co-ordinated strategy[24] and enhancing both public and private

---

[19] Barlow and Duncan, above, n. 17, 25.

[20] On moralism in New Labour's Communitarian strategies, see ibid.; and Smith, and Driver and Martell, above, n. 5.

[21] See especially the work of the Women's Unit (www.womens-unit.gov.uk), and the National Family and Parenting Institute (www.nfpi.org), both New Labour creations.

[22] See, e.g., *Supporting Families* (above, n. 3), paras. 24–28 and *WorkLife Balance* (above, n. 6), ch. 2 .

[23] For details, see www.dti.gov.uk/work-lifebalance.

[24] DfEE, *Meeting the Challenge of Child-care: A Framework and Consultation Document* (London: DfEE, May 1998). On the legacy of inattention to childcare provision in the UK before 1997 see Fredman, S., *Women and the Law* (Oxford: Clarendon, 1997) 209–17. Further details on the National Childcare Strategy are available at www.dfes.gov.uk/childcare.

provision, with the promise, *inter alia*, of free nursery care for all three-year-olds by 2004. Indeed, the National Childcare Strategy, comprised, as it is, of a broad variety of measures which cross-cut government departments (tax, education, employment, trade and industry) and involve the deployment of both legal and non-legal mechanisms, demonstrates the extent to which a family-friendly stance has permeated government policy. It evidences a sense of coherence and creative experimentation, a willingness to try new approaches, and work in concert to achieve the desired goal(s). Indeed, taken together with the widespread legislative developments considered below, it has all the appearance of a radical programme.

However, it is important to put things in context. In particular, it must be recognized that, in comparison to most other EU countries at any rate, Britain starts from a very low baseline—a working environment that is historically far from family-friendly. The British workplace is still characterized by long hours,[25] poor maternity provision,[26] and highly gendered patterns of employment in which low pay and sex discrimination persist[27] and 'flexible' working arrangements are more associated with job insecurity, labour market polarization, and exploitation than a better balance between work and family life.[28] Public childcare provision in the UK, while improving, remains inadequate, and is reflected in the low labour market participation of UK lone parents compared with other countries.[29] Unsurprisingly, a recent survey of British parents revealed a perception of Britain as one of the least family-friendly countries in Europe.[30]

New Labour's radical programme must also be set against the backdrop of Britain's EU obligations; much of the recent employment legislation addressing work/family issues has been compelled by European directives.[31] While the strong EU commitment to the reconciliation of

[25] For details and inter-European comparisons see TUC, *Work Smarter: An End to Burnout Britain* (London: TUC, 2000).

[26] A 1998 European Commission memorandum placed Britain at the bottom in terms of the number of weeks during which maternity leave is paid. See further McColgan, A., 'Family-Friendly Frolics? The Maternity and Parental Leave etc Regulations 1999' (2000) 29 *ILJ* 125, 143.

[27] On pay, see Rake, K. (ed.), *Women's Incomes over the Lifetime: Explaining the Female Forfeit* (London: Women's Unit, 2000). On discrimination against women with family responsibilities see EOC, *Work/Life Balance Tipped Against British Workers* (Manchester: EOC, 2000).

[28] See generally Purcell, K., Hogarth, T., and Simm, C., *Whose Flexibility? The Costs and Benefits of Non-standard Working Arrangements and Contractual Relations* (York: York Publishing Services, Joseph Rowntree Foundation, 1999).

[29] For comparisons see *Work and Parents*, above, n. 3, para. 2.6.

[30] *Is Britain Family-friendly? The Parents' Eye View* (London: National Family and Parents Institute, 2000).

[31] Specifically the Working Time Directive 93/104 [1993] OJ L307/18, the Parental Leave Directive 96/34 [1996] OJ L145/4, and the Part-Time Work Directive 97/81 [1998] OJ L14/9.

work and family life[32] provides a highly propitious political and legal environment in which to pursue a family-friendly agenda, in most cases, the UK government has introduced only the minimum level of provision required by European law, even where it is apparent that this is less than adequate to achieve the stated objectives.[33] This raises reasonable questions about the depth of New Labour's commitment. Nevertheless, as current developments in labour, tax, and social security law clearly demonstrate, it cannot be denied that things are happening.

Strengthening employment rights

Since its accession in 1997, New Labour has conferred a host of new employment rights with a 'family-friendly' dimension in a reform process which remains ongoing.[34] The legislative focus here comprises both measures aimed at working parents (and, to a limited extent, other carers) as a specific group, and family-friendly initiatives which apply to workers generally. The primary objective has been *to change workplace practices* in order to facilitate the successful combination of work and parenting: 'We need to achieve a society where being a good parent and a good employee are not in conflict'.[35]

To this end, the government has focused in particular on the improvement of maternity rights: the basic maternity leave period has been extended from fourteen to eighteen weeks with plans for further extension under review;[36] and the scope and amount of income replacement

On the pending implementation of Directive 99/70 on Fixed-Term Work [1999] OJ L175/43, see DTI Consultation Paper on Fixed-Term Work Proposals (London: DTI, Mar. 2001) and the Draft Fixed-Term Employees (Prevention of Less Favourable Treatment) Regulations (available at www.dti.gov.uk/er). The Pregnant Workers Directive 92/85 [1992] OJ L348/1, laying down minimum requirements for maternity provision, was implemented by an earlier Conservative administration in the mid-1990s.

[32] An EU concern with work–family issues predates the UK government's current stance and is evident, e.g., in the 1989 Social Charter. EU policy now comprises three strands: (i) protecting pregnant workers; (ii) parental rights (e.g., parental leave); and (iii) post-leave policies, e.g., enhancing part-time and fixed-term work and promoting childcare arrangements (see Council Recommendation on Childcare 92/241 [1992] OJ L123/16). See generally Barnard, C., *EC Employment Law* (2nd edn.) (Oxford: OUP, 2000) 266–80; Caracciolo di Torella, E., 'A Critical Assessment of the EC Legislation Aimed at Reconciling Work and Family Life: Lessons from the Scandinavian model?' in Collins *et al.*, above, n. 8, 441.

[33] See, e.g., Aileen McColgan's trenchant criticisms of the government's implementation of the Part-Time Workers' Directive in 'Missing the Point? The Part-Time Workers (Prevention of Less Favourable Treatment) Regulations 2000' (2000) 29 *ILJ* 260, as well as widespread criticism of the failure to provide a right to *paid* parental leave (discussed below).

[34] The precise state of legislative play (with accompanying documents) can be ascertained from the DTI website (www.dti.gov.uk/er/review.htm).

[35] Stephen Byers, Secretary of State for Trade and Industry during the 1997–2001 Labour administration, 'Foreword', *Work and Parents*, above, n. 3.

[36] The reforms to date are effected by the Employment Relations Act 1999 (ERelA) and the

during leave marginally increased.[37] As it is automatically unfair to dismiss on grounds of pregnancy or childbirth, pregnant employees have also benefited from the increase—from £12,000 to £50,000—in the maximum compensatory award for unfair dismissal,[38] while legislators have endeavoured to iron out the doctrinal difficulties women encounter in establishing dismissal after a (failure to) return from additional maternity leave.[39]

Further family-friendly measures include the introduction of new rights to leave and time off for parents and (to a lesser extent) other carers.[40] Working parents can each take up to thirteen weeks' leave during the first five years of a child's life, subject to restrictions and qualifying conditions: the provisions cover only employees; they must have one year's continuous service; and leave can only be taken in blocks—a minimum of one week and no more than four weeks in any given year. In addition, employers can postpone parental leave for up to six months (except in the period immediately after the birth or adoption of a child). Most significantly, leave is unpaid (subject, of course, to any contractual arrangements).

Maternity and Parental Leave etc Regulations 1999, SI 1999/3312 (MPL Regs.), amending the Employment Rights Act 1996 (ERA), Part VIII. All pregnant employees are entitled to ordinary maternity leave (OML) regardless of length of service. Longer serving employees are entitled to additional maternity leave (AML) of up to 29 weeks after the baby is born subject to one year's continuous service (formerly, two). The reforms have also sought to streamline the relationship between OML and AML and simplify the notice requirements, which were notoriously complex and confusing. For an overview and critique of the main changes to date see McColgan, above, n. 26. On proposed further changes, including the extension of OML and AML to provide a year's leave in total, see DTI Consultation Paper, *A Framework for Maternity Pay and Leave* (London: DTI, May 2001).

[37] Most pregnant employees are entitled either to Statutory Maternity Pay (SMP) from their employer or Maternity Allowance (MA) from the state, but qualifying conditions apply. To qualify for SMP—paid at 90% of a woman's weekly earnings for 6 weeks, followed by a flat-rate weekly amount (currently £60.20) for 12 weeks thereafter—the applicant must be an employee with 26 weeks' continuous employment and minimum weekly earnings of (around) £67. To qualify for MA, the main obstacle is a minimum earnings threshold which Labour has reduced from around £60 to £30 a week, thus increasing the number of low-paid workers entitled to some income replacement. See generally the Social Security Contributions and Benefits Act 1992, Part XII, and the Statutory Maternity Pay (General) Regulations 1986, S.I. 1986/1960, as amended. The government has since announced plans to increase the flat-rate of SMP to £100 by 2003 (see further DTI Consultation Paper, above, n. 36).

[38] ERelA 1999, s. 34(4). In practice, many pregnant claimants avoided the low compensation ceiling by bringing a simultaneous claim under the Sex Discrimination Act 1975, where no financial limit applies.

[39] As illustrated in the House of Lords judgment in *Halfpenny* v. *Ige Medical Systems Ltd.* 14 Dec. 2000.

[40] The Parental Leave Directive, above n. 31, was the legislative outcome of the EU 'social dialogue' procedures involving the direct participation of the 'social partners'—management and labour—in lawmaking. Thus, many of the detailed arrangements operate by way of default in the event that employers and workers do not agree their own scheme in a collective or workforce agreement. See MPL Regs, 1999, scheds. 1 and 2.

Employees may also take reasonable (unpaid) time off to deal with family emergencies, for example, bereavement, injury, or illness, or the unanticipated care needs of a 'dependant'.[41] Both the rights to parental leave and time off for dependants are protected by a supplementary right not to be dismissed or subject to any detriment for family reasons.[42]

Viewed internationally, Britain's current arrangements for working parents are far from poor. However, they still remain well below the EU average. Unsurprisingly, therefore, they have attracted criticism from those who think the government can and should do more. A chief focus of attack has been the failure to provide any paid element to parental leave which the TUC (and others) argue prevents most parents from taking up the entitlement.[43] The TUC has also criticized the provisions for their inflexibility—in particular, because parents cannot use them to reduce their working week or day.[44] A further feature of the provisions, limiting their application to children *born* after 19 December 1999—when the EU directive came into force—attracted such critical comment (as well as a TUC legal challenge) that the government has now agreed to extend parental leave to the parents of all children *under five* on 19 December 1999.[45]

The maternity provisions, too, have come under fire for their continued restriction to employees[46] and the general inadequacy of maternity pay.[47] There has also been disquiet about the continuation of the 'automatic trigger' whereby a woman taking time off for any reason in the six weeks before her expected due date is deemed to have commenced her

---

[41] ERA 1996 (as amended), s. 57A. The definition of 'dependant' is not unduly restrictive and would include, for example, a gay cohabiting partner (s. 57A(3)).

[42] Where 'family reasons' are defined in line with the primary rights conferred on parents and carers—ERA 1996, s. 99 (as amended) and MPL Regs., regs. 19 & 20.

[43] Critics here have included the TUC, politicians, academic commentators, a House of Commons Select Committee, the EOC, the Low Pay Unit, Maternity Alliance, and the National Society for the Prevention of Cruelty to Children. As McColgan observes, citing the government's own statistics, 'the firm evidence is that uptake of leave turns on whether it is paid or not', above, n. 26, 139. The government has since responded (Apr. 2001) by proposing the introduction in 2003 of a two-week period of paid *paternity* leave mirroring the current SMP arrangements. However, parental leave in general will remain unpaid.

[44] See, generally, TUC, *Response to the DTI Consultation on Paternity and Maternity Leave and the Draft Maternity and Parental Leave Regulations* (Oct. 1999), available from the TUC website (www.tuc.org.uk).

[45] On the TUC legal challenge, see *R v. Secretary of State for Trade and Industry ex parte TUC* [2000] IRLR 565, where the question of compliance was referred to the ECJ. The government capitulated in a press release on 25 Apr. 2001.

[46] TUC, above, n. 44.

[47] The EOC, e.g., criticizes the absence of maternity pay for most of the additional leave period: *New Maternity Rights* (London: EOC, 2000). To the government's credit, it has met criticisms here with plans significantly to enhance maternity leave and pay: see DTI Consultation Paper, above, n. 36.

maternity leave.[48] A number of these concerns have since been considered in the DTI Green Paper, *Work and Parents*, and the *Framework for Maternity Pay and Leave*, and it is clear that the government intends to address at least some of the criticisms with further legislative reform.

Apart from the introduction and/or strengthening of the rights of working parents *per se*, there have also been a number of more general employment enactments, including national minimum wage provision, new regulations on working time, and enhanced protection for part-time workers, all of which are characterized as family-friendly initiatives.[49]

The National Minimum Wage Act 1998 (NMWA) introduced, for the first time in the UK, a national minimum wage entitlement. The right, which applies to 'workers',[50] not just employees, was viewed from the outset as a strategy, *inter alia*, to enhance women's employment opportunities and reduce the gender pay gap, and there is evidence that, in this respect, it is having some effect.[51] The Working Time Regulations 1998[52] impose restrictions on working time, including the establishment of a basic forty-eight hour week, limitations on night work, new rights to daily and weekly rest, and paid annual leave.[53] Among the stated goals of the regulations are 'tackl[ing] excessively long hours' and 'ensur[ing] that all parents are better able to balance work and family life'.[54]

In similar vein, the Part-Time Workers (Prevention of Less Favourable Treatment) Regulations[55] promise to deliver 'better quality part-time jobs and more choice, which will help parents, women and men, to combine work with family life'.[56] In fact, through the creative application of

---

[48] TUC, above, n. 44 and McColgan, above, n. 26, 131. The 'trigger' operates even if a day is taken off due to some minor viral infection, reducing the length of leave *after* childbirth. The government is now proposing to reduce it to 4 weeks (DTI Consultation Paper, above, n, 36).

[49] See *Fairness at Work*, above, n. 1, para. 5.5.

[50] A 'worker' is 'an individual who has entered into or works under . . . (a) a contract of employment; or (b) any other contract . . . whereby the individual undertakes to do or perform personally any work or services for another party to the contract whose status is not by virtue of the contract that of a client or customer of any profession or business undertaking carried on by the individual . . .': NMWA 1998, s. 54(3). Additional provisions (ss. 34–35) ensure the inclusion of homeworkers and agency workers.

[51] According to the 3rd Report of the Low Pay Commission, *The National Minimum Wage: Making a Difference* (London: British Government Publications Collection, 2001), 70% of the beneficiaries of the NMWA have been women and two-thirds are part-time workers. See also *Work and Parents*, above, n. 3, para. 2.9.

[52] SI 1998/1833, enacted in compliance with EC Council Directive 93/104 [1993] OJ L307/18, the legality of which was unsuccessfully challenged by a then Conservative UK government: Case C–84/94, *United Kingdom* v. *EU Council* [1997] ICR 443.

[53] For a critical overview see Barnard, C., 'The Working Time Regulations 1998' (1999) 28 *ILJ* 61.

[54] *Fairness at Work*, above, n. 1, para. 5.5.

[55] SI 2000/1551, implementing EC Council Directive 97/81 [1998] OJ L14/9.

[56] *Fairness at Work*, above, n. 1, para. 5.5.

European sex equality law, part-time workers had already made some legal gains, successfully challenging, for example, the legislative restrictions on part-time workers' access to employment protection.[57] Part-time workers also invoked European and UK law to challenge practices which adversely affected their pay,[58] access to benefits,[59] and even access to part-time work itself.[60] However, such protection was haphazard and highly dependent upon statistical showings of gendered disparate impact, which, in turn, gave rise to complexity and inconsistent outcomes.[61] The new regulations purport to eliminate such difficulties by prohibiting employers from treating part-time workers less favourably than 'comparable full-time workers' (regulatory 5(1)). There is no need to show (indirect) sex discrimination. However, the provisions remain subject to a justification requirement—employers can avoid liability if they can show that less favourable treatment is 'justified on objective grounds' (regulation 5(2)(b)).

While there can be no doubt that these developments offer British workers greater protection than could ever have been envisaged in the earlier Conservative era, they have, nevertheless, been subject to a barrage of criticism. Leaving aside proponents of deregulation who view the whole New Labour employment programme as an attempt to burden employers with a mountain of 'red tape',[62] many who are supportive of enhanced protection do not consider the government's current enactments to have gone anything like far enough. The Part-time Workers Regulations, in particular, have been widely condemned because they are drafted so narrowly and represent such an ungenerous interpretation of the EU directive upon which they are based, excluding around 90 per cent of existing part-time workers from the scope of protection.[63] The provisions have also been criticized for failing to confer any right of *access* to part-time work, viewed by

---

[57] In *R* v. *Secretary of State for Employment ex parte the EOC* [1994] ICR 317, the House of Lords held that the statutory 16 hours a week threshold to unfair dismissal and redundancy pay protection indirectly discriminated against women, contrary to European law. The part-time bar was formally removed by the Employment Protection (Part Time Employees) Regulations 1995, SI 1995/31.

[58] Case 96/80, *Jenkins* v. *Kingsgate* [1981] ECR 911, [1981] IRLR 228.

[59] Case 170/84, *Bilka-Kaufhaus* v. *Weber von Hartz* [1986] ECR 1607, [1986] IRLR 317.

[60] *Home Office* v. *Homes* [1984] IRLR 299 and, generally, Conaghan, above, n. 8.

[61] See, e.g., *Pearse* v. *Bradford Metropolitan Council* [1988] IRLR 379; *Barry* v. *Midland Bank plc* [1999] IRLR 581.

[62] See, e.g., the British Chamber of Commerce's 'Burdens Barometer' which 'costs' the government's employment provisions in terms of the burdens imposed on business, available at the BCC website (www.britishchambers.org.uk).

[63] McColgan, above, n. 33, 263, citing the results of the government's own Regulatory Impact Assessment. The main difficulty seems to be the requirement of an *actual* full-time comparator (reg. 2(4)), given the segregated nature of part-time work. An earlier proposal to confine the regulations to employees was abandoned in favour of the broader concept of 'worker' after consultation.

many as fundamental to the success of a family-friendly strategy.[64] In fact, the government has dithered over whether or not to introduce a right of access to reduced working hours arguably because of the strength of business opposition to the idea.[65] Although the EU Part-Time Workers Directive does not directly require the introduction of such a right, it does charge Member States to 'identify and review obstacles of a legal or administrative nature which may eliminate the opportunities for part-time work and, where appropriate, eliminate them' (clause 5(1)(a)), and employers to, 'as far as possible . . . give consideration to' requests by workers to transfer from full-time to part-time work (clause 5(3)). Despite this strong exhortation, however, as well as extensive discussion in *Work and Parents* of ways in which a right to reduced hours might be implemented,[66] the government has still not committed itself and the signs are that, if a right to reduced hours *is* introduced, it is likely to be narrower in some ways than the contingent right of access to family-friendly working hours which has emerged from the strategic deployment of disparate impact arguments under the Sex Discrimination Act 1975.[67]

The national minimum wage and working time provisions have also been criticized by organizations friendly to workers' interests. The NMW was initially set considerably below the level recommended by the TUC (£4.94 an hour, based on half male median earnings) and debate has been intense about whether or not it is sufficient at current levels (£3.70 an hour) to make substantial inroads into the problem of low pay.[68] This is

---

[64] See, e.g., the report in *The Guardian*, 8 Dec. 2000, 1, stating that the (then) employment minister, Margaret Hodge, and women's ministers, Tessa Jowell and Baroness Jay, were allegedly pressing hard for a 'reduced hours plan' in the course of the DTI review.

[65] Hence the conflicting media reports, e.g., 'Mothers May Get Part-time Working Rights', *The Guardian*, 23 Mar. 2000; and 'Mum's Right to Cut Job Hours Axed', *The Guardian*, 15 Oct. 2000. See the lengthy discussion of ways to implement a right of access in *Work and Parents*, above n. 3, paras. 4.15–4.25.   [66] Above, n. 3, paras. 4.13–4.25, 6.28–6.40.

[67] See above, n. 60. A significant difficulty with the current disparate impact approach is that it is not easily invoked by men because they cannot show they are statistically disadvantaged by a full-time work requirement. An independent right to reduced hours would clearly solve this problem. On the other hand, *Work and Parents* suggests various restrictions on such a right, including exemptions for small businesses (paras. 6.38–6.40), and a time limit on exercise, possibly until a child is 5 (para. 4.24) or, more narrowly, during the maternity leave period only (para. 4.16). None of these restrictions applies to arguments based on disparate impact. The government has recently announced its intention to introduce a right to *request* flexible working hours (Nov. 2001).

[68] The government-created Low Pay Commission has so far given the NMW a fairly clean bill of health in terms both of implementation and enforcement but has recommended a significant increase in the level of payment to £4.10 in Oct. 2001, and £4.20 in Oct. 2002, proposals which the government has accepted (see above, n. 51 and government press release of 5 Mar. 2001). However, the campaign group, The Low Pay Unit, continues to criticize the level of payment, arguing that, while undoubtedly having some impact, it will do nothing in the long term to address low pay and the social problems accompanying it. See Low Pay Unit, 'Minimum Wage Campaign: The Case for a Higher Minimum Wage' and LPU press release of 6 Mar. 2001 (www.lowpayunit.org.uk).

crucial because the prevalence of low pay tends either to price many workers with family responsibilities out of the labour market (because they
cannot cover the costs of childcare) or encourage them to work excessive
hours (to make a living wage). The minimum wage and working time provisions must, therefore, be viewed together: restrictions on working time are
unlikely to benefit families who, as a result of low pay, are financially dependent on long working hours. Unsurprisingly, perhaps, figures produced
since the introduction of working time restrictions suggest that British workers are working longer hours than ever,[69] evidencing the continued widespread dependence of UK workers and employers on long hours and the
ineffectiveness of the provisions supposed to curb that dependence.
Particularly controversial is the individual opt-out from the forty-eight hour
week, which many argue makes a nonsense of any legislative attempt to
combat the long hours culture.[70] In this context, the government's attempt
to placate the business lobby by making it easier for employers and employees to 'agree' an opt-out (by removing specific record-keeping obligations)
seems to belie their stated commitment to tackling the problem.[71] More
generally, the Working Time Regulations, with their wide range of derogations and limited enforcement provisions, seem insufficiently robust to
impact significantly on working life, apart, perhaps, from extending annual
paid leave to workers formerly lacking such an entitlement.

Restructuring tax and social security provision

While the introduction of new and improved employment rights is
primarily concerned with *facilitating* parental participation in paid work
by changing workplace practices, tax and social security reform reveals
an additional concern to *encourage* such participation. The object is to
create conditions in which it is reasonable to expect virtually all adults to
engage in labour market activity. This involves a radical restructuring of
the traditional relationship between work and family, in which the
economic participation of one parent presupposes the limited or non-
participation of the other. It is this 'housewife' model of employment,
upon which tax and social security policy in the UK has long been based,
that New Labour seeks to displace.

---

[69] Institute for Employment Research, University of Warwick, *Work-Life Balance 2000
Survey* (London: DfEE, Nov. 2000).

[70] Britain is the only EU country to take advantage of the individual opt-out in the
Working Time Directive, due to be reviewed in 2003: see Collins, this volume. For criticism
see TUC report, above, n. 25. For a more positive assessment of the opt-out and the WTR
provisions based on the need to enhance competitiveness see Collins, in this volume.

[71] See Barnard, C., 'The Working Time Regulations 1999' (2000) 29 *ILJ* 167 for a discussion
of these changes.

This is apparent in the combination of 'carrots and sticks'—incentives and disincentives—which recent changes reflect. The idea is to reward parents who participate in paid work with favourable tax and social security benefits (as well as the benefits of improved employment rights) while discouraging parents from choosing not to work by minimizing social security provision. This is a difficult path for the government to negotiate as, on the one hand, it wishes to increase the economic incentives to work but, on the other hand, does not want to be seen to be subjecting unemployed families with children to unacceptably low levels of income support. Hence, New Labour has so far retained and increased child benefit, a universal social security benefit which, in the company of other welfare entitlements, including housing benefit, income support, and council tax benefit, meet the minimal needs of unemployed families. Similarly, it has refrained from outright coercion of single parents into work through withdrawal of benefit. However, while the 'New Deal for Lone Parents'—a state scheme providing comprehensive back-to-work help for single parents on income support (including help with childcare costs)—does not yet require full participation as a condition of continued welfare provision, this may soon change, not least because coercive welfare-to-work tactics appear to have been effective in relation to other categories of the unemployed, for example, young people.[72]

The government focus on increasing the labour market participation of lone parents is, in fact, a good example of the difficulties posed by the housewife model of employment in a society where lone-parent families increasingly abound.[73] Clearly, any concerted attempt to enable lone parents to get off benefits and into paid work must tackle the organizational, structural, and economic obstacles posed by paid work to those who also engage in unpaid, caring work. Improved employment rights and the informational and financial support which the New Deal offers go some way to address these concerns. At the same time, the recent introduction of an initial interview requirement and the setting of a government target of 70 per cent labour market participation for lone parents by 2010 (it is currently about 50 per cent) is expressive of more than a policy

---

[72] Six 'New Deal' programmes have been set up since 1998 to facilitate the return to employment of particular targeted groups, including young people, the long-term unemployed, partners of unemployed people (often women living with unemployed men), disabled people, and people over 50. Some but not all contain an element of compulsion, in the form of withdrawal of benefit for non-compliance. In Dec. 2000, the government announced its intention to require lone parents on income support with children aged 5 to attend a New Deal interview or risk forfeiting benefit. It also expanded the scheme to cover lone parents not on income support. See 'Brown Aims at Lone Parents after Hitting Youth Jobs Target', *The Guardian*, 1 Dec. 2000, 14.

[73] Almost a quarter of UK families with dependent children are headed by lone parents (*Work and Parents*, above, n. 3, para. 2.5).

of enablement; while couched in the rhetoric of 'support' and 'choice',[74] the government's family-friendly stance here evidences a growing element of compulsion. This is perhaps most starkly demonstrated by the withdrawal of Lone Parent Benefit (an additional social security benefit to which lone parents were entitled) in 1998, just as the New Deal scheme was launched nationally.

Changes in social security provision designed to encourage workforce participation are complemented by a range of measures designed to ease the tax burden of low-income, economically active, families. Chief among these is the new Working Families' Tax Credit (WFTC), introduced by the Tax Credits Act 1999 to replace Family Credit, a social security benefit previously paid out to low income working families. WFTC[75] represents an attempt by the government to co-ordinate the tax and social security systems in order to eliminate the 'poverty trap' arising when the interaction of taxation eligibility and social security withdrawal render it uneconomical for families to work. Additionally, from April 2001, a new Children's Tax Credit replaces the existing married couple's allowance, signalling a shift in emphasis in tax policy away from privileging marriage *per se*, towards supporting families. Both measures can be seen as part of a longer-term strategy of tax and social security integration.[76]

A policy of co-ordinating tax and social security provision to eliminate the 'poverty trap' condemning many families to a life on benefit makes obvious sense. However, again, misgivings have been expressed about the strategies and mechanisms adopted. In particular, many commentators have raised questions about the gendered effects of a shift from social security benefit to tax credits in the context of low-income families, arguing that WFTC may effectively transfer income from mothers (previously the common recipients of Family Credit) to fathers who, evidence suggests, are less likely to spend it on family needs.[77] Experience of family

---

[74] Note the titles of new labour policy documents, e.g., 'Work and Parents: Competitiveness and Choice',' Supporting Families' (above, n. 3).

[75] WFTC comprises the following elements: (i) a basic tax credit for each family; (ii) an additional tax credit where one family earner works over 30 hours a week; (iii) a child tax credit; and (iv) a child care tax credit. For details of the eligibility criteria as well as a general ssessment see Lee, N., 'The Working Families' Tax Credit: An Integration of Tax and Benefit Systems (2000) 7 *Journal of Social Security Law* 159.

[76] See generally HM Treasury, *The Modernisation of Britain's Tax and Benefit System, Tackling Poverty and Making Work Pay—Tax Credits for the 21st Century*, Report No 6 (London: the Stationery Office, 2000).

[77] Lister, R., Goode, J., and Callender, C., 'Income Distribution Within Families and the Reform of Social Security' (1999) 21 *Journal of Social Welfare and Family Law* 203. The government's response to this criticism was to permit couples in one-earner families to 'opt' for direct payment of the credit to the partner at home. However, Lister *et al.* suggest that this may not solve the problem in 'inegalitarian' families where the woman does not feel empowered to express a preference (ibid., 214–15).

tax credit systems elsewhere, for example, Canada, supports this assessment.[78] In addition, Natalie Lee speculates that WFTC is no more likely to reduce the risks and effects of the poverty trap than its predecessor. She also questions the degree of integration achieved by current and projected reforms of tax and social security.[79] There is an element of inconsistency, for example, in introducing a tax credit based on the notion of a family income (reflecting the tendency of social security provision to treat the family as a single economic unit) and the prevailing trend towards the individualization of taxation which many feminists, for example, have long advocated.[80] Thus, although there is a consensus that tax and social security provision must adapt to changing patterns of family and working life, disagreement prevails about the precise way forward. There remains, too, a concern that some goals—for example, equality of access to household income or easing the heavy burden of responsibility that falls on single parents (usually mothers)—may be subordinated to others which fit more comfortably with the government's desire to reduce levels of public support for families by encouraging private, market-based alternatives.

IV TRANSFORMATIVE POSSIBILITIES AND PROBLEMS IN THE FAMILY-FRIENDLY DEBATE

I began by offering reasons why labour lawyers should pay particular attention to New Labour's family-friendly approach. I suggested that the gender benefits were by no means self-evident, requiring careful assessment. I also intimated that the pursuit of family-friendly policies revealed a feature of labour law that rarely surfaced but was, nevertheless, a constant presence—its schematic and conceptual dependence on women's unpaid labour. Finally I speculated about the extent to which New Labour's programme could be characterized as politically progressive—perhaps transformative—in the light of its compatibility with, indeed deference to, economic imperatives. Could this be an instance where social and economic aspirations happily align, where, in the words of Sylvia Walby,[81] no 'trade-off' is necessary?

In fact, the implementation of New Labour's family-friendly agenda has been accompanied by a great deal of 'trading-off', in which the more progressive and radical elements of social policy have been seriously

---

[78] See here the Joseph Rowntree Foundation study by Mendleson, M., *The WIS That Was: Replacing the Canadian Income Supplement* (Layerthorpe: York Publishing Services, 1998).
[79] Lee, above, n. 75, 179–82.
[80] Ibid., 181. See also Brannen, J., 'Caring for Children' in Walby, above, n. 16, 47.
[81] See text accompanying n. 16 above.

undermined by restrictions designed to placate the 'business lobby'. Hence, for example, the initial absence of a *paid* element to parental leave, the limited scope of the Part-time Workers' Regulations,[82] the relatively low level of the National Minimum Wage, and the derogations and opt-outs which all but disable the Working Time Regulations.[83] Hence, too, government wobbling over crucial issues such as whether to introduce a right to reduced working hours in the face of strong business hostility to the idea.

Of course, to be fair, these limitations can and, perhaps, should be understood as problems of transition. The government has frequently emphasized the need to change the *culture* of work, so that family-friendly initiatives are viewed as acceptable, and, indeed, welcomed by businesses. This cannot be achieved overnight and, in the meantime, it is surely counterproductive to impose radically family-friendly agendas on implacably hostile employers. It may have the opposite effect to that intended by creating a working environment in which employers are chary of employing workers (women) with family responsibilities. In any case, many of the limitations characterizing the current batch of family-friendly initiatives are likely to be relaxed by future legislation. The DTI Green Paper, *Work and Parents*, and subsequent policy documents reveal a willingness to reconsider issues such as paid parental leave and a right to reduced working hours. Maybe a little patience is in order.

Still, it always pays to be vigilant and, in particular, to monitor the extent to which the process of transition brings with it problematic assumptions and practices from the past. The risk is that what looks like change—transformation even—is merely the reproduction of old oppressions in new guises. Such a risk pervades New Labour's family-friendly agenda and it derives from a fundamental assumption which links the old policies with the new—the assumption that paid 'market' work produces value and unpaid 'home' work does not.

It is this assumption which most threatens the progressive credentials of New Labour's current stance. It also renders problematic the advantages to women of policies which devalue much of the 'work' which they, predominantly, continue to perform.[84] At the same time, the assumption becomes much more difficult to sustain when the interdependence of family and market is rendered explicit, as when state policy seeks to redraw the boundaries demarcating the two spheres. This is why New Labour's policies have run into trouble. There seems to be a glaring contradiction between a family policy which purports to value parenting

---

[82] SI 2000 No. 1551.   [83] SI 1993 No. 1533.

[84] Despite the popular rhetoric of the 'New Man', the evidence is that women still carry most of the burden of housework and caring responsibilities. See, e.g., Lister, R., 'What Welfare Provisions do Women Need to Become Full Citizens?' in Walby, above, n. 16, 18–19.

and an employment policy which clearly does not—or, more accurately, values it only under certain conditions, namely when it is complemented by participation in 'productive', that is, paid work.

The implications for women of such an approach are highly problematic. As primary carers, their path to social citizenship—achieved, New Labour insists, through earning—is strewn with obstacles not faced by the majority of men. The government may purport to remove some of these obstacles but has done little or nothing to address the conditions giving rise to them. Women's path to employment may be smoother but they are still likely to carry a heavy load along the way. Nor is there anything in current government policy which encourages men to share the load. Why, for example, should men accept the economic deprivations of parental leave when, until now, their role as parents has not carried with it any workplace disadvantage whatsoever? And why should they take on more domestic work in the absence of incentives to do so? The government may contend that as women's participation in paid labour increases, men will, of necessity, assume a greater domestic burden. However, there is little evidence to suggest that this will happen and plenty to suggest it will not.[85]

The government may also insist that the path to paid work is the only path out of 'social exclusion'. Therefore, it must be taken by women— even those without partners with whom they might notionally share caring responsibilities—because the alternative is poverty and dependence. However, this is true only to the extent that the government chooses to define social *inclusion* in terms of paid work. It is the product of a political choice to deny the economic value of the unpaid caring work women typically carry out in the home and the community. There are many ways, in fact, by which the economic value of such work might be socially and politically recognized. Adequate state benefits conferring direct entitlements on carers is one possibility.[86] Requiring employers to internalize more of the costs of reproduction—which are, after all, also costs of production—is another. So far, the UK government has taken few tentative steps in the direction of reallocating costs as between parents and employers. However, in relation to the state, it has sought to confine direct subsidies—as far as is possible—to carers who are also earners. Caring *per se* attracts little or no economic recognition and the carer only 'contributes' to the economic welfare of society when she is in receipt of a wage. In short, New Labour's concept of social citizenship, a pre-condition to social inclusion, is largely predicated on the devaluation of unpaid domestic labour.

---

[85] See above, n. 9.
[86] See further Lister, above, n. 82.

In the same vein, the notion of 'work' upon which current family-friendly policies are based remains rooted in the traditional demarcation of the productive and reproductive spheres. 'Work' is posited in opposition to 'family' and the object is to 'reconcile' the conflict that ensues when two spheres collide. In fact, it is not the collision of two distinct spheres which has given rise to New Labour's family-friendly programme. Rather, it is the coming apart of a system of production in which the family and workplace were deeply implicated, and in which women's work in the family facilitated men's participation in the workplace. In both the 'old' housewife model and the new family-friendly one, unpaid work subsidizes paid work and although, in the latter model, there may be more opportunity for women to recoup some benefits of the subsidy they provide, the subsidy itself continued to go unacknowledged. Hence, the supreme irony of a political rhetoric in which 'work' remains external to and distinct from 'family' and a political programme in which their mutual interdependence has become glaringly apparent.

A final consequence for women of New Labour's privileging of paid work is that it reinforces the construction of non-earners as *dependent*. The implicit assumption is that unpaid caring work is without economic value and that those who engage exclusively in such work are not contributing to the general economic welfare of society. Not only do they produce nothing but, in sustaining themselves financially though their partners or the state, they are *consuming* resources they have not themselves generated. In effect, they are parasites who feed off the labour of others. While New Labour would probably shrink from portraying the situation of non-earning carers in such stark terms, the implication is there to be drawn.

There is, however, nothing natural or inevitable about the dependent status of unpaid carers which is the product of a set of legal rules and social practices constructing them as such. In particular, their 'dependence' on the state derives from a rhetoric and a set of policy choices in which social security has been re-presented as responding to 'need' rather than conferring 'entitlement'.[87] It is the existing distribution of resources and the rules supporting it that render women who care as dependent; and it is an unwillingness to engage in *redistribution* in ways which acknowledge the economic dimensions of care work which prevents New Labour's family-friendly programme from being truly radical or transformative.

---

[87] This is evident, e.g., in the government's 'new contract for welfare' which is explicitly premised on the 'twin pillars of work and security': 'work for those who can; security for those who cannot': DSS Green Paper, *New Ambitions for Our Country*, above, n. 3. 'Work' here clearly means wage-earning work. On the competing discourses of 'need' and 'entitlement' in welfare law see Williams, L. A., 'Welfare Law and Legal Entitlements: The Social Roots of Poverty' in Kairys, D. (ed.), *Politics of Law* (3rd edn., New York: Basic Books, 1998).

This does not mean that progressive labour lawyers should turn away from the policies New Labour currently espouses. Indeed, the signs are that much of its future programme is still uncertain, leaving open the possibility of more radical measures in the future.[88] It does, however, compel a much closer scrutiny of the UK government's family-friendly policies and critical evaluation of their compatibility with progressive/feminist concerns to redress women's social, economic, and political disadvantage. In this context, one cannot but speculate about the extent to which a redistribution of resources in ways which acknowledge the economic value of women's unpaid work can co-exist with policies seeking to reduce the costs of caring borne by the state by passing them on to carers themselves. In the same vein, one is left to wonder whether policies aimed at redesigning the labour market in order to enhance the competitiveness of businesses in a global economy will happily tolerate a more equitable distribution of the costs and benefits of reproductive work in a world where, for the most part, they remain most unequally distributed. It may be that a truly transformative family-friendly policy requires much greater disruption of the boundaries of family, state, and market than New Labour has yet envisaged.

[88] Consider, e.g., the report in *The Times*, 29 Dec. 2000, 'Treasury studies £500m baby credit' in which a proposal to pay mothers to stay at home during the first 3 years of their babies' lives life are, apparently, under consideration.

4

Who Needs Labour Law? Defining the Scope of Labour Protection

PAUL BENJAMIN

I INTRODUCTION

Defining an employee is perhaps the most fundamental question in labour law. How a legal system poses and answers this question generally determines who does or does not receive the protection of labour law. Writing in 1966, Lord Wedderburn described the approach of the British courts to defining an employee as an 'elephant test'—'an animal too difficult to define but easy to recognise when you see it'.[1] It is highly unlikely that anyone writing on the state of early twenty-first century labour law would describe the test of employee in these terms. Factors such as globalization, deregulation, and technological change have combined greatly to increase the variety of forms of employment. Many employers have adopted strategies to disguise employment. An increasing number of employees are located in a grey area on the fringes between employment and self-employment. We are no longer able to say with such confidence that we recognize an employee when we see one. At the same time the science of identifying the employee has not kept pace with this labour market evolution. Old tests are still used to classify new forms of employment.

Increasing numbers of workers, particularly the vulnerable and the unorganized, are not protected by labour law. A policy paper published by the Department of Labour described the consequences of the lack of protection in the South African labour market in the following terms:

The current labour market has many forms of employment relationships that differ from full-time employment. These include part-time employees, temporary employees, employees supplied by employment agencies, casual employees, home workers and workers engaged under a range of contracting relationships. They are usually described as non-standard or atypical. Most of these employees are particularly vulnerable to exploitation because they are unskilled or work in sectors with little or no trade union organisation or little or no coverage by collective bargaining. A high proportion are women. Frequently, they have less

---

[1] Lord Wedderburn, *The Worker and the Law* (3rd edn.) (Harmondsworth: Penguin, 1986) 116.

favourable terms of employment than other employees performing the same work and have less security of employment. Often they do not receive 'social wage' benefits such as medical aid or pension or provident funds. These employees therefore depend upon statutory employment standards for basic working conditions. Most have, in theory, the protection of current legislation, but in practice the circumstances of their employment make the enforcement of rights extremely difficult.[2]

Similarly, the ILO has noted that globally during the last two decades of the twentieth century there has been 'a general increase in the precarious nature of employment and the reduction of workers' protection'.[3]

Defining an employee raises two related but distinct issues. The first is an issue of legislative policy—what legal instruments and institutions should determine who receives the protection of labour law. The second is a question of judicial interpretation—how courts and other arbitral forums interpret legal definitions of who should be covered by labour law. This chapter seeks to address both these issues by examining the manner in which the ambitious and innovative programme of labour law reform introduced by South Africa's first democratic government has defined the employment relationship and how the courts interpret that definition. It will be suggested that the legislators have retained the traditional approach of placing the responsibility for determining who should receive the protection of labour law in the hands of the courts. The courts have in turn continued to use traditional approaches to defining the employment relationship. A lack of judicial imagination has resulted in a significant proportion of the workforce being denied the effective protection of these labour statutes.

II POST-APARTHEID LABOUR LAW REFORM IN SOUTH AFRICA

South Africa's first democratic government embarked on a comprehensive overhaul of the legislation underpinning labour market regulation. Its first five-year term of office saw the enactment of four major new statutes—the Labour Relations Act 66 of 1995; the Basic Conditions of Employment 75 of 1997; the Employment Equity Act 55 of 1998; and the Skills Development Act 97 of 1998. The Labour Relations Act (LRA) came into effect in late 1996 and the Basic Conditions of Employment Act (BCEA) approximately a year later. The Skills Development and Employment Equity legislation came into effect during 1999.

---

[2] Department of Labour, 'Green Paper: Policy Proposals for a New Employment Standards Statute' (Government Gazette, 23 Feb. 1996).

[3] ILO, 'Meeting of Experts on Workers in Need of Protection: Basic Technical Document' (Geneva: ILO, 2000) 4–6.

The LRA of 1995 comprehensively restructures the legal and institutional basis of collective labour law and unfair dismissal law. It creates for the first time a single legal framework for labour relations applicable to all sectors of the economy, including the public service. It establishes two new institutions for dispute resolution and adjudication: a para-statal Commission for Conciliation, Mediation and Arbitration (CCMA), and a specialist system of labour courts with an exclusive labour law jurisdiction. It also codifies the law of unfair dismissal in a manner consistent with the ILO's Convention 156 of 1982, and seeks to promote orderly collective bargaining, by entrenching key trade union organizational rights and, at the same time, establishing a protected positive right to strike.[4]

While the LRA promotes collective bargaining as a mechanism for determining conditions of employment, the BCEA guarantees all South African workers certain minimum standards of employment while, at the same time, creating mechanisms and institutions for varying the application of these standards to particular workplaces or sectors. This tension between setting minimum standards and permitting them to be varied in appropriate cases reflects a policy of 'regulated flexibility' which is a central tenet of South African labour market policy.

The Employment Equity Act (EEA) is the government's primary response to the heritage of racial discrimination and inequality that is a defining feature of the South African labour market. The Act prohibits discrimination in the workplace while at the same time requiring larger employers to take affirmative action to achieve diversity in their workforces. The Act does not set quotas but does require employers to develop a plan which will ensure the employment of adequate numbers of blacks, women, and disabled persons. The Skills Development Act (SDA) seeks to address the low skill-base that is a feature of the South African labour market by systematizing and creating incentives for the provision of education and training to employees and new entrants into the labour market.

III CONSTITUTIONAL LABOUR RIGHTS

The Labour Relations Act was the first labour legislation enacted during South Africa's new constitutional era. The transition to the democratic era was regulated by the 1993 Interim Constitution. In 1996, the Interim

---

[4] Its approach has been compared to that of the Italian Workers' Statute: Hepple, B., 'Can Collective Labour Law Transplants Work? The South African Example' (1999) 20 *ILJ (SA)* 1, 2. For a discussion of the Italian Workers' Statute, see Lord Wedderburn, 'The Italian Workers' Statute: British Reflections on a High Point of Legal Protection' (1990) 19 *ILJ* 154.

Constitution was replaced by the final constitution which was enacted by a Constitutional Assembly consisting of the members of the country's two legislatures elected to office in 1994.

Both Constitutions contain a Bill of Rights, including a set of fundamental labour rights.[5] The terms of these rights and the beneficiaries to whom these rights are extended are cast in wide terms. The right to fair labour practices is extended to everyone.[6] All workers are granted the right to form, join, and participate in the activities of a trade union and the right to strike.[7]

The Constitution describes the Bill of Rights as the cornerstone of South African democracy. The state is required to respect, protect,

[5] S. 23 of the Constitution reads as follows
'23(1) Everyone has the right to fair labour practices.
(2) Every worker has the right—
(a) to form and join a trade union;
(b) to participate in the activities and programmes of a trade union; and
(c) to strike.
(3) Every employer has the right—
(a) to form and join an employers' organisation; and
(b) to participate in the activities and programmes of an employers' organisation.
(4) Every trade union and every employers' organisation has the right—
(a) to determine its own administration, programmes and activities;
(b) to organise; and
(c) to form and join a federation.
(5) Every trade union, employers' organisation and employer has the right to engage in collective bargaining. National legislation may be enacted to regulate collective bargaining. To the extent that the legislation may limit a right in this Chapter, the limitation must comply with section 36(1).
(6) National legislation may recognise union security arrangements contained in collective agreements. To the extent that the legislation may limit a right in this Chapter, the limitation must comply with section 36(1).'

[6] S. 23(1).
Commentators have queried the appropriateness of including a right to fair labour practices in the Constitution. The term is open-ended and is generally used as a basis for regulating the conduct of employers and employees rather than as a basis for evaluating the constitutional sufficiency of legislation. Politically it was introduced into the Interim Constitution as one of a number of provisions aimed at securing the support of the apartheid public service for the constitution. See Cheadle, H., 'Labour' in Davis, D., Cheadle, H., and Haysom, N., *Fundamental Rights in the Constitution: Commentary and Cases* (Cape Town: Juta, 1997) 212–17. The concept of unfair labour practice was introduced into South African labour law in 1979 when an industrial court was created with broad equity-based powers to declare workplace conduct an unfair labour practice. The industrial court used these powers to create a right not to be unfairly dismissed as well as developing collective bargaining jurisprudence to include a 'duty to bargain'. The LRA 1995 does not expressly incorporate an unfair labour practice jurisprudence—it codifies the unfair dismissal jurisdiction. Collective bargaining is regulated by granting trade unions various organizational rights and by the statutory entrenchment of a positive right to strike. The Labour Court cannot rule on the fairness of conduct during collective bargaining or direct an employer to bargain with a trade union. The Act retains a limited 'residual' unfair labour practice jurisdiction dealing with disciplinary action short of dismissal and unfair conduct in relation to aspects of the individual employment relationship such as promotion or demotion.

[7] S. 23(2).

promote, and fulfil the rights contained in the Bill of Rights. Rights contained in the Bill of Rights are not absolute; they may be limited by a law of general application if the limitation is 'reasonable and justifiable in an open and democratic society based on human dignity, equality and freedom'.[8] The Constitutional Court has adopted a purposive or value-orientated approach to the interpretation of the Bill of Rights. Its approach is similar to the manner in which the Canadian courts have interpreted the Canadian Charter of Fundamental Rights. The meaning of a right guaranteed by the Bill must therefore be ascertained from an analysis of the interests the right is meant to protect. A purposive interpretation may lead to a liberal and generous interpretation of the rights, but it will not always do so as in some instances a general or liberal interpretation may overshoot the purpose of the rights.[9]

The commitment to a democratic constitutional order is reflected in the LRA. One of the Act's primary objects is to give effect to and regulate the fundamental labour rights entrenched in the Constitution.[10] The Act must be interpreted to give effect to its primary objects and in compliance with the Constitution as well as South Africa's public international law obligations.[11] The effect is to require a purposive approach to the interpretation of the Act in which the objects of the Act and the constitutional labour rights must inform the interpretative process.[12]

The constitutional labour rights are significant factors in determining the scope of labour legislation for at least two reasons. First, the broad terms of the fundamental labour rights created by the Constitution and, in particular, the broad terms in which these beneficiaries of these rights are described (everyone, all workers) may provide a basis for arguing for an extensive interpretation of the definition of an employee.[13] If such an

---

[8] S. 36(1). In assessing any limitation of a right the court must take into account all relevant factors including the nature of the right; the importance of the purpose of the limitation; the nature and extent of the limitation; the relation between the limitation and its purpose; and less restrictive means to achieve the purpose.

[9] Chaskalson, M., Kentridge, J., Klaaren, J., Marcus, G., Spitz, D., and Woolman, S., *Constitutional Law of South Africa* (Cape Town: Juta, 1996 updated to 1999) 11–25 to 28.

[10] LRA s. 1(a).   [11] LRA s. 3.

[12] See du Toit, D., Woolfrey, D., Murphy, J., Godfrey, S., Bosch, D., and Christie, S., *Labour Relations Law: A Comprehensive Guide* (3rd edn., Durban: Butterworths, 2000) 59–62.

[13] In *South African National Defence Union* v. *Minister of Defence* 1999 (4) SALR 469 (CC) the Constitutional Court had to consider whether members of the armed forces, who are expressly excluded from labour legislation, were workers as contemplated by s. 23(2) of the Constitution. O'Regan J stated that s. 23 used the term 'worker' in the context of employers and employment and therefore concluded that the term referred primarily to those who were working for an employer in terms of a contract of employment to provide services to that employer. While members of the Defence Force did not have contracts of employment, she found that their conditions of enrolment in the Defence Force in many respects mirrored the conditions of persons employed under contracts of employment and she therefore concluded that they were workers (paras. 20–29).

argument were accepted, it would allow the courts to use the principles of purposive interpretation to give a broader interpretation to the term 'employee' than is presently the case. Secondly, an argument can be mounted that the restriction of labour legislation to persons falling within the conventional definition of an employee represents an unjustifiable and unreasonable limitation on the rights of persons who are granted these rights by the Constitution but denied these rights by labour legisla- tion. If an argument of this type were to succeed, the Constitutional Court could direct parliament to enact legislation extending those statutory labour rights that are protected by the constitution to a broader group of workers.

IV THE INTERNATIONAL CONTEXT

Before proceeding to examine South African legislation more closely it is necessary for two reasons to place the issue of the scope of labour law in an international context. First, South African public international law obligations are a factor to be taken into account in interpreting labour legislation. Secondly, recent work by the ILO has begun to document the extent to which workers are slipping through the net of labour protection.

The major source of South Africa's public international law obligations in the area of labour law will be the Conventions of the ILO, particularly those that South Africa has ratified. The ILO's core instrument, Convention 87 of 1948 (Convention concerning Freedom of Association and Protection of the Right to Organize), guarantees the right of 'workers and employers, without distinction whatsoever' to establish and join organizations of their own choosing without previous (state) authoriza- tion. The Freedom of Association Committee of the governing body of the ILO has held that the criterion for determining whether persons are covered by this right is not based on the existence of an employment rela- tionship and that self-employed workers in general should enjoy the right to organize.[14] Recent international instruments have shown a conscious policy to extend their application to workers not employed in conven- tional employment relationships. For instance, the Convention on Maternity Protection, 183 of 2000, applies to all women 'including those in atypical forms of dependent work'. A country ratifying this Convention would be required to extend its legislation dealing with maternity protection to these workers.

As early as 1990, the International Labour Conference adopted a reso- lution calling for the protection of workers who are nominally self-

---

[14] ILO, *Freedom of Association* (4th edn., Geneva: ILO, 1996) 51.

employed from exploitative sub-contracting arrangements and labour contracts.[15] In 1997, proposals to adopt an international Convention regulating contract labour were tabled at the International Labour Conference. The aim of the proposed Convention was to promote the extension of employment protection to persons working in conditions of subordination or dependency but who did not have an employment relationship recognized by the laws of their country. These proposals did not lead to the adoption of a Convention. The reason for this lay in terminological difficulties and conceptual ambiguity concerning the term 'contract labour', as well as employer opposition to the development of an international instrument on this topic.

Subsequently, the ILO commissioned a series of country studies aimed at identifying the extent to which workers needing the protection of labour law were unprotected by or received inadequate protection from labour law. On the basis of these studies, the ILO concluded that there has been a world-wide decrease in workers' protection. The ILO also concluded that internationally there has been what it terms a 'loss of focus' of labour legislation due to the increasing concealment of employment relations and the rise of ambiguous terms of employment.[16] It has therefore proposed the adoption of a 'promotional' instrument which would require states to clarify which workers are covered by labour legislation and adjust these definitions in response to changes in employment relationships.[17]

V DEFINING AN EMPLOYEE

The LRA 66 of 1995 defines an 'employee' as:

any person, excluding an independent contractor, who works for another person or for the State and who receives, or is entitled to receive, any *remuneration*; and any other person who in any manner assists in carrying on or conducting the business of an employer.

This definition has been replicated in the BCEA, EEA, and SDA. The term 'independent contractor' is not defined in any of the statutes or in any other statute.

Whether a worker is classified as an employee or an independent contractor has immense consequences. Independent contractors are excluded entirely from the ambit of labour and employment legislation. The definition reflects a distinction between an 'employee' and an 'independent contractor' that has its origins in Roman law, the source of much

---

[15] See above, n. 3, 4–6.   [16] Ibid., 26.   [17] Ibid., p. ix.

of South Africa's common law. The contract of service (employee) and the contract for services (independent contractor) are both viewed as forms of lease.

The statutory definition of an employee is open-textured. The legislation does not prescribe the factors or criteria that courts should use to distinguish employees from other categories of workers. The courts have a blank cheque to determine the criteria to be used in drawing this distinction. As a result, the central labour market policy issue of who should be covered by labour law has been handed to the courts. As will appear, the courts have adopted a 'business as usual' approach to determining who is an employee under the new labour law.

Historically, the approach of the South African courts to determining who is an employee shows a trend found in many countries. Initially, the courts sought a single definitive touchstone of the employment relation. Until the 1950s, the courts regarded the employer's right of *control* over the employee as the defining element. Later the conventional wisdom accepted that an employment contract could exist (particularly in the case of highly skilled or senior employees) in the absence of control, and the courts asked whether the employee was integrated into the employer's *organization*.[18] The vogue of the 'organization' test was short-lived, and in 1979 it was rejected as 'vague and nebulous'. For the last two decades, the South African courts have applied a multi-factoral approach—the 'dominant impression' test.

VI RELYING ON DOMINANT IMPRESSIONS

The central thesis of the 'dominant impression' test is the assertion that there is no single factor that decisively indicates an employment contract. The court must evaluate all aspects of the contract and classify it on the basis of the 'dominant impression' formed in that evaluation. The existence of a right of supervision or control, while an important consideration, is not conclusive proof of the existence of a contract of employment.[19]

---

[18] As in other countries, these tests evolved in cases that were concerned not with the scope of labour legislation but the issue of the employer's liability to third parties for damages. The relevant litigation generally concerned motor vehicle accidents and, particularly in the South African case, police assaults.

[19] The 'dominant impression' was first articulated in *Smit v. Workmen's Compensation Commissioner* 1979 (1) SALR 51 (AD). In that case, the court held that the plaintiff, a travelling insurance salesman, was not employed in terms of a 'contract of service' and therefore not entitled to claim statutory worker's compensation. Those who are not familiar with the system of Roman-Dutch law that forms the common law of South Africa will be astonished that these distinctions flow from an extensive analysis of Roman law and the law of certain

The courts have identified the following factors[20] as the most important legal characteristics of the contract of service (employee) and the contract of work (independent contractor):

Table 4.1 *Features of Employment and Self-employment*

	Employee	Independent contractor
1.	Object of the contract is to render personal services.	Object of contract is to perform a specified work or produce a specified result.
2.	Employee must perform services personally.	Independent contractor may usually perform through others.
3.	Employer may choose when to make use of services of employee.	Independent contractor must perform work (or produce result) within period fixed by contract.
4.	Employee obliged to perform lawful commands and instructions of employer.	Independent contractor is subservient to the contract, not under supervision or control of employer.
5.	Contract terminates on death of employee.	Contract does not necessarily terminate on death of contractor.
6.	Contract also terminates on expiry of period of service in contract.	Contract terminates on completion of work or production of specified result.

The dominant impression test can be criticized on a number of jurisprudential and policy grounds. As early as 1980, a commentator made the point that the test fails to say anything about the legal nature of the contract of employment[21] and that it amounts to nothing more

provinces of Holland in the 17th century. The discussion informs us that, in Rome, independent contractors were used to train slaves, and that Roman-Dutch law permits the employers of domestic servants, as well as shipmasters, a right to inflict moderate physical chastisement on their employees.

[20] These factors were first identified by the Appellate Division of the Supreme Court of South Africa (now the Supreme Court of Appeal) in *Smit* (above, n. 19). They were subsequently confirmed by the Labour Appeal Court in *SA Broadcasting Corporation* v. *McKenzie* (1999) 20 ILJ (SA) 585 (LAC)—a case arising out of the Labour Relations Act 28 of 1956. The Labour Relations Act 66 of 1995 gives the labour courts exclusive jurisdiction in respect of matters concerning the interpretation or application of the Act, thereby ousting the jurisdiction of the Supreme Court of Appeal. The Supreme Court of Appeal retains the jurisdiction to hear matters arising out of the interpretation of contracts of employment.

[21] Mureinik, E., 'The Contract of Service: An Easy Test for Hard Cases' (1980) 97 *South African L. Journal* 246, 258.

than saying that the decision must be taken in the light of all relevant factors.[22]

The test has become a largely formalistic consideration of the differences between the contracts of service and the contract for service. In particular, the evaluation of 'independence' is concerned with the traditional legal nomenclature of 'independent contractor', and not with the presence or absence of real economic or other dependence of the worker on the employer. As has been pointed out, the test of employment performs a number of functions in legal systems, in particular, to determine an employer's liability for the unlawful conduct of its employee. It does not take into account those factors that should most concern a court when deciding whether a worker should be protected by labour law. In particular, the test does not require a court to concern itself with the relative bargaining strengths of the parties to the contract. The *absence of a purposive approach* to defining an employee has prevented the courts from considering the policy considerations that may determine whether it will be appropriate for a particular category of workers to, for instance, have a protected right to form or join trade unions, or to strike, or to be protected against unfair dismissal, or be a beneficiary of the requirement for affirmative action in the Employment Equity Act.

The failure to elevate the presence of control to a dominant factor allows an employer to seek to arrange employment relationships so as to avoid labour law. Simulating the absence of control is, for instance, very much more difficult than arranging patterns of remuneration or working time so as to create the impression of independent contracting. The test, with its mantra that each case be evaluated on its circumstances, creates a realm of uncertainty that prevents many workers from asserting their rights. It also gives insufficient guidance to enforcement officials such as labour inspectors who are required to determine whether workers fall within their jurisdiction. Even the courts have had great difficulty understanding it. The Labour Court, a specialist court created to oversee a new era of constitutionally inspired labour law, has without a second thought adopted this common law approach as the method by which to determine its jurisdiction.[23]

In retrospect, the evolution of the tests for identifying the employment relationship has resulted in the baby being thrown out with the bath water. The organization test was favoured because of the concern that there was a category of employment relationships in which the traditional factor of

---

[22] Brassey, M., 'The Nature of Employment' (1990) 18 *ILJ (SA)* 528.

[23] *SABC* v. *McKenzie* (1999) 20 ILJ (SA) 585 (LAC). Significantly, a number of arbitrators deciding cases in the Commission for Conciliation, Mediation and Arbitration (CCMA) have shown a more imaginative approach to determining who is an employee.

control was not present. But, by any reckoning, this group represents a relatively small portion of the workforce. Even with the level of diversity found in contemporary labour markets, the presence or absence of control should be able to determine whether there is an employment relationship in a significant number, if not the majority, of cases. While the use of a multi-factoral approach restores the element of control it fails to accord it an appropriate primacy. Both the 'organization' and the 'dominant impression' tests were devised to provide a jurisprudential basis for determining the existence of an employment relationship in those 'difficult' cases in which 'control' as traditionally understood is not present.

A shift to some form of multi-factoral approach which recognizes the variety of employment relationships is, therefore, inevitable. However, the test must accord with the reality of the factors present in employment relationships. The test that has evolved in South Africa fails to give sufficient weight to the dominant criteria such as control and does not address whether or not it is appropriate for the worker to be protected by labour law.

VII IDENTIFYING THE UNPROTECTED

The growth of forms of atypical employment has meant that an increasing number of workers are clustered on the border between employment and self-employment. Many of these workers are vulnerable workers, employed in atypical forms of employment such as part-time work, homework, or casual work who are effectively excluded from protection. A high proportion of vulnerable workers will fall into those categories of employees who in practice may not be in a position to assert their rights, even though they may be employees. Accordingly, both the definition of 'employee' and its interpretation by the courts undermine the effective protection offered to vulnerable workers.

The manner in which legislation defines an employee and the tests that the courts have developed to interpret these definitions result in the exclusion of many categories of vulnerable workers from the ambit of labour legislation. In examining these patterns of exclusion, it is necessary to distinguish two categories of workers excluded from labour legislation. The first group are workers who would be viewed by the courts as employees but are in practice unable to assert or enforce their rights as employees because they are not in a position to counter the assertion by their employer that they are independent contractors; in other words, they are employees in law but are excluded in fact from the protections of labour law. The second group consists of workers whom the courts would classify as independent contractors but who nevertheless are in a position of dependence on the persons or organizations for whom they work.

VIII UNPROTECTED EMPLOYEES

Unprotected employees are generally unorganized or poorly organized. The reasons for the lack of organization may be the weakness of the trade union movement or trade union indifference to particular groups of workers. However the lack of organization may also flow from the structure of the sector in which they work, particularly if it consists of small businesses or, as in the case of agriculture, remote locations.

In the best of all possible worlds these excluded employees would be able to obtain rulings from the appropriate courts or administrative authorities that they are indeed employees entitled to receive the protection of labour law. But in practice this does not occur. Workers in this group who assert their rights as employees will generally be met with the threat that their services will be terminated if they either make a complaint to an inspector or trade union official or bring legal proceedings. The employee who proceeds despite the threat runs the risk of being unemployed and receiving no income until the dispute is resolved. When the matter proceeds to adjudication, the employer will raise the issue of the employee's status as a preliminary issue. This may extend the length of the case. Even if the employee is successful, the employer may appeal to or seek a review by a higher court. This will usually suspend the initial decision and the employee will remain without income until the final decision. There is no guarantee, particularly in the case of small employers, that the business will still be in existence when judgment is finally obtained or that the employer will have the assets to satisfy the judgment. The cumulative effect is that it is a high-risk strategy for a worker to resist an employer's assertion that he or she is not an employee. The level of risk is enhanced by the fact the courts casuistic approach to this issue makes it difficult to predict the outcome in all but the most blatant of cases.

Strategies to 'convert' employees into independent contractors have become a central aspect of contemporary South African labour debates. An employers' organization, the Confederation of South African Employers (COFESA) recruits its members on the basis of its expertise in this area.[24] COFESA claims to have assisted employers in transforming one million employees into independent contractors and entrepreneurs, thereby excluding them from labour law. While this figure is no doubt exaggerated rhetoric, COFESA's ideological and overtly political opposition to the ANC labour law reforms has received enthusiastic support from many small and medium-sized enterprises.

---

[24] The origins of COFESA lie in apartheid South Africa when it was set up with financial support from the Nationalist Government's Security Police to counter the growth of trade unionism among black workers.

While COFESA calls for labour law deregulation, its attack on labour regulation is painted in broad strokes and it seldom identifies particular provisions in the law as hampering business activity. Its criticisms also ignore the significance of any impact that the labour legislation may have on small businesses when evaluated against other factors. A series of studies has indicated that the most significant factors determining whether small businesses succeed or fail are access to capital, managerial capacity, and product demand.[25] It is likely that in most cases the claimed transformation is no more than a sham in terms of which workers are described in their contract as 'independent contractors' but the actual conditions of work remain unchanged. It is difficult to conceive of many small labour-intensive operations running with a staff consisting entirely of genuine self-employed persons not obligated to follow instructions from their employer about the manner in which they perform their work.

Much of the responsibility for the lack of protection of these workers can be attributed to factors such as lack of organization and enforcement. But the legislature and the courts are not wholly without blame. There is little doubt that the uncertainty concerning the borderline between an employee and an independent contractor that flows from an open-ended statutory definition of an employee that has been imprecisely interpreted by the courts gives employers considerable scope for avoiding the requirements of labour law. It is these circumstances that have permitted an organization such as COFESA to thrive.

However, treating genuine employees as independent contractors can have disastrous consequences for the employers concerned, particularly where there is effective enforcement. Recently, certain bargaining councils (sectoral bargaining institutions) have succeeded in having employers who do not register with the council jailed for contempt of a court order requiring them to register.[26] Potentially, an employee can bring a claim for underpayment under the terms of the Basic Conditions of Employment Act or a bargaining council collective agreement for a period of three years. Department of Labour and bargaining council inspectors also have the power to bring these claims on behalf of workers. This may include claims for overtime payment, premium rates for work on Sundays or public holidays, annual leave, or contributions to pension or provident funds operated by bargaining councils. Employers who, on

---

[25] Horton, C., Honderich, K., and Modise, K., 'Small Business What's Holding it Back' (2000) 17/1 *Indicator South Africa* 45, 46–7.

[26] *Business Day*, 8 June 2000. These employers refused to register with a bargaining council within whose scope they fell on the basis that, as they had no employees, they were not employers. The Labour Court rejected this argument accepting that their workers were employees. Ultimately, they were given prison sentences for being in contempt of a court order to register with the bargaining councils. It is anticipated that this decision will seriously dent the membership of COFESA.

the advice of an organization such as COFESA, do not contribute to social security funds such as the Unemployment Insurance Fund and the Compensation Fund may also face claims for arrears in payments from these bodies. In practice, it appears that many employers hedge their bets and contribute to these funds despite regarding their workers as independent contractors for the purposes of other labour laws. Moreover, recasting employees as independent contractors can have unseen consequences for employers. Unlike employees, independent contractors are not precluded by the Compensation for Occupational Injuries and Diseases Act from instituting civil actions against the employer arising out of occupational accidents or diseases.

IX DEPENDENT SELF-EMPLOYMENT

The defining feature of dependent self-employment is that these workers are formally 'independent' of their employer but their relationship is marked by a real dependence. That dependence may take a number forms, for instance, economic, organizational, or technical. Those workers have been variously described as dependent contractors, semi-independent workers, or as being in dependent self-employment. The use of this terminology breaks with the traditional view that the world of work is neatly demarcated by the two classifications of employee and independent contractor and recognizes that the term 'independent contractor' is no longer adequate to cover all work relationships outside formal employment. The notion of dependent contracting as a distinct and identifiable work relationship requiring appropriate protection has also been recognized by the ILO,[27] and is reflected in the legislation of some countries.[28]

One of the key issues facing the South African courts when considering whether to offer protection to workers in dependent self-employment is the weight that should attach to any description that the parties have agreed to give to their relationship. The Supreme Court of Appeal has held that the terms of a written contract are decisive unless they have

---

[27] 'Contract Labour', Report to the 85th Session of the International Labour Conference, Geneva, 1997.
[28] E.g., the Ontario Labour Relations Act which defines a dependent contractor as '[a] person, whether or not employed under a contract of employment, and whether or not furnishing tools, vehicles, equipment, machinery, material, or any other thing, or any other thing owned by the independent contractor who performs work or services for another person for compensation or reward on such terms and conditions that the dependent contractor is in a position of economic dependence upon, and under an obligation to perform duties for, that person more closely resembling the relationship of an employee than that of an independent contractor'.

been varied or a party can bring evidence that the contract is a 'sham'.[29] The authors of a leading labour text have suggested that 'in the absence of a specific pleading that the employment contract has been amended, it does not avail an employee that, in practice, the relationship is something different from that specified in the employment contract'.[30]

It is suggested that this approach is both wrong and undesirable. It is not in keeping with the objects of South African labour legislation to permit an employer to avoid legal protection by pressurizing an employee to accept a characterization of their relationship in the contract that is at variance with the reality of the relationship. Before deciding what weight to give to a contractual term that characterizes the relationship as one of independent contracting, the courts should make an informed assessment of the relative bargaining strength of the parties. There are numerous contracts in which a lengthy series of duties and undertakings to obey instructions is followed by the stipulation that the worker agrees that he or she is not an employee but an independent contractor falling outside labour law. Where this concession has been obtained by the exercise of the employer's economic muscle, the courts disregard it. On the other hand, there are situations where skilled or highly paid employees may agree to a certain presentation of their employment relationship to obtain advantages that may flow from self-employment, such as tax benefits. In such a case, the courts have been less keen to assist the employee, particularly where the complaint is brought after a period of enjoying the benefits of self-employment once the employer has terminated the relationship.

The complexities of regulating self-employment are revealed by an examination of the road transportation sector which, internationally, has seen a significant development of new forms of employment relationship. Many employers in the sector have required wage-earning drivers to agree to become self-employed-drivers who are required to hire or purchase a vehicle as a condition of retaining their employment. This category is generally referred to as 'owner-drivers' or 'owner-operators'.[31] The consequences of these changes in the form of employment relationship include cost-cutting and other forms of cost reduction, enormously long hours of work, drivers taking inadequate rest periods while on the road, overloading of vehicles, and the inadequate maintenance of vehicles.[32] This, in turn, has serious consequences for the health and

[29] *Liberty Life Association of Africa Ltd* v. *Niselow* (1998) 19 ILJ (SA) 752 (SCA).
[30] Du Toit *et al.*, above, n. 12, 73.
[31] ILO, above, n. 3, 39.
[32] See Cheadle, H., and Clarke, M., 'Study on Worker's Protection in South Africa' and Clayton, A., and Mitchell, R., 'Study on Worker's Protection in Australia'. These are unpublished country studies commissioned by the ILO.

safety of drivers, their economic security, and their family lives. It also poses serious dangers to the public by significantly increasing the risk of harm due to traffic accidents involving vehicles driven by professional drivers.

Driving dramatically illustrates the social costs of this form of flexibility. One of the major purposes of protective legislation, such as those setting minimum conditions of employment or regulating workplace health and safety, is to prevent employers transferring costs that may flow from long hours of work, dangerous work practices, or unsafe working conditions to the state or the community. The successful exclusion of professional drivers from the realm of labour law means that many of the hazards that flow from professional driving become unregulated, unless some other authority steps in to require appropriate preventive action.

Traditionally, drivers' hours of work have been subject to regulation by labour departments. In South Africa, maximum hours of work set for drivers apply only to drivers who are employees. The creation of owner-drivers effectively deregulates this. There are a number of responses open to regulators. The jurisdiction of labour and health and safety inspectorates can be extended to cover workers such as 'owner-drivers', even though they may be employers for other purposes. Alternatively, traffic authorities can prescribe maximum permissible hours of driving.[33] Ultimately, any attempt successfully to police an issue such as the hours of work of professional drivers will require concerted and co-operative action by the authorities responsible for labour and traffic regulation.

How to classify owner-drivers raises complex issues. On the one hand, their contracts contain clauses indicative of their economic dependence on their former employer. Many are obliged to provide services to their former employer only, for a period of up to five years. Some are required to park their vehicles on the employer's premises when not in use. But, at the same time, the contract to purchase the vehicle is a commercial transaction involving a considerable amount of money and many owner-drivers are themselves employers of assistants.

X RECENT LEGISLATIVE DEVELOPMENTS

The evolution of South African legislative policy does reflect a gradual recognition of the shortcomings of traditional methods of defining an

---

[33] Three reports commissioned by the Department of Transport between 1986 and 1992 recommended that the Department take steps to regulate maximum driving hours. However, the Department rejected this proposal on the basis that hours of driving were a matter for labour legislation and collective bargaining: see Henwood, N., 'The Long Road: Hours of Work in the Transport Industry' (1998) 22/4 *South African Labour Bulletin* 32, 33–4.

employee. The first articulation of this is in the Government Policy Paper that preceded the publication of the BCEA. This 1996 Green Paper proposed that the Employment Conditions Commission should have the power to recommend the extension of employment standards to workers who fall outside the formal definition of an 'employee' but who are engaged in a dependent contracting relationship.[34]

This proposal was incorporated into the Act. The Minister of Labour has the power, on the advice of the Employment Conditions Commission, to extend provisions of the Act on a sectoral determination made in terms of the Act to persons other than employees. The Act does not make use of the term 'dependent contractor', nor does it set criteria for the Minister to take into account in exercising this power. It provides an administrative basis for extending the protection of labour standards to workers in dependent self-employment. This method avoids the pitfalls and uncertainties of relying exclusively on judicial interpretations in individual cases to determine the scope of the employment relationship. A determination by the Minister applies automatically to the groups of workers identified in the notice. Although the BCEA has been in operation for almost three years, during which the protection of vulnerable workers has been a central concern, the Minister of Labour has not used this power.[35] This is considered to reflect a lack of capacity within the Department of Labour.

More recently, during 2000 the Department of Labour published draft Bills to revise both the LRA and the BCEA. These contain certain proposals aimed at addressing the issue of who is an employee. The Department has proposed incorporating into the two statutes a series of rebuttable presumptions to assist workers to establish that they are covered by labour law. If one of these factors is present, the worker is presumed to be an employee and therefore covered by legislation unless the employer brings evidence to establish the contrary. These factors are: the worker's manner or hours of work are subject to control or direction; the worker forms part of the organization he or she works for; the worker has worked for the same person for an average of at least forty hours per month over the last three months; the worker is economically dependent on the person for whom he

[34] The endorsement of the extension of labour protection can also be found in the South African government's macro-economic strategy document, *Growth, Employment and Redistribution* (14 June 1996). Although this has been intensely criticized by the trade union movement for promoting labour flexibility, the policy does support a labour market policy that extends 'the protection and stability afforded by (the) regulatory framework to an increasing number of workers' vol. (6).

[35] The Occupational Health and Safety Act 85 of 1993 also contains administrative processes permitting the Minister of Labour to extend the protections of the Act to persons falling outside the definition of employees. Again, these powers have never been utilized. This failure is particularly striking as there are numerous situations (for instance, contract cleaners working in a chemical factory) when an organization other than the employer is in a position to protect the health and safety of workers.

or she works or provides services; the worker is provided with his or her tools of trade or work equipment; the worker only works or supplies services to one person.

The factors which bring the presumption into play are in the main those that have been relied upon in traditional multi-factoral approaches to identifying the employment relationship. However, the presence of one of the factors will be sufficient to trigger the presumption in favour of the employee. The employer will then have to lead evidence concerning the nature of the employment to disprove it. The approach seeks to balance a recognition of the diversity of employment relationships with the need to assist vulnerable workers to establish that they are employees.

Following its publication the draft legislation was subject to an intensive process of tri-partite consultation. This resulted in an agreement between organized business, organized labour and the state to include this provision in legislation which is to be passed by Parliament in early 2002. As a concession to the concerns of business that the presumptions would be abused by skilled consultants, it will apply only to employees earning below a defined wage threshold. A further feature of these consultations was an agreement that the Minister of Labour's administrative power to extend the scope of laws to non-employees should be extended to all labour legislation.

The agreement represents a significant recognition of the need to prevent employers using disguised employment relationships as a device for avoiding the cover of labour law.

XI CONCLUSION

Given the innovative content of South Africa's new labour legislation, it is striking that the application of these statutes depends on a combination of a distinction between two forms of lease that evolved more than two millennia ago and a judicial test developed to determine employer liability for motor accidents involving employees. This has significantly restricted the number of workers who receive the effective protection of these laws and denied them the promised benefits of political liberation. Strategies by some employers aimed at avoiding labour legislation have focused attention on the need to delineate the protected groups with greater certainty. More recent legislative policy has sought more creative mechanisms to extend these laws to workers requiring protection. For these policies to succeed, they will have to ensure that vulnerable workers have the confidence to assert their statutory rights. However, the border between employment and self-employment is likely to remain a contested terrain for many years to come.

5

Beyond Labour Law's Parochialism: A Re-envisioning of the Discourse of Redistribution

LUCY A. WILLIAMS

I INTRODUCTION

Left labour and welfare law constitute two primary fields of discourse about redistribution. However, each has traditionally seen itself as isolated, not only from one another but also from the critically related fields of immigration, family, and international law. The failure of each to engage with the other results in theoretical and political gaps that have contributed to both fields' inability to envision redistribution strategies sufficient to measure up to the power and pervasiveness of the conservative/neo-liberal agenda.

This chapter seeks to draw threads between fields of inquiry and practice that progressives, especially labour and welfare lawyers, must understand as intimately linked. I argue that any progressive transformation of labour law requires intense engagement with welfare law. With notable exceptions, labour law still largely situates questions of power and income distribution within the framework of labour markets. Its perspective on work remains limited to wage labour. And it still privileges collective bargaining by unions within a nation-state as the primary site of progressive initiatives for economic and social redistribution. These internalized ways of thinking guarantee that labour law will become increasingly stultified and marginalized as the new century progresses, and that labour lawyers will have steadily less to contribute to economic redistribution and social change.

Likewise, progressive welfare lawyers have traditionally focused almost exclusively on central government transfers as the redistributive hub, failing to engage with and expose the state's role in constructing labour markets. More recently, since the 1996 US 'welfare reform', discussed below, progressive welfare lawyers have often focused on developing social services to help poor families 'overcome barriers to employment', instead of challenging the structure of low-wage labour markets. Activists in both welfare and labour law, viewing their constituencies within nation-state boundaries, have not infrequently voiced protectionist rhetoric.

Privileging nation-state waged work as the site for redistributional politics ignores and devalues the needs and concerns of millions of productive, low- and non-waged workers in the globalized economy. Likewise privileging government transfers as the primary site of redistribution, counterintuitive as this may sound, contributes to the dominant discourse of a 'free market' by failing to expose the politically chosen, legally constructed labour market structures that reinforce income disparity. Left lawyers certainly do not intend their theoretical formulations and political stances to render disempowered populations invisible. But often, through lack of interdisciplinary and cross-border dialogue, we fail effectively to criticize our own positions and re-imagine broad-based redistributive political agendas.

This chapter attempts to expose ways in which many left labour and welfare lawyers have unwittingly played into a discourse that reinforces the economic *status quo* by validating the economic structures creating poverty. The left's default can be seen particularly in a failure fully to appreciate and expose the reinforcing links between three seemingly disparate legal-theoretic discourses that feed into the dominant political consensus on social policy. Together these discourses privilege and naturalize waged labour within a free market as the arena for productive participation in society, thereby justifying the assault on the welfare state.

The first is the discourse of the public and private distinction. Mainstream legal thought, both conservative and liberal, conceives private law as arising more or less naturally, rather than being a contingent product of state policy. Within this understanding, private law and the institutions it structures, such as market and family, arise 'prior to' and independent of state power. This conceptual framework naturalizes the existing distribution of wealth and power in these social arenas, which then appear to have nothing to do with and, indeed, to require protection from state intervention. In addition, it necessarily marginalizes welfare law and policy by portraying it as government 'intervention' into natural market outcomes and family arrangements. When welfare lawyers focus on government transfers and when labour lawyers marginalize welfare law as state intervention, both are contributing to the legitimization of the 'free market'.

Similarly central within the dominant legal and policy framework is the conception of a 'worker' as someone engaged in wage labour. Social protection laws connected to waged work frequently further narrow the meaning of 'worker' to those in full-time, high-wage, long-term jobs. This definition identifies as 'non-workers' and therefore excludes many individuals who are, in fact, active in waged work as well as the many who work but do not receive a wage. These definitions reinforce the socially constructed identities upon which mainstream discourse and political rhetoric are founded. By pursuing a traditional social welfare agenda[1] primarily connected to an anachronistic image of the waged worker, and by distancing other members of society as 'non-productive', labour contributes to the stigmatization of millions of low-waged and non-waged workers, including welfare recipients and immigrants.

Finally, there is the notion of social citizenship, to which some progressive welfare and labour policy-makers have subscribed, often as a repository of democratic and egalitarian aspirations, without critically assessing the gender, racial, and economic biases of traditional citizenship discourse. In addition, they typically view their fields within the boundaries of nation-state citizenship, without engaging with the current social reality of global economic integration or the class, racial, and alienage implications of a citizenship paradigm that fails to incorporate a cross-border perspective.

By failing critically to analyse our roles in perpetuating these discourses, left labour and welfare theoreticians have, albeit inadvertently, ceded discursive and political ground to the conservative/neo-liberal consensus, contributing by default to the hegemonic discourses that portray the social *status quo* as natural. Through interdisciplinary and cross-national dialogue by and among progressives working in the fields of labour, welfare, immigration, and international economic organization, we can strengthen our critiques, and better position ourselves to disrupt the 'naturalness' and self-fulfilling quality of dominant discourse.

My particular focus is on the perceived lack of connection between labour and welfare law, primarily in a US and UK context. I then draw threads from labour and welfare to the areas of family, immigration, and international economic law. My hope is that by elucidating theoretical and political gaps in and among these fields, we can develop a more sophisticated redistributive agenda—one that is multicultural and gender-sensitive, allowing, indeed encouraging, transformation of social roles, and one that incorporates a re-imagined, globalized conception of citizenship, attentive to racial and gender differences. Finally, it should be one that reclaims and re-legitimates redistribution, moving beyond the mere redistribution of income to facilitate the redistribution of power, resulting in self-actualization and active citizenship within the market, family, and political community. One (although only one) step toward developing the theoretical tools needed to revitalize transformative politics is for labour

---

[1] In the USA, 'welfare' is commonly used to refer to Aid to Families with Dependent Children (AFDC), replaced in 1996 by Temporary Assistance to Needy Families (TANF). Throughout this chapter I use the term 'welfare' to refer to *social assistance* programmes, the eligibility for which is means-tested, not conditioned on a requisite tie to waged work. I use the term 'social welfare' in a broader sense, to include both social assistance and *social insurance* programmes, in which eligibility is defined by a sufficient attachment to waged work.

lawyers and others thoroughly to engage with the insights and innovations of modern welfare law.

II THE LEGAL CREATION OF POVERTY

Welfare law is premised upon and uniquely illuminates fundamental
teachings of critical legal thought first developed, in the USA, by the
Legal Realists. The core insight is that all legal rules are contingent products of human choice that have distributive consequences. That is, legal
rules affect the distribution of wealth and power, whether vertically
among classes, horizontally among races and genders, or internationally
among regions, communities, and nation-states. For a century, traditional
legal thinkers have engaged in intense ideological work to suppress or
marginalize these insights. Left-legal theorists and practitioners have
resisted this hegemonic view. But they have never fully appreciated the
theoretical contributions of welfare law or its potential as a forum to
expose the legal means by which poverty is perpetuated. By uncritically
accepting the mainstream view that welfare law takes market outcomes
as its starting point, left-legal theory has implicitly validated the mainstream view that the background rules structuring market behaviour are
not really acts of government.

The dominant political discourse in Western nations, reinforced by our
legal culture, teaches that poverty arises naturally and that the legal
system bears no responsibility for causing it. Private law concepts of
family, tort, property, and freedom of contract are made to appear as the
necessary and neutral framework of social and economic power relations,
arising independently of law. The dominant political culture denies that
these background rules privilege any group or have anything to do with
allocating wealth or income. The role of law in distributing property,
valuing waged labour, and consequently devaluing family work is almost
always invisible.

In fact, the stubborn persistence of poverty, in both developed and
developing countries, largely results from political and legal decisions
and institutions that generate and sustain a sharply unequal distribution
of wealth and resources. Far from being natural or neutral, legal rules,
norms, and practices play a central part in maintaining poverty by according privilege to and legitimating certain values, interests, and concerns
over others. Legal precepts shape social roles by assigning power and
responsibility in social relationships, whether within the family or in the
workplace.

For example, the everyday common sense of modern, democratic,
political, and legal cultures—that the family is a private haven from the

public realms of market and government—ignores the intimate, indispensable, and legally constructed connections between these social spheres. As discussed below, the production of goods and services for the market by *paid* workers depends on the subsidy of *unpaid* care-givers'—predominantly women's—labour. Similarly, family wealth and income could not exist without the full range of property rules entrenched by government. The rules that comprise freedom of contract, referring to rich and poor, male and female, and employer and employee as 'equals' because they formally share the power to contract, ratify steeply unequal access by individuals and families to the economic means of life-enjoyment. The state is not independent from other social structures. The state entrenches those structures.

Nor is the existing array of background legal rules inevitable. Human actors, making implicit or explicit moral and political decisions about who is and is not deserving of reward, create legal entitlements that reflect and enact distinct political values. All of the ways in which society sustains income inequality and poverty—whether through government programmes funded by general taxation, market structures, familial responsibility, or private charity—reflect politically chosen regulatory policies.

Welfare law, whose *raison d'être* is to question the existing distribution of wealth and income, provides a forum for exploding the neutrality of these background rules of entitlement. It is, therefore, at least potentially, a permanent threat within mainstream jurisprudence because it reveals the false pretense or illusion that the bedrock common law of property, market, and family is distributionally neutral and exists prior to and independent of governmental action. From a critical perspective, welfare discourse sees every legal artefact as crafted by officials in a given historical and institutional framework. Thus, welfare law persistently threatens to reveal the contingency and political character of all law.

Mainstream politicians, at least subliminally alert to the Trojan-horse nature of welfare law and its potential to explode the most basic assumptions of the legal culture, periodically go to considerable lengths to suppress its critical aspect and to recast welfare law in a manner consistent with *status quo* assumptions. Just as labour law's potentially radical implications for wealth and power distribution, even within the limited waged work sphere, were blunted by a functional reinterpretation of the discourse,[2] so, too, have progressive ideas in welfare law needed to be domesticated or marginalized. Thus, mainstream policymakers and

---

[2] Klare, K. E., 'Workplace Democracy and Market Reconstruction: An Agenda for Legal Reform' (1988) 38 *Catholic University L. Review* 1, and 'Judicial Deradicalization of the Wagner Act and the Origins of Modern Legal Consciousness' (1978) 62 *Minnesota L. Review* 1049.

jurists face the intellectual challenge of creating a conception of welfare law that, while moderately re-distributive, does not disrupt or delegitimate core institutions.

To accomplish this goal, a modicum of procedural due process, and thus a perception of fundamental fairness, was incorporated into welfare law.[3] But this concession, important as it was, has been ultimately overwhelmed in significance by increasingly vitriolic debate about the welfare system's very purpose. The normative foundations of welfare state theory are ideas about equality and minimum material circumstances for a meaningful life-experience. Over the last twenty years, the 'new' welfare theory, legitimated and promoted by a policy consensus of conservatives (for example, Thatcher and Reagan) and liberal/neo-liberals (for example, Blair and Clinton), has promoted different assumptions and commitments.

One normative baseline of this strange alliance is a modernized version of the old ideal of liberty, meaning freedom from governmental interference. Advancing under the banner of the so-called 'Washington Consensus' and espousing the virtues of deregulation, limited government spending, and free trade, politicians in many Western nations[4] have attacked and dismantled previously well-established welfare programmes. Most varieties of the neo-liberal tradition take the position that social provision is a sometime necessary evil to correct market failures and imperfections, just as sometimes the state must 'intervene' in domestic matters because of family breakdown.[5] Many New Right theorists and politicians acknowledge the possibility of market failure in theory but doubt its existence in practice. Accordingly, social provision for them is simply an interference with the free market and has no legitimate purpose. But the various wings coalesce around so-called free markets and the two-parent heterosexual family as the appropriate institutions for distributing wealth and power.

In sum, the intellectual achievement (if one can call it that) of the conservative/neo-liberal 'welfare reform' consensus is to formulate social policy as an adjunct to private law. Questions of income, wealth, and power inequality—let alone redistribution—fade from the picture.

---

[3] See, e.g., *Goldberg* v. *Kelly*, 397 US 254 (1970) and its progeny.

[4] Of course, many European countries continue to maintain more expansive welfare states, including additional family supports, albeit still retaining elements of gender bias as well as racist connotations in terms of immigration law and immigrant access to benefits. The role of social protection and labour in many Latin American, African, and Asian countries is, in many ways, even more complex. This chapter does not attempt to highlight and problematize the labour and social welfare debate throughout the world, but focuses rather on US/UK discourse, which currently forms the basis of discussion in many other countries, in part because of World Bank and International Monetary Fund structural austerity measures.

[5] Olsen, F. E., 'The Myth of State Intervention in the Family' (1985) 18 *University of Michigan Journal of Law Reform* 835.

Moreover, the consensus is also built on historical ambivalence over how much the poor are responsible for their own plight, resurfacing the causation issue with intensely pejorative rhetoric. Welfare benefits, the consensus holds, generate pernicious social consequences, as well as inefficiencies, and must be eliminated because they foster a culture among the poor that does not reflect majoritarian values.[6] This discourse attributes poverty to individual fault, characterized as a lack of the work ethic in the first world and a lack of acquaintance with or mastery of entrepreneurial values and skills in developing countries. The common assumption is that individual agency can always overcome cultural, societal, and economic obstacles. The argument continues that these individual character flaws are largely created and sustained by the institution of welfare. Thus it is argued, without a trace of irony, that because the welfare state creates dependency, welfare actually causes poverty rather than ameliorating it. Without state intervention, the free market would create the incentives for mainstream attitudes and behaviour, by which is meant those consistent with waged work and the patriarchal family. The rhetoric of individual responsibility and institutional dependency legitimates the inevitability of growing disparity in the distribution of wealth both within and between nation-states and underwrites the policy imperative of dismantling the welfare state. The hegemonic success of this rhetoric has led to a significant retrenchment in availability of and entitlement to social protection benefits.

Despite differences, mainstream political discourses about welfare, from moderate-liberal to the far right, have come to share a common thread in recent decades by subsuming welfare policy into private law. At best, welfare smooths out rough edges of the free market (what are technically called 'market imperfections' or 'externalities'). This theoretical ploy cried out for a progressive response aimed to show that the background rules and assumptions by which law regulates the free market, themselves constitute a site of distributive conflict. Instead, most left-legal criticism has pursued one of two alternative avenues.

Progressive welfare theorists have largely seen their task as that of defending the legitimacy of state 'intervention' to achieve egalitarian redistribution. Of course, they make strong arguments against welfare retrenchment, for example, skilfully rebutting the argument that welfare is an addictive drug, and exposing the racism and sexism inherent in the

---

[6] For discussions of the history of welfare theory from various sub-movements of the right see Williams, L. A., 'Welfare Law and Legal Entitlements: The Social Roots of Poverty' in Kairys, D. (ed.), *The Politics of Law: A Progressive Critique* (3rd edn., New York: Basic Books, 1998); *ead., Decades of Distortion: The Right's 30-Year Assault on Welfare* (Somerville, Mass.: Political Research Associates, 1997); *ead.,* 'The Ideology of Division: Behavior Modification Welfare Reform Proposals' (1992) 102 *Yale L. Journal* 719.

welfare reform consensus. But their ultimate solution to poverty and inequality is still framed as a system of central government transfer payments, criticized by some politicians as a 'tax and spend mentality'. The Achilles heel of this approach is that it concedes the mainstream's central premises, that free markets and governmental regulation are diametrically opposed modes of social ordering, and that family and markets are autonomous from state power. Progressive welfare advocates' method of redistribution assumes a conceptual framework in which a 'regulatory' state intervenes in a 'free market'. That focus contributes to the belief that the legal background rules governing the market and the family have no part in the distribution of income and power and operate in a totally separate realm from welfare law. In other words, welfare law is about state intervention in a normally 'free' realm, while background legal rules arise more or less spontaneously in private spheres. Thus welfare law's traditional, bounded assumption that central government transfer policy is the primary arena of redistribution has frustrated its efforts to counter the centre/right consensus and challenge the overall legal structure of inequality.

While labour lawyers take for granted that labour markets are sites of distributive conflict, they customarily fixate on increasing waged workers' bargaining power. Unable to think very far beyond labour market conflict as the engine of redistribution, left labour academics and activists have unwittingly reinforced the naturalization of family, contract, property, and tort law. Rarely do they deploy their critical arsenal against the background rules of private law that give existing labour markets their highly inegalitarian shape. Like most practitioners and legal academics, they fail to appreciate the importance and theoretical richness of welfare law or to develop its connections with and implications for labour law. By marginalizing welfare law as separate from labour law, they have contributed to a discourse that frames welfare law as comprising isolated acts of 'state regulation', thereby naturalizing the free market.

This limited view of welfare law as anomalous state intervention, and the artificial conceptual divisions between family, state, and market,[7] regrettably mirrors the ideas behind the current welfare reform consensus. The hegemonic rhetoric, in both the USA and UK, deflects attention from the political underpinnings of income inequality, and instead focuses on an alleged breakdown of the natural *family* and the failure of poor people, particularly lone mothers, to participate in the 'free' *market*. The prevailing political consensus relies on this unchallenged belief in the

[7] See generally Orloff, A. S., 'Gender and the Social Rights of Citizenship: The Comparative Analysis of Gender Relations and Welfare States' (1993) 58 *American Sociological Review* 303.

neutrality of private law to support the dismantling of welfare programmes, articulated as public interventions in the natural order but which are really ameliorative adjuncts to alienated waged work. Critical welfare and labour law must expose the state's presence in structuring and distributing power in families and markets, and it must reclaim welfare law as a site of redistributional politics. It must engage with and undermine the central premise of the contemporary welfare reform consensus (and its historical antecedents) that poverty can be alleviated simply by strengthening families and pushing people into wage labour. And it must expose and challenge the class, gender, and racial biases of the legal rules structuring family life and market processes.

III SOCIAL WELFARE LAWS CONSTRUCT IDENTITIES AND EXCLUSIONS

Having artificially distinguished public and private realms, placing welfare in the former, the next challenge for mainstream political discourse was to explain why some central government income transfers are legitimate without exposing the contingency of all socio-economic structures. Why choose some income transfers and not others that are just as easy to imagine (for example, a guaranteed minimum income funded by steeply progressive taxation)? One solution has been to define 'legitimate' income transfers so as to reinforce the core institutions and understandings of the social *status quo*, made 'natural' by common law background rules. Thus, social welfare laws and policies were crafted in the shadow of an assumed model of alienated wage labour, comprised of breadwinners who were subsidized by unpaid work in the home based on a gendered division of labour. In the process, social welfare law built upon and added its own nuances to law's naturalizing and legitimation projects.

An area of doctrine that illuminates this process concerns the legal designation of eligible claimants for various social welfare programmes. In legal fiction, drafters of social welfare statutes develop policy based on a population consisting of people with fixed identities independent of law (for example, a person who is, in medical terms, permanently disabled from waged work). But drafting and administering welfare laws are political practices with discursive as well as instrumental consequences. In short, legal work creates meanings. Social welfare-related legal practices partially construct the identities of deserving and undeserving claimants.

By way of illustration, one of the most fundamental distinctions in social welfare law is between programmes for 'workers' who suffer income interruption (due, for example, to unemployment, accident, or retirement) and programmes for 'non-workers'. Social insurance programmes for 'workers' or ex-workers are typically financed by employer–employee contribution schemes. Social assistance programmes for 'non-workers' are commonly financed from general revenues, and are less generous and highly stigmatized. An elaborate body of statutory rules and doctrines determines who is a 'worker' and who is not.

The worker versus non-worker distinction is highly ideological. It draws upon and develops the messages of the legal culture generally— the public/private distinction, the disjuncture of family and market, and the privileging of market activity. The highly negative popular image of welfare beneficiaries is largely a self-fulfilling prophecy of general social welfare law and policy, built upon long-standing prejudice against the poor, whether in waged or non-waged work.

To begin with, the fundamental, and fundamentally gendered, assumption of mainstream theory is that 'work' means paid work, and 'worker' means someone who works almost exclusively in waged labour. Traditional theories of 'productivity' largely exclude the value of unpaid labour as an integral factor, a cost of production. Workplace productivity assessments are based on factors that isolate one's role in paid work and ignore other parts of life that influence, contribute to, or detract from productivity. While economists and lawyers speculate about increased 'efficiency' or 'productivity' as if these were fixed or 'natural' concepts, they ignore production costs currently absorbed by the household, such as the provision of health care and childcare. The production of value outside and apart from paid work for employers does not 'count' (it is valuated at zero), so policy makers take this form of subsidy largely for granted.[8]

In addition, since everyone (including, by the twentieth century, women) owns his or her labour power and has freedom of contract, everyone potentially can work (that is, earn wages). So if a woman does not earn wages, and also fails to marry and make a home for a wage-earning spouse, her poverty is attributable to her social deviancy. Such a person becomes 'dependent' on 'the state'. The main point of this rhetoric is, of course, to stigmatize the victim, but there are several powerful subtexts. First, since waged work is the opposite of non-waged work, and since non-waged work is 'dependent', waged work must be 'independent'. Therefore mainstream theory complacently ignores or actively suppresses the alienated, subordinate, often authoritarian character of waged work, and most waged workers' utter dependence on how well their employers manage and cope with technological and market shifts.

---

[8] On the economic interdependence of paid and unpaid work and its invisibility in dominant discourse see, further, Rittich, in this volume.

Secondly, since 'non-worker' recipients of social assistance are dependent on the state, everyone else must be independent of the state. Therefore, mainstream theory ignores the role of government in creating and protecting the 'entitlement programmes' of the well-to-do, namely, the background laws of property, contract, family, and tort, not to mention tax and other subsidies to business and to middle and upper-class households.

The mainstream framing of social welfare policy in terms of the worker/non-worker distinction produces many unfortunate consequences for both general public debate and the left's ability to imagine transformative alternatives. Among the most damaging is that this perspective renders invisible the population who are *both* 'workers' (that is, waged workers) and 'non-workers' (welfare recipients, most of whom do massive amounts of unpaid family work).

Large numbers of people cycle between low-waged work and welfare programmes. Studies within the USA, immediately preceding the 1996 US 'welfare reform', document welfare and waged work as inextricably intertwined, thereby challenging the widely held assumption that welfare recipients are a category separate and distinct from paid workers. A majority of women receiving welfare move in and out of low-waged work on a regular basis.[9] One study found that of the 64 per cent of women on welfare for the first time who left the rolls within two years, almost half left for work. But of those who left, three-quarters eventually returned; 45 per cent returned within a year.[10] Another study found that 70 per cent of welfare recipients participated in some way in the waged labour force over a two-year period: 20 per cent combined paid work and welfare, 23 per cent worked intermittently, receiving welfare between jobs, 7 per cent worked limited hours and looked for more paid work, and 23 per cent searched for, but could not obtain, paid work. The women in this study held an average of 1.7 paid jobs over the two-year period and spent an average of sixteen weeks looking for paid work.[11]

As in most Western nations, the US legal rules concerning eligibility for

[9] If one used 'point in time' data, i.e. counting the percentage of those *on a given day both* receiving welfare *and* participating in waged work, there appears to be very little overlap, figures showing only about 7% of welfare recipients are also in paid labour. Staff of House Committee on Ways and Means, *Background Material and Data on Programs. Within the Jurisdiction of the Committee on Ways and Means*, 104th Cong., 2d Sess. (Washington, DC: US Government Printing Office, 1996), 474. But this type of data collection does not take into account the 'cyclical welfare/work population'.

[10] Pavetti, L. D., 'The Dynamics of Welfare and Work: Exploring the Process by Which Young Women Work Their Way Off Welfare', unpublished Ph.D. dissertation, JFK School of Government, Harvard University (1993).

[11] Spalter-Roth, R., *Making Work Pay: The Real Employment Opportunities of Single Mothers Participating in the AFDC Program* (Washington, DC: Institute for Women's Policy Research, 1994).

benefits under the Unemployment Insurance (UI) system reflect the false dichotomy between waged workers and welfare recipients. Although low-waged workers contribute to the UI benefit pool in the sense that employers pass payroll taxes onto them in the form of lower wages, UI rules exclude many low-waged workers, particularly women[12] and people of colour, from the definition of 'employee'.[13] Minimum past earning requirements in many states[14] render ineligible many part-time, low-wage workers.[15] Thus most of the single mothers who moved from welfare to waged labour and then lost their jobs found they were *ineligible* for the UI Program. In one study of women-maintained families in which the mother was employed for at least three months, almost three times as many families turned to welfare as to UI. In another study of 1,200 single mothers who received welfare for at least two months in a twenty-four month period, 43 per cent also worked, averaging just about half-time. However, only 11 per cent of those who worked later qualified for UI. By denying many low-wage-earning mothers transitional support when they become unemployed, forcing them to resort or return to welfare, UI law *constructs* them as persons who are 'not attached to the labour force', that is, as social deviants who cause their own poverty by refusing to work and who are, therefore, unworthy of assistance from society.

Far from welfare recipients demonstrating an unwillingness to work, these studies suggest that most welfare recipients prefer and endeavour

---

[12] Twenty per cent of women were excluded based on minimum weeks of prior employment as opposed to 8% of men. Ten per cent of women were disqualified based on the required amount of earnings in the highest earning quarter compared to 4% of men. Minimum earnings requirements disqualified 4% of women as opposed to 2% of men. Taken together, prior earnings requirements excluded 34% of women as opposed to 15% of men: Yoon, Y. H., Spalter-Roth, R., and Baldwin, M., *Unemployment Insurance: Barriers to Access for Women and Part-Time Workers* (Washington, DC: National Commission for Employment Policy, 1995) 24.

[13] E.g., UI coverage requires not just a connection to waged work, but a *sufficient* connection, disadvantaging low-waged and contingent workers. To meet monetary eligibility minimums, low-waged workers must work more hours than higher paid workers. Advisory Council on Unemployment Compensation, *Report and Recommendations* (Washington, DC: US Government Printing Office, 1995) 17. In 9 states, a half-time, full-year (1040 hours of work) worker who earns the minimum wage is completely ineligible for benefits, while the worker who earns $8.00 an hour for the same hours of work is eligible (ibid.). Likewise, a two-day a week, full-year worker earning the minimum wage would be ineligible in 29 states, but the same worker earning $8.00 an hour would be eligible in all but two states (ibid.).

[14] Thirty-three states require that a minimum amount of earnings be received in an individual's high-waged quarter. Thus, workers who concentrate their work hours in a shorter period are more likely to meet the eligibility requirements (ibid., 94, 98). E.g., 9 states would disqualify a half-time, full-year minimum wage worker (who worked 1040 hours), but only one state would disqualify the same worker if she worked the same number of hours full-time for 26 weeks and did not work at all for the rest of the base period (ibid., 98).

[15] One study found that 10% of all unemployed part-time workers received unemployment insurance, as opposed to 36% of full-time workers (Yoon *et al.*, above, n. 12, 34).

to earn wages even under the most trying personal circumstances. Their efforts are frequently frustrated by barriers for which legal rules and public policies are responsible. Often, they cannot find employment for which they are qualified. Even in times of low unemployment, low-waged work conditions are so precarious as to guarantee that many low-waged earners will periodically cycle through periods of unemployment. Low-waged jobs in the USA, UK, and many other developed nations pay below-subsistence wages (thereby ensuring that workers cannot provide for their families), provide little or no training or advancement opportunities, and typically have inflexible work schedules allowing no adjustment for the family-care needs of low-income families who do not have nannies or other family members available to care for their children and elders. Low-wage employers often induce employee turnover as a wage-depression strategy. Far from providing a forum for self-actualization, independence, autonomy, and empowerment, these jobs generate self-alienation, depression, poverty within wage work, and disempowerment.

The perceived bifurcation of waged work and welfare receipt allows the idea of dependency to be severed from any connection with the sale of labour power in the market, discursively erasing the alienation and subordination within low-waged work. The legal system defines who is a worker and who is independent, thereby stigmatizing adults who do not meet the legal definition of worker as trapped in dependency. The legally constructed identity of welfare recipients as shiftless non-workers, rather than as 'autonomous' wage earners, reinforces the negative images of welfare recipients that resonate so deeply with much of the US and UK public. This 'reality' drives the debate about welfare reform, as, for example, during the US debates leading to the passage of the 1996 Personal Responsibility and Work Opportunity Reconciliation Act (PRWORA). The PRWORA limits a family's ability to obtain welfare to a maximum of five years in a lifetime, and mandates stringent work requirements even during the eligibility period. In other words, the Orwellian power of legal discourse to portray workers as non-workers creates a disconnection between people's *experience as workers* and their *recognition as workers*. Like the background rules that divide the family and the market into independent 'private' spheres, both separated from 'state-imposed' welfare, social welfare laws create and reinforce identities and images that deeply influence labour and welfare policy debates.

Unfortunately, progressive labour lawyers have often played into this discourse, again privileging labour markets as the site for redistributive politics and wage labour as the arena of productivity. The dominant consensus treating 'dependency' as a condition located outside waged work helps sustain a cultural and psychological framework that encourages the labour movement and waged workers to deny or overlook their dependency and subordination. Labour movements can and do view government transfer programmes serving paid workers as legitimate entitlements for those who contribute to society, not for those dependent on society.

For example, UI laws in the USA often reflect hard fought victories for the labour movement. But traditionally, as US unions lobby for improvements in and expansion of UI laws, they have consciously distanced themselves from welfare recipients. Indeed, in urging UI reform, unions have often explicitly invoked the rhetoric of the 'worthiness' of UI as an earned entitlement, specifically juxtaposed against a view of welfare as an unearned 'dole' for non-workers. Perhaps they have done so under an assumption that union members or prospective members will never need to rely on welfare or be out of waged work for substantial periods of time because of family responsibilities, or that *incremental* victories for waged workers within the bargaining unit can be achieved only by valorizing a certain 'self-reliant' image of earner. However justified, this approach has deflected labour's attention away from government social policy as an arena of redistributive politics separate from ameliorating market imperfections.

Thus, organized labour plays into the fundamentally conservative vision that even favoured social programmes like UI (as we have seen for welfare programmes as well) are simply an adjunct to market outcomes, rather than potentially redistributive programmes. And, however unwittingly, labour reinforces the social exclusion of non-waged workers.

IV WHO IS A CITIZEN?

Recently, activists and theorists on both the left and right have embraced a refurbished discourse of citizenship as a paradigm for developing welfare policy. Despite some rhetorical appeal, this turn to citizenship discourse has not avoided, and, in some ways, has deepened, the problems arising from more traditional framings of social policy questions: privileging the market as a site for self-actualization and independence, while often ignoring, misunderstanding, and, on occasion, rendering invisible invidious class, gender, racial, and alienage biases, thereby devaluing subordinated social groups.

Advocates of the New Right have advanced claims about the obligations of citizens to support arguments for reducing or eliminating social protection programmes. They pose 'active citizenship', by which they mean participation in waged work, as an alternative to social protection. This rhetoric has been generously incorporated into current policy thinking in the USA and UK and lends support to the welfare reform consensus. Ironically, many left activists and theorists in the USA and UK are also embracing a discourse of citizenship, in part as a medium for developing arguments to defend social protection in the face of the welfare reform consensus. At times, they rely on an aspect of the idea of social citizenship,[16] that communal provision of basic needs is critical to human flourishing and self-actualization. The democratic and republican overtones are appealing, and revitalizing the concept of social citizenship may be seen as a helpful way to move beyond the liberal conception of formal equality based on acquisition of property, the franchise, and the right to associate. On the other hand, the concept of citizenship carries considerable ideological baggage. The willingness of progressive activists and theorists to work within an unreconstituted, unchallenged discourse of citizenship can be dangerously misleading in two important ways: first, within most political and theoretical discourse to date, the idea of citizenship is premised on one or another version of the public/private distinction, with the obligations of citizenship, albeit couched in neutral terms, incorporating racial and gendered models of white male productivity in the public sphere; secondly, classical concepts of citizenship rest on a model of political community that most theorists, including most left theorists, have been unwilling or unable to detach from the notion of the 'nation-state'. The modern nation-state is the product of historical forces, including conquest, imperialism, exclusion, and genocide. Nationalism is sometimes an emancipatory discourse of self-determination, but is often a platform for racism and domination. Thus the left should interrogate, not valorize, the nation-state or build a political theory on it.

Citizenship discourse encompasses both rights and obligations within the 'public' sphere. In its traditional, more limited, version, 'public' means 'governmental', and 'private' includes the realms of market, waged work, and family. Public/private corresponds to state/civil society. Under this model, citizenship entails entitlements and duties to participate actively in the political affairs of the day (for example, by voting and the exercise of expressional rights). People of colour, women, children, and individuals without real property—groups which have historically suffered political disenfranchisement—have been to a significant extent excluded from this traditional conception of citizenship.

Progressives fought a long, uphill battle to bring the concept of citizenship into the paid workplace in the form of collective bargaining rights, minimum labour standards, and equal employment opportunities.

---

[16] See generally Marshall, T. H., 'On Citizenship and Social Class', in his *Class, Citizenship and Social Development* (New York: Doubleday & Co., 1964), defining citizenship as 'a status bestowed on those who are full members of a community' and developing three stages of citizenship: civil, connoting liberty and property rights, political, connoting the franchise and right to organize, and social, connoting economic welfare and security (71–2).

Even so, the expansion of citizenship rights into paid work, as progressives traditionally fought for it, has incorporated a racialized, gendered breadwinner model. In other words, traditional progressivism effectively promotes a second version of the public/private distinction, in which 'public' means government *and* economic activity, whereas 'private' denotes the family. Although the boundary between the public and private has shifted, citizenship obligations continue to incorporate racial and gender hierarchies and bias by excluding those who are economically disenfranchised, that is, insufficiently attached to waged work. Little conceptual progress has been made to imagine viable alternative forms of citizenship participation in other arenas. Specifically, citizenship obligations until heretofore have not included care-giving, and, correspondingly, the image of the citizen does not include care-givers, whether wives, servants, or slaves.

As previously disenfranchised groups have acquired formal, political status as citizens, with rights to vote, contract, own property, and associate, the dominant political culture has embraced the assumption that 'equality' has been achieved—that all individuals, regardless of race, class, and gender, stand on an equal playing field and can negotiate in markets and family structures as equals in the pursuit of economic welfare and security. Thus, the traditional discourse of citizenship reinforces formal conceptions of equality, individualism, and self-reliance, and the view that individual responsibility (merit and effort) is the primary method for correcting economic and power imbalances. An imagery of citizenship focused on independent and autonomous individuals possessing rights and obligations within the public sphere legitimizes the correlative imagery of 'dependants'— people who are not full citizens because they are not in waged work. Paid work becomes the forum within which social citizenship can be recognized. In other words, the 'private' pre-legal rules of the market become the 'public' cultural sphere through which citizenship obligations can be fulfilled.

It is very difficult to erect a broad, multi-layered programme for economic redistribution on such a platform. Indeed, from this, it is a short step to rhetoric emphasizing the need for welfare recipients to be active and productive participants of society within the public sphere of waged work. This concept of citizenship—the white male breadwinner version— excludes welfare recipients cycling in and out of low-waged employment, juggling the demands of paid work and family responsibility, as well as care-givers who are not in the paid labour market. Like the statutory definitions of 'worker' that exclude low-waged workers and home-makers, building 'social citizenship' on the foundation of an unproblematized, liberal conception of who is a citizen risks excluding welfare recipients

and others considered outside mainstream society.[17] Because the dominant discourse embraces formal, ahistorical conceptions of the individual,
the citizen, and equality, concepts of social citizenship uncritically
derived therefrom will not be sufficiently sensitive to the structural limitations of civic rights and entitlements in societies permeated by illegitimate racial, gender, and class domination.

Yet often left labour and welfare theorists have not attended to the
highly gendered and racialized nature of citizenship as we know it, nor
have they done much to re-envision the concept to include the life experiences and needs of the millions of people who cannot meet the conventionally defined obligations of citizenship.[18] The forum for fulfilment of
citizenship, even among progressive labour and welfare advocates,
remains the public realm. Labour's conception of social citizenship refers
largely to collective action and minimum guarantees in the labour market.
Jurists interpreting welfare laws valorize waged work as the privileged
site of human self-realization.[19] Not surprisingly, since the PRWORA,
many progressive welfare lawyers have focused on assisting poor families to overcome barriers to participation in paid work. They have done
so, however, without seriously challenging the mainstream tenet that
government 'interventions'—like welfare programmes—are presump-
tively inefficient and should be carefully limited to the role of ameliorating the contradictions, and correcting the imperfections, of the market. A
left political agenda that merely grafts some socio-economic rights onto
the model of citizenship, albeit within discourses of workplace democracy and egalitarian family relations, fails to problematize its foundational concepts.

Even if we were to develop a richer conception of participation, for
example, by including care-giving activities currently denigrated because
of the privileged place of politics and waged labour, it remains the case

---

[17] Note the current rhetorical deployment by the UK government of notions of 'exclusion'
and 'inclusion', often designating lone mothers as 'excluded' from society, reminiscent of
the poverty discourse in Elizabethan times that viewed the pauper as outside the community, i.e., in the poor house. On current UK welfare policy see further Conaghan, in this
volume.

[18] Notable exceptions include O'Connor, J. S., 'Gender, Class and Citizenship in the
Comparative Analysis of Welfare State Regimes: Theoretical and Methodological Issues'
(1993) 44 *British Journal of Sociology* 501; Yuval-Davis, N., 'Women, Citizenship and
Difference' (1997) 57 *Feminist Review* 4; Orloff, above, n. 7; Lister, R., 'Citizenship: Towards
a Feminist Synthesis' (1997) 57 *Feminist Review* 28.

[19] See, e.g., *New York State Department of Social Services* v. *Dublino*, 413 US 405 (1973), and
Brief of the Appellants, New York State Departments of Social Services and Labor and their
Commissioners: 'But work is not an obligation that makes less of a man[sic], but rather it
makes more of a man. Tub work is more than doing a job, putting in time and collecting pay.
Work is a source of interest, of friendship, and of activity that gives meaning and fulfillment
to life' (36).

that citizenship discourse rests historically on notions of membership and participation in a particular polity or nation-state.[20] Although this may not be logically entailed, membership is taken to imply exclusion, whether by social or geographic boundaries. But the nation-state as we know it owes more to conquest, racial exclusion, imperialism, and genocide than to the liberal-democratic revolutions and the progressive appeal of self-determination.[21] When labour and welfare academics and activists take the national context for granted, we fail to grapple with the intricate connections linking social protection, labour, mobility of capital, and immigration, often, in ostrich-like fashion, hiding our heads in the sand in a time of increasing global economic integration.

Of course, in light of the crisis of declining union power and the intensity of assaults on the welfare state, US labour and welfare advocates and theorists have understandably focused attention on their domestic scene. However, in so doing, our rhetoric often reflects a nostalgia for isolationism. Labour's nation-state focus is most evident in its fixation on collective bargaining as the privileged site of redistributional possibility. While this model has yielded many important victories, it rests on several increasingly problematical assumptions, including, for example, the assumption that nation-states can control the impact of capital flight and currency fluctuations; that immigration can be regulated through border enforcement of legal prohibitions established by nation-states; and that union density, even within a nation-state, will reach worker-majority levels and incorporate waged workers not currently included within any collective bargaining framework, so that vertical redistribution (from management to labour) through collective bargaining poses only limited risks of exacerbating horizontal inequalities (between higher paid unionized and non-unionized, low-wage workers).

While perhaps some of these assumptions were plausible in the post-war years, for reasons discussed below, social reality is rapidly pushing in a different direction. Labour and welfare law cannot be viewed as 'domestic issues' within any nation-state. In light of currently unfolding trends toward global economic integration, a concept of citizenship anchored solely in the nation-state is anachronistic. The expansion and liberalization of trade, increased volume and mobility of capital and financing, breakdown of the Bretton Woods mechanisms for currency control, portability of many production techniques and equipment, and

---

[20] For additional discussion of the idea of citizenship within the discursive framework of the nation-state see, further, Bosniak, in this volume.

[21] Recent US critical approaches to international law have begun to articulate more complex, multi-layered notions of borders. See, e.g., Buchanan, R., 'Border Crossings: NAFTA, Regulatory Restructuring, and the Politics of Place' (1995) 2 *Indiana Journal of Global Legal Studies* 371.

the emergence of third-world manufacturing all sharply call into question the assumption that employment and social policy can be made within a nation-state framework. All of this is in addition to the moral and political imperative for people in the developed world to accept responsibility for addressing the gross maldistribution of wealth and resources on a world scale.

Mainstream US politicians and, regrettably, many progressive critics discuss 'transitioning' welfare recipients to work under the PRWORA within a framework based not only on a dichotomized image of welfare recipient versus waged worker, but also on a domestic labour market, as if the USA had no links to the rest of the world. But economic life in the USA involves massive cross-border capital and labour flows and integrated, cross-border production chains. Changes in labour or welfare laws in other countries often have important ramifications in the USA (and vice versa), whether in the form of human migration, capital migration, or rising naturalizations of legal immigrants. More restrictive immigration policy, rather than reducing migration, may produce more undocumented immigrants, creating a quite different impact on US low-wage labour markets than that produced by legal immigration. Progressive lawyers attempting to develop new institutional mechanisms for redistribution must grapple carefully with the tension between capital mobility and restrictions on the free movement of persons.

The relationship between the USA and Mexico highlights the implications of cross-border labour, welfare, immigration, and trade interactions, particularly the impact of anti-NAFTA and anti-immigrant rhetoric on US welfare policy and naturalizations, and the artificiality of borders *vis-à-vis* citizenship. US labour union opposition to the NAFTA in 1994 was often voiced as a fear of 'losing US jobs to Mexico'. Two years later, the PRWORA terminated the eligibility of *legal* immigrants, whether or not in waged work, for virtually all welfare programmes. Mexicans formed the largest group of US legal immigrants by far, who had chosen not to naturalize as US citizens. Labour and welfare academics and activists condemned PRWORA, but there was virtually no self-critique as to whether labour's anti-NAFTA position might have, however unintentionally, fed into racist, anti-Mexican, and anti-immigration attitudes that culminated in the disqualification of thousands of legal immigrants.

In ratifying the NAFTA, one bone that Congress threw to labour was the NAFTA–Trade Adjustment Act providing additional weeks of UI benefits for retraining workers (excluding workers not covered by UI laws) who lose their jobs due to increased imports or capital flight generated by the NAFTA. As a result, US taxpayers are funding the extended UI and retraining of workers dislocated by US trade policy, at the same

Lucy A. Williams

time as they are defunding many welfare benefits to low-waged welfare recipients and legal, often Mexican, immigrants.

PRWORA's targeting of immigrants and similar political developments (such as California's Proposition 187 barring undocumented immigrants from receiving almost all education, social services, and health benefits) prompted the emergence of a new consciousness among legal Mexican immigrants in the USA to become naturalized US citizens so that they could vote and participate fully politically. This development in turn has brought about profound changes in the political landscape. Until 1994, the number of naturalizations by Mexicans legally residing in the United States was fairly stable at about 20,000 per year. In 1994, the year that Californians adopted Proposition 187, naturalizations surged to 46,186, and in 1995 to 79,614. Most dramatically, in 1996 (the year the PRWORA was being debated and enacted), Mexico was the leading country-of-birth of persons naturalizing, with 254,988 or 24.4 per cent of total naturalizations.[22] As naturalized citizens, these individuals enjoy greatly expanded legal rights to bring family members into the USA. Thus the ironic result of anti-immigrant politics in the 1990s may be that even greater numbers of Mexican immigrants will settle in the USA, naturalize, and vote. This, in turn, raises questions about the effect of this additional supply of waged workers on both union density and decisions of companies to relocate cross-border.

Juxtapose these developments to dramatic new changes in Mexican laws relating to dual citizenship and the ability of non-residents to vote in Mexican elections. Recent legal changes allow Mexican non-residents to maintain dual nationality. In particular, Mexican immigrants who are naturalized US citizens are now permitted to reclaim their Mexican nationality.[23] Mexico's Constitution was modified to allow non-resident Mexican citizens to vote in Mexican elections without returning to Mexico.[24] Although not yet implemented at the time of the 2000 election (in which the Institutional Revolutionary party (PRI) was defeated for the first time since 1920 by the National Action Party (PAN)), almost 10 million Mexicans, more or less permanently residing in the USA, could be

---

[22] US Dept. of Justice, Immigration and Naturalization Service, *1996 Statistical Yearbook of the Immigration and Naturalization Service* (Washington, DC: US Department of Justice, Immigration and Naturalization Service, 1997) 152. Of course, there were other legal changes which factored into this increase, most specifically the numbers of undocumented immigrants allowed to naturalize pursuant to the Immigration Reform and Control Act of 1986, Pub. L. No. 99–603, 100 Stat. 3359 (1986).

[23] Constitucion Politica de los Estados Unidos Mexicanos, Art. 37 (amended 1997). There are nuances between nationality and citizenship that are beyond the scope of this chapter.

[24] Although the Chamber of Deputies had approved a package implementing this election reform, the Senate (controlled by the PRI) allowed the measure to die in July 1999: Smith, J. F., 'Vote Denied to Mexicans Living Abroad', *Los Angeles Times*, 2 July 1999, at A1.

eligible to vote in Mexican elections. They are expected to support either the PAN or the Party of the Democratic Revolution (PRD), Mexican political parties advocating the democratization of labour unions in Mexico.[25] Thus the huge increase in US naturalizations by Mexicans (in turn opening the door for further immigration by family members) and the emergence of dual citizenship and dual voting privileges in Mexico could have broad implications for social protection and low-wage labour in both the USA and Mexico, exemplifying why citizenship attached to the nation-state is an increasingly antiquated concept.

Most lawyers working to revivify the concept of social citizenship and enlist it in the service of progressive causes reflexively and unconsciously adopt the nation-state perspective or, at best, leave that aspect of citizenship discourse unexamined. But 'social citizenship' will never become the emblem of redistributive politics and transformative aspirations until it is re-imagined from a thoroughly globalized perspective.

V CONCLUSION

The three legal discourses discussed in this chapter individually and cumulatively privilege labour markets and waged work, marginalize broad redistributive agendas as exceptions, and obscure the understanding that all legal questions have distributive implications. Family and market are constructed as private, pre-legal, and autonomous from the state. The role of background legal rules in entrenching power imbalances within those societal spheres is ignored. Labour lawyers and welfare lawyers have both contributed to the discursive construction of income distribution as somehow independent of state action: labour lawyers by valorizing labour markets and collective bargaining as the privileged site of income distribution while at the same time viewing welfare law as a 'special case' of state intervention, and welfare lawyers by fixating on government transfer policy and largely ignoring private law. Thus welfare law becomes a market corrective technique, an adjunct to private law, rather than a redistributive hub. Likewise social insurance and social assistance statutes, often fought for and defended by the left, separate 'workers' and 'non-workers' through artificial definitions that support the creation of partial identities. When labour lawyers argue for enhanced UI benefits on the ground that society should protect and reward primary-sector wage-earners, they are 'othering' many potential allies

[25] McDonnell, P. J., 'US Votes Could Sway Mexico's Next Election', *Los Angeles Times*, 15 Feb. 1999, at A1. On labour politics in a Mexican context see further, De Buen Unna, in this volume.

within waged work and denigrating non-waged work, thereby perpetuating a hierarchy of market work over family care-giving performed
primarily by women. The discourse of citizenship perpetuates a male
model of participation in the 'public' spheres of liberal democratic institutions and waged work as the means of fulfilling citizenship obligations
and therefore acquiring full social status. And traditional citizenship
discourse legitimates first-world protectionist policies and attitudes that
perpetuate gross global inequalities, while ignoring the implications of
increasing global interdependence. The discourses of these quite
disparate fields reinforce one another. However unwittingly, progressive
legal advocacy often reaffirms the prevailing political 'consensus'—that
policies privileging the nation-state, market, and traditional family are
natural and those dismantling the welfare state are inevitable.

   In other words, the rhetoric of many progressive labour and welfare
theoreticians and activists assumes that the identities constructed by
statutory social welfare programmes accurately reflect a pre-legal order
providing the appropriate framework for self-fulfilment and citizenship
activity. The reaffirmation of the free market and the traditional family as
the 'correct' framework for dealing with domestic and global income
disparities—without challenging and transforming the background rules
that structure markets and families—perpetuates class, racial, and gender
inequality and disempowerment.

   I do not suggest that we must devise a single, integrated, cross-border
low-wage labour and poverty policy. But we must challenge ourselves to
look beyond our limited or narrowly defined constituencies, to frame new
questions about labour and welfare strategy within an increasingly globalized economy. My hope is that, by increasing the amount and sophistication of dialogue among social welfare, low-wage labour, immigration,
family, and economic globalization discourses, scholars and activists in
these linked fields can begin to disrupt and undermine the ways legal
culture legitimates and reinforces the social and economic *status quo*. This
chapter challenges both labour and welfare lawyers to enter more rigor-
ously into interdisciplinary self-critique as a basis for intellectual renewal
and the creation of a transformative vision of the politics of redistribution.

Part III

Globalization and its Discontents

6

Feminization and Contingency: Regulating the Stakes of Work for Women

KERRY RITTICH*

Among the most dramatic transformations in the world of work in the last generation has been the steep rise in the number of women in the paid labour force. This trend, already well-established virtually everywhere at least ten years ago,[1] has become even more entrenched,[2] showing no signs of reversal; on the contrary, everything points to a decisive and fundamental shift in the face of the labour force.

The gendered transformation of work has taken place alongside the emergence of the new economy and the growing salience of what is commonly identified as contingent, non-standard, or atypical work. It is characteristic of all industrialized countries that the rate at which part-time, casual, temporary, own account or self-employed, homework, and contract work are growing, outstrips the growth in full-time, long-term work in the service of a single employer or sector, with regular pay, hours, and working conditions. Nor are these developments restricted to the industrialized parts of the global economy. Rather, atypical arrangements have come to represent standard modes of organizing work in global production. The result is the 'feminization'[3] of labour: an unfolding landscape of work in which, as women have entered the labour force, the forms and structures of the work traditionally associated with women have increasingly become normalized.

This process has been profoundly important, not simply to women but to the path of economic development and the transformation of work relations in general. For example, no country has successfully industrialized via export promotion without drawing on a large pool of low-wage female workers.[4] Indeed, women are often the preferred workers in both

* I am very grateful to the Social Sciences and Humanities Research Council of Canada for their generous support of the reseach in connection with this project.
[1] With the exception of Central and Eastern Europe and the CIS, which already had relatively high labour force participation rates for women. See ILO, *Yearbook of Labour Statistics* (Geneva: ILO, various years).
[2] Standing, G., 'Global Feminization through Flexible Labor: A Theme Revisited' (1999) 27 *World Development* 583.
[3] Standing, G., 'Global Feminization through Flexible Labor' (1989) 17 *World Development* 1077.
[4] Standing, above, n. 2, 585.

service work and production, not least because they can often be compelled to accept terms and conditions that cannot be successfully imposed upon men. Most industrialized countries also rely on low-waged women workers, a disproportionate number of whom are immigrants or racial and ethnic minorities, for increasing amounts of service and production work.

Much of this work is either definitionally excluded or badly served by labour standards, employment regulations, and collective bargaining laws. In the industrialized world, this is partly due to the constituency toward which such rules and standards were originally targeted, and the particular work relations and structures that were affected as a result. Now, the absence or repeal of legislation, the creation of 'regulation-free' production zones, the exclusion of particular types of work, the failure to adjust standards, and weak enforcement have created a growing cadre of workers who derive little benefit from the matrix of labour and employment rules and are subject to the cost-benefit calculus governing other commercial transactions. As work is subcontracted, the distinction between formal and informal work becomes increasingly blurred and difficult to sustain. The rise in non-standard or contingent work is, along with a deformalization of work, also associated with the expansion of the 'unregulated' or underground economy.

The feminization of labour is an ambiguous term,[5] signaling both the perils and the possibilities of the new economy for workers. Despite the obvious attractions of labour force participation, it is clear that access to flexible work is far from an unmitigated benefit for many women. In the face of low wages and job insecurity, impediments, both legal and practical, to collective action, and poor prospects for acquiring greater skills or control over the workplace, it often represents, at best, an improvement over unhappy local alternatives, a choice exercised by those with few better options.

While labour scholars and progressive policy-makers everywhere are currently preoccupied with the flexibilization of work and the deterioration in the position of workers it seems to imply, attention to the gendered character of this phenomenon and its connection to the ongoing reorganization of work is often curiously absent.[6] Yet although it now attracts attention because a growing number of men do it too, atypical work,

---

[5] Standing, above, n. 2, 585.

[6] One exception is European Commission, Directorate-General for Employment, Industrial Relations and Social Affairs, *Transformation of Labour and Future of Labour Law in Europe* (Luxembourg, EC Commission, June 1999) [the Supiot Report]. This report looks explicitly at the feminization of labour; it also considers shifting conceptions of working time and advocates the adoption of a new concept of 'occupational status' that would reflect time spent both outside and inside the labour force.

particularly at the low end, remains deeply associated with women, suggesting that the simultaneous appearance of more atypical work, more women workers, and declining worker power is not merely fortuitous. Some of the concerns generated by the feminization of labour are not altogether new. However, current productive strategies have intensified their effects and importance in ways that make them integral to contemporary debates over the rights, rules, standards, and practices that govern the operation of labour markets. As a result, the concerns and agenda that labour scholars and activists seek to promote need to be refocused in the effort better to understand what lies between the transformed structure of work and those who now do it.

While neither has disappeared, both 'normal' work and the average or ideal worker in whose image the organization and regulation of productive activity, as well as much of the wider social policy agenda in industrialized states, was crafted are increasingly difficult to locate. It seems unavoidably clear that there is no longer any single, prototypical worker; continued reliance on an outmoded ideal is the source of but one of the many misalignments that lie at the heart of the regulatory conundrum in the new economy.[7] The old deal, which mandated a 'family wage' for the protected male worker and unpaid domestic labour for his wife, is in disarray, if not completely undone. Many men in industrialized states no longer earn a family wage; those in developing countries cannot safely aspire to do so. Most women in the west, even those with very small children, now do labour market work as well as domestic work; most others, have never contemplated market work on any other terms. Moreover, many families do not look anything like the nuclear unit upon which the old deal rested; everywhere, single parent families, almost always headed by women, are proliferating.

There have always been demonstrably partial and unsafe assumptions about the identity, interests, and circumstances of workers underpinning the regulation of work. However, the feminization of labour and the subversion of the 'normal' worker in its wake have made these assumptions progressively more unsound, placing new items on the agenda and heightening the significance of many that have long hovered in the wings. Foremost among these are the intersecting, and often conflicting, demands of productive and reproductive work.

'Feminization' has therefore brought to the surface yet another misalignment in the emerging economy. Both trade unions and labour academics have typically concerned themselves exclusively with paid

---

[7] For a discussion of other misalignments in the new economy, in particular, the discontinuities between political, economic, and juridical space, see Arthurs, H. W., 'Labour Law Without the State?' (1996) 46 *University of Toronto L. Review* 1.

work. Indeed, feminist scholars apart, the idea that 'work' denotes market work is such a deep background assumption that it is rarely subject to comment, let alone question. However, the feminization of work casts doubt on the problematic division between market and non-market work. It also disturbs the longstanding tendency of both market reformers and the labour movement to treat such issues as the special concerns of women, separate from 'hard' economic issues and marginal to the concerns of labour as a whole.

The feminization of labour also stands as a direct challenge to the emerging narrative about the worker in the global economy. Once it is recognized that women with obligations of care represent highly plausible workers in the new economy, many of its operative assumptions seem questionable, if not absurd; the idea that it represents a progress narrative and model to which workers should aspire is seriously undermined.

In market reform agendas of various stripes,[8] workers are increasingly figured as entrepreneurs who, facing the inexorable imperatives of the new economy, must invest in their 'human capital' and sell their talents to the highest bidder. As the new forms of discipline and flexibility that the emerging labour market both permits and requires are celebrated, the model worker becomes one who conforms to its demands. Embracing risk, eschewing the siren call of security, and casting off reliance on labour market regulations and traditional worker strategies such as collective action, he adopts a posture of co-operation rather than conflict toward his employers. Adjusting continually to the changing landscape of work and armed only with 'core' individual rights, he remains mobile and ready to exploit the ever more attractive opportunities generated by the market.

In many such accounts, there is little attention to the gendered organization of work and production, the omnipresent stratification of labour markets along such lines as ethnicity, race, and national origin, and the disadvantage this generates for different groups of workers. Instead, the story proceeds as if there are simply 'workers' who, apart from individual talents and preferences, enter the labour market and compete among each other on essentially similar terms. The non-market activities and circumstances of these workers are treated as if they were of no concern. Indeed, one of the major assumptions underlying the entrepreneurial model is that workers are not seriously encumbered by obligations that cannot be subordinated to the demands of paid work.

Strikingly muted in, if not absent altogether from, such narratives are references to the historic disadvantage of workers in their encounter with capital and, by extension, the *raison d'etre* for the regulation of labour

---

[8] See, e.g., World Bank, *World Development Report 1995: Workers in an Integrating World* (New York: Oxford University Press, 1995); and Collins, in this volume.

markets. Instead, at the very moment when workers appear to have become intensely vulnerable and discussion about disparities in power unusually relevant, distributional conflicts have been eclipsed. In many places, the use of labour market regulation and collective worker action to redress such conflicts is discredited.[9] There are new calls for refocusing attention on 'core' or fundamental labour rights such as freedom from slavery, the abolition of child labour, freedom of the individual to associate, and freedom from discrimination.[10] However, at the same time, labour standards, employment regulations, and collective action through unions, the traditional vehicles by which workers have captured greater economic returns and a measure of control over their working lives, are newly subject to scrutiny and criticism. They now have an uncertain, if not illegitimate, place in the architecture of the new economy.

Given the reconstructed ideal worker and the general displacement of distributional questions, it is perhaps unsurprising that there is also little discussion of the structural reasons why some groups of workers, including many groups of women, cannot readily perform according to the emerging ideal. Although the constraints of families and households on labour market participation have long formed the basis for regulating the working conditions of women, now such particularities and complications, and the solutions to them, are often simply written out of the script.

This changing ideology surrounding labour market regulation is embedded in a concurrent shift in expectations about the state. At the same time as the organization of work is undergoing transformation, dependence on the state is being discouraged, if not pathologized, and individuals increasingly induced, if not coerced, to rely on the market to secure their welfare.[11] As the worker is idealized and private responsibilities increase, participation in the market thus increases exponentially in importance.

The decline of the redistributive state means that the conditions determining how particular groups of workers fare in the market have become of paramount importance. However, the potential effects of different market regimes may be markedly different for men and women. Apart from the differences caused by ongoing gender disparities in wages and the vertical and horizontal stratification of labour markets, much of the

---

[9] However, there still remains significant variation among states, visible in particular between the USA and Europe, in the role accorded to unions and the legitimacy of labour market regulations.

[10] ILO, Declaration on Fundamental Principles and Rights at Work, 86th Session, Geneva, June 1998, available at http://www.ilo.org/public/english/standards/decl/index.htm (accessed 2 June 2000).

[11] Fraser, N., and Gordon, L., 'A Genealogy of "Dependency": Tracing a Keyword of the U.S. Welfare State' in Fraser, N., *Justice Interruptus: Critical Reflections on the 'Postsocialist' Condition* (New York: Routledge, 1997).

risk for women lies beyond the workplace in the gendered division of labour in households and in the boundaries which are (re)constituted between economic and social or political concerns, and productive and non-productive activity.

I UNPACKING WORK

In the new economy, it is easy to lose sight of the fact that what matters is not simply what changes, but what is held stable in the background. Making sense of the prospects for women in emerging labour markets, as well as the claim that a fundamental reconfiguration of the labour agenda is in order, requires drawing into the foreground some of the most fundamental facts and assumptions about the nature and organization of productive activity. While these facts and assumptions almost always pass without comment, it is here that the keys to the relative fortunes of men and women in emerging labour markets reside.

First, despite the feminization of labour, work remains a deeply gendered activity. Labour markets are routinely organized according to the real and perceived characteristics of particular groups of workers and everywhere remain hierarchically segregated according to gender. Despite considerable variation, it is characteristic of all societies that men and women undertake different types of work and that gender is one of the major axes around which work is organized.[12] Indeed, this phenomenon is so pervasive as to suggest that if gender identities are produced as they are enacted,[13] gender takes its meaning in important ways from the performance of different tasks and activities by men and women. Secondly, productive activity comes in paid and unpaid varieties. Although unpaid work is conventionally differentiated from 'real' work and excluded from mainstream discussions about labour markets, it is, in fact, integral to the performance and structure of productive activity in the market. Thirdly, the performance of unpaid work is, like market work, markedly gendered; women do most of it, a fact of great significance for the feminization of labour markets. The short explanation is that the image of the worker, the manner in which paid work is organized, the jobs women occupy, and women's ability to respond to incentives and opportunities of the market have everything to do with the roles men and women tend to assume and the tasks they perform, or are exempt from

---

[12] Hadfield, G., 'A Coordination Model of the Sexual Division of Labor' (1999) 40 *Journal of Economic Behaviour and Organization* 125–53.

[13] Butler, J., *Gender Trouble: Feminism and the Subversion of Identity* (New York and London: Routledge, 1990).

performing, outside the market. Consequently, no probing investigation of the operation of labour markets is possible without an examination of the way that they are formed by and articulated with other institutions such as the family or household. Indeed, given the concurrent feminization and deformalization of labour markets, any analysis that ignores these issues, both in the organization of production and in the lives of workers, seems unlikely to capture some of the central characteristics and dynamics of current labour markets.

The limits of imagining work as co-extensive with certain types of employment relations are fast upon us. Even in 'regulated' sectors, entrepreneurs and enterprises, by exploiting the boundaries of firms, have rather easily found modes of circumventing employment rules and standards and mitigating or avoiding the obligations they incur as employers. Less obvious are the limits to focusing on paid work alone. Work in the new economy not only tends to cross the boundaries between firms and traverses the borders of the formal and informal sectors, it also increasingly troubles the established boundaries between 'productive' and 'reproductive' tasks. Emerging forms of work are now as likely to obscure as to respect distinctions between public and private time and space, and market and non-market activities.[14] Telecommuting, industrial homework, and increased subcontracting, self-employment, and informal work all signal, among other things, new pressure on the conventional geographic separation of work from non-work space, work from non-work time, and costs of production from costs of living. All such transformations potentially entail economic consequences for individual workers. As market and non-market time and activities become intermingled, workers, particularly those at the bottom end, are at risk of absorbing more of the costs and risks of production.

Although technological innovations play a role, these developments are also related to the demands of unpaid work. Many of those engaged in atypical work do not conform to the new entrepreneurial ideal but have household activities and obligations that preclude some employment options and render others attractive. While this has always been true of atypical workers, the increase in such work may indicate that employers are now more innovative and aggressive in exploiting the circumstances of particular workers and the opportunities they present to shift and lower costs.

Even where the lines between work and other activities remain relatively clear, however, unpaid obligations remain important to the structure of paid work and the prospects of different workers. Because they routinely affect the hours of paid work, the mobility of workers, the type

---

[14] See Supiot Report, above, n. 6.

of work, the degree of responsibility that workers feel able to assume and that employers are prepared to assign them, they seriously affect the position of many women, and some men, in the labour market. Freedom from such obligations, by contrast, confers a concomitant advantage, allowing those without them to focus on market work and reap the attendant rewards.

On reflection, it is not obvious why only certain types of work should be of interest, while others—domestic work, volunteer work, subsistence work, or community work, for example—remain largely neglected. As non-controversial and deeply normalized as it seems, this state of affairs was rendered possible in part because the mainstream labour agenda became consolidated around the concerns of workers for whom work simply meant paid work. The relative freedom men enjoyed, and still continue to enjoy, from unpaid household and family obligations meant that, except to the extent that they affected wage levels, non-work obligations could be treated as irrelevant to the conflicts and concerns of work.

The result was that the concerns and interests of significant numbers of workers, many of whom were women, were not reflected in the rules and conventions regulating work.[15] Trade unions historically failed actively to press these concerns; indeed, often they bluntly traded them off against those of men. The result was a set of regulations that produced both privileged forms of work and privileged workers. The active and successful lobby for a family wage, for example, positioned men and women as workers with greater or lesser entitlements to remuneration simply by virtue of their sex and status, and simultaneously enabled both employers and male workers to exclude women from many forms of employment. The priority given to seniority and job security for full-time workers systematically disadvantaged those with intermittent or more tangential connections to the paid workforce. This history casts a long shadow. Had there been serious engagement with the situation of women in the labour market, it seems highly unlikely that the world of production would have been defined as it is, and the intersection of unpaid work and market work placed beyond the concerns of labour.

The current instability surrounding the employment relationship in the new economy has prodded labour activists, scholars, and policy-makers into rethinking the category and definition of employee. The progressive disintegration and fragmentation of the ideal worker compel a similar reconsideration of productive work and the boundaries of workplace concerns. They also enable us to see more clearly how labour market regulations help organize work, producing not only advantage and

---

[15] See Conaghan, J., 'The Invisibility of Women in Labour Law: Gender-neutrality in Model-building' (1986) 14 *International Journal of Sociology of Law* 377.

disadvantage for different groups of workers but particular types of workers.

Effective state regulation is a marker of the boundary between formal and informal work. However, in important ways, law also helps determine the boundary between paid and unpaid work. Unpaid work is not simply 'found', it is made. It is a function of how production in total is organized, a legacy of the separation of industrial from home production and the radical reconceptualization and devaluation of household labour.[16] The differential recognition and compensation for varying forms of work is both reflected in and produced by the rules and institutions that govern employment, production and exchange. Legal entitlements not only allocate resources and powers to various parties in labour market transactions and influence the way that market work is structured and the degree to which workers and employers benefit; the regulation of labour and production is one of the mechanisms by which the very boundary between production and reproduction, and market and non-market activities, is produced. Myriad laws, standards, policies, and regulations determine whether, and to what extent, certain risks are shared and which tasks and activities, both market and non-market, are compensated or cross-subsidized by other workers, employers, and consumers. Thus, unpaid work is actually produced, to an extent that resists easy or certain calculation, by the regulation of work and the laws governing markets. So too are gender norms around work, which are themselves continually reconstituted and reinforced by the incentives which these regulations provide.

The amount of compensation different parties enjoy and the risks they absorb in connection with particular activities are affected as much by the absence as by the presence of legal rules, employment policies, and other norms, as the lack of entitlements imposes costs on workers and confers corresponding benefits on employers. The close connections between legal entitlements, the allocation of resources, and the distribution of income means that the laws governing production are continually implicated not just in the organization of paid work but in the structure and welfare of households as well. Because direct access to external resources appears to improve the position of women within the household, the presence or absence of legal entitlements can affect both the behavior and

---

[16] Folbre, N., 'The Unproductive Housewife: Her Evolution in Nineteenth Century Thought' (1991) 16 *Signs: Journal of Women in Culture and Society* 463.

relative power of different parties within the household,[17] and thus the structure of gender norms, as well. Current debates on the regulation of markets are thus a promising site from which to consider the making of work, both valuable and worthless. Within those debates, what counts as an economic, business, or productive issue, and which forms of work are compensated have now become inseparable from the labour market prospects of large numbers of workers.

III THE NEXUS BETWEEN PAID AND UNPAID WORK

As a consequence of the recent work of feminist and development economists,[18] it has become more broadly recognized that unpaid work has independent economic value. As numerous reports have documented, unpaid labour, the vast majority of which is undertaken by women, contributes substantially to national economies. It appears that at least as much unpaid as paid work is performed; if its value was included in systems of national accounts, estimates suggest that indices of growth would be increased somewhere in the order of 30 to 50 per cent.[19]

Whatever its other uses, the attempt to draw attention to unpaid work is a strategy to subvert a number of commonly held assumptions, the most basic of which is that unpaid work is irrelevant to economic life. Despite the fact that unpaid work is widely styled as 'reproductive' and distinguished from 'productive' or market-based work, the calculation of its value makes clear that it is not intrinsically less productive than market work. Indeed, for many purposes, reproductive work is not inherently different from productive work. Its domestic location and the fact that it often involves the care of people with whom the caregiver has an intimate relationship tends to obscure the fact that it is still 'real' work. Despite the widely held intuition that certain tasks are naturally or properly done for free, where they are not, services must be either purchased in the market or foregone, sometimes at significant cost.

[17] Agarwal, B., ' "Bargaining" and Gender Relations: Within and Beyond the Household' (1997) 3 *Feminist Economics* 1; Sen, A., 'Gender and Co-operative Conflict' in Tinker, I. (ed.), *Persistent Inequalities: Women and World Development* (New York: Oxford University Press, 1990).

[18] Boserup, E., *Women's Role in Economic Development* (London: Allen and Unwin, 1970); Waring, M., *If Women Counted: A New Feminist Economics* (San Francisco, Cal.: Harper and Row, 1988); Elson, D., 'Male Bias in Macroeconomics: the Case of Structural Adjustment' in Elson, D. (ed.), *Male Bias in the Development Process* (Manchester: Manchester University Press, 1990), 164; Beneria, L., 'Accounting for Women's Work: the Progress of Two Decades' (1992) 20 *World Development* 1547; Beneria, L., 'Conceptualizing the Labour Force: the Underestimation of Women's Economic Activities' in Pahl, R. E. (ed.), *On Work: Historical, Comparative and Theoretical Approaches* (Oxford: Blackwell, 1988).

[19] See UNDP, *Human Development Report 1995* (New York: Oxford University Press, 1995), 97.

Apart from redrawing the boundary of productive activity, part of the point of tabulating the time involved in unpaid work and calculating its value is to unsettle conclusions about the dependent status of those who perform it and the consequent direction in which subsidies flow. While those who specialize in unpaid work may be dependent on others for providing the financial wherewithal to purchase other goods and services, it is also the case that those workers, often men, who engage in market work free of such obligations normally receive a substantial benefit or subsidy from those who perform unpaid household services for them or their children.[20] In short, the ability of 'autonomous' market actors to function in an entrepreneurial manner, or simply to function at all in labour markets, often depends on the presence of someone to do un- or under-paid work. Yet, the feminization of labour typically means that these workers increasingly *are* also those unpaid workers.

Calculating the extent of unpaid work allows a more comprehensive picture to be drawn of the scope of economic activity than does measuring market growth alone. It also provides a mechanism, as yet largely unexploited, for tracing the aggregate economic effects of policy and regulatory shifts in the state or the market. Although typically excluded from measurements of economic growth, unpaid work is routinely affected by and relied upon as a cost-saving strategy and unacknowledged safety net in market reform and restructuring plans. For example, contractions in the monetized economy that often follow the implementation of fiscal austerity measures may increase the amount of unpaid work performed. Conversely, increases in economic growth indicated by measures such as the Gross Domestic Product may simply indicate a shift from subsistence or home to market production, rather than any real increase in the level of productive activity. Measures that are efficiency enhancing from the perspective of the enterprise or state may simply impose new costs on households. They may also exact hidden costs, such as increased unpaid work and/or reduced ability to engage in market activity, thus actually suppressing sources of economic growth. At the end of the day, many strategies conventionally identified as economically efficient, and thus deemed unequivocally beneficial, may turn out principally to shift burdens and redistribute economic returns. The pursuit of efficiency may have real, if hidden, costs, including costs that cast the very efficiency of the strategies concerned in doubt.

Some of these effects are foreseeable, given that whether a strategy is costly or efficient for a particular party is partly a function of the manner

---

[20] This is an old, if neglected, observation. See, e.g., Hindman, M., 'Who Will Support You?', *New Northwest*, 10 Oct. 1878, quoted in Siegel, R., 'Home as Work: The First Woman's Rights Claims Concerning Wives' Household Labor, 1850–1880' (1994) 103 *Yale L. Journal* 1073, 1156–7.

in which legal entitlements are allocated.[21] Economic value and determinations about efficient economic strategies are artifacts, rather than facts, that result partly from a given structure of legal entitlements. If the dichotomy between work and non-work is largely socially constructed,[22] it is in part due to the way that productive activity is regulated. For example, if there is no legal requirement compelling enterprises to internalize the costs of child-care or maternity leave, employers may be strongly inclined to externalize them and the labour becomes unpaid as a result.

Despite current policy and regulatory efforts to promote the creation of markets organized principally around the logic of efficiency, these insights complicate the claims that economic issues are different from social and political issues, and that productive activities and expenditures can easily be separated from unproductive, valueless, or burdensome activities and expenditures. They also subvert the argument that the enhancement of efficiency can be unproblematically advanced through regulatory and institutional reforms without contravening or even engaging other social or political projects. Because the concerns and activities of enterprises and households are interrelated and the structure of production and reproduction interconstitutive, decisions about reform inevitably affect the operation of households and the individual prospects of their members.

From this perspective, the ongoing if not growing disadvantage to women working beyond the reach of labour and employment regulation is entirely explicable: it is a function of presence and absence of particular legal entitlements in the market and the strategies those entitlements encourage. Because women perform the bulk of unpaid tasks, the displacement of a growing number of costs and responsibilities to the 'private' sphere, whether by the employer or the state, is likely to increase burdens and have significant negative distributional effects for women.

The effects of differential unpaid work obligations are not confined to workers. Although the ways in which employers and enterprises benefit are neither well-delineated nor widely accepted, they too derive significant value both directly and indirectly from unpaid household labour. Indeed, this value has increased to the extent that they are no longer providing even limited compensation for unpaid work through family wages. Absent either significant increases in wages sufficient to replace unpaid services through the market or subsidized services provided by

[21] Kennedy, D., 'Law and Economics from the Perspective of Critical Legal Studies' in Newman, P. (ed.), *The New Palgrave Dictionary of Economics and the Law* (London: Macmillan Reference, 1998).

[22] Tzannatos, Z., 'Women and Labor Market Changes in the Global Economy: Growth Helps, Inequalities Hurt and Public Policy Matters' (1999) 27 *World Development* 551.

the state, both of which run counter to the new economy narrative, few workers can easily accommodate intensified work demands. As a result, like natural resources such as air or water, a substantial part of the cost of providing and sustaining the labour force is taken for granted but in fact heavily subsidized by the unpaid or under-compensated labour of women, women who are themselves increasingly likely to be also market workers.

There is nothing natural or inevitable about the boundaries between productive and reproductive activity or the ability of different parties to pass on or absorb greater or lesser parts of the costs of production. Indeed, struggle over these very issues is one way to conceptualize the current debate over the scope and legitimacy of labour rights and standards. Current employer and worker entitlements represent not the immutable order of things but the outcome of earlier social and political struggles that have been institutionalized in formal rights and informal norms. They reflect among other things the relative power of workers and employers, and the relatively weak position of women *vis-à-vis* men; at the same time they help constitute that power and position. As they represent the contingent settlement of the conflicts surrounding work, production, and exchange of an earlier era, there is no reason to expect that they should stand untransformed, or at least uncontested, during the current transformation of work.

More specifically, the terms of employment may convert unpaid work into labour that is at least partly compensated. If, as already occurs in some states, maternity and child-care leave were both extensive and well-compensated, we could expect a significant reduction in both the number of women with intermittent employment status and the amount of time that women spend on unpaid work. However, the relative freedom of male workers from such obligations has enabled the organization of work around a worker who is unencumbered by unpaid duties. This is reflected most directly in the absence of a robust set of laws and work norms accommodating the time, expense, and career disruption these duties almost inevitably involve. If, by contrast, all workers were assumed to have obligations of care during at least part of their paid-working lives, the organization of production and compensation for such risks and costs would necessarily be very different. The interaction of the two worlds of work would be prioritized by trade unions and some settlement concerning their intersecting and often competing demands would be reflected in labour and employment norms and regulations.[23]

Thus the feminization of labour brings to the surface the gap between

---

[23] On recent regulatory efforts in the UK to address the work–family intersection and their consequences for women see Conaghan, in this volume.

the work that is the object of regulatory attention and the varied forms of work, paid and unpaid, that people actually do. Establishing the economic value of unpaid work and its nexus to other productive activities, while hardly guaranteeing automatic compensation, provides a basis from which to challenge the established boundaries between workplace and non-workplace concerns, and the distribution of power and resources in the new economy. This is a pressing need, given the growing reliance on the false ideal of the unencumbered worker. It also calls into question contemporary claims that labour regulations such as maternity leave are necessarily a drag on efficiency.

If the average worker is as likely to be female as male and now engages in extensive amounts of both paid and unpaid work, then the presumption that workers are normally available for work unencumbered by significant non-market concerns is mistaken. Moreover, if the performance of that unpaid work is not unrelated but necessary to economic activity, it is also a mistake to treat it as a purely private, non-market issue. Finally, if market participation is to be the *sine qua non* of welfare and security in the new economic order, the question is why a response to these issues is not central to the policy and regulatory debates in the new economy.[24]

There are myriad rules and policies in fields as diverse as family law, taxation, social welfare policy, and health care that have a potentially significant impact on the structure and amount of unpaid work performed. However, in a climate in which greater taxation and spending on social programmes are increasingly resisted on both normative and economic grounds, the question remains how to ensure that workers, all workers, can participate and garner an adequate income in the market. Clearly, labour and employment regulations cannot function as a solution to all the issues thrown up by unpaid work. They would do nothing to assist those outside the labour market entirely. Nor would they reach those who work in informal markets, or the large numbers of female workers engaged in non-standard work. But this is only to say that exploring the impact of labour market regulation on production in general and using it to compensate those now providing an unpaid contribution is connected to a larger debate. Its fate is tied to the success of initiatives to exert governance over labour markets in the new economy and bridge the regulatory gap around non-standard work.

---

[24] There is considerable jurisdictional variation among even industrialized countries on this point, with states ranged along a continuum from an almost total no-support model in the USA to relatively elaborate systems of support for caregiving labour in the Nordic countries.

IV REGULATING WORK: TOWARDS AN INTEGRATED VISION OF WORK

Employers, states, and international organizations have long recognized that many women have household and family obligations that impinge on their ability to engage in paid work. Since the advent of industrialization, regulations and standards have been introduced to 'protect' women by mitigating the conflicts between market and non-market demands. Some of the first battles between the courts and legislatures around industrial capitalism in the USA, for example, concerned the regulation of the hours of women at work.[25] One of the earliest conventions adopted by the ILO concerned night work by women.[26]

Many of the traditional forms of labour market regulation directed at women were deeply problematic, resting on assumptions about the limits and vagaries of (some) women's bodies and defended in the name of the sanctity and demands of maternal roles. They were motivated both by paternalism and, to no small degree, by self-interest on the part of men. For those reasons, large classes of workers, such as domestic workers, were routinely excluded from protection and at the same time defined out of the category of women in need of protection. By consigning women to the periphery of labour markets, such regulations helped produce the very persons they purported to protect: a class of economically dependent and vulnerable persons with weak participation rates, marginal attachment, and only contingent entitlement to paid work. They also induced, if not compelled, such women to invest deeply in their roles as housewives and mothers. Hence, labour market regulations were mechanisms for the discipline, domestication, and maternalization of women.[27] Over time, however, they also become mechanisms of redistribution, a means of shifting resources, such as time and income, to women, usually in connection with their child-bearing or family activities.

Within neoliberal ideology regarding labour rights and standards, special labour market regulations for women have been subjected to a range of efficiency-based criticisms. While basic 'rights' such as non-discrimination entitlements have become acceptable, indeed *de rigueur*, in the new economy, other regulations are regarded as suspect or undesirable market 'interventions' that undermine employers' need for flexibility. Because they impose costs on employers, render women 'expensive' to employ, and therefore function as disincentives to hiring women,[28] it is

[25] The famed constitutional challenge to early employment standards legislation, the case of *Muller v. Oregon*, 208 US 42 (1908), concerned maximum hours legislation for laundresses.

[26] ILO, Convention no. 3, Maternity Protection Convention (1919); ILO, Convention no. 4, Night Work (Women) Convention (1919).

[27] See Frug, M. J., *Postmodern Legal Feminism* (New York: Routledge, 1992).

[28] World Bank, *World Development Report 1996: From Plan to Market* (New York: Oxford University Press, 1996).

argued that they either cost jobs or depress women's wages, hurting those they are intended to help, thereby falling prey to the perversity argument identified by Hirschmann.[29]

It is at this point banal to suggest that gender equity requires that women have access to labour markets. However, the persisting patterns of female disadvantage in current labour markets, ranging from lower wages to exclusion from high-skill jobs and management positions as well as pregnancy-related career derailments and dismissals,[30] all reinforce the intuitive conclusion that formal access alone is no panacea. Given the historically gendered allocation of unpaid work, part of what labour market equity for women requires is not simply formal means of non-discrimination, but access to labour markets under terms and conditions that do not disadvantage those who undertake unpaid work. This is not solely, or essentially, a gendered issue; even in a world of shifting gender roles, unpaid obligations remain a source of labour market disadvantage. Yet, however obvious this may seem, it is an argument that meets with persistent resistance. As some litigation over sex discrimination discloses,[31] a robust concept of non-discrimination may compel a re-interpretation of the traditional boundary between work and family, as well as the employer's responsibility to accommodate the demands of unpaid work. However, the dominance of neo-classical reasoning concerning labour market regulation often serves to impede such a comprehensive analysis.

It might be easier to make the stakes clear if the issue were characterized as an economic conflict and the case for labour market regulation to compensate unpaid domestic work articulated expressly in distributive terms. This would have the virtue of placing it squarely within the traditional concerns of labour, even if at the same time it highlighted the contemporary difficulties surrounding the issue. Neither traditional arguments about women and work, which are classically conducted in the language of protection, nor contemporary equality arguments, which are usually framed in terms of enhancing women's choices, make reference to the distributive function that such regulations perform. Arguments that refer to the 'special needs' of women and the 'choices' that women face suggest that women's encounter with and relation to the labour market is somehow fundamentally different from that of

---

[29] Hirschmann, A., *The Rhetoric of Reaction: Perversity, Futility, Jeopardy* (Cambridge, Mass.: Harvard Belknap, 1991).

[30] Standing, above n. 2; Compa, L., 'NAFTA's Labour Side Agreement Five Years On: Progress and Prospects for the NAALC' (1999) 7 *Canadian Labour and Employment L. Journal* 1.

[31] For a discussion see Conaghan, J., 'The Family-friendly Workplace in Labour Law Discourse: Some Reflections on *London Underground* v. *Edwards*' in Collins, H., Davies, P., and Rideout, R. (eds.), *Legal Regulation of the Employment Relation* (The Hague: Kluwer International, 2000) 161.

men. However, the precise nature of this difference is often obscured, even mystified.

What the traditional discourses largely fail to convey is that labour market regulations allocate resources and power to women, and thus can be usefully approached as both mechanisms of (re)distribution and sets of economic incentives. Regulations such as paid maternity leave not only protect women's jobs and entitlements to time off, but also protect women from foregoing all of their income when reproductive or domestic work prevents them from engaging in paid work. They permit women not simply to choose to work but structure some of the costs and opportunities in doing so, largely by reducing the massive disadvantages and disincentives to entering the labour market faced by those required single-handedly to absorb and accommodate non-market work as well. Whatever their other properties and functions, regulations mandating paid parental or maternity leave are modes of compelling other parties to cross-subsidize or underwrite costs that are otherwise borne largely by women. Unless this economic cost is acknowledged and compensation is incorporated into regulatory and policy choices, 'respecting women's choices' and 'protecting women' risk remaining sentimental moralizing that is completely compatible with continuing labour market disadvantage for women.

Once the nexus of unpaid to market work is highlighted, such regulations can be regarded as 'expensive' only in the sense that they make visible and pass on to other parties more of the costs of production and the risks associated with performing market work. Moreover, in these respects they are not unique. Pensions, unemployment insurance, vacation pay, and sick leave all do similar things, by ensuring that some compensation continues to flow to workers when they are prevented by generally foreseeable events from directly engaging in paid work. The question then becomes why these regulations in particular tend to draw criticism.

The naturalization of women's maternal roles and the gendered division of household labour prevent them from being demanded by, or even in the interests of, all workers. The idea that the family is 'private' and separate from the market[32] underwrites the legitimacy of excluding them from the domain of labour or market concerns. However, such practices rest on contestable claims about the boundaries of work and the nature and demands of 'real' workers. Moreover, the resulting policy and regulatory decisions themselves help to make, and remake, these boundaries and to reconfigure the image of the normal worker.

Many jurisdictions appear to be moving toward the adoption of a new

[32] Olsen, F., 'The Family and the Market: a Study of Ideology and Legal Reform' (1983) 96 *Harvard L. Review* 1497.

set of institutional and political norms which hold that, absent a providing spouse, all adults must earn a living through participation in the
labour market. The massive shift from single to double income families
and the increase in single-parent families headed by working women are
both causes and effects of profound changes in the ideological landscape
concerning who is entitled and obligated to work. However, as the widespread neglect of the non-market sphere on the part of policy-makers
discloses, in the main we have yet to trace the implications or document
the effects of this shift.

There are vast amounts of unpaid family, community and volunteer
work performed by those who have traditionally had limited or no
engagement in market work. Despite the low regard in which it is held,
this work remains central to economic activity and social life as a whole.
Conclusions that paid maternity leave or subsidized child-care are 'too
costly', whether for firms or governments, simply amount to the conclusion that those with care-giving obligations should continue to carry the
costs of discharging them, notwithstanding the feminization of the labour
market now underway. As Ingrid Palmer observed, this is equivalent to
compelling women to pay a tax on participation in the labour market,[33]
thus starkly raising the question how this could be considered a fair,
reasonable, or even workable deal.

Part of what makes it appear fair, reasonable, and workable are the
beliefs that value resides unproblematically in market prices; that the
nature of productive work is uncontroversial and self-evident; that the
regulation of markets is properly separated from political, social, and
distributive considerations; and that non-market work is irrelevant to
economic activity in the market. Thus, the background legal and
economic assumptions which form the terrain upon which questions of
market regulation are now debated function as a formidable barrier to
even discussing the organization and compensation of work.

The simultaneous shift toward 'core' labour rights and away from standards motivated by distributive considerations, the de-emphasis on the
historic problem of worker disempowerment, and the primacy given to
the creation of a regulatory environment aimed at enhancing 'efficiency',
all mark a concerted attempt at reconfiguring the legal entitlements and
institutions within which work and production occur. However, the
language used—that of the protection of rights and the promotion of efficiency—has so far largely served to obscure the shift in resources and
power from workers involved. Despite the nod in the direction of non-
discrimination norms, it is difficult to locate a place in the new economy

---

[33] Palmer, I., 'Public Finance from a Gender Perspective' (1995) 23 *World Development*
1981.

for market regulations that are frankly (re)distributive in design and effect. As a result, emerging labour markets are likely to marginalize and/or penalize those with unpaid obligations. There are other less unhappy scenarios however, and, given that the regulatory debate is ongoing rather than closed, they are worth exploring.

While the conventional response is to say that the solution lies in social transfers and subsidies, there are now obvious reasons to resist confining the list of available strategies in this way, or to imagine the issue as solely a question of need, poverty, or charity with respect to women. Just as labour scholars and activists would find social safety nets, however desirable and necessary, an inadequate answer to the loss in power and income many workers are experiencing in the current transformation of production, so they are at best half an answer to this issue. We need instead to examine more closely how market rules and institutions become implicated in the making and valuing of different types of work and how they might become instruments to remake and revalue it, and, by extension, to improve the prospects of all workers.

Recognizing the interconstitutive relationship between markets and households and charting the flows of resource across their boundaries provides a basis from which to challenge the current arguments against labour regulations and to explore the role they might play in altering the terms and conditions of unpaid work. Assessing the impact of unpaid work on labour market participation highlights the issue of income distribution and sharpens the sense of alarm around economic security, particularly with respect to women. It also illustrates the inadequacy of the claim that regulation necessarily impedes the efficient allocation of labour.[34] Were we to pay more attention to the role of regulation in dispersing the costs of unpaid work and enhancing the ability of such workers to pursue income-generating opportunities, it seems unlikely that such arguments would continue to persuade.

Whether because of assumptions about the inevitability of women's marginal participation in labour markets, lingering hopes that women will altruistically continue to discharge domestic obligations even as they engage in more and more market work, an unarticulated moral or cultural agenda which holds that they should remain unpaid caregivers, or simple indifference to gender inequality, market reformers have expressed little interest in, let alone investigated, the effects of non-market obligations on market work. Given the promotion of the entrepreneurial worker, this is a striking omission. While it might be explained simply by

---

[34] There is a well-established internal critique of such assertions. See, e.g., Sengenberger, W., and Wilkinson, F., 'Globalization and Labour Standards' in Michie, J., and Grieve Smith, J. (eds.), *Managing the Global Economy* (Oxford: Oxford University Press, 1995) 111.

a commitment to a particular vision of the market and the state, it also discloses elements of that vision that remain submerged in the official story.

Despite the rhetorical shift toward greater self-reliance and market participation, economic dependence and disadvantage for some seem to remain institutionalized in the new labour markets in powerful although covert ways. The entrepreneurial work model shows signs of both producing and relying on elements of a traditional gendered family structure, including much unpaid work by women. If this is not in fact what is envisaged, several contradictions need to be confronted. The first arises from the new emphasis on performance-based pay and the increase in wage inequality and reduction in risk-sharing it entails: it is unclear how this will not penalize those who must limit their involvement in paid work and function as a disincentive to re-allocating unpaid work between women and more highly compensated men? The second relates to wage levels: apart from increased rewards to the most productive, wage restraint is the order of the day. If the majority of workers have no reasonable expectation of purchasing services as a substitute for unpaid work, then absent some other source of income, ongoing unpaid work, along with constraints on paid work, for some have to be presumed. For many women, this is likely to mean continued over-representation in low wage, low-skilled, atypical work. In short, as long as the border between paid work and unpaid work is maintained in its traditional form, the stripped down, reinvented labour markets promise to create dependent and relatively impoverished workers, many of whom will continue to be women.

7

Seeking Post-Seattle Clarity—and Inspiration

BRIAN A. LANGILLE

I INTRODUCTION

The post-Seattle[1] beating of the pro- and anti-globalization war drums goes on, and on. From Seattle, to Quebec City, to Genoa, to countless sites of contest around the globe, promoters and opponents of globalization regularly relieve themselves of what are now almost ritualistic slogans, both pro and con. Occasionally a third set of voices is heard amid the resulting din—a set of voices seeking neither the triumph nor the demise of globalization as an end in itself, but rather the construction of a humane world economy. The headlines I read every day reflect all this: 'The case for globalization' (*The Economist*); 'In Prague, capitalism with a human face: world financial leaders heed warnings' (*International Herald Tribune*); 'The west's globalization drive is proving a massive failure' (*International Herald Tribune*); 'Two cheers for sweatshops' (*New York Times Magazine*); 'International lenders' new image: a human face' (*New York Times*); 'The charade of sustainability' (*Financial Times*); 'Foreigners home in a pool of cheap labour' (*Financial Times*); 'MIT report says international auditing firms overlook factory abuses' (*New York Times*); 'Globalization in a nutshell at a Nicaraguan jeans plant' (*International Herald Tribune*); 'Globalization done right is what developing countries want' (*International Herald Tribune*); 'Prague police prepare for protestors' (*Financial Times*); 'Professors take on campus protestors: US academics are in conflict with student anti-sweat shop activists' (*Financial Times*).

And so it goes. And, it seems, in common with many of the important issues of our time, rational reflection and discussion are at risk of being drowned out by a combination of provocative visuals on TV news, unreflective sound bites, self-indulgent and self-interested moralizing, and, sometimes, thuggery.

How then are we to make sense of all of this? In what follows, I seek not to answer the vital questions which globalization poses, but rather to clarify them—to show what is at stake and what is not. Then, I reveal my hand as an optimist. I believe that we live in interesting times—times in

---

[1] This is a reference to the WTO Ministerial Meeting held in Seattle, Washington, in 1999, and to the street demonstrations and other events surrounding those meetings.

which our normative thinking is shifting and in which a new and integrated view of globalization is ascendent, or at least possible to imagine.
This is a world in which the economic and the social are increasingly seen
as integrated and mutually reinforcing, and not as mutually exclusive
alternatives to be traded off in a zero-sum game.

Before turning to a brief discussion of the basis for an optimistic view
of the state of our normative thinking, I first attempt to clarify the current
debates about globalization—debates about races to the bottom, level
playing fields, social dumping, regulatory competition, protectionism,
loss of sovereignty, the need for multilateral agreements, and democratic
deficits. My thinking about these arguments and the often unsatisfactory
conversations in which they are invoked has led me to adopt an heuristic
device which may help in thinking through the issues involved. It
involves a thought experiment in which the reader is invited to imagine a
world, not of economic integration, free trade, foreign direct investment,
interchange of goods, people, and ideas, but of isolated 'island' jurisdictions with no economic or other interaction at all—no trade, no investment, no immigration. The reader is then asked to think through the
process by which labour regulation would, ideally, be established in such
island jurisdictions. Then, in a series of steps, the hypothetical reality of a
world of island jurisdictions is altered by introducing, one at a time, the
various elements comprising the new global reality—trade, foreign
investment, and so on. The idea is that by moving step by step away from
the unreal world of island jurisdictions towards the real world of deep
economic integration, we will be able to disentangle many of the complicating elements in current debates, to clarify them, and to map the controversies surrounding them. This is not a sufficient condition to answering
all the questions, but is surely a necessary one.

II SEEKING CLARITY POST-SEATTLE

One should not embark upon this venture in map-making totally
unequipped. Experience teaches that those setting out upon this sort of
inquiry must come prepared with the following three basic considerations and understandings in place as prerequisites to further exploration.

First, one must enter into debates about labour law and globalization
equipped with a well thought out view of what domestic labour law is
and what it is for; one must have a view of what labour law is about 'at
home' before taking on the world. One must also have a well thought out
view of what kind of society one wishes to live in and what labour law's
role is in constructing that society. This entails having an account of both
the virtues and limitations of labour markets in general, and individual

labour contracts in particular. Is labour a commodity or not? If not, why not? In particular, one must address the 'pro-market', 'deregulation', or 'neo-liberal' agenda. Even if one disagrees with some or all of that agenda, reasons must be offered which address pro-market arguments both on their own economic terms and on other conceptual and normative grounds. In short, one needs a story that one can tell oneself, credibly, which answers what is commonplace in the United States and other parts of the world—a view of the market 'triumphant'.

Secondly, one must embark upon the thought experiment equipped with the idea that labour laws are embedded in complex social, cultural, and economic systems. Labour law systems, for example, are located within industrial relations systems, which are in turn part of, and help construct, larger structures which may be called 'modes' of capitalism. The view that the oft-compared capitalisms of Japan, the United States, and Germany are profoundly different is right. Until recently, the US economy was 'booming'—and its unemployment rate had fallen to 4.7 per cent. The Japanese economy, on the other hand, is in 'dire straits' and its unemployment rate is at an all-time post-war high—around 5 per cent. As this suggests, the ways in which different systems are in crisis (or not) are deeply dependent upon the structural differences between various economies and systems of organizing labour markets.

Finally, one must embark with what I would refer to as a certain sort of moral generosity; that is, one must embark upon these debates with a view of global, not just local, welfare. One of the great tragedies of the recent past is that the poorest nations in the world have systematically been making massive payments to the world's richest nations. Wealth in the world is grotesquely maldistributed. In thinking about globalization it is important to think about the role of trade and investment in directing resources to those parts of the world which most desperately need them. This is not a simple or easily accomplished task, but to adopt a purely domestic account of welfare would be a recipe for further global injustice. Those interested in labour's fate in the world economy should not become agents of distributive perversity. In what follows I hope it becomes clear why these three items are prerequisites to clear thinking about globalization and labour.

We need to recognize too that the debate is not about 'free trade' and labour. Trade is not the problem. No one believes that it is a good idea for Canada to attempt to grow its own mangoes. The problem lies elsewhere, in what many have referred to as global economic integration, or global production. We can get at this most basic of points using the thought experiment. Instead of tackling the real world of free trade and economic integration, imagine its opposite, a world of isolated 'island' jurisdictions. Furthermore, imagine that each of these island jurisdictions is an advanced 'OECD-type' economy, with a tolerably well-working liberal democracy and basically 'good' labour standards, including respect for freedom of association and collective bargaining. I am tempted to say that we should imagine the world populated by a bunch of Canadas, but it is probably more appropriate for these purposes to conjure up a world populated by a bunch of Hollands or Denmarks. These nations are island jurisdictions because there is no economic interchange between them—no trade in goods, no foreign investment, direct or otherwise, no immigration, no links at all.

What kind of labour law would and should each of these island jurisdictions have? Their democratic governments would, of course, aim at fair, productive, distributively just, democratic labour laws conducive to the development of a decent and flourishing civil society in which citizens are offered the maximum set of opportunities to live long, healthy, and full lives. In constructing its own particular model of industrial relations and labour law, each jurisdiction would, in effect, be fulfilling the first prerequisite, creating for itself an understanding of the virtues and limits of market ordering in labour as preconditions to an economically successful and just society.

Within each such isolated island jurisdiction, precisely *how* would such a labour law regime be created? It would be a joint process in which labourers, investors, and consumers had equal access to a fair, democratic political regime. Certainly, both capital and labour would have equal access to the democratic fora. Neither side could threaten, in the long run, to refuse to participate in such a regime. Each would be forced to use its political 'voice' in the construction of an appropriate model of labour relations. And, of course, given our second prerequisite, the exact shape of the system created would vary with local conditions, history, and culture.

Now, what difference would free trade in goods[2] make to this world of isolated island jurisdictions, with their democratically constructed, fair, and efficient models of labour law? First, some international trade is clearly beneficial. My ability to buy fresh produce in downtown Toronto in the middle of February (our mid-winter) is a good thing. But what of situations in which goods can be grown both here in Canada and abroad? The central idea of the theory of comparative advantage is that international trade allows countries to secure gains from trade by virtue of specialized production, even in circumstances in which one country is

---

[2] By free trade here I mean what Adam Smith and Ricardo did—free trade in goods. A large problem with the debates about globalization and labour, at least early on in the free trade/fair trade debate, is that they ignored this limit on classical free trade theory and did not address other key issues, such as investment or government regulation. I return to this point below. Often free trade discussions which focus upon the relationship between labour standards and free trade in goods miss the most crucial dynamics.

comparatively less efficient at producing everything. In a recent economics textbook this point is intuitively made clear by posing the following question—'Should Michael Jordan (the famous basketball player) mow his own lawn?' The answer is 'no'. The theory of comparative advantage is a theory of specialization. One should maximize benefits flowing from one's relatively advantageous talents. Thus, even if Michael Jordan is a better basketball player and lawn mower than anyone else (in all probability true), he is much better off if he concentrates on playing basketball rather than going into the lawn mowing business. And vice versa for the rest of us.

What difference does this view of the world, common and indeed fundamental to trade economics, have upon our island jurisdictions? Here we need to distinguish between the *direct* impact of engaging in trade in goods upon *labour* (jobs), and the *indirect* impact of free trade upon *labour law* policy and social policy more generally.

Recall that in our experiment all the other countries of the world are OECD-type economies with 'civilized' and 'humane' labour law regimes. Within such regimes the decision to engage in free trade will have an impact upon jobs. There will be winners and losers within various sectors. That's the point according to the theory. In this connection, we should recall our third consideration, that we should take a *global* distributive perspective on debates about free trade. The normative argument would be that jobs should go to those liberal democracies which are poorer and less developed, enabling them to secure the resources to finance better education and health systems and provide real progress for their citizens.

The key questions for each jurisdiction should be how to deal with 'adjustment', for moving from autarky to free trade will necessitate debates about how to distribute the gains from trade. Again, this debate will be a democratic one in which consumers, workers, and investors have equal voice and access to the process. There is widespread agreement that the best policy is to secure the gains from trade but to ensure that the 'losers' within each jurisdiction are compensated—through adjustment policies which assist in their transition to 'winning' sectors.

But is there any *indirect* impact involved in the shift from island jurisdiction to free-trader status? Recall that each of our competitors is, like us, a liberal democracy with fundamentally fair and efficient labour regimes. If we, in our home jurisdiction, decide to compete on the basis of lower wages with other less advanced (but still liberal/democratic) regimes, there may be some pressure to lower labour standards—such as minimum wages. But if we are consistent there is no reason why this should occur. If another, less developed jurisdiction has an advantage in 'low priced labour', then the whole point of the theory of trade is for them and us to benefit from that advantage. A rich liberal/democratic regime might decide to 'lower' its labour policy in order to compete with poorer regimes, but this would seem a short-term and unsound strategy, given the possibility of greater gains from a 'high road' strategy in which it plays to its comparative strengths.

Now, let us relax another assumption. Thus far we have assumed that all countries engaging in free trade in goods are liberal democratic regimes with sound labour policies: in short, that all the countries are just like (insert your favourite example). But what if there were oppressive, anti-democratic, anti-labour regimes, in which we found bonded labour, forced labour, bonded child labour, or the shooting of union organizers? In such circumstances we might well say that any resulting comparative price advantage in such nations was unfairly created; that it was an unfair trade advantage whose impact—goods made by forced labour appearing on our store shelves—was unappreciated. To say this would be to miss an important point, however. Within a strictly economic view of the world, we might well be indifferent to the reasons why other jurisdictions pursued certain policy choices. We might just take the gains from trade, however created. But this seems unlikely in a civilized liberal democratic regime. There are two ways in which this intuition can be captured. First, even within economic theory we are not operating in a non-normative world but in a profoundly normative one. The appeal of markets to liberty, respect for autonomy, equality, and freedom of choice is deeply normative and ultimately grounds any political theory of economic ordering centred on markets. We can say that even *within* economic theory we have no reason, or need, to respect, or to take as given or credible, the coerced choices of others.

But to view this version of our thought experiment through the lens of economics and comparative advantage is probably to miss the point. Our concern is best viewed directly. The problem is not that vicious regimes elsewhere may gain a comparative advantage, but simply that they are doing terrible things to their own citizens. The need or desire to assist victims, including victims of oppressive labour law policies *there*, may become more publicized *as a result of* free trade. We may not want our children kicking around a football hand-stitched by bonded child labour. But the key problem here is not that unfairness leads to a comparative advantage in the production of footballs but the unfairness itself. And the best arguments here are straightforward human rights arguments. To be sure, one can expect and will get arguments about, for example, 'Asian' values. But when it comes to debates about core labour or human rights, most such appeals are simply smoke-screens for oppression. The best evidence of this comes from the mouths of the oppressed, not from the oppressors who speak of 'Asian' values.

The key question in this new version of our thought experiment—

where we are engaging in the free trade of goods between otherwise island jurisdictions some of which are oppressive—would be how to assist the victims of those regimes by advancing their labour rights, human rights, and the democratic agenda. We should view any conditioning of trade upon improvement in local human rights processes as just one weapon in an arsenal. That is, we should view it, for example, as on a par with conditioning humanitarian assistance, or military intervention, or diplomatic protests. There is no *necessary* link between the human rights agenda and the conditioning of trade. It is simply one weapon or device which happens to be available. There are other carrots and sticks available as well. Any intervention will have to be thought out carefully— so that it actually helps people there and is not simply a counterproductive exercise in self-righteousness, aided and abetted by vested interests.

On further reflection, it will become apparent that *unilateral* efforts to affect policies elsewhere will be deeply problematic: the offending regimes will play individual states off against each other. Unilateral action against China, say, is commonly observed to be ineffectual. While it might obviously be right to attempt to improve human rights recognition in China, it is in the individual interests of no nation state to do so alone. In fact it may put a state at a distinct disadvantage. China may play off jurisdictions one against the other when accepting investment or awarding contracts. Here the best example is, perhaps, Rupert Murdoch, or, more substantially, that of Boeing versus Airbus (if the USA presses the human rights agenda, China shifts orders from Boeing to Airbus). The problem here is *unilateral* action—not action itself—and the obvious solution is multilateral action.

But we have still to reach the more complex, real world. Our initial scenario was of a world populated by island jurisdictions, all of which are liberal democratic regimes with 'civilized' labour policies. We then moved to a world in which these democratic, rights-respecting regimes exchanged goods with one another; and then to a world in which some of these regimes were not civilized regimes.

To get to the real phenomenon of globalization, however, we must shift from a world of goods-exchanging, island jurisdictions, only some of which are liberal democracies, to a world of *global economic integration*. That is, we must shift from a world in which not only goods, but services, ideas, money, markets, and production are truly global and mobile by virtue of advances in communication and transportation technologies. We must move from the model of *shallow* economic integration to a model of *deep* economic integration in which advancements in transportation and technology enable capital to see the whole world as its stage. The key insight is that this new world represents a potentially radical re-alignment of political and economic realities. For labour law the key change is that capital has become mobile; labour has not. For both *de jure* and *de facto* reasons, capital has acquired the ability to exit the nation-state, while labour has not. Even in a world, unimaginable as it may be, of zero restrictions on immigration, people—as Polanyi said, 'labour is the technical term for human beings'—will still find it more difficult to move from one country to another than money. Money flickers on a computer screen and is gone. Not so people.

What this brings home to us is that our old story is challenged. Recall that we started off with a world of island jurisdictions which were all liberal democracies and in which labour law policies were established through democratic dialogue. In this dialogue both labour and capital had 'voice' within the democratic process, but, because these are *island* jurisdictions, lacked the alternative strategy of 'exit'. The decision to engage in free trade in goods did not disturb this reality. It is, however, disturbed by a world of global economic integration. This is the source of the sense of democratic unease, the loss of democratic dialogue between capital and civil society, the 'democratic deficit' which pervades many of the debates about 'globalization'. Of course, there is a debate about the extent to which capital actually is mobile, but in our model it is not so much the actual exit of capital as its new ability credibly to threaten exit which alters the bargaining dynamic.

Recall, however, that we began our thought experiment with the idea that every regime is a liberal democratic one, relaxing it to take account of oppressive regimes. But so important is the move from a free trade world to a world of global economic integration that even if every state or nation were liberal/democratic, there would still be 'collective action' problems for states in a world in which capital was mobile and states and labour immobile. In such circumstances, it might well be rational for an individual state to attempt to attract (or retain) investment by altering its hitherto democratically established, fair, and efficient labour laws. Additional investment, jobs, and taxes might more than compensate for a slight lowering of labour standards.[3] The collective action problem arises because every other nation would also see that it would be in its interest to do exactly the same. The end result *for all* is a lowering of standards and *no* extra investment. The rational pursuit of self-interest by all leads to a socially sub-optimal result.

Now we come to the final step in our thought experiment. We must imagine a world in which nation-states engage in free trade, and in which all factors of production, except labour, are mobile. These nation-states

---

[3] The reality is, of course, that we see this as part of our political rhetoric every day. Democratic regimes, such as provinces within Canada, compete with one another for investment on precisely this basis.

exist in a world of increasing economic integration and global production; and in a world in which not all nation-states are liberal/democratic ones. Some are oppressive, anti-labour regimes which deny the fundamental rights of their citizens to freedom of association. This is the real world.

In such a world, then, we have three concerns. First, there is our direct concern for the labour and human rights abuses occurring elsewhere in the world. We are legitimately concerned with the cause of democracy, say, in Burma, to use a current example. Second, is our concern with the 'collective action' problems associated with a *unilateral* approach. Thirdly, there is the concern, even within the liberal democratic regimes of the world, with the sense of democratic disempowerment and unease. The results—or possibility—of mobile capital playing off immobile regimes has altered our basic understanding of how to address labour law or many other domestic policy issues.

If the human rights problems in such a world are well understood, the third problem is often misunderstood. Some people take it as an objection to free trade across the board, arguing that those who object to lower labour standards elsewhere are ignoring the theory of comparative advantage. Clearly, this is not the basis of the objection at all. If all the nation-states in the world are liberal/democratic ones, and there is no independent reason to object or to consider their labour policies the results of human-rights 'wrongs', there is no across-the-board comparative advantage-type argument. There is, however, even in a world in which all states are liberal democratic ones, a legitimate concern about collective action problems. This is not a concern about comparative advantage but a concern about the fact that individual pursuit of self-interest by all individual states often results in global sub-optimality. This is the well-known lesson of the Great Depression. Individual nation-states pursued beggar-thy-neighbour policies on trade, currency pricing, and so on, which may have been a perfectly rational thing to do individually but which led to global disaster. The key to overcoming such collective action problems lies, as is well known, in multilateral agreement and action. It is also possible to argue within the existing free trade regime that the lowering of labour standards could constitute a 'subsidy'. Trade theorists, such as Michael Trebilcock and Paul Krugman, say that this is a conceptual error and advise scrapping the whole idea of subsidies within international trade theory. It may be that within the theory of international trade any factor of advantage should be taken at face value and that there should be a market in everything. But there *is* a concept of subsidies within the world trading order as it now exists, whether trade theorists like it or not; and there is, therefore, no consistent way of avoiding the argument for subsidies that is being made. Moreover, the fundamental idea behind scrapping subsidies is that there should be a market in everything, including an international market in labour law.[4] What are we to make of this position?

Thus far, I have described a world of immobile labour and nation-states, with mobile capital posing 'collective action' problems. The problem could, however, be conceptualized differently in terms of a new world order which offers a market in labour laws. Rather than a socially sub-optimal, beggar-thy-neighbour situation, what we have is a perfectly straightforward example of law as a 'product' which various jurisdictions use to compete for investment—a market in labour law for which investment shops. And this market, the argument goes, is as beneficial as any other. There is no way out of this conceptual conflict except by normative argument; both modes of conceptual analysis are entirely appropriate. The question which to deploy is normative, and this will in turn depend upon whether there is some definition of the socially optimal beyond that determined by the market mechanism. Recall our first general prerequisite consideration—that one needs a theory of what labour law is for. And recall that this will involve a firm understanding of both the virtues and limits of market ordering in labour. The one answer that *cannot* be given to the question 'what are the limits of market ordering?' is 'it is for the market to decide'. This is conceptually a question that cannot be answered from *within* market theory. It is a question *about* market theory. But that conceptual point rests upon the normative point that there is a requirement for a democratic dialogue about the appropriate scope of market ordering. That is what labour law is for. That is why the new world order is problematic from the labour law point of view. The new world order threatens the very idea of labour law by threatening to substitute market ordering for democratic decision-making about the appropriate scope of market ordering. It attempts to answer the question with one possible answer and to remove debate about other possible answers. The answer which 'old' labour law gave to proponents of market ordering was 'labour is not a commodity'. The answer which 'new' labour law must give in a globalized economy is that it also follows that 'labour *law* is not a commodity'. This is a central conceptual point.

All of this will be, of course, complicated by the fact that we are constantly reminding ourselves of our third general consideration as well—that is, that from a global distributive perspective it is a good thing, all else being equal, that jobs and investment flow to those parts of the world where they are most needed. Foreign direct investment and job

---

[4] Of course, there will be lots of room for debate about the extent to which this picture actually represents the world as we know it. For example, there are empirical disagreements about the responsiveness of capital and foreign direct investment to 'lower' labour standards. Recall, however, that a large part of the question rests, not upon actual investment flows in response to 'lower' labour standards, but upon the threat of such activity.

creation in South Africa are a good thing. Of course, South Africa knows that it is 'threatened' by Mexico, Indonesia, China, etc. While we know that this is true, we also know that *not all else is equal*; that not all nations are liberal democratic ones; that there are human rights abuses elsewhere; and that there are collective action problems confronting countries respecting labour rights.

So, at the end of the day, we still have three real problems: first, how to render assistance to ameliorate human rights/labour abuses elsewhere; secondly, how to solve collective action problems in order to address problems *there*; and, thirdly, how to solve collective action problems and the pressure to lower labour policies *here*.

The real world is, of course, highly complex and a long way from a starting point of imagined island nation-states having no economic links or interaction with other island jurisdictions. As a result, there is probably no single solution and lots of potential objections to any proposed solutions. However, a lot of problems can be circumvented by avoiding simplistic 'race to the bottom', 'level playing field' types of argument. The ideas of trade and global economic welfare depend upon the transfer of resources around the globe. That is to be expected and desired. We need to avoid unwanted protectionism and the unhelpful alliances between employees in the developed world and employers in the developing world in the continuance of global moral wrongs. We need to address the real issues of human rights abuses and collective action problems both among states respecting fundamental labour rights, and *vis-à-vis* those states which do not do so.

In addressing these problems it is probably useful to distinguish supra-national (ILO, WTO, OECD, IMF, and World Bank) and sub-national (trade unions, firms, consumers, NGOs) strategies; and the use of carrots on the one hand and sticks on the other, both of which are available at the supra-national and sub-national levels. For example, trade or other economic and non-economic sanctions can be issued against offending regimes, but so can the inducements of additional trade benefits and investment. Consumers, unions, and NGOs can engage in boycotts, or in positive 'consumer labelling' campaigns designed to give market recognition and advantage to conforming products, firms, or regimes. But these large issues of strategy are the subject matter for another essay. The aim here is simply to clarify why we need any such strategies at all.

III SEEKING INSPIRATION POST-SEATTLE

Clarity about controversial issues is one thing, agreement on them quite another. Some may think the clarifications of the thought experiment merely make even more explicit the extent of the differences over labour policy, agreement about which is a prerequisite of both domestic and multilateral policy initiatives. Even if we focus solely on core or fundamental labour rights such as freedom of association and the right to collective bargaining, surely the lesson of the recent period of intensive global economic integration is that these rights are even more hotly contested, resisted, and denied, both in action and in argument. What sources of optimism are there in light of events in Seattle, and Genoa?

The very naïve may point to the recent adoption by the ILO of its *Declaration of Fundamental Principles and Rights at Work* as clear evidence of widespread and renewed agreement on the importance of core labour rights such as freedom of association and the right to collective bargaining. In the Preamble to the ILO Declaration, the world community staked itself to a number of normative claims about the link between such rights and economic progress and development.

The claims contained in the Preamble begin with the Constitutional reminder of the most fundamental of ILO beliefs—'that social justice is essential to universal and lasting peace'. Following this direct echo from the original 1919 Constitution, the Preamble goes on to make other claims about our understanding of the world:

Economic growth is essential but not sufficient to ensure equity, social process and the eradication of poverty . . .

. . . in the context of a global strategy for economic and social development, economic and social policies are mutually reinforcing components in order to create broad-based sustainable development . . .

In seeking to maintain the link between social progress and economic growth, the guarantee of fundamental principles and rights at work is of particular significance in that it enables the persons concerned to claim freely and on the basis of equality of opportunity their fair share of the wealth which they have helped to generate, and to achieve fully their human potential . . .

. . . it is urgent, in a situation of growing economic interdependence to reaffirm the immutable nature of the fundamental principles and rights embodied in the Constitution of the organization and to promote their universal application . . . [1998]

But the fundamental question for the non-naïve is how are we to read these claims? One view, the shallow view, is that these claims contain no challenge to the view which has recently dominated and structured much public policy debate, both domestically and internationally. On this view there are two segregated spheres—the economic and the social—and the projects of economic and social development are both autonomous and sequenced in a certain way. From this perspective, economic growth is a self-contained problem, to be managed on its own terms which, if achieved, will generate the assets with which to purchase 'luxury goods' in the social sphere, should we wish it. In practical terms this has resulted in an apartheid in policy debates. On this shallow reading, the claims contained in the Declaration's Preamble, declaring a connection between the economic and the social, is merely pragmatic and strategic. Any perception of a 'link' or a 'mutually reinforcing relationship' between the two spheres is based upon nothing more than a perceived need to avoid a 'backlash' at the maldistribution of the benefits and costs flowing from an integrated global economy. On this view, the normative foundations of the economic and the social are different, and indeed contradictory, and the problem of governance is one of strategically managing these fundamental contradictions. From this perspective, the economic is prior to the social, and social policy has a purely redistributive role rather than a role in creating economic success. Moreover, there is often a 'big trade off' between fairness and efficiency—one comes at the cost of the other. This is a view held not only by those pursuing the economic agenda but by those in opposition, who also see a zero-sum game at stake, but desire a different outcome.

A second, and deeper, view of the Declaration's normative claims rejects this interpretation, seeing the preamble as accurately reflecting a deeper understanding, which has recently gained recognition and affirmation. On this view, there is an integration not a segregation of the economic and the social. The economic is not prior to the social; rather recognition of fundamental social rights and principles is both and simultaneously the necessary precondition to, and the goal of, human development. Our normative architecture does not rest upon two foundations but one. Our normative commitments are not in contradiction and our task in managing them is not merely strategic. Rather, we need to be true to our deep human commitments which are comprehensive and unified in nature.[5] This is not a triumph of the social over the economic, nor of the economic over the social. It is about seeing both clearly. To get at this deeper understanding of the normative claims of the Preamble involves going back to first principles, and sorting out our means from our ends. We are fortunate in these times to be offered a clear chance to undertake this normative reassessment. But there is a danger, evident in the aftermath of Seattle, that entrenched interests *on both sides* will dig in and become more blinkered. The task is to convince both sides, hitherto segregated, that they share common ground.

The optimistic view is that fundamental labour rights, such as those of

---

[5] This richer understanding reveals that, properly conceived, our economic and social goals cannot be traded off for they are the same.

freedom of association and effective recognition of collective bargaining, are increasingly important to effective and sustainable economic and human development. Further, the optimist holds that this is true not just as an academic matter, but as a real world, public policy phenomenon. It is increasingly the case that these fundamental values are conceived as constitutive of, and not merely as instrumental to, human progress.

For many this claim will appear as radical, and as radically incoherent as a statement either of reality or ambition. This is because in the latter part of the twentieth century much public policy was informed by a normative view dominated by markets and market ordering. The normative case for markets has been largely perceived in consequentialist terms in which their value lies in their ability to maximize utility, most commonly expressed as efficiency, which in turn is most commonly expressed in terms of wealth, such as GDP *per capita*. Atomistic, self-interested individuals maximizing their own utility in a sparsely constructed space of the free market will allocate scarce resources to highest valuing users, maximizing overall benefit to society. This view has found domestic expression in a distrust of government, the public and social (conceived often as mere redistribution, as structuring perverse incentives to productive market activity), and regulation; in short, of any interference with the operation of the free market not aimed at correcting some defect in the operation of the market itself. In the labour market in particular, this view demands the rejection of much labour regulation and much of the ILO's international labour code on the basis that they constitute perverse public policy, unless and to the extent that they are legitimate legislative attempts to cure market defects such as information asymmetries between employers and workers. Traditional public defences of labour market regulation, in terms of equitable redistribution or the need to correct for 'inequalities of bargaining power', have been rejected as structuring perverse incentives or as conceptually incoherent. Within the economic approach, the idea of inequality of bargaining power as a prime justification for freedom of association, unions, and collective bargaining is perceived as a simple misunderstanding of certain fundamental tenets of economic theory. On this view, economic efficiency is perceived as the adequate, indeed the dominant, metric of social success.

At the international level this neo-classical or neo-liberal economic perspective has found expression in the so-called 'Washington Consensus', which held that good economic performance required liberalized trade, macro-economic stability, and 'getting prices right'. In essence, this involves dramatic shrinkage of the role of the state and a corresponding increase in the role of markets—sometimes simply put as 'getting governments out of the way'. The typically mandated macro-economic stabilization policy included expenditure reductions to eliminate or contain budget deficits and high rates of inflation, exchange rate devaluations, trade and foreign investment liberalization, privatization of state-owned enterprises, and the deregulation of price and entry controls in many sectors. In its more extreme versions, the whole project is to marginalize the state, confining its role to the facilitation of markets through the adequate structuring and enforcing of property and contract rights, and the construction of space for private exchange. While the exact bounds of the Washington Consensus are contested, its overall policy orientation is unmistakable, representing the rejection of the post-war paradigm of 'embedded liberalism'[6] with its pursuit of full employment and its social contract between capital and labour. On this view, institutions of labour market regulation, including the ILO, are part of the problem, not part of the solution.

The Washington Consensus constituted, in part, what has been called the 'globalization of the mind'. That is, it became the dominant paradigm for understanding how best to structure and react to the forces of globalization and economic integration. It represents, again, a view of the link between the economic and the social, and a view of development in which there are two autonomous realms serving different and contradictory ends. The Washington Consensus thus makes possible a separation of debates about economic progress and debates about social justice and human rights. On the neo-liberal view, these are 'luxury goods', which adherents to the Consensus will be better able to afford, should they wish to do so. The concern is that adherence to the second agenda undermines the first order agenda of economic progress.

The contrasting, optimistic view is that the segregated approaches to domestic and international public policy are deeply problematic and shallow. They are *deeply* shallow not because of some strategic and/or empirical miscalculation about the degree of social solidarity required to advance the agenda of economic progress, but because they misunderstand of what human progress consists. Moreover, there is evidence that this is increasingly being recognized; that the normative framework of the Washington Consensus and its domestic counterpart is shifting. Its architects now openly consider what a 'post-Washington Consensus' might look like[7] and there is much discussion of a new approach to development—the Comprehensive Development Framework of the World Bank is an explicitly integrated approach to our issues. Discussions of 'second generation reforms' are the order of the day. 'Integrated' and 'holistic'

---

[6] Ruggie, J. G., 'International Regimes, Transactions, and Change: Embedded Liberalism in the Postwar Economic Order' (1982) 36 *International Organization* 195.

[7] Stiglitz, J., 'More Instruments and Broader Goals: Moving Towards the Post-Washington Consensus', World Institute for Development Economics Research (WIDER) Lecture 1998, available from the WIDER website (www.wider.unu.edu).

approaches to economic and social development, 'good governance', 'social capital', 'legal capital', and 'process' are being discussed and analysed as necessary ingredients of successful development. Institutions matter again. There is a richer understanding of the link between the market and the institutions—both explicit and implicit—which structure it and in which it is embedded.

Much of this is encouraging, but also equivocal. There is a view, still dominant in some of these new discussions, that these new ideas merely imply that the Washington Consensus is necessary but not sufficient to achieve global justice, a view which is consonant with a continuation of a segregation of the economic and the social. The view taken here, however, is that these developments are not a mere addition to our agenda, not a mere discovery of an additional ingredient or two to add to our recipe for successful development, but rather a reconceptualization of what development comprises. This involves a fundamental and deep reassessment of our ends and our means and the discovery of a unity in realms hitherto considered separate and not part of a coherent whole.

What, then, is the deep, unified, understanding which is implicit in the developments we see all around us at the turn of the millennium? What is the deep understanding of the normative claims contained in the Preamble to the ILO Declaration? More specifically, how do the fundamental principles of freedom of association and collective bargaining cohere with that unified understanding?

Freedom of association is constitutive of the essence of humanity and, as an aspect of freedom in general, has the deepest normative salience for humans, as Nobel Laureate Amartya Sen has made so clear.[8] The significance of Sen's contribution lies in his articulation of a deep and unified foundation for an integrated view of human progress and development. In Sen's view, human freedom is both the end of, and a crucial set of means to, human development. It is the destination and the way. Development is the very process of expanding the real freedoms that people have. Our goal is not the construction of markets or global integration, or macro-economic stability or increasing GDP per head, or the creation of an International Labour Code, *for their own sakes*, but rather as ways of enabling people to live longer, better, more meaningful, and productive lives. This is a substantive view of freedom as the real 'capability' to lead lives 'we have reason to value'. The process of development is the process of removing obstacles to this real human freedom. As Sen points out, these obstacles come in a variety of forms:

Sometimes the lack of substantive freedoms relates directly to economic poverty, which robs people of the freedom to satisfy hunger, or to achieve sufficient

---

[8] Sen, A., *Development as Freedom* (New York: Alfred A. Knopf, 1999).

nutrition, or to obtain remedies for treatable illnesses, or the opportunity to be adequately clothed or, sheltered, or to enjoy clean water or sanitary facilities. In other cases, the unfreedom links closely to the lack of public facilities and social care, such as the absence of epidemiological programmes, or of organized arrangements for health care or educational facilities, or of effective institutions for the maintenance of local peace and order. In still other cases, the violation of freedom results directly from a denial of political and civil liberties by authoritarian regimes and from imposed restrictions on the freedom to participation in the social, political and economic life of the community.[9]

The point of public policy both domestically and globally is the removal of obstacles to human freedom so conceived. This is the one foundation stone of our normative architecture. Sen's great achievement lies in his demand that we begin thinking about development in human progress by first sorting out our goals as distinct from the means we use to achieve them. This is a basic and important point. It is unfortunately all too common in human history for social and political systems to take on a life of their own, detached from the ends they were initially constructed to advance, serving only their own internal demands, sometimes terrifyingly so. Sen's starting point is required to break out of the dead end of such self-serving ideologies.

If freedom is what development advances, then there is a major argument for concentrating on that overarching objective, rather than on some particular means, or some specially chosen list of instruments. Viewing development in terms of expanding substantive freedoms directs attention to the ends that make development important, rather than merely to some of the means that, *inter alia*, play a prominent part in the process.[10]

But Sen's accomplishment is still greater. Not only does he remind us of the fundamental goal of removing sources of unfreedom, he observes that human freedom is itself a means to the goal of human freedom and that there are mutually reinforcing interconnections between different sorts of human freedoms. That is, while 'what people can positively achieve is influenced by economic opportunities, political liberties, social powers, and the enabling conditions of good health, basic education and the encouragement and cultivation of initiatives', it is also true that 'the institutional arrangements for these opportunities are also influenced by the exercise of people's freedoms, through the liberty to participate in social choice and in the making of public decisions that impel the progress of these opportunities'.[11] So, for example:

Political freedoms (in the form of free speech and elections) help to promote economic security. Social opportunities (in the form of education and health facilities) facilitate economic participation. Economic facilities (in the form of

---

[9] Ibid., 4.   [10] Ibid., 3.   [11] Ibid., 5.

opportunities for participation in trade and production) can help to generate personal abundance as well as public resources for social facilities. Freedoms of different kinds can strengthen one another.[12]

This is not a view which is in any way antithetical to the value of the market ordering of human affairs, and it would indeed be strange if a theory of freedom were so. Rather, it is a unified view which sees free markets as part of the goal of expanding human capacities in general, and as an important means to that end. It is, in fact, a vital reminder of the moral foundations of markets—of the core values on which they are constructed and which they serve. Markets are often defended in terms of their consequences, but there is a common grounding for economic policies and social policies, which is prior to their consequences and which rests on the inherent value of human freedom. The economic and the social stand in common cause, not in autonomous realms. They cohere in support of our overall objective, they do not stand in contradiction. We do not have a strategic or pragmatic problem in balancing our fundamental objectives and they are not to be sequenced or traded off. The relationship between the economic and the social is not a zero-sum game, because they are one.

Core labour rights represent the most basic level of freedom—the ability to enter the labour market on terms of freedom. A freedom-based perspective demands that we focus upon this truth, something often overlooked by theories of development which focus only upon outcomes. The fixed star of our overarching goal also forces us to recognize that as important as true market freedoms are, both as ends and means, other economic, social, and political freedoms play crucial roles in enhancing the lives that people are able to lead.[13] Truly to take freedom seriously, we must, as Sen says, take it as a social commitment.

The significance of free association and collective bargaining by workers also has complex interconnections with other freedoms and social arrangements, bearing out its significance not simply as a freedom in and of itself but as a means to other freedoms and societal arrangements. Recently available analyses of the differential responses of various nations to the Asian financial crisis by Lee[14] and Rodrick[15] point to complex preventive and curative roles played by organized labour. In part these studies bear out the logic of one of Sen's famous observations— that famines do not occur in democracies. But these studies go further in

---

[12] Sen, A., above, n. 8, 11.

[13] In particular, it is necessary to pay attention to what Sen identifies as five other types of freedom: political freedoms, economic facilities, social opportunities, transparency guarantees, and protective security.

[14] Lee, E., *The Asian Financial Crisis: the Challenge to Social Policy* (Geneva: ILO, 1998).

[15] Rodrick, D., *The New Global Economy and Developing Countries: Making Openness Work* (Washington, DC: Overseas Development Council, 1999).

their observations about the roles of unions and collective bargaining, and of democratic institutions in general, to our understanding of both the causes of, and the reaction to, significant financial disruptions.

Moreover, the complex interplay of the various human freedoms in general, and freedom of association and the right to collective bargaining in particular, is increasingly understood by reference not simply to their relevance to traumatic economic disruptions, but to the evolutionary process of development itself. At the heart of this new appreciation, increasingly and explicitly articulated by the Bretton Woods and other international and global institutions, is the idea that free human participation is both an end in itself and important means to securing sustainable progress. The robustness of the connections between participation, freedom of association, and the existence of free and viable trade unions, on the one hand, and development is comprehensive and multifaceted. Unions and institutions of collective representation are increasingly seen and understood not just as institutions dedicated to their expressly articulated goals, but as having general and beneficial side effects. Foremost among these would be the increased appreciation of the role of institutions and, in particular, of institutions of conflict management. As Rodrick puts it:

Healthy societies have a range of institutions which make . . . colossal coordination failures less likely. The rule of law, the high-quality judiciary, representative political institutions, free elections, independent trade unions, social partnerships, institutionalized representation of minority groups and social insurance are examples of such institutions. What makes these arrangements function as institutions of conflict management is that they entail a double 'commitment technology': they warn the potential 'winners' of social conflict that their gains will be limited, and they assure the 'losers' that they will not be expropriated. They intend to increase the incentives for social groups to cooperate by reducing the payoff to socially uncooperative strategies.[16]

Trade unions and the institutions of collective bargaining are also understood as prime sites, and at the same time generators, of 'social capital' and 'civil society'. Even more fundamental is the understanding of participation as an essential element of sustainable development. If development is viewed as a 'transformation' of society, then participatory *processes* are important on a number of dimensions and in complex, interconnected ways.[17] Development involves, at its core, a transformation in

---

[16] Rodrick, D., 'Institutions for High-Quality Growth: What They Are and How to Acquire Them', IMF Conference on Second General Reforms (Nov. 1999) 8.

[17] Stiglitz, J., 'Participation and Development: Perspectives from the Comprehensive Development Framework', remarks at the International Conference on Democracy, Market Economy, and Development, Seoul, South Korea, 27 Feb. 1999, available from the World Bank website (www.worldbank.org/knowledge/chiefecon/stiglitz.htm).

the way people *think* about change and human agency. In this perspective, participation and voice not only legitimize policy decisions by securing the consent of the governed, not only make them more durable by securing the political 'buy-in' of those who will live by them, but are essential to the *very idea* of development understood as a 'transformation'. This sort of transformation of a society in its orientation to the world is definitionally possible only with the participation of the members of that society.

The empirical data continue to mount to confirm our deep and long-held intuition that justice and freedom are not the enemies of economic development and social progress. Freedom of association and the effective recognition of the right to collective bargaining are now increasingly viewed not only as valuable aspects of human freedom in and of themselves, but as contributing in complex ways, perhaps not of all which we yet understand, to the reinforcement of other human freedoms and to a world which is both the result of, and the necessary precondition to, real human freedom.

The deep truth of Sen's insight is increasingly clear and widely accepted—'the overall achievements of the market are deeply contingent on political and social arrangements'.[18]

IV CONCLUSION

There is an obvious human tendency to read the current state of affairs as inevitable, and to believe that the recent past provides all of the data required to understand what is necessary to predict the future. This is often appallingly the case with proscribers of economic and social policy. The view expressed here suggests that, while for the past decade or so those concerned with labour rights have been preoccupied with measuring the threat and costs of globalization to their cause, the future offers the possibility of the promise of globalization—of, as our headlines say, 'Globalization with a human face'. Yet as the events occurring in the streets of Seattle and Genoa show, there is a very real risk that this possibility will be thwarted. Many in the streets are simply segregationists of a different stripe from those they believe they oppose. They reject the integrationist's view, see the social and economic as locked in a zero-sum game, and simply seek a different outcome from the segregationists on the other side.

If we can put aside this brace of segregationist views, how does the integrationist and optimistic view match up with our efforts at clear

[18] Sen, above, n. 8, 142.

thinking? It does so by providing the basis for addressing the three problems we identified. First, we now have a robust account of why we are concerned about labour rights, both domestically and abroad. It also provides the basis for the solution to the two collective action problems which nation-states face both in addressing problems elsewhere and in sustaining labour rights at home. This, the integrated view does in a number of ways, the most important of which is to force us to reassess the incentives required to attract and retain investment. In so far as there remain any incentives to defection from the optimal strategy, the new view provides the underpinning for the multilateral agreements required to overcome them. Finally, the deeper view provides the normative and external fixed star which enables us to break the conceptual deadlock of trying to figure out whether we should see invisible hands or prisoners' dilemmas in the efforts of individual nation-states to deal with the reality of the global economy.

A plea for clarity of thought can help expose a lot of humbug on both sides—by exposing the arguments invoked to clear scrutiny and by refusing to discussants the luxury of talking past one another. This creates both the need and the room for a more honest assessment of values and global realities. In this light my view is not a claim that if only the world would read Sen that all would be well. It is, rather, the assertion that he may just be right, and that some are coming to see it that way.

8

Death of a Labour Lawyer?

DENNIS M. DAVIS

He had the wrong dreams. All, all wrong.[1]

This chapter is a direct response to two apparently different yet similarly pessimistic analyses of the effect of globalization upon labour law. In a speech to the Intell Conference 2000, Harry Arthurs effectively pronounced the death of labour law.[2] The dreams of American Professor Willy Loman may have been the correct ones during the 1940s, 1950s, 1960s, and, indeed, 1970s, but they are now decidedly the wrong dreams. Similarly, Jeremy Baskin, who had at one time had played an important role in the Congress of South African Trade Unions, has, within the context of the South African economy, warned against any transformative role for labour law outside a framework of the 'third way'.[3] While Baskin's contribution to the debate is, perhaps, more hopeful than Arthurs's, the purpose of this intervention is to explore whether either of these responses to globalization is all that is left for the left.

I THE POSITION OF DESPAIR—LABOUR LAW(YERS) AS REDUNDANT

Harry Arthurs has previously raised the spectre of despair in a typically learned contribution to the debate about the development of labour law in a global era.[4] In his Intell address, he pulls no punches. As he writes:

With neo-liberalism comes the end of Keynesian strategies to control the business cycle and maintain full employment; comes deregulation of the labour market; comes dramatic reductions in public employment; comes a scarcity of administrative and judicial resources to enforce labour laws which remain on the books; comes the weakening of the social safety net for workers who are displaced by economic restructuring. . . . With globalisation come legal constraints on the regulatory power of states; comes an exit option for capital, which discourages states from using their remaining power to protect workers . . .[5]

---

[1] Miller, A., *Death of a Salesman* (London: Heinemann, 1968) 106.

[2] Arthurs, H., 'What is Left of Labour Law?', unpublished paper delivered at Intell 2000, University of Toronto, 22–24 Sept. 2000.

[3] Baskin, J., 'South Africa's Quest for Jobs, Growth and Equity in a Global Context' (1998) 19 *ILJ (SA)* 986.

[4] Arthurs, H., 'Labour Law Without the State' (1996) 46 *University of Toronto L. Journal* 1.

[5] Arthurs, above, n. 2, 2–3.

The inevitability of these developments means that managerial prerogative expands at the expense of legal principles enforcing a culture of
managerial justification, thereby heralding the destruction of labour law's
fundamental premise—that it provides a framework within which workers can build a countervailing power to that of management. Rights for
labour which were previously knitted into the system rapidly unravel.

Within this climate, industrial pluralism and collective bargaining no
longer form part of a hegemonic project, having been replaced by productivity gains, labour flexibility, and the inherent mobility of capital. The
problem not only encompasses the collapse of the model so superbly
articulated generations ago by Otto Kahn-Freund, namely, that 'the main
object of labour law has been and . . . will always be, to be a countervailing force to counteract the inequality of bargaining power which is inherent and must be inherent in the employment relationship'.[6] There is a
general crisis of law, for law 'cannot call states to account for their regres-
sive social policies, for recalcitrant corporations to treat their workers
decently, or curb the disruptive tendencies of marginalized workers who
can see no way to defend themselves except by resorting to direct social
action'.[7] As the disjuncture between labour law, the dominant industrial
relations system, and the political economy in which both are located ultimately grows, the claim that labour law has any transformative potential
becomes all the more hollow. Law in general and labour law in particular
have little to offer in acting as an effective countervailing mechanism
against the power of capital in the global world. On the basis of this
analysis the best that labour law can do is to obfuscate reality by making
claims to transformation that are unsustainable.

II THE THIRD WAY FOR THE VICTORS OF THE APARTHEID STRUGGLE, OR
SOCIALISM IS DEAD—LONG LIVE TONY GIDDENS[8]

Baskin begins his analysis with an observation concerning the severe limitations which globalization places upon national governments. Investors
into the developing world demand a sound economic framework—
modest rates of tax, no exchange control, minimal deficits on the
budget—together with a sound system of governance and incentives for
investment. Within this context, a fall in living standards is all too often
accompanied by a rise in inequality which only compounds the problems

---

[6] Davies, P., and Freedland, M. (eds.), *Kahn-Freund's Labour and the Law* (3rd edn.,
London: Stevens & Sons, 1983) 18.
[7] Arthurs, above, n. 2, 9.
[8] Giddens, A., *The Third Way* (London: Polity Press, 1998).

for a government in a country with massive patterns of inequality. But upward pressure on wages is accompanied by growing levels of unemployment. So, what to do? Baskin suggests that two agendas have been placed before the public—one being to resist the 'race to the bottom' and demands for greater labour flexibility; the other being to embrace the global world as defined by the World Trade Organization, deregulate our labour markets, and 'take our chances' in the new world economic order. According to proponents of this option, there is no realistic alternative.

Baskin suggests there is a third way—one recognizing that although labour market regulation can be blamed for but 25 per cent of the unemployment in South Africa, labour market reform is necessary if growth and job creation are to make a serious dent in the unemployment and poverty problems that loom as major obstacles to the long-term future of a developing country such as South Africa. Accordingly, Baskin suggests a review of legislation that may protect workers but the complexity of which burdens small- and medium-sized employers excessively. Labour policy must err on the side of more rather than better jobs. Although it may not be necessary to trade equity for jobs as a rule, the consequences of protective legislation for job growth must be raised to a major policy priority.

Relying upon a study by Fallon and Lucas,[9] Baskin argues that a 10 per cent increase in real wages is associated with a 7 per cent decline in employment. The challenge is to deal with those growth sectors such as tourism, construction, and services where there is great sensitivity to trade-offs of equity for wage cost. This means that if there is to be minimum wage legislation it must be set at low rates and that collective bargaining must be reduced in its scope—particularly, in the number of issues regulated by collective agreements.

III THIRD WAY AND NO WAY

Baskin's analysis provides a useful foundation for my argument in that his intention is to explore the way in which a middle-ranking country such as South Africa can develop a progressive labour agenda in a global world. Unlike Arthurs, Baskin does not interpret the effect of globalization as constituting a reason to give up on any form of legal agenda. The question arises whether the responses to his concerns are justifiable.

A reply is not difficult to find. In its country study on South Africa, the ILO has found that the reasons for unemployment in post-apartheid

---

[9] Fallon, P., and Lucas, R., 'South African Labour Markets: Adjustments and Inequalities', World Bank Discussion Paper # 12 (Washington, DC: World Bank, 1998).

South Africa lie far beyond claims of labour inflexibility caused by protective legislation. The study suggests that the loss of jobs in the post-apartheid era has been caused to a considerable extent by a process of production rationalization which has occurred as a result of international competition. Further, the study refers to empirical evidence which associates levels of investment with employment levels.[10] At present, fixed investment represents only 17 per cent of Gross Domestic Product, a low level when compared with middle-income countries which have succeeded in decreasing levels of unemployment. Accordingly, the study concludes that 'the capital stock is presently insufficient to absorb more employment'.[11]

Unquestionably, the lack of skilled labour—itself a reflection of the historical legacy of apartheid—has contributed to negative economic growth and may well have hindered the development of labour-intensive sectors. But, as the authors of the ILO report make clear, the answer to the problem lies in the development of training programmes to enhance skills, as well as in a change of emphasis upon incentives that encourage certain forms of capital-intensive industry rather than the development of labour skill. For example, only the mining sector enjoys a tax deduction of capital expenditure as opposed to all other industries where a five-year depreciation allowance is allowed.[12] A further problem which has been observed by the ILO is that 'instead of investing in training, many enterprises prefer to attract trained workers by offering marginally higher wages'.[13] The main reasons for a lack of functional adaptability in the labour market is to be found in the inadequate patterns of work and profound skill shortages. The study concludes that the present labour legislation has promoted a certain and fair framework for collective bargaining. It also finds that 'existing regulations do not appear to be stringent by international comparison'.[14]

In a society which is confronted with glaring income inequality and alarming levels of unemployment,[15] it is hardly surprising that the study recommends that core labour standards be maintained, as well as the development of an adequate safety net to protect workers from dislocation

---

[10] ILO Task Force on Country Studies on Globalization, *Studies on the Social Dimension of Globalization: South Africa* (Geneva: ILO, Feb. 1999) 16–18.

[11] Ibid., 20.

[12] The level of expenditure upon training is low and does not appear to have increased in recent times. Thus, the ILO study reports that on average only 3.3% of payroll was expended upon training by South African public companies, compared with 3.2% in 1995 (ibid., 28).

[13] Ibid.

[14] Ibid., 34.

[15] In 1993, the poorest 20% of households accounted for only 3.3% of total household consumption while the richest 20% accounted for 63.3%. A comparison with other middle-income countries reveals that only Brazil and Botswana have a more unequal distribution of wealth than does South Africa (ibid., 45).

and exclusion from the formal economy. This latter recommendation accords with an earlier finding by Standing *et al.* that a vital component of policy should be 'raising the incomes and self-sufficiency of rural areas [which] would tend to lower the social wage of urban-industrial workers as well as benefit the poorest groups in society'.[16]

The ILO recommendations hardly represent a blueprint for social revolution but they are revealing in that they serve to emphasize the importance of core labour standards and a legislative framework for a social safety net, as key components of a policy to protect, in this case, the overwhelming majority of the population from the ravages of unfettered globalization. In addition, the findings question the all too easy conclusion, drawn even by sympathetic commentators like Baskin, that changes to labour legislation are required for a middle-ranking developing country like South Africa to survive in the global world. The state should respond to global pressures, but this is best achieved in the context of social dialogue, to put it in the terms of the ILO report, or as a framework within which both the power of management and organized labour are restrained, to employ the older formulation of Kahn-Freund.[17] Without a social safety net which protects the most impoverished sections of the population, core labour standards, and a concentrated programme to develop skills and empower workers, South Africa can never respond to global challenges. Ultimately, this is the message which emerges from the ILO report. It is a far cry from the conclusion of those like Baskin who appear almost obsessed with labour flexibility, and hence changes in the legislative regime.

IV THE DEBATE WRIT LARGE

The point of this comparison between Baskin and the ILO is that it offers an indication of the intellectual and political hegemony enjoyed by the right in the global world. The conventional wisdom about wage levels and flexibility dominates debate. Take, for example, the comparison between Europe and the United States. The conventional wisdom has it that employment has risen at a much faster rate in the USA than in either Japan or Europe.[18] It is suggested that these differences can be explained in terms of macro-economic growth and labour market reforms. In

---

[16] Standing, G., Sender, J., and Weeks, J., *Restructuring the Labour Market: The South African Challenge* (Geneva: ILO, 1996) 216.

[17] Davies and Freedland, above, n. 6, 16.

[18] This summary of the conventional view is derived from an analysis by Merrill Lynch distributed to its clients as an occasional report entitled 'Benchmarking the New Economy: Europe in Context' (2000).

support of this view, it is argued that whereas the Netherlands, for example, has been vigorous in the introduction of reforms such as increasing part-time work, wage restraint, and more stringent eligibility conditions for benefits—and hence the Dutch unemployment rate has declined from 11 per cent in 1993 to less than 3 per cent in 2000—Germany has been hampered by trade union activity, high wage deals, a sharp rise in social security contributions, and a shift towards more capital-intensive production, such that, over the period 1995–9, Germany has experienced negative employment growth. This argument is then extended to conclude that where there is a stricter system of employment regulation, employment growth is more sluggish—a phenomenon most evident in Southern European countries as well as in France and Germany. Thus, it is argued that there is good evidence to suggest that high levels of non-wage labour costs such as social insurance contributions and generous unemployment benefits have been partly, if not chiefly, responsible for the rising unemployment rate.

The conventional view has come under some compelling scrutiny.[19] Thus, James Galbraith *et al.* argue that high-income countries subsidize and support the pay of low-productivity people. They do not rely solely upon markets in that they provide high minimum wages, buyers for farm produce, jobs in vast bureaucracies, free health care, and higher education. Accordingly, low productivity people stay put in their jobs. There is no incentive for people in such jobs to migrate in search of higher pay, thereby overloading labour supply. On this basis, Galbraith *et al.* argue that the real rigidities in contemporary Europe have 'nothing to do with supposed inflexibility of relative wages inside any particular country'.[20] Were relative wage differentials to be increased, even more low productivity workers would abandon their present employment in favour of the dole. By contrast, the rigidities in Europe are caused by the reluctance of governments to foster the development of macro-economic policy that can build the peripheral economies of Europe through national programmes of full employment, as well as by the lack of vast income transfers across national lines.

Galbraith *et al.* argue that, at present:

European policy is designed to work in just the opposite direction. Through monetary union and the Maastricht treaty, Europe has moved to restrict the autonomy of both monetary and fiscal policies and impede the achievement of full employment on a national scale. Meanwhile barriers to migration and resettlement obstruct the citizens of the European periphery from taking full advantage of the

[19] Galbraith, J., Conceição, P., and Ferreira, P., 'Inequality and Unemployment in Europe: the American Case' (1999) 237 *New Left Review* 28.
[20] Ibid., 48.

more generous social welfare systems to their north. This concentrates unemployment in Spain, Italy, and Greece and reduces the pressure on Northern Europe to pursue full employment policies. And, of course, European fiscal policy places relentless pressure on individual countries to cut back on their welfare states.[21]

On the basis of this analysis, Galbraith *et al.* recommend that interest rates be lowered in Europe; that the use of private, business, and government credit be promoted; that 'middle class public consumption goods'—particularly health care, urban services, and education—be expanded; and that social security benefits be improved, along with the introduction of a minimum wage. In short, a continental version of a welfare state would begin to resolve the employment problem suffered by many European states.

The implications to be drawn from this critique are similar to those which flow from the South African example, namely that the claim that unemployment is a product of labour inflexibility sourced in labour legislation is suspect in the extreme, and that the extension of a social democratic infrastructure, as opposed to its erosion, may well contribute to greater employment and welfare, rather than the converse.

V RIGHTS TALK

While the voluntarism of Kahn-Freund may have been submerged under the sheer weight of the global imperative, the concept of rights has not suffered the same fate. The rebuttal to the conventional market view or the pessimism of much of the traditional left as articulated in this chapter, has opened the way to a reconsideration of rights talk. A number of different motivations are offered for this development. For example, when Amartya Sen delivered his address to the ILO in 1999, he referred to his earlier findings suggesting that famines do not occur in democracies.[22] According to Sen, famines are easy to prevent and a government in a multi-party democracy with a free press and elections has strong incentives to undertake famine prevention. In short, democratic governance ensures not only political freedom but, in addition, a form of economic freedom, that is, freedom from extreme starvation and death by famine. Viewed in a broader context, the lack of discipline in financial management and the lack of democratic protective power in a financial crisis can be sourced in such a lack of democratic government.

Hugh Collins has adopted an innovative response to the global imperative and its effect on the Kahn-Freund model of labour law. Thus, the law

[21] Ibid.
[22] Sen, A., *On Economic Inequality* (Oxford: Clarendon Press, 1997).

needs to respond to the requirement of flexibility in the employment relationship in order to enhance competitiveness in a knowledge-based economy. In a knowledge-based economy, the nature of the organization of
work changes. The employee is vested with a considerable measure of
discretion not only to achieve a particular task but to innovate and thus
define tasks and change work goals. The organization becomes more of a
partnership. Within this context, the ambition of regulation changes from
the traditional emphasis on labour standards; instead, it focuses upon
steering 'the organization of business in ways that promote transformations of relations of production in directions suitable for the knowledge-
based economy'.[23]

While Collins cautions that the effects of mandatory labour standards
upon competitiveness are unpredictable and that the threat of capital
flight to a more deregulated environment cannot be discounted, regulating for competitiveness can create a regime in which the rights of employees are protected. For example, training is often in the interests of both
parties. Employers are often disposed to making a strong commitment to
training only to honour the commitment more in the breach than in the
observance when it proves to be inconvenient or expensive. If an
employee had a right to paid time off for training, the employee would be
placed in a position where she could resist the short-term perspective of
her employer. In this way, the right would disempower the employer
from unilaterally reneging on the earlier commitment but would leave
open a measure of flexibility as regards the implementation of the right.

Within a flexible model, employees will require greater access to information about business plans, production methods, and staffing policy. In
a knowledge-based economy, an employer could be held to be in breach
of organizational regulation for failure to provide information within a
reasonable period where she proposes to change the nature of the organization. Similar rights could be created in respect of job security. A legally
enforceable collective agreement could provide for a sanction in the event
that the employer breaches the legitimate expectation of the parties in
respect to the nature and duration of the relationship.

Collins represents an attempt to ground the possibility of a new form
of labour law in the changing nature of relations of production and the
consequent effect upon the nature of the organization of work. By
contrast, the question whether adherence to international labour standards will impede competitiveness and growth is somewhat more uncertain. One recent study has concluded that core labour standards do not
play a significant role in shaping trade performance. Thus, the view

---

[23] Collins, H., 'Regulating the Employment Relationship for Competitiveness' (2001) 31
ILJ 1.

contending that countries with less regulation will enjoy a greater share of an export market does not find empirical support.[24] Another study, however, indicates that lax labour standards are associated with lower costs and, further, that they significantly affect economic performance in that the more relaxed the standard, the larger the comparative advantage in labour-intensive goods.[25]

The argument of the pessimists can thus be anticipated. Collins may well have a point in the carefully targeted, knowledge-based sector. But the vast majority of firms will respond to regulation by exercising the exit option, thereby denuding the economy of much needed capital whenever the imposition of some form of minimum standard is introduced. Yet, even the studies that support this view are not unequivocal. For example, the Rodrick study also found that countries with poor labour standards received less foreign investment than would have been predicted on the basis of their other characteristics.[26] To a considerable measure, this conclusion fits with that of the ILO study on South Africa that the solution to the unemployment problem is not to be found in deregulation. This should be coupled with an argument which extends Collins's position. The introduction of minimum labour standards can reinforce the development of co-operative work organization, more emphasis upon training, and skill development, which, in turn, represents a commitment to following the high road of the knowledge economy.[27]

VI THE LACK OF COUNTERVAILING POWER

While the argument developed concerning standards and the knowledge economy represents a response to the guarded pessimism of Baskin and similar third way supporters, it would most certainly not satisfy advocates of the position taken by Harry Arthurs. Fundamentally, extreme pessimism about the future of labour law is located in a conception of the new sovereignty. Whereas nineteenth and earlier twentieth century political thought was based upon the principle of territoriality of states, it is now predicated upon a world of financial capital where the borders are no longer policed by border guards but by a global network of banking institutions. In this world, the competition between currencies determines

---

[24] OECD, *Trade, Employment and Labour Standards: A Study of Core Workers' Rights and International Trade* (Paris: OECD, 1996).

[25] Rodrick, D., *Has Globalisation Gone Too Far?* (Washington, DC: Institute for International Economics, 1997).

[26] Ibid., 46.

[27] See Lee, E., 'Globalisation and Labour Imposed Standards' (1997) 136 *International Labour Review*, 173.

the social standards which are implemented nationally, including wages, employment protection, and the regulation of work. Global financial markets determine the market for goods and services through the pricing of interest rates and currency rates, and by the effect of these developments upon local markets. Within this context, the nation-state operates within tight constraints. It must do the bidding of international financial markets, including deregulation of labour markets, liberalization of prices and exchange rates, privatization of public utilities, restrictive monetary and fiscal policies, and maintenance of stable currencies.

Much of this has been a long time in coming. More than twenty-five years ago, Poulantzas observed that the fiscal crises of the national state were being accompanied by a change in power relations. The cost of social welfare, including education, exacerbated the problem. Scientific developments, particularly in the area of information technology, contributed to changes in the nature of work. Thus, as Tsoukalis writes, relying on the work of Poulantzas, 'the combination of the overaccumulation of capital, growing intercapitalist competition, and soaring social costs led to a universal trend towards a renegotiation of the overall terms of labour contracts and for a concomitant reorganization of the exploitation patterns in the world economy'.[28] These changes held vital implications for the nation-state—implications that cannot simply be reduced to the bland conclusion that the nation-state is no longer of any significance. In short, whereas in the past the nation-state has traditionally had the responsibility for the protection of law and order within its borders, it is now involved in the promotion of international competitiveness in a global context. Previously a buffer between the demands of international markets and the interests of its citizens, the new role of the nation-state is to facilitate the adaptation of society to the demands of borderless markets.[29] As Poulantzas observed:

[28] Tsoukalis, K., 'Globalisation and "the Executive Committee"': Reflections on the Contemporary Capitalist State' [1999] *Socialist Register* 57, 63. See also Poulantzas, N., *Classes in Contemporary Capitalism* (London: New Left Books, 1975). Significantly, in other areas of law, there has been a recognition of the manner in which international instruments are mediated by national states as a result of domestic 'moral' agendas and 'normative priorities'. Whatever their political source, these influences shape national acceptance, e.g., of international instruments dealing with criminal justice. See, e.g., Henham, R., 'Sentencing Theory, Proportionality and Pragmatism' [2000] *International Journal of Sociology of Law* 239. While Henham's argument may well be about the manner in which the nation-state's criminal-justice priorities shape the manner in which international human rights guarantees are incorporated into domestic law, the point remains that the national state has not been hollowed into a skeleton but continues to be a powerful mediator in shaping the law which applies within the nation-state. Once this is accepted, then the argument must turn to the forces shaping the politics and institutions of the nation-state. This is the very basis of my critique of Arthurs and others who share his position.
[29] See Mahnkopf, B., 'Between the Devil and the Deep Blue Sea: The German Model under Pressure of Globalisation' [1999] *Socialist Register* 142, 147.

Relations between the imperialist metropolises themselves are now being organised in terms of a structure of domination and dependence within the imperialist chain. The United States hegemony is not analogous to that of one metropolis over the others, as in the previous phases, and it does not differ from this in a merely quantitative way. Rather it has been achieved by establishing relations of production characteristic of American monopoly capitalism and its domination inside the other metropolises ... [I]t similarly implies the extended reproduction within them of the ideological conditions for this development of American imperialism.[30]

Leaving aside the accusation that Poulantzas is guilty of over-egging the American pudding, his analysis represents a compelling argument against the conclusion that the national state has been hollowed out. Indeed developments have been to the contrary, as national states have removed restrictions on cross-border flows of money and introduced massive programmes of privatization of assets and policies of deregulation.

This approach to the role of the national state holds significant implications for a reply to Arthurs and other who argue there is nothing left of left law. If the nation-state is a crucial site for the reproduction of international capital, then less has changed than appears to be the case at first blush. During the heyday of the voluntarist model of Kahn-Freund, it could hardly have been contended that national capital had not penetrated the formation and shape of the state. Yet, it was still considered that law could create some space for the possibility of political activity and, hence, for the exercise of countervailing social power against the power of national capital. Suddenly, the argument alters and it is now contended that law has not fulfilled its promise, or, to employ the words of Arthurs, 'law can't seem to do the jobs it sets its mind to: not protecting the environment, not keeping our streets safe, not maintaining integrity in government. It can't transform society or trump powerful economic, political, and cultural forces'.[31] It is surely an act of profound social amnesia to suggest that law ever accomplished these tasks in an unequivocal way and without extreme contradiction between purpose and outcome. But this is not the place to debate the contradictions of law as they manifested themselves during the period of the dominance of national capital.[32] The assertion is that law invariably operates in contradictory ways and that this still holds true.

The internationalization of the national state has brought about numerous contradictions. As Tsoukalis comments:

---

[30] Poulantzas, above, n. 28, 47.

[31] Arthurs, above, n. 2, 8.

[32] For a classic exposition of the contradictory nature of law see Thompson, E. P., *Whigs and Hunters* (Harmondsworth: Penguin, 1975).

deregulation is the new dominant theme, and unlimited performative deregulation is not only a specific form of active intervention but also the main ideological
tenet that must prevail. Intervention in the deregulatory process is, however, an
internally contradictory process. The constant public attention required to bring
about appropriate institutional and legal deregulatory reforms calls for increasingly authoritarian forms.[33]

This authoritarianism holds implications for a multitude of national institutions, including schools and universities, health and welfare institutions, and the courts. For all of these institutions a new discourse has
replaced that with which they worked and in terms of which they were
developed. The imperative of establishing international competitiveness,
flexible labour markets, and increased productivity has replaced
autonomous and sustained national development as the framework for
the operation of these institutions. This change has affected the very core
of what public organizations traditionally understood to be their role.
Institutions that operated within the (perceived) context of national
autonomy are now being constrained to function within a global
discourse which strips away even the pretence of autonomy. But globalization is not about the disappearance of the nation-state; rather, the
nation-state produces a cohesion required for the new dominant form of
capital accumulation. So we reach the contradiction—the nation-state
ensures the conditions for the functioning of the global market place,
while the professed aims of many of the key public organizations are at a
fundamental variance with this new discourse.[34]

These contradictions have important consequences for my argument.
As Tsoukalis writes:

the national state, still the fundamental instance ensuring the reproduction of
social cohesion, has been led to modify spectacularly the form of its specific interventions as well as its functional role in neutralising the dominant forms of class
struggles, both on the economic and on the political/ideological level. In this
context, new contradictions between the various components and functions of the
state apparatus have appeared, endangering its internal cohesion.[35]

These contradictions do not herald the beginning of some social democratic millennium, but they do reveal that new forms of resistance and
struggle are possible and, indeed, are occurring within this context. Left
pessimism which dismisses any possibility for law acting as a means (as
opposed to the means) by which to conduct such struggle, on the basis
that, like some Foucaultian nightmare, global capital has developed seam-

[33] Tsoukalis, above, n. 28, 66.
[34] See Panitch, L., 'The New Imperial State' (2000) II/2 *New Left Review* 5.
[35] Tsoukalis, above, n. 28, 74.

lessly, is guilty of ignoring the very contradictions inherent in the global economy and the institutions which promote world economic integration.

The World Bank has understood these contradictions. This is reflected in the manner in which it has reversed its position on the importance of the state. In its 1997 World Development Report, *The State in a Changing Society*, it identified five fundamental tasks for the so-called 'hollowed out' national state—the establishment of the foundation of law; maintenance of a non-discriminatory policy environment including macroeconomic stability; investment in basic social services and infrastructure; protecting the vulnerable; and protecting the environment. That institutions such as the World Bank grant a key role for the nation-state in the vision of the development of the global economy supports the very point of my earlier analysis. But inherent in this vision are the very same contradictions manifest in the legal system, which flowed from the earlier version of the national state—the national state as experienced and envisaged by Kahn-Freund and his contemporaries. Thus, when the World Bank observes that economic growth depends on the maintenance of market confidence, which is in turn based upon a free flow of information, which is itself based on transparent corporate governance, open press, and transparent governmental institutions, it opens the possibility of space for political struggle against corruption and arbitrary decision-making.[36] Similarly, when Collins's analysis of the knowledge-based economy leads him to outline a labour law model which is congruent with such an economy, he opens the possibility for a labour law which *can* perform some of the purposes for the system Kahn-Freund had in mind.

VII CONCLUSION

The third way and 'no way' approaches to labour law are both predicated upon the idea that law is inextricably linked to a particular political project, roughly speaking, post-war social democracy. Consequently, labour law has no purchase outside the parameters of such a project. Perceiving that the monolithic imperative of free market globalization is the political project of our times, it follows for Arthurs, for example, that labour law is permanently enfeebled.

We need to see, however, that other oppositional political projects remain viable, including critical projects focused on law itself. We can build on Duncan Kennedy's work on adjudication which 'reveal[s] the large role played by the legal system'. He refers to the importance of being able to:

[36] World Bank, *Development and Human Rights* (Washington, DC: World Bank, 1998) 17–18.

delegitimate the outcomes achieved through the legal system by exposing them as political when they masquerade as neutral; to show that they are in some sense unjust and that their injustice contributes to the larger injustice of the society as a whole; to be, thereby, a radicalizing force on those who read and accept the analysis; and to suggest ways that a radicalizing project should approach the task of making the system less unjust through political action.[37]

While the outcomes of a legal system are hardly designed to promote social justice over the long run, the powerful point made by Kennedy is that legal texts are shot through with apparent gaps, actual contradiction, and ambiguity. Thus, legal texts do not generate clear meanings; the consequence of a legal result does not jump from the page in a neatly folded package of meaning. While the text represents a constraint such that it is a fallacy to imagine that 'anything goes', the work undertaken in arriving at a legal meaning has deep political significance. As Kennedy observes, 'fidelity to law kicks in only when there is a law to be faithful to. Any legal actor, advocate or judge can influence what the law is through legal work'.[38] So when the legal texts of labour law change to accommodate the knowledge economy and flexibility, the meaning of these texts is the subject of legal and indeed political work. Depending upon the outcome, progressive or conservative consequences will follow. This is hardly a new or dramatic conclusion, notwithstanding a recent bout of social amnesia.

Capital and labour have invariably contested the nature and purpose of labour law. On their own, labour struggles through the law have not achieved the distributional aims of social democratic aspirations. Labour litigation has never been labour struggle by other means. But whatever the contradictions of the labour law of the Wagner Act and Kahn-Freund may have been, labour lawyers did contribute to restraining the power of capital and creating the possibility for struggles to prefigure a more egalitarian social organization.

Some will argue that progressive legal interpretive work is not possible within the global economy because, where a national court progressively interprets the provisions of a labour code, capital can always exercise its exit option and move to a jurisdiction where a conservative outcome is certain. What I have sought to show is that neither the nation-state, which is not yet hollow and, indeed, cannot be, nor global free-market imperatives are so free of fundamental contradiction that exercise of the exit option—from a stable society with established rules, independent courts, and educated, healthy employees, to the instability and

---

[37] Kennedy, D., *A Critique of Adjudication (fin de siécle)* (Cambridge, Mass.: Harvard University Press, 1997) 280.

[38] Kennedy, D., 'Strategizing Strategic Behaviour in Legal Interpretation' [1996] *Utah L. Review* 785, 787.

uncertainty of an authoritarian regime—can be regarded as axiomatic. While there are many shades of political and economic grey between these parameters, the point remains—the exit option is not free of cost or risk.

What this chapter has sought to do is emphasize that history is not yet dead and to illustrate how the contradictions of international capital open up different, if not dissimilar, possibilities for legal development. As the international system responds to the mobility of capital and labour, to the escalation of the knowledge economy, as well as to social instability and environmental threat, the contradictions become less obfuscated than they may have been in the earlier high-water mark of global rhetoric. These possibilities of the future will be missed if we fetishize models from the past.

Part IV

Same as the Old Boss? The Firm, the Employment Contract, and the 'New' Economy

9

The Many Futures of the Contract of Employment[1]

SIMON DEAKIN

I INTRODUCTION

'Myth'[2] or 'figment';[3] 'riddle';[4] source of conceptual 'anarchy' and 'crisis',[5] and of 'artificial and unpersuasive doctrinal explanations';[6] 'indeterminate' and 'dysfunctional' in its effects:[7] all these things and worse have been said of that 'fundamental legal institution of Labour Law',[8] the contract of employment. British labour lawyers, in particular, have maintained a 'sceptical discourse'[9] on the matter more or less continuously since the early 1950s.[10] More recently, social scientists have added their voices to the chorus of discontent. The contract of employment, or its close equivalent the 'standard employment relationship',[11] heads the list of those labour market institutions whose continued usefulness is called into question by what appear to be fundamental changes in the world of

---

[1] With apologies to Ian Macneil (see below, n. 17).

[2] Foster, K., 'The Legal Form of Work in the Nineteenth Century: the Myth of Contract?', paper presented to the conference on *The History of Law, Labour and Crime*, University of Warwick, 1982, 2.

[3] Davies, P., and Freedland, M. (eds.), *Kahn-Freund's Labour and the Law* (3rd edn, London: Stevens & Sons, 1983) 8.

[4] Hepple, B. A., 'Restructuring Employment Rights' (1986) 15 *ILJ* 69, 71.

[5] Clark, J., and Wedderburn, Lord, 'A Crisis in Fundamental Concepts', in Lord Wedderburn, Lewis, R., and Clark, J. (eds.), *Labour Law and Industrial Relations: Building on Kahn-Freund* (Oxford: Clarendon Press, 1983) 110, 153.

[6] Collins, H., 'Market Power, Bureaucratic Power, and the Contract of Employment' (1986) 15 *ILJ* 1, 2.

[7] Collins, H., 'Independent Contractors and the Challenge of Vertical Disintegration to Employment Protection Laws' (1990) 10 *OJLS* 353, 369.

[8] Lord Wedderburn, *Cases and Materials on Labour Law* (Cambridge: Cambridge University Press, 1967) 1.

[9] Freedland, M., 'The Role of the Contract of Employment in Modern Labour Law' in Betten, L. (ed.), *The Employment Contract in Transforming Labour Relations* (Deventer: Kluwer, 1995) 17, 19.

[10] In this respect, Kahn-Freund's early contribution ('Servants and Independent Contractors' (1951) 14 *MLR* 504) appears to have been highly influential.

[11] On the standard employment relationship or SER as a sociological concept see Mückenberger, U., and Deakin, S., 'From Deregulation to a European Floor of Rights: Labour Law, Flexibilisation, and the European Single Market' (1989) 3 *Zeitschrift für ausländisches und internationales Arbeits- und Sozialrecht* 157.

work. Vertical disintegration of production, the decline of the 'male breadwinner' family, the ending of 'full employment' as a goal of government policy, and the rise of global regulatory competition are, it seems, combining to undermine the value of the open-ended employment relationship in which 'subordination' is traded off in return for security. The conceptual inadequacies identified by legal scholars are, perhaps, merely symptoms of a deeper malaise, a basic lack of fit between the techniques of courts and legislators, on the one hand, and the changing reality of employment relations on the other.

Amidst the clamour for a new conceptual framework which accompanies calls for reform from all sides of the policy debate, it is easy to forget that the contract of employment has been 'a remarkable social and economic institution, as important as the invention of limited liability for companies'.[12] The flexibility inherent in the idea of a 'managerial prerogative' or 'authority relation' was an important source of savings on transaction costs in large, vertically integrated organizations.[13] Equally important was the implicit promise of economic security which the employee received in return for becoming subject to the bureaucratic power of the enterprise.[14] This was never a cost borne completely or even principally by individual employers. In most systems, the state became the implicit third party to the contract, channelling the risks of insecurity throughout the workforce as a whole through the social insurance system, and using social security contributions and income taxation to support the public provision of welfare services. The complex interaction of these different governance mechanisms was reflected in the juridical form of the contract of employment. Given the multiple tasks of classification, regulation, and redistribution which it was called on to perform, it is perhaps the durability of the contract of employment, rather than its supposed ineffectiveness, which requires explanation.

Part of the explanation may lie in the *evolutionary* character of the contract of employment, that is to say, its capacity for adaptation in the face of changes in economic relations and political imperatives. The contract of employment, as we know it today, is a very *recent* innovation.[15] The concepts used by nineteenth century judges and legislators to

---

[12] Marsden, D., 'Breaking the Link. Has the Employment Contract had its Day?', *Centrepiece* (1999, winter) 20. See also Marsden, D., *A Theory of Employment Systems: Micro-Foundations of Societal Diversity* (Oxford: Oxford University Press, 1999).

[13] Coase, R. H., 'The Nature of the Firm' (1937) 4 *Economica* (NS) 386.

[14] Simon, H., 'A Formal Theory of the Employment Relation' (1951) 19 *Econometrica* 293.

[15] Deakin, S., 'The Evolution of the Contract of Employment 1900–1950: the Influence of the Welfare State' in Whiteside, N., and Salais, R. (eds.), *Governance, Industry and Labour Markets in Britain and France: The Modernising State in the Mid-Twentieth Century* (London: Routledge, 1998), 212 [The Contract of Employment and the Influence of the Welfare State], and 'Legal Origins of Wage Labour: the Evolution of the Contract of Employment from

describe employment relationships—independent contractor, casual worker, servant, labourer, workman—do not map neatly on to the 'binary divide'[16] between employees and the self-employed with which we are familiar today. As I explain below, that distinction took the whole of the first half of the twentieth century to emerge, and was clearly established only in national insurance legislation of the 1940s. It was also only in the 1940s that, in Britain at least, intermediate forms of labour subcontracting finally faded away in major industries such as coal and steel. The contract of employment was the result of these parallel processes, in the political and economic spheres, which at this time tended towards the standardization and stabilization of the employment relationship.

Understanding the evolutionary processes at work in forming the modern-day contract of employment helps us to see precisely why it is that the unravelling of the post-war consensus, in politics as in the workplace, has placed the standard model under strain. The re-appearance of subcontracting and outsourcing, now strongly encouraged by the state through measures aimed at extending 'market testing' to previously integrated organizations, is one of the factors which removes the ability of employers to make credible promises of long-term employment. To the extent that short-term and part-time employment become more widespread, the employment relationship becomes less suitable as a vehicle for sharing and redistributing risks among the working population. The idea of a 'breadwinner' wage becomes inappropriate when traditional relations of inter-dependence and division of labour within the family are breaking down. Finally, with globalization occurring on terms which favour the mobility of capital over that of labour, the state appears to be confined to offering its citizens 'competitiveness' as a proxy for the 'security' which they previously enjoyed, in the hope that footloose capital can thereby be persuaded to stay put.

These developments may give us reason to believe that the employment contract is unlikely to continue indefinitely in its current form. However, it does not follow that the employment contract has no future. The employment contract is best understood as a governance mechanism which links together work organization with labour supply in such a way as to make it possible to manage long-term economic risks. This highly useful function will be no less useful as a result of the developments referred to above. Viewed in this way, it is possible to envisage a number of different futures for the employment contract,[17] according to the way

---

Industrialisation to the Welfare State' in Clarke, L., de Gijsel, P., and Jansenn, J. (eds.), *The Dynamics of Wage Relations in the New Europe* (Dordrecht: Kluwer, 2000) 32.

[16] This expression is used by Freedland, above, n. 9.

[17] Ian Macneil's use of the term contract 'futures' in the title of his seminal article 'The Many Futures of Contracts' (1974) 47 *Southern California L. Review* 691, has a dual sense

in which these risks are regulated and distributed. It is also possible to identify movements within existing labour law systems, 'mutations' within the conceptual framework of employment law, which suggest possible directions of future change. Some of these tendencies are mapped out below.

II THE CONTRACT OF EMPLOYMENT AS AN EMERGENT INSTITUTION

Alain Supiot has described the nature of the employment relationship which emerged out of the growth of the welfare state in the following terms:

Under the model of the welfare state, the work relationship became the site on which a fundamental trade-off between economic dependence and social protection took place. While it was of course the case that the employee was subjected to the power of another, it was understood that, in return, there was a guarantee of the basic conditions for participation in society. It is the very foundations of this compact which are now being called into question: economic pressures are stronger than ever (both for those who are in work and for those who are not), but they are no longer compensated for by security of existence.[18]

Supiot describes here a societal 'contract of employment' whose effects were felt far beyond the immediate parties to the individual employment relationship. The 'trade-offs' involved were extensive and complex. On the one hand, there was the norm of 'subordination', which reserved for the employer a space for discretion in decision-making, beyond any express agreement for the performance of the contract. In common law systems the juridical form of this idea can be found in the 'master–servant' model which reached its height in the mid-nineteenth century while in civilian systems, during the same period, the employer's unilateral powers were grafted on to the traditional concept of the contract of hire.[19]

In time, the employer's right to give orders became rationalised, in the English common law and in systems closely influenced by it, as an implied contract term, so cloaking managerial prerogative in contractual

which is also relevant to the present chapter: the sense in which contracts operate as mechanisms for the governance of long-term risks, through the technique which Macneil called 'presentiation'; and the sense in which the institution of contract will continue to perform this role in the future, notwithstanding widespread predictions of its imminent demise.

[18] Supiot, A., 'Préface' in Supiot, A. (ed.), *Au-delà de l'emploi: Transformations du travail et l'avenir du droit du travail en Europe. Rapport pour la Commission Européenne* (Paris: Flammarion, 1999) 7, 10.

[19] Veneziani, B., 'The Evolution of the Employment Relationship' in Hepple, B. (ed.), *The Making of Labour Law in Europe* (London: Mansell, 1986).

form. However, this was a twentieth-century development which occurred only some time after the point (in the 1870s) at which criminal sanctions for breach of the contract of service were repealed. It is highly doubtful that nineteenth-century judges regarded the source of the employer's unilateral power as contractual, at least in the sense that it is now understood.[20]

The 'contractualization' of the employment relationship was associated with the gradual spread of social legislation in the fields of workmen's compensation, social insurance, and employment protection. The terms 'contract of employment' and 'employee' came into general use as a description of wage-dependent labour only as a result of this process. Contractualization had two central aspects: the placing of limits on the employer's legal powers of command, limits which were given a contractual form as either express or implied terms; and the use of the employment relationship as a vehicle for channelling and redistributing social and economic risks, through the imposition on employers of obligations of revenue collection, and compensation for interruptions to earnings.

As we have seen, for many labour lawyers, particularly those influenced by a public law viewpoint, the common law courts' characterization of the employment relationship as contractual has always struck a false note. However, the model of the open-ended or indeterminate employment contract, based on reciprocal commitments of loyalty and security and lodged within a dense network of organizational and societal rules, is in many ways the paradigm case of what Ian Macneil has termed a 'relational' contract. Here, the 'classical' contract law of discrete market exchange gives way to a model in which exchange is governed by the 'political and social processes of the relation, internal and external', so that the relation becomes situated within 'a mini-society with a vast array of norms centred on exchange and its immediate processes'.[21]

Macneil's idea of the relational contract was taken up in the 1970s and 1980s by the proponents of 'new institutional economics' in a way which may not have been particularly faithful to his essentially inductive and taxonomical methodology, but which nevertheless initiated an important debate on the comparative efficiency properties of different types of contractual form. Oliver Williamson's influential arguments synthesized elements from the earlier contributions of R. H. Coase[22] and Herbert Simon.[23] Coase argued that where long-term, repeated exchange was conducted under the 'authority relation' of the firm, it was possible to save on the search and information costs which would arise under conditions

---

[20] For a more extensive defence of this claim see the works cited above, at n. 15.
[21] Above, n. 17, 801. [22] Above, n. 13.
[23] Above, n. 14.

of decentralized market trading, although he also acknowledged that there was an important role for contract in setting the limits of managerial power. Simon suggested, conversely, that certain features of the employment relationship in large organizations, such as regular, salaried income and career progression, could be seen as the employee's *quid pro quo* for agreeing to be subject to the employer's instructions. In bringing these ideas together, Williamson and his co-authors[24] were able to offer an explanation both for the pattern of vertical integration and for the spread of institutions of collective employee representation, which were seen as serving to minimize the danger, from the employee's point of view, of employer 'opportunism' during the performance stage of the contract.

The approach of new institutional economics is explicitly functionalist in the sense that it involves an attempt to explain the emergence and persistence of institutions in terms of their adaptiveness to particular environmental conditions. On this basis, the contract of employment may be said to be an 'efficient' response to the particular conditions of contracting in the modern, vertically integrated enterprise. New institutional economics sees institutions as emerging through a process of competitive selection and deselection: as forms are thrown into competition with one another, the more efficient (in the sense of adaptive) will win out. The most extreme forms of this idea associate adaptiveness with optimality. While individual deviations from optimal forms of organization are possible, 'over tens of years and thousands of firms' those forms which survive best under the pressure of competition will outlast their rivals.[25] Adherents to this approach often end up asserting that the rules which we observe, if they are of long standing, must have 'survival value' and therefore must be efficient. This is an argument made, for example, in relation to the doctrine of employment at will,[26] despite the fact that this particular juridical form is almost completely unique to the United States—just about every other developed system of labour law has some version of unjust dismissal legislation. It seems that the conditions for its 'survival' are, at best, highly system-specific, and far from generalizable.

A comparative and historical perspective would immediately suggest an alternative point of view to the strongly functionalist one just outlined.

---

[24] See Williamson, O., Wachter, M., and Harris, J., 'Understanding the Employment Relation: The Economics of Idiosyncratic Exchange' (1975) 6 *Bell Journal of Economics and Management Science* 250; Williamson, O., *The Economic Institutions of Capitalism* (New York: Free Press, 1985) ch. 9.

[25] Easterbrook, F., and Fischel, D., *The Economic Structure of Corporate Law* (Cambridge, Mass.: Harvard University Press, 1991) 6.

[26] See Epstein, R., 'In Defense of the Contract at Will' (1984) 51 *University of Chicago L. Review* 947; Rock, E., and Wachter, M., 'The Enforceability of Norms and the Employment Relationship' (1996) 144 *University of Pennsylvania L. Review* 1913.

This is that even over long periods of time and with large populations of actors, the pattern of institutional change is not the linear process of adjustment postulated by the accounts of mainstream law and economics analyses; rather, it is historically-contingent, context-specific, and cumulative. Among the processes which account for the emergence of institutions are mechanisms of social learning and cultural transmission. While competition may also have a role in rooting out less useful practices, its effects depend on, and are mediated through, the institutional framework provided by social and legal norms.

The evolution of rules of the workplace can be analysed from this point of view. David Marsden[27] has suggested that as vertical integration replaced sub-contracting as the predominant form of economic organization during the first half of the twentieth century, workplace rules emerged to deal with the problem of how to specify the limits to managerial prerogative within the context of the open-ended employment relationship. These rules can be seen as a response to the dangers of employer opportunism which arose with the end of the subcontracting system, and the removal of many traditional forms of workers' control over the pace and organization of work.[28] The solutions found—such as the categorization of grades according to work tasks, craft skills, professional qualifications, and, more recently, to flexible job functions—were context-specific in the sense that they differed according to the degree to which work in different countries and industries was organized along the lines of 'occupational' or craft labour markets or according to bureaucratic or enterprise-based systems of control. The process was also both contingent and cumulative, in the sense that existing rules and practices were put to new purposes. Hence, in the cumulative manner of 'path-dependent' evolution, rules which had initially been deployed for the purposes of management, such as job classification rules, were then used by unions to defend established working patterns, since 'defining people's jobs also makes clear the limits on their obligations'.[29]

Labour law supported many of the norms arrived at by labour and management by codifying them in the form of terms incorporated from collective agreements, common law implied terms, and statutory employment protection rights. The growth of large-scale enterprise provided both the opportunity for redistributive policies which operated through the taxation and social security system, and also the need for such interventions, as individuals and households became increasingly dependent on continuous, waged employment for access to income, and vulnerable

---

[27] Above, n. 12.
[28] Ibid., 21. In similar vein see Saglio, J., 'Changing Wage Orders: France 1900–1950' in Clarke *et al.* (eds.), above, n. 15, 44.
[29] Marsden, above, n. 12, 22.

to the effects of any prolonged interruptions to earnings. State intervention, by imposing responsibility for these wider social risks on employers,
provided further strong incentives for the growth of the vertically integrated firm, which was best placed to deal with the costs of regulatory
compliance.

The early solutions provided by the state in Britain took the form of
statutory schemes for workmen's compensation and social insurance.
These forms of intervention attached mandatory obligations to the
employment relationship: employers were required to make compensation payments to injured workers, the risks of which they could then
spread through employers' liability insurance, and to pay contributions
on behalf of themselves and their workers into national insurance funds,
from which state pensions and unemployment compensation were then
paid out. The combination of regulation with both private and social
insurance meant that the enterprise became the main conduit for the
wider process of risk-sharing at which the laws were aimed.

Social insurance contained the potential for extensive pooling and
redistribution of risks within the working population. At the turn of the
twentieth century, private insurance schemes for sickness and injury, and
occupational arrangements relating to retirement pensions, completely
excluded a significant segment of the working population from coverage.
The proponents of social insurance aimed to bridge the gap by bringing
certain of the excluded groups into state-run systems for unemployment,
retirement, and illness, while at the same time broadening the contribution base to include groups already in higher-income and more stable
employment. However, the state schemes did not initially displace those
of the private sector. In the thirty years following the National Insurance
Act 1911, state and private schemes operated alongside each other, with
private welfare arrangements continuing to cover higher-status employees, and the state schemes being reserved for lower-income earners and
others who were unable to gain access to employer-based or occupational
schemes. Many categories of casual employment remained excluded. Just
as the period between 1875 and 1950 was one of the increasing integration
in the sphere of production, it was also the period during which the state
system of social security and income taxation was gradually extended
to cover all wage-dependent workers. It was only with the National
Insurance Act of 1946 that the single status of the 'employee' subsumed
the older categories of wage-dependent workers (labourer, servant, and
workman), and that, as a result, the modern contract of employment was
born.[30]

Prior to that point, the models of employment used by the courts were

[30] See the works cited above, at n. 15.

based, in part, on conceptions of the business enterprise, but also on conventional understandings of social status. The term 'employee' signified professional or managerial status, in contrast to the term 'workman', which was used for manual workers and others employed under a 'contract of service'. The modern 'binary divide' between employees and the self-employed can be traced to the Beveridge report on social insurance of 1942.[31] In an attempt to expand the contribution base so that it would finally cover the entire labour force, Beveridge envisaged just two categories of contributor: in the language adopted by the National Insurance Act of 1946, these were 'employed earners', a category which included all those 'gainfully employed in employment . . . being employment under a contract of service', and those employed on their own account. The latter group—the 'self-employed'—paid a lower contribution rate but were, in return, excluded from the unemployment compensation scheme. Tax legislation around the same time adopted essentially the same division between employees, who were subject to compulsory deduction of income tax at source under Schedule E, and the self-employed who, under Schedule D, paid their own tax, in effect retrospectively, while also being able to benefit from various fiscal subsidies not available to employees, such as the right to set off work-related expenses against income.[32] Once the binary divide was established by statute, the courts gradually began to discard the status-based distinctions which were associated with the old 'control' test, in favour of the more inclusive 'integration' and 'economic reality' tests for identifying the contract of employment.[33]

This overview of the development of the contract of employment suggests a number of insights into the processes by which social and legal institutions emerge. An 'institution' of this kind is in essence a complex bundle of conventions and norms of varying degrees of formality, ranging from tacit understandings which are acted on in everyday situations in the workplace, to juridical concepts which are deployed to various ends by civil servants, courts, and legislators. As descriptions or classifications of the social world, institutions may be thought of as 'encoding' information about solutions to co-ordination problems which have been successful in the past, in the sense of being widely followed and observed. In order for a particular set of social conventions to be encoded in juridical form, they must first be filtered through the processes of litigation and legislation, which are subject to various selective pressures which include the relative strength of particular social groups which support actions

---

[31] *Social Insurance and Allied Services*, Cmd. 6404 (London: HMSO, 1942), para. 314.
[32] See Deakin, 'The Contract of Employment and the Influence of the Welfare State', above, n. 15.
[33] Ibid.

before the courts and attempts to change the law through statutory intervention, as well as factors internal to the juridical process. The institution
of the 'contract of employment' may therefore be said to be 'emergent', in
the sense that it is not the product of any single advocate, judge, policy-
maker, or drafting committee, but of the sum total of a large number of
interactions in terms of economic organization, dispute resolution, and
political mobilization.

It follows that the pattern of institutional emergence is far more
complex than a linear account of the competitive selection and deselection
of rules would allow. The cumulative nature of institutional development
means that conceptual tools which were appropriate for one purpose end
up being adapted for a different one, with results that may be both positive and negative.[34] 'Network' effects—simply, the benefits to relying on
widely-observed standards and guidelines for behaviour—increase the
costs of institutional change even when there is general agreement on the
limitations of existing arrangements. The speed of environmental change
may far outstrip the capacity of norms and legal rules to adjust. For all
these reasons, the best we can expect of institutions is that they have a
qualified adaptiveness—they may be adaptive to the needs of yesterday
rather than today, or to the circumstances of one particularly influential
enterprise, industry, or country-specific model which has, perhaps for
reasons of historical accident as much as anything, served as a model for
others to imitate. The non-optimality of institutions means that there will
be continuous pressure for redesign, for example, through legislative
intervention. However, it is in the nature of such interventions that they
result in solutions which fall short of the theoretical optima which their
designers envisaged, so that the process begins again under a new set of
constraints and possibilities.

Viewed in this way, it is possible to see why it is that the contract of
employment could be, at one and the same time, the 'cornerstone'[35] of the
modern labour law system, joining the enterprise to the welfare state just
as it connected the common law of contract and property to social legislation, *and* the source of anachronisms, confusions, and dysfunction in the
application of the law. On the one hand, it spoke to the inclusive agenda
of the welfare state, aiming for an ideal of social citizenship which could
mirror the notion of political and civil rights, completing the democratic
project by extending the conditions of social existence in the same way
that the conditions of civil and political participation were extended

---

[34] See Balkin, J., *Cultural Software: A Theory of Ideology* (New Haven, Conn.: Yale
University Press, 1998), in particular chs. 1 and 2.

[35] The expression used by Kahn-Freund in 'A Note on Contract and Status in Modern
Labour Law' (1967) 30 *MLR* 635.

through the franchise. On the other, it was constructed on a set of contingent social and economic circumstances which soon began to unravel, thereby endangering the very project of democratic emancipation which it embodied.

This was because, in the first place, the contract of employment looked back to the model of economic subordination contained in the master–servant relation. This meant, among other things, that the objectives of economic democracy and participation in decision-making within the enterprise remained unfulfilled; they were addressed neither by the reforms to employment law which aimed to regulate the employer's powers of discipline and dismissal, nor by the predominant emphasis on wage determination and related distributional issues within collective bargaining. At the same time as subcontracting and outsourcing of production were revived in the 1980s, in large part as a consequence of government measures aimed at cutting public expenditure and undermining the floor to wages and conditions of employment, the traditional protective model became a source of weakness: the ability of employers to avoid the indirect employment costs of regulation and taxation was now a major factor of competition in the product market.

Secondly, the contract of employment, at least in its classic form, incorporated an anachronistic notion of the division of household labour. This was done by formalizing the notion of the male breadwinner wage through collective bargaining, and by ensuring the primacy of the single (male) earner within social insurance. In the traditional model of social insurance, women were rarely in a position to claim unemployment or retirement benefits in their own right, either because their occupations were excluded from the coverage of the contributory schemes, or because their contributions records were inadequate on account of low earnings and interruptions to employment. Conversely, their most substantial rights were those derived from dependence on a male earner through marriage or other family connection. The gradual abolition of discriminatory provisions in state and occupational social security which began, under the influence of European Community law, in the late 1970s, has just as often assisted male workers as female,[36] while doing little or nothing to improve the position of many millions of part-time female employees whose earnings fall around the minimum earnings level for national insurance contributions or whose periods in paid employment lack the continuity necessary to claim benefits which were adequate replacements for earnings.

[36] This is one curious effect of the judgment of the European Court of Justice in Case 262/88, *Barber* v. *Guardian Royal Exchange Co. Ltd.* [1990] ECR I–4389, [1990] IRLR 240, particularly as interpreted in Case C–408/92, *Smith* v. *Avdel Systems Ltd.* [1990] ECR I–4435, [1994] IRLR 602.

Finally, the contract of employment was premised on a model of the nation-state as a more or less self-contained political entity, insulated from the pressures of transnational economic migration and integration. 'Full employment in a free society', Beveridge's programme for economic inclusion, was a strategy addressed to national government. *National* insurance, the *National* Health Service, the *National* Minimum Wage set clear jurisdictional limits to the notion of social inclusion which the contract of employment was capable of representing. When, in the late 1970s, governments began to liberalize rules on the movement of capital, the bases upon which they had previously assumed powers of regulation and taxation were undercut. The increasing inter-dependence of national economies from the point of view of trade made it, paradoxically, more difficult for governments to co-ordinate their national macroeconomic policy interventions. These were among the factors encouraging governments to replace the post-war goals of demand management and full employment with those of competitiveness and a high employment rate. As this occurred, a vital form of government support for the traditional employment model—the use of employment policy measures to support the indeterminate or open-ended employment relationship and actively to suppress casual hirings[37]—went into reverse, with access to short-term and insecure employment now seen as factors likely to promote the 'employability' of those seeking work.[38]

III FROM DISINTEGRATION TO RECONSTRUCTION?

So much for the decline, and prospective fall, of the contract of employment. Reactions fall into two broad categories. On the one hand, it is possible to envisage a 'de-socialization' of the employment contract, as governments lift fiscal and regulatory costs from employers in an effort to encourage flexibility and entrepreneurship. A strongly functionalist view would associate such a change with 'selective' pressures derived from global regulatory competition and the adoption of new technologies which shift the boundaries between the firm and the market.

The Supiot report to the European Commission, *Beyond Employment: The Transformation of Work and the Future of Labour Law in Europe*, recently offered a different perspective. While its authors took as their point of departure 'the crisis in the socio-economic model of governance around which labour law has been constructed since the beginning of the

[37] On this aspect of Beveridge's full employment policy see Deakin, 'The Contract of Employment and the Influence of the Welfare State', above, n. 15, 224.

[38] On 'employability' as part of the 'Third Way' in contemporary British labour law see Collins, in this volume.

[twentieth] century',[39] they did not use this as the occasion to propose the rapid dismantling of systems of social protection. Nor did they consider that a system of fundamental social rights could be put in place without any regard to economic issues. The report accordingly declared itself in favour of a 'third way'[40] which would be based on 'those democratic imperatives which motivated the construction of social law'.[41]

It is not possible here to do justice to the full set of proposals advanced, with this end in view, by the Supiot report. For present purposes, the focus will be the report's suggestions with regard to the future of the standard employment contract or relationship. The report rejected the continuation of the existing model on the grounds that, when combined with 'the inexorable flexibilisation of work', this would simply offer encouragement to a dual labour market, in which privileged 'insiders' were required to entrench themselves ever more deeply against excluded 'outsiders'. The group argued instead for 'a reconfiguration of the notion of security', along three lines. The first involves redefining the idea of the worker's *labour market status*[42] so as to focus on participation over the life cycle, rather than on employment stability as such; the second is concerned with the articulation of an extended concept of 'work' in place of the narrow notion of 'employment' as the basis for access to social rights and protections; and the third introduces the idea of 'social drawing rights' which individuals can use to 'manage their own flexibility', making it possible for them to achieve an 'active security under conditions of uncertainty'.[43]

The Supiot report offers a welcome corrective to rigidly deterministic accounts which insist that labour law must 'adjust' to superior technological and global economic forces if it is to remain relevant. The implicit theoretical position of the report is that these supposedly overwhelming forces do not exist in a state of nature; they themselves are the product of a process of institutional change which has altered the shape and force of competition, and which, in turn, may be susceptible to influence through public action. In this vein, the report argues[44] that the most appropriate

[39] Above, n. 18, 291.
[40] It is clear that the 'third way' proposed by the authors of the Supiot Report differs radically from the version which Hugh Collins (above, n. 38) associates with the labour law policies of the present Labour government in Britain.
[41] Above, n. 18, 293.
[42] The term used in the French-language version of the Supiot Report is *'statut professionel'* which literally translates as 'occupational status', but this does not quite capture the sense in which this new form of status would link social and economic rights to an individual's history of training, education, and participation in socially useful but non-waged work, in addition to their record of waged employment. Accordingly, 'labour market status' is suggested as an (imperfect) alternative.
[43] Above, n. 18, 297–8.
[44] Ibid., 12–13.

role for analysis is 'to identify existing evolutionary tendencies, put them in perspective, and determine their strength; not to assert that a particular future is inevitable, but to outline a number of possible futures'.

What then are the possible futures of the contract of employment: is it destined to be discarded, or can it transform itself in such a way as to renew the project of social inclusion and democratic participation? The evolutionary perspective developed earlier in this chapter suggests that, just as the traditional model built on existing concepts at the same time as adapting them to new ends, so barring major discontinuities in the institutional framework, a similar process of cumulative change will occur in response to the present transformation of work relations. Signs of this happening will be briefly examined in three related areas: vertical disintegration and the definition of the employment relationship; the importance of changing patterns of labour supply; and the impact of changes in collective bargaining. The analysis will draw on recent empirical research on the changing nature of employment contracts in the British economy.

Vertical disintegration and the employment relationship

The problem which vertical disintegration poses for labour law is not so much the growth of self-employment at the expense of protected forms of labour; rather it is the blurring of the 'binary divide' itself. As the Supiot report recognized,[45] the growth of a 'grey zone' of workers who are neither clearly employees nor self-employed affects all systems which are required to grapple with definitions of the work relationship for fiscal and protective purposes. As recent empirical research in the UK shows,[46] the idea that employees receive security and stability of employment in return for adherence to the rules and requirements of the organization, while the self-employed trade off security in return for the chance of profit, with some assistance from tax subsidies, is becoming irrelevant for workers in this position (now approaching one-third of the working population). This is because, on the one hand, many employees find themselves excluded both from the 'implicit' employment contract of job security and from the legal categories to which employment protection rights are formally granted, in particular, as the numbers employed on fixed-term contracts or through intermediary or agency organizations are increasing very quickly.[47] Conversely, there are many nominally

---

[45] Above, n. 18, ch. 1.

[46] Burchell, B., Deakin, S., and Honey, S., *The Employment Status of Workers in Non-standard Employment*, EMAR (Employment Market Analysis Research) Research Series No. 6 (London: DTI, 1999).

[47] See ibid., ch. 5, suggesting that the figures on fixed-term employment contracts collected by the Labour Force Survey seriously understate their extent.

self-employed workers who do not employ others, have little or no access to working capital, and have few business assets other than their own know-how and expertise. For many of them, the opportunities of earning a secure and stable income through contracting are often quite remote. Worse still, many individuals find themselves being classed as self-employed for labour law purposes, but as dependent workers for the purposes of tax and national insurance, so denying them fiscal support.

Most of those most seriously affected do not work in new technology industries. The problem is, in essence, an institutional rather a technological one, and to some extent it has generated an institutional response in the form of the 'worker' concept which broadly corresponds to civil law notions such as that of 'parasubordination'. The 'worker' concept involves an attempt to shift the boundary of the legal category of dependent labour so as to encompass those apparently self-employed workers who, while they may lack a contract of employment based on 'mutuality of obligation', are not genuinely in business on their own account (the so-called 'dependent self-employed'). The concept was used, in the British context, in the National Minimum Wage Act 1998 and the Working Time Regulations 1998. The Employment Relations Act 1999[48] also contained a significant new power making it possible for the employment status of particular groups of workers to be reclassified by delegated legislation. Assessing the numbers of 'dependent' and 'independent' self-employed in the workforce without depending on self-reporting is, inevitably, a hazardous exercise. However, one estimate is that the numbers of independent self-employed could be as few as 8 per cent of the working population, leaving over 90 per cent in the 'worker' category (which includes both employees and the dependent self-employed).[49]

In one sense, the 'worker' concept looks back to old ideas of the form of the contract for personal services; indeed, it draws directly on existing statutory precedents. At the same time, it can be seen as a contemporary mutation within employment law, a response to the particular problems of definition which have arisen from the growth in precarious and insecure employment forms since the late 1970s. The longer-term implication of its use may be to dissolve entirely the traditional boundary between employees and the self-employed, leaving only independent entrepreneurs (those with business assets and the opportunity to capture residual profits) outside employment law. However, what is of particular interest is that the response has not taken the form of a de-socialization of the employment relationship. On the contrary, it is an attempt to extend the logic of social protection to certain forms of self-employment.

---

[48] S. 23.   [49] Burchell, Deakin, and Honey, above, n. 46.

Changing patterns of labour supply, working time, and social insurance

Rising levels of female labour market participation and the diffusion of the principle of equal treatment in employment and social security evidently necessitate a radical rethink of the post-war model in which full employment and social insurance were constructed on the foundations of the 'male breadwinner' wage. However, it has not been possible to move straightforwardly from an insurance system based on the single male earner to one incorporating a dual-earner system in which men and women acquire effective earnings-replacement rights on the basis of their individual employment records.

The household continues to be the site for extensive cross-subsidization of economic activity between family members, on the basis of an uneven division of labour. Few married women have earnings records based on continuous full-time employment across the life cycle. Most households accordingly operate on the basis of a 'one and half times earner' model.[50] Notwithstanding the removal of the more obvious forms of discrimination against part-time workers in respect both of employment practice and of the fiscal system, many women who work part-time remain significantly dependent on male earnings for security of income. More flexible working patterns for men, of the kind envisaged by laws on parental leave, have, as yet, barely made an impact. The uneven division of household labour is evident from the reasons given by women for seeking out casual and precarious forms of employment which, while providing little or no income security, nevertheless give them the opportunity to strike a better balance between family commitments and working time than they could achieve if they were employed under an open-ended contract of employment.[51]

Signs of change in the employment relationship may however be seen in the recent strengthening of pregnancy protection laws, in the form of providing better protection for the right to return to work after the period of maternity leave.[52] In one sense, these laws reinforce the role of the stable, continuous employment relationship as the principal basis for long-term income security and career fulfilment, for women as it is for men. At the same time, they contain elements of the 'labour market status' idea of the Supiot report. The right to return to work could be

[50] Lewis, J., 'Reforming Social Insurance and Social Protection', paper presentation to SASE (Society for the Advancement of Socio-Economics) seminar on *The Transformation of Work and the Future of the Employment Relationship*, London School of Economics, 8 July 2000.
[51] Burchell, Deakin, and Honey, above, n. 46, ch. 7.
[52] These reforms were introduced through the Employment Relations Act 1999 and the Maternity and Parental Leave etc. Regulations, SI 1999/3312.

seen as a kind of social drawing right, which is in abeyance during the period of absence from the workplace, but can then be exercised when the period of maternity leave comes to an end. As in the case of the 'worker' concept, then, this recent statutory reform looks both forwards and back.

Collective bargaining, trade union influence, and legal regulation of managerial prerogative

The transformation in the influence of collective bargaining in Britain since the early 1980s has been three-fold: first, a reduction in the influence of multi-employer, sectoral bargaining, which in some senses may be traced to the 1960s, but which accelerated rapidly in the mid-1980s; secondly, a fall in the coverage of collective agreements and other forms of wage determination from over 80 per cent of the employed labour force at the start of the 1980s to around a third of the workforce twenty years later; and, even within organizations where trade unions continued to be recognized for the purposes of collective bargaining, a loss of union influence over traditional areas of negotiation, in particular pay.

How did these various changes affect the employment relationship? It would be easy to jump to the conclusion, from the raw figures on the decline in collective bargaining coverage, that collectivism has given way to a greater emphasis on individual bargaining and hence to some kind of 'recontractualization' of the employment form. Closer study of organizations in which collective bargaining rights were withdrawn during the 1980s, and a comparison of their experience with that of firms retaining union recognition reveal a different picture.[53]

The employment contract has, if anything, become more standardized at enterprise level, not less, as a result of the diminution of union influence. There is only limited evidence of greater individual differentiation of contract terms. In both unionized and de-unionized firms, the contractual terms of the employment relationship, in terms of job definition, working time, and the composition of the wage, now tend to take the form of a standard-form agreement which is largely set by the employer. In many cases, job definitions have been widened and controls on working time removed. The main difference is that this process has gone further in the de-unionized firms. Individual *bargaining* is exceptionally rare, and the performance appraisal systems now widely used to set individual pay, replacing the annual pay round, tend not to take a contractual

---

[53] Brown, W., Deakin, S., Hudson, M., Pratten, C., and Ryan, P., *The Individualisation of Employment Contracts in Britain*, EMAR (Employment Market Analysis and Research) Research Series no. 4 (London: DTI, 1998).

form. Instead, they are administered under terms which give employers a very wide, extra-contractual discretion.

Given that the role of contract within the open-ended employment relationship was, however imperfectly, to set limits to managerial prerogative, these developments signify a retreat from the relational contract model of employment, and, in that sense, a *'de*-contractualization' of employment.[54] The weakening of trade union influence has encouraged employers to reassert control over the pace and direction of work by rewriting job classifications and categorizations which previously protected workers. This is one of the factors contributing to the greater intensification of work in a number of sectors.[55]

This process has, nevertheless, been partially offset by the continuing formalization of contract terms and conditions, under the influence of employment protection legislation, and by the growing recourse of individual employees, with union assistance, to employment tribunals as a source of protection. Rather than seeing regulation give way completely, then, there has been a shift in the *level* of regulation from the collective sphere to that of the individual relationship. This has been accompanied by a change of emphasis in the role of unions, from co-regulators of terms and conditions of employment to monitors and enforcers of employees' legal rights.[56] In short, the open-ended employment contract continues to be a principal focus of regulation of enterprise-level relations, albeit under conditions where the weakening of union power has exposed 'core' employees to the dangers of unfettered managerial prerogative and growing work intensification. If employees' legal rights are to be made effective in practice, the restoration of collective influence within the workplace seems to be an essential next step.[57]

IV CONCLUSION

In order to assess the future of the contract of employment, it is necessary to understand its past. The contract of employment emerged at a particular

---

[54] Deakin, S., 'Organisational Change, Labour Flexibility and the Contract of Employment in Britain' in Deery, S., and Mitchell, R. (eds.), *Employment Relations, Individualisation and Union Exclusion: An International Study* (Annandale, NSW: Federation Press, 1999) 130.

[55] Burchell, B., Day, D., Hudson, M., Ladipo, D., Mankelow, R., Nolan, J., Reed, H., Wichert, I., and Wilkinson, F., *Job Insecurity and Work Intensification: Flexibility and the Changing Boundaries of Work*, Joseph Rowntree Foundation *Work and Opportunity Series* (York: York Publishing Services, 1999).

[56] Brown, W., Deakin, S., Nash, D., and Oxenbridge, S., 'The Employment Contract: From Collective Procedures to Individual Rights' (2000) 38 *BJIR* 611.

[57] Ibid.

historical juncture at the mid-point of the twentieth century, when changes in economic organization, the structure of the family, and the regulatory power of the nation-state came together to favour the standardization and stabilization of labour market relations. The fiscal and regulatory techniques which were used at this time were designed to channel the risks of economic insecurity more widely throughout the working population, at the same time as underpinning relations of production at the level of the enterprise. The normative force underlying this process was a conception of social citizenship, which would extend the bases for social and economic participation in the same way that rights of democratic participation had been extended through political reform.

In evaluating the impact of current transformations in the world of work, it is essential not to confuse the normative aims which are embodied in the institution of the contract of employment, the means chosen to achieve them, and the historical conditions under which they were first put in place. It does not follow, from the unravelling of the historical conditions, that the aim of social citizenship has ceased to be legitimate. Nor is it necessarily the case that the means used—in particular, the channelling and redistribution of social risks and the control of economic power through fiscal and regulatory intervention—are no longer appropriate. The regulatory mechanisms in question must respond to changing environmental conditions if they are to remain of use; but this process is already occurring.

The transformation of the contract of employment into an extended form of 'labour market status', as envisaged by the Supiot report, is one of the many possible futures which can be imagined by extrapolating from recent developments in labour law. These include the use of the 'worker' concept to extend the range of employment protection legislation and the recognition of limited 'social drawing rights' in the context of the balance between work life and family life. More negative implications of the current changes include the intensification of working conditions at organizational level, resulting from the decline of collective employee representation. The future laid out here is one in which contractual restraints on managerial prerogative are further stripped back, and the implicit contract of job security in return for open-ended commitment is finally revoked. For those outside the organizational 'core', there is the prospect that fiscal controls will be extended without corresponding guarantees of access to the means of economic participation.

There is nothing inevitable, then, about the transformation of the contract of employment. It is, nevertheless, worth remembering that the process of institutional construction which culminated in the mid-twentieth century welfare state had begun half a century earlier amidst

conditions of growing economic insecurity and the casualization of work
under a globalized trading regime. The aim of a 'public organisation of
the labour market'[58] may have seemed just as remote to that earlier generation as it sometimes appears to us today. There is good reason to believe,
however, that our own experience of engagement and reconstruction will
be similar to theirs.[59]

---

[58] The expression used by the Minority Poor Law Report of 1909, which was heavily
influenced by the reforming agenda of Sidney and Beatrice Webb and other Fabian thinkers.
[59] See Supiot, '*Préface*', above, n. 18, 14, referring to the role of 'engagement, conflict and
collective negotiation' in the formation of labour law.

10

From Amelioration to Transformation: Capitalism, the Market, and Corporate Reform

PADDY IRELAND

In recent years, Anglo-American labour lawyers have been much exercized by what Karl Klare has called the 'current difficulties' facing the discipline,[1] difficulties seen as emanating from changes in the process of production which have 'profoundly transformed the world of work'.[2] These changes have been variously described but are generally seen as revolving around a shift from vertically-integrated, nationally-based, standardized, Fordist production to increasingly transnational, post-fordist, 'flexible' production.[3] While there are inevitable disagreements about the precise nature, extent, and depth of these structural changes, there is general agreement that the replacement of earlier production processes, which gathered together large numbers of hierarchically organized, full-time workers in one location, by modern processes of 'flexible specialization',[4] with their shorter-run, more customized production and their vertical disintegration and geographical dispersal of firms from single to multiple sites, has undermined the foundations of post-war labour law, with its ideal-typical full-time male worker with secure job tenure, its emphasis on collective bargaining and its essentially sociological, 'industrial relations' model of the discipline. Together with the increasing mobility of capital and growing international competition, these changes are also seen as having undermined the power of the working class and of the nation-state itself. The overall result, says Harry Arthurs, is that one simply cannot avoid questioning 'whether familiar labour law concepts are capable of capturing the emerging paradigm of

---

[1] Klare, K., 'Countervailing Workers' Power as a Regulatory Strategy', paper delivered to the W. G. Hart Workshop, 6–8 July 1999.

[2] Hepple, B., 'New Approaches to International Labour Regulation' (1997) 26 *ILJ* 353.

[3] The changes tend to be described and explained in technological terms rather than in terms of social and class relations. One vital but neglected aspect of 'globalization', however, has been the huge increase in the size of the proletariat. Not only have certain strata of workers within established capitalisms been expanded (women, immigrants), whole new proletariats have been created in areas where once only subsistence peasantries were to be found. 'Globalization in its modern form', suggests David Coates, 'is a process based less on the proliferation of computers than on the proliferation of proletariats'. *Models of Capitalism* (Cambridge: Polity Press, 2000) 256.

[4] Piore, M. J., and Sable, C. F., *The Second Industrial Divide* (New York: Basic Books, 1984).

employment in "the new economy" ', with its 'globalization, . . . incongruent spaces and diminished role [for] the nation-state, [and] reorganization of production, management, and work'.[5] Hugh Collins echoes this, writing of the 'disintegration' of labour law, meaning the gradual erosion of the previously dominant labour law discourse and the rise of a multiplicity of rival discourses based around economic efficiency, individual rights, and social justice.

I FLEXIBILITY AS A TRANSFORMATIVE OPPORTUNITY

Contractual versus organizational flexibility

It is significant, however, that Collins considers the disintegration of labour law to have been 'productive' in the sense that the new discourses are more sensitive and responsive to 'the key developments' which have occurred in the last few decades,[6] for, as this suggests, not all labour lawyers view the difficulties facing the discipline in an entirely negative light. First, it is argued, on reflection, collective bargaining has never been all it is cracked up to be, tending to focus rather narrowly on full-time male employees[7] and on issues concerned with 'exploitation' (such as pay and redundancy), but doing little to 'address [the] broader range of issues connected to redressing disrespect and alienation at work'. Collective bargaining, it is claimed, has left management's right to govern largely unchallenged, marginalizing the goals of job enrichment and self-realization, and neglecting the desire of workers to be treated with dignity and respect.[8] Secondly and more positively, it is argued that while the changes which have occurred in the process of production may have undermined traditional labour law, they have also created *new* transformative possibilities and *new* routes to worker empowerment by making co-operative, trusting relations between companies and their workers a prerequisite of efficiency and competitiveness.

In the 'new economy', this argument runs, constant innovations in design and production techniques have been rendered necessary by ongoing technological advance and the forever changing demands of consumers. As a result, the rules of the competitive race have been rewritten: in order to

---

[5] Arthurs, H., 'Labour Law without the State' (1996) 46 *Toronto L. Journal* 1, 8, 16, and 18.
[6] Collins, H., 'The Productive Disintegration of Labour Law' (1997) 26 *ILJ* 295.
[7] See Conaghan, J., 'The Invisibility of Women in Labour Law: Gender Neutrality and Model Building' (1986) 14 *International Journal of Sociology of Law* 377.
[8] Collins, H., 'Flexibility and Empowerment' in Wilthagen, T. (ed.), *Advancing Theory in Labour Law and Industrial Relations in a Global Context* (Amsterdam: Royal Netherland Academy of Arts and Science, 1998) 117.

survive, both individuals and firms need to be, in Tony Blair's words, 'adaptable, flexible, [and] open to change'.[9] The organizational and managerial forms adopted by corporations[10] are thus said to be increasingly important to competitive success. It is possible, it is argued, for corporations to seek adaptability and flexibility through contract, a technique (applicable to methods of financing and technologies as well as to the employment of labour) which emphasizes dispensability and keeping long-term ties and commitments to a minimum. But flexibility achieved in this manner, it is claimed, undermines long-term relationships of cooperation, destroying 'organisational surplus value' at a time when 'deepened relationships with and between employees, customers, suppliers, investors and the community' are ever more essential.[11] Only an 'organizational' approach to flexibility—'a legal conception of corporate governance based upon a micro-corporatist coalition of producers' in which neither labour, capital, nor management is regarded as having a 'natural claim' to control of the company[12]—can preserve the long-term relationships with workers (and others) which are necessary for an organization to flourish in modern conditions. Far from constituting barriers to adaptability and flexibility, therefore, enhanced workers' rights and greater worker involvement in management are posited as potential aids to the realization of corporate goals, as contributing to the creation of the conditions of trust and security within which innovation and change can be most effectively achieved and managed. In short, then, the suggestion is that in the new global economy, capital needs inclusive relations with workers in order to remain competitive and that this is something that labour can exploit for its own benefit.[13] A glimmer of optimism thus emerges from what might otherwise appear to be a globalized, flexible, post-fordist, post-socialist gloom.

From profit and conflict to efficiency and partnership

Capital's alleged need for co-operation from workers has rekindled the interest of labour lawyers in company law and corporate governance reform.[14] The very same changes have, however, simultaneously

[9] Speech delivered at the Trade Union Congress, 9 Oct. 1997.

[10] In this chapter, the terms 'corporation' and 'corporate' are used to refer to large publicly quoted companies.

[11] Royal Society of Arts, *Tomorrow's Company* (London: RSA, 1995) 6.

[12] Teubner, G., *Law as an Autopoeitic System* (Oxford: Blackwell, 1993) 139–41.

[13] For a perceptive and more sombre account of the consequences of 'flexibility' for workers both individually and collectively see Sennett, R., *The Corrosion of Character: The Personal Consequences of Work in the New Capitalism* (New York: Norton, 1998).

[14] In most English-speaking jurisdictions, what in the UK is called company law is generally called corporate law.

prompted them to lower their horizons so far as corporate reform is concerned. In the post-war period, progressive labour lawyers regularly advocated 'worker participation' or 'industrial democracy', usually meaning the introduction of worker representatives on corporate boards along the lines found in Germany and a number of other European countries. This commonly involved seeking radical company law reform: a relaxation of the goal of profit maximization, a diminution of shareholder rights, a re-orientation of corporate goals and so on. There was, however, by no means unanimity on the desirability of German-style co-determination, either within the labour movement or among left-leaning intellectuals. For Sir Otto Kahn-Freund, the doyen of British labour law, for example, the choice was between a 'pluralist' model of industrial relations based around labour law and collective bargaining, a model which recognized the fundamental conflict of interest between capital and labour, and a less desirable 'unitary' model based around company law and industrial partnership in which the fundamental conflict between capital and labour was implicitly denied. He was deeply sceptical about the benefits of worker participation. However, most labour lawyers believed that it was possible to have the best of both worlds, using worker participation to supplement collective bargaining to provide workers with a forum in which to address the wider questions of job-enrichment and self-realization in a relationship with capital of 'conflictual partnership'.[15]

Although the issue of worker participation slipped down the agenda during the post-1970s economic downturn, it resurfaced a decade or so later, particularly in the debates about 'stakeholding'. Thus, in the late 1980s, more and more radical labour lawyers once again began to advocate the extension of democratic values into economic life. In the United States, for example, Karl Klare asserted that the expansion of democracy at work had to be a 'guiding principle of our labour laws' and had to be extended beyond the more mundane levels of a firm's day-to-day operations to the upper tiers of its governance and strategic decision-making processes.[16] And in the UK at about the same time, Hugh Collins similarly suggested that the source of the 'the subordination of labour to capital, or of employee to employer' was not, as collective bargaining mistakenly assumed, inequality of bargaining power, but the 'fundamental institutional framework of capitalist relations of production' and the 'institutional design of firms'. This framework, he claimed, 'establish[ed] a hierarchy of employees from the chief executive down to the shop-floor

---

[15] Kahn-Freund, O., 'Industrial Democracy' (1977) 6 *ILJ* 65; Davies, P., and Wedderburn, W., 'The Land of Industrial Democracy' (1977) 6 *ILJ* 197.

[16] Klare, K., 'Workplace Democracy and Market Reconstruction' (1988) 38 *Catholic University L. Review* 1.

worker' which was 'only challenged weakly and indirectly by collective bargaining'. So far as empowering workers was concerned, legal techniques and social practices which 'grant[ed] control to workers over the nature of their work' and which 'reduc[ed] or blunt[ed] the power exercised through institutional hierarchy' were just as important as collective industrial relations. In Collins's view, therefore, labour lawyers needed to pay much greater attention to issues of worker ownership and democratic participation; to 'shift [their] sights slightly towards the terms on which organisations of capital are established and alternative patterns of governance within those organisations'.[17]

In the years following, however, there was a tempering of ambition. The more radical proposals for 'stakeholding corporations', with their democratic aspirations, gave way to more modest proposals which did not seek direct board representation for workers, merely consideration of their interests by directors. More recently, as the traditional redistributive objectives of social democracy have been diluted (if not abandoned) in favour of the goals of competitiveness and 'efficiency', even these diluted versions of stakeholding have fallen from favour, displaced by a human-resource-management notion of 'partnership at work' which is decidedly *non*-conflictual.[18] In the UK, for example, the TUC now champions 'workplace partnerships' founded on mutual trust and respect and a 'joint commitment to the success of enterprises', arguing that companies are 'communities of interest'.[19] The result is that in recent years, even on the left, the case for workers' rights within both labour and company law has increasingly come to be couched in terms of enhancing competitiveness rather than in terms of justice, fundamental rights, fair distribution of wealth, and self-realization. Discursively, 'capitalism' has been ousted by 'globalization', 'profit' by 'efficiency', and 'conflict' by 'partnership'.

Within the European Union (EU), the increasingly ubiquitous idea of 'partnership' has found one of its most influential expressions in the growing support for worker representation in the form of compulsory 'Works Councils' through which employees are to be consulted and provided with information on a wide range of issues. Such Councils, Collins argues, offer a 'new, simple and pragmatic' way forward in face of the 'withering' of more radical proposals for employee involvement in management. Indeed, he suggests, by disengaging the issue of company

[17] Collins, H., 'Labour Law as a Vocation' (1989) 104 *LQR* 468, and 'Market Power, Bureaucratic Power, and the Contract of Employment' (1986) 15 *ILJ* 1.
[18] See Wilson, G., 'Business, State and Community: "Responsible Risk Takers"', New Labour, and the Governance of Corporate Business' (2000) 27 *Journal of Law and Society* 151.
[19] Monks, J., 'Corporate Governance and Stakeholding: The New Agenda', speech to the Institute of Public Policy Research (IPPR) Conference, 29 Feb. 1996. See TUC, *Your Stake at Work: TUC Proposals for a Stakeholding Economy* (London: TUC, 1996).

law reform from that of worker representation, the European Works Councils Directive[20] gives the Commission 'a realistic chance of introducing the institutional framework for a European company'. Precisely because of the changes which have taken place in the process of production, it is, he believes, politically possible to sell proposals of this sort to business and achieve a 'structural coupling' which aligns capital's growing need for co-operative relations with labour's desire to achieve greater self-determination in the workplace.[21]

Despite their acknowledged limitations, then, reforms of this sort are still thought worthwhile and valuable. The slide from industrial democracy to stakeholding to partnership—and the accompanying decline of interest in truly radical company law reform—is presented as an essentially pragmatic, tactical move along the same political axis, rather than a fundamental change in aspiration: even if workers are only kept informed and consulted rather than actually represented on decision-making bodies, it is still a step in the direction of 'democratization' which will better enable them to protect and further their interests. Works Councils may be limited in scope, but they still hold out the possibility of greater worker input into and influence over working conditions, for in implicitly recognizing workers as stakeholders in firms if not as full members akin to shareholders, they offer a mechanism whereby the neglected issues of disrespect and alienation, 'those aspects of work which turn it into drudgery rather than an opportunity to confront challenges', can be addressed.[22] Despite their politically expedient emphasis on efficiency and competitiveness, therefore, one still finds in these arguments traces of the idea that institutions such as Works Councils will serve to temper the unfettered rule of capital in the workplace; that they might operate so as to alter the balance of class power in the productive process in workers' favour.

II THE IMPERSONAL IMPERATIVES OF THE CAPITALIST MARKET

Market dependence and its compulsions

There is no doubt that to those anxious to further the interests and welfare of workers the idea of the stakeholding company provides a more attractive model for company law than the shareholder-oriented model which currently prevails; and that the proposals for compulsory Works

[20] Council Directive 94/45/EC of 22 Sept. 1994 [1994] OJ L254/64.
[21] See Collins, above, n. 8. On Works Councils more generally see Villiers, C., *European Company Law: Towards Democracy* (Aldershot: Ashgate, 1998).
[22] Collins, above, n. 6.

Councils, modest though they are, constitute a move in the right direction. But how great is the potential of reforms of this sort, desirable though they are? The writings of the historian, Robert Brenner, provide a useful starting point for theoretical consideration of this question, for Brenner's work on the emergence of capitalism,[23] and, more recently, on the post World-War II world economy[24] has added significantly to our historical understanding of the development of capitalism, providing important new insights into its nature, dynamics, and specificity as a mode of production.[25]

In brief, Brenner's work suggests that, in the first instance at least, the origins of capitalism are to be found in the emergence and growth of market dependence and that, historically, this dependence pre-dated the general commodification and proletarianization of labour. The pressure to increase the productivity of labour associated with capitalism, Brenner argues, did not initially flow from the relation between wage-labour and capital, but from the competitive pressures imposed by growing market dependence on direct producers, whether or not they employed wage-labour. In Brenner's account, indeed, the pressures exerted on the productivity of labour by growing market dependence was a cause, rather than an effect, of proletarianization and the generalized relation between capital and wage labour. It follows that, in his view, while it is true that the market imperatives which compel individual capitals to compete and accumulate also lead them to exploit labour as intensely as possible, these imperatives are not actually constituted by the relation between capital and wage-labour but are historically independent of it. For Brenner, therefore, capitalism is defined not only by the capital–wage labour relation but by the market dependence of productive units. And while there

[23] See, e.g., Brenner's contributions to Aston, T. H., and Philpin, C. H. E. (eds.), *The Brenner Debate: Agrarian Class Structure and Economic Development in Pre-Industrial Europe* (Cambridge: Cambridge University Press, 1985), 10, 213.

[24] Brenner, R., 'The Economics of Global Turbulence' (1998) 229 *New Left Review* 229.

[25] The crucial thing about Robert Brenner's work is that he seeks to explain the transition from feudalism to capitalism without assuming the very thing that needs to be explained. In other words, he does not read capitalist principles and values back into pre-capitalist societies or presuppose an underlying transhistorical capitalist logic, thus enabling us better to understand the specificity of capitalism. Indeed, he critiques accounts which see the rise of capitalism as occurring when constraints on market exchange were lifted and opportunities for trade expanded, on the grounds that they tend to see capitalism as 'always there', waiting to be liberated. In these accounts, which are increasingly prevalent today, the rise of modern capitalism becomes the outcome of 'natural' processes, an expression of immutable laws. The implication is that as a result of their nature, people have always, given the chance, been guided and driven by the principles of capitalist rationality—profit, increasing labour productivity, and so on. When this assumption is made, of course, history becomes, to a large extent, simply the story of the lifting of the barriers to the universalization of this (natural) rationality. Contemporary liberal ('globalized') capitalism thus comes to appear as the 'end of history' to which there is no alternative.

are vital connections between market dependence and exploitation, he argues, there is also a fundamental contradiction in the relationship between capitals that is independent of that in the relationship between capital and labour. Brenner thus gives an explanatory status to market dependence and competition which is quite separate from—and, indeed, historically prior to—the relation between capital and wage-labour.[26]

This colours Brenner's analysis of the end of the long post-war boom and the subsequent failure of capitalism decisively to emerge from the long downturn which has followed. He does not deny that class struggle affects profits, but it is not to a labour-induced 'profit squeeze'—to a change in the balance of class power operating in labour's favour—to which Brenner attributes the modesty of the recovery. He attributes it, rather, to the increasingly competitive relationship between capitals and its generation of chronic over-capacity on a system-wide scale, especially in manufacturing. This, he suggests, accounts for the failure of the recent decline in working class power to bring the downturn unequivocally to an end. For Brenner, the competition between capitals is a source not only of dynamism but of overcapacity, economic stagnation, and recession, whatever the prevailing balance of power between capital and labour.

This is significant both theoretically and politically, for Brenner's analysis underlines and emphasizes that it is quite possible for significant changes to occur in the content of the immediate workplace relations between capitalists (corporations) and their workers—or in the general balance of power between classes—without eradicating either the tendency of the accumulation process towards crisis or the subjection of the production process to the destructive effects of competition. The dynamics of competition operate whatever the balance of class power. Even if workers were to gain more managerial 'say', therefore, as long as the market continues to regulate the economy, subjecting productive units to its abstract imperatives, the scope for making the production process more responsive to the needs and interests of workers would still be limited. Whether in corporations or co-operatives, whether capitalists or workers, those managing production would still be subject to the power of the market and compelled to treat labour instrumentally and exploitatively as they tried to compete and survive. Ultimately, workers lack power over the process of production not so much because of their exclusion from managerial decision-making or their subordination to the personal authority of capitalist corporate managers (important though these things are) but because all economic actors are subject to the *impersonal* laws of capital and the market. For this reason, the scope for

---

[26] See Meiksins Wood, E., *The Origin of Capitalism* (New York: Monthly Review Press, 1999).

developing truly democratic self-determination within market capitalism is limited: even if firms were to be 'democratized', the demands of capital and the market would continue to take precedence over the needs of workers and the well-being of society as a whole. Indeed, in recent years, as the market has become more than ever a coercive instrument for capital—the ultimate mechanism for controlling labour—it has emerged as a major terrain of class struggle.

Democracy and the autonomous 'economy'

The limitations on what can be achieved by democratizing productive enterprises within capitalism highlights the separation of the 'economic' and 'political' spheres in capitalist societies—a separation which has important consequences for all democratizing projects, within production and beyond. Whereas under historically preceding modes of production, surplus labour was appropriated by means of such things as labour services, taxes, and rents, so that the 'economic' and the 'political' were (so to speak) fused, in capitalist societies the process of appropriation does not rest immediately upon political, legal, and military coercions. This is not to say that the exploitation of labour within capitalism is not ultimately dependent on the political or legal sphere. On the contrary, capitalist social relations of production exist in particular legal and political forms—most notably, forms of property—which have to be constituted and sustained. It is, rather, to say that within capitalism the exploitation and appropriation of surplus labour are effected through the mechanism of commodity exchange rather than by direct 'political' means; that 'economic' power is based not on direct relations of juridical or political subjugation but on contractual relations between formally free and equal individuals. In other words, the coercive power which underpins capitalist exploitation has, in effect, been relocated into a 'private' (purely 'economic') sphere of supposed freedom and voluntary activity (the market) which, unlike the coercive, 'public' ('political') sphere, is not supposed to be in need of democratizing—as, it is claimed, it is inherently democratic.[27] The resulting differentiation of the economic and the political in modern capitalist societies is, therefore, both real and apparent. It is a historical reality in the sense that there *is* something in the nature of capitalism that is manifested in a differentiation of these spheres, but merely an appearance in the sense that the 'economic' (private) in capitalism is legally and politically (and, therefore, publicly) constituted.

The rigid conceptual separation of the economic from the political (like

---

[27] For an extended discussion of this point see Meiksins Wood, E., *Democracy Against Capitalism* (Cambridge: Cambridge University Press, 1995), upon which this section is based.

the separation of the political from the legal) has long been one of the cornerstones of capitalist ideology. Indeed, in recent years, as 'the economy' seems more than ever to have taken on a life of its own (the increasing coerciveness of the seemingly autonomous, self-regulating market lying at the heart of much of the discourse on globalization), it has played an especially important role in cleansing capitalism of social and political content. So much so that the existence of capitalism as a set of politically and legally constituted, structured, material processes is now not even recognized by many, let alone seen as something to be critiqued. In the fragmented postmodern world, the systematic unity and totalizing imperatives of the capitalist market—which shape our prospects, choices, relationships, and identities—have been conceptually and discursively dissolved. The effect has been largely to exempt them from critical evaluation, while at the same time elevating them, by default, to the status of *de facto* universal laws of nature.[28]

Historically, then, the relinquishment by capital(ists) of direct political power over labour—most vividly reflected, perhaps, in the legal shift from a master–servant to an employment–contract conception of the relationship between capital and labour—has been accompanied by (and, indeed, was arguably made possible by) a process in which not only productive activity but social life as a whole has been drawn ever more deeply into the orbit and field-of-force of the capitalist market and its seemingly neutral, transhistorical imperatives. Indeed, in recent years, because, in particular, of developments in financial markets, the productive process has become ever more sensitive to the demands of (money) capital, to the requirements of what has come to be called in the corporate context 'shareholder value'.[29] If anything really does decisively distinguish the present era from that preceding it, then, it is the fact that in a world in which the power and mobility of capital in its impersonal, intangible, mobile, liquid, financial forms has grown, market imperatives have extended and tightened their grip, remorselessly subordinating human needs to its demands. In so doing, they have reduced the room for manœuvre not only of individual capitalists and corporate managers but of nation-states. Indeed, it is arguable that it is precisely the increasing intensity and reach of the *impersonal* imperatives of the market—something sponsored by those very same nation-states—that is making some measure of worker participation more imaginable than was the case a few decades ago. Put simply, capitalism, with its separation of the economic and the political, can increasingly permit greater 'democracy', not only in

---

[28] See Ireland, P., 'History, Critical Legal Studies and the Mysterious Disappearance of Capitalism' (2002) 65 *MLR* (forthcoming).
[29] See Dore, R., *Stock Market Capitalism: Welfare Capitalism* (Oxford: Oxford University Press, 2000), ch. 1.

the workplace but in the institutions of civil society as a whole, without putting at risk its constitutive relations and their market-imposed coercions. Indeed, in certain respects the changes in productive organization and working methods associated with post-fordist flexibility have accentuated the perceived classlessness, impersonality and neutrality of the imperatives of capital and the market. As Richard Sennett has observed, one aspect of the rise of the ideas of 'workplace partnership', 'co-operation', and 'adaptability' has, superficially at least, been the erosion of authority in the workplace. In the flexible firm, he explains, managers are less bosses and more 'facilitators', 'leaders of group processes', 'on your side rather than your ruler', something which has generated the emergence of the 'fiction' that 'workers and bosses aren't antagonistic' but are, rather, members of the 'same team'. Ultimately, Sennett suggests, this idea of 'community at work' merely serves the relentless drive for greater productivity and profits. But in a world of global competition and seemingly neutral (albeit remorseless) market imperatives, managers are in a position to declare that all are equally 'victims of time and place'.[30]

In short, then, while democratic principles have, in certain senses, been extended under capitalism, this extension has come at a price, for democracy has simultaneously been redefined and its reach attenuated as it has been excluded from the 'economic' sphere. Indeed, so circumscribed is the meaning and scope of democracy in the modern world that greater 'democracy' is now increasingly commonly associated not with participation in policy-and-decision-making but with the extension of market principles,[31] something which has contributed to the debasement of contemporary western politics. Recognition of these realities is vitally important to those trying to use labour law and company law as vehicles for social transformation, not least because in these circumstances 'industrial partnership', wrongly cast, might easily become less a springboard for radical change and more a mechanism whereby workers are encouraged to internalize the market imperatives faced by managers and made more responsive to them. As, for example, the adaptable, flexible, and co-operative workers at the Longbridge Rover plant in the UK recently discovered, neither industrial partnership nor Works Councils offered protection from closures and job cuts when the executives of BMW were confronted by the imperatives of capital and the global market for cars. On the contrary, they merely served to explain their inevitability.

---

[30] See Sennett, above, n. 13, 108–17.
[31] See Frank, T., *One Market Under God* (New York: Doubleday, 2000).

III STRATEGIES FOR REFORM

'Progressive' strategies for competitiveness: market as opportunity versus market as imperative

From this perspective, 'globalization' and the other developments which have so troubled radical labour lawyers in recent years mark not so much an epochal change, the emergence of entirely new forces, but more an extension and intensification of the well-established logic of capitalism— an empirically observable, systematic, and historically specific logic mani- fested in and imposed by the imperatives generated by market dependence and competitive production, and characterized by a compul- sive search for increased labour productivity, relentless technological advance, and the ruthless exploitation of labour.[32] It is in this light that the various proposals for industrial partnership and the new efficiency-based arguments for enhanced workers' rights need to be viewed. For they are, in essence, aspects of a wider centre-left strategy—associated in Britain with 'New Labour' and the so-called 'Third Way', elsewhere with the idea of 'comparative' or 'shaped advantage'—aimed at improving the lot of working people by trying to accommodate the intensification of this logic and its imperatives rather than by trying to change and, eventually, replace it.

Conceived in an era in which the strategies associated with Keynesianism are no longer thought to be available and as an alternative to neo-liberal strategies of 'competitive austerity', these 'left competitive- ness' strategies purport to have a progressive bent, in that they seek to underline the importance to competitiveness and efficiency of high labour standards, proper training, good working conditions and decent pay. '[H]igh productivity, workers rights, flexibility, unionization and economic competitiveness', claim Mishel and Voos, 'are not incompatible, . . . [in fact] they may be highly compatible components of a high perform- ance business system'.[33] By tapping into the alleged need for co-operation from workers and by purporting to offer benefits to both labour *and* capi- tal, these strategies are portrayed as not only economically viable but politically realistic, unlike the utopian aspirations of more traditional socialists with their emphasis on the need for militant class struggle. They offer, it is argued, a politically feasible way of revitalizing social democ- racy, of combining economic efficiency with social equity within capital- ism.

---

[32] See Ireland, above, n. 28.
[33] Mishel, L., and Voos, P. (eds.), *Unions and Economic Competitiveness* (Armonk, NY: Sharpe, 1992) 10.

Originating, as they generally did, in the 1980s and early 1990s, these strategies were usually constructed with the 'corporatist' or 'welfarist' models of capitalism of countries like Germany and Sweden (and in some versions Japan[34]) in mind. On the basis of their sustained periods of relative economic success and on their seeming ability to combine steadily improving workers' rights and social services with strong growth, many thought, and some still think, that these models provide a viable and progressive model of capitalism worth emulating. From this perspective, the key is the adoption of the *right kind* of capitalism and the establishment of a mutually beneficial balance between capital and labour. As this entails, *inter alia*, staving off capitalism's tendency towards stagnation and recession, it follows that workers should not to be too militant and demanding as this will serve only to undermine competitiveness and, with it, profitability, employment, and social provision.

Unfortunately, the 1990s were a bad decade for the 'trust-based' capitalisms of Germany, Sweden, and Japan, all of which now appear to be in relative decline. As capital has become more internationally mobile, the character of the local employing classes in these countries has changed, weakening the national class compacts upon which their particular versions of capitalism were founded. The reality is that nowadays no models of capitalism appear to be working particularly well, at least so far as working people are concerned. On the contrary, all seem to be suffering from remarkably similar difficulties. Earlier social settlements are being ratcheted down, so that in the 'established capitalisms' of the west (even those thought recently to have been relatively 'successful', like that of the USA) white male workers 'have now experienced between fifteen and twenty-five years (depending on where they are) of frozen (or falling) real wages, increased job insecurity and intensified work processes'.[35] Indeed, it is arguably precisely because of the inadequacies of strategies for 'progressive competitiveness' that neo-liberalism is being embraced by governments of all political colours. It is difficult to escape the conclusion that in many sectors it is perfectly rational for capital to seek to restore competitiveness by downsizing, diminishing workers' rights, devaluing labour, and intensifying work, and that this is the real message hidden in the discourse on 'flexibility' and 'efficiency'. So while it cannot be doubted that competitive advantage shifts between nations, it is increasingly apparent that capitalisms exist in a state of mutual interaction and interdependence; and that in an era in which barriers to capital

---

[34] For an account of the dark side of the Japanese 'economic miracle', particularly its labour repression and exploitation of women workers, see Henderson, J., 'Against the Economic Orthodoxy' (1993) 22 *Economy and Society* 200; see also Ishida, in this volume.

[35] Coates, above, n. 3, 250.

mobility have been lowered both technologically and politically, for the system as a whole progressive strategies for competitiveness are essentially a zero-sum game: one national capital's gain is another's loss. As David Coates observes, '[y]ou cannot get off the treadmill simply by running faster. All you can do . . . is temporarily pass others, until they respond by running faster too, with the long-term consequence of having the whole field increase their speed just to stand still'.[36] The victor in this race is not the runner, but the treadmill.

Put slightly differently, and to draw on a distinction drawn by Ellen Meiksins Wood, progressive strategies for competitiveness and the belief that flexibility might be a positive force are both premised on a conception of the market as an *opportunity* rather than as an *imperative*. In other words, they focus on the opportunities which the market offers rather than on the imperatives it imposes.[37] Thus, from the New Labour/Third Way perspective, the old problems addressed by labour law—those associated with class conflict and the distribution of wealth—need to be consigned to (the end of) history. The regulation of the employment relationship is now about efficiency and creating opportunities for employment. In the New Labour dictionary, therefore, 'social exclusion' is a reference not to poverty but to a lack of labour market opportunity, the solution to which is a workforce which is more flexible, better trained and educated, and anti-discriminatory measures such as family-friendly employment policies. In similar vein, the alleged competitive need of firms for workplace partnership is now increasingly portrayed as an opportunity for labour to participate in decision-making in pursuit of the goal of efficiency rather than of greater democracy, justice, or empowerment. The suggestion, in other words, is that 'globalization' and 'flexible specialization' have created *new* market opportunities for labour that might be exploited in a progressive manner; and that the market opportunities available to capital might simultaneously be obstructed through such things as the imposition of high international labour standards and the insertion of social clauses into trading agreements (to prevent destructive competition), and the introduction of 'Tobin taxes' (to throw sand into the wheels of financial markets). The growing strength of market *forces* is recognized ('globalization'), but these forces are seen in many ways as manipulable and, indeed, as beneficent—as compelling economic rationality and efficiency. As Wood observes, however, what is peculiar and historically specific about the *capitalist* market is precisely that its dominant characteristic is not opportunity or choice but compulsion.

---

[36] Coates, above, n. 3, 254.

[37] Meiksins Wood, E., 'From Opportunity to Imperative: The History of the Market', *Monthly Review* (July–Aug. 1994) 46.

What needs to be recognized is not so much how people can respond to the market (how it *enables*), but how they are compelled to respond to it (how it *coerces*); how it *disempowers* rather than *empowers*; how it closes off rather than opens up opportunities.

Ultimately, then, strategies of progressive competitiveness cling to the belief—developed during the course of the long post-war boom which provided the foundations for social democracy and the welfare state— that the self-regulating market can be regulated and controlled in such a way as to fashion a humane capitalism. The problem is that history increasingly suggests that the long post-war boom was *exceptional*, a conjunctural product of highly specific historical circumstances; that the problem lies not with the particular model of capitalism adopted but with capitalism itself; and that, notwithstanding events in Eastern Europe, the 'crisis' that has hit the left in recent years is as much a crisis of social democracy as it is of socialism. Indeed, the current demand for flexibility is, arguably, the closest we have ever got to admitting that it is simply not possible to construct a permanently house-trained capitalism and that high labour standards, let alone true industrial democracy, are simply incompatible with it.

Redistributive reform strategies

Where does this leave progressive strategies for labour and company law reform? Well, it certainly does *not* mean that the kinds of changes currently being advocated—high national and international labour standards, improved individual employment rights, social clauses, voluntary corporate codes, Works Councils, stakeholding companies, and the like— are not worth fighting for. On the contrary, they are vitally important. Precisely because of the way that it subordinates human needs to the imperatives of productivity and profitability, capitalism is not only a uniquely dynamic but a uniquely destructive way of organizing material life. Its wastefulness, its failure to satisfy the basic material needs of billions of people worldwide, its degradation of the environment, and its heightening of sexual, racial, and national oppressions are not accidental by-products of its workings, unfortunate 'externalities', but the systematic results of its inner logic. Strategies aimed at eradicating these consequences are indispensable. But it does mean that these strategies are, *in themselves*, essentially ameliorative rather than transformative.[38] For they do not address, as a genuinely transformative strategy must, the structural conditions which subject social and material life to the ruthless imperatives and logic of the market. In this context, it is vital that we

---

[38] See Meiksins Wood, E., 'The Politics of Capitalism' (1999) 51 *Monthly Review* 12.

recognize, with Brenner, that the capitalist market and its imperatives are *not* part of some transhistorical natural law but are based on human agency; that they are rooted in historically specific social property forms and relations which are amenable to change. As Gregory Albo observes, 'the only thing that obliges us to conclude that there is no alternative to the pursuit of international competitiveness is the *a priori* (and unexamined) assumption that existing social property relations—and hence the structural political power sustained by these relations—are sacrosanct'.[39] It is in relation to the reform of these relations that company law once again comes into play, for it not only protects but constitutes one of the key property forms upon which these relations are now based—the share, which enables essentially functionless corporate shareholders to exert both income and control rights over productive activity.

The issue of property rights, and of corporate property rights in particular, has, in fact, recently risen to prominence, with many calling for a radical redistribution in the ownership of shares and other intangible forms of financial property. In the UK, for example, Richard Minns,[40] observing that pension funds already control assets to the total value of shares quoted on the world's three leading exchanges, has argued that much financial wealth is already held on behalf of workers and that it would be possible to increase further their influence over the production process by transferring ownership of still more through something resembling the scheme proposed by Rudolf Meidner in Sweden in the mid-1970s.[41] Andrew Gamble and Gavin Kelly have similarly argued for a major redistribution of property rights in pursuit of 'an egalitarian market economy'.[42] In the USA, Jeff Gates, lamenting the growing concentration of wealth and income, and the tendency of 'ownership benefits to flow into the hands of a few', has also advocated a substantial redistribution of capital assets, arguing that the main problem with capitalism is that it does not create enough capitalists.[43] And Samuel Bowles and Herbert Gintis have recently added their voices to the call for a democratization of the economy through a major redistribution of capital assets to workers.[44]

While there is no doubting the radicalism of these proposals, however, they would leave unaffected the *forms* and *nature*, as opposed to the *distribution*, of property rights. And, as a result, it is doubtful whether they

[39] Albo, G., 'A World Market of Opportunities? Capitalist Obstacles and Left Economic Policy' in Panitch, L. (ed.), [1997] *Socialist Register* 5, 27.

[40] Minns, R., 'The Social Ownership of Capital' (1996) 219 *New Left Review* 42, 43.

[41] See Meidner, R., 'Why Did the Swedish Model Fail' [1991] *Socialist Register* 219.

[42] Gamble, A., and Kelly, G., 'The New Politics of Ownership' (1996) 220 *New Left Review* 62.

[43] Gates, J., *The Ownership Solution: Towards a Shared Capitalism for the Twenty-First Century* (London: Penguin, 1998).

[44] Bowles, S., and Gintis, H., *Recasting Egalitarianism: New Rules for Communities, States and Markets* (New York: Verso, 1998).

would have a significant impact on social production relations and the destructive, exploitative, and competitive dynamics—the logic of process—that they engender. Indeed, one of the hallmarks of many of these proposals is their broad acceptance of private ownership and the logic of free, self-regulating markets.[45] The project of an egalitarian market economy, write Gamble and Kelly, 'combines the moral argument for spreading rights of ownership more widely on the grounds of social justice and individual autonomy with the economic argument that the way in which property rights are distributed has economic consequences for efficiency and equality'.[46] Similarly, for Bowles and Gintis, the redistribution of property rights would help to deal with the problems surrounding labour discipline. For all their overt radicalism, therefore, these strategies do not propose fundamentally to alter the property relations of capitalism, nor its dynamics and imperatives.

To a certain extent this deficiency is recognized in that the call for a redistribution of property rights is commonly accompanied by assertion of the need to refashion the 'culture' of 'ownership'. Minns, for example, observes that while the rise of pension funds has enabled some privileged workers to become capital owners, it has also aggravated the 'characteristic vices' of Anglo-American stock exchanges and forms of corporate governance: a tendency towards ruthless shareholder-oriented short-termism. The savings of workers are 'hostages to a financial regime which systematically searches for the highest rate of return regardless of the consequences for employment, the environment, or the state of the social infrastructure'.[47] Like Gamble and Kelly, Gates, and many others, Minns therefore calls for more active, socially responsible, shareholding—more participatory 'ownership'—to ensure that corporations take account of broader social and welfare considerations. There is a need for a more 'democratic voice' in financial systems, for greater 'collective influence over the deployment of financial capital'. Or, as Gamble and Kelly put it, we need 'measures which can deliver accountability in the way in which companies and institutional investments are run' so that 'the preferences of the ultimate owners are reflected in the behaviour of their agents'.[48]

The periodic re-emergence of proposals of this sort—variations on

---

[45] In this respect see Roberto Unger's *Democracy Realized: The Progressive Alternative* (New York: Verso, 1998) which, for all its political and institutional radicalism (calling for a transformative state engaging in a constant process of democratic experimentalism), is economically conservative, advancing a self-consciously post-fordist strategy for economic growth based on 'progressive competitiveness' and 'flexible specialisation', in which workers and managers will work together on a 'partnership principle' governed by 'co-operation and innovation'.

[46] Gamble and Kelly, above, n. 42, 81.   [47] Minns, above, n. 40, 48.

[48] Ibid., 55; Gamble and Kelly, above, n. 42, 95, 90.

Peter Drucker's 'pension-fund socialism'[49]—is testimony to their attractions. But, again, what is their potential? They seek to build on the growing 'class duality' of the minority of more privileged (western) workers who, with 'deferred labour income' becoming a major source of the new money flowing into capital markets, are not only wage-labourers but beneficial owners of stocks and shares.[50] The hope is that the capital 'ownership' power of workers can be used not only to achieve greater income equality but to tame and socialize increasingly rapacious corporations. Despite the recent widening of the base of the financial pyramid, however, the richest households still hold a hugely disproportionate share of financial property.[51] Moreover, worker-investors, with their relatively small holdings, tend to be concerned even more than those with larger holdings with maximizing their returns, hardly surprising given that for most of them (myself included) these investments are simply a way, in an era of declining social provision, of trying to guarantee a reasonable standard of life when wage-earning ceases. Even more importantly, while it is true that institutional investors now exercise greater power *in* financial markets, they are also subject to the growing competitive disciplines imposed *by* those markets. In the search for the highest possible returns, the relative performance not only of different investment funds but of money managers within particular funds are placed under constant scrutiny. Contrary to the hopes of pension-fund socialists, then, historically, 'shareholder activism' in its various forms has not generally operated as a force for the general good. Its effect has, rather, been to tighten market imperatives and, as Doug Henwood observes, 'to increase the profit share of national income, and to claim a larger portion of that profit share for *rentiers*'.[52]

Towards transformation: reconceptualising corporate rights

How, then, does one begin to develop a strategy for company law reform that might have greater transformative potential? The problems, outlined above, faced by strategies for corporate reform based on the redistribution of existing corporate property rights, underline the fact that shares and other financial instruments are forms of property which, *by their very nature*, do not lend themselves to the socially and environmentally sensitive use and development of productive resources, including

---

[49] See Drucker, P., *The Unseen Revolution: How Pension Fund Socialism Came to America* (London: Heinemann, 1976).

[50] Seccombe, W., 'Contradictions of Shareholder Capitalism' [1999] *Socialist Register* 76, 91.

[51] See Gates, above, n. 43.

[52] Henwood, D., *Wall Street* (London: Verso, 1997) 293.

labour. It is this, the essential nature of forms of property such as the share—a bundle of intangible rights to appoint and dismiss directors and to receive an income derived from unpaid labour—and the logic of process that they engender that a transformative corporate strategy needs to address. What must be challenged is not simply the distribution but the very legitimacy of this form of property and the rights that it confers, rights which are not only protected but constituted by company law. Over time, the grounds for mounting such a challenge have become stronger.

Historically, the rights of corporate shareholders have traditionally been legitimated by reference to their 'ownership', through the share, of either the company's assets or 'the company' itself, enabling shareholders to enlist in their support the powerful justifications of natural right, liberty, and moral desert.[53] Until the mid-nineteenth century, when joint stock corporations were relatively small, much less impersonal associations, and when there was no developed share market, shareholders were conceptualized as the co-owners of assets who were actively involved in either management or its monitoring. In similar vein, companies were conceptualized not as 'completely separate' entities from their shareholders but as those shareholders merged into one body: the shareholders *were* the company and entitled to its surplus product by virtue of their ownership rights. Gradually, however, as a result of changes in the nature of corporate shareholding and in the legal rights attached to it, these 'ownership' claims have become harder and harder to sustain. As companies became larger, the number of shareholders grew and a sophisticated market in shares rapidly developed, with the result that most corporate shareholders became passive *rentiers* completely detached from the companies in which they held shares. In law, this was reflected in the emergence of the modern doctrine of separate corporate personality (whereby 'the company' came to be regarded as a completely separate entity from its shareholders) and in the legal constitution of shares as forms of property in their own right, as saleable titles to revenue quite separate from the assets of companies. In keeping with the fact that shareholders now took little or no active interest in management, the rights attached to share ownership were gradually diminished, while the rights and powers of managers were extended. The result is that, today, despite the enduring myth of shareholder 'ownership', in both economic reality and law corporate shareholders own neither productive assets, nor, in any meaningful sense, companies.[54] They are, rather, functionless, parasitic, *rentier* owners of shares—an attenuated but valuable 'bundle of

---

[53] See Christman, J., *The Myth of Property* (Oxford: Oxford University Press, 1994).

[54] See Ireland, P., 'Company Law and the Myth of Shareholder Ownership' (1999) 62 *MLR* 32.

rights', most importantly to residual profits (part of the unpaid labour of the workforce) and to appoint and dismiss directors. Severed from productive purpose and from most of the rights and responsibilities traditionally associated with 'ownership', the moral basis for these rights has, for those who bother critically to consider them, long been difficult to discern. In short, for the same reasons that these *rentier* property forms are ill-suited to ensuring the just, responsible, and effective use of society's productive resources, they are also difficult to justify and defend. Nowhere is the impermanent, socially constructed, and contingent nature (as well as the 'public' and political character) of private property rights more vividly illustrated than by corporate history.[55]

It is precisely because of the erosion of traditional ownership-based justifications for shareholder rights that in recent decades new justifications for them have been developed, justifications which seek to establish the role of these rights in ensuring productive (and especially capital-market) 'efficiency'. Quite apart from the spuriousness of many of these claims, however, as soon as one begins to offer instrumental justifications for shareholder rights, one highlights their social nature and origins, and invites not only an empirical assessment of their effectiveness in achieving the alleged goals but an evaluation of those goals relative to other competing ones.[56] Put bluntly, shareholder corporate rights effectively permit a relatively small parasitic minority to appropriate the surplus labour of workers world-wide. They have generated, with the assistance of international agencies such as the International Monetary Fund and the World Trade Organization, new financial forms of imperialism. Moreover, through the operation of contemporary financial markets— which insist on the highest possible returns on financial assets ('shareholder value') whatever the consequences for workers, society, and the environment—they have come to play an increasingly important role in subjecting material life to the ruthless imperatives of exploitation and profitability. In short, hidden behind the seemingly neutral concepts of 'efficiency' and 'market forces' are social relations, social processes, and forms of property which are, ultimately, expressions of class power and exploitation.

Challenging these forms of property, whose socially disembedded liquidity and mobility have played such an important role in intensifying market imperatives, is a prerequisite of developing a transformative strategy capable of disrupting the destructive internal dynamic of capitalism and the market. It will not be sufficient merely to exhort capital

---

[55] See Ireland, P., 'Defending the *Rentier*: Corporate Theory and the Reprivatization of the Public Company' in Parkinson, J., Gamble, A., and Kelly, G. (eds), *The Political Economy of the Company* (Oxford: Hart, 2001) 141.

[56] See ibid.

to be more 'patient', or to try to regulate capital movements, or to establish Works Councils and universal labour standards. Worthwhile though such reforms would be, there are profound limits to what they can achieve. Transformation will require, among many other things, nothing less than a fundamental reconceptualization, reconstitution, and reallocation of rights in and over corporations. It will require a gnawing away at the rights of *rentier* shareholders, the abandonment of the ideas that corporate assets are private property capable of being 'owned', and that labour is nothing more than a commodity, a gradual reconceptualization of corporations as social institutions, and a process of experimentation in which they are increasingly placed under a combination of worker, community, supplier, and consumer control. As Doug Henwood says, this will be 'technically and politically . . . difficult as hell',[57] particularly in an era in which even modest reforms are viewed by financial markets with horror and not just the political effectiveness but the very existence of the working class is doubted. But even amelioration will prove difficult without challenging the power of capital and the financial instruments which now constitute the dominant forms of property and class exploitation. At the end of the day, the more ambitious goal of social transformation might prove rather less utopian than forlornly trying to create a kinder capitalism from the wreckage of social democracy.

The left needs not only to recognize but to *emphasize* that the virtual universality of capitalism is an expression not of its conformity with human nature but of its own internal dynamic, its logic of process, its historically specific, expansionary drive, a drive which has wrought a transformation in the relationships of human beings with themselves, with one another, and with nature. As it becomes ever clearer that the remarkable expansion in productive capacity that capitalism has generated has not been, and is not going to be, matched by an improvement in the quality of life that it delivers to the great majority, the search for a new, rational, humane, and democratic material logic for society is becoming more, not less, pressing. In this context, whatever their reservations about collective bargaining, progressive labour lawyers would be ill-advised to abandon, in the current swell of postmodern fragmentation, the politically vital concepts of class and collectivism, not least because the changes in the composition of the workforce and the nature of working that have transformed their discipline have also made labour a potentially more inclusive agent for social change. They would also be well-advised to revive their earlier aspiration to radical company law reform, for it is company law that constitutes the *rentier* property forms

---

[57] Henwood, above, n. 52, 320.

which are now not only the principal sources of economic power in society but increasingly responsible for sustaining and intensifying the dynamics which are subjecting not only the workplace but all aspects of human life to the ruthless imperatives of the capitalist market.

11

Death and Suicide from Overwork: The Japanese Workplace and Labour Law

MAKOTO ISHIDA

I INTRODUCTION

Workplaces in each country have their own peculiar bright and dark sides. Japanese workplaces have been regarded as a model of democratic and participatory workplaces[1] but, as the 1993 ILO World Labour Report showed, Japanese workers are not only harmed by long hours of work, but are also victims of *karoshi*, or death from overwork.[2] Instances of *karojisatsu*, or suicide from overwork, were not widely known at the time the ILO Report was written, but now suicide from overwork is also a social issue, alongside death from overwork.

Death and suicide from overwork have become a grave social problem not simply due to the increased number of lawsuits and the active reporting of the facts by the media. Rather, contrary to the image projected by the democratic and participatory workplace model, the process by which victims die from overwork and overwork-induced suicide is indicative of the underlying cause of the problem, the grim severity of the Japanese workplace. What is more, one must focus on the fact that such extreme overwork, described by a court as 'beyond the pale of common sense',[3] is not only the result of employer compulsion, but is also reinforced by weaknesses in Japanese labour law.

I will attempt to do two things in this chapter. First, I will analyse the problem of overwork-induced death and suicide while focusing on the role of labour law in relation to worker health, and, through this analysis, elucidate the connection between the characteristics of the Japanese workplace and labour law. Secondly, I will look at the problem of overwork-induced death and suicide in relation to the characteristics of Japanese society, and ascertain its place in the international trend towards the recognition of work-related diseases.

---

[1] Kato, T., 'The Political Economy of Japanese KAROSHI' (1994) 26 *Hitotsubashi Journal of Social Studies* 41.

[2] *ILO World Labour Report 1993* (Geneva: ILO, 1993), 65–7.

[3] *Oshima v. Dentsu, Inc.*, Tokyo Dist. Ct., 24 Mar. 1996, 692 Rodo Hanrei (Labour Cases) 13.

Death from overwork (*karoshi*) means that fatigue accumulates because of too much work, resulting in death. The word *karoshi* was invented by physicians trying to have overwork-induced brain and heart disorders certified as labour accidents. They gave the name *karoshi* to 'the overwork-induced collapse of biorhythms, leading to a state engendered by the fatal failure of a person's life support functions', and the term was the title of a book they published in 1982.[4] This was the first appearance of the word.

Thus *karoshi* was, from the outset, a socio-medical term that came to be used in connection with labour accident certification for cerebrovascular and other circulatory disorders: it was a concept which indicated that an excessive workload and work-related stress were involved in bringing about the(se) condition(s). Initially, cerebral and cardiac disorders such as subarachnoid haemorrhages and cerebral infarctions were viewed as the typical forms of death from overwork, but, recently, an increasing number of cases deemed as death from overwork involve asthma and other respiratory system disorders, as well as suicide.

Karoshi, as a socio-medical term, has found rapidly widening use as a word that symbolizes an overworked Japan, and the term has made its way around the world to describe the obscure part of a country that had achieved astonishing economic growth. In this respect, a major role was played by the *Karoshi* Hotline Network, which was established in June 1988, mainly by lawyers and physicians. From its inception until June 1998 this counselling service received nearly 5,000 requests for counselling, and almost half of those concerned actual deaths. Although there are no official government statistics or studies on death from overwork in Japan, we can ascertain the characteristics of *karoshi* by examining the specifics of cases reported to the Hotline Network. A compilation of the cases reported to the network from June 1988 to June 1998 is shown in the Table opposite.

The first characteristic we can glean from this Table is that, judging by the job types and positions of the victims, *karoshi* can happen to anybody regardless of those two attributes. It does not matter if they are blue- or white-collar workers. Victims are found everywhere from workers on the front line to middle managers, and even among executives. In that sense, *karoshi* represents 'classless death'. The second characteristic, revealed by the victims' ages and gender, is that although *karoshi* is common among male workers in the most productive years of their 40s and 50s, it is, at the same time, not uncommon among younger workers in their 20s and 30s. Additionally, while there are fewer victims among female workers than

---

[4] Hosokawa, M., Tajiri, S., and Uehata, T., *Karoshi (Death from Overwork)* (Tokyo: Toyokeizaisha, 1982).

TABLE 11.1 *Summary of cases reported by the Karoshi Hotline Network from 1988 to 1998*

1 Contents of Consultation	Total	4911
	Worker's Compensation	3299 (67.2%)
	[Death Cases]	[2047] [41.8%]
	Health Care	1373 (27.9%)
	Others	239 (4.9%)
2 Clients	Total	4652
	Workers	914 (19.6%)
	Wives	2207 (47.5%)
	Other relatives	1001 (21.5%)
	Trade unions	64 (1.4%)
3 Occupation	Total	3233
	Directors	130 (4.0%)
	Managers	768 (23.8%)
	Manufacturing workers	721 (22.3%)
	Office workers	757 (23.4%)
	Drivers	298 (9.2%)
	Technical workers	304 (9.4%)
	Government employees	255 (7.9%)
4 Age	Total	4672
	Under 30 years old	411 (8.8%)
	30–39 years	685 (14.7%)
	40–49 years	1169 (25.0%)
	50–59 years	1121 (24.0%)
	over 60 years old	247 (5.3%)
	Unknown	1039 (22.2%)
5 Gender	Total	3299
	Male	3032 (92.0%)
	Female	162 (5.0%)
	Unknown	105 (3.0%)
6 Type of disorder	Total	3303
	Cerebral haemorrhage	468 (14.2%)
	Subarachnoidal haemorrhage	479 (14.5%)
	Cerebral thrombus, infarction	205 (6.5%)
	Myocardial infarction	339 (10.3%)
	Suicide	264 (8.0%)
	Heart failure	508 (15.8%)
	Others	1040 (31.5%)

Source: Summary of Karoshi Hotline Cases as of 20 June 1998.

males, there are recently increasing reports of *karoshi* among women, and it is said to be spreading among female teachers, nurses, clerical workers, and the like.[5]

The third characteristic, as indicated by the victims' specific disorders, is that while cerebrovascular and cardiac disorders make up the overwhelming majority, suicide has been quickly increasing. Requests for counselling on overwork-induced suicide numbered about forty at most until 1997, but in 1998 the number jumped to 180, the reason being the 1996 decision of the Tokyo District Court in the *Dentsu* case which served as the trigger turning overwork-induced suicide into a social and legal issue. The *Dentsu* case[6] involved the suicide of 24-year-old Mr Ichiro Oshima, who worked for the world-famous advertising company, Dentsu, Inc. His parents claimed damages from Dentsu on the grounds that 'the cause of our son's suicide was depression induced by fatigue from long hours of work'. On 28 March 1996, the Tokyo District Court, in the first decision of its kind, recognized Dentsu's responsibility and ordered it to pay 126 million yen in damages.

What is suicide from overwork (*karojisatsu*)? It is a form of *karoshi*, but according to Hiroshi Kawahito[7] the following characteristics distinguish it from other kinds of *karoshi*. First, although *karojisatsu* affects a broad array of workers through cerebral and cardiac disorders just as *karoshi* does, it differs in that the proportion of male victims is far higher. Reasons for this gender-based difference are that there are fewer full-time female workers over 30, and even full-time female workers usually do not work as many hours as their male counterparts. Secondly, the cause of overwork-induced suicide is not only the physical burden caused by excessive work such as long hours; for a high proportion it is also the mental stress arising from frustration, at being unable to attain a goal. Underlying such stress are draconian cost-cutting practices and personnel reductions made by many Japanese companies since the collapse of the bubble economy in the early 1990s.

Thirdly, the process leading to suicide often involves depression and other mental disturbances. Because one characteristic of depression is that its sufferers plan suicide, it is often the case that *karojisatsu* victims follow a course from overwork and stress, to mental disturbances like depression, and then to planning suicide. Fourthly, when a *karojisatsu* incident occurs, almost all companies have a strong tendency to disregard problems of working conditions and labour management, and see the suicide

---

[5] Kawahito, H., 'Karoshi: Death from Overwork', paper presented at the Joint Symposium on Employment, 14–22 Feb. 1988, in Osaka and Nagoya, Japan.
[6] Above, n. 3.
[7] Kawahito, H., *Karojisatsu (Suicide From Overwork)* (Tokyo: Iwanamishoten, 1998).

as the personal responsibility of the worker. Companies assume a high-handed attitude toward the survivors of *karojisatsu* victims, claiming that the victims 'caused trouble' for their companies, which forces survivors into an apologetic position. The result is a reversal of places, in which the wrong-doer who has created the cause of suicide rebukes the victim's survivors.

III LABOUR LAW AND THE CAUSES OF OVERWORK-INDUCED DEATH AND SUICIDE

At the foundation of all human rights is the freedoms of life and self. The freedom to be born into this world and live freely until a natural death without being deprived of one's life and health is fundamental to human beings. *Karoshi* and *karojisatsu* infringe these fundamental human rights. But Japanese companies, which are unified communities of labour and management, have resisted involvement in, and, sometimes, even inter-fered with, requests for co-operation in saving workers from *karoshi* and *karojisatsu*, and in obtaining workers' accident compensation. The labour law system, too, has neglected redress for individual workers because it gives precedence to respecting the autonomy of these company commu-nities. In this sense, Japan's labour law system has reinforced and repro-duced the social despotism of the unified company community of labour and management. Here, I would like to show, from several perspectives, the 'accomplice' relationship between the occurrence of *karoshi* and *karo-jisatsu* and labour law.

Long working hours and law on working hours

The primary cause behind *karoshi* and *karojisatsu* is, needless to say, extremely long working hours. Case precedents for litigation over *karoshi* and *karojisatsu* show that the victims work 3,000 hours a year or more. If we use the term extremely long working hours for the 3,000 or more hours a year that cause *karoshi* and *karojisatsu*, then how many extremely long-hour workers are there in Japan? Using the government's statistics on working hours to answer this question turns up something peculiar. Japan's government releases two kinds of statistics on working hours, but their figures are different. One set of statistics comes from the Monthly Labour Survey prepared by the Ministry of Labour (now, the Ministry of Health, Labour, and Welfare) according to surveys using data provided by companies, and the other set comes from the Labour Force Survey, which is prepared by the Management and Co-ordination Agency (now, the Ministry of Public Management) using data obtained from workers. Normally one would expect the figures to match no matter what survey method is used, but the Labour Force Survey is 200 to 350 hours higher than the Monthly Labour Survey in total annual working hours. The reason for this large statistical difference is that the Monthly Labour Survey, which uses company-provided data, does not include so-called 'free overtime'. Although collective agreements and work rules stipulate that workers are to receive overtime premiums, some overtime is in fact unpaid. This is 'free overtime'. Because companies do not pay for this overtime, they do not report it as hours worked. But because the Labour Force Survey is based on data from workers who honestly report their free overtime as hours worked, those additional hours raise the total. The difference between the two kinds of government statistics shows that Japanese workers are donating between 200 and 350 hours a year to their companies for no pay. Thus labour economists point out that the Labour Force Survey shows the true state of working hours in Japan in connection with *karoshi* and *karojisatsu*.[8] Using the Labour Force Survey to determine the approximate number of people working extremely long hours of 3,000 or more annually reveals that in 1996 there were 4,690,000 non-primary industry male workers whose average working hours per week were sixty or more, coming to 3,120 hours or more annually, and that those male employees accounted for 16.3 per cent of the whole.[9] Even now, one in six Japanese workers works extremely long hours. The number and proportion of such workers has indeed declined from the 1989 peak of 6,850,000, but because, on the other hand, labour density is thought to be definitely increasing year by year, if we take this labour density increase into consideration, the extremely long working hours as reflected in Labour Force Survey statistics are the macroscopic factor behind *karoshi* and *karojisatsu* becoming social problems.

Japan's labour law system and its implementation impose few limitations on overtime work under labour-management agreements, leaving no way to deliver workers from extremely long working hours. Article 32 of the Labour Standards Act, as a general rule, limits working time to forty hours a week, but there is a crucial exception. Article 36 of the same law provides that if the representative of a labour union composed of over half the workers, or the representative of over half the workers if there is no such union, enters into an agreement with the employer (a so-called Article 36 agreement), and the employer pays a 25 per cent overtime premium, then working hours may be lengthened over the legal limit of forty hours per week, and employees may have to work on holidays, too. These represent highly relaxed overtime working restrictions in

[8] Tokunaga, Y., 'Hatarakisugi to Kenkoshogai (Overwork and Health Injuries)' (1994) 133 *Keizaibunseki (Economic Analysis)* 1.
[9] 'Annual Report on the Labour Force Survey' (Tokyo: Nippon Tokei Kyokai, 1996) 104–5, *Rodoryoku Chosa Nenpo*.

comparison with the legal restrictions of France and Germany, whose laws set hourly limits on working time per day, week, or other time period, and the 50 per cent overtime premium common in Western countries.[10] Because nearly all companies have such Article 36 agreements, these agreements transpose the general rule and exceptions on working hours, so that, in fact, abiding by the legal limit on working hours is the exception. What is more, even overtime restrictions under these Article 36 agreements are not effectively implemented, with the result that it is very common for companies to exact overtime labour for which they pay no premiums, and in fact pay nothing at all.

This labour law system and the consequence of its implementation have created two grave problems. One is that whether business conditions are good or poor, owing to the low-rate premiums paid for overtime work and 'free' overtime, the cost of overtime is low, and, sometimes, non-existent. Here we find the underlying reason that overtime work in Japan has deviated from its role as a buffer for employment adjustment and has become routine.

Secondly, overtime work is performed by agreement between employers and representatives of labour unions or of over half the workers, and not necessarily with the consent of individual workers. Even if a disgruntled worker protests individually by refusing to work overtime and is dismissed as a consequence, there is, in reality, no way that a worker can win restitution in court. This is evident from the 1991 Supreme Court First Petty Bench decision in *Hitachi*,[11] in which it was held that in the event that an Article 36 agreement has been made, and there are work rules prescribing overtime labour within the scope of that agreement, then, as long as the provisions of those work rules are reasonable, they constitute an explicit labour contract and, as such, a worker has the duty to perform overtime work regardless of whether there has been an individual agreement. In this case, the seven reasons specified for extending working hours by the Article 36 agreement that established the provisions of the work rules at Hitachi's Musashi Plant consisted of extremely vague and sweeping rules, such as 'when necessary to attain production targets'. The Supreme Court stated of such reasons that:

It is undeniable that [the rules] are somewhat general and sweeping, but the need for companies to properly and smoothly implement production plans that respond quickly to the supply and demand situation is anticipated by Article 36 of the Labour Standards Act.[12]

It judged that 'the reasons cannot be said to lack appropriateness'. In

---

[10] Sugeno, K., *Japanese Labour Law* (Tokyo: University of Tokyo Press, 1992) 231–2.
[11] *Tanaka v. Hitachi, Inc.*, Supr. Ct. 1st Petty Bench, 28 Nov. 1991, 45 Civ. Cases 1270.
[12] Ibid. 1274.

other words, because the Supreme Court recognized the reasonableness of Hitachi's work rules in relation to the 'the need to attain production targets', this means that as long as Article 36 agreements exist, the obligation of workers to perform overtime work will be affirmed in nearly every instance, closing avenues by which individual workers who resist requests for overtime work might seek redress in the courts.

Restitution for workers and the workers' accident compensation law

Karoshi and *karojisatsu* are worker accidents (meaning death, injury, or illness incurred by a worker while on the job), but the Ministry of Labour, which is Japan's agency for certifying workers' accident compensation, has been loathe to recognize *karoshi* and *karojisatsu* as workers' accidents. The upshot is that not only have *karoshi* and *karojisatsu* victims and their survivors not received adequate restitution, the Workers' Accident Compensation Law has also not played a sufficient role in preventing *karoshi* and *karojisatsu*.

There are two ways to obtain workers' accident compensation under Japanese labour law. One is insurance benefits under the Worker's Compensation Insurance Act. The worker's accident insurance system is an employer-paid, government-administered, insurance system whose purpose is to establish clearly employers' responsibility for workers' accident compensation. Employers must pay insurance premiums into this government-run insurance programme, while workers who suffer workers' accidents, or their survivors, can receive benefits if they claim them from the Labour Standards Inspection Office and their accidents are certified as injuries or death on the job.[13] The other way is employer-paid damages. When the employer is at fault for a worker accident, that employer is liable for damages under civil law. Under Japan's labour law system, worker's accident victims or their survivors can obtain compensation not only as workers' accident compensation, but also as civil damages from employers. This reflects a legislative policy called the coexistence of workers' compensation and damages, a policy that is not common internationally.[14]

The institutional defect cited with respect to *karoshi* and *karojisatsu* is the attitude of the Ministry of Labour toward certification of 'death or injury on the job' for *karoshi* or *karojisatsu* to obtain workers' accident compensation. The Labour Ministry had established a strict administrative coverage formula and would hardly ever recognize death from overwork as a work-related accident. The basis for that refusal was the

---

[13] See Sugeno, above, n. 10, 318–34.   [14] Ibid., 335–43.

administrative coverage formula of November 1987.[15] This formula required two conditions for the recognition of the *karoshi* causes of cerebral and cardiac disorders as 'death or injury on the job': first, that prior to death the worker must have been under an 'excessively heavy burden', meaning the worker was subject to an unusual circumstance or engaged in excessively onerous work; and, secondly, that the 'excessively heavy burden' arose at most one week before death. With this formula the government looked at only the working conditions immediately before death, thereby hardly ever awarding insurance benefits for *karoshi* as the cumulative effect of excessively onerous work over a long period. This resulted in a huge reduction in the number of eligible claimants, the number of applications, and the number of awards. While it is difficult accurately to ascertain the annual number of *karoshi* and *karojisatsu* victims, it is said there are about 10,000 victims a year.[16] And although there are 500 applications annually for workmen's accident insurance benefits, from 1987 to 1994 only twenty to thirty awards were made annually.

However, criticism of the Labour Ministry's negative attitude increased, and, at the same time, a series of court cases overturned decisions made by the Labour Standards Inspection Office not to pay workers' accident insurance benefits for *karoshi*.[17] In bowing to this criticism the Labour Ministry partly revised its administrative coverage formula in February 1995, taking into account an 'excessively heavy burden' during a period of time earlier than in the week before *karoshi*.[18] This resulted in a 2.5-fold jump in the number of awards in 1995. Yet, despite this increase, it amounted to only about eighty cases per year, falling far short of the estimated 10,000 victims and the 500 or more applications per year. An administrative coverage formula for *karojisatsu* was finally created in September 1999. The figures for 1998 were twenty-nine applications with only four awards.

As this discussion shows, even though the Workers' Accident Compensation Law and its implementation are supposed to help victims of worker accidents and prevent the reoccurrence of such accidents, in actuality they are reproducing *karoshi* and *karojisatsu* by doing nothing about them.

---

[15] 26 Nov. 1987, Kihatsu No. 620.

[16] Kawahito, H., *Karoshi Shakai to Nihon (Death from Overwork Society and Japan)* (Tokyo: Kadensha, 1996) 3.

[17] Ishida, M., ' "Sagyokanrenshikkan" (Work-related Diseases)' in Wada, H., Nishimura, K., and Ishida, M. (eds.), *21 Seiki no Rodo-ho [Labour Law in the 21st Century]* (Tokyo, Yuhikaku, 2000) vii, 95.

[18] 1 Feb. 1995, Kihatsu No. 38.

IV *KAROSHI, KAROJISATSU,* AND JAPANESE SOCIETY

Sometimes the way people die highlights the contradictions and dilemmas inherent in the societies in which they lived. Suicide in particular has long been researched by sociologists as something that expresses the crises of relationships between society and the individual. Emile Durkheim's *Suicide: A Study in Sociology* (1897) is a well-known classic sociological study of suicide. Instead of seeing suicide as an isolated and personal act by individuals, Durkheim conceived it as a tendency that is found in a certain time and a certain society or group, and tried to understand its characteristics in connection with social structures. According to Durkheim:

There is ... for each people a collective force of a definite amount of energy, impelling men to self-destruction. The victim's acts which at first seem to express only his personal temperament are really the supplement and prolongation of a social condition which they express externally.[19]

When we attempt to examine *karoshi* and *karojisatsu* in connection with the structure of Japanese society, Durkheim's study offers us many hints.

Durkheim divides suicide into four types in relation to the social conditions that underlie suicide. The first is egoistic suicide, and is a product of 'excessive individualism',[20] that is, as social integration and solidarity weaken, and the individual is separated from group life, he becomes isolated, the consequence being suicide. The second type is altruistic suicide. Contrary to egoistic suicide, this type 'occurs because ... society holds him in too strict tutelage'.[21] The third type is anomic suicide. Anomy is a state in which the common values and morals that order people's daily behaviour are lost, and society becomes dominated by the absence of norms and by chaos. Anomic suicide 'results from man's activity's lacking regulation and his consequent sufferings'.[22] The fourth type is fatal suicide, which, contrary to anomic suicide, happens when oppressive restrictions on people's wants are too strong, giving them feelings of bafflement and despair. These four suicide types, however, are conceptual types meant for the sociological analysis of suicide. They will not necessarily appear in their independent and pure forms. The 'different social causes of suicide themselves may simultaneously affect the same individual and impose their combined effects upon him'.[23]

If we use Durkheim's suicide types to analyse *karoshi* and *karojisatsu* in Japan, what sort of social structure contradictions and dilemmas will

---

[19] Durkheim, E., *Suicide: A Study in Sociology* (trans. Spaulding, J. A., and Simpson, G., London: Routledge and Kegan Paul Ltd., 1952) 299.

[20] Ibid., 209.   [21] Ibid., 221.

[22] Ibid., 258.   [23] Ibid., 287.

appear? The first thing one notices from such a perspective is that *karojisatsu* in Japan is similar to altruistic suicide. Durkheim cites an incident of *harakiri* by a Japanese as an example of altruistic suicide, and sees there an illustration of the moral state of uncivilized societies, such as contempt for an attachment to life. But *karojisatsu* differs from *harakiri* in the sense in which Durkheim speaks. Nevertheless, reading the following suicide letter, left behind by a *karojisatsu* victim, reveals a connection with suicide in the military, cited by Durkheim as an example of altruistic suicide. Let us begin with the letter:

Dear Department Chief,

I'm sorry you had to have a lax subordinate like me. I tried hard to live up to your expectations, but I just wasn't up to the job. In addition to apologizing with my life, I extend my sincere apologies to the president, the Personnel Department, other company people, the union people, and to associates. I'm very sorry this had to happen at such a trying time.[24]

Durkheim says the reason that the military has many suicides is 'this aptitude for renunciation, this taste for impersonality develops as a result of prolonged discipline'.[25] When workers are in Japan's corporate society for a long time their sense of dependency on their corporate organizations heightens, resulting in a tendency toward self-sacrifice and impersonality. While, on the one hand, this leads to workers being subjected to 'excessive' stress and overwork, it also leads workers to believe that it is their own responsibility when their work does not go well. By the apology in the suicide letter quoted above, the writer disregards the former problem (stress and overwork), while showing that he can see the situation only in terms of the latter (his own responsibility). Certainly this is an example of altruistic suicide.

On the other hand, *karoshi* is not suicide, so Durkheim's four suicide models do not apply to it. However, his sociological insight on altruistic suicide, that is, that such suicide happens when society very forcefully makes the individual dependent upon it, throws light on the underlying cause of *karoshi*. Not only *karojisatsu*, but also *karoshi*, have something basic in common with altruistic suicide. Professor Tatsuo Inoue provides an excellent description of the deep relationship between *karoshi* and altruistic suicide.

Karoshi is not an isolated personal tragedy. Just as egoistic and anomic suicides symbolize the anxiety and despair of the individualistic society, karoshi symbolizes the tension and distress of a hyperindustrialized and secularized communitarian society, not of a primitive and religious community. It symbolizes the deep-seated dilemma of contemporary Japanese society.[26]

---

[24] Kawahito, above, n. 7, 85.   [25] Above, n. 19, 234.
[26] Inoue, T., 'The Poverty of Right-Blind Communality: Looking Through the Window of Japan' (1993) 2 *Brigham Young University L. Review* 538.

Karojisatsu, which has characteristics likening it to altruistic suicide, is also related to anomic suicide. Durkheim says:

Anomy may likewise be associated with altruism. One and the same crisis may ruin a person's life, disturb the equilibrium between him and his surroundings, and, at the same time, drive his altruistic disposition to a state which incites him to suicide.[27]

Specifically he notes that:

a bankrupt man kills himself as much because he cannot live on a smaller footing, as to spare his name and family the disgrace of bankruptcy. If officers and noncommissioned officers readily commit suicide just when forced to retire, it is also doubtless because of the sudden change about to occur in their way of living, as well as because of their general disposition to attach little value to life.[28]

Post-war Japan's suicide and unemployment rates closely coincide. Research exploring Durkheim's anomy theory in relation to unemployment has demonstrated from empirical data that 'sudden social changes encourage suicide when those changes involve unemployment'.[29] Examining the factors behind *karojisatsu* while bearing such research in mind, it seems safe to say that *karojisatsu* arises when the anomy generated by the economic deterioration that followed the collapse of the economic bubble is combined with the altruistic feelings of workers who are excessively dependent on their companies, while at the same time it also happens when concern about unemployment reinforces workers' dependency on their companies, and the workers, driven by their tasks, end up suffering from overwork and stress.

Thus while *karoshi* is caused by the altruistic nature of Japan's corporate society, *karojisatsu* manifested itself amid the worsening of the economy as *karoshi* then combined with social anomy.

IV *KAROSHI* AND *KAROJISATSU* FROM AN INTERNATIONAL PERSPECTIVE

As analysed above, one distinctive facet of *karoshi* and *karojisatsu* is the pathology of Japan's corporate society, while another is the universal facet of work-related diseases, which have become an international issue in the field of industrial health. 'Work-related diseases' was proposed at the 1976 World Health Organization (WHO) Twenty-ninth Congress as a concept that indicates ordinary diseases that are somehow related to

---

[27] Above, n. 19, 288.   [28] Ibid., 289.
[29] Yamamoto, T., 'Shitsugyo to Jisatsu' (Unemployment and Suicide)' (1982) 12 *Shakaikagaku Kenkyu Nenpo (Yearbook on Social Science Studies)* 139.

work.[30] The reason for the proposal of this concept is that even though so-called 'occupational diseases' are decreasing, there are, as labour undergoes qualitative changes and the median age of workers increases, an increasing number of general diseases that have some assumed connection to work. The emergence of the work-related disease concept is a sign of the times, in which industrial health and workers' accident compensation must also now address ordinary diseases that from an international perspective are distinguished from 'occupational diseases' with a clear connection between illnesses and the harmful elements of work.

Disorders to be considered as work-related diseases are cerebrovascular diseases, cardiac diseases, stress-related diseases, and others. Many of the clinical diseases of *karoshi* and *karojisatsu* fall into this category. In this light it seems that through the problem of *karoshi* and *karojisatsu*, Japan has built a store of advanced experience on workers' accident compensation for work-related diseases, and one would expect that the same kind of phenomena are occurring in many other countries as well, although the specific manifestations and causes may differ. Henceforth it will perhaps be necessary to make international comparisons of *karoshi* and *karojisatsu* using, as a common element, the internationally emerging concept of work-related diseases.

[30] WHO, *Identification and Control of Work-related Diseases* (WHO Technical Report Series no. 714, 1985).

12

A Closer Look at the Emerging Employment Law of Silicon Valley's High-Velocity Labour Market

ALAN HYDE

The spectacular technological and economic growth of the high-technology sector in the United States owes much to its employees as well as to employment laws that, in unappreciated ways, treat employees as intellectual contributors to production and facilitate new forms of employee organization. This combination suggests that aspects of working in American high technology deserve attention from political progressives who might otherwise dismiss them out of hand.

In the 1980s, economists explored the fact that a significant proportion of the American workforce held implicit contracts for lifetime employment. These contracts had a predictable profile: they lasted a long time; compensation increased over the job cycle; and the contract would terminate with the separation of the employee (usually through retirement or, rarely, discharge for cause), rather than wage reduction.[1] This discovery proved to be a powerful lens before the eyes of legal scholars. It brought into focus such disparate legal problems as age discrimination, wrongful termination, and other workplace causes of action, and from this focus came specific legal and policy recommendations.[2] Contrasts between the

---

[1] The discovery of the reality of stable employment in the USA is generally attributed to Hall, R. E., 'The Importance of Lifetime Jobs in the U.S. Economy' (1982) 72 *American Economics Review* 716. Forerunners include earlier work on internal labour markets such as Doeringer, P., and Piore, M., *Internal Labour Markets and Manpower Analysis* (Lexington, Mass.: Heath, 1971). The idea that such contracts normally precluded downward wage adjustment and thus were subject to termination, whether or not such termination rights had been reserved *ex ante*, was developed by Lazear, E. P., 'Why Is There Mandatory Retirement?' (1979) 87 *Journal of Political Economy* 1261. See generally Rosen, S., 'Implicit Contract: A Survey' (1985) 23 *Journal of Economic Literature* 1144.

[2] Wachter, M. L., and Cohen, G. M., 'The Law and Economics of Collective Bargaining: An Introduction and Application to the Problems of Subcontracting, Partial Closure, and Relocation' (1988) 136 *University of Pennsylvania L. Review* 1349 (duty to bargain under National Labor Relations Act s. 8(a)(5) should extend only to managerial decisions likely to reflect opportunism left open by implicit employment contract); Stone, K. V. W., 'Employees as Stakeholders Under State Nonshareholder Constituency Statutes' (1991) 21 *Stetson L. Review* 45 (labour law implications); O'Connor, M. A., 'Restructuring the Corporation's Nexus of Contracts: Recognizing a Fiduciary Duty to Protect Displaced Workers' (1991) 69 *North Carolina L. Review* 1189; Schwab, S. J., 'Life-Cycle Justice: Accommodating Just Cause and Employment At Will' (1993) 92 *Michigan L. Review* 8; Weiler, P. C., *Governing the Workplace: The Future of Labor and Employment Law* (Cambridge, Mass.: Harvard University

American and Japanese economies, it was said, had been exaggerated. Many Americans—professionals, managers, and production workers—could expect stable, lifetime employment, and economic and legal institutions had been built around this reality.

Even as the legal framework was synthesized, its social basis was eroding. While stable careers within firms have by no means disappeared, they do not appear to be growing in importance. The median US employee has been with his or her current employer for 3.6 years (an historic low). The median US employee in the service sector has been with his or her current employer for 2.4 years (note these are 'employees' and exclude the 7 per cent or so of the workforce who are self-employed, many of whom contract to supply their services to firms).[3] Study after study has now made clear that average tenure on the job is growing shorter, with notable drops in very long tenures (over ten years) and particular groups (men with no education past high school).[4] Particularly

Press, 1990), 48–104 (wrongful termination); Hyde, A., 'In Defense of Employee Ownership' (1991) 67 *Chicago-Kent L. Review* 159, 179–95 (employee ownership as remedy for strategic non-disclosure of information and high costs of monitoring associated with implicit employment contracts); Howse, R., and Trebilcock, M. J., 'Protecting the Employment Bargain' (1993) 43 *University of Toronto L. Journal* 751 (worker participation institutions evaluated as enforcement devices for implicit employment contracts); Charny, D., 'The Employee Welfare State in Transition' (1996) 74 *Texas L. Review* 1601 (employee insurance against risk presupposes implicit contracts; discussion of alternatives given decline in those contracts); Issacharoff, S., and Worth, E., 'Is Age Discrimination Really Age Discrimination?: The ADEA's Unnatural Solution' (1997) 72 *New York University L. Review* 780; Worth, E., 'Note, In Defense of Targeted ERIPs: Understanding the Interaction of Life-Cycle Employment and Early Retirement Incentive Plans' (1995) 74 *Texas L. Review* 411; Willborn, S. L., Schwab, S. J., and Burton, J. F., *Employment Law: Cases and Materials* (2nd edn Charlottesville, Vir.: LEXIS Legal Publishing, 1998), *passim*, e.g., 8–10, 88–103, 174–5 (explaining numerous workplace contract and tort actions as protection of employees in lifetime employment contracts). The assumption of a stable career with a single employer was not gender-neutral but reflected employment patterns much more typical of men than women: Conaghan, J., 'The Invisibility of Women in Labour Law: Gender-neutrality in Model-building' (1986) 14 *International Journal of Sociology of Law* 377.

[3] Bureau of Labor Statistics, Current Population Survey, Employee Tenure Summary, USDL 98–387, 23 Sept. 1998, http://www.bls.gov.news.release/tenure.news.htm.

[4] Aaronson, D., and Sullivan, D., 'The Decline of Job Security in the 1990s: Displacement, Anxiety, and their Effect on Wage Growth' (1998) 22 *Federal Reserve Bank of Chicago Economic Perspectives* 17 (Displaced Worker Survey; increasing rates of job loss for individuals with more than 5 years' tenure); Bernhardt, A., Morris, M., Handcock, M. S., and Scott, M. A., 'Job Instability and Wages for Young Adult Men' (1999) 17 *Journal of Labor Economics* 565 (National Longitudinal Surveys; significant increases in job instability, declining returns to job changing); Boisjoly, J., Duncan, G. J., and Smeeding, J., 'The Shifting Incidence of Involuntary Job Losses from 1968 to 1992' (1998) 37 *Industrial Relations* 207 (panel data from Panel Study of Income Dynamics and National Longitudinal Study: increases in involuntary job loss for all groups); Farber, H., 'Trends in Long Term Employment in the United States 1979–96', Princeton University Industrial Relations Section, Working Paper No. 384 (1997); Farber, H., 'The Changing Face of Job Loss in the United States 1981–1993' (1997) 55 *Brookings Papers on Economic Activity: Microeconomics* (Displaced Worker Surveys; higher overall rates of job loss in the 1990s, particularly for older workers); Rose, S. J., 'Declining Job Security

in industries facing global competition, wages now respond much more readily to market factors and are much less likely to reflect orderly increases from a given baseline.[5] Moreover, with hindsight, the wave of successful US lawsuits brought in the 1980s by dismissed managers appears not to have reflected a new wave of contracts for stable employment.[6] Rather, it reflected the repudiation by employers of employment contracts that had seemed efficient *ex ante* when entered into in the 1950s and 1960s, but came to seem inefficient *ex post* in the increased global competition of the 1980s and 1990s.

American legal scholars have just begun to consider the implications of this decline in internal labour markets and stable employment. If their earlier scholarship was correct, as I believe it was, in asserting that embedded in much of US labour and employment law is an unexamined assumption that normal work consists of a lifetime career at a single place of employment, then numerous aspects of labour, discrimination, pension, and other employment laws are likely to come under pressure. In this context, political progressives and friends of working people, roughly

---

and the Professionalization of Opportunity', Res. Rep. No. 95–04, National Comm. for Emp. Pol., May 1995 (Panel Study on Income Dynamics: pronounced decline in men reporting only one change of employer over 10-year study); Swinnerton, K. A., and Wial, H., 'Is Job Stability Declining in the U.S. Economy?' (1995) 48 *Industrial & Labor Relations Review* 293 (Current Population Survey: declining probability 1983–91 that workers at given level of seniority will remain with their employer for four more years). Cappelli, P., Bassi, L., Katz, H., Knoke, D., Osterman, D., and Useem, M., *Change at Work* (New York: Oxford University Press 1997), 173–93 review the evidence. Scholars who study only tenures of a year or two sometimes question whether there has been an overall drop in job tenure although all agree that some identifiable groups, notably men with no education beyond high school, have seen such drops. Jaeger, D. A., and Stevens, A. H., 'Is Job Stability in the US Falling? Reconciling Trends in the Current Population Survey and Panel Study of Income Dynamics' (1999) 17 *Journal of Labor Economics* S1 (increase in the number of workers aged 30 and over with less than 10 years' tenure; little change in share of employed individuals with less than one year); Neumark, D., Polsky, D., and Hansen, D., 'Has Job Stability Declined Yet? New Evidence for the 1990s' (1999) 17 *Journal of Labor Economics* S29 (Current Population Survey: modest decline in job stability in first half of 1990s; sharp declines in stability for workers with more than a few years of tenure, but not clear that this is a long-term trend). For a comprehensive discussion of contingency see Lester, G., 'Careers and Contingency' (1998) 51 *Stanford L. Review* 73.

[5] Bertrand, M., 'From the Invisible Handshake to the Invisible Hand?: How Import Competition Changes the Employment Relationship', National Bureau of Economic Research Working Paper 6900, http://www.nber.org/papers/w6900, Jan. 1999. This is a particularly remarkable finding. As noted, a staple of the analysis of implicit employment contracts was that wages could almost never be decreased; consequently, if the contract had become *ex post* inefficient, there was no alternative to terminating it. Lazear, above, n. 1; Bewley, T. F., 'A Depressed Labor Market as Explained by Participants' (1995) 85 *American Economics Association Papers & Proceedings* 250; Johnson, W. R., 'The Social Efficiency of Fixed Wages' (1985) 100 *Quarterly Journal of Economics* 101.

[6] See, e.g., *Pugh v. See's Candies, Inc.*, 171 Cal. Rptr. 917 (Ct. App. 1981) (Grodin, J) (termination of vice-president after 32 years of employment may violate implied-in-fact promise) and generally Schwab, above, n. 2.

speaking, face two choices. They can attempt to use labour and employment law and other kinds of labour market regulation to withstand or reverse the trend toward shorter employment periods, and re-establish the stable careers of an earlier era. While I do not generally favour this option, I fully recognize it as an option. It is not part of my argument that high-velocity, American-style labour markets are inevitable. Job separations can be regulated or taxed; career jobs subsidized; trade competition restricted. The reason these measures will not be taken in the United States is not because they will not occur to American minds gripped by neo-liberal ideological hegemony. Rather, there is little US political constituency for the old labour market because the new labour market has been such a stunning success. In the words of the most recent Economic Report of the President:

the number of workers employed is at an all-time high, the unemployment rate is at a 30-year low, and real (inflation-adjusted) wages are increasing after years of stagnation. Groups whose economic status has not improved in the past decades are now experiencing progress. The real wages of blacks and Hispanics have risen rapidly in the past two to three years, and their unemployment rates are at long-time lows; employment among male high school dropouts, single women with children, and immigrants, as well as among blacks and Hispanics, has increased; and the gap in earnings between immigrant and native workers is narrowing.[7]

While real incomes were stagnant for most Americans during the early years of the current recovery, they are, as the report indicates, now increasing. The unemployment rate has been below 5 per cent for several years, and both employment and earnings continue to rise.[8] Now, these happy results reflect many factors besides legal flexibility in job creation and extinction; it is wrong to think that such flexibility automatically yields low unemployment, or even that economists have an agreed-on model of the relationship.[9] Nevertheless, the US reality in the last few years has combined low unemployment, real earnings gains, declines in lifetime jobs, and low legal regulation, and there is no political likelihood of changes in that package in the near future.

While high-tech employment declined in 2001, and stock prices declined sharply, my interviews have disclosed no Silicon Valley firms

---

[7] *Economic Report of the President 1999*, ch. 3, 'Benefits of a Strong Labor Market', 99, available at http://www.gpo.ucop.edu/catalog/erp99.html (text only) or http://www. gpo. gov/usbudget/fy2000/maindown.html (text and tables).

[8] Bureau of Labor Statistics, The Employment Situation News Release: Nov. 1999, http://www.bls.gov/news.release/empsit.news.htm

[9] Krueger, A. B., and Pischke, J. S.,'Observations and Conjectures on the US Employment Miracle', National Bureau of Economic Research Working Paper 6146 (1997) (http://www.nber.org/papers/w6146); Blank, R. M., 'Contingent Work in a Changing Labor Market' in Freeman, R. B., and Gottschalk, P. (eds.), *Generating Jobs: How to Increase Demand for Less-Skilled Workers* (New York: Russell Sage Foundation, 1998).

reverting to traditional, long-term employment. There are no firms instituting private pensions. The few that had policies against layoffs (Hewlett-
Packard, Cisco) have abandoned them. Flexible compensation through
stock options is still universal in the Valley. Most employers have concentrated job elimination among temporary employees and employees on
temporary visas, but these sectors remain large, and some large employers
(like Cisco) have evaluated all staff irrespective of formal status.

A second option for political progressives then is to learn more, much
more, about how such high-velocity labour markets work: what are the
most important features that support rapid technological and economic
growth; how do such markets work for people who are successful in
them; and, how could they be made to work better for people who find
themselves in them against their preference? While such labour markets
are, as I have said, not inevitable, there is a certain sort of rapid technological development that can probably not be achieved in any other sort
of labour market. Law can either facilitate or retard the development of
such markets, or it can adjust the distribution of their rewards.

My focus here is twofold, namely to consider the implications of a
labour market with rapid employee turnover and consequent re-employment by other firms, for the meaning of equal employment opportunity,
and the operation of post-employment restrictions governing, for example, trade secrets or covenants not to compete. In fact, the picture of the
labour market I will sketch has implications for many other aspects of
labour and employment law not here addressed.[10] Drawing on my
research into the labour market of 'Silicon Valley', California (the portion
of the southern San Francisco Bay region centered on Palo Alto and San
Jose), I will emphasize the way in which today's labour markets are also
information markets. Employees moving rapidly among firms can spread
information across formal and informal networks that make possible a
kind of economic growth and firm and employee organization not achiev-
able in any other way. These networks offer a solution to legal problems
of employment discrimination and trade secrets that is quite different
when posed against the assumption that employees have stable careers
inside isolated firms. I will therefore argue that friends of working people
should embrace rather than resist this kind of labour market flexibility,
and focus on building and extending effective network organization by
employees.

---

[10] I am currently writing a book with the working title *Working in Silicon Valley: Legal and Economic Analysis of a High-Velocity Labor Market* (Armonk, NY: Sharpe, M. E.) and a projected publication date of 2002.

I SILICON VALLEY AS A HIGH-VELOCITY LABOUR MARKET

The claim that Silicon Valley is marked by particularly rapid employment turnover is familiar and not controversial, but it turns out to be surprisingly difficult to document given existing statistical sources. The claim is familiar from well-known work by AnnaLee Saxenian, who attributes Silicon Valley's economic triumph, over the similar high technology district along Route 128 around Boston, precisely to what is termed here Silicon Valley's high-velocity labour market. In brief, Silicon Valley's engineers broke off to form start-ups in garages, while their counterparts in the East pursued orderly, less innovative careers inside the internal labour markets at Digital or Wang.[11] Careers in Silicon Valley are rarely defined within the boundaries of a single firm, and individuals report loyalty to teams or technologies rather than to individual companies.

While these observations are not controversial and tend to ring true to those familiar with both Silicon Valley and Route 128, there is no easy way of obtaining comparative data on job tenures or turnovers for such small geographic units. One can measure direct employment by temporary help agencies or self-employment (sometimes used as a proxy for contracted labour) although both these measures are notoriously unreliable. Most importantly, they miss the crucial fact, often misunderstood by Americans and non-Americans, that *most contingent jobs in the United States—however defined—are held by 'employees'*. The basic American contract of employment is barely regulated at all—it contains no required terms on benefits, vacations, or termination, and requires only a minimum wage (essentially irrelevant in high technology) and a requirement of premium pay for more than forty hours a week, full of exemptions for most technology workers.[12] Thus, it is feasible and common in the USA for people to hold jobs as employees even though the job carries few benefits and will be eliminated in the foreseeable future. (In many other countries, such contingent arrangements may not be described as relations of employment and must be structured as relations of independent contracting.) Much statutory employment in Silicon Valley is of this highly contingent type. While there are no sources of data on job tenures broken down by county or locality, it is certainly suggestive that only 21 per cent of Californians in the workforce have been with their current employer

---

[11] Saxenian, A., *Regional Advantage: Culture and Competition in Silicon Valley and Route 128* (Cambridge, Mass.: Harvard University Press, 1994).

[12] Congress has expressly provided that computer programmers and software engineers do not have to be paid premium pay for overtime work, PL 101–583 (1990), 29 USC s. 213 (17). Uncompensated overtime work may thus be required of individuals without a college degree, without regular employment or guaranteed salary, and making as little as $150 a week (29 CFR s. 541.3(a)(4)).

for ten years or more, compared to a national figure of 35.4 per cent.[13] And, as mentioned, along with these figures on short-term employment relations, one may examine figures on workers directly employed by temporary help agencies, which are computed at the county level. In Santa Clara County, California, direct employment by temporary help agencies is 3.5 per cent of the workforce, perhaps twice the national rate.[14]

The percentage of county residents who describe themselves as self-employed, by contrast, is around the national figure of 6.7 per cent. (There is much confusion and misinformation about self-employment in the USA, which, contrary to much media coverage, has been stable for decades and is currently at a *low* point.[15] Many have been struck by the fact that a number of business services, formerly provided only by career corporate employees, including management services, are now provided by independent contractors. However, statistically this is offset by professionals such as doctors and lawyers who are considerably more likely to be employees today than were their predecessors two or three decades ago.) Interviews confirm that most of the self-employed in Silicon Valley are self-employed by choice, at least if they are at the high end. They see little advantage in so-called regular or permanent employment that is neither regular nor permanent.[16]

---

[13] The national figure for employees with the same employer for 10 years or more has been dropping rapidly, though not as rapidly as California's. As recently as 1979, 50% of US men between the ages of 35 to 64 had been with their current employer for 10 years or more. Today, nationally, that figure is down to 40%: Farber, H. S., 'Trends in Long-term Employment in the United States, 1979–96', *Working Paper #384*, Industrial Relations Section, Department of Economics, Princeton University, July 1997.

[14] Benner, C., 'Silicon Valley Labor Markets: Overview of Structure, Dynamics and Outcomes for Workers', prepared for conference on Work, Labor Organizations, and Labor Market Institutions in the New Economy: Lessons from Silicon Valley, San Jose, Cal., 29–30 Jan. 1999, 12, quoting from California Economic Development Department, Labor Market Information Division. This paper is available at http://mitsloan.mit.edu/ iwer/ SiliconWPS.html. Confusions over counting temporary employees in the USA are discussed in Houseman, S. N., 'Flexible Staffing Arrangements: A Report on Temporary Help, On-Call, Direct-Hire Temporary, Leased, Contract Company, and Independent Contractor Employment in the United States' (Aug. 1999), http://www2.dol.gov/dol/asp/ public/futurework/conference.htm 8–11.

[15] A press release summarizing the most recent Supplement on Contingent and Alternative Work Arrangements to the Current Population Survey is at http:// www.bls.gov/news.release/conemp.new.htm.

[16] In one set of interviews of 52 technical contractors, only four expressed a desire to return to permanent employment. Most had never experienced significant time between contracts, although some anticipated such problems in the future. Nearly all made substantially more money as contractors than they had as permanent employees (Kunda, G., Barley, S., and Evans, J., 'Why Do Contractors Contract? The Theory and Reality of High End Contingent Labour' (unpublished manuscript, 26 Jan. 1999, available from Center for Work Technology and Organization, Department of Industrial Engineering and Engineering Management, Stanford University) 29–36 and at http://mitloan.mit.edu/iwer SiliconWPS. html). By contrast, most in a small sample of low-end temporary workers wanted more

II EMPLOYMENT EQUITY IN SILICON VALLEY AND THE SOLUTION OF NETWORK ORGANIZATIONS

What does equal employment opportunity mean in a labour market with such rapid turnover and high proportions of temporary work? Much of the current apparatus of US equal employment law assumes stable careers inside hierarchical firms and maps poorly onto Silicon Valley. Plaintiffs' lawyers in discrimination cases ask: 'Have any women ever been vice-presidents at this company? How many African-Americans serve above [some specified salary/level]?' If the company has rapid turnover at all levels, including managerial, subcontracts out important managerial functions to independent contractors and consultants, and maintains few meaningful promotion ladders, what does the plaintiff's counsel even want to ask? Is it meaningful to ask the race or sex of 'all persons providing services to the company'? Is it legally relevant if many of those services are provided by individuals who are independent contractors, not employees? There is no federal or state civil rights statute governing discriminatory outcomes in the private award of service contracts.

Should Americans be concerned about this lack of fit between their discrimination law and emerging high-velocity labour markets? Much may depend on whether Silicon Valley is perceived to present particular problems of discrimination. It is no paradox to assert that Silicon Valley is both a highly segregated labour market and simultaneously one of the least discriminatory yet observed. Moreover, as I will argue, the very technologies and work organization that encourage the economic growth of the Valley—that is, mobility and networks—show considerable promise in addressing issues of employment equity as well.

Earnings are unquestionably unequal and apparently growing more unequal over time. While the average annual income in Silicon Valley was $46,000 in 1997—quite a bit higher than the national average of $29,900[17]— inequality is also great. Consider four typical employees in Silicon Valley, each the subject of anthropological studies to which I will refer.

permanent employment, at least at points in their lives when health benefits were particularly important (Darrah, C. N., 'Temping at the Lower End: An Incomplete View from Silicon Valley', presented at the conference Work, Labor Organizations and Labor Market Institutions in the New Economy: Lessons from Silicon Valley, San Jose, Cal., 29–30 Jan. 1999 available on the above website). These figures are roughly comparable to those in Cohany, S., 'Workers in Alternative Employment Arrangements: A Second Look', 121 *Monthly Labor Review* no. 11 (Nov. 1998), 3 (84% of independent contractors prefer that arrangement to a traditional job), 6 (only one in three workers employed by temporary agencies preferred that arrangement), 14. A charming account of the life of some independent contractors in Silicon Valley is Bronson, P., *The Nudist on the Late Shift and Other True Tales of Silicon Valley* (New York: Random House, 1999) 98–138.

[17] Benner, above, n. 14, 18, citing Joint Venture: Silicon Valley Network 1998 Index, http://www.jointventure.org.

At the top, the top 100 executives in the Valley's largest companies made almost seven million dollars each in 1996. Their average compensation grew 390 per cent from 1991–6, and the ratio of their income to that of the average production worker rose during that time from 42:1 in 1991 to 220:1 in 1996.[18] Next, consider someone working in the software industry, where the average wage was $90,380 in 1997, or semiconductors, $83,690.[19] For reasons to be made clear in a moment, I will assume this individual is an engineer or scientist born in Taiwan or India. In the 1990 census, one-quarter of the engineers and scientists employed in California's technology industries were foreign-born—more than twice that of Massachusetts or Texas. In Silicon Valley, one-third of engineers and scientists in 1990 were foreign-born. Most observers anticipate that the 2000 census will reveal an even higher percentage. By most standards, these engineers and scientists have done extremely well. They make more than their white counterparts in either professional or managerial positions. Yet two-thirds of Asian professionals in the Valley believe that their advancement to managerial positions is limited by race, and they remain (in comparison to whites with similar education) more likely to hold professional positions and less likely to hold managerial positions.[20]

My third and fourth stereotyped employees are also foreign-born.[21] My third is a manufacturing worker in Silicon Valley who fabricates chips or assembles communication equipment.[22] She is, to quote the title of a book currently in progress by Karen J. Hossfeld, 'Small, Foreign, and

[18] Ibid., 20.

[19] Ibid., 18, citing Joint Venture, above, n. 17.

[20] Saxenian, A., *Silicon Valley's New Immigrant Entrepreneurs* (San Francisco, Cal.: Public Policy Institute of California, 1999). Those surveyed attributed this less to 'racial prejudice and stereotypes' than to the perception of an 'old boys network that excludes Asians' and 'lack of role models'. See also Fernandez, M., 'Asian Indian Americans in the Bay Area and the Glass Ceiling' (1998) 42 *Sociological Perspectives* 119.

[21] Twenty-three per cent of the population of Santa Clara County in 1990 was foreign-born, surpassing San Francisco County (Saxenian, above n. 20, 6), citing Alarcon, R., 'From Servants to Engineers: Mexican Immigration and Labor Markets in the San Francisco Bay Area', University of California at Berkeley, Chicano/Latino Policy Project Working Paper, Jan. 1997.

[22] Most manufacturing by Silicon Valley companies is performed overseas, but production workers physically in Silicon Valley are still needed for prototypic and other short-term projects that must be completed rapidly. 'Although manufacturing done on-site in Silicon Valley involves "higher-tech" stages of the production process, the assembly work that immigrant women engage in closely resembles the same "low-tech" labor done by their "sisters" overseas'. (Hossfeld, K. J., ' "Their Logic Against Them": Contradictions in Sex, Race, and Class in Silicon Valley' in Ward, K. (ed.), *Women Workers and Global Restructuring* (Ithaca, NY: ILR Press, 1990) 153. Increasingly, the local manufacturing employees are employed by subcontractors. Benner, above, n. 14, 13, cites an estimate that for a typical manufacturer of personal computers or related equipment (like Hewlett-Packard or Sun), the cost of components, software, and services purchased from outside has increased over the last decade from less than 60 to more than 80 % of total production costs: Ernst, D., 'From Partial to Systemic Globalization: International Production Networks in the Electronics Industry', *Berkeley Roundtable on the International Economy Working Paper 98* (1997).

Female'. The average hourly earnings of a manufacturing worker in Santa Clara County were $16.70 in 1998, which represents a *decrease* of 2.2 per cent since 1990 ($17.07).[23] Our Filipina or Vietnamese woman working for the manufacturing subcontractor is unlikely to be making that much.[24] Fourthly, imagine the janitor cleaning the headquarters at night. He or she is likely to be a Mexican immigrant employed by a building services contractor and may earn $5.88 an hour.[25]

Now, from one standpoint this *is* a very unequal labour market, with the possibility of discrimination at every level. But from another, it is the 'most meritocratic labour market anywhere in the world',[26] and has the potential to be even more so. This partly reflects its rapid growth and the enormous demand for skilled professionals and semi-professionals, of all racial and ethnic backgrounds. But, perhaps surprisingly, it also reflects effective employee organization, as the author of the 'most meritocratic' characterization has recently shown. By employee organization, I do not necessarily mean a labour union. Ironically, one of many things uniting the Taiwanese or Indian engineer, the Filipina manufacturing worker, and most Mexican janitors is that none of them has a union. Instead, I mean network organization. While the economic success of immigrant Chinese and Indian scientists and engineers reflects their hard work and educational achievements, it also, importantly, reflects their employment of a new organizational form: the identity-based network organization that transcends firm boundaries and helps advance careers in an industry. As we shall see, possible adaptation of this form holds great potential for the Filipina in the computer chip fabrication shop or the Mexican polishing the floor.

[23] Benner, above, n. 14, 22, citing Bureau of Labour Statistics, *Annual Report on Employment, Hours and Earnings*, calculated from data at www.bls.gov/oes/1999/oes_7400. htm# 651–0000.

[24] When Hossfeld, above, n. 22, 154–5, conducted her interviews in 1982–6, Silicon Valley manufacturing operatives were 90% female, 80% foreign, and made entry wages of $4–$5.50 an hour, rising to $5.50–$8 an hour after some experience.

[25] Zlolniski, C., 'The Informal Economy in an Advanced Industrialized Society: Mexican Immigrant Labor in Silicon Valley' (1994) 103 *Yale L. Journal* 2305, 2312–16, divides Silicon Valley's janitors into three groups: janitors who work for unionized companies under contract with Service Employees International Union Local 1877 and normally earn around $7 per hour with health insurance and some other fringe benefits; janitors who work for non-union contractors and make less than $5.50 an hour with no medical or fringe benefits; and women (mostly) working in small crews for self-employed contractors, paid in cash and earning around $3.30 an hour, violating legal standards for wages and also health and safety conditions. Zlolniski does not estimate the proportion of the janitorial workforce in each of the three groups. The figure in text is a median average for janitors' wages, from Benner, above, n. 14, 10, citing California Economic Development Department.

[26] AnnaLee Saxenian, personal communication, 9 Mar. 1999.

Network organizations for Chinese and Indian engineers

I mentioned above that two-thirds of Asian-born professionals in Silicon Valley believe that advancement to managerial positions is limited by race.[27] Yet I have been unable to locate a single lawsuit under Title VII of the Civil Rights Act of 1964 brought by an Asian-born professional in Silicon Valley. Saxenian shows that when Asian-born professionals in the Valley feel their advancement blocked within the company, they leave to start their own—what she terms a response in 'typical Silicon Valley fashion'—'[b]y 1997 Chinese and Indian engineers were running one-quarter of the region's technology businesses started since 1980, and . . . these companies collectively accounted for more than $12.5 billion in sales and 46,290 jobs'.[28]

An earlier stereotype for the Silicon Valley start-up was Bill Hewlett and David Packard (or Apple's Steve Jobs and Steve Wozniak) building machines in a garage. By contrast, today's entrepreneurs, particularly the Asians, draw on extensive formal and informal networks of other professionals built around ethnicity. Saxenian lists thirteen formal professional associations of Chinese or Indian engineers fostering networking and support along fairly narrow ethnic lines. For example, there are distinct associations of engineers with origins in Taiwan (who speak Mandarin at meetings), Hong Kong (Cantonese), and mainland China. Another association was named 'The Indus Entrepreneur' to include Pakistanis, Bangladeshi, and Nepalese; however its members are in fact almost all Indian. Saxenian carefully discusses the role of these associations in facilitating members' career development. They put professionals in touch with role models and sources of venture capital; they serve as important sources of information about markets for labour or products, and offer formal and informal lessons in basic facts of entrepreneurship, management, and (for Chinese) English communication.[29]

This is an important finding. Earlier writing about Silicon Valley, including Saxenian's first book, had emphasized rather the isolation of Silicon Valley engineers, normally portrayed as classic loners who joined no formal associations, even professional associations, had trouble staying married, and bowled (if at all) alone.[30] This picture, although not

---

[27] Saxenian, above, n. 20.   [28] Ibid., 2.
[29] Ibid., 21–43.
[30] Saxenian, above, n. 11, discusses informal networks among engineers (30–7), and formal associations among company executives (47–9 and 163–4); conspicuous by their absence are formal professional or other associations of engineers and professionals. The image of the Silicon Valley manager or engineer, who belongs to no formal organizations and has trouble with marital commitment, is central to such popular books as Bellah, R. N., Madsen, R., Sullivan, W. M., Swidler, A., and Tipton, S. M., *Habits of the Heart: Individualism and Commitment in American Life* (Berkeley, Cal.: University of California Press, 1985) 3–8.

totally inaccurate, was perhaps ethnocentric. Formal professional associations are alive and well in Silicon Valley, although not in the form of labour unions or traditional engineering societies. The successful form is rather the identity-based network organization that transmits information about markets and facilitates career development through entrepreneurial opportunity.

Saxenian's paper on these organizations is essential reading for anyone interested in the organization or legal regulation of a high-velocity labour market, but rather than quote more extensively from it here, I would like briefly to suggest some possible applications, calling for future research. They reflect my belief that law can do more to address employment equity issues in high-velocity labour markets like Silicon Valley's by encouraging network organizations and ease of starting a business, than it can through employment discrimination laws as we know them.[31] Two groups that might make more effective use of the network organizational model than they do at present are women professionals in Silicon Valley and low-wage workers such as Mexican immigrants cleaning the floors. Let me propose a research agenda for studying these groups.

Network organizations for women?

My own preliminary and unsystematic interviews with women professionals in Silicon Valley suggest that they do not currently make effective use of network organizations, at least, not in any sense as effectively as the Chinese and Indian engineers who have founded so many successful companies. It is possible, however, that such organizations could be adapted to make entrepreneurial opportunities more available to women professionals.

There does not appear to be much published research on women professionals in the Valley.[32] A survey on how women professionals perceive employment equity in a high-velocity labour market is urgently needed, and should include questions—suggested by Saxenian's paper

---

The 'bowling alone' synecdoche, for the supposed general decline in Americans' voluntary affiliations, is from Putnam, R. D., *Bowling Alone: The Collapse and Revival of American Community* (New York: Simon & Schuster, 2000).

[31] This is not a proposal to repeal any US employment discrimination laws although I do think some of them could be usefully amended in ways that this chapter will not address. On the basic issue of the effect of globalization on employment equity, I think that access to networks, job mobility, and entrepreneurial options are simply more relevant responses than any conceivable changes in the legal definition of discrimination. My entire discussion, however, presupposes the continued presence, not repeal, of existing statutes on discrimination.

[32] Saxenian, above, n. 20, does not discuss gender at all, but all the individuals mentioned in her paper are men.

on Asian engineers—on how they plan careers transcending firms, and how they use both networks and formal organizations. My unscientific guesses, based on my unscientific interviews to date, follow. Women professionals in the Valley are still unlikely to be engineers or scientists. They are more likely to work in law, marketing, finance, or personnel relations. Some women professionals have spent quite a bit of time with one employer (like Hewlett-Packard or Intel); many have moved among many employers; the proportional breakdown is probably no different from that for male professionals. For most of these women, Silicon Valley is an outstanding place to work. Companies are relatively open to new ideas and free of prejudices and stereotypes. More women work in really top jobs, as general counsel or in finance, than would be true in any other US industrial sector. Moreover, the acceptance of self-employed contracting creates enormous freedom to custom-design combinations of work and family responsibilities.

I would further guess that women professionals employ informal networking arrangements to help learn about openings for consultants or managers at other firms and that they do not employ formal organizations in the way that Chinese or Indian engineers do. Formal organizations of women professionals are probably smaller and provide fewer services than the organizations that Saxenian studied. They are probably rarely the source of capital. I think too that women professionals would be interested in greater use of inter-firm formal networks as vehicles for portable health insurance and other benefits, training, and industry information. Finally, I would guess that although these women will attribute some lack of success in attaining managerial positions to discrimination, they, like Chinese and Indian engineers, will find networking for inter-firm career advancement, and greater opportunities for self-employment, to be more relevant solutions than traditional discrimination lawsuits. For example, my women informants tend to describe companies that are 'good companies' or 'bad companies' for women in terms of organizational culture. 'Bad companies' do not let you have a family or private life, make unreasonable time demands, and cut you out of the decisional loop if you were not in the building at 4 a.m. for the frisbee game. While I do not minimize the impact of this kind of organization (if that is the word) on opportunities for women and others who want to raise children, these are not the kinds of issues with which current US discrimination laws are equipped to deal.

Network organization for unskilled immigrants?

Now it may seem that a labour market organized around rapid mobility and network organization must necessarily reward the nimble professional and offer little to the ordinary worker. I want to challenge just that view. Thinking about how to improve life for the Mexican or Central American immigrant, cleaning bathrooms or assembling boards, is when one really sees the power of network organization. While from some perspectives they face stratified and segregated labour markets, it is impossible to imagine them as victims of any imaginable, legally-cognizable discrimination. It is not unlawful discrimination or pretextual to discriminate against the unskilled or poorly-educated. Even if it were, the kinds of remedies for discrimination now part of US law would not get our janitor out of his or her dead-end job. The most able and ambitious cleaner at Sun Microsystems has nowhere to advance at Sun. He or she is probably not a Sun employee. Sun probably does not employ any of its own maintenance staff. Neither his employer nor Sun will train him for more skilled maintenance work. The turnover rate of employees at all levels of Sun does not provide an obvious way to imagine a stable career there for our immigrant. Yet these are the traditional legal remedies for discrimination.

A union solution is excellent, as far as it goes, and I favour the kinds of legal changes discussed elsewhere that would facilitate unionization among low-wage service workers.[33] The economy of Silicon Valley appears robust enough to pay janitors $7.00 an hour with health insurance, instead of $5.50 an hour without it. A strong union might also concern itself with educational support for the janitor's children or other social services. However, the only kind of career advancement that a union might facilitate is career advancement within an employing establishment (which does not exist in the kind of labour market Silicon Valley tends to produce—whether the employer is Intel or Bright Cleaning Services) or within the union itself.

Many of our janitors will stay janitors for their working lives and should be able to do so in dignity, able to support a family. But some might like to establish their own building services contracting firms, employing others, or branching into more challenging and remunerative building or other business services. Increasingly, it is recognized that successful careers for low-wage service workers require ladders from dead-end jobs to better jobs, and that those ladders require training and mobility among firms.[34] One part of this story will turn out to be precisely the kind of ethnic-based networking organizations already employed by Chinese and Indian immigrant engineers and already employed, much

---

[33] See generally Wial, H., 'The Emerging Organizational Structure of Unionism in Low-Wage Services' (1993) 45 *Rutgers L. Review* 671. This may involve more scope for secondary action by labour organizations: see Zlolniski, above, n. 25, 2334–5.

[34] See generally Herzenberg, S. A., Alic, J., and Wial, H., *New Rules for a New Economy: Employment and Opportunity in Postindustrial America* (Ithaca, NY: ILR Press, 1998).

more informally, by Mexican and other immigrants in low-wage jobs.[35] The best strategy for the economic advancement of those janitors and production workers are organizations that put them in touch with successful contractors of building service or manufacturing labour, train them in new skills, teach basic business skills, including the English language, and transmit information about market opportunities. There is no reason why unions could not take on the functions of preparing members for successful self-employment or business ownership, however untraditional this might be.

III POST-EMPLOYMENT LEGAL PROBLEMS IN SILICON VALLEY: RECOGNIZING EMPLOYEES AS SOURCES OF INFORMATION[36]

A second area of law, placed under substantial pressure by the decline of implicit employment contracts, concerns post-termination obligations such as covenants not to compete, loyalty, and trade secrets. In a labour market in which careers involve successive stops at multiple employers, these problems increase in importance. While it is perhaps intuitive that 'trade secret' cannot mean the same thing in an economy of rapid turnover as in an economy of implicit lifetime jobs, modelling the economic implications of different definitions of 'trade secret' is in fact quite difficult.[37]

In Silicon Valley, nearly everybody is a former employee, or former independent contractor, of a competitor. In such a labour market, termination of employment is normal, expected, and not necessarily a big deal. Termination rarely raises any issues of breach of express or implied contract, breach of implied obligations of good faith and fair dealing, or public policy. Engineers or marketing consultants understand that they will be back on the job market when the current project ends. They want to be sure, however, that when they re-enter that market, they will be able to trade on the experience gained in all their previous jobs.

---

[35] See generally Zlolniski, above, n. 25.

[36] A much fuller treatment of this subject is my unpublished paper, 'The Wealth of Shared Information: Silicon Valley's High-Velocity Labour Market, Endogenous Economic Growth, and the Law of Trade Secrets', available on my web page http://andromeda.rutgers.edu/~hyde.

[37] The under-appreciated role of information in economic growth, specifically, 'non-rivalrous' information that is shared with others and from which competitors cannot legally be excluded, is modelled in Romer, P. M., 'Endogenous Technological Change' (1990) 98 *Journal of Political Economy* S71. Romer does not focus on the mechanisms of spreading such information or the precise role of employee mobility, as opposed to other means of spreading shared information (such as technology licensing, academic publication). There is no good economic model of the relationship between employee mobility and economic growth.

In most states other than California, the law of post-termination obligations forms a major obstacle to economic growth. Outside California,
employers can and do insert standard covenants not to compete and trade
secrets agreements into standard-form employment contracts. The effect
is to reinforce the more traditional, internal labour markets associated
with US East Coast high-technology districts such as Boston's Route 128
in which employees pursue predictable careers inside firm hierarchies.

Most Silicon Valley start-ups—the centrepiece of the remarkable entrepreneurial culture that so many immigrant engineers have worked
successfully—are founded by former employees of another Valley
employer, who leave to develop products that will be compatible with,
and may compete with, their former employer's.[38] If Californian courts
enforced covenants not to compete, or routinely enforced agreements not
to disclose trade secrets with injunctions against changing jobs, none of
these start-ups could have been founded. The unenforceability of
covenants not to compete in California is a happy historical accident that
undoubtedly helped bring about Silicon Valley.[39] In 1872, California
adopted a massive codification of its laws that included a provision
making covenants not to compete unenforceable.[40] Obviously, this has
nothing to do with policy on high technology. However, in some other
Western states adopting the same Field Code prohibition on covenants
not to compete, the courts have construed the statute as if it enacted only
the common law's prohibition of 'unreasonable' covenants.[41] So perhaps
a deeper explanation is needed of why Californian courts did not eviscer-
ate its statute but continue to deny enforcement to covenants.

The trade secrets story is even more complicated, for here California
has adopted, along with forty-two other jurisdictions, the Uniform Trade
Secrets Act.[42] Here again, some courts construe this statute in a way that
would prohibit the ordinary Silicon Valley start-up. A particularly horri-
ble example is *Pepsico, Inc.* v. *Redmond*, construing the Uniform Act to
enjoin a regional manager from Pepsico from taking a job as Vice

[38] Saxenian, above, n. 11, 25–7; Bankman, J., 'The Structure of Silicon Valley Start-Ups'
(1994) 41 *UCLA L. Review* 1737, 1739.

[39] This thesis is developed in more depth in Gilson, R. J., 'The Legal Infrastructure of High
Technology Industrial Districts: Silicon Valley, Route 128, and Covenants not to Compete'
(1999) 74 *New York University L. Review* 575.

[40] Now Cal. Bus. & Prof. Code, s. 16600. The statute permits covenants not to compete
when a business is sold but forbids them in most employment settings.

[41] See, e.g., *Dobbins, DeGuire & Tucker, P.C.* v. *Rutherford*, 708 P 2d 577 (Mont. 1985); *Bayly,
Martin & Fay* v. *Pickard*, 780 P 2d 1168 (Okla. 1989) (dictum). Both Montana and Oklahoma
have statutory bans on covenants not to compete that are identical to California's but are
construed by the courts to permit 'reasonable' restriction. On those common law restrictions
see generally Trebilcock, M. J., *The Common Law of Restraint of Trade: A Legal and Economic
Analysis* (Toronto: Carswell, 1986).

[42] 14 ULA 438 (1990). The California version is Cal. Civ. Code s. 3426.

President for Field Operations of what was then the Gatorade division of Quaker Oats. Although Pepsico was unable to identify any particular trade secret that was jeopardized, a federal appeals court granted the injunction on the ground that Redmond would 'inevitably disclose' *some* trade secret or other on the new job.[43] This is an unusually pro-plaintiff decision. Trade secrets plaintiffs normally have to identify the precise secret that they fear will be disclosed—that is, courts have mostly refused to adopt plaintiffs' arguments that there is a doctrine of 'inevitable disclosure'—and few, if any, cases actually enjoin defendants from taking a job. Still, if generally adopted as the correct construction of the Uniform Trade Secrets Act, this would almost completely prohibit start-ups in the Valley, most of which involve at least some former employees or contractors of competing firms who *might* be called on to disclose something they learned at the last job.

Californian law is rather unsettled on these points, as there are no important decisions of its Supreme Court, and few of its Courts of Appeals, construing the Trade Secrets Act. Until recently, the interesting story was that relief was unavailable to Silicon Valley employers even when employees went out of the door with diskettes or files. Courts and juries tended to find that the relevant information was not a trade secret, was general knowledge in the industry, or hardly different from information that had been published, or information that the plaintiff had not kept secret.[44] The effect was to permit the well-known Silicon Valley phenomenon, already discussed, in which employees leave their employer and obtain venture capital for a new venture, manufacturing software or hardware designed to be compatible, or to compete, with their old employer's. More recently, however, some Californian courts, in unreported decisions, have issued injunctions prohibiting departing employees from working in particular areas as competitors,[45] whilst two

---

[43] *Pepsico, Inc.* v. *Redmond*, 54 F 3d 1262 (7th Cir. 1995). On remand, the district court narrowed the injunction, permitting Redmond to take the job at Quaker, but merely enjoining any disclosure of Pepsico confidential information or trade secrets, 1996 WL 3965 (ND Ill., 1996). The decision has been criticized: Gilson, above, n. 39, 622–6; Merges, R. P., 'The Law and Economics of Employee Inventions' (1999) 13 *Harvard Journal of Law & Technology* 1, 59, n. 179; Whaley, S. S. (student author), 'Comment: The Inevitable Disaster of Inevitable Disclosure' (1999) 67 *University of Cincinnati L. Review* 809; Bui-Eve, H. (student author), 'To Hire or Not to Hire: What Silicon Valley Companies Should Know About Hiring Competitors' Employees' (1997) 48 *Hastings L. Journal* 998–1000.

[44] One that received a great deal of publicity was Intel's completely unsuccessful litigation against ULSI Technology, Inc., both criminal and civil. See Jackson, T., *Inside Intel* (New York: Dutton, 1997) 284–93.

[45] *Advanced Micro Devices, Inc.* v. *Hyundai Electronics America*, No. CV752679 (Cal. Super. Ct., Santa Clara County, 5 Apr. 1996), discussed in Goodin, D., 'AMD, Hyundai Resolve Litigation Over Trade Secrets', *The Recorder*, 19 Nov. 1996, 1 (available in LEXIS, News data base), and Hardie, C., 'AMD, Hyundai Settle Flash Squabble', 42 *Electronic News*, 25 Nov. 1996, 16 (available 1996 WL 13933861); Ballon, I. C., 'Keeping Secrets', *IP Magazine*, Mar.

Alan Hyde

recent decisions strongly criticize the doctrine of 'inevitable disclosure' as incompatible with California's policy favouring 'employee mobility'.[46]

This dominant California approach—identifying public policy with mobility of employees—carries a hazy notion that these engineers and executives bring their minds to work; that their spread of information across networks of firms is a crucial element in economic growth; and that public policy supports this mobility and information spillover. This concept, at best latent in the cases, may seem, even if strengthened, to offer little to our hypothetical janitor or production worker. Still, we would not want to discard this tender shoot—treating employees as the source of critical intellectual capital—just yet. US progressives have waged a battle for decades, mostly a losing one, to have labour and employment law recognize (for example, in defining collective bargaining) the intellectual contribution that ordinary working people bring to their jobs.[47] When law finds a public interest in employee mobility, it recognizes that information is being carried among firms, and may evolve into a broader recognition of the role of employee intellect in economic growth.

So progressives, like employers, have reason to think carefully about the American trend away from careers and toward high-velocity labour markets. Surely employers cannot have it both ways on the definition of a 'trade secret'. Obligations of loyalty and confidentiality may have meant something in the days when employers implicitly promised a lifetime career, and kept that promise. They necessarily mean something different, if they mean anything at all, when the employer makes no reciprocal promise to the employee, express, implied, or implicit. Along with this argument from fairness, however, is the economic argument that I have been developing. There is a kind of economic growth (and job creation) that can be achieved only when internal labour markets erode; when

---

1998, available on-line at <http://www.ipmag.com/98-mar/ballon.html>, reporting on *GTE Government Systems Corp v. Patrick*, No. 770111; Feinberg, I. N., 'Inevitable Disclosure of Trade Secrets: A New Problem for Companies Hiring Experienced Technical Employees', available on-line at <http://www.gcwf.com/articles/interest/interest_5.html>, reporting on *IBM v. Read-Rite, Inc.* An intermediate court of appeal in California has recently 'adopted' the doctrine of inevitable disclosure of trade secrets in dictum, although the actual holding carefully examined all the plaintiff-employer's asserted 'trade secrets', concluding that none was really such, and denied any relief. Thus, the case's holding, as opposed to its dictum, is the antithesis of the doctrine of 'inevitable disclosure': *Electro Optical Industries, Inc. v. White*, 90 Cal. Rptr. 2d 680 (Ct. App. 1999). A recent order prohibits any citation of this decision, 2000 Cal.LEXIS 3536 (Supreme Ct. of Cal., 12 Apr. 12000).

[46] *Bayer Corp. v. Roche Molecular Systems, Inc.*, 72 F Supp. 2d 1111 (ND Cal. 1999); *Intel Corp. v. Broadcom Corp.*, Cal. Super. Ct., Santa Clara County, No. CV 788310 (20 May 2000).

[47] See, e.g., Klare, K., 'The Bitter with the Sweet: Reflections on the Supreme Court's *Yeshiva* Decision' (1983) 13/71 *Socialist Review* 9; Stone, K. V. W., 'Labor and the Corporate Structure: Changing Conceptions and Emerging Possibilities' (1988) 55 *University of Chicago L. Review* 73, 138–47; Hyde, above, n. 2.

employees move freely among firms, spreading information as they go. As I have argued above, there is also a kind of equal employment opportunity that can be achieved only in such a labour market. So other jurisdictions, seeking to emulate Silicon Valley by renaming some random geographical feature 'Silicon', might be better advised to examine the extent to which their law of restrictive covenants and trade secrets impedes the formation of a high-velocity labour market and growth district. And progressives might want to re-examine their dream of an orderly world of stable careers that will never return. Instead, we might want to consider, as foundation for a new employment law, the twin pillars: working people who make unique contributions to economic growth through their intellectual input and the networks that bind employees and convey information across the boundaries of the firm.

13

'A domain into which the King's writ does not seek to run': Workplace Justice in the Shadow of Employment-at-Will

RICHARD MICHAEL FISCHL*

I LOSING MY RELIGION

I was in my second year with the National Labor Relations Board when I began to grow self-conscious about the boilerplate with which a generation of Board attorneys had opened the argument section of their appellate briefs:

Section 7 of the National Labor Relations Act guarantees employees the right to engage in union organizing and other concerted activities. Section 8(a)(1) of the Act implements that guarantee and prohibits an employer from interfering with, restraining, or coercing employees in the exercise of their section 7 rights. Section 8(a)(3) of the Act further implements the section 7 guarantee and prohibits an employer from discharging or otherwise discriminating against employees for engaging in union activities.

As I recall, it was the *verbs* that brought about the first wave of concern. The more labour law I learned, the less comfortable I felt painting with a broad brush about the rights that section 7 purportedly 'guarantees' for employees. To be sure, the statutory provision itself is sweeping and unambiguous: 'Employees shall have the right to self-organization, to form, join, or assist labor organizations, to bargain collectively through representatives of their own choosing, and to engage other concerted activities for the purpose of collective bargaining or other mutual aid or protection.'[1]

But the case law I encountered told a different story. The Board and the courts had repeatedly invoked various employer-friendly policies (like the primacy of property rights and the need for unfettered managerial control) to deny section 7 protection to such literally 'concerted activities' as sitdown strikes and slowdowns.[2] Indeed, I quickly surmised that

---

* The author would like to thank Joanne Conaghan and Jeremy Paul for their thoughtful critiques of an earlier draft.
[1] 29 USC. § 157.
[2] For a collection of illustrative cases see Fischl, R. M., 'Self, Others, and Section 7: Mutualism and Protected Protest Activities under the National Labor Relations Act' (1989) 89 *Columbia L. Review* 789, 790 n. 4.

someone could write a book about the long and ever-growing list of 'concerted activities' for which section 7 did not 'guarantee' any protection at all—our ingenuous boilerplate to the contrary notwithstanding.[3]

'Prohibits' had begun to trouble me as well. Even in those instances in which section 7 did appear to provide legal protection—covering, for instance, employees who neither sit down nor slow down but who dutifully leave the workplace altogether and conduct a full-fledged strike in support of their union's economic demands—the effect of sections 8(a)(1) and 8(a)(3) of the Act on the prerogative of employers to retaliate turned out, on closer examination, to be surprisingly equivocal. Once again, the underlying statutory provisions were seemingly unambiguous, broadly condemning as an unfair labour practice any 'interfer[ence]' with section 7 activities and any anti-union 'discrimination'.[4] But once again, the cases provided a complicating countertext, and I knew I was really getting the hang of labour law when I could explain with a straight face that the Act prohibited an employer from interfering with and discriminating against employees pressing an economic strike by *firing* them, but did not prohibit the same employer from interfering with or discriminating against such strikers by *permanently replacing* them.[5]

By the time I left the Board for academia, I had lost faith in even the boilerplate's nouns. This was largely the product of five years spent attempting to convince sceptical federal judges to reinstate employees fired for engaging in one or another of the 'concerted activities' that continue to enjoy section 7 protection. When the typical case reached my desk, it had already cleared a long series of administrative hurdles: the discharged employee—or perhaps her union representative—had filed an unfair labour practice charge with one of the Board's regional offices; after investigation, region officials had determined that there was reasonable cause to believe the discharge was unlawful and, having failed to secure a settlement with the employer, had issued a complaint; after a hearing, one of the Board's administrative law judges had concluded that the complaint had merit and issued a decision ordering reinstatement of the

---

[3] As it turned out, at about that time there were two individuals writing at some length—and with great insight—on just that subject: see Atleson, J., *Values and Assumptions in American Labor Law* (Amherst, Mass.: The University of Massachusetts Press, 1983), and Klare, K., 'The Judicial Deradicalization of the Wagner Act and the Origins of Modern Legal Consciousness, 1937–1941' (1975) 62 *Minnesota L. Review* 265.

[4] 29 USC. §§ 158(a)(1), 158(a)(3).

[5] See *NLRB* v. *Mackay Radio & Telegraph Co.*, 304 US 333 (1938). On the difference between discharge and permanent replacement—which is somewhat more significant than it may seem at first blush—see Fischl, above, n. 2, 804–5 n. 43. For the classic critique of *Mackay* see Atleson, above, n. 3, 1–34. For a more recent critique—which insightfully explores the interaction between the *Mackay* rule and doctrinal developments during the 1980s—see Finkin, M. W., 'Labor Policy and the Enervation of the Economic Strike' [1990] *University of Illinois L. Review* 547.

dismissed employee; and, on review of the record, a three-member panel of the five-member NLRB itself had affirmed the judge. It was only then that those of us who served as the Board's appellate lawyers got into the (A)ct. But the stakes were high: If our briefs and oral arguments did not persuade a majority of the judges on a panel of the US Court of Appeals that the Board had it right, then all of the earlier work by our agency colleagues seemingly went for naught.

Like most NLRB lawyers over the years, I was fortunate enough to win more cases than I lost. But in the process my confidence in our boilerplate took another blow, for I learned first hand that it was not section 7 or section 8(a)(1) or section 8(a)(3) or any other provision of the Act that provided employees with whatever legal protection they had; nor, for that matter, was it the hardworking and dedicated staff of the NLRB. Instead, it seemed that Holmes had it right all along, at least when it came to labour law: The legal protection employees enjoyed was nothing more than a prediction of what two out of three judges would or would not do on their behalf in a particular case.[6]

My disenchantment became complete during my final months with the agency, when I discovered that, even discounting for the Holmesian gloss, our boilerplate still promised more than it could deliver. I learned, to my great surprise, that *courts* did not provide employees with much legal protection either. Pride came just before the fall when the briefs I had drafted helped to persuade the Supreme Court to uphold the Board in *NLRB* v. *Hendricks County REMC*.[7] At issue in *Hendricks* was the Board's challenge to the discharge of Mary Weatherman, the personal secretary to the general manager of a rural electric membership co-operative in Indiana. The employer had fired Weatherman—who had been with the firm for nine years and had held the personal secretary position for the last four—for engaging in a classic 'concerted activity': signing a petition protesting against her employer's decision to dismiss a colleague on the basis of a disabling injury the latter had sustained in an on-the-job accident. But what we won in the highest of courts—by persuading a five-to- four majority to reject the employer's claim that Weatherman's potential access to company secrets made her a 'confidential employee' outside the coverage of the NLRA—we quite nearly lost back in the world of work life.[8]

The Board's remedial order required the employer to offer Weatherman 'immediate and full reinstatement to her former job or, if such job no longer exists, to a substantially equivalent job', and to 'make

---

[6] See Holmes, Jr, O. W., 'The Path of the Law' (1987) 10 *Harvard L. Review* 457, 461 ('The prophecies of what the courts will do in fact, and nothing more pretentious, are what I mean by the law').

[7] 454 US 170 (1981).

[8] The 'confidential employee' issue is discussed in Fischl, above, n. 2, 821–6.

her whole for any loss of earnings' she suffered by reason of the discharge.[9] This 'reinstatement-with-backpay' order is as much as the typical employee can expect to get in a retaliatory discharge case under the Act. Under section 10(c), the Board can authorize reinstatement, back pay, and other compensatory, 'make-whole' relief; but, under a long-standing rule, 'punitive' remedies—in the form of enhanced money damages or otherwise—are prohibited.[10] In any event, the Supreme Court directed the Court of Appeals to enforce the Board's remedial order, which it did in due course.[11] But the employer was not as complaisant. In what struck me as an unbelievably transparent ploy, the firm purported to eliminate Weatherman's former position in order to create a new one: the general manager would now have an 'executive assistant' rather than a 'personal secretary'. As luck would have it, the individual who had replaced Weatherman for the duration of the litigation was promoted to the new slot, where she continued to perform the lion's share of Weatherman's former duties.

Meanwhile, Weatherman—reinstated to the firm, but in effect demoted to the position of receptionist/typist—looked on in disbelief. She had waited over five years for the day she would win back the job she had held for nearly half a decade before her dismissal. She had participated enthusiastically in the hearing before the Board; she had followed the internal agency appeal and judicial-review proceedings with cautious optimism; she had even driven cross-country to see her case argued before the Supreme Court on the first Monday in October. And she had experienced her fabled fifteen minutes of fame when the decision in her favour came down and what seemed like every journalist in the Midwest sought out her story. So she certainly did not expect it all to end *this* way—just out of reach of her goal, but just close enough to watch someone else do her job while her employer enjoyed a last and most sardonic laugh.

My efforts to interest responsible Board officials in these developments were met with sympathy but little action. The employer had, after all, rehired Weatherman at her former rate of pay and was co-operating with the agency in the calculation of her back pay and lost benefits. In the absence of retaliatory conduct considerably more egregious than mere 'haggling' over the precise scope of Weatherman's duties, I was told, we could scarcely expect a busy Court of Appeals to respond favourably to a claim that the employer was in contempt of the reinstatement order. 'Look', explained a senior colleague, who knew how much I cared about the case and was trying to calm me down after I had received one of

---

[9] *Hendricks County REMC*, 236 NLRB 1616, 1621 (1978).
[10] 29 USC. § 160(c); see, e.g., *Republic Steel Corp.* v. *NLRB*, 311 US 7, 10 (1940).
[11] *Hendricks County REMC* v. *NLRB*, 688 F 2d 841 (7th Cir 1982).

Weatherman's periodic reports. 'We took her case all the way to the Supreme Court. We won it. We got her back on the job, where she's basically doing the kind of work she did before. And she's going to get a lot of back pay. Beyond that, there's really not much we can do, and we certainly can't expect the court to police every little workplace slight. She's going to have to get used to the fact that, from here on out, she's pretty much on her own.'

The irony of the situation was extraordinary. As the case had wound its way to the Court, I had frequently regaled family and close friends with accounts of Weatherman's courageous stand in support of her disabled colleague; of her heartless discharge by a callous employer; and of our vigorous efforts on her behalf. And while most listened patiently with some mixture of pride and amusement, more than a few had spotted the issue long before I had. What, they would ask, would it be like for Weatherman to go back to work for an employer who had fired her, had spent countless hours and thousands of dollars fighting her reinstatement, and had then been humiliated by a very public defeat in, of all places, the Supreme Court of the United States? But three years of legal education had taught me to ignore such questions and to focus instead on the task at hand: if only we could secure a decision in Weatherman's favour, then the rest would take care of itself. And besides, I would respond to my doubting interlocutors, some little electric co-operative in rural Indiana was not going to defy a ruling by the United States Supreme Court!

And so it was, as I prepared to leave my job at the Board for a career in legal academia, that I began to wonder whether all those things Americans call 'labour law'—section 7 and the other provisions of the NLRA; the NLRB and its lawyers; the briefs, the boilerplate, and the Supreme Court itself; 'all the King's horses and all the King's men'— could in the end actually *do* anything to put someone like Mary Weatherman back in the job to which the same law said she was entitled.

II (DON'T GO BACK TO) ROCKVILLE

Mary Weatherman's plight is by no means unique. Empirical studies reveal what one commentator has aptly described as 'dismal' success rates for employees reinstated under the NLRA.[12] Indeed, the problem of

---

[12] Weiler, P. C., *Governing the Workplace: The Future of Labor and Employment Law* (Cambridge, Mass.: Harvard University Press, 1990), 86; see West, M., 'The Case Against Reinstatement in Wrongful Discharge' [1988] *University of Illinois L. Review* 1, 28–30 (discussing studies revealing that only 40–50% of employees offered reinstatement under the NLRA attempted a return to their firms, and among those only 20% were still with their firms two years later).

in-kind remedies in the employment setting is an old and seemingly intractable one in American law. Consider the common law rule, dating back to the nineteenth century, that courts will not order specific performance of personal service contracts—a rule that, at least in theory, applied with equal force to employers seeking to compel employee performance and employees seeking reinstatement.[13]

The conventional arguments in support of the traditional rule are familiar enough. For one thing, the employment relationship—characterized, as it is, by conflicting mutual bonds of loyalty and distrust, emotional commitment and economic self-interest—is perhaps second only to marriage in its complexity as an associational form, and were the law to force an employee upon an unwilling employer, the resulting relationship would likely resemble a productive and mutually beneficial employment contract about as much as a 'shotgun marriage' resembles living happily ever after.[14] For another, courts have neither the time nor the competence for distinguishing the fair from the foul in the multitude of conflicts that typically arise in the employment setting—let alone in those one would expect to encounter in the context of a relationship already suffering the strains of the original discharge and the ensuing litigation.[15] And for yet another, since a court cannot order an employee to return to a job against her wishes, then it would not be fair to force her employer into the ideological—if not precisely the practical—equivalent of involuntary servitude either.[16]

These arguments resonate deeply in American legal culture and continue to this day to be invoked by lawyers and judges alike as reasons to deny reinstatement, even in the face of unambiguous statutory provi-

---

[13] See, e.g., Labatt, C., *Commentaries on the Law of Master and Servant, Including the Modern Laws on Workmen's Compensation, Arbitration and Employers' Liability* (Rochester, NY: The Lawyers Co-operative Publishing Company, 1913) §§ 322, 335. The development of this rule—and its connection to the emergence of the modern conception of 'free labour'—is analysed in fascinating detail in Steinfeld, R. J., *The Invention of Free Labor: The Employment Relation in English & American Law and Culture, 1350–1870* (Chapel Hill, NC.: The University of North Carolina Press, 1991).

[14] See, e.g., *H.W. Gossard Co.* v. *Crosby*, 132 Iowa 155, 164 (1906). The marital analogy is suggested by the famous opinion of Atkin LJ in *Balfour* v. *Balfour* [1919] LR 2 KB 571 (CA 1919), which is also the source of the quotation appearing in the title of this chapter: '[p]romises [between spouses] are not sealed with seals and sealing wax. The consideration that really obtains for them is that natural love and affection which counts for so little in these cold Courts. . . . In respect of these promises each house is a domain into which the King's writ does not seek to run, and to which his officers do not seek to be admitted.'

[15] See, e.g., *Fitzpatrick* v. *Michael*, 177 Md. 248, 255 (1939).

[16] See, e.g., ibid., 259. To be sure, even outside the institution of slavery, American labour had not always been quite this 'free'; through the middle of the 19th century, many US jurisdictions authorized specific performance—and in some cases criminal sanctions—for contract-breaching employees. See Steinfeld, above, n. 13 (*passim*) and more generally Orren, K., *Belated Feudalism: Labor, the Law, and Liberal Development in the United States* (Cambridge, New York: Cambridge University Press, 1991).

sions authorizing just that remedy.[17] But a fourth argument may have even more bite than the first three, and—as the saga of Mary Weatherman suggests—it is the employee who typically gets bitten. The conventional arguments defend the personal services rule by stressing the interpersonal complexity of the employment relationship, the limits of judicial competence, and the importance of individual freedom for both parties. But they scarcely acknowledge that a fundamental reason the 'shotgun marriage' will not work—and that courts cannot seem to do anything about it—is that one of the parties to a reinstatement order typically has a degree of 'freedom' within the relationship that the other does not. Indeed, the absence of any principled basis for distinguishing between the employer who is attempting to thwart a reinstatement order by 'mistreating' a returning employee (on the one hand) and the employer who is simply doing what the common law permits him to do to his employees in virtually *any* setting (on the other) reveals more about the sorry nature of that common law baseline than it does about the supposed inability of the courts to detect deviations from it.

To be sure, we have come some distance from the days in which corporal punishment was a legally sanctioned form of American human resource management.[18] But—to take a not quite random example—there is nothing in US common law to prevent an employer from targeting an employee with nearly half a decade's tenure as the general manager's personal secretary (and twice that time with the firm) and demoting her to receptionist/clerk with neither notice nor prior consultation, but just, as they say, for the sport of it. Her position in the firm, like the job itself, is utterly 'at will'. What the conventional arguments about reinstatement miss, then—indeed, what the invocations of relational complexity and reciprocal autonomy actively obscure—is that the principal reason it is so difficult to enforce a 'right of return' for a wrongfully discharged employee is that *she had no right to be there in the first place.*

III YOU CAN'T GET THERE FROM HERE

This instance of a yawning chasm between 'the law on the books' and 'the law in action'—of a 'little electric co-operative in rural Indiana' that did indeed 'defy a ruling by the United States Supreme Court'—seems to me to render vivid an increasingly important dimension of the American 'employment-at-will' rule that has thus far received only occasional attention. In numerous ways, large and small but typically hidden from view, the rule—under which an employer enjoys the privilege of firing at any time, with or

---

[17] See West, above, n. 12, 51–6 and nn. 250–1, 260–2.
[18] See Steinfeld, above, n. 13, 11, 16, 152 and nn. 17–18.

without advance notice, 'for good cause or for bad cause, or even for no cause'[19]—undermines the 'exceptions' to it and with them efforts to bring justice to the American workplace through law and legal institutions.

Today, of course, those 'exceptions' include not only the NLRA's protection for union organizing and other concerted activities, but also the large and growing list of prohibitions against retaliation for other forms of oppositional conduct (such as 'whistleblowing'[20]) as well as discharges and other adverse action on the basis of 'status' (such as race, gender, or religion[21])—the latter more commonly known as the law of employment equity, by some distance the most prolific source of wrongful discharge litigation in the contemporary American workplace.[22] But the real story lies not in what the exceptions have changed but in what they have left intact, and what they have left intact is a rule that threatens to swallow the exceptions to it at nearly every turn.[23] I am for this reason profoundly sceptical of efforts in the USA and elsewhere to enhance employment equity protection while at the same time reducing job security.[24] The burden of my argument is that there can be no workplace

---

[19] *Payne* v. *Western & Atl. RR*, 81 Tenn. 507, 518 (1884), overruled on other grounds by *Hutton* v. *Watters*, 132 Tenn. 527, 544 (1915).

[20] See, e.g., Florida Whistleblowers Act, Fla. Stat. §§ 448.101–105 (statute prohibiting retaliation against employees who report or refuse to participate in unlawful employer conduct); *Tameny* v. *Atlantic Richfield Co.*, 27 Cal 3d 167 (1980) (common law decision providing similar protection in tort).

[21] See, e.g., the Civil Rights Act of 1964, § 703, 42 USC § 2000e-2.

[22] There is also a third category of claims—those alleging that a discharge violates the 'implied' terms of the individual employment contract—a theory of liability the widespread judicial acceptance of which during the 1980s prompted a flurry of litigation that substantially abated as employers learned how to draft around the problem in personnel manuals, employment policy statements, and the like. A management lawyer who spoke to one of my classes offered an extraordinary example of this latter trend, noting that he had advised one client to programme the firm's computer network so that employees would encounter a pop-up reminder that they were employed at will as they signed on at their work station each morning. With as straight a face as I could muster, I asked him how the client's human resources personnel had reacted to this suggestion, and he responded that he thought they had all been 'downsized'.

[23] Scholarly debate over the American employment-at-will rule during the past quarter century has for the most part focused on 'residual' cases—dismissals thought to be unjust but which do not fit within any of the established exceptions to the rule—and on whether such cases ought to be governed by the traditional rule or by an alternative standard such as a 'just cause'. Compare, e.g., Epstein, R., 'In Defense of the Contract At Will' (1984) 51 *University of Chicago L. Review* 947, with, e.g., Weiler, above, n. 12, 48–104. In attempting to shift the focus to the effect of the rule on the legal regime created by the exceptions—an effect almost entirely ignored by the participants in the conventional debate—I continue the work begun by Cindy Estlund and Ann McGinley. See Estlund, C. L., 'Wrongful Discharge Protections in an At-Will World' (1996) 74 *Texas L. Review* 1655, and McGinley, A. C., 'Rethinking Civil Rights and Employment at Will: Toward a Coherent National Discharge Policy' (1996) 57 *Ohio State L. Journal* 1443.

[24] A particularly forceful argument along these lines was presented by Jeremy Baskin of South Africa at the Intell conference in Cape Town in 1999.

equity without workplace justice and that there can be no workplace justice in the shadow of employment at will.

Perfect circle: effects on litigation strategy and party attitudes

Perhaps the most dramatic illustration of this hidden interplay between 'rule' and 'exception' is what might be usefully described as the 'square peg/round hole' problem. Under the background rule, a discharge—no matter how unfair or egregious—is *damnum absque injuria*, and that is very much the point of employment-at-will. Accordingly, if an employee is to secure relief, she must characterize her dismissal to fit one of the exceptions. In the event that she has a 'round peg'—that is, that she was discharged in clear violation of one of the exceptions and (important qualification here) she has both the evidence and the resources to prove it—she may well have a winning case. But what happens if instead she has a 'square peg'—a claim that may be compelling as a matter of simple fairness, but just does not quite fit the 'round hole' of an at-will exception?

It is my impression—borne of countless discussions over the past decade with former students and other lawyers working the respective sides of the employer/employee fence—that the 'square peg' problem is an extremely common one in the contemporary practice of US labour and employment law, particularly in the context of employment equity claims. Employee-side lawyers believe that juries will generally be receptive to 'square peg' stories, whether or not the stories actually fit the 'round hole' of the relevant legal doctrine, and on that point those working management-side would readily agree. But the trick is getting past the judge to the jury—or at least making a credible threat that you will be able to do so—and the only way to accomplish that goal is to present the case as a plausible fit for the 'round hole' established by law.

While employers and their lawyers are likely to view such framing efforts as disingenuous or worse, the reality is quite a bit more complex. For one thing, as countless progressive critics have argued, there is a considerable gap between the lived experience of racism, sexism, and other forms of subordination (on the one hand) and the legal vehicles available for the vindication of employment equity claims (on the other).[25] While the relevant doctrines reflect dominant

---

[25] See, e.g., Freeman, A., 'Legitimizing Racial Discrimination through Antidiscrimination Law: A Critical Review of Supreme Court Doctrine' (1978) 62 *Minnesota L. Review* 1049; Lawrence, C. R., 'The Id, the Ego, and Equal Protection: Reckoning with Unconscious Racism' (1987) 39 *Stanford L. Review* 317; Crenshaw, K., 'Demarginalizing the Intersection of Race and Sex: A Black Feminist Critique of Antidiscrimination Doctrine, Feminist Theory and Antiracist Politics' [1989] *The University of Chicago Legal Forum* 139; Krieger, L. H., 'The Content of Our Categories: A Cognitive Bias Approach to Discrimination and Equal Employment Opportunity' (1995) 47 *Stanford L. Review* 1161.

cultural understandings and thus tend to portray discrimination as the product of discrete and intentional actions by errant individuals, the plight of those in subordinated groups is frequently the result of unreflective habits, complex social structures, and entrenched institutional practices. Indeed, even in cases in which there is a strong suspicion that something more virulent is in play, admissible evidence may be hard to come by; the requirement of proof of 'intentional' discrimination—with its focus on the subjective dimension of employer decision-making—forces employees to find their way in the dark. As a consequence, in order to satisfy the legal requirements for an employment equity claim, the employee has a strong incentive to recharacterize the subtle or the unconscious as blatant and purposeful.

There are likewise many cases in which the racial or gender dimension of the saga that eventuated in dismissal is real but attenuated; or in which there is a story of racial or gender conflict, but the conflict played no readily discernible role in the challenged discharge decision; or in which neither the employee nor her counsel can really tell whether such conflict played a role or not. Indeed, it is frequently the unfairness of the discharge itself that leads the employee to suspect a racial or gender aspect—but (as American judges so often remind us) the law of employment equity does not prohibit unfairness, just discrimination, so it is the suspected discrimination rather than the obvious unfairness that must be emphasized. In these situations as well, then, the employee who would challenge her dismissal will be forced to tell a story that may differ from 'what really happened'.

Let me emphasize that in doing so she is fabricating neither the racial/gender dimension of her employment experience nor the injustice of her dismissal, but there are nevertheless risks associated with this strategy. There is first, of course, the prospect that she will not pull it off—that the judge will decide that her 'square peg' claim just does not fit the law's 'round hole' and therefore grant summary judgment for the employer. But there are other costs as well, and they are not insignificant.

To state the matter bluntly, the need to repackage unjust dismissal claims as discrimination claims needlessly racializes many employment disputes while at the same time trivializing the real but subtle and complex role of racial domination in the workplace. It leads employers and their lawyers to conclude that minorities and *their* lawyers are dishonest—a perception that is itself in large part the product of the same dominant cultural understandings that construct the law's ill-suited 'round hole' in the first place. Thus, a charge of racial or gender discrimination is likely to be viewed by the one so charged as an accusation of intentional racism or sexism, and—especially in the rancorous context of the typical legal dispute—efforts to explain that the problem is more complicated are less likely to succeed in that endeavour than to convince the employer that the charge is an exaggeration and the claimant acting in bad faith. The prospect of such consequences would surely diminish were the employee to focus instead on the unfairness of the dismissal, but that focus is precluded by employment at will.

These developments are obviously unlikely to promote a happy resolution to the case at hand, nor are they likely to further the cause of employment equity more generally. Indeed, as 'square peg' claims proliferate, they shape the attitudes of employers and personnel managers, of their lawyers, and of the judges who hear these cases—judges who are, it is worth noting, infinitely more likely to be recruited from the ranks of the management bar than from the other side. The attitudes thus generated are likely to influence, and not in a good way, the views of these repeat players toward those in subordinated groups and toward employment equity issues in general, and those are decidedly not the attitudes with which we would like persons in positions of power over working people to operate. In the USA in any event, these repeat players do not just exert influence over our system of employment equity; *they run it*.[26]

I stress that the problems I have outlined here are the product of a regime in which the prohibition against discrimination is an 'exception' to a rule that otherwise permits discharges willy-nilly—however unfair or outrageous they may be—and that I should not be understood to be advocating abandonment of the salutary goals of employment equity. The point is rather that those goals are more likely to be accomplished in a context in which victims of unjust dismissals—whether and to whatever extent those dismissals are racially based—are not required to distort their claims in order to see them vindicated.

Feeling gravity's pull: effects on judicial ideology and on worker responses

A second consequence of the interplay between rule and exception lies in its effect on the way American judges understand and frame the stakes in employment cases. When I was handling retaliatory dismissal claims for the NLRB, we could always tell we were in serious trouble when the court's opinion began with what was in the late 1970s a most familiar

---

[26] As Cindy Estlund has argued, experience with (or fear of) employment equity claims may well prompt employers to undertake defensive measures that exacerbate the problems outlined in the text and further undermine the goals of employment equity law. On the one hand, employers may attempt to minimize the prospect of such claims by discriminating against minorities at the entry level. At the same time, employers may 'bend over backwards' in their treatment of incumbent minorities, thus simultaneously patronizing the latter and generating hostility and resentment among their non-minority colleagues. See Estlund, above, n. 23, 1678–82.

refrain—an invocation of 'the established principle that an employer legally may discharge for any cause, whatever others may think of its adequacy, so long as his motivation is not interference with rights protected under the National Labor Relations Act'.[27]

Perhaps the most remarkable point about the refrain is that *it was not true*, for even then there were a host of reasons (race, gender, colour, national origin, religion, age, and pregnancy among them)—quite apart from 'rights protected under the National Labor Relations Act'—for which an employer was decidedly *not* free to fire at all, or so at least the law said. The refrain was wrongheaded in a more fundamental respect as well, for the casual deployment of a common law rule with its source in state law to establish the boundaries of federal statutory claims represented a striking and utterly unexplained reversal of the usual hierarchies of authority in American law.[28]

There was, moreover, something oddly celebratory, even giddy, about the errant formulation. It is difficult to fathom a judge in a murder case, for example, reminding the government that 'the defendant is free to fire guns, wield knives, detonate explosives, release poisonous gas, and otherwise produce mayhem, so long as the activity in question does not result in death'; or a judge in a securities fraud case going out of his way to emphasize the right of a broker to 'misstate, misrepresent, wheedle, cut corners, puff, connive, and mislead, so long as he doesn't actually violate Rule 10-b(5)'.

Although I have not encountered the old refrain for some time—at some point the proliferating exceptions to the discharge privilege no doubt finally began to intrude on the consciousness of opinion writers—the cavalier attitude toward unfair dismissals that it reflected continues in full force. As Ann McGinley has observed, contemporary judges seem to view the rule as granting employers a 'licence to be mean', and one consequence of this judicial mindset is that employees and their representatives frequently face an uphill battle in persuading judges that a particular dismissal is the result of a prohibited motive rather than simply a privileged exercise in animosity, contrariety, or whimsy.[29] Irrational exercises of authority are normalized—they are accepted as the 'rule' rather than treated as an 'exception'—and as a consequence they raise no red flag when judges encounter them. Rather than viewing such instances as

---

[27] *NLRB* v. *Eastern Smelting and Refining Corp.*, 598 F 2d 666, 669 (1st Cir 1979).

[28] Striking and utterly unexplained, to be sure, but hardly unprecedented; indeed, the staying power of common law values and assumptions notwithstanding legislative revision is the central theme of Jim Atleson's wonderful book, above, n. 3. For a more recent instance see *Lechmere, Inc.* v. *NLRB*, 502 US 527 (1992) (state common law property right to exclude trespassers trumps federal statutory right to organize).

[29] McGinley, above, n. 23, 1459–62; see also Estlund, above, n. 23, 1671–2.

exceptional and therefore suspicious behaviour, judges in the thrall of employment at will may well perceive them as simply a legitimate exercise of employer privilege.

But there is, I think, a more basic problem, and it is this: the fundamental structures of proof in American employment law—from the three-part *McDonnell Douglas* test for disparate treatment under Title VII to the *Wright Line* burden-shifting test for mixed motives under the NLRA[30]—rest on a series of highly contestable assumptions: that 'employers' are individuals rather than hierarchies, bureaucracies, committees, and networks; that such concepts as 'intent' and 'motive' can usefully capture the rich complex of behaviours that prompt us to do the things we do, let alone the things we do collectively rather than individually; and that these subjectivities can be neatly and usefully divided into dichotomous categories of permissible 'good' (or 'legitimate' or 'non-discriminatory') reasons and 'bad' reasons prohibited by law.[31] My sense is that these assumptions—each of them the product of a mindset organized by the rule/exception relationship of discrete legal prohibitions operating against the backdrop of employment at will—have played a significant role in the construction of the 'square peg'/'round hole' problem described in the previous section. The legal forms thus misunderstand and misdescribe the dynamics of the employment relationship every bit as much as they misunderstand and misdescribe the problems of racism and other forms of subordination.

Unlike judges—whose awareness of the employment-at-will rule induces them to undermine the exceptions—American workers seem to think that the exceptions *are* the rule. The recent fascinating survey by Richard Freeman and Joel Rogers of contemporary worker attitudes across a broad range of topics strongly suggests that a substantial majority of American employees wildly overestimates the legal protection available against unfair dismissals.[32] This finding is closely corroborated

---

[30] See *McDonnell Douglas Corp.* v. *Green*, 411 US 792 (1973) (once an employee establishes a *prima facie* case of discrimination, the employer must offer a legitimate reason for the challenged decision, and the plaintiff may prevail by establishing that the reason offered was a pretext for discrimination); *Wright Line*, 251 NLRB 1083 (1980), upheld in *NLRB* v. *Transportation Management Corp.*, 462 US 393 (1983) (once the employee establishes that one of the reasons for the adverse action was employer opposition to union activities, the employer must prove that it would have reached the same decision even in the absence of the anti-union motive).

[31] See Fischl, R. M., 'Fear and Loathing on the Picket Line: Labor Law and the Social Dimension of Workplace Protests' (describing the difficulty in distinguishing between 'good' and 'bad' reasons for retaliatory discharges under the NLRA) (forthcoming); McGinley, above, n. 23, 1466–73 (describing similar difficulties in discrimination cases under Title VII).

[32] Freeman, R. B., and Rogers, J., *What Workers Want* (Ithaca, NY: ILR Press, 1999) 118–19 (reporting, among other things, that 83% of their respondents said it would be illegal for an employer to fire an employee 'for no reason').

by Pauline Kim,[33] who conducted an empirical study specifically designed to test the assertion by employment at will's most ardent defender that the rule simply reflects the actual preference of employees and employers alike.[34] As these and other studies confirm,[35] the at-will rule is utterly at odds with the ground rules most employees assume to be governing the employment relationship, and thus the widespread failure to 'opt out of the default rule' cannot fairly be read as the result of informed choice among alternative benefit packages.

Freeman and Rogers attribute the misperception they report to 'a kind of "there's got to be a law" syndrome' where 'people think that anything that is blatantly unfair at the workplace must be illegal'[36]—and that is surely a large part of the story. But the reason so many working people think that 'there's got to be a law' proscribing unfair dismissal may well be that the 'exceptions' (which seem to confirm that view) are visible to them in ways that the 'rule' (which would contradict it) is not. Thus, the exceptions are for the most part legislative interventions (for example, civil rights statutes or whistleblower laws) that are the end product of various forms of political activism, and both the intervention and the activism have typically taken place in the public eye; likewise, the stories of individual employment cases that are most likely to garner widespread media coverage and public attention are the stories of large settlements and dramatic courtroom victories by David against Goliath. In stark contrast, the employment-at-will rule is the product of common law decisions that are now over a century old, and working people who are not judges, lawyers, or law students are for the most part unlikely to find out about the rule until it is too late.

Whether and to what extent workers would behave differently if they were more aware of employment at will is obviously difficult to say. Perhaps they would attempt to opt out of it during individual bargaining—although the impediments to doing so are formidable.[37] Perhaps such awareness would instead generate political action in support of reversal. Or perhaps it would lead many to take a second look at the

---

[33] Kim, P. T., 'Bargaining with Imperfect Information: A Study of Worker Perceptions of Legal Protection in an At-Will World' (1997) 83 *Cornell L. Review* 105.

[34] Epstein, above, n. 23.

[35] See, e.g., Forbes, F. S., and Jones, I. M., 'A Comparative, Attitudinal, and Analytical Study of Dismissal of At-Will Employees Without Cause' (1986) 37 *Labor L. Journal* 157 (reporting that fewer than a quarter of their respondents were aware of the fact that an employer could fire workers without cause); see also Sunstein, C., 'Human Behavior and the Law of Work' (2001) 87 *Virginia L. Review* 205, 229–31 (analysing studies on this topic).

[36] Freeman and Rogers, above, n. 32, 120; to the same effect see Sunstein, above, n. 35.

[37] For an excellent discussion of the difficulties see Weiler, above, n. 12, 74–7 (citing, among other things, the psychodynamics of the job interview and significant problems of agency and collective goods); for a similarly insightful discussion see Sunstein, above, n. 35, 220–31.

potential benefits of union representation—a collective 'opt out' option that comes with its own enforcement mechanism, more about which I will have to say in a moment. The point, then, is not just the one we ordinarily associate with critical studies of common law background rules—that such rules appear to be 'natural' or 'necessary' and thus resist the virus of democratic revision[38]—but rather that, in this instance, the common law establishes a baseline that disappears altogether, albeit only from the view of those to whose working lives it most matters.

There she goes again: effects on the feasibility of reinstatement

Let us return to the problem of in-kind remedies, the problem with which the chapter began. There is, of course, a setting in the American context in which such remedies are not a problem at all: unionized employment. Scholars who report 'dismal' success rates for administrative agency- and court-ordered reinstatement paint a far brighter picture when employees are reinstated pursuant to arbitration in the shadow of collective bargaining.[39]

What accounts for the considerable differential in success rates? The most obvious factor is institutional, for the presence of a union can have strong deterrent and remedial effects on employer non-compliance with reinstatement orders, and this point will rightly loom large in any analysis. But there is another less obvious factor, and once again it is the background role of employment at will.

Thus, the employee who is reinstated in the union setting will almost invariably be the beneficiary of a provision in the underlying collective-bargaining agreement that prohibits discharge or discipline in the absence of 'just cause'. As a consequence, any subsequent mistreatment—from blatant abuse at the hands of a supervisor embittered by the reversal of his discharge decision; to subtler slights (like lukewarm evaluations); to subconscious acts of petty retribution—will, if challenged, be evaluated on the basis of substantive fairness and procedural regularity. Indeed, since the employer is contractually obligated to ensure that all of its discharge and disciplinary decisions conform to the 'just cause' standard—and typically bears the burden of establishing that the standard

[38] See generally, Kennedy, D., *A Critique of Adjudication (fin de siècle)* (Cambridge, Mass.: Harvard University Press, 1997), especially ch. 10.

[39] See West, above, n. 12, 38–9 (in union context, more than 85% of employees who are offered reinstatement accept the offer, and up to three-quarters of those who accept the offer remain on the job two years later); Weiler, above, n. 12, 86 and n. 72 (70–80% of reinstated employees in union context remain on the job 'for an appreciable period' thereafter). West and Weiler report that in the administrative- and court-ordered setting, fewer than half of those offered reinstatement attempt a return and about a fifth of those who make the attempt are still with their firms by the two-year mark.

has been satisfied in a particular instance—it is likely to have policies and procedures in place that will, to some extent, constrain the impulse for vengeance and, in any event, establish a track record that will make deviant treatment stick out like a sore thumb.

The contrast to reinstatement in the absence of a 'just cause' guarantee could scarcely be starker, for in that context the returning employee enters hostile territory to confront an employer who is armed with the employment-at-will rule. She will already be in a more precarious position than the employee reinstated in the union setting, for she will have secured her return through agency and/or court proceedings, thus visiting on the employer a more protracted, more expensive, and more public reversal of fortune than would have occurred in the arbitration context. But her ability to challenge adverse action by the employer—a demotion, say, from a position as the general manager's personal secretary to mere receptionist/typist—will depend not on the fairness or the regularity of the employer's conduct, but entirely on whether a retaliatory motive can be established. And, as Mary Weatherman learned, that is a mighty thin reed on which to hang one's hopes for a successful return to a job from which one was unlawfully dismissed.[40]

The consequences of the limited feasibility of the reinstatement remedy should not be underestimated. As a practical matter, the alternative is money damages. If they are capped—under the NLRA, for example, the discharged employee is almost invariably limited to back pay less interim earnings—then the employee's dignitary, social, and professional losses will go entirely uncompensated. But even if greater damages are permitted—as is the case in employment equity suits—in the typical case the party who will benefit the most is her attorney, and the likelihood that her recovery will come anywhere close to compensating her for the full value of her loss is virtually nil.[41]

Taken together, the various consequences of the employment-at-will rule produce for American labour and employment law a whole that is considerably worse than the sum of its constituent parts. Judges in the thrall of the rule have developed requirements of proof that bear scant resemblance to the employment decision-making under challenge; faced with those requirements—and with the looming threat of the employment-at-will default—employees are required to reframe their claims to

---

[40] To be sure, reinstatement remains an elusive remedy in some jurisdictions that do provide legal protection against unjust dismissal. See Collins, H., *Justice in Dismissal* (Oxford: Clarendon Press, 1992), ch. 7 (analysing the UK experience); but see Roccella, M., 'The Reinstatement of Dismissed Employees in Italy: An Empirical Analysis' (1989) 10 *Comparative Labor L. Journal* 166 (reporting far greater success with reinstatement under Italian law).

[41] See Summers, C., 'Effective Remedies for Employment Rights: Preliminary Guidelines and Proposals' (1992) 141 *University of Pennsylvania L. Review* 1457.

fit artificial legal standards if they are to have any hope of securing relief; those reframing efforts contribute to an atmosphere of mistrust and suspicion between the parties, who have little incentive to moderate their mutual antagonism since—given the infeasibility of reinstatement—there is no need to worry about what kind of relationship they will have when the dispute is over; the antagonism is further exacerbated because the employee has an incentive—since, once again, in-kind relief is out of the question—to raise the stakes by inflating the claim for money damages, and management attorneys are paid by the hour and thus have little incentive to resist escalation of the conflict; employee claims are heard by judges who are increasingly sceptical both because of their prior experience with 'square peg' claims and because they view arbitrary dismissals as an employer privilege rather than as a social vice; employers and their lawyers develop hardened views of employment equity claims and those who make them; and employees with no way of knowing about employment at will grossly overestimate the legal protection they enjoy and are therefore far less likely to turn to the one institution that can help them escape its grasp.

IV IT'S THE END OF THE WORLD AS WE KNOW IT

I close with a few observations about two developments that threaten to reduce my chapter to a critique of questionable relevance to the present predicament of the legal regulation of employment.

Automatic for the people: mandatory arbitration of individual employment claims

The first development is the latest rage in US human resource management: requiring workers—as a condition of hire or continued employment—to sign agreements to submit any and all disputes with the employer to binding arbitration. In a reversal of the usual order of things, the law led the way on this front, when the Supreme Court shocked the employment bar in 1991 and issued an opinion suggesting that such agreements were enforceable in spite of a venerable precedent from the early 1970s that had been widely read to hold that employment equity claims could not be forced into arbitration against the wishes of the claimant.[42] The earlier case had arisen in the context of collective bargaining, and—one might have thought—a rule prohibiting employees with

---

[42] Compare *Gilmer* v. *Interstate/Johnson Lane Corp.*, 500 US 20 (1991) with *Alexander* v. *Gardner-Denver Co.*, 415 US 36 (1974).

the bargaining power of their union behind them from binding themselves to the use of arbitration would apply *a fortiori* in the context of the
lone, unrepresented employee. In any event, the 1991 decision encouraged numerous employers to try their luck, and the gambit paid off in the
spring of 2001 when the Court issued a decision that removed any doubt
about the legality in principle of what Katherine Stone has aptly referred
to as the 'new yellow-dog contract'.[43]

One way of viewing this development is to conclude that this is just
another instance of nineteenth century employment contract principles
displacing the rule of law and that arbitration systems unilaterally
designed by employers and imposed on their employees are the workplace equivalent of the cat guarding the canary cage. Now both workers
and their right to a judicial forum to vindicate the few rights they have are
seemingly employed at will. There is certainly anecdotal evidence to
support this view[44] and very little in the current rush to adopt these
systems to suggest that employers are doing so in order to improve the lot
of their workers.

My own reaction is a bit more complex. On the one hand, the assumption that an arbitration agreement entered into as a condition of employment is in any meaningful sense voluntary is, I think, as wrongheaded as
the potential reach of the practice it sanctions is frightening. But I am
reluctant to head for the barricades over the right of access to a forum
whose principal contribution to American workplace law is the employment-at-will rule. Indeed, I think Roberto Corrada is right to caution that
we should not unreflectively cede the terrain of individual arbitration to
employers and thus ignore the progressive—perhaps even transformative?—potential in this development.[45]

For one thing, as a practical matter the economics of legal representation
will preclude many, perhaps most, employees from using the judicial
forum to secure relief in an employment case; for them, the arbitration alternative may be the only realistic avenue they ever have for pressing their
claims.[46] Moreover, the relative expeditiousness of arbitration may offer
real and substantial benefits. If you live paycheque to paycheque—as most
US working families do—the prospect of a protracted period of uncertainty

---

[43] *Circuit City Stores, Inc.* v. *Adams*, 532 US 105 (2001); Stone, K. V. W., 'Mandatory
Arbitration of Individual Employment Rights: The Yellow-Dog Contract of the 1990s' (1996)
73 *Denver University L. Review* 1017.

[44] See, e.g., Jacobs, M. A., 'Men's Club', *Wall Street Journal*, 9 June 1994, A1 (reporting difficulties faced by female employees in the securities industry whose sexual harassment claims
were heard by male-dominated arbitration panels appointed and paid by an industry organization).

[45] Corrada, R. L., 'Claiming Private Law for the Left: Exploring *Gilmer's* Impact and
Legacy' (1996) 73 *Denver University L. Review* 1051.

[46] See ibid., 1052–3; Summers, above, n. 41.

and contentiousness may itself foreclose the option of challenging a dismissal. Expeditious dispute resolution may also improve the prospects of success for in-kind remedies such as reinstatement—remedies that, when they are workable, may give the claimant something far closer to a just result than any award of money damages for which she can hope under current law.

The model of justice that is emerging in the individual employment arbitration context is still very much a work-in-progress, as courts, lawyers' groups, bar associations, and private arbitration providers (such as the American Arbitration Association) have begun to have their say about procedures that depart significantly from traditional notions of due process and from the dictates of substantive law.[47] Naturally, the one constituency from whom we have not heard much in this regard comprises those whose lives these systems will most affect. Yet the Freeman and Rogers study offers some intriguing data in this respect. On the one hand, it suggests that American employees are more receptive to employer-based arbitration systems than one might have predicted, with fully a quarter viewing the alternative as a 'very effective' method for resolving workplace disputes and more than half responding that they would willingly choose it over litigation.[48] On the other hand, however, the respondents overwhelmingly voiced a preference for a system in the design and development of which employees have a say and almost as overwhelmingly opposed systems that impose a choice of forum on employees, requiring them to give up their day in court as a condition of employment[49]—that is, the kind of system to which the Supreme Court just gave its imprimatur.[50]

To be sure, there is an institution in American work life that could provide employees with a 'say' in the design of these emerging systems and at the same time offer them competent and affordable representation in individual cases, and that is organized labour. Promoting 'legal services' memberships for unrepresented workers—and leading legal and economic challenges to employers who maintain unfair dispute resolution systems—may well turn out to be a highly effective tool for recruiting and organizing, providing labour unions with the opportunity to expose the considerable gap between the legal rights employees imagine they have and the realities of life in a non-union workplace. Indeed, my sense is that the progressive potential for employer-imposed arbitration

---

[47] See Corrada, above, n. 45, 1067–8; see *Cole v. Burns International Security Services, Inc.*, 105 F 3d 1465 (DC Cir 1997) (Edwards J) (rejecting requirement that employee pay arbitrator's fees).

[48] Freeman and Rogers, above, n. 32, 132.

[49] Ibid., 135–6 (reporting support for employee input at 95% and opposition to mandatory arbitration at 78%). [50] *Circuit City*, above, n. 43.

lies far less in success in persuading courts and arbitration associations to establish increasingly elaborate due process guidelines for reluctant employers than in taking up the challenge to provide working people with their own voice in the matter.

Whatever the forum, what is not likely to change any time in the near future is the continued role of employment at will as the background rule in the legal regulation of employment—at least for those employees who do not enjoy the benefits of union representation. It remains very much to be seen whether and to what extent the arbitration model will simply replicate the vices I have described from the litigation context (for example, moving the 'square peg'/'round hole' problem to a new forum); or avoid them (for example, by making reinstatement a viable remedy); or (truly scary thought) develop new ones altogether.

Shiny happy people: law and the death of the job

I turn, then, to a second line of argument—offered in a recent article by Katherine Stone[51] and in Alan Hyde's contribution to this collection[52]—that poses a challenge to my critique. The real problem with employment at will (the argument goes) is that it constituted an insidious bait-and-switch. On the one hand, the central if implicit assumption of what was in the mid- to late-twentieth century the dominant (if by no means universal) model of American work life was a guarantee of 'career' employment.[53] As Stone explains, this implicit guarantee was the key provision of the 'old psychological contract' between employers and their employees, the *quid pro quo* given in exchange for the trust and loyalty of the latter.[54] But here's the rub: under the traditional at-will rule neither an 'implicit' assumption nor a 'psychological' contract is worth the paper it is printed on, so the law would not force an errant employer to make good on the implicit guarantee, thus leading to a striking discontinuity between what employees fairly expected and what the law would actually deliver.

But that problem (the argument continues) is rapidly disappearing because 'career' employment is itself in steep and swift decline and the world of work once only imagined by the employment at will doctrine is finally upon us. Progressive scholars and labour lawyers ought therefore to 're-examine their dream of an orderly world of stable careers that will never return'[55]—and, one is tempted to add, stop writing quaint articles

[51] Stone, K. V. W., 'The New Psychological Contract: Implications of the Changing Workplace for Labor and Employment Law' (2001) 48 *UCLA L. Review* 519.

[52] Hyde, in this volume.

[53] Ibid., 233–4; Stone, above, n. 51, 526–39.   [54] Ibid.

[55] Hyde, in this volume, 251.

about employment at will. We are urged to focus instead on legal developments (such as post-employment disputes over the mobility of human capital) more relevant in a world of 'high-velocity labour markets', in which individuals change firms as frequently as teenagers do their dating partners,[56] and to a workplace governed by a 'new psychological contract', under which employees are promised not job security but skills development, and thus the prospect of improved employability for their return trips to the labour market.[57]

Although we have much to learn about the contemporary workplace from these authors, I am more sceptical than either of them appears to be about the degree to which developments they report are or will any time soon be as widespread in American work life as their provocative analyses suggest. Indeed, Stone acknowledges a lively scholarly debate on this topic,[58] and other labour scholars have forcefully called into question predictions of the 'death of the job'.[59]

To whatever extent Stone and Hyde are right about the demise of 'career' employment, though, I confess that I am far less sanguine than they about either the 'new psychological contract' or the legal developments that may accompany it. Stone's intriguing picture of 'competency-based organizations', 'total quality management' systems, and workers with 'boundaryless careers' is drawn largely from the writings of organizational behaviour theorists,[60] corporate executives,[61] and management consultants.[62] By contrast, ethnographic studies that focus on what life is actually like in some of these brave new workplaces—rather than on what management officials *say* life is like or what their consultants tell them life *ought* to be like—suggest that the new boss may well turn out to be an awful lot like the old boss and that the implicit promise of skills training and enhanced employability may turn out to be not worth the paper it is printed on either.[63]

Even when employees do gain highly marketable skills on the job—as is clearly the case for high-tech workers in Silicon Valley—the way that American courts are answering the question of who 'owns' those skills suggests that the common law may play the same ignoble role with respect to the supposed guarantee of enhanced employability as it played in the past with respect to the implicit promise of job security. The body

---

[56] Ibid., 238–9, 247–51.
[58] Ibid., 539–49.
[60] See, e.g., Stone, above, n. 51, 551–2.
[62] See, e.g., ibid., 565–8.

[57] Stone, above, n. 51, 549–72.
[59] Freeman and Rogers, above, n. 32, 8–11.
[61] See, e.g., ibid., 541.

[63] Compare ibid. (describing W. Edward Deming's 'total quality management' theories) with, e.g., Graham, L., *On the Line at Suburu-Isuzu: The Japanese Model and the American Worker* (Ithaca, NY: ILR Press, 1995) (ethnographic study of life in a US auto plant implementing those theories).

of law that enables high-tech workers to participate in a labour market where 'nearly everybody is a former employee, or former independent contractor, of a competitor'[64]—and to do so over the objections of employers who claim that they are expropriating trade secrets and violating covenants not to compete—turns out to be the law of exactly one American jurisdiction; as Stone reports, the law virtually everywhere else is moving in precisely the opposite direction.[65] One is left with the impression that California is well on the way to becoming to the developing law of human capital what Montana is to employment at will.[66]

But I have a far more fundamental reservation about the analyses offered by these authors, and it lies in what is missing from their respective accounts. Stone's story of the development of the 'old psychological contract' with its promise of job security—and of its ongoing/impending replacement by a new one—is a story in which employees and labour unions have played an almost entirely passive role. With the help of organizational theorists and management consultants, employers devise and revise employment contracts to suit their own needs and cope with changing markets; employees learn to live with what they are offered; and the union's function in this connection is to negotiate formal agreements that enable workers to hold management to the promises and guarantees—implicit, psychological, and otherwise—that are then in vogue.[67]

One would scarcely guess from this account that American workers and their unions have played an important historical role in the development of a world in which job security has been a core value and in which conflicts over arbitrary dismissal have been the central feature of labour relations; one would scarcely guess that the protection (*de facto* as well as *de jure*) that many workers still enjoy is in no small measure the result of workplace struggles, of union organizing campaigns, of strikes supporting demands made during collective bargaining, of litigation strategies and successes, and of employers who have only agreed to the so-called implicit contract as a prophylactic against unionization.[68] Indeed, the story with which I began this chapter—of Mary Weatherman's unlawful discharge and the difficulties encountered in securing her reinstatement—is the story of just such a struggle, for Weatherman herself had been fired for courageously protesting the

---

[64] Hyde, in this volume, 247.

[65] See, e.g., Stone, above, n. 51, 577–97.

[66] Montana is the only current American jurisdiction to reject the employment-at-will rule, adopting in its stead a statutory prohibition against discharge without 'good cause'. See Weiler, above, n. 12, 96–9.

[67] See, e.g., Stone, above, n. 51, 572.

[68] See, e.g., Weiler, above, n. 12, 141, 151.

unfair dismissal of a colleague.[69] In my own experience, nothing is more likely to prompt an otherwise quiescent group of employees to take collective action—or indeed to give serious consideration to the prospect of union representation—than an employer who ignores the value that they place on their jobs, and we should not underestimate the extent to which the norms of contemporary workplace life are the result of such protests.[70]

To be sure, worker agency does play a prominent role in Hyde's account of recent developments in Silicon Valley. The workers whose world he explores are in a very real sense 'voting with their feet' and doing so in the context of a body of California law with genuinely subversive (if thus far jurisprudentially isolated) potential, recognizing as it does that the 'feet' in question belong to workers rather than to their employers. But we part ways when Hyde offers a stark choice between reinventing labour regulation in a manner that simply accepts the demise of stable employment relationships (on the one hand) and mounting a rearguard legal action in order to thwart or retard that demise (on the other)[71]—as if the development itself were just a fact of life rather than terrain that has long been contested by workers themselves. At the risk of overdoing the metaphor, it seems to me that the larger struggle is still very much for a world of work in which you do not need to have 'feet' in order to get to 'vote', that is to say, a struggle over whether and to what extent democratic values have a role to play in a world of market ordering.

V STAND: EPILOGUE

A few years back—when I first began thinking about the difficulties of labour regulation in the shadow of employment at will—I decided to try to track down Mary Weatherman to see how it had all turned out. The best place to start, I figured, was with what I assumed would be her former employer—the rural electric co-operative whose general manager was messing her about when last we had been in touch. The co-operative is located in a small town in rural Indiana, and I was certain that someone working there would know how I might find her. Much to my surprise, not only was Weatherman still on the job, but she had also returned to her former position as personal secretary to the general manager. As it turned out, Weatherman had outlasted both the man who had fired her and the

---

[69] I recount this part of Weatherman's story in greater detail in Fischl, above, n. 2, 793–8.
[70] See ibid., 858–61.
[71] Hyde, in this volume, 235–7.

assistant he had hired in her place—the tenacity and resilience she had demonstrated during the many years of litigation had obviously served her well—and so it was she who was enjoying the last laugh after all. She never gave up her fight for the job from which she was unlawfully dismissed; it seems to me that we should not presume to do so on her behalf.

Part V

Border/States: Immigration, Citizenship, and Community

14

The Limits of Labour Law in a Fungible Community

GUY MUNDLAK

I INTRODUCTION: A TALE OF TWO CITIES

The two towns are only twenty kilometres apart. In many ways they are similar, although a fence separates them. On both sides of the border the residents are, for the most part, industrial workers in labour-intensive industries such as textiles and food. Were it not for the fence, economists would predict the creation of a single local labour market in these two towns. But a fence there is, and the average cost of labour on one side of the border is approximately ten times the average labour costs on the other. On one side there is a minimum wage law, anti-discrimination legislation, and even an active union. On the other side there is little regulation (by the state or through collective bargaining) of the labour market. On the 'expensive' side of the border, economic measures indicate a higher level of human capital, but not sufficiently high to justify the labour costs differentials, nor is this advantage always useful for the low-skilled industrial work performed in the region's factories. The two sides of the border are also culturally, linguistically, and socially distinct and quite separate.

Recently the union on the 'regulated' side decided to initiate industrial action in protest against the employer's intention to shut down a textile factory and move it across the border. The strike has failed. Legally, it is the management's prerogative to relocate. The strike is allowed as long as it is confined to the economic outcomes of the decision to relocate, for example, regarding additional severance pay to cushion the bleak prospects of re-employment near the border. Economically, the union's bargaining power in this situation is weak. The little power it can still exert remains only because the employer may still have other plants in the country, or because the employer still cares, for whatever reason, about the social response to the removal of the plant across the border. The social responsibility the employer portrays to the media is accompanied by diffusing the blame to the state and the union. Their insistence on raising the minimum wage, rigidifying work routines, and constantly imposing on managerial prerogative are the causes of the transfer of the factory across the border. For those who remember the panoply of issues negotiated in detail during past negotiations, the image of the current strike seems somewhat desperate.

The two towns can be on the US–Mexico border, or on the border between Eastern Europe and Western Europe. Yet, the two particular towns described here are Beth-Shaan in Israel and Irbid in Jordan. The striking differences in terms of labour costs and industrial relations systems are typical of many borders. Some borders are fenced, others are not. Many towns on the 'costly' side of the border have experienced the employer's relocation a few kilometres away to an economically segmented labour market which can be physically observed at a short distance. The scenario is not new.

Discussion of globalization has dominated much of the social sciences and legal academic discourse in the last decade. It has been suggested that the new process of globalization indicates, or requires, a paradigm shift, or that it is a new mode of regulation.[1] What does this rather all-encompassing notion of globalization hold in store for the residents of Beth Shaan and Irbid? In this chapter I will try to justify a rather pessimistic prediction regarding the promise of peace for the residents of these two towns. The challenges of globalization in general, and regionalization in particular, are not unique to the Middle East. However, the very partial solutions that have been developed to address the traditional objectives of labour law are currently inapplicable in the developing Middle Eastern region. Labour law in particular, and social law in general, necessarily relies on a sense of community that is perceived by its members as more than a market place. The fragile state of peace has yet to provide a new sense of a regional community, but the current movement of capital across borders distances the possibility of its establishment in the future. Consequently, the evolving peace process, with its emphasis on geo-political borders and disregard for the unique socio-economic conditions in the region, destabilizes existing institutions, but does not provide any alternative to those who relied on them for their welfare.

II TWO TYPES OF LAW, TWO TYPES OF COMMUNITY

Consider Mohammad from Jordan who wants to contract with Moses from Israel. In negotiating this transnational contract the parties must bargain for the *lex contractus*. Mohammad prefers to apply the Jordanian law of contracts, while Moses prefers the Israeli law. Moses may demand a higher price in exchange for agreeing to the applicability of the

---

[1] See Boyer, R., 'State and Market: A New Engagement for the Twenty first Century?' in Boyer, R., and Drache, D. (eds.), *States Against Markets* (New York: Routledge 1996) 84.

Jordanian law of contract. The outcome will reflect the parties' relative bargaining power. They may also compromise by adopting the law of the Netherlands, or any other national law of contract for that matter. National laws of contract are therefore traded commodities. A national law of contract is associated with national values, but for the parties to the contract who seek to adopt the most convenient law, based on their mutual interests, this association is of little concern. Adopting the Dutch, Jordanian, or Israeli law does not bind them to the community that authored the law. The community, and its law of contract, are fungible.[2]

Corporate law is similarly attached to a fungible community. Although there is no explicit bargain between two parties over the preferred choice of law, corporate headquarters can locate their offices at the venue that offers the most attractive corporate law. The choice of venue need not require that production or sales or any other substantial activity take place at that venue. Delaware's attraction for corporations is not in the great view it offers, nor in the exceptionally skilled workforce that resides in the state. Other areas of commercial law, such as banking and even taxation, also assume a fungible community.

By contrast, labour law cannot be sold or priced.[3] It cannot be traded and adopted without association to the community authoring the law. Statutory standards are, by nature, mandatory, and are applied territorially, and occasionally even extra-territorially, by the authoring country. The law of collective bargaining is inseparable from the social institutions of the authoring country. Mutual shopping for a collective labour regime can only be described as a category-mistake. Employers shop for a labour regime by becoming insiders of the authoring state. They cannot do so while remaining outside the authoring community, as Mohammad and Moses did in the above example. Nor can they adopt one state's labour law regime in another, merely by locating headquarters in the former, as is the case in corporate law. Theoretically, workers, like corporations, can shop for their most preferred venue as well.[4] There is however an asymmetry between workers and corporations. First, unlike a corporation that can establish its manufacturing in one state and its corporate headquarters in another, workers' choice of venue is indivisible. Moreover, while employers are courted worldwide to introduce their business into the fungible community, migrant workers 'shopping' for a labour law regime

---

[2] I draw on Margaret Radin's distinction between fungible and non-fungible commodities in Radin, M. J., *Contested Commodities* (Cambridge, Mass.: Harvard University Press, 1996).

[3] See Langille, B., 'Labour Law is not a Commodity' (1998) 19 *ILJ (SA)* 1002.

[4] Crouch, C., 'The Globalized Economy: An End to the Age of Industrial Citizenship?' in Wilthagen, T. (ed.), *Advancing Theory in Labour Law and Industrial Relations in a Global Context* (Amsterdam: Koninklijke Nederlandse Akademie van Wetenschappen, 1998) 151.

are often treated as a threat to the non-fungible community. They are looked upon as defectors in the labour-exporting states and as rent-seekers in the labour importing states.

Labour law seeks to remedy the inherent difference between capital and labour in a capitalist market, yet when the market expands and globalizes, the balance is lost.[5] The law governing capital is a commodity, the community authoring the law can be substituted, and capital's forum-hunting improves the price capital pays. By contrast, social law (including both labour and welfare law) remains immutable and attached to the non-fungible community, and the absence of markets for labour law (or more accurately, the fact that only one side of the employment relationship is capable of doing the shopping) renders it at a disadvantage. When some laws can be traded, and others are left outside the market place, the former marginalizes the latter. When the community has both a fungible and a non-fungible face to it, the former destabilizes the latter. The two images of the community, as reflected in two types of law, cannot cohabit in the same space. In other contexts, this has been designated as the domino theory which points to the inability of two regimes to co-exist, leading to the marginalization of non-market or co-operative regimes by markets and adversarial arm's-length arrangements.[6]

Although the often-stated argument on the 'death of labour law' is overstated, it is arguable that labour law can no longer rely on the nation-state as the sole relevant community. Given the need of labour law for a non-fungible communal context, it must seek an alternative, or a complementary community, in addition to the nation-state. If no such context can be formulated, labour law merges into the commodifiable legal instruments, most notably the law of contract. The process of globalization suggests two non-exclusive alternatives to the nation-state: extra-national communities and small intra-national communities. The heralded global village as the peak of extra-national communities is only one example,

---

[5] I intentionally invoke here a particular, yet common, definition of labour law, which highlights its distributive, rather than merely regulatory, objectives. See Collins H., 'Labour Law as Vocation' (1989) 105 *LQR* 469.

[6] See Radin, above, n. 2, 95–107. I find this theory useful in the present context and make no claim regarding its truism or universality in diverse contexts. Contrary to many references to this term in legal literature, I do not read it as synonymous with the more familiar 'slippery slope'. Radin's domino theory should be classified together with other 'multiple equilibria' theories where the adversarial and competitive equilibrium eventually outweighs the cooperative and community oriented one. See, e.g., Levine, D. I., and Tyson, L. D., 'Participation, Productivity and the Firm's Environment' in Blinder, A. (ed.), *Paying for Productivity* (Washington, DC: Brookings Institute, 1990) 183; Samuelson, P., 'Altruism as a Problem Involving Group Versus Individual Selection in Economics and Biology' (1993) 83 *American Economic Review* 143. I agree with Radin that the solution to the commodified realm's imperialism is not necessarily to prohibit it altogether. Instead, the solution must be, in her words, 'to foster the non market aspect of much of what we buy and sell' (Radin, above, n. 2, 107).

and, in fact, geographic regions are currently the more predominant venues. At the same time, the breakdown of the national community has increased the need for small communities that serve as the source for self-regulation and the constitution of the individual's identity as part of a communal context. These can be sorted into geography-based communities, such as municipalities or industrial regions, or identity-based communities founded, for example, on gender or race.[7]

The growth in importance of alternative communities poses the potential for reclaiming some of the objectives served by social law, which was traditionally authored solely by the nation-state. The multiple alternatives also interact in different ways, thus suggesting a new type of individual and communal influence on the regulation of labour markets. Common to all potential solutions is the quest for a sense of community that is more than a venue for law-shopping. The stronger the sense of community, the greater is the likelihood that labour law will survive the process of globalization, albeit in a non-traditional form. Weak communities such as the 'global village' imply diminished expectations, as was well demonstrated in the ILO's recent decision to define and concentrate on core labour rights at the expense of the more ambitious agenda of the past.[8]

On the basis of these assumptions it is now possible to examine the expected future of labour law in the evolving region of the Middle East. As will be argued, the socio-economic aspects of peace in the Middle East are currently being shaped by the commodifiable perspective of both the nation-states and the newly established region. Labour law is therefore currently in search of an alternative communal context.

III TOWARDS PEACE IN THE MIDDLE EAST AND THE ECONOMIC CONSTRUCTION OF A REGION

The peace process in Israel has been slow, starting with the peace negotiations between Israel and Egypt in 1977. The region is fraught with conflicting interests and charged with historical arguments and religious convictions that cannot be rationally untangled. The possibility of creating

---

[7] Several scholars have observed the nexus of labour law (or industrial relations) /community/ democracy. A thorough analysis of this nexus can be found in Held, D., *Democracy and the Global Order* (Stanford, Cal.: Stanford University Press, 1995). See also Crouch, above, n. 4, and Sciarra, S., 'How "Global" is Labour Law? The Perspective of Social Rights in the European Union' in Wilthagen, above, n. 4, 99. The problem of the non-fungible community is therefore closely related to the problem of the 'democratic deficit'.

[8] ILO Declaration on Fundamental Principles and Rights at Work (86th Session, June 1998). On the implications of this decision see Langille, B., 'The ILO and the New Economy: Recent Developments' (1995) 15 *International Journal of Comparative Labour Law and Industrial Relations* 229.

Guy Mundlak

an economic region that will bring about a greater level of prosperity to the partners in peace is expected to provide some legitimacy to a process that cannot suffice with controversial accounts of history for solutions. In this region, inter-state economic activity can potentially aid in deflating the strong sense of nationalism and creating mutual interests that can ease the national partners towards peace. In the Middle East, economic activity is a first step to the structuring of a regional community, unlike other regions where recent efforts to co-ordinate economic activity were legitimized by an existing sense of regional community (be it loose as in South East Asia or stronger as in Europe).

In the ongoing multilateral peace negotiations, regional prosperity and co-ordination in the Middle East are commonly discussed solely as a trade issue. There are currently debates regarding how much the regional partners will enjoy free trade arrangements, contingent on an analysis of the comparative advantages of the various national partners.[9] In a consideration of the movement of both capital and labour across the open borders in the region, it is necessary to bear in mind the grave inter-state inequalities that prevail in the region.[10] These are a result of several factors, including Israel's higher rate of investment *per capita* and differences in human capital, both resulting in a higher productivity in Israel. The conventional economic argument, tracing differences in pay to differences in either supply or demand, does not capture the significant role of labour market institutions in Israel. Employment and labour standards in the neighboring countries cannot match those of Israel. There are trade unions in most of the neighboring countries, although their independence, capacity, and interest to act as the autonomous voice of workers range from largely independent, as in the Palestinian entity, to wholly subservient in Syria.[11] All states in the region are far from the paradig-

[9] Cf., 'Symposium: Israel and the Regional Economy' (1994) 41 *The Economic Quarterly*, 574–711 (Hebrew); Fischer, S., Rodrik, D., and Tuma, E. (eds), *The Economics of Middle East Peace: Views From the Region* (Cambridge, Mass.: MIT Press, 1993); Gross, O., and Sagi, E., 'Separation Versus Integration: Comments on the Economic Aspects of the Israeli–Palestinian Permanent Status Agreement', in (2000) 47 *The Economic Quarterly* 50 (Hebrew); Gross, O., 'Mending Walls: The Economic Aspects of Israeli-Palestinian Peace' (2000) 16 *American University International L. Review* 1539.

[10] The factual information in this section is based on Feiler, G., Fishelson, G., and Nathanson, R., *Labour Force and Employment in Egypt, Syria and Jordan* (Tel Aviv: The Histadrut's Institute for Economic and Social Research, 1993); Feiler, G., Fishelson, G., and Nathanson, R., *The Labour Market in the Territories* (Tel Aviv: The Histadrut's Institute for Economic and Social Research, 1993); Freeman, R., Abu-Shokor, A., El-Ahmad, A., and Klinov, R., 'Palestinian–Israeli–Jordanian Labour Mobility: The Current Situation and Issues for a Peaceful Future' in Fischer, S., Hausman, L., and Karrasik, A. (eds.), *Securing Peace in the Middle East: Project on Economic Transition* (Cambridge, Mass.: MIT Press, 1994) 69; Drake, L., 'Arab–Israeli Relations in a New Middle East Order: The Politics of Economic Cooperation' in Wright, J. W. (ed.), *The Political Economy of Middle East Peace* (London: Routledge 1999) 11.

[11] ILO Committee of Experts (annual publication); US Department of State, *Country*

matic, unfettered assumptions of the neo-classical analysis. The difference is between regimes in which governments intervene in the operations of markets with an eye to the protection of workers (for example, Israel), and centrally administered regimes (for example, Syria) with little or no protection of workers. Empirically, in the Middle East, the more developed the economy is, the more developed are the protective labour market institutions.

A simple neo-classical economic analysis can predict that with the elimination of economic borders in a peaceful Middle East, workers and capital will move across the borders until a new peaceful regional equilibrium is reached. Where production or services are not dependent on a particular locality (proximity to oil, language, etc.), capital will move to those places that offer entrepreneurs the best conditions for running the business. These can include lower labour costs and diverse arrangements ranging from tax relief and subsidies to relaxed statutory standards in areas such as corporate, antitrust, environmental, and labour law. At the same time, there will be movement of workers to those locations where there is a demand for workers and (relatively) advantageous opportunities. A continuum lies between the non-permeable borders of the past and the removal of economic borders, and it is frequently assumed that the stronger peace is, the weaker economic borders are.

Economic regionalization is expected to aid in constructing a new postnational sense of community in the Middle East. At least some of the effects of displacement with the reallocation of production in the region will be compensated by the peace dividend.[12] The expected peace dividend is composed of the discount on security-related expenditures and the predicted region's advantages that will attract foreign capital, consequently expanding the overall share of the region in world production and trade. This analysis lends itself to statements such as: 'we are likely to see increased Palestinian exports of, *inter alia*, cement, workers and olives'.[13] The problem with this analysis is that, unlike olives, workers are reflexive and respond to changing conditions, while at the same time part of the population that shapes these conditions. They provide or deny the legitimacy basis of the peace process itself.

The commodification of labour in the peace negotiations leads the parties to neglect certain political components of the regionalization process. First, the institutional barriers to the creation of a regional

Reports on Human Rights Practices (annual publication); Ziskind, D., *Labour Laws in the Middle East: Tradition in Transit* (Los Angeles, Cal.: Litlaw Foundation, 1990).

[12] On the 'peace dividend' see Seliktar, O., 'The Peace Dividend: The Economy of Israel and the Peace Process' in Peleg, I. (ed.), *The Middle East Peace Process: Interdisciplinary Perspectives* (New York: SUNY Press, 1998).

[13] Symposium, above, n. 9, 575–601, and, in particular, 596–7.

unitary market are enormous.[14] It is sufficient to observe past patterns of labour migration in the region to realize that cross-border migration of workers is not merely a process of push and pull economic forces. Palestinian labour in Israel,[15] or labour migration from Egypt, Jordan, and Syria to Kuwait, Saudi Arabia, and Iraq,[16] has aided the labour-importing countries, and to a lesser extent the labour-exporting countries, but has not brought about a new equilibrium of wages. In both patterns of migration, domestic labour market institutions and social norms have succeeded in replicating national boundaries by way of segmenting the local labour markets. Economic transnational activity in the region has always been subordinated to nationalist interests. The movement of labour across borders has hardly blurred the economic boundaries in the region; in fact, it has gone toward reaffirming them.

Secondly, the allegedly efficient allocation of production factors across the region does not reveal the potential for *social dumping*.[17] All the phenomena associated with social dumping are already observable in the region. The textile workers in Beth-Shaan are paying a significant price for sponsoring the economic regionalization of the Middle East. The unemployment caused by the flight of capital from Israel is aggravated by the influx of foreign workers into the country. The two processes exert grave pressure on all labour market institutions within Israel, as employers argue against the extent and level of minimum wage legislation, collective bargaining agreements, extension orders, and the costs of national insurance. Consequently, there is a potential for a *race to the bottom*.[18] This

---

[14] Garvey, J. I., 'Regional Free Trade Dispute Resolution as Means for Securing the Middle East Peace Process' (1999) 47 *American Journal of Comparative Law* 147; also see Gross and Sagi, above, n. 9.

[15] Semyonov, M., and Epstein, N. L., *Hewers of Wood, Drawers of Water* (Ithaca, NY: ILR Press, 1987); Mundlak, G., 'Power Breaking or Power-Entrenching Law: The Regulation of Palestinian Workers in Israel' (2000) 20 *Comparative Labor Law and Policy Journal* 569.

[16] Shtayyeh, M. (ed.), *Labor Migration: Palestine, Jordan, Egypt and Israel* (Ramallah: Palestine Centre for Regional Studies, 1998).

[17] On social dumping see Mosley, H., 'The Social Dimension of European Integration' (1990) 129 *International Labour Review* 147.

[18] This is the process whereby the nation-states compete among themselves to attract foreign investment. In the process, a country with a costly regulatory regime in the region may relax its standards to avoid the flight of industry to a country with a more industry-friendly legal infrastructure. For reasons of collective action problems, the outcome of this jurisdictional competition may be grossly inefficient, and undesirable for sustaining long-term, high value added growth within the region. A more efficient regional alternative may be reached by means of regional co-ordination. See generally Olson, M., *The Rise and Decline of Nations* (Cambridge, Mass.: Harvard University Press, 1982). The evidence on the race to the bottom is debatable. One of the major objections to this theory is that when firms consider the most appropriate location for production, labour costs present only one consideration among others. Moreover, higher labour costs may sometimes be compensated by higher productivity. These arguments indicate the need to distinguish among different industries. The threat of the race to the bottom is most severe in industries that are managed

process is not yet actively observable because the asymmetry among the countries is so great that Israel has very little to offer in the competition, and the neighbouring countries are already offering much, merely by remaining passive.

While the movement of labour and capital in the region stagnated for some time, Israeli firms acknowledged the advantage of relocating in the mid-1990s. Acknowledging the narrow political importance attributed to the socio-economic aspects of the peace process by the negotiating states, and the fact that the peaceful borders in the Middle East have produced a hinterland, Israeli industrialists started to shut down factories in Israel and to relocate to Egypt and Jordan. This pattern has been observed most strikingly in the textile sector, and to a lesser extent in light industry and food. At the same time, the movement of labour across the borders is almost non-existent. Israel, which depended on Palestinian labour from the territories for many years, has limited the number of workers allowed to enter Israel and replaced them with foreign workers from the rest of the world. The share of foreign workers in Israel coming from Egypt and Jordan is minuscule. The growing movement of industry out of Israel and the declining movement of labour across borders are complemented by a very partial fulfilment of the expected peace dividend, in terms of a growing share of the region in global production and trade. The peace process with the neighbouring countries is at present too cold, and with the Palestinians it is too slow, to promote a significant co-operative venture in building a true sense of an economic region.

The very partial reality of open borders in the region at present strongly affects the nature of both national and regional communities. While capital responds to the simple economic prescription, engaging in unilateral forum-hunting that renders national communities fungible, labour still perceives the nation-state as a non-fungible community. The Middle East region and the states within it are therefore perceived differently by different groups. Workers in Israel still hold the state responsible for cushioning the blow of displacement. Israeli workers in development towns where work has disappeared throughout the last decade are generally more strongly opposed to peace. Israeli policy with regard to Palestinian workers is coloured by interests based on an inseparable mixture of capitalist and nationalist interests. Jordanian and Egyptian workers do not hurry to cross the borders into Israel, and it does not seem that they will desire to do so, in significant numbers, in the near future. Trade unions in Egypt and Jordan are vocal leaders in the opposition to peace. Palestinian workers who lost hope of finding steady employment

on the basis of employing low-waged, low-skilled workers, and which are labour intensive, as is the case with the Israeli textile industry.

in Israel or in the underdeveloped Palestinian entity are finding relief, economically and spiritually, in the fundamentalist organization Hamas, which leads a strong opposition to peace in the Palestinian Entity. All these workers, throughout the region, are seeking a remedy for their hardship in one community or another—the small community, the nation-state, or religion.

The opening of borders, deemed to be efficient from the economic perspective, has the potential for introducing a distributional impact that will hurt those who are the worst off to begin with. While this tension can be observed in the global village, unrelated to the current peace process in the Middle East, the problem becomes acute at the regional level because economic integration is necessary for the advancement of the peace process itself. The necessary tool for integration is also its Achilles' heel. The more economic regionalization advances in accordance with the economic perspective, the more there is a risk that the legitimacy basis of peace will erode. However, it is risky to presuppose that the peace process will reach the economic long term unless there is a short-term distributional response. Arguments on the efficiency of long-term policies are inadequate because the Middle East's long term is contingent on very short-term horizons. This is the paradox of peace.

IV IS THERE A PLACE FOR LABOUR LAW IN THE MIDDLE EAST?

What is the future for labour law in the evolving region? The domino theory predicts that commodifiable law will suffocate non-commodifiable law. The latter includes standardization, through statutes or case law that impose on (or improve) the freedom of contract, or through the statutory infrastructure of a collective bargaining regime. Economic regionalization of the Middle East need not be coterminous with individualization of the employment relationship. Regional movement of commodities, production factors, and labour is conducted in an institutional setting far removed from the image of unfettered markets. The problem with the region is that the institutional setting has thus far failed to compensate for the eroding significance of national communities that were strengthened by the state of warfare in the region, and is yet to create a new regional community on the pillars of peace. Given this twilight zone created in the course of the regionalization process, the traditional means of labour law are for the most part ineffective.

The breakdown of the national system: the case of Israel

To demonstrate the breakdown of labour law at the national context, Israel provides the more interesting case study in the region. Among the nation-states constructing the new region, Israel has the most developed labour market institutions, which have evolved to an almost comprehensive corporatist system.[19] Its institutions are therefore the most vulnerable to the effects of regionalization.

The Israeli industrial relations system was premised in the past on a combination of one strong union (the *Histadrut*) that represented most of the workforce in Israel, an almost comprehensive voluntary membership of employers in the federated employers' associations, and the active intervention of the state in regulation of the labour market through negotiated pacts with the social partners. The stability of the Israeli industrial relations system was based on its totality. Its boundaries coincided with the national boundaries of the state. It thus relied on a very strong non-fungible sense of community. The tripartite structure preceded the evolution of the state and was intended to promote not only social democratic values but also nationalist values.[20] The Histadrut was established at first to mediate between Jewish capital and labour and to promote Jewish work in an Arab-dominated land. After the state of Israel was established as a homeland to the Jewish people, the social pact continued to advance the objective of strengthening the Jewish homeland. The corporatist pact was made possible because all three sides were committed to the national agenda.

The wisdom of the trilateral pact was that it did not rely merely on ideological commitment, but also succeeded in creating the necessary win-win solution that made ideology a benefit to all.[21] To this end, employers consented to wage escalation and received from the state in return a tariffs policy that protected them from foreign competition. The Histadrut retained, with the endorsement of the state, its almost monopolist position as a health-care provider, ensuring comprehensive membership of the population in the Histadrut. Its centralized structure was intended to stifle wage demands of small groups. The Histadrut's position as the second largest employer in the state also ensured for government that it would restrain wage demands so as not to damage its own economic wellbeing. The state strengthened both the employers' associations and the Histadrut, because their strong presence allowed negotiated economic policy with a relatively strong leverage for the state to intervene. Moreover, the state secured relative industrial and political peace. The win-win pact resulted in a system that relied on a domestic parcel of

[19] Shalev, M., *Labour and the Political Economy in Israel* (Oxford: Oxford University Press, 1992); Grinberg, L. L., *Split Corporatism in Israel* (Ithaca, NY: SUNY Press, 1991).

[20] Sternhell, Z., *Founding Myths of Israel: Nationalism, Socialism and the Making of the Jewish State* (Princeton, NJ: Princeton University Press, 1998); also see n. 19.

[21] Mundlak, G., 'The New Labour Law as a Social Text: Reflections on Social Values in Flux' (1998) 3 *Israel Studies* 119.

attributes: most domestic labour worked for domestic enterprises, which, with the co-operation of the state, blocked external competition and therefore provided most of the domestic consumers' needs. While the 1973 economic crisis brought about the new reality of globalization, which by the 1980s had become a central concern for labour worldwide, the Israeli industrial relations system remained insulated from the global trend until the late 1980s. This was partially a result of its geo-political position in the Middle East, but also a result of the internal system's comprehensive coverage and stability. Consequently, the role of labour law was relatively minimal, and intended mostly to secure the stability of the corporatist pact.[22] Other components of labour law, including the law of contract and statutory standard setting, were present, but given the comprehensive reach of collective agreements and extension orders that covered the majority of workers in Israel, their importance was marginal.

By the 1990s the industrial relations system had experienced several shocks. The forces of globalization knocking at the Israeli door were complemented by a neo-liberal ideology that started growing unchecked in response to the suffocating totality of the social and economic system. Tariffs were gradually reduced and employers were no longer assured that they would be insulated from competition. Consumers sought cheaper commodities regardless of where they were manufactured. Starting from 1977, when the Labour party lost the general election for the first time to the Likud party, there was a gradual erosion in the legitimacy of the Histadrut that in the past had kept it safe from public critique. As the peace process emerged, the industrial relations system was awaiting a general recognition of its weakness. In 1994, when the first industrial undertakings were moved across the border to Egypt, the strong sense of community, the encompassing solidarity, and the mutual commitment of the social partners to the stability of the system were all too weak to inhibit the profit maximization interest of the industrialists. If in the past such a move would have been perceived as defection, it was now viewed simply as a matter of rational profit maximization. Moreover, the move across the border was in line with the vision of a new Middle East and a necessary step toward the normalization of the relationship between the countries. Yet, co-ordination of wages and employment conditions requires that the union's span of control be at least as broad as the product and labour markets.[23] Once the assumption of a domestic parcel of attributes that served as the focal point of the old system was dropped, the system destabilized.

[22] Mundlak, above, n. 21.
[23] Reder, M., and Ulman, L., 'Unionism and Unification' in Ulman, L., Eichengreen, B., and Dickens, W. (eds.), *Labour and an Integrated Europe* (Washington, DC: Brookings Institute, 1993) 13.

The only body of law to be so strongly disrupted with the breakdown of the old social and economic system was labour law. The inadequacy of current labour law is twofold. First, there is a mismatch between the old doctrines and the problems that currently appear. The old labour law assumed a strong union negotiating the wages and working conditions of most workers in Israel. Once the union has been weakened, there is little in Israeli labour law to accommodate new types of negotiations. There are no other institutionalized modes of labour-management consultation, such as works councils. Unorganized workers have very slim protection as well. There are hardly any restraints on employers' withdrawal from collective bargaining. There is no law on organizing workers and, more problematic, no practice of organizing. Currently, any effort to provide a greater level of protection to the Israeli labour force merely serves as a catalyst to the flight of capital across the border.

Secondly, for Israeli workers who rely on the nation-state for socio-economic protection, the destabilization of the corporatist system has left them with a much weaker level of protection. Because the social pact had much influence on the social welfare system as well, the unemployed and the poor are generally experiencing a less favourable environment as welfare schemes come under attack. At the same time, employers' commitment to Israeli industrial relations has been diminished because, unlike the past, it is in tension with their economic self-interest. They can easily migrate across the borders. They do not have to do so in fact, because the mere threat of relocating serves the purpose of weakening the power of organized labour. The opening of borders weakens the non-fungible community and strengthens its fungible dimension. Where, in the past, labour and capital constructed together the non-fungible nature of the Israeli industrial relations system, their ways have now parted and the two perceptions of the community no longer cohabit.

The breakdown of the national system in the sense described so far is applicable only to Israel. A common argument in the debate on free trade and global standardization of labour standards is that the desire to strengthen labour law in general, and labour standards in particular, is merely a protectionist measure that seeks to privilege labour in the stronger countries. The process of regionalization in the Middle East aids workers in neighbouring countries, and from the point of view of both regional efficiency and regional justice, the shifting of jobs from Beth Shaan to Irbid does not hurt labour *as such*. It primarily hurts *Israeli* labour. If there is a true interest in establishing a regional community, the welfare of labour cannot be calculated from only one side of the border. This regional perspective however is somewhat myopic.

The movement of employers across the borders is motivated by the relative absence or weakness of labour market institutions in the

neighbouring countries. Yet forum-hunting on this basis creates a problem in the long run. Even if the welfare of workers in the less well-off
states improves, as predicted, the process of regionalization will not allow
workers in the neighbouring countries to affect its distributive outcomes.
Benefits to workers in other countries are all contingent on the employers'
continuous control over wages and working conditions. The asymmetrical perception of the community suggests that any effort to use the
regionalization process as a method of establishing a more convenient
non-fungible community for workers will also make the venue less attractive for 'hunting' employers. In this sense, the state of war that prevailed
in the region is being substituted by economic competition in which
Israeli capital and industrialists are setting the terms. There is little in
these terms to aid the creation and stability of the post-national effects
attributed to peace in the region.

Developing the regional: standardization

Can the new region be structured as a non-fungible community, drawing
on the same legal instruments that were used to create the non-fungible
nation-state? Various regional, and, to a lesser extent, global, efforts have
been critically studied.[24] One of the more common methods is to establish
cross-national standardization of labour rights. While it is possible to
imagine the development of regional directives by the neighbouring
governments in the Middle East, this approach is ineffective at best, and
more likely incoherent.

Theoretically, standardization of wages (and fringe benefits) in the
region can prevent some of the effects of social dumping and the race to
the bottom. However, wage differentials in the region are not only a result
of historically non-permeable borders, but also of different productivity
levels, attributed to differences in the available human capital and the
given utilization of labour and technology. Moreover, wages must be
adjusted to the significant differences in the cost of living. Wage standardization requires a more comprehensive change in the background
conditions and could take place only in conjunction with a wholesale

---

[24] Stone, K. V. W., 'Labor and the Global Economy: Four Approaches to Transnational
Labor Regulation' (1995) 16 *Michigan Journal of International Law* 987; *ead*, 'To the Yukon and
Beyond: Local Laborers in a Global Labor Market' (1999) 3 *Journal of Small and Emerging
Business Law* 94; Bercusson, B., 'Globalizing Labour Law: Transnational Private Regulation
and Countervailing Actors in European Labour Law' in Teubner, G. (ed.), *Global Law
Without a State* (Aldershot: Dartmouth, 1997), 133; Arthurs, H., 'The Collective Labour Law
of a Global Economy' in Engles, C., and Weiss, M. (eds.), *Labour Law and Industrial Relations
at the Turn of the Century* (Deventer: Kluwer, 1998), 143; Kyloh, R., *Mastering the Challenge of
Globalization: Towards a Trade Union Agenda* (Geneva: ILO, 1997); Trebilcock, M., and Howse,
R., *The Regulation of International Trade* (2nd edn., London/NY: Routledge, 1995) 441.

opening of all social and economic borders.[25] In the short term, such a process is not feasible for political reasons, and its effects on the social sphere in the region are likely to be devastating. As the proposed peace paradox suggests, the distributional outcomes may be so harsh that the region will not succeed in reaching a stable long-term peace. Any standard set without the use of market mechanisms will either be too low to be of any significance in Israel, or too high to be taken seriously in the neighbouring countries. Here is where the market's advantages must be taken at face value, and regarded as the optimal (second best) mode of setting wages.[26] Regional efforts need to focus on defining the rules of the game according to which the markets function, rather than eradicate market mechanisms altogether. This is especially true in the Middle East region, where it has been demonstrated that a market economy is better equipped to provide labour rights and powers than the heavily administered economies.

The major standardization challenge lies in the non-wage components. Although any kind of standardization can be quantified in terms of economic costs, there is still a difference in the economic and social perception of various standards, including: restrictions on child labour, protection against health and safety abuses in the workplace, restrictions on excessively long working days, and prohibition of discrimination in employment. Common to all of these areas of employment regulation is that they are conceived as exceeding merely the realm of labour compensation, and reflect the more consensual perception of human rights, including rights to dignity, life, and equality.[27]

There is however a fundamental problem with regard to at least some of the potential areas for regulation. In light of cultural differences and differences in labour market conditions, restrictions on child labour (assuming they are enforced) may serve as an oppressive form of regulation with regard to parts of the population. Those families who rely on their children's labour as an important means for survival, or where there are no norms for completing twelve years of formal (including vocational) education, will experience the regional efforts as reducing, rather than augmenting, their opportunities to advance. Thus, while the logic of

---

[25] See, e.g. the complex relationship between the single currency adopted in the EU and the industrial relations system, documented in Jauppinen, T. (ed.), *The Impact of EMU on Industrial Relations in European Union* (Helsinki: Finnish Industrial Relations Association, 1998).

[26] Compare Reynolds, C., 'Will a Free Trade Agreement Lead to Wage Convergence?' in Bustamente, J., Reynolds, C., and Ojeda, R. H., *US–Mexico Relations: Labour Market Interdependence* (Stanford, Cal.: Stanford University Press, 1992) 477.

[27] Leary, V., 'The Paradox of Workers' Rights as Human Rights' in Compa, L., and Diamond, S. (eds.), *Human Rights, Labor Rights and International Trade* (Philadelphia, Penn.: Pennsylvania University Press, 1996) 22.

directing children to school rather than to work is economically and socially sound, it requires a complementary, comprehensive, reform in the area of education. Similarly, anti-discrimination norms, especially with regard to women, are very different in Israel and in its neighboring countries. It is here that some of the more delicate issues are involved, because the setting of anti-discrimination norms is strongly linked with issues of religious tolerance, and with secular tolerance for religious norms. These problems exist within Israel as well, but their expansion into the regional arena, with its strong religious orientation, is likely to augment the sensitivities involved. The tension between legitimate relativism and non-compromisable human rights requires the development of cultural co-ordination or harmonization in the region. Such a process requires a strong non-fungible sense of regional community. However, the peace paradox suggests that the disintegration of economic boundaries in the region, which renders both the region and the national communities much weaker, does not aid in constructing this kind of communal deliberation and is in fact antithetical to it.

Developing a regional industrial relations system

Ideally, with the opening of borders, national unions need to adjust and expand their activities to match the changing scope of the labour markets. The most ambitious regional agenda is to reach a cross-national representation of workers to match the movement of capital and to eliminate some of the differences that affect the employers' choice of venue. There are however less ambitious strategies that can address more particular patterns of intra-regional activity. First, unions can negotiate inter-union agreements for the representation of migrant labour in the region. Secondly, unions in adjoining countries can co-operate in organizing workers in the proposed free export or industrial zones that may mushroom in the region.[28] Thirdly, with the establishment of joint labour and product markets, unions can co-operate to promote cross-national harmonization on issues such as pensions' portability across borders. Similarly, unions can establish the position of social partners by creating joint training programmes to the benefit of workers, employers, and the national communities. Common to all of these potential avenues for a new unionism is the quest to trace the employers' steps across the economic boundaries and to reclaim a non-fungible sense of community at the regional level.

---

[28] Israel has enacted the Law on Free Industrial Trade Zones (1994), which holds, *inter alia*, that not all Israeli statutory standards will apply in the free zones (i.e., a derogation clause).

An example of such inter-union alliance can be found in the agreement which was signed in 1995 between the Palestinian Federation of Trade Unions (PGFTU) and the Histadrut.[29] The agreement stipulates that the Histadrut will collect trade union agency fees for Palestinian workers employed in Israel and remit half of the sum collected to the PGFTU. The other half will fund trade union representation of Palestinian workers employed in Israel. The agreement also establishes a liaison committee whose members will be senior officers from the two unions. However, efforts to extend this example of regional co-ordination to other unions and to other tasks seemingly face serious problems of implementation.

The major obstacle to regional co-ordination is that Egypt's and Jordan's unions (not to mention the unions of countries that have not yet entered into a peace agreement with Israel) resist co-operation with the Histadrut. Unions in the region's Arab countries still grasp the peace process from a highly nationalistic point of view as a political and economic threat. The Palestinian federation of trade unions is the only exception. A second obstacle to cross-national union representation (of any form) is the union structure in the neighbouring Arab countries. While Jordan and Egypt have relatively progressive unions compared with some other Middle Eastern countries (except perhaps Lebanon), their unions are politically sycophant and still dominated by government. The weak position of unions in these countries is indicative of an even more serious problem that strikes at the heart of the effort for regional co-ordination. Many points on the agendas of regional unions, or unions that function in a region, such as the European unions, aim at harmonizing different systems. However, the differences in the Middle East are such that they make the international portability of pension plans, social security benefits, and similar safety net protections impossible. Some countries still do not have a social security system or an institutionalized system of pensions, and any effort by one nation or local union to harmonize is viewed as a gross infringement of sovereignty, rather than a workable ironing out of differences.

The highly unequal position of the potential partners for regional co-ordination indicates that much needs to be done prior to the regional effort. It is unlikely that much co-operation can be established when the partners (that is, the national unions) are not on equal footing. Unions or other intermediate-level organizations need to be developed before there can be a meaningful effort to develop a regional industrial relations system. Just as it was demonstrated that in the Middle East, market states are associated with a more developed system for labour law, market

---

[29] The Agreement on the Framework for Cooperation between the Histadrut and the Palestine General Federation of Trade Unions (PGFTU), of 5 Mar. 1995.

activity in the region has to be tied with newly developed social institutions, rather than with industrialists' unilateral initiatives. However, the peace paradox indicates that the development of social institutions is not likely to take place as the nation-state is losing its power, and the region is being structured on the assumption that it is fungible and unco-ordinated, just like unfettered markets. The peace paradox therefore requires a hesitant position regarding the development of a regional industrial relations system.

V NEW FRONTIERS FOR TRANSFORMATIVE LABOUR LAW—LOOKING FOR THE NON-FUNGIBLE COMMUNITY IN THE SMALL COMMUNITY

The harsh effects of globalization on labour law world-wide have led some to ask whether we need a new theory.[30] It seems that there is a lot of theory. We know why labour law is facing a crisis, but it is very difficult to provide solutions that can be translated into action. For years labour law scholars have sought to remedy the effects of globalization of labour law by shifting the conventional instruments of labour law (most notably various types of standardization and cross-national collective representation) from the nation-state to the regional or the global arena. The praxis of this strategy has not been too promising. Reliance on the conventional instruments used by labour law, at the national or regional level, has been argued to be ineffective. Admittedly, the Middle East is an idiosyncratic region, and the peace paradox does not affect other regions of the world in the same way. Yet, the underlying argument about the making of both national and international communities fungible seems to account for the futility of many efforts to establish the regional or to cling to the national.

I do not intend to conclude with an optimistic scenario. But I do think that the quest for the non-fungible community must direct some new academic and practical efforts in the region, and perhaps elsewhere. Labour law's need for a non-fungible community is not met because neither the nation-state nor the region is successfully overcoming the peace paradox. The weakness of traditional venues may potentially be compensated by nesting labour law in the small community, in the very local, or in the non-geographical identity groups. What are the implications of reversing the direction of inquiry from the supra-national to the local?

---

[30] Cf., Wilthagen, above, n. 4; Creighton, B., 'The Internationalisation of Labour Law' in Mitchell, R. (ed.), *Redefining Labour Law* (Melbourne: Centre for Employment and Labour Relations Law, 1995) 90.

First, to develop regional standards, some alliances across borders are needed. Anti-discrimination standardization in the region will be possible only once women's groups formulate a cross-national coalition. There is unlikely to be any standardization of occupational health and safety standards, unless unions or health care providers push for such standards in both the national and regional political venues. Only when unions or other forms of collective voice are strengthened (although not to the extent of the Histadrut's power in the corporatist regime) can there be a significant effort to structure a regional labour law in the Middle East. If the municipalities in Beth-Shaan and Irbid can co-ordinate a local policy to aid the workers in the region, on both sides of the border, perhaps with the aid of governmental agencies and NGOs, a sense of local community will arise in which a new type of labour law can develop. Admittedly, none of these ideas is easy to implement. Still, they do require attention for a practical and a theoretical reason. Practically, examples do exist of the quest for the local, rather than for the regional. These experiments are often ignored, because they are not as impressive as multinational directives or a new ILO convention. Meetings between women's groups in the Palestinian entity and in Israel, joint training programmes for tourism workers in the adjoining cities of Akaba (Jordan) and Eilat (Israel), and the first agreement between the Histadrut and the PGFTU are all very small efforts, that are only partially successful, but their importance should not be understated.

For the nation-state these ideas translate into a counter-intuitive idea that makes their development difficult. The idea that the making of a regional economy requires states to encourage the development of civil society and labour market institutions can be attacked from both left and right. The right argues that reviving this kind of institutions is archaic and out of tune with the expansion of markets and globalization. Yet the local is not identical with the national, and it is as post-national and globally oriented as the one worldplace vision. This paper has argued that any effort to liberalize the region and increase its peace dividend is dependent on resolving the loss of the non-fungible community. The single market place vision relies on strengthening social institutions and may not be able to afford their absence.

On the left, it may be argued that if labour law moves to promote civil society, education, social movements, and the like, there is not going to be much left of the direct effort to correct the power imbalance in the labour market. Labour law is going to lose its vocation. Yet problems in the labour market are symptomatic or inter-related to problems in other social spheres, and cannot be detached from them. For the same reason that solutions for pre-labour market discrimination may sometimes need to avoid direct market regulation and tend to the social and legal structures that construct the discriminatory practices in the labour market, the solutions for the evolving regional labour market may require a preliminary correction of communities' weakness. Only after tending to the structuring of a new sense of community can labour scholars and practitioners tend to the appropriate means for the creation of a new labour law.

15

Immigration Policies in Southern Europe: More State, Less Market?

BRUNO CARUSO

... If we could look deeper than our obsession with development allows us to, if we could just sit quietly and listen to places every now and then, if we could think of the desert as not only a place without water, perhaps we would be more able to understand the drama of the South, its refugees and clandestine inhabitants ... [1]

I NON-EU IMMIGRATION TO EUROPEAN COUNTRIES: NEW CONDITIONS AND OLD ISSUES

Recent interdisciplinary studies on immigration in Europe have remarked on the social upheaval it has brought about, referring to a process of 'management crisis' in major European countries.[2] Social relations, the senses of national identity and values, and the structures of Europe's various welfare and labour law systems are all bursting at the seams under the strain. The global nature of the phenomenon, linked to the North/South divide, cannot, however, conceal its differential impact. In European states with imperial and colonialist histories, such as France, Great Britain, and Holland), the collective experience is one of historical nemesis, for which full and proud responsibility should be taken.[3] Even these old colonial states, however, find themselves having to face problems of rights to

---

[1] Cassano, F., *Paenisula, L'Italia da ritrovare* (Bari: Laterza, 1998) 10–11.

[2] See Baldwin-Edwards, M., 'The Emerging European Immigration Regime: Some Reflections on Implications for Southern Europe' (1997) 35 *Journal of Common Market Studies* 497, 513; Papademetriou, D. G., and Hamilton, K. A., *Managing Uncertainty: Regulating Immigration Flows in Advanced Industrial Countries* (Washington, DC: Carnegie Endowment for International Peace, 1995). For recent data see OECD, *Trends in International Migration*, 1999 edition (Paris: OECD). In fact, a crisis in the system of immigration control, increasingly seen as inadequate, inefficient, or excessively liberal, was identified as early as the 1980s: see Sciortino, G., 'Troppo buoni? La politica immigratoria tra controlli alle frontiere e gestione del mercato del lavoro' (1996) 64 *Sociologia del lavoro* 50.

[3] See Blanc-Cheléard, M. C., 'Des logiques nationales aux logique ethniques?' (1999) 188 *Le Mouvement Social* 3. This does not mean that different immigration and citizenship policies regarding inclusion/exclusion criteria have not been applied in these countries over the years, cf. Bonifazi, C., *L'immigrazione straniera in Italia* (Bologna: Il Mulino, 1998) 199 ff.; Reyneri, E., 'Le politiche per l'inserimento degli immigrati' (1992) 54 *Giornale di diritto del lavoro e delle relazioni industriali* 243, 254 ff.

asylum and the integration of ethnic minorities that would have been hard for policy-makers to imagine only few decades ago.[4]

On the other hand, in Southern European states, such as Italy, Portugal, Spain, and Greece, with histories characterized by emigration rather than immigration, the impact is more contradictory and sociologically less easy to interpret.[5] Commonly defined as 'transit areas', these countries have now become the final destinations for non-EU immigrants. Researchers investigating migration in Southern Europe agree that these countries, historical inexperienced in dealing with immigration, have adopted restrictive immigration policies under the influence of those found in Northern Europe and the USA.

Central European countries, such as Germany, Belgium, Switzerland, and Austria, are also currently having to cope with waves of immigrants from the former Soviet Union—in some cases like Germany, with specific legal problems relating to the acquisition of citizenship and the associated social rights—alongside the massive traditional presence of non-national residents from places such as Turkey.[6] In these countries, too, as the current situation in Austria confirms, the enormous scale of the phenomenon has given rise to disturbing political and institutional unrest.[7]

Moreover, as the collective European imagination links this new phenomenon directly to the problem of 'borders', and their defence against the continuous flow of clandestine immigrants, southern European countries increasingly feel under pressure from their northern counterparts. Following the Schengen agreement and its insertion into the *acquis communautaire*, their task within an integrated EU immigration policy is to 'hold' the southern border. This has clearly led to a state of convulsion and political neurosis in countries like Italy, where the problem of borders means controlling five thousand miles of coastline in an environment which has traditionally been 'indulgent towards immigrants'. The fear that Italy would become the weak link in the chain, and the point of entry

---

[4] See Favell, A., 'The Europeanisation of Immigration Politics' (1998) 2/10 *European Integration Online Papers* 1, 2.

[5] In Italy, public opinion oscillates between an excess of 'charitable good-heartedness'— i.e. 'accept everything and everyone'—above all, among Catholic volunteer groups, radical environmentalists and the far left, and attitudes of racism and xenophobia. See Spicacci, V., 'Coscienza civile, Coscienza cristiana e Immigrazione clandestina in Italia' (1999) I *La Civiltà Cattolica* 425.

[6] On Germany see Hönekopp, E., 'Labour Migration to Germany from Central and Eastern Europe—Old and New Trends' (1997) 23 *IAB Labour Market Research Topics* 1. For the different impact of the immigration phenomenon in Northern and Southern Europe see King, R., and Black, R., *Southern Europe and the New Immigrations* (Brighton: Sussex Academic Press, 1997).

[7] In Austria over 10% of the population is represented by immigrants and, according to demographic experts, this is the critical threshold beyond which dangerous tension may be unleashed.

for immigrants heading towards central Europe, probably precipitated recent domestic legislation, which is much closer to that found in America, with its controlled opening up of borders and processes of rational immigration planning. The problem of correct and efficient application of the law is, however, quite another matter.

Faced with these phenomena, observers of migratory flows have divided into two main camps: those who stress its extraordinary, exceptional nature; and those who, placing it in historical context, tending to see it as a normal cyclical occurrence.[8] However, an overall picture of the new migratory situation which has arisen in Europe at the dawn of the new millennium can be drawn. Originally an essentially economic issue linked to labour market dynamics, immigration in Europe has become increasingly dependent on demographic forces (a drop in the birth rate in Europe and an uncontrolled increase in other countries) and other political, ethnic, and religious factors, such as local wars and consequent dispersions. In addition to its economic implications, immigration has, therefore, taken on political and cultural dimensions, affecting not only social rights and the management of the labour market, but political rights, meaning basically the rights to asylum and to citizenship in a formal legal sense.[9]

In considering the immigration, increasing weight is also now given to the 'anti-crime policies' of the various states involved. Connected in this way to penal repression and domestic security policy, immigration is increasingly perceived by public opinion as a matter for the Ministries of the Interior rather than the Ministries of Labour. The co-existence within the EU of countries with experience of immigration with others for whom the problem is new has not prevented the search for a common political response. In this sense the trend can be said to be one of harmonization, or rather co-ordination or approximation of immigration and asylum policy. However, in the context of the policies of southern European countries, and drawing a distinction between *policies for immigration*[10] and

---

[8] Messina, A., 'The Not So Silent Revolution: Postwar Migration to Western Europe' (1996) 49 *World Politics* 130; Sassen, S., 'The De Facto Transnationalizing of Immigration Policy' in Sassen, S. (ed.), *Globalization and its Discontents* (New York: The New Press, 1998); Sassen, S., *Migranti, coloni, rifugiati. Dall'immigrazione di massa alla fortezza Europa* (Milan: Feltrinelli, 1999); Randall, H., 'Migration, Citizenship and Race in Europe: Between Incorporation and Exclusion' (1999) 35 *European Journal of Political Research* 415.

[9] On economic reductionism in approaches to the study of migratory flows see Borjas, G. J., Freeman R. B., and Katz L. F., *Searching for the Effect of Immigration on the Labor Market* (Cambridge, Mass.: National Bureau of Economic Research, 1996). On dual citizenship in social/symbolic and juridical/formal terms see Lo Faro, A., 'Immigrazione, lavoro, cittadinanza sociale: appunti per una ricerca' (1997) 4 *Giornale di diritto del lavoro e relazioni industriali* 535.

[10] Including provisions regarding immigrants already living in a country.

immigration policies,[11] a distinction typical of immigration law in the USA, the 1990s can be said to have been characterized by the introduction of essentially restrictive and regulatory laws, while provisions regarding the status of immigrants already living in these countries—in particular, integration and anti-discrimination policies—have been made almost an after-effect of the former and are not particularly innovative. Finally, in relation to the labour market, it is significant that the phenomenon of immigration in the last decade has coincided with high European rates of unemployment thus demonstrating the continuing validity of classical economic explanations of unemployment, based on the dual segmented structure of domestic labour markets.[12] The persistence of high unemployment rates means that several European countries will have to continue to cope with immigration from other countries over the next few years.[13] In the 1990s, however, the mechanisms regulating the flow of immigrants in the major European nations has passed from the market into the hands of the state.[14] While, therefore, immigration is still experienced in various contexts as an economic necessity, this is accompanied today by 'political' fear on the part of states about the potentially destabilizing impact of uncontrolled immigration on welfare systems (such as health systems guaranteeing universal assistance) which are already widely considered financially too burdensome. The dialectic between the increasingly fragmented and discontinuous economic requirements of the market, and the political and financial headaches of state welfare systems, underlies an unusual new relationship between migratory movements on the supply side, the black economy, and the increasing segmentation of the European labour markets.

This last point highlights the mutual links between instruments for border control and instruments of control which use the labour market; and the question of their relative effectiveness in contemporary conditions as instruments of immigration policy.[15] I will therefore offer an

---

[11] Including provisions to counteract the pressure of immigration and regulate the influx of new immigrants.

[12] See Bonifazi, above, n. 3, 260. See also the classic Piore, M. J., *Birds of Passage: Migrant Labor and Industrial Societies* (Cambridge/New York: Cambridge University Press, 1979).

[13] The number of immigrants needed to compensate for the rigidity of the domestic labour market in Germany has been calculated as 200,000 units a year: Hönekopp, above, n. 6, 22. A recent UN study, which did not gain the public attention it deserved, calculated that the number of immigrants needed in Italy to compensate for the dramatic negative increase in the population was 300,000 units.

[14] See Spire, A., 'De l'étranger à l'immigré. La magie sociale d'une catégorie statistique' (1999) 129 *Actes de la recherche en sciences sociales* 50, 51.

[15] According to reliable analyses, the complexity of immigration policies also depends on the types of control instruments in relation to three different aims: (a) reduction or construction of migratory potential; (b) control of the size of the migratory flow; (c) control of the labour market: Sciortino, above, n. 2, 53.

interpretative hypothesis which, while laying no claim to general validity, seems particularly appropriate to Italy and other southern European countries. The hypothesis can be stated as follows. First, the emphasis laid, from the mid-1980s onwards, on the problem of security and public order primarily represents an attempt by liberal-democratic states to assert new, discretionary, political powers over the acceptance of immigrants and to deal with domestic political pressures, rather than their inability to control immigration. Secondly, the loss of control that these states have experienced is not to be viewed in absolute terms, as the ability to control remains, to all intents and purposes, high but relative to unrealistic expectations based on a notion of *total* control. It seems likely that the relative inefficiency of the control systems in Italy and other countries such as Greece does not derive from an excess of legal guarantees in favour of immigrants, but from a calculation of the benefits involved: the high rate of irregular and clandestine immigration provides labour for the shadow economy, not only ensuring flexibility in various sectors of the labour market but also safeguarding the welfare system.[16] In Italy, in particular, the phenomenon of clandestine immigration is closely linked to the shadow economy, providing its 'structural backbone'. The growth of a vast informal economy is tolerated, or, at least, is not tackled through an application of the tools typical of labour market regulation: the application of effective sanctions against employers, the involvement of the trade unions, and the consequent effect of transparency on the labour market. In countries such as Sweden and Norway, where the control of clandestine immigration is more thorough as a result of labour market control—involving trade unions in accordance with the Scandinavian tradition—the shadow economy seems less prominent.[17] It appears that the problem of regulating immigration, which began with the labour market and then became a firm item on the agenda of external security and public order policies, is now recursively affecting important issues regarding labour market regulation.

II THE 'EUROPEAN FORTRESS': EU POLICIES ON IMMIGRATION

There is, therefore, a homogenizing trend in EU immigration policies, and, perhaps, across the world. Nevertheless, European states still jealously

[16] The paradox is that clandestine immigrants are excluded from the welfare system but contribute towards funding it, at least via indirect taxation. For an almost perfect balancing of this paradox in the Greek labour market see Reyneri, E., 'Inserimento degli immigrati nell'economia informale, comportamenti devianti e impato sulle societa di arrivo: alcune ipotesi di ricerca comparativa' (1996) 64 *Sociologia del Lavoro* 9.

[17] See Brochmann, G., *European Integration and Immigration from Third Countries* (Oslo: Scandinavian University Press, 1996).

claim powers and prerogatives over certain issues, giving rise to lasting differences in their respective legal systems—in relation, for example, to the admission of foreigners and the granting of citizenship. Moreover, the fact that the phenomenon of migration is increasingly recognized within the conceptual framework of the EU has not affected the categories of thought applied to the problem. Paradoxically, while the globalization of markets, deregulation, and the opening up of borders are now parts of economic debates world-wide, the logic typical of the nation-state, based on the defence of national sovereignty, still permeates 'state thought on immigration'.[18] Even more surprising is the fact that this kind of logic has permeated a supranational body like the EU, the political and cultural premises of which are supposedly based on downplaying national sovereignty and territoriality in favour of multilateral and federal relations.

The symptoms of the persistence of this 'state thought' in the construction of immigration policies in the EU can be traced. First, from the 1980s up to the Treaty of Amsterdam in the mid-1990s, the logic of inter-governmental co-operation prevailed over communitarian logic in defining common immigration policies. As a result, it was states themselves, with no intervention by EU institutions, that attempted to standardize EU immigration policies on the basis of a rigorous defence of national sovereignty. Intervention by the Commission and even the European Court of Justice was thus necessarily low-profile and limited.[19] Until the Treaty of Amsterdam, core EU migratory policies had, therefore, legal bases that were, by definition, 'extraneous' to the competence of the EU. The turning point marked by the Treaty of Amsterdam, more promise than reality, saw the EU undertake to enunciate in the near future a social policy regarding non-EU immigrants. This is by virtue of Article 12 (formerly Article 6) of the Treaty, which in solemn, almost emphatic, terms asserts the general principle of non-discrimination on the basis of nationality, and which might be seen as constituting an embryonic common Union policy on the matter. The undertaking, postponed until five years after the Treaty came into force, and with many restrictions and procedural constraints,[20] was to introduce common policies and specific EU competencies regulating entry and migratory flows, the granting of visas, freedom of movement for non-EU citizens inside the EU borders, the right to

[18] See Sayad, A., 'Immigration et "pensée d'état" ' (1999) 129 *Actes de la recherce en sciences sociales* 5, 7.
[19] This was basically due to the insufficiency of legal bases prior to the Amsterdam Treaty. This chapter does not take into account the Nice Treaty modification of the issue, since it is not yet in force.
[20] Specifically, the adoption of the principle of unanimity, with some exceptions regarding the issue of visas.

asylum, and the fight against illegal, clandestine immigration.[21] These limitations, however, cannot conceal the importance, at least at a symbolic/formal level, of the fact that competence regarding issues of immigration, asylum, and freedom of movement for non-EU citizens have been transferred from the third pillar (concerning provisions on police and judicial co-operation in criminal matters) to an autonomous title inserted into the Amsterdam Treaty (Part III, Title IV).[22] Finally, the prerogatives concerning the acquisition of European citizenship are still jealously reserved for the citizens of EU states, and there remains a reluctance to grant to non-European citizens political rights, such as the rights to vote and stand in local elections. In this way, in the terminology of legal scholars, alongside the notion of European citizenship based on a peculiar dual mechanism (in that it is complementary citizenship, derived from national citizenship), there is now a notion of '*Non-EU citizenship*' which is increasingly being evoked. It does not refer to a proper, autonomous juridical status, but to a *non-status*, something other than European citizenship. At a theoretically more refined level, the concept of 'immigrant', to which a certain social stigma is attached in Europe, is abandoned in favour of the more aseptic, neutral concept of 'foreigner', typical of legal and statistical sciences.[23]

In short, it seems clear that EU immigration policies are still strongly inspired by a purely functionalistic view of immigration and are typically gradualist in nature, despite the fact that immigration is raising with increasing vigour questions of democratic political legitimacy and social citizenship, connected as it is with the right to freedom of movement within the EU and access to the fundamental rights associated with European citizenship. In the near future, EU immigration policies are destined to move along the narrow ledge which separates the fears of the Member States, market requirements, and the democratic legitimacy of the Union. However, awareness that immigration policies represent a significant aspect of EU social and employment policies is timidly starting

[21] A vast amount of literature exists on the Schengen agreement and the complex provisions of the Treaty of Amsterdam concerning immigration and asylum: for analytical comment see Simpson, G., 'Asylum and Immigration in the European Union after the Treaty of Amsterdam' (1999) 5 *European Public Law* 91; Wagner, E., 'The Integration of Schengen into the Framework of the European Union' (1998) 25/2 *Legal Issues of European Integration* 1; Hailbronner, K., and Thiery, C., 'Schengen II and Dublin: Responsibility for Asylum Applications in Europe' (1997) 34 *Common Market L. Review* 957.

[22] See Wagner, above, n. 21, 2. It is significant that the Italian Constitutional Court (judgment no. 31, 3 Feb. 2000) should have recognized the substantial Europeanization of national norms regulating immigration and foreigner status. It is on the grounds of this recognition that the High Court declared the inadmissibility of the request for abrogation, by means of a repealing referendum on the legislative decree 286/98 which regulates immigration, put forward by the Lombard League, a political party suspected of xenophobia.

[23] See Spire, above, n. 14.

to surface. This new sensibility is confirmed in, at least, three important documents. First, in the December 1999 proposal for a European directive on the re-uniting of the families of migrant workers;[24] secondly, in the *Avis* of the Committee of the Regions, November 1999,[25] where reference to planning migratory flows through direct liaison with the countries of origin of immigrants becomes a measure of basic importance; and, finally, in the 2000 Commission guidelines on employment policies,[26] developed in the context of the European employment strategy outlined by the Treaty of Amsterdam, which contain a reference, albeit generic, to the insertion of immigrants into the single European labour market.

III IMMIGRATION POLICIES IN SOUTHERN EUROPEAN COUNTRIES:
BETWEEN CONTROL AND THE PROMOTION OF WELFARE

As far as southern European states are concerned, a period characterized by an almost total lack of mechanisms for intervention—the 1980s—has been followed by a period of widespread intervention. In all four Mediterranean countries—Italy, Greece, Portugal, and Spain—the interventions have been broadly the same in three fundamental ways: in the fight against illegal immigration, the increasingly cautious and conditional handling of asylum policies, and the handling of visas and entry permits, including bilateral admission agreements.[27]

What is most surprising is the counter-trend, relative to other continental European countries, with respect to the naturalization of immigrants and the acquisition of formal, juridical citizenship. In Greece, Portugal, and Italy, progressively more restrictive provisions were introduced in the 1990s, with hardly any public debate on either the bureaucratic procedures or the requirements for acquiring citizenship. In almost all Northern European countries, on the other hand, there has been a progressive acceptance of dual nationality and a gradual slackening of the requirements for naturalization.[28] Indeed, it is doubtful whether the supine adaptation of immigration policies in southern European countries to models that have

---

[24] COM (1999) 638 final.

[25] *Avis du Comité de régions*, 16 Nov. 1999, *Flux migratoires en Europe*, Com-7/019.

[26] Proposal for a Council Decision on guidelines for Member States' employment policies for the year 2000, COM (1999) 712 final.

[27] For a detailed analysis of the provisions introduced in Southern European countries in the 1990s see Baldwin-Edwards, above, n. 2, 506 ff. Only in visa policies, for obvious economic reasons connected with tourism, do the policies of Southern European states appear to be less restrictive than those of their Northern European counterparts.

[28] Germany represents an exception among European countries in that the norms regulating the acquisition of citizenship remain rigidly tied to the *ius sanguinis*, with cultural reminiscences of the idea of *Volk*.

been tried and tested in the north would be effective, given important differences in geography, administrative apparatus, state bureaucracy, and economic context.

As far as immigration policies are concerned, analogies can be seen in the normative structure of the most recent and significant provisions. For example, laws introduced in Italy and Spain combine measures to control entry with measures affecting the social and juridical status of immigrants in the host country. They make a clear attempt to reorganize the instruments available to control immigration through the labour market in order to plan and regulate immigration flows. Although the *external* control dimension is not neglected—hence the attempt to render the means of expulsion of illegal migrants more effective—new emphasis is given to *internal* control through specific interventions in the labour market. Most significant in this regard is the development of national migration policies through the establishment of annual flow rates and the planning of the number of immigrants to be inserted into the labour market. This has been accompanied by requiring immigrants to obtain ministerial authorization to work—to obtain so-called 'work permits', a complicated process in Italy. The aim of Italian legislators is to achieve almost complete transparency in the immigrant labour market through constant certification and monitoring. It is, however, doubtful whether the great flexibility required by labour markets—which are increasingly volatile and unstable—can be reconciled with complex administrative procedures and a normative system that clearly threatens rigidity. For example, the sanctions levied against those who aid and abet clandestine immigration, including collusive employers, have been revised and clearly hinder flexibility. The instruments regulating legal entry and settlement, such as residence permits and visas, have also been defined more clearly (pending EU harmonization). An organic system regulating the re-uniting of families has also been worked out, anticipating in both the Italy and Spain future EU trends as outlined in a proposed directive proposal submitted by the European Commission. In both countries, important provisions have also been introduced on the social and welfare rights of immigrants: the right to strike and to join trade unions, the provision of education, housing, health assistance, social security, equal access to public services, etc.[29] These may make more acute certain contradictions in national and regional labour markets: the flourishing of the informal economy in Italy is, in some ways, a distorted response to the economic crisis of the welfare state and the refusal to fund it, while the

---

[29] Spanish legislation has been tightened up by Act 8/2000 of 12 Dec. 2000, which restricts some of these rights to foreigners who obtain a residence permit or become domiciled in Spain.

heavy presence of immigrants in certain areas of the country, especially the larger cities, gives rise to paradoxical social stigmatization.[30] At the same time, they mark, symbolically, a historic moment in the process whereby immigration law in countries in which immigration is relatively new is brought into line with that of countries in which it is well-established. *Last but not least*, an absolute, but hardly effective, principle enshrined in the provisions is non-discrimination in access to employment on the ground of race, nationality, or religion—indirect discrimination being ascertained and eliminated by means of legal procedures that have been widely tested in legislation concerning equal opportunities for women. These legal procedures are well known in Italy for their capacity to combine subtlety and technical precision—for example, the partial inversion of the burden of proof—with a dearth of practical results. The new cluster of anti-discrimination norms is completed by civil procedural rules aimed at neutralizing infringements of anti-discrimination rights, by promoting collectively agreed schemes aimed at preventing discriminatory behaviour and removing discriminatory effects—and, lastly, by allowing for the payment of damages. It is of interest to note that in Italy and Spain the flow of positive action policies against indirect discrimination is exactly the opposite of that in the USA: from sex discrimination to race discrimination, rather than vice versa. The normative apparatus involved is, therefore, extremely well articulated. Its regulatory complexity reflects the social phenomenon it is intended to regulate, for immigration is becoming more and more like a mirror in which are reflected the legal and cultural structures, development dynamics, and labour market conditions of the host societies concerned. Notwithstanding the questionable effectiveness of the legal and administrative tools used, the policy line of Spanish and Italian legislators is clear.

The difficult, but commendable, goal is to find a balanced trade-off between the need to control immigration flows—through public-order measures and external border control, as well as through instruments typical of the labour market—and the need to develop policies promoting the insertion and integration of immigrants into the labour market. In other words, there is a renewed conviction that the labour market cannot do without the contribution of immigrants, but that their insertion should be

---

[30] 'As long as immigrants occupy the lowest positions and above all work in the unofficial labour market, they are stigmatised, whereas when they get better, steady jobs and become economically better integrated, they are seen as dangerous rivals for the local population and discriminatory attitudes and behaviour intensify': Reyneri, E., *Sociologia del mercato del lavoro* (Bologna: Il Mulino, 1996) 18 ff; 'This reinforces the typical vicious circle of economic crisis and welfare crisis, the growth of irregular employment, the increasing insertion of immigrants into the shadow economy, a more and more negative attitude towards immigrants and an increasingly rigid entry policy': Reyneri, E., 'Immigrazione ed economia sommersa' (1998) 53 *Stato e Mercato* 277 ff.

gradual and regulated so as to avoid the socially and politically negative effects that an unregulated flow of immigration might have. There is, therefore, a new awareness that work, 'although deprived of ideological emphasis and palingenetic hopes of renewal, is a basic factor in legitimizing cohabitation, social integration, and access to citizenship rights'.[31]

The immigration issue, in any case, highlights the typically Italian contradiction between the 'good-hearted' intentions of the legislators, the inefficiency of the results, and harsh reality. How can the policy declared by the government and legislators, embodied in a substantial set of norms and entrusted not only to the Ministries of Labour and the Interior but also to local administration, be reconciled with the reality of a prosperous, flourishing informal labour market that is regularly fed by flows of clandestine immigration? Is it a case of inefficient control mechanisms, or is it part of a more general sphere of unworkable policies and of the obsolete structural features and rigidity with which the Italian labour market is regulated? To try to sketch a possible answer to these questions, it is necessary to conduct a close investigation of the shadow economy in Italy and its relationship with immigration.

IV THE CONTRADICTIONS OF THE ITALIAN LABOUR MARKET SEEN THROUGH THE 'KALEIDOSCOPE' OF IMMIGRATION: THE CASE OF THE SHADOW ECONOMY

The link between immigration and the shadow economy obviously does not just concern southern Europe. The persistent increase in the flow of immigrants from the southern hemisphere and the former Communist countries, combined with the simultaneous tightening of immigration legislation, has caused the shadow economy to be supplied with a steady stream of clandestine or irregular immigrants, who find 'opportunities' in the increase in demand for poor, low-cost, unskilled, and insecure jobs in the more developed Western countries.

Some argue that it is not immigration itself that generates or nourishes the shadow economy, but that, on the contrary, the roots of the shadow economy are endogenous to the economies of developed countries, lying in the organizational and productive restructuring resulting from the shift from manufacturing to service-based industries. According to this view, there is a peculiar cause and effect relationship between the post-Fordist economy and the spread of the various components of the informal, shadow economy.[32] Others, however, tend to stress the inexhaustible

---

[31] Ambrosini, M., *Utili invasori* (Milan: Angeli, 1999) 13.

[32] See Sassen, S., 'The Informal Economy: Between New Developments and Old Regulations (1994) 103 *Yale L. Journal* 2289.

nature of the immigration flows sustaining the shadow economy, choices of destination being more conditioned by social and family ties than by a favourable legal or economic context.[33] In short, sociological investigations indicate that the presence of an irregular economy of varying proportions is a founding feature of the functioning of contemporary economic systems, and immigrant labour seems to fit the bill, especially if it is prevented from entering the labour market through more regular channels. The underworld of irregular labour can be considered a perfect environment in which immigrants, with paradoxical efficiency, meet the new requirements generated by transformations in the systems of production.[34]

If this is generally true, the vicious circle of illegal immigration and the shadow economy is likely to appear more evident in southern Europe, where it is sustained by even closer mutual ties. In this context, the needs of workers and their lack of alternative sources of income are often the main, if not the only, factors underlying the shadow economy. The specific structural features of the labour market, together with the regulatory anomalies in policies governing the issue of residence permits, the successive waves of regularization of immigrants who have entered the national territory illegally, and the atavistic inefficiency of the control apparatus have done the rest: these structural conditions have inevitably become the cultural context in which irregular immigration and the shadow economy are conjoined. These factors have ended up producing wide sectors of shadow economy sustained by irregular or clandestine immigration, the dimensions of which cannot be compared with those of central and northern Europe, In Italy, in particular, a deeply rooted shadow economy based on endogenous structural factors—not least the widespread presence of small family-run enterprises and artisan workshops, and the fragmentation of local labour markets (linked, among other things, to the great North/South divide)[35]—has favoured the flow of irregular immigration, especially in the last decade. A permanent feature of the domestic labour market, these irregular immigrants have become a strong underground stream flowing into the catchment basin of the shadow economy. The factors behind this vicious circle are predom-

---

[33] See Massey, D. S., and Espinosa, K., E., 'What's Driving Mexico–US Migration? A Theoretical, Empirical and Policy Analysis' (1997) 102 *American Journal of Sociology* 939, exploring the factor of 'social networks' in relation to Mexican immigration in the USA.

[34] See Ambrosini, above, n. 31, 103; for the situation in the USA and Japan respectively see Foo, J. L., 'The Vulnerable and Exploitable Immigrant Workforce and the Need for Strengthening Worker Protective Legislation' (1994) 103 *Yale L. Journal* 2112, and Stalker, P., *Les travailleurs immigrés. Étude des migrations internationales de main–d'œuvre* (Geneva: BIT,1995).

[35] For recent data concerning the different geographical shadow economy rates in Italy and the rest of Europe see Berretta, G., Caruso, B., and Ricci, G., *Lavoro sommerso (dossier)*, *DMLonLine* 1 (1999), http://www.lex.unict.it/dml-online/archivio/archivio.htm.

inantly economic and social in nature, interactively linked with not only the demand for but also the supply of labour. Legal and institutional factors, however, have also contributed to the phenomenon, especially in Italy: the poor functioning of the control instruments concerned with the general regulation of the labour market and its endemic rigidity and inefficiency; the particular character of immigration policies and the connected systems of external control and public order; and the malfunctioning of the policies regulating entry, control, expulsion, recurrent regularization, and so on.

The economic and social factors at the root of the peculiar relationship between irregular immigration and the shadow economy can be summarized as follows. First, in Italy the development of domestic and personal services (cleaning, catering, care of the elderly, childcare) and the restructuring of certain traditional, low-technology sectors (building, agriculture, small enterprises) have caused an increase in the demand for unskilled, low-cost labour endowed with a flexibility that the official labour market cannot provide; what is more, Italian citizens are becoming increasingly unwilling to take on such menial tasks. To this situation we must add a particular feature of the Italian labour market concerning young people with qualifications: their employment rate is lower than the European average but they tend to stay at home longer and refuse, *pour cause*, offers of jobs not considered appropriate to their social and professional status and, indeed, thought harmful to career prospects. This specific feature of the Italian labour market accounts for the greater availability of unqualified job opportunities for both regular and irregular immigrants. It also explains the essentially complementary and non-competitive nature of the immigrant workforce.

Secondly, on the labour demand side, the high costs of tax and welfare contributions (due to the great national debt amassed, above all, in the 1980s) favour not only the widespread evasion of tax and welfare payments, but also violation of the minimum wage standards laid down by national collective agreements; in this way, whole sectors and individual enterprises, especially the smaller ones operating in *labour intensive* fields, can maintain levels of productivity and competitiveness that would otherwise be unattainable. The result is that irregular immigrants are particularly exposed to these evasive practices, or, rather, are 'privileged' for reasons of mutual convenience since, to safeguard their irregular or clandestine status and avoid expulsion, they do not apply to labour inspectors or to the judicial authorities for recognition of their salary and pension rights. This gives rise to connivance between employers and employees—and recruitment by word of mouth—and fosters a peculiar chain of illegal immigration. It is more convenient to take on clandestine or irregular immigrants than to offer jobs 'off the books' to both Italian

citizens and immigrants in possession of residence permits, both categories having the same rights as regards wages and welfare contributions.
The only way, therefore, for businesses operating in sectors such as the
retail trade, agriculture, domestic and personal services, building, transport, and tourism—all labour-intensive sectors with low levels of technological innovation and productivity growth, and ones in which it is also
difficult to bring about externalization and extension beyond national
borders—to reduce their costs has been to dip into the reservoir of irregular or clandestine immigrant labour.[36] Faced with such a distortion of the
labour market, Italian legislators have offered purely repressive
responses, the latest provisions introducing quite a substantial increase in
the administrative and penal sanctions against employers who take on
clandestine or irregular immigrants 'off the books', and against the immigrants themselves, who may face expulsion. But it is clear that increasing
sanctions does not in itself mean more effective control, as the peculiar
combination of mutual convenience between employers and employees
leaves the task of detecting irregular immigration to the inspection
authorities, or, in more serious cases (such as forced labour, which is
widespread among the Chinese community), to the police. Moreover, the
perverse economic balance that the shadow economy creates in certain
areas of the country has held back not only public inspections but also
trade union interventions aimed at tackling the problem at source. There
must, therefore, be doubts about the likely effectiveness in Italy of a strategy to deal with clandestine immigrant workers which is based only on
repression—even if in Northern European countries such as Sweden and
Norway repressive measures to control the labour market have been
widely and effectively used to counter irregular and clandestine immigration.

A further factor that, historically, has supported the vicious circle of
irregular immigration and the shadow economy in Italy is the composition of immigrant labour and the chains of migration that have attracted
flows of non-regular immigrants in the last ten years, not in very large
numbers—there has not been the 'invasion' that certain anecdotes
suggest—but certainly in numbers larger than in the past. Beyond the
sociological data confirming that immigrants tend to overestimate
the opportunities and underestimate the difficulties of insertion into the
labour market, it is well established that many immigrants, searching for
an improvement in their standards of living, tend to consider Italy as a
country that is easy to get into and even easier to stay in because of the
ineffectiveness of its control mechanisms; and also a country where relatively well-paid jobs are available and where levels of racist and xeno-

---

[36] See Reyneri (1998), above, n. 30, 331.

phobic intolerance are still quite low, albeit increasing. The attractiveness of the Italian shadow economy for irregular immigrants is, therefore, evident: it is the only way, besides more risky illegal or criminal activities, for people without residence permits to remain in Italy and to earn an income. Far from being an effect of illegal immigration in Italy, therefore, the shadow economy is more likely the cause. The supply of and demand for labour thus give rise to a direct correlation between work by irregular and clandestine immigrants and the shadow economy. Paradoxically, the stiffening of sanctions against both employers and workers introduced by the 1998 legislative reforms has actually brought the interests of these groups closer together, and represents a major obstacle to detection, becoming, perhaps counter-intuitively, an important factor in inducing the submersion of immigrant labour.

Finally, it should be noted that the equality of wages and normative treatment of immigrant and native workers—implied by the legal mechanisms regulating the administrative authorization to work and the employers' duty to respect collective agreements—produce a convergence of working conditions for native and immigrant workers in the regular labour market. This hinders any strategy aimed at uncovering clandestine and immigrant labour by offering employers incentives based on the possibility of less rigid treatment, or derogation from existing legal and contractual provisions. However, the abstract, prescriptive aspect of the constitutional principle of equality, especially in its negative dimension—the prohibition of discrimination—cannot be questioned. Indeed, it is widely held among legal scholars that obligatory equal treatment of both national workers and immigrants has indirect regulatory effects on the labour market: on the one hand, protecting immigrants; on the other, operating as a way of regulating the labour market in relation to the effectiveness of citizens' right to work, tempering domestic social dumping phenomena. From this perspective, equality and equal treatment are absolute and non-derogatable rules, particularly if seen in terms not only of banning unequal treatment but also of securing substantial equality.

When applied to immigration, this rigid and egalitarian model of labour law, widespread in continental Europe, presupposes the mechanical transfer of a series of rights envisaged for a uniform national labour market to a type of work whose very *raison d'être* is mobile, fragmented, territorialized labour markets. In these markets, the need for flexible adaptability derives not only from the demand and the need for flexibility in norms and salaries to enhance the competitiveness of the businesses involved, but also from the social characteristics of the labour supply: from its the need for seasonal, provisional work, for income during particular periods, and its lack of interest in comprehensive welfare coverage; in other words, from the life plans of individual immigrants.

However, the difficulties involved in envisaging a modification of the principle of equality (the possibility of a derogation from the rigid system of rights guaranteed by law and collective agreements), although perhaps justifiable in terms of revealing at least some of the various aspects of irregular immigration, has recently been the source of disagreements, even within the Italian trade union movement, over the most appropriate strategies for a less comprehensive application of the principle of equality. These strategies are legitimated by reference to a model in which labour law rules are differentiated. The goal is to identify the most effective and efficient regulatory dynamics for the labour market and involves the broader question of the relationship between the integration of immigrant workers in the host society and the concrete essence of social citizenship, with particular reference to the actual enjoyment of fundamental rights and the principle of equal opportunity.

V EQUALITY OF TREATMENT AND ADAPTATION OF THE RULES: WHAT ARE THE PROSPECTS OF 'SOCIAL CITIZENSHIP' FOR IMMIGRANTS IN THE LABOUR MARKETS OF SOUTHERN EUROPE?

The contrast between the egalitarian and the adaptive (or differentiated) models has, in a sense, been the main topic in the debates relating to the evolution of labour law, and even European constitutional systems themselves, faced as they are at the turn of the millennium with the challenge of globalization. The debate has involved the more general question of equality, the latter serving as a mirror reflecting both the genesis and the various stages of development of the discipline. The dialectic between the egalitarian and adaptive models, between formal and substantive equality, has become the 'very essence of rationality in labour law'.[37] In this way, the thread of equality has brought together the various public policies needed to cope with a growing conflicts of interest and values that are increasingly difficult to reduce to the trade-off between capital and labour that has been the unifying feature of modern European social constitutions. As Massimo D'Antona, writing on the destiny of labour law at the end of the second millennium, pointed out, the phenomenon of immigration, along with the prospect of federalism (at supranational and infranational levels) and intergenerational justice, is one of the main elements of constitutional complexity that labour law—as a result of its heritage of interconnected principles, values and policies—has to face.[38]

---

[37] See Supiot, A., 'Principio di eguaglianza e limiti della razionalità giuridica' (1992) 2 *Lavoro e Diritto* 211, 216.

[38] D'Antona, M., 'Diritto del lavoro di fine secolo: una crisi di identità?' (1998) 2 *Rivista giuridica del Lavoro* 311, and English translation, in this volume. See also Supiot, A. (ed.), *Au delà de l'emploi* (Paris: Flammarion, 1999).

The growth of the informal, shadow economy, copiously fed by immigration, is a challenge not only to equality *in* labour law but to the very effectiveness *of* labour law and its regulatory apparatus, effectiveness being one of its main aims. The scale of the shadow economy in southern European countries, especially Italy, is a clear indication of the inefficiency and obsolescence of the rules governing the labour market and the systems safeguarding employment rights, not to mention the inefficiency of the tax and contributions systems. The figures provide irrefutable proof against any attempt to search for a solution to the problem elsewhere. It is true that sociological research tells us that important phenomena of this sort are rarely rooted in a single cause but are symptomatic of systemic complexity. And it is also true that in terms of practical policies a low level of tax and contributions and a high level of deregulation—as in the USA—are not in themselves sufficient to eliminate all interaction between the shadow economy and immigration. This is why, as the moral limits of utilitarian rationalism become ever hazier, the claim that 'the shadow economy may not look good but is useful', is no longer just murmured but almost raised as a bludgeon against all that remains of the American system of labour law.[39] Extreme ideologies apart, however, serious investigations in the field seem to have confirmed that the more coercive, rigid, and homogeneous the rules, the more likely that they will be found intolerable and the more frequently they will be broken.[40] In Italy, the *de facto* alternative to the egalitarian model turns out to be social fracture and, consequently, a dualistic model: on the one hand, egalitarian rules (irrespective of legal citizenship) for regular workers (native workers, EU citizens, and foreigners with proper authorization); and, on the other hand, a total lack of application of those rules to 'off the books' workers, with no formal discrimination but statistically evident effects of indirect discrimination towards non-EU citizens and native workers in certain areas of southern Italy.

It is likely that the absence of trade union strategies for adapting labour law will result in its becoming increasingly ineffective for a growing sector of the labour market, a large slice of which is represented by immigrants occupied in the informal sector and consensually engaging in the so-called 'right to self-exploitation'. Moreover, when adaptation of the rules governing labour law to the particular features of labour markets and to the particular characteristics of the labour supply—or, to put it

---

[39] See Priest, G. L., 'The Ambiguous Moral Foundations of the Underground Economy' (1994) 103 *Yale L. Journal* 2259; and further references in Caruso, B., 'Lavoro sommerso e ruolo del sindacato' (1999) 3 *Rivista Giuridica del Lavoro* 79 ff.

[40] See generally Paglin, M., 'The Underground Economy: New Estimates from Household Income and Expenditure Surveys' (1994) 103 *Yale L. Journal* 2239; for immigrant work in Italy, see Ambrosini, above, n. 31.

differently, when identification of a new balance between safeguarding the rights of those who have a job and providing opportunities for those who do not—involves the question of immigrants, anti-discrimination policy immediately springs to mind. The mechanisms for banning discrimination are understandably set at very high levels of sensitivity.

New trade union strategies for the social integration of immigrants through the right to work

The difficulties involved in integrating immigrants, the dramatic statistics on the informal economy, and the ineffectiveness of administrative and legal anti-discriminatory measures in Italy and also in Spain,[41] have induced some Italian trade unions to seek to adapt the rules to favour the social integration of immigrant workers. The decision to do this was probably dictated by the belief that a legislative framework based exclusively on equality and respect for minorities is no longer, in itself, sufficient to ensure social citizenship through work, and that more articulated, active employment policies are required. In local-level social pacts, in particular, agreement has been reached between certain trade unions, employers associations, and local administrators—the so-called Milan pact of 1 February 2000, signed without the agreement of the CGIL (Confederazione Generale Italiana del Lavoro), the main Italian trade union confederation which is left-wing oriented—with the specific aim of promoting jobs for immigrants and other marginalized groups, albeit in temporary positions and in unskilled, labour-intensive sectors. In exchange, the unions obtained a public commitment to improve vocational training for the groups involved and a promise on the part of the enterprises concerned to implement employment stabilization processes. Two questions arise out of the Milan pact. First, can policies aimed at uncovering non-regular, immigrant labour, or at inserting into the labour market a regular but unemployed immigrant workforce—regarded in the same way as other weak segments of the native workforce (ex-convicts, the long-term unemployed) who have been excluded from the official labour market—legitimate channelling of these workers into flexible, unskilled, labour-intensive jobs (housework, care, etc.), without violating the principle of non-discrimination? That is, does social citizenship obtained through work that is flexible, initially temporary, but regulated, legitimate an institutional and legal strategy aimed at placing workers on the first step of the employment ladder in jobs that do not necessarily

---

[41] See Perez Molina, R., *Labour Market Discrimination Against Migrant Workers in Spain, Part B, Discrimination Against Immigrant Workers in Access to Employment in Spain: From Worthless Paper to Effective Legislation* Geneva: ILO, 1998), http://www.ilo.org/public/english/protection/migrant/publ/index.htm.

belong to the 'three Ds' category—*dirty, dangerous,* and *dull*? If so, it would represent an active employment policy, a conscious, deliberate choice, rather than a policy which leaves things in the hands of a deregulated free market. Secondly, can the aim of social citizenship and integration through work legitimate the adaptation of general labour rules—still, of course, under the protection of the principle of anti-discrimination—for immigrant workers, both within the limits contemplated by the general legislation (the short-term contracts authorized by the pact) and in further local-level pacts (through negotiated planning in other areas at occupational risk) with the possibility, for example, of derogating from nationally agreed wage standards to favour the insertion or regularization of immigrants? Put bluntly and provocatively, is it possible to envisage positive action for employment in terms of pejorative treatment for a category of workers otherwise condemned to unemployment or black market labour?

In this case, the trade union strategy presupposes that access to social citizenship and the principle of equality of treatment for immigrants are closely connected with getting them over the threshold separating them from work (by law, the status of legal worker is followed by regularization so as far as immigration norms are concerned). In choosing between strengthening equality of treatment measures, which are symbolically important but constantly run the risk of ineffectiveness,[42] and instruments that promote the demand for labour and active employment policies for the immigrant workforce, the Milan Pact definitely opts for the latter.

VI THE RIGHT TO WORK, SOCIAL CITIZENSHIP, NEW TERMS OF EQUALITY: OUTLINES FOR A RESEARCH AGENDA

The two questions outlined above raise problems concerning values and relative policy choices. The legitimacy of such a strategy cannot be based only on a new functionalist paradigm of labour law (efficient labour policies, a market that functions, as measured through quantitative indices and results). These and other similar choices can be legitimated only by developing a theoretical paradigm based on a new trade-off between the values and principles present in European constitutions inspired by the principle of social welfare. It is probable, however, that the order of priority of these values and principles should be changed, and that a revised

---

[42] In Italy there are no empirical studies on the judicial application of anti-discrimination measures in the treatment of immigrant to compare with the research conducted by Molina Perez in Spain; if such studies were available, the conclusions reached would probably be quite similar in terms of ineffectiveness.

view of equality is needed to support a concept of social citizenship permeated by the constitutional principle of the right to work, which in Continental juridical culture has quite a different significance from what it has in Anglo-Saxon culture and American legislation. This suggests that a new constitutional compromise is needed.

The impact of globalization on the nation-state, in fact, legitimates a new interpretation of the constitutional right to work in the light of the multi-ethnic and multi-racial, if not multicultural, dimensions acquired by both societies and their domestic labour markets. This new reading would extend international provisions (specifically, ILO Convention 47), in as much as the right to work should be recognized as a universal social right and not be limited to the citizens of the state in question. In other words, the methodology used should be similar to that which suggests a multicultural reconsideration—albeit in an extreme version of cosmopolitanism and deconstructivism—of basic human rights, based on a vision of globalization that is not purely economic, but social, political, and cultural.[43]

In Italy, the recent law on immigration has repealed earlier provisions allowing 'reasonable discrimination' based on a 'priority test' guaranteeing native and EU workers precedence in access to work. In this way, it is recognized that the objective needs of labour markets, in countries where immigration has only recently become a problem, have revived the historical emancipatory and egalitarian significance of the right to work, extended not only to native and EU workers but also to non-EU citizens. The functional complexity of the relationship between immigration and the labour market, in fact, allows for a different ordering which connects recognition of identity through inclusion in the labour market and the acquisition of differentiated social citizenship and cultural integration. The prospect is thus one in which, in Touraine's words, *'diversity and equality are not only not contradictory but inseparable'*. Within this framework, adaptation of the rules—reducing the risk of the colonization of life worlds[44] implicit in imposing an egalitarian model on subjects whose personal plans are migratory, variable, volatile, and differentiated— makes it possible to legitimate *active strategies* to correct the marginalized conditions of immigrants, handled collectively on a territorial basis but with the full involvement of the individuals concerned, as an antidote to the evident risk of segregation and the ethnicization of marginality.

The heart of the matter can thus be put in the following terms: it is a

---

[43] See de Sousa Santos, B., 'Toward a Multicultural Conception of Human Rights' (1997) 1 *Sociologia del Diritto* 27.

[44] Habermas, J., *Teoria dell'agire comunicativo* (Bologna: Il Mulino, 1986); Simitis, S., 'Il diritto del lavoro e la riscoperta dell'individuo' (1990) 12 *Giornale di diritto del lavoro e di relazioni industriali* 87.

question whether the right to work legitimates differential treatment, justified as a means to an end; and, therefore, whether it is recognized that trade unions have not only the power to bring out differences in identity, subordinating the right to difference to the principle of *tolerance* and *respect* for universally recognized individual rights (and thus against any form of cultural holism), but also the power to modify legal and contractual regulations where explicit adaptation is needed to reflect the specific characteristics and particular requirements of various types of immigrants. The prospect opens up the question of trade union representation in relation to policies of differentiated recognition applied to the problematic relationship between trade unions and immigrants. This, in turn, raises questions of identity and of the function of trade unions in multiethnic societies; and of the crisis of the general class-based trade union model (typical in particular of southern European countries) when faced with the challenge of differences, multiple representation strategies, and classless inequalities. The *right to work* could thus become a launching pad for a new constitutional compromise, based on a milder, less Manichaean, vision of flexibility, seen as differentiation that is not in conflict with a new interpretation of the constitutional principle of equality.

16

The Imagined European Community: Are Housewives European Citizens?

MARGRIET KRAAMWINKEL*

'We have an urgent need for identity, for a European self image.'[1]

I THE EUROPEAN IDENTITY

It has been argued that a nation-state needs some idea of national identity and national culture—an 'Imagined Community', as Benedict Anderson calls it.[2] The creation of a nation-state cannot be achieved without (creating) ties between the people living in that state. In modern Europe, the borders have been drawn rather arbitrarily and have changed over and over again. Alsace Lorraine, for example, has been alternately French and German territory. Thus, the nation-state is not a natural phenomenon but a construction. It is necessary to stress both its singularity and special characteristics to separate one state from another and to tie bonds between those who live in a state. This is especially the case if the nation-state develops into a welfare state. Indeed, De Swaan[3] argues that since the modern northern European welfare states presuppose some form of solidarity and redistribution of income, the distinction between the in-group and the out-group becomes even more important. Thus, inclusion and exclusion are the basis of the Northern European welfare nation-states and the construction of community through the imagination of national identity and culture lies at the heart of the welfare state.

* Parts of this paper were originally presented as 'E non voglio più servir—an Essay on Soccer and the Welfare State', presented at the fourth Damwoude conference, Bergen aan Zee, the Netherlands, 31 May–2 June 1996; 'Prostitutes, Housewives and Soccer Players: The Economic Identity of the European Worker', presented at the Critical Legal Conference, University of East London, Sept. 1996; and, under the current title, at a workshop on The Sociology of European Community Law, International Institute for the Sociology of Law, Oñati, 25–26 Sept. 1997. I would like to thank Jim Bergeron, Joanne Conaghan, Thomas Spijkerboer, and Maaike Wienk for helpful and critical comments on previous drafts of this paper, and Deborah Maranville, for her encouragement.
    [1] Bishop Muskens of Breda as cited in *De Volkskrant*, 29 Oct. 1996, 3.
    [2] Anderson, B., *Imagined Communities: Reflections on the Origin and Spread of Nationalism* (London: Verso, 1983).
    [3] De Swaan, A., *In Care of the State: Health Care, Education and Welfare in Europe and the USA in the Modern Era* (Cambridge: Polity Press, 1988).

This imagination can consist of several aspects. Habits or structures can be called 'typically Dutch' to make clear that they are elements of Dutch national identity. A variety of things can be claimed to be constituents of national identity: ranging from sports, via food, to the organization of the welfare state, or from soccer, via French fries with mayonnaise, to the unpaid care tasks women perform. Common ideas about family and gender relations play an essential role in creating national identities.[4] For example, in the Netherlands, governmental policy officially promotes part-time work both for women and men in order to enable them also to perform unpaid care tasks. The creation of greater possibilities for paid (public or private) care like flexible day-care centres is rejected as not fitting with 'the Dutch culture of self-care' (read: the fact that Dutch women have so long performed care tasks without being paid).[5] Thus, self-care (unpaid labour of women) is constructed as a constituent of Dutch national culture and identity.

Nationality and national identity are most visible in a passport, and, with that, in citizenship. Citizenship is also characterized by inclusion and exclusion. The citizen is included and the non-citizen excluded from the national community.[6] Inclusion of a citizen means more than just the emotional aspects of belonging.[7] This emotional sense of belonging to a community, the identity-based link between the citizen and the community (or citizenship as an identity-generating element), is the first aspect of the dynamic relation between the citizen and the polity to which s/he belongs. The second is the political link between citizen and community or the primal citizenship of political participation (citizenship practice). Citizenship practice is first and foremost linked with political rights. Citizens have more rights than non-citizens. The most important example of a citizenship right is the right to vote. But there is more to citizenship than political rights[8]—T.H. Marshall,[9] for example, divided citizenship into civil, political, and social rights. Like De Swaan later, he thus

[4] See the papers collected in: Yuval-Davis, N., and Anthias, N. F. (eds.), *Woman—Nation—State* (London: MacMillan, 1989); and: Kofman, E., and Sales, R., 'The Geography of Gender and Welfare in Europe' in Monk, J., and García-Ramon, M. D. (eds.), *Women of the European Union. The Politics of Work and Daily Life* (London: Routledge, 1996) 37.

[5] Kraamwinkel, M., 'Herverdeling van zorg en arbeid. Bespreking rapport "Onbetaalde zorg gelijk verdeeld"' ('Redistribution of Labour and Care. A Critique of the Report "Unpaid Care Distributed Equally"') [1996] 2 *Nemesis* 50–6.

[6] Dahrendorf, R., *The Modern Social Conflict* (London: Weidenfeld and Nicolson, 1988) 25–47.

[7] Wiener, A., 'Citizenship in a Non-State' in Wiener, A., *'European' Citizenship Practice—Building Institutions of a Non-state* (Boulder, Col.: Westview Press, 1997), 3–18.

[8] Van Gunsteren, H., *A Theory of Citizenship: Organizing Plurality in Contemporary Democracies* (Boulder, Col.: Westview Press, 1998).

[9] Marshall, T. H., *Citizenship and Social Class* (Cambridge: Cambridge University Press, 1950).

connected the nation-state and the welfare state with a broad concept of citizenship as glue, there to hold everything together.

Both national citizenship and national identities are challenged by the development of larger entities like the European Union and, indeed, the fear of losing one's national identity in the expanding European Union continues to grow. At the same time, it is arguable that a European identity is now gradually developing. This is a quite difficult project as the European Union lacks concrete aspects of identity which appeal to the imagination of its inhabitants, like French fries with mayonnaise. The European identity is an abstract concept. The emotional sense of belonging to a group is fairly non-existent. 'You can't love a market', claimed Jacques Delors, and, although the rise of free market economics may seem to contradict this statement, I think most Europeans would agree with Delors.

Like the nation-state, the developing European Union takes shape through a process of exclusion and inclusion. Explicitly excluded from the European image are so-called third-country nationals. Even legally established immigrants are kept out of the imagined community of Europeans and cannot, for instance, invoke the non-discrimination clauses in the Treaty to complain about discrimination against them (the Treaty is meant to abolish discrimination only between nationals of Member States). 'Fortress Europe' is closing its gates. You are in if you are a national of one of the Member States of the European Union and you are out if you are a third country national.[10] And once you're in, the citizenship of the Community, established by the Maastricht Treaty in Article 17(1) [8(1)] EC,[11] and solemnly declaring that: 'Citizenship of the Union is hereby established', descends upon you. Lacking the emotional ties, EC citizenship is the inclusionary process through which a European identity is developed. But the notion of European citizenship is not unproblematic, as we will see.[12]

In this chapter I will look at the gender dimension of European citizenship. By now, a vast body of literature exists exploring gendered aspects of European welfare states and notions of citizenship in that context.[13] Most of this literature is written by political scientists and

---

[10] Curtin, D., and Geurts, M., 'Race Discrimination and the European Union Anno 1996: From Rhetoric to Legal Remedy?' (1996) 14 *Netherlands Quarterly of Human Rights* 147–71.

[11] The Amsterdam Treaty changed the numbers of the Articles of the EC Treaty. In this chapter I will add the old numbers in square brackets: [O].

[12] I will not discuss the question whether the dual belonging to a community—both national and European—is possible. See generally Aron, R., 'Is Multinational Citizenship Possible?' (1974) 41 *Social Research* 638–56; see also Wiener, above, n. 7, 3–18.

[13] See, e.g., the papers collected in: Sainsbury, D. (ed.), *Gendering Welfare States* (London: Sage, 1994). See further: Hoskyns, C., *Integrating Gender* (London: Verso, 1996) and Meehan, E., *Citizenship and the European Community* (London: Sage, 1993), 26–9 and 101–2. On social rights and citizenship see also Marshall's classic work, above, n. 9.

sociologists. What I want to do is to analyse European citizenship from a legal point of view, restricting my analysis to the contents of European citizenship as it has developed in the Maastricht Treaty and the case law of the European Court of Justice (ECJ). I will argue that in EC law, the word 'citizen' in effect means 'worker'. Thus, if we want to understand the nature of European identity and citizenship, an analysis of the legal construction of the European worker is imperative.

In pursuit of this analysis, I will focus on three decisions of the ECJ, addressing the economic status of prostitutes, soccer players, and house-wives respectively. Each case contains a discussion of the concept of worker and all reveal a conception of the European worker as more than just an employee in a standard employment relationship. Outlining the European identity, I will sketch the consequences of this case law for the future position of women in Europe. In this context, it is worth drawing attention to the growing analsyis of EC case law from a feminist perspective, exemplified in the recent work of Clare McGlynn,[14] Tamara Hervey, and Jo Shaw.[15] These authors point to ways in which the ECJ has used its relative freedom in interpreting the Treaty to restrict the equality concept, suggesting, therefore, that the ECJ, by strictly limiting the utility of sex equality law, has failed to bring about any significant improvement in women's lives. This chapter has a slightly different focus, using the economic background of the Union as a framework for analysis, and comes, too, to a different conclusion. My conclusion is that EC case law has a huge effect on women's lives and can be very helpful in achieving improvement in women's lives.

II THE EUROPEAN CITIZEN

As a true act of creation, the Maastricht Treaty declares European citizen-ship established and thus expresses in formal terms what Europe can give its people: citizenship. By naming the phenomenon, the Maastricht Treaty, in a way, creates citizenship. Thus, it is the starting point for this analysis. In the section on citizenship of the Union[16] (Articles 17–22 [8–8e]), the content of European citizenship is elaborated in terms of a series of individual rights. Article 18 [8a] confers a right to free movement (which is subject to the limitations and conditions in the Treaty); Article

[14] McGlynn, C., 'Ideologies of Motherhood in European Community Sex Equality Law' (2000) 6 *European Law Journal* 29–44.

[15] Hervey, T., and Shaw, J., 'Women, Work and Care: Women's Dual Role and Double Burden in EC Sex Equality Law' (1998) 8 *Journal of European Social Policy* 43.

[16] See generally Weatherill, S., and Beaumont, P., *EC Law* (Harmondsworth: Penguin, 1993) 9–13.

19 [8b] the right to vote and stand as a candidate in municipal elections and elections for the European Parliament in the community of residence; and Article 20 [8c], the right to protection by diplomatic or consular authorities in countries where one's own Member State is not represented. Article 21 [8d] contains the right to address a petition to the European Parliament, and Article 22 [8e] obliges the Commission to report to the Parliament, the Council, and the Economic and Social Committee on the implementation of the section. The first right of the European Citizen is thus the right to free movement. Mobility is the central right around which the others orbit. Without the right to free movement, Articles 19–21 make no sense at all and are merely ornamental. What good would it do to be able to vote in a community of residence other than in your country of nationality if you cannot go there? So, if freedom of movement is the central characteristic of European citizenship, what does this right to mobility mean? More pertinently, who qualifies for this right?[17]

The first group of nationals of Member States who have the right to residence in other Member States are the 'rich': nationals of Member States of independent means,[18] elderly people with a sufficient pension,[19] and students,[20] provided there is no fear that they will have to apply for subsistence income in the country of residence. The second group consists of those who can invoke Articles 39 [48] (free movement of workers), 43 [52] (freedom of establishment), and 49 [59] (free movement of services) of the EC Treaty. For the freedom of movement of persons, Article 39 is by far the most relevant provision.[21] The term 'worker' in Article 39 has a Community law content and has been developed by the Court. Thus, at the core of the right to freedom of movement in Article 19 [8a], is the concept of worker as elaborated in the Court's case law. The rights that come with European citizenship predominately descend upon the worker, as workers can invoke not only the protection of Article 39 and the Regulations, but also the equal treatment provisions in the Treaty and the Directives, as we will see below. This citizenship entitles European migrants[22] to a set of rights.[23] European migrants are entitled to social

---

[17] Although the *Martinez Sala* decision (C–85/96 [1998] ECR I–2691) has by some authors been heralded as the beginning of something new, as nationals of other Member States do get citizenship rights, its main statement is that a national of another Member State—being a citizen of the Union—has the right 'not to suffer discrimination on grounds of nationality within the scope of application *ratione materiae* of the Treaty' (paras. 61–62). Also, *Sala* is mainly decided on the basis of Art. 39, not on the basis of Art. 18 which contains European citizenship.   [18] Directive 90/364 [1990] OJ L180/26.
[19] Directive 90/365 [1990] OJ L180/28.   [20] Directive 93/96 [1996] OJ L317/59.
[21] See generally Bercusson, B., *European Labour Law* (London: Butterworths, 1996), 386–96.
[22] By 'European migrants', I mean migrants who are nationals from a Member State, to distinguish them from migrants who are third-country nationals.
[23] Weatherill and Beaumont, above, n. 16, 481–4.

security on the same basis as nationals of the Member States where they reside. Furthermore, Regulation 1612/68 stipulates that, under certain conditions, the European migrating worker can take his family with him if he moves to another EC country. However, the rights of these dependent family members are derived from the rights of the worker, and are not independent rights for his family members. According to the ECJ, it is the worker who has the right 'to be accompanied in the territory of the latter State by his spouse'.[24]

Through Article 19 [8a], the right to mobility of workers has—at first sight—been expanded to all European nationals. However, limitations on the free movement rights of Article 19 are to be found in the Treaty, more precisely, in the same Article 39 [48] which can be seen as Article 19's concrete elaboration. Therefore, the notion of the worker is at the heart of the imagined European Community.

The European worker is entitled not only to freedom of movement and the social security rights that go along with it, based on Regulations 1408/71 and 1612/68, but also to equal treatment regarding sex in the fields of employment and social security. Hence, the notion of a worker applies to social security. In the *Nolte* decision,[25] the Court, citing the *Unger* judgment,[26] stated that the notion of worker in the field of social security has a Community content similar to that within the scope of Article 39 [48]. Therefore, the Court was able to rely on cases concerning Article 39 of the Treaty to decide that *Nolte* fell within the scope of Directive 79/7[27] (concerning equal treatment of men and women in statutory social security) although the applicant worked very few hours. In the field of equal treatment in social security, there is a large body of case law expanding the scope mainly of Directive 79/7.[28] Hence, the concept of worker within Community law relies on case law, on Article 39 and Regulations 1408/71 and 1612/68, and on Directive 79/7.[29]

The background of free movement of workers and equal treatment of men and women is parallel. The prohibition of discrimination on grounds of nationality is aimed at abolishing obstacles to the Single Market. The lofty aim of abolishing sex discrimination against employees likewise has an economic rationale. Article 141 [119], for instance, was introduced at

---

[24] Case C–370/90 *The Queen* v. *Immigration Appeal Tribunal, ex parte Surinder Singh* [1992] ECR I–4265 para. 21.

[25] Case C–317/93 *Nolte* v. *Landesversicherungsanstalt* [1995] ECR I–4625.

[26] Case 75/63 *Hoekstra (née Unger)* v. *Bestuur der Bedrijfsvereniging voor Detailhandel en Ambachten* [1964] ECR 371; see also Case 444/93 *Megner and Scheffel* v. *Innungskrankenkasse Rheinhessen-Pfalz* [1995] ECR I–4741.   [27] [1979] OJ L6/24.

[28] See Pennings, F., *Introduction to European Social Security Law* (Deventer: Kluwer, 1994) 263–86.

[29] Kuijer, A., and Steenbergen, J. D. M., *Nederlands Vreemdelingenrecht* (Dutch Immigration Law), (revised edn, Utrecht: NCB Utrecht, 1996), 110–16.

the initiative of France. French law already required equal pay for men and women, and the French therefore feared unfair competition from cheap women's labour in other European countries.

That an economic rationale underlies both the free movement of persons and the European elaboration of the equality principle is no coincidence. Economic mobility is the central goal of the European Treaty: free movement of workers (Article 39 [48]), services (Article 49 [59]), and capital (Article 56 [73b]), and the freedom of establishment (Article 43 [52]) form the core of the European Community. Hence, one of the four freedoms underpinning the European Economic Community has become the core of European citizenship and, thus, of European identity.[30] And yet, if 'you can't love a market' neither can you love the circulation of goods and capital. In this functional core of the European Community, free movement of persons is the only thing which can appeal to the imagination and which can create the sense of community and belonging, fulfilling the emotional aspect of European citizenship. Sipping wine in Nice, having Tapas in San Sebastian, doing your Christmas shopping in London while you earn a living in Berlin with your Danish passport are the great hopes Europe holds out to its citizens.

So the worker-citizen embodies the imagined European Community, and fulfils a central role in the developing European identity. The concept of the European worker is further developed by the case law of the Court. The next sections address three cases concerning the question who is a worker. In addition, I will use case law both from cases on Article 39 [48] and from cases from the field of equal treatment of men and women to provide an overview of the concept of the European worker.

III SEX AS WORK: REZGUIA ADOUI AND DOMINIQUE CORNUAILLE

The freedom of movement of prostitutes

On 18 May 1982, the ECJ decided the joined cases of *Adoui and Cornuaille.*[31] Central to these cases was the question whether a Member State could derogate from the right of free movement of workers on the basis of public policy. Adoui and Cornuaille were French citizens who worked in Liège in a 'bar which was suspect from the point of view of morals and in which waitresses displayed themselves in the windows and were able to

---

[30] See D'Oliveira, H. U. J., 'European Citizenship: its Meaning, its Potential' in Monar, J., Ungerer, W., and Wessels, W. (eds.), *The Maastricht Treaty on European Union: Legal Complexity and Political Dynamic* (Brussels: European Interuniversity Press, 1993) 87–92, for a more extensive analysis.

[31] Cases 115 and 116/81 *Adoui and Cornuaille* v. *Belgium* [1982] ECR 1665.

be alone with their clients'. The Belgian State refused them residence permits on grounds of public policy. This is permitted in Article 39(3) [48] of the EC Treaty, which is further explained in Directive 64/221. Prostitution as such was—and still is—permitted in Belgium, although it was severely restricted and regulated.

National values and freedom of movement

Belgium claimed that the personal conduct of Adoui and Cornuaille made them undesirable for reasons of public policy encompassed by Article 39(3) [48] of the Treaty. The Court considered that 'Community law does not impose upon the Member States a uniform scale of values as regards the assessment of conduct which may be considered as contrary to public policy' (paragraph 8 of the Judgment). Thus, Member States have a certain freedom in choosing their moral values. However, while a state *can* restrict admission to or residence in the territory of the Member State on grounds of public policy, the Court held that this cannot be done if the state does 'not adopt, with respect to the same conduct on the part of its own nationals repressive measures or other genuine and effective measures intended to combat such conduct' (paragraph 8). In other words, the European equality principle requires that nationals of other Member States should be treated in many respects in the same way as home nationals. The women's right to freedom of movement was thereby upheld by the Court.

Prostitutes are workers

While the ECJ accepted the claim of *Adoui and Cornuaille*, it did not deal *explicitly* with the question whether prostitutes are workers within the meaning of the Treaty. However, it appears to follow from the Judgment, as the Court applied Article 39 [48] and Directive 64/221 to determine the case. As Adoui and Cornuaille can invoke the rights imbedded in both Article 39 and the Directive, they are, apparently, workers within the scope of EC law. The nature of the work does not seem important in deciding whether they are workers or not. They receive wages for their work in the bar and that seems sufficient. The fact that Belgium tries to restrict work in prostitution because it is considered contrary to public policy is not important enough. Maybe Belgium does not like prostitution, but work is work. As long as the worker gets paid, the prerequisites of the concept of the European worker are fulfilled.

IV THE CULTURAL DEFENCE: JEAN MARC BOSMAN

Free movement of soccer players

On 15 December 1995, the ECJ decided the *Bosman* case.[32] Central to this case was the question whether UEFA (the European soccer association) and FIFA (the international soccer association) transfer rules and nationality clauses were consistent with the principle of freedom of movement for workers.

The transfer rules came down to the obligation of a soccer club to pay a transfer sum to other clubs from whom it acquired players. Without this payment the transfer could not take place. The lack of a transfer sum prevented Belgian professional player, Jean Marc Bosman, changing from a Belgian to a French soccer club, and he claimed that the system was contrary to Article 39 [48] of the Treaty. The nationality clauses restricted the extent to which foreign players could be fielded in a match. A club might field three foreign players in a match plus two players who had played in the country of the relevant national soccer association for an uninterrupted period of five years (the three plus two rule). Bosman argued that the nationality clauses were contrary to Article 39(2) [48] of the Treaty which prohibits discrimination on the basis of nationality between workers of the Member-States.

Transfer rules

First, the applicability of Article 39 [48] to the transfer rules was addressed by the Court. The question was essentially whether Article 39 [48] applies to sporting activities. The Court explained that for Article 39 to be applicable, the employer did not have to be an undertaking: 'all that is required is the existence of, or the intention to create, an employment relationship' (paragraph 74). Furthermore, citing the 1976 *Donà* judgment,[33] the Court held that freedom of movement cannot be restricted to exclude the whole of a sporting activity from the scope of the Treaty. Thirdly, the Court stated that although 'the practical consequences of any judicial decision must be weighed carefully, [when it comes to the effect on the organization of soccer as a whole] this cannot go so far as to diminish the objective character of the law and compromise its application on the ground of the possible repercussions of a judicial decision' (paragraph 77). Fourthly, the cultural defence, stating that soccer is culture and, therefore, sportsmen

---

[32] Case C–415/93 *Union Royale Belge des Sociétés de Football Association* v. *Bosman* [1995] ECR I–4921.
[33] Case 13/76 *Donà* v. *Mantero* [1976] ECR 1333.

are not workers, was rejected because Article 39 [48] contained a fundamental freedom in the Community system (paragraph 78).

Thus, Article 39 [48] did apply to the rules laid down by sporting associations determining the terms on which professional sportsmen could
engage in gainful employment (paragraph 87) and, when applied, Article
39 [48] led to the conclusion that the transfer rules were contrary to freedom of movement.[34] From this case it can be concluded that professional
soccer players are to be considered as workers falling within the scope of
the Treaty. Although soccer has some cultural aspects as well, the bottom
line is that players have an employment relationship with their club and
thus fall within the scope of the concept of worker as developed in EC
law.

Nationality clauses

The second aspect addressed by the Court concerned the nationality
clauses. Citing the *Donà* judgment again, the Court stated that Article 39
[48] applied to clauses contained in the regulations of sporting associations which restrict the participation of nationals of other Member States
in soccer matches (paragraph 119) as these obviously also restricted the
chances of employment of the player concerned (paragraph 120).

UEFA, among others, argued before the Court that the nationality
clauses were justified on non-economic grounds, concerning only the
sports as such. According to the Court, the nationality clauses 'cannot be
deemed to be in accordance with [Article 39 [48]] of the Treaty, otherwise
that Article would be deprived of this practical effect and the fundamental right of free access to employment which the Treaty confers individually on each worker in the Community rendered nugatory' (paragraph
129). The Court did not accept UEFA's arguments concerning the importance of the nationality clauses in order to maintain good national teams
and, in paragraph 137, concluded that Article 39 [48] precluded the application of the nationality clauses with respect to soccer players of other
Member-States. The Court's response to UEFA's sombre expectations on
the organization of soccer as a whole was no more than to limit the
temporal effects of the judgment.

---

[34] Although the transfer rules also applied to transfers between clubs within the same
country, they were still seen as obstacles to freedom of movement (paras. 98–100). As long as
freedom of movement is restricted in such a way that migration to another Member State is
hindered, it is, apparently, contrary to Art. 39. This could mean that other national measures
restricting the changing of jobs might be contrary to Art. 39 as they also restrict European
migration, in which case *Bosman* has a potentially far-reaching effect on, for instance, non-
competition clauses. However, this issue falls beyond the scope of this chapter.

The culture of sports and the freedom of movement

The *Bosman* judgment has been heralded as the end of 'slavery' for professional soccer players. It did not, however, surprise lawyers working in the field of EC law as it is consistent with previous case law. And it did not end the 'slavery' of third-country players: in the summer following the *Bosman* judgment, Nwankwo Kanu, possessing a Nigerian passport, switched from Ajax to Inter Milan by means of a large transfer sum.[35] Nevertheless, apart from the above mentioned possible consequences on non-competition clauses, the *Bosman* case is also important in terms of the Court's reasoning.

In defending both the transfer rules and the nationality clauses, several arguments cloaked in moral and cultural terms—like the autonomy of sports, cultural aspects of soccer, identity of clubs, and the interests of the national team—were invoked. Accepting that soccer has aspects of culture and the framing of national identity, the Court responded in the same way to these arguments: EC law cannot be set aside on any possible ground when it is applicable. EC law comes first; soccer, culture, and whatever come later. If EC law is considered this important, it is not surprising that other values mentioned above are not decisive. Just as public policy provides only limited exception grounds for compromising the rights of the European worker, so also do considerations of national culture and identity.

The priority of EC law has invoked bitter reactions, rather surprisingly stating that the economic character of EC law should not reign over soccer which is merely an innocent pastime for nice boys, and yet soccer is to a large extent a commercial product delivered by undertakings which we still call soccer clubs but which are quoted on the stock exchange. One of the protesters was the then Belgian Prime Minister, Jean-Luc Dehaene, who suggested introducing a sports exception to the EC Treaty because 'sport cannot be treated like a market share'.[36]

V THE HOUSEWIFE: ELSIE JOHNSON

The social security of housewives

On 11 July 1991, the Court decided the *Johnson* case.[37] This case did not concern free movement of workers, but contains, nevertheless, an important

---

[35] Swaak, C. R. A., 'Kanu—Ajax, arbitraire toepassing van EG kartelrecht' (1996) 30 *Nederlands Juristenblad* 1212.

[36] *Agence Europe*, no. 6647, 18 Jan. 1996, 8.

[37] Case C–31/90 *Johnson* v. *Chief Adjudication Officer* [1991] ECR I–3723.

decision on the nature of the European worker. Elsie Johnson was a single mother who gave up her job to take care of her daughter and was unable to return to work years later because of back problems. She applied for a disability allowance which was denied due to some prerequisites she did not meet. She complained that this was contrary to EC law, specifically to the obligations of EC Directive 79/7, concerning equal treatment of men and women in statutory social security. Before the Court, two points were addressed: the question of the direct effect of Article 4(1) of the Directive containing the principle of equal treatment in social security matters, and the question of the scope of the Directive. The direct effect of Article 4(1) had been well established since December 1984[38] so this point did not lead to much discussion. The scope of the Directive, however, offered some interesting observations.

Scope of the Directive

The scope of Directive 79/7 is, according to Articles 2 and 3, limited to persons who are available on the labour market or who have ceased to be so owing to the materialization of one of the risks specified in the Directive, for instance, disability. A person may still be regarded as falling within the scope of Directive 79/7, as a person seeking employment whose search is made impossible by the materialization of one of the risks specified in Article 3(1)(a) (paragraph 21). Thus, the protection of EC law also reaches those who are not actually working but who are seeking work.[39] And even if you become ill when looking for work, you may still fall within the scope of the European worker. How many hours one works hardly matters—from *Nolte* it is clear that somebody working very few hours falls within the scope of the Directive. This is consistent with the case law on Article 39 [48] of the Treaty where the Court has decided that the notion of a worker is not restricted to those who work full time.[40] In those cases, the Court decided that part-time workers are workers falling within the scope of the Treaty. Furthermore, in *Drake*[41] the Court concluded that someone *who gave up her job* to take care of an invalid parent could still invoke the protection of the Directive. Those who do not fall within the scope of the Directive are housewives. And giving up your work to bring up a child is not one of the risks mentioned in the Directive; thus, in *Johnson*, the Court stated it was not covered (paragraph 19).

[38] Case 71/85 *Nederlandse Staat* v. *FNV* [1986] ECR 3855.
[39] Case C–292/89 *Antonissen* [1991] ECR I–745 in which the Court stated that someone looking for work falls within the scope of Art. 39 [48] of the Treaty.
[40] Case 53/81 See *Levin* v. *Staatssecretaris van Justitie* [1982] ECR 1035, Case 139/85 *Kempf* v. *Staatssecretaris van Justitie* [1986] ECR 1741, and Case 2/89 *Bestuur van de Sociale Verzekevingsbank* v. *Kits van Heijningen* [1990] ECR 1755.
[41] Case 150/85 *Drake* v. *Chief Adjudication Officer* [1986] ECR 1995.

The housewife as a worker

What becomes clear from *Johnson* is that a housewife *can* be considered as a worker as long as she also works part-time or is looking for work. Apart from the deduced rights for dependent spouses (above), 'just' staying at home is not enough, but only a little effort is needed to fall within the scope of the Directive and the Treaty.

It is, however, possible to interpret the notion of a worker in such a way that the 'mere' housewife does fall within the scope of EC law. In *Steymann*[42] the Court considered work in a religious community. Mr Steymann worked in the kitchen of the community of which he was a member. He was not paid wages but received food and lodging instead. According to the Court, these provisions could be considered an indirect *quid pro quo* for 'real work', and thus Steymann could invoke Article 39 [48] of the Treaty. In other words: a wage is not necessary to be considered a worker within the scope of EC law. Compare this reasoning with the provisions of Dutch matrimonial law. The Dutch Civil Code obliges spouses to provide for each other in Article 1: 81. These provisions also include food and lodging and the basic necessities of life and can also be seen as a *quid pro quo* for the housework a housewife does. Following *Steymann*, the *quid pro quo* for the work a housewife performs would arguably be enough to establish that a housewife is a European worker. Except that housework is not considered real work because it is not an 'occupational activity'.[43] Once the link between wage and work is broken, the key issue in deciding whether 'work' is to be considered work under EC law seems to be what constitutes an occupational activity. In the *Züchner*[44] case, the Court held that a *housewife* who takes care of an invalid family member and whose labour would have to be done by a paid worker if she did not do it cannot invoke Directive 79/7 as she is not considered a worker falling within the scope of the Directive. The difference between *Drake* and *Züchner* is that Ms Drake was a worker and Ms Züchner a housewife before taking care of the invalid family member.

VI THE EUROPEAN CITIZEN WORKS

In the cases analysed above, some common strands of reasoning can be found from which we can deduce European identity. European citizenship and, therefore, European identity are largely economic. As I have

---

[42] Case 196/87 *Steymann* v. *Staatssecretaris van Justitie* [1988] ECR 6159.

[43] See, e.g., Case 300/84 *Van Roosmalen* v. *Bestuur van de Bedrijfsvereniging voor de Gezondheid, Geestelijke en Mastachappelijke Belangen* [1986] ECR 3097.

[44] Case 77/95 *Züchner* v. *Handels (Ersatzkasse) Bremen* [1996] ECR I-5689.

argued, free movement as established in Article 19 [8a] is the core of European citizenship. Free movement has two aspects. First it is, at bottom, an economic freedom, as are all Community rights. It improves the possibilities for labour mobility, essential to free market economies. Secondly, only those who are economically active can invoke EC law and these most important citizenship rights of Europe. The European citizen is first and foremost a worker:[45] a worker has this most important citizen's right of free movement. To be considered a worker within the scope of EC law, the nature of the work does not matter, neither do the number of hours worked or wages paid. Looking for work is enough to become a worker for the purpose of equal treatment protection.

The economic orientation of the Community can also be seen in the superiority of EC law to other values. According to the Court, the economic rationality of EC law is superior to the moral and cultural values that constitute the various national identities of the Member States. The supremacy of EC law over national values and morals is not total, although supremacy over the autonomy of certain fields of work (sports for instance) or over the cultural aspects of certain sectors (like soccer) is taken for granted. Thus, the Court contributes to an economic European identity. In stressing the freedom of movement of workers, it claims the superiority of this freedom above other values the cases raise, such as the cultural aspects of soccer. This economic orientation should not come as a surprise. From the beginning, the economic collaboration of Member States was the important goal of the Community. The system of Community law is oriented to free market economics and supports free market interests, like the free movement of workers. The European interpretation of citizenship means that those who are not workers are excluded from full citizenship. Furthermore, the Court prefers to decide questions of citizenship and freedom of movement on the basis of Article 39 [48], the freedom of movement of workers, and not on the basis of Article 18 which still does not have direct effect.[46]

In constituting the European citizen as a *homo economicus*, the Court does not interfere with the other parts of the lives of citizens. It affects them only in so far as they go out into the labour market. The European citizen as a culturally, socially, or politically active human being is far from sight. Critics of the Treaty of Amsterdam complained about this economic orientation and the substance of European citizenship is, thereby, attracting more attention. But, while the vocabulary is alluring, from a legal point of view, nothing much has changed. Even in its

---

[45] Meehan above, n. 13, 147, concludes that in so far as citizenship has a Community dimension, citizens are citizens-as-workers.
[46] See Case C–378/97 *Criminal proceedings against Wijsenbeek* [1999] ECR I–6207.

Steymann judgment, while accepting food and lodging as a *quid pro quo* for work, the Court always uses the concept of occupational activities to distinguish between work and non-work. The *Züchner* judgment shows how little has been gained. Housewives still do not count as full citizens because they are not workers. Their labour is not commodified and is not available on the labour market. If the housewife were a prostitute, *she* would be commodified, and if she worked in a day-care centre for one day a week her labour would be. But being at home does not give her labour a market value. Housewives who are nationals of a Member State are considered European citizens. However, they have only second-rate citizenship as they are bereft of their most important citizen's right of free movement and the ability to invoke the equal treatment Directives.

This glorifying of the citizen-as-worker fits perfectly with the free market economics of the Union, but it is arguable that it will have negative effects on perceptions of citizens. Because this construction of citizen values work and work ethics, it will, for example, diminish the value of other things; other activities will be held in lower estimation. The devaluation of housework and cultural, political, or other activities, and the corresponding valuation of paid labour, prepares people for the labour market. The images conveyed by Europe are that only 'work' counts,[47] perhaps leading to more women becoming economically active.

The question will then be what is considered a proper job. We have seen in the discussion of the cases that the EC does not have any moral attitudes about the kind of jobs people perform and that, for instance, prostitution is seen as work falling within the scope of the Treaty. In the Netherlands, prostitution has been legalized since 1 October 2000 and thus another problem arises. Pimps—whether they exploit brothels, clubs, or street corner prostitutes—want Eastern European and Asian women to work for them. These women need work permits, as they are not coming from within the EC. Work permits are delivered only if there are no Dutch or other EC women available to perform the jobs.[48] Although the general feeling is still that you cannot 'force' women to work as prostitutes any more than you can 'force' them to work in factories or shops by denying them (full) welfare benefits as long as there is work in factories and shops, with the legalizing of prostitution the sector gets a certain air of decency. I wonder how long it will be before prostitution is considered suitable work

---

[47] This is also conveyed by national policy measures. The breaking down of the Dutch welfare state leads to a growing pressure on people on welfare to accept all sorts of jobs.

[48] See for an overview of the current discussions: Haveman, R., Wijers, M., Scholtes, H., and Timmermans, R., 'Bemiddeling buitenlandse prostituées. Uitzendformule toegepast bij de toelating' (Mediating for foreign prostitutes. Temporary employment strategies for admission) [1996] 5 *Nemesis* 156–62.

for women on welfare and how long it will take women to discover they can become full European citizens by becoming prostitutes.[49]

The rationale behind this emphasis on paid work is an economic one: the process of flexible accumulation and flexible specialization leads to the need for a large flexible workforce in which women, as the folding chair workers of the Community, can become the reserve army of labour. The changes in modes of production induce employers to develop a small core group of employees with specific skills and tasks and good labour and wage conditions. Apart from the core groups, two other groups of employees are developing in a less favourable position. First, there is a group of employees doing relatively simple tasks like typing. The second group is a far more flexible group on temporary contracts with bad labour and wage conditions.[50] The jobs women secure are not generally long-term employment relationships with beautiful career prospects but flexible short-term part-time jobs; however, they do offer citizenship. These same jobs, be it not part-time but more than full-time, at even lower wages are done by third-country immigrants and illegals. So through labour which is largely done by third-country immigrants and illegals to survive, women can become real European Citizens. For housewives, paid work thus fulfills the function of naturalization for third-country nationals.

VII INCLUSION THROUGH SEX, RACE, OR WORK

Citizenship is an 'invention' of the French Revolution. Often, the core of citizenship is seen in political rights,[51] but, as we have seen, other rights have been included. In Europe, the core of citizenship is paid work.

According to Wallerstein, liberalism induced working class co-operation in three ways. First, working people were granted increasing political participation through universal suffrage. Secondly, they were involved in the redistribution of surplus value through the development

---

[49] The first pimp, exploiting a brothel in Leeuwarden, has already come to a job centre looking for women to become prostitutes as working with illegal prostitutes becomes more difficult—*Vrij Nederland*, 14 Dec. 1996, 8. Furthermore, the first residence permit has been delivered to a third-country national prostitute as she was considered a self-employed person under the meaning of the Treaty between the EC and the Czech Republic: District Court, The Hague, 18 July 1997, AWB 97/1016VrW (not reported; text on file with the author). A woman who worked as a prostitute was denied a welfare benefit when she left the job and had no other means of subsistence as she had left the job voluntarily; on appeal she did get the benefit. See Haveman, R., 'Sekswerk passende arbeid' [1999] 1 *Nemesis* 31–2.

[50] See for a more extensive analysis Harvey, D., *The Condition of Postmodernity. An Enquiry into the Origins of Cultural Change* (Cambridge/Oxford: Blackwell, 1989), especially 150–4; van Walsum, S., 'Mixed Metaphors: the Nation and the Family' (1994) 22/23 *Focaal* 199–218.

[51] Meehan, above, n. 13, 107.

of the welfare state. Thirdly, through the development of the nation-state and the creation of national identities, a bond between working-class people was forged.[52] The European Union is destroying all three. Political participation in the Union is fairly non-existent. The Parliament, the only directly chosen body, has little power.[53] In the elections in the spring of 1998, only half the voters turned out to vote. Apparently, the citizens of Europe do not consider it important to choose their representatives. Meanwhile, European welfare states have been deteriorating at high speed since the economic crises of the 1970s and 1980s and many state welfare cuts are presented in terms of European Union requirements. Finally, the Union is making national identities and national states less and less important. Indeed, the one thing the European Union renders is freedom of movement for the economically active and an economically oriented citizenship. The European citizen is thus imagined as a worker. But what does this imaginative construct entail?

Inclusion in European citizenship is achieved through paid work. The rights of freedom of movement and equal treatment are closely connected. Free movement existed before the foundation of the nation-state. War, the plague, hunger, love, and adventure induced people to move and find a living elsewhere. As the European Community in the end means the end of the nation-state, free movement should return. Equality has been pursued since the French Revolution. While largely limited to equality among white men, increasingly (particularly since the 1960s), and together with other human rights, it has been invoked by women and people of colour. It was, however, never intended for all and is restricted again.[54] The restriction now is not to be found in traditional sexist and racist categories but in the facially neutral requirement of paid work. But the opportunities to fulfil the requirements for the European worker are unevenly spread and the highest rates of failure are amongst migrants of third countries and women. A gender-neutral content of citizenship is not enough to achieve full citizenship for all.[55] Equality still cannot be realized, as racism and sexism are cloaked in the requirements of nationality and occupational activities.

Something, however, *has* changed. Citizenship is about inclusion and exclusion.[56] Traditionally, for men, being a citizen meant full political rights and the duty to serve in the army. For women however, citizenship

---

[52] Wallerstein, I., *After Liberalism* (New York: The New Press, 1995) 97–101, 151–3, and 236.
[53] See Weatherill and Beaumont, above, n. 16, 85–114 for a description of the limited powers of the European Parliament.
[54] Wallerstein, above, n. 52, 153.
[55] See Meehan, above, n. 13, 102–5 for a detailed analysis of the literature on this point.
[56] Dahrendorf, above, n. 6, 25–47.

implied only the duty to bear and raise children.[57] Inclusion in society used to operate along blatantly sexual (and racial) lines. Inclusion in Europe now operates through paid work. Although this can also be seen as a veiling of sexist practices, in the same way as meritocratic demands can be interpreted as sexist demands,[58] it can also be interpreted as a step forward in combating sexism. Discrimination on grounds of nationality and sex is prohibited. Together with the relatively small requirements which must be met to qualify as a European worker, citizenship—however limited in scope—is open to all who are willing to make themselves available on the labour market.[59]

The economic interpretation of citizenship delivers at least a way of disregarding sex when it comes to distributing rights. Europe does not adequately solve the worse labour conditions of women compared to men nor does it really try to take into account the difficulties women encounter when they try to combine paid labour with care tasks. What we have gained, however, is a notion of a citizen imagined not only as a man but also as a woman who engages in paid work. This image is new and radically different from the old images of women as, for instance, mothers. It does not mean that all women's problems will be solved through Europe or that Europe's high hopes are held out to men and women alike. But it does offer possibilities of inclusion and possibilities for combating discrimination even as, at the same time, the neutral wording of citizenship cloaks existing discrimination. The point is that progressive possibilities *can* be found for participation in the imagined European Community.

[57] Meehan, above, n. 13, 3.

[58] Wallerstein, above, n. 52, 159.

[59] An interesting comparison can be drawn between the way illegal entrants can be legalized in the Netherlands and in a few other European countries. Those who have worked for 6 years without a residence permit but have paid taxes and social security contributions can be legalized if they can prove they have been working and paying. Here, the racism of the closed borders of 'Fortress Europe' can be overcome by work, and work again functions as a way to secure your place in society.

17

Critical Reflections on 'Citizenship' as a Progressive Aspiration

LINDA BOSNIAK

Citizenship has become a very hot topic in academic discourse lately. In 1994, the journal *Ethics* published a review essay by political theorists, Will Kymlicka and Wayne Norman, announcing the 'return of the citizen' to normative political thought,[1] and, since then, interest in the subject has only intensified, not merely in political theory but across the disciplines.[2] The idea of citizenship has become particularly ubiquitous in the field of labour studies, where analysts increasingly speak of 'economic citizenship', 'workplace citizenship', and 'citizenship unionism', among other things.[3]

Given the breadth of its attraction and uses, it is hardly surprising to find substantial disagreement on what the idea of citizenship actually means. There is a strikingly wide range of different understandings or discourses of citizenship in circulation. Some of these are concerned with citizenship as rights, in the tradition of British sociologist, T.H. Marshall;[4] others focus, in the republican tradition, on citizenship as political activity—as active engagement in the life of the political community.[5] Still others emphasize citizenship as a mode of cultural or political identity.[6] And, of course, citizenship continues to denote formal legal status in a political community.

---

[1] Kymlicka, W., and Norman, W., 'Return of the Citizen: A Survey of Recent Work on Citizenship Theory' (1994) 104 *Ethics* 352.

[2] Notably, interest in citizenship has not been confined to legal and political theorists. The new preoccupation with citizenship is highly interdisciplinary, with citizenship serving as a major conceptual category for sociologists, historians, and, increasingly, cultural theorists as well.

[3] See, e.g., Forbath, W., 'Civil Rights and Economic Citizenship: Notes on the Past and Future of the Civil Rights and Labor Movements' (2000) 2 *University of Pennsylvania Journal of Labor and Employment Law* 697 ('economic citizenship'); Ross, G., 'Labor vs. Globalization' (2000) 57 *Annals of the American Academy of Political and Social Science* 78 ('citizenship in the workplace'); Stone, K. V. W., 'Employment Regulation in a Boundaryless Workplace', paper presented at INTELL Conference, University of Toronto, Canada, 22–24 Sept. 2000 ('citizenship unionism').

[4] Marshall, T. H., *Citizenship and Social Class* (Cambridge: Cambridge University Press, 1950).

[5] This Aristotelian, virtue-oriented understanding of citizenship has been invoked increasingly by participatory democrats and civic republicans in the past two decades.

[6] Citizenship-as-identity has been described as citizenship in its 'psychological dimension': Carens, J., 'Dimensions of Citizenship and National Identity In Canada' (1996–7) 28 *Philosophical Forum* 111, 113.

There is, however, one thing that almost everyone *does* seem to agree on, and that is that citizenship is something very significant and desirable. Today, citizenship stands as an aspirational touchstone for civic republicans, radical democrats, cultural radicals, and liberals alike. It is a term, moreover, that has been adopted with special enthusiasm by progressives of various stripes. The idea of citizenship somehow manages to evoke a sense of community well-being, democratic engagement, and personal fulfilment simultaneously.

This resurgence of interest in citizenship as an aspirational ideal in progressive discourse, including progressive labour discourse, raises a variety of questions. I will touch on two of them in this chapter. The first is the question of who gets to be counted as belonging among the community of citizens to which this literature refers. This is a question concerning the class of citizenship's subjects. The other is the related question of where citizenship should be understood to take place. This is a question concerning citizenship's location, actual and ideal. Both these questions are concerned with what I consider to be the mostly unexamined and unjustified nation-centredness of citizenship discourse—something I have sought to challenge in my own work.[7]

I CITIZENSHIP FOR WHOM?

I begin with the 'who' question. When you examine most of the recent literature on citizenship in legal and political theory, you see that scholars of citizenship assume that citizenship should ideally entail universality—universal membership. Particularly in the American rights-based literature, the idea of citizenship—the idea of equal citizenship—is portrayed as the antidote to a history of racism and other status-based exclusion in the USA. It is well known that the United States' history of racial subordination is inextricably linked with the exclusion of African Americans and other national groups from formal recognition as citizens. Given the advent of formal equality, however, the focus today is not so much on the denial of citizenship *qua* formal status as on the imposition of what we often call 'second-class citizenship' on racial minorities in our society. This critique of second-class citizenship is also articulated in a variety of emancipatory movements and appears in feminist, gay-rights, and class-based (including labour rights) discourses. But the challenge is most often heard, and probably carries the most resonance, in the context of race.

---

[7] This chapter draws to some degree on two of my earlier articles: 'Universal Citizenship and the Problem of Alienage' (2000) 94 *Northwestern L. Review* 963 and 'Citizenship Denationalized' (2000) 7 *Indiana Journal of Global Legal Studies* 447.

Stating one's opposition to second-class citizenship is meant to express a couple of ideas. First of all, it conveys an opposition to the existence of structured inequalities, or caste-like stratification, in society. It condemns treatment of an individual as a 'member of an inferior or dependent caste or as a nonparticipant', in Kenneth Karst's terms.[8] Opposition to second-class citizenship is also, implicitly, a protest against hypocrisy: it represents a challenge to deeply entrenched inequalities in a society which purports to be egalitarian.

Notice, however, that opposition to second-class citizenship is not purely a negative stance. Implicit in the critique is an embrace of a contrasting ideal of citizenship. This is a full and equal citizenship; a one-class or universal citizenship; a full and meaningful membership for 'each individual'.[9] In fact, in this discourse, universal or equal citizenship is presumed to be citizenship in its genuine form, in contrast to second-class citizenship, which is understood as a failure or distortion of citizenship in practice. As Iris Marion Young has written, the contemporary ideal of citizenship stands for 'the inclusion and participation of everyone'.[10]

So full and equal citizenship for all is an ideal. And this ideal of universal and egalitarian citizenship (which, again, is the negation of second-class citizenship) is a deeply resonant one; it has been fundamental in shaping modern political thought. The idea of full and equal citizenship has taken on even greater significance for many on the left in the post-Marxist era, as evidenced by the emergence of the themes of 'social citizenship' or 'economic citizenship' in much legal and sociological literature.[11] Full and equal citizenship is often described as out of reach as a practical matter in capitalist and patriarchal societies, but there is never any question that citizenship—full and equal citizenship—is a fundamental requirement of political and economic justice.

Now, when I began reading some of this literature several years ago, I was very ambivalent about it. On the one hand, I found it attractive because I identified with its trenchant critique of exclusion and its demand for universal social justice. But, at the same time, I came to this

---

[8] Karst, K., *Belonging To America: Equal Citizenship and the Constitution* (New Haven, Conn.: Yale University Press, 1989) 3.

[9] Ibid.

[10] Young, I. M., 'Polity and Group Difference: A Critique of the Ideal of Universal Citizenship' (1989) 99 *Ethics* 250, 251.

[11] The concept of social citizenship was originally set forth by Marshall, above, n. 4. For more recent invocations of social/economic citizenship see, e.g., Fraser, N., and Gordon, L., 'Civil Citizenship Against Social Citizenship?' in van Steenbergen, B. (ed.), *The Condition of Citizenship* (London: Sage, 1994); Held, D., 'Between State and Civil Society: Citizenship' in Andrews, G. (ed.), *Citizenship* (London: Lawrence & Wishart, 1991); Handler, J., 'The Moral Construction of Social Citizenship and the Crisis of the Welfare State' (draft on file with the author); Forbath, W., 'Caste, Class and Equal Citizenship' (1999) 98 *Michigan L. Review* 1; Karst, K., 'The Coming Crisis of Work in Constitutional Perspective' (1997) 82 *Cornell L. Review* 523.

literature as someone concerned about specifically national forms of exclusion, particularly the exclusion of immigrants. And it struck me that most of the citizenship literature is utterly oblivious to the fact that the idea of citizenship embodies not only inclusionary but also deeply exclusionary impulses.

The idea of citizenship is exclusionary in a couple of different ways. First, the literature almost always assumes that citizenship takes place within a national political framework—and, that being the case, it implicitly excludes from its scope of concern national outsiders (people located outside the nation). The universal citizenship that Kenneth Karst is talking about, for example, is a specifically American citizenship. This means that citizenship's claimed universality is actually a bounded universality. I will further explore this nation-centred assumption below.

But even accepting that citizenship is going to be confined to the nation-state—even assuming a citizenship restricted to a national territory—the idea of citizenship *still* falls short of its universalist aspirations. The problem is that citizenship is not just about rights and inclusion; it is also a legal status that designates formal membership in the nation-state. And this is an exclusive status denied not only to foreigners but also to large numbers of immigrants who reside within the country as aliens ('alien' being the technical legal term for non-citizen). As a result of their legal status, in turn, aliens are treated as 'second-class citizens' in a great variety of ways, even in the most liberal democratic states. In most countries, aliens are denied the vote, many are now ineligible for a number of important social benefit programmes, and all are subject to deportation from the country under a variety of circumstances.[12]

Progressive theorists of citizenship, I have argued, have advanced powerful critiques of social and economic exclusion. But for all their concern with a variety of exclusions, theorists of citizenship almost never recognize and condemn exclusion based on citizenship status. Again, their conception of universality is bounded; it is bounded both by territory, and also by exclusive, nationalist conceptions of membership within the territory.

One of the questions that emerges is whether citizenship's exclusionary commitments necessarily taint or contaminate the idea of citizenship as a progressive ideal. I have sometimes thought that it does and that we need to come up with other language that does not implicitly smuggle in a nationalist vision of political life. It comes down to this: in the context of immigrants' rights advocacy, 'citizenship' is simply not the unmitigated

---

[12] There is a vast literature on this subject. For a recent volume on the status of aliens in various receiving countries see Joppke, C. (ed.), *Challenge to the Nation-State: Immigration In Western Europe and the United States* (Oxford: Oxford University Press, 1998); see also Bosniak, 'Universal Citizenship', above, n. 7, 970–80.

object of desire that it is in anti-racist and other progressive discourses. Here, it is more of a double-edged sword. Certainly, non-citizen immigrants (aliens, in legal discourse) very often aspire to legal citizenship, and regard the denial to them of citizenship status as a form of injustice. So, for example, recent efforts by the US government to limit eligibility for naturalization, or to deny citizenship to children born in that country of undocumented alien parents, have been strongly opposed and criticized.

But while they seek greater access to citizenship status, immigrants and their defenders are also engaged in battle on another front: they want to displace citizenship from its privileged place in our political imaginations. This is because, as they point out, citizenship as an idea and as an institution is not always emancipatory. In fact, it often works to exclude people from the enjoyment of rights and recognition. Immigrants' rights defenders thus often want to decouple the idea of citizenship from those of rights and recognition—precisely because they are pressing for rights and recognition for immigrants who specifically lack citizenship status—for aliens. What they argue is that rights and recognition should be based on an individual's personhood or her social participation, rather than on citizenship.

From this vantage point, then, the idea of citizenship is problematic as an aspirational ideal and should perhaps be abandoned. I am not entirely convinced of this, however, because I have also been intrigued by the possibility that the ideal of citizenship in its universalist, inclusionary mode could be used to challenge citizenships more exclusionary conceptions. One way to express this rhetorically might be to argue on behalf of 'alien citizenship'. Calling for 'alien citizenship' is not the same thing as arguing for citizenship status *for* aliens, via naturalization (although this is certainly worth pressing for as well). It is, rather, a demand for the extension of full rights and recognition to aliens *qua* aliens. Of course, if such a demand were to be met, the citizen/alien divide would collapse into meaninglessness—which is why the idea is deeply paradoxical. But this is an instructive paradox because it underlines how narrow and how exclusionary our conventional understandings of universality ordinarily are.[13]

II CITIZENSHIP WHERE?

The second question about citizenship I want to touch on here is the 'where' question—the question where citizenship is located and where it

---

[13] Judith Butler has persuasively pointed out how highly contingent and contested our understandings of universality are. Advocating 'the citizenship of aliens' could be regarded, in this spirit, as a means of 'exposing the parochial and exclusionary character of a given historical articulation of universality, [thereby] extending and rendering substantive the notion of universality itself': Butler, J., 'Sovereign Performatives in the Contemporary Scene of Utterance' (1997) 23 *Critical Inquiry* 350, 366–7.

should it be located. As I stated earlier, most theorists of citizenship assume that citizenship is a national project. They regard citizenship as a set of political and social relationships that take place among the members of a national state. This nation-centred premise in the literature raises at least two kinds of questions. The first of these is whether citizenship is, in fact and by definition, a national (nation-state) enterprise.

Obviously, this has been the conventional understanding, and it describes much of the current state of affairs in institutional terms. But I would submit that there is nothing necessary about it. As a historical matter, first of all, citizenship was presumed to be located in sites other than the state; citizenship got its start, after all, in the city. Furthermore, in analytical terms, it seems perfectly plausible to say that aspects of citizenship are located both above and below the state and across states, as well as within the state.

For example, some of the rights we associate with citizenship are no longer guaranteed exclusively at the nation-state level. It is well known that the international human rights regimes that have taken shape in the post-World War II period are designed to implement standards for the treatment of individuals by states. These standards, which include civil, political, social, and cultural rights, serve as an alternative source of rights—one that transcends the jurisdiction of individual nation-states. Of course, there are real limits to the international human rights system, and people still face serious obstacles to enforcing their rights. But it remains the case that the rights commonly associated with citizenship are no longer entirely constrained by national boundaries.

Similarly, the kind of political activity and engagement we associate with republican citizenship is certainly not always conducted at the level of the state. Increasing numbers of people are, in fact, engaged in democratic political practices not only below but across national boundaries, in the form of transnational social movements of environmentalists, feminists, human rights workers, and trade unions, among other groups.[14] Some will no doubt argue that such activity, however transnational, cannot be described in the language of citizenship since citizenship can be meaningfully practised only in the context of a formal, organized, territorially-based community with some degree of sovereign self-governance. In response, however, one can draw on rich, anti-statist conceptions of politics—conceptions which urge recognition of citizenship and its practices in the economy, in the workplace, in the neighborhood, in

---

[14] For a comprehensive account of such transnational activism see Keck, M. E., and Sikkink, K., *Activists Beyond Borders: Advocacy Networks in International Politics* (Ithaca, NY: Cornell University Press, 1998).

professional associations, even in the family.[15] In this conception, citizenship is practised in the realm of civil society and not merely the state—often by way of the 'new social movements'.

We may take this conception one step farther by looking at political practices in the domain of what some have called global civil society. There is no logical reason why such activity should not be described in the language of citizenship as well. Indeed, transnational political activity arguably fulfils the normative criteria of republican and participatory democratic conceptions of citizenship very well: it is robust and engaged, and it reflects 'commitment to the common good and active participation in public affairs'.[16] The difference is simply that the notions of 'common good' and the public domain involved are drawn more expansively than they usually are within the tradition.

When we talk, finally, about citizenship as a mode of collective identity or solidarity, it is hardly controversial that people sustain fundamentally important connections and commitments to various non-national (transnational and subnational) political communities. Anthropologists and others have recently made clear that people frequently maintain identities that transcend or traverse national boundaries. This is particularly true of cross-national migrants who live in various diasporic and other cross-national communities.[17]

Undeniably, citizenship is harder to divorce from the nation-state when we are concerned with citizenship *qua* legal status. But even here there are some departures, like the development of a regionally framed, supra-national citizenship in the European Union (EU). The advent of EU citizenship has begun to challenge the conventional correspondence that we assume exists between citizenship status and the nation-state—although it is also true that Union citizenship remains

[15] E.g., Pateman, C., *Participation and Democratic Theory* (Cambridge: Cambridge University Press, 1970) 45–102; Dahl, R., *Democracy and Its Critics* (New Haven, Conn.: Yale University Press, 1989) 324–32; Okin, S. M., 'Women, Equality and Citizenship', *Queens Quarterly* 99 (Spring 1992) 56, 69; Jones, K. B., 'Citizenship In a Woman-Friendly Polity' in Shafir, G. (ed.), *The Citizenship Debates* (Minneapolis, Minn.: University of Minnesota, 1998).
[16] Dagger, R., *Civic Virtues: Rights, Citizenship and Republican Liberalism* (New York: Oxford University Press, 1997) 99.
[17] There is a growing empirical literature in anthropology and sociology on such communities. See, e.g., Basch, L., Glick Schiller, N., and Szanton Blanc, C., *Nations Unbound: Transnational Projects, Postcolonial Predicaments and Deterritorialized Nation-States* (Toronto: University of Toronto Press, 1994): Smith, R. C., 'Transnational Localities: Community, Technology and the Politics of Membership Within the Context of Mexico and U.S. Migration' in Smith, M. P., and Guarnizo, L. E. (eds.), *Transnationalism From Below* (New Brunswick: Transaction Publ., 1998) 196–240; Portes, A., 'Global Villagers: The Rise of Transnational Communities', *American Prospect* (Mar.–Apr. 1996) 74; Soysal, Y., 'Changing Parameters of Citizenship and Claims-Making: Organized Islam in European Public Spheres' (1997) 26 *Theory and Society* 509, 519–21.

346 Linda Bosniak

subordinate to European national citizenships in several important respects.[18]

My contention is this: that the idea of citizenship possesses multiple meanings; it represents, at once, a variety of different social and political institutions and practices. To determine whether citizenship is necessarily national in character, therefore, we ought to determine whether the practices and institutions ordinarily designated by the term are actually constrained by the bounds of the nation-state. By this measure, the premise that there is a necessary relationship between citizenship and the nation-state is questionable, at least in some contexts.

On the other hand, even if citizenship is not necessarily national in character as a matter of *fact*, we may still want to ask whether it ought to be. Is the relationship between citizenship and nationality a desirable one? *Should* citizenship be national? Or should we aspire to what some recent commentators have described as emerging forms of 'postnational citizenship'?[19]

Of course, asking where citizenship should be located is to ask several questions at once, as, given citizenship's various associated meanings or discourses, we are asking about the proper locus of rights, politics, legal status, identities, and solidarities simultaneously. I have been interested in citizenship solidarity and citizenship, in particular, because they inform our experience of citizenship in its other aspects. I will therefore limit my focus to this dimension.

Especially under conditions of globalization, we are faced all the time with questions about where (and with whom) our identifications and solidarities should lie. In particular, we are often pressed by events of the day—those concerning immigration or trade, for example—to consider whether our primary commitments lie with co-nationals or elsewhere. The significance and the difficulty of this question, however, is not always reflected in our scholarship. Most of the citizenship literature, in particular, simply presumes, without argument, that our primary political and ethical commitments are to fellow nationals. As one example, a number of progressive American legal scholars have recently been

---

[18] For further discussion see Bosniak, 'Citizenship Denationalized' above, n. 7, 456–60; see also Kraamwinkel, in this volume.

[19] Yasemin Soysal is the best-known exponent of the idea of postnational citizenship (see Soysal, Y., *Limits of Citizenship: Migrants and Postnational Membership in Europe* (Chicago, Ill.: University of Chicago Press, 1994)). Soysal, however, purports to deploy the idea descriptively. For more normative, aspirational invocations see, e.g., Linklater, A., *The Transformation of Political Community* (Columbia, SC: University of South Carolina Press, 1998); Falk, R., 'The Making of Global Citizenship' in Brecher, J., Brown Childs, J., and Cutlr, J. (eds.), *Global Visions* (Boston, Mass.: Beacon Press, 1993); Spiro, P., 'The Citizenship Dilemma' (1999) 51 *Stanford L. Review* 597. See also the comprehensive discussion of this idea in Bosniak, 'Citizenship Denationalized', above, n. 7.

urging recognition of the importance of 'economic' aspects of citizenship. William Forbath and Ken Karst, for example, have argued that 'the right to decent work' and 'the right to earn' are essential features of any defensible conception of equal citizenship.[20] Bruce Ackerman and Ann Alsott, Joel Handler and Charles Reich have all written about the need to guarantee to Americans what they call 'economic citizenship'—by which they mean a decent standard of living—via government and community action.[21]

This literature is clearly to be welcomed for bringing distributional concerns into discussions about citizenship. Citizenship studies have tended to emphasize status-based and political concerns, and it is important to bring matters of economic justice back onto the table. Yet it is also clear that these scholars are exclusively concerned about the economic condition *of Americans.* They do not pause to ask about the working or living conditions of anyone else anywhere else. They simply assume that the universe of normative concern is national. (And, I should add, they pay virtually no attention at all to the ways in which the economic problems they are concerned about are linked to various processes of economic globalization. Their approach is strikingly insular, not just normatively but analytically.)

These scholars, as I have noted, never actually defend their nationalist commitments; they are unspoken and simply assumed. There are some progressive scholars, however, who *have* affirmatively made the case for primary national loyalties. These scholars—often called liberal nationalists—make two kinds of arguments on behalf of the priority of national citizenship affiliations. First, liberal nationalists argue that, as a practical matter, the kinds of redistributive values that political liberals and progressives usually support can be realized only in the context of a bounded, national society. According to political theorist David Miller, 'the welfare state—and . . . programmes to protect minority rights—have always been *national* projects, justified on the basis that members of a community must protect one another and guarantee one another equal respect'.[22] Richard Rorty has declared, in this vein, that 'the primary responsibility of each democratic nation-state is to its own least advantaged citizens'[23] and on that basis has supported trade protectionism and

---

[20] See Forbath, above, n. 11; Forbath, W., 'Civil Rights and Economic Citizenship: Notes on the Past and Future of the Civil Rights and Labor Movements' (2000) 2 *University of Pennsylvania Journal of Labor and Employment Law* 697; Karst, above, n. 11.

[21] Handler, above, n. 11; Ackerman, B., and Alsott, A., *The Stakeholder Society* (New Haven, Conn.: Yale University Press, 1999); Reich, C. A., 'Property Law and the New Economic Order: A Betrayal of Middle Americans and the Poor' (1996) 71 *Chicago-Kent L. Review* 817.

[22] Miller, D., *On Nationality* (Oxford: Oxford University Press, 1995) 187.

[23] Rorty, R., *Achieving Our Country: Leftist Thought in Twentieth Century America* (Cambridge, Mass.: Harvard University Press, 1998) 88.

immigration control. Many liberal nationalists also argue in a more communitarian mode that not only is nationalism necessary for liberal democratic outcomes, but it is intrinsically desirable because the nation-state is the only large-scale contemporary institutional setting in which people may develop the sense of 'common good' or 'shared fate' which is so vital for collective human flourishing.[24]

There are, of course, other ways to conceive of citizenship identity and solidarity. One alternative is the cosmopolitan outlook of people like philosopher Martha Nussbaum, who recently declared herself a 'citizen of the world', and argued that we should 'work to make all human beings part of our community of dialogue and concern'.[25] Support for international human rights and—sometimes—world-wide redistribution of resources[26] is defended in humanitarian terms. Then there are those who are trying to figure out a way to articulate some sort of less totalizing transnational citizenship identity—some kind of updated left internationalism, perhaps, best represented by the movement on behalf of 'globalization from below'.[27] Here, the object of solidarity is not humanity in general so much as the marginalized and subordinated, however precisely defined. Theoretical work on this project is much less developed than on liberal nationalism and cosmopolitanism—partly because those sympathetic to it are cautious about avoiding various fundamentalist habits of thought, and partly because it often seems as if we are stuck in a zero-sum game in which solutions for some mean worse conditions for others across national lines.

Still, there are some recent developments that may seem cause for optimism. One is the AFL-CIO's recent call for amnesty for undocumented immigrants in the USA; another, the burgeoning student anti-sweatshop movement, and the demonstrations against the WTO in Seattle. In each case, one can see forms of transnational, anti-corporate solidarity at work—something which could be described as a kind of incipient transnational citizenship in action.

Of course, the question remains whether we really want to use the language of citizenship to describe these developments. In the end, I remain ambivalent, mostly because it is not at all clear that the idea of

---

[24] Taylor, C. 'Cross-Purposes: The Liberal-Communitarian Debate' in N. L. Rosenblum (ed.), *Liberalism and the Moral Life* (Cambridge, Mass.: Harvard University Press, 1989) 170.

[25] Nussbaum, M., 'Patriotism and Cosmopolitanism' in *ead, For Love of Country: Debating the Limits of Patriotism* (Boston, Mass.: Beacon Press, 1996).

[26] See, e.g., Barry, B., 'Statism and Nationalism: A Cosmopolitan Critique' in Shapiro, I., and Brilmayer, L. (eds.), *Global Justice* (Nomos XLI) (New York: New York University Press, 1999) 12–13.

[27] For a suggestive discussion of some of the dilemmas entailed in such a project see Robbins, B., *Feeling Global: Internationalism In Distress* (New York: New York University Press, 1999).

citizenship can be divorced from its long association with the national state. At the same time, however, I am inclined to think that the term's tremendous rhetorical power and its sometimes progressive history mean that we ought to hang on to it and to try to redefine it in post-national terms. At the very least, describing the post-national ethical impulse in the language of citizenship serves as a rhetorical form of critique of nationally-centred modes of political thought—especially in otherwise progressive discourse.

Part VI

Labour Solidarity in an Era of Globalization: Opportunities and Challenges

18

The Decline of Union Power—Structural Inevitability or Policy Choice?

FRANCES RADAY*

Collective labour power has become something of an anathema in politically correct societal and academic discourse. After close to a century of collective labour relations in the developed world, accompanied by the vigorous growth of trade unions and the regulation of employment conditions by collective bargaining, there is clear evidence of a reversal, a return to individualism and free market forces. The idiom of the *fin de siècle* has been individualism and liberalism. Francis Fukuyama sees this as the final phase, the end of history, with liberal democracy and modern capitalism here to stay as the mode of social organization consistent with people's 'nature'.[1] And so Fukuyama joins forces with Friedman and Posner who have gone before him to reinforce the popular ideology that social systems should conform to individualistic competitive instincts. The delegitimization of collective power and of the unions in which it is concentrated is part of this liberal ideology. Thus, Posner condemns unions as cartels,[2] Estreicher argues that global competition has made unions anomalous,[3] and Basset and Cave attribute the fall of unions to rampant individualism amongst workers.[4]

This ideological attack on welfare socialism and, with it, collective labour power, is, I believe, not to be conceded. There are competing worldviews: co-operation *vis-à-vis* competition; responsibility *vis-à-vis* right; and equality *vis-à-vis* elitism. John Kelly describes the replacement of class-conscious collectivism with self-interested individualism, and of adversarial collective bargaining with co-operative social partnership as 'fashionable and beguiling notions which are seriously flawed and misleading'.[5] The human costs of competition and of resulting social

---

* My thanks go to Daniel Elan for his research assistance in preparing this article and for his insightful comments.

[1] Fukuyama, F., 'Women and the Evolution of World Politics' (1998) 77 *Foreign Affairs* 24.

[2] Posner, R., 'Some Economics of Labor Law' (1984) 51 *University of Chicago L. Review* 987.

[3] Estreicher, S., 'Labor Law Reform in a World of Competitive Product Markets' (1993) 69 *Chicago-Kent L. Review* 3, 13.

[4] Bassett, P., and Cave, A., *All for One—the Future of the Unions* (London: Fabian Pamphlet, 1993).

[5] Kelly, J., *Rethinking Industrial Relations—Moblization, Collectivism and Long Waves* (London: Routledge, 1998) 1.

inequality have been well documented by Amartya Sen, and the importance of non-market considerations restored to the current map of political philosophy.[6] I suggest that although liberalism and free market ideology have challenged welfare socialism, they have not succeeded in exorcizing it.

The liberal attack on collective labour power must, of course, fail in so far as the attack on welfare socialism fails, for both are part of the same class-conscious collectivism targeted by competitive individualism. But, even on the ideological grounds of liberalism itself, the attack on unions should fail. In collective bargaining, unions act not as external interveners in market forces but as market actors, negotiating transactions under the pressures of economic exigencies. The transactions negotiated by unions are market transactions based on the relative economic bargaining strength of the negotiating parties. The argument that unions are cartels undermining market efficiency seems somewhat strange in view of the unquestioning acceptance of joint interest negotiation throughout economic markets. The joint interest negotiation of employees via unions is no more monopolistic than the transactions negotiated by other composite market actors, such as partnerships, shareholding companies, governments, and states. Furthermore, just like other negotiating parties, unions have an economic interest in the mutual success of the transaction. They need to reach a transaction that is viable not only for them but also for the firm because, without the firm, there are no jobs and, without jobs, no union. In this sense, unions are an integral part of the free market.

The collective bargaining function of unions straddles the ideologies of welfare socialism and free market capitalism. Using market techniques, negotiating on behalf of comparatively powerless individuals, and righting a socio-economic imbalance, unions perform an important welfare function. As Kelly points out, 'worker collectivism is an effective and situationally specific response to injustice, not an irrelevant anachronism'.[7] This welfare role of unions is challenged, however, not only by the neo-liberals as being contrary to free market ideology, but also by some critical left theorists. Collective *laissez faire* has been taken to task for 'persistently failing to embrace certain categories of workers (largely populated by women) or advance their interests' and for representing the workplace as a largely autonomous, self-governing entity which presupposes a conceptual and practical separation of the realms of work and family.[8] However, this criticism, though in part valid, is not an argument against the essential welfare

---

[6] Sen, A., *Inequality Re-examined* (Oxford: Clarendon Press, 1992).

[7] Above, n. 5, 1.

[8] Conaghan, J., 'Feminism and Labour Law: Contesting the Terrain' in Morris, A., and O'Donnell, T. (eds.), *Feminist Perspectives on Employment Law* (London: Cavendish, 1999) 13. See also Crain, M., 'Feminism, Labor and Power' (1992) 65 *Southern California L. Review* 1819.

value of unions. The failure to take women workers' interests into account and seek ways of integrating the family and the workplace has been shared by almost all policy-making institutions, and unions should not be singled out from other social actors as the transgressors. Indeed, in some countries, the unions' record has been better than that of other policy-makers: union negotiation of childcare leave or maternity benefits beyond the statutory minimum is an example of this.[9]

The campaign to herald the demise of trade unionism is being conducted at an empirical as well as an ideological level. The empirical claim is made, with overtones of finality, that unions are declining everywhere. This decline is perceived as structural. It is perceived as resulting from globalization, changes in workers' education and expectations, the move to individualism, the changing character of work from traditional life-time employment to transient and contingent labour, the shift from industrial and manufacturing jobs to services, and so on. These—the decline of unions and the reasons for it—are all presented as social facts, engendered by objective forces. However, the very fact of universal decline is a questionable proposition, as is also the attribution of any decline, which does exist, to structural change.[10]

First, it seems to be an overgeneralization to say that union membership is declining everywhere. It is clear from the ILO World Labour Report 1997–8 that, although over the years 1985–95, there is an overall trend towards decline in union membership, some countries show no change: for example, Belgium, Canada, Denmark, Finland, Malta, Norway, Spain, and Sweden. These are not marginal examples, in view of the importance of the countries involved as developed free market economies with distinctive socio-political ideologies. Secondly, even where there is a decline in union membership, this does not tell the whole story about the deterioration of union power. There is no necessary direct correlation between the two. In France, for instance, union membership is as low as 6 per cent of the workforce and yet the influence of French unions is considerable.[11] The decline in union membership may or may not be co-extensive with a decline in collective agreement coverage; this will depend on the structure of collective bargaining, the basis of union representation in bargaining units, and the scope of application of collective bargaining agreements. Thirdly, it is not clear that the decline of union power is evolutionary and irreversible. Kelly argues that, 'contrary

---

[9] See ILO-ICFTU Survey, *The Role of Trade Unions in Promoting Gender Equality and Protecting Vulnerable Women Workers* (Geneva: ILO, 1999) 26.

[10] See Cella, G., and Treu, T., 'National Trade Union Movements' in Blanpain, R., and Engels, C. (eds.), *Comparative Labour Law in Industrialised Market Economies* (The Hague: Kluwer, 1998) 281, 303.

[11] *World Labour Report 1997–1998* (Geneva: ILO, 1998) 7.

to postmodernist claims that the classical labour movement is in terminal decline, long wave theory suggests that it is more likely to be on the threshold of a resurgence'.[12]

The presentation of the decline of union power as if it were ideologically and empirically predetermined pre-empts searching examination of the issues of choice involved in that decline. Policy choices frame the legal context in which unions thrive or fail. The acceptance of union decline as a fact impedes inquiry into ways of avoiding such a decline. The project of this chapter is to analyse the extent to which the maintenance of union strength or its decline is to be attributed to political-legal choices rather than viewed as the inevitable result of socio-economic structural exigencies. One of the most significant analyses of the impact of legal regulation on trade union bargaining power is the Weiler analysis of the differences between the USA and Canada.[13] Here, I shall attempt—on the basis of a wider comparative analysis as part of which I shall examine the Israeli experience—to show various political-legal policies that contribute to the rise or fall of unions.

The Israeli experience might be considered to present the pathology of the interaction of law and union power. It is instructive to note (and the implications will be discussed below) that Israel union membership exhibited the most drastic decline in density of all the countries listed in the World Labour Report. It showed a decline of 77 per cent—as compared with the fairly severe decline of 27 per cent of union membership density in the UK, and 17.6 per cent in Germany.[14] This decline has coincided with changes in legislative policy. The major piece of legislation, which clearly and directly affected union membership, was the National Health Insurance Law, which came into effect in 1995. This law severed the connection between the Histadrut General Federation of Employees in Israel and the General Sick Fund, which it had established at the time of its inception. The General Sick Fund had provided many of the functions of a national health insurance scheme. Membership of the Fund had been conditional upon membership of the Histadrut itself. Hence, the Fund had acted as a method of attracting union membership. Indeed, at the beginning of the 1980s, 90 per cent of salaried employees were members of the Histadrut. By the beginning of the 1990s, however, there had been a drop in this high level of membership. This may have been caused by many

---

[12] Above, n. 5, 1.

[13] Weiler, P., 'Promises to Keep: Securing Workers' Rights to Self-Organization under the NLRA' (1983) 96 *Harvard L. Review* 1769 and 'Striking a New Balance: Freedom of Contract and the Prospects for Union Representation' (1985) 98 *Harvard L. Review* 351. See also Schiller, R. E., 'From Group Rights to Individual Liberties: Post-War Labor Law, Liberalism, and the Waning of Union Strength' (1999) 1 *Berkeley Journal of Employment and Labor Law* 2.

[14] See above n. 11, 239–40.

factors: general global economic and structural factors, the development of alternative private health insurance funds, and the shift from a socialist to a capitalist political-legal climate in Israel which will be discussed below. According to some reports, by 1992, Histadrut membership had dropped to as low as 42 per cent;[15] but it seems hard to reconcile this figure with the continued presence of the General Sick Fund as the largest of the health insurance funds in Israel, with a membership of 70 per cent of all households. When the 1995 Law came into effect, Histadrut membership dropped immediately to 23 per cent, and by 1998 was down to 19 per cent of salaried employees. In spite of this severe blow to membership numbers, the Histadrut still retains some political power. The Histadrut leadership has attempted to transpose its traditional strength into direct political power by running as a political party in the Knesset, winning two seats in the 1999 elections. It remains to be seen how long this historically derived power will be sustained.

It is in light, *inter alia*, of the sudden and dramatic decline in union membership in Israel that I pose the question whether the decline of union strength is the inevitable result of socio-economic structural evolution or can be attributed to political-legal choices. The polarization of these two options is in itself problematic since, amongst other things, a deconstructive view of either option could lead us to the other as a causal factor. Political-legal choices may be the result of socio-economic change, and socio-economic change may be engendered by political-legal choices. The aim then is not to attempt to isolate political-legal choices as a sole or even major cause of union decline but merely to re-establish their importance as among the possible determinative factors. The argument is anti-determinist, intended to counterbalance the currently predominant view according to which unions are defunct, by act of God and the market.[16]

---

[15] Natanson, R., and Zaiser, G., 'The Impact of Trade Unions in Times of Economic Change' (1997) 47 *Economics Quarterly* 373 (in Hebrew).

[16] For the sake of clarification, I draw attention to the fact that this inquiry into the ways legal policy may directly or indirectly affect unions is informed by the assumption that union bargaining power fulfils a unique function in preserving the political, social, and economic well-being of free market economies. In the political sphere, the power of unions to represent employees makes an important contribution to democracy at both state and industrial levels. At the state level, it is a vital component of political democracy, allowing the inchoate voice of the working community to be focused and heard. At the industrial level, it is the vehicle for industrial democracy, allowing representation of employee interests in decisions fundamentally affecting their lives. In the social sphere, it is union power that moderates the gap between entrepreneurial or managerial incomes and the incomes of the rank and file, making a unique contribution to the equalizing of the distribution of resources. Union influence on legislative and governmental policy is directed to the promotion of economic and social rights and maintenance of higher levels of welfare benefits. Finally, unions have the greatest potential for effectively policing the workplace, for securing observance of employees' statutory rights and preventing the neglect of health and safety measures.

I POLITICAL-LEGAL POLICIES

Policy regarding trade unions falls into three rough modes: deterrent, neutral, or supportive. A deterrent policy is one that limits or deters union formation, growth, or collective bargaining activity. A neutral policy is non-interventionist, allowing unions and management to form their own rules of the game and provide their own sanctions for breach. A supportive policy is one under which the political or legal system provides incentives for union development or collective bargaining activities.

There is a general perception that policy in the industrialized world developed in a linear fashion through these three modes. Cella and Treu trace an evolution, in almost all developed nations, from 'repression', to 'tolerance', to 'intervention', and they regard the interventionist phase as having 'support[ed] the formation and growth of trade unions'.[17] The culmination of this linear trend—the current period—is regarded as a period of support and benevolence towards trade unions. In this perception, there may be a 'mix of promotion versus restriction', with registration and recognition procedures imposed by the state as a condition for the increased state support for their activities.[18] Diversions from this linear trend are regarded as specific and exceptional, not counter-trends.[19] If this perception is correct, it lends support to the argument that the current decline of unions cannot be attributable to shifting policy patterns. It is this premise that I re-examine here.

There is no doubt that a severely deterrent approach ('repression') was the 'founding' policy for trade union law in the nineteenth and early twentieth centuries. I would also agree that the development of labour law for the hundred years between 1875 and 1975 entailed a shift in industrialized democratic countries from a deterrent to a neutral (or ostensibly neutral) policy ('tolerance'), with measures of *supportive* policy. However, in current post-1975 labour law, I question whether the new interventionism can be classified as generally supportive. Current labour law is, rather, in a modern (or post-modern) phase in which there appears to be a smorgasbord of all three policies—deterrent, neutral, and supportive.

In this chapter, I seek to explore some current examples of deterrent, neutral, and supportive policies in democratic regimes with developed economies, where the provision of basic guarantees freely to organize,

---

[17] See above n. 10, 321–3.

[18] Ibid., 323–4, 339.

[19] Ibid., 322. The authors regard the Thatcher period in the UK and the Reagan era in the USA as temporary digressions from the *laissez-faire* (tolerance) and intervention (promotion) models typical of those countries (at 339).

bargain collectively, and engage in strike action are taken as a given. This exploration should serve to dismantle the myth of political-legal support for unions, or at least tolerance, as the uniform backdrop for the decline of union power. This project is subject to two caveats. First, the evidence is obviously selective and is offered only in an anecdotal or suggestive way as a framework for future analysis. Secondly, I do not presume to establish which is cause and which effect—political policy or union power—either may be the causative factor: strong unions may produce benevolent political policy or vice versa. This said, the discovery of a correlation may, at the very least, indicate that political-legal policy has a part to play in strengthening or weakening unions and is likely to be used by whichever side has the power to deploy it. It may also demonstrate the possibility that any structural trends toward union decline are being either slowed down or accelerated by legal policy measures.

Deterrence

Current deterrent policies can be divided into three categories: the undermining of union power to organize and strike; the legitimization of an inherently non-unionizable or extra-collective bargaining workforce; and the facilitation of employer exit from the collective bargaining framework. Some of these deterrent policies are direct and some merely contribute indirectly to the decline of unionism by creating a deterrent environment.

Undermining union power to organize and strike

A prime example of legal policy that directly undermines union power to organize has been the delegitimization of union security arrangements. The shift in attitude to union security arrangements is one of the outcomes of the constitutionalization of labour law. The constitutionalization process has engendered a move from collective rights to individual justice.[20] Thus, for example, the freedom to organize has gradually been expanded to include an equal freedom not to organize, and, although the European Court of Human Rights in the (in)famous decision of *Young, James and Webster* stopped short of such a conclusion on the ground that it was not necessary to the decision at hand, their holding that the closed shop arrangements under scrutiny, requiring union membership as a condition of employment, were a violation of the freedom of association

---

[20] I have developed this argument more fully elsewhere in Raday, F., 'Constitutionalisation of Labour Law' in Blanpain, B., and Weiss, M. (eds.), *The Changing Face of Labour Law and Industrial Relations, Liber Amicorum in Honour of Professor Clyde Summers* (Baden-Baden: Nomos Verlagsgesellschaft, 1993) 83–108; Raday, F., 'Privatising Human Rights and the Abuse of Power' (2000) 13 *Canadian Journal of Law and Jurisprudence* 103.

provision of the European Convention, effectively recognized a 'negative' right not to be compelled to associate.[21]

Weiler, emphasizing the individualistic quality of the constitutional lens, describes union security arrangements as anathema to market libertarians and romantic liberals alike:

> They see a lone gallant dissenter struggling against a large bureaucratic union organization, fighting a cause that is intuitively appealing to a judge observing the contest through the lens of the Charter. To my mind, though, that image of these cases is too formal and individualistic in tone; it ignores the real social context for which these labour practices and policies have been devised.[22]

The shift from collective to individual justice and the resulting delegitimization of union security arrangements directly undermine union organizing power.[23] Where the union's achievements in collective bargaining become a public good, freely available to all employees in the bargaining unit, the union has no economic leverage by which to attract fee-paying members on an individual cost-benefit basis. Hence, if deprived of the right to establish effective union security arrangements, the union must rely on employees' enlightened self-interest. It is significant that in the Scandinavian countries, the constitutional freedom of association has not been considered to incorporate a negative freedom to disassociate.[24]

Although it is beyond the scope of this article systematically to examine variations in the basic freedom to organize, bargain collectively, and strike, I shall very briefly draw attention to measures taken to restrict the right to strike during the decade of union decline, between 1985 and 1995. There was not a general trend to restrict the freedom to strike in this period and the restrictive measures seem to have been something of an exception. However, not surprisingly, strike restriction formed an intrinsic part of UK labour policy during the Thatcher years and in subsequent Conservative administrations (throughout the 1980s and most of the 1990s). In particular, restrictions were imposed on secondary action, and strike action was conditioned upon a strike vote majority with highly

---

[21] *Young, James and Webster* v. *United Kingdom* [1981] IRLR 408. The decision of the Court did not entirely prohibit all forms of union security arrangement: while it prohibited the closed shop, it left the legitimacy of the union shop unclear and failed to refer to agency shops. It is pertinent that the Scandinavian justices wrote a dissenting opinion in which they strongly rejected the idea that a freedom not to organize is an integral part of the freedom to organize.

[22] Weiler, P., 'The Charter at Work: Reflections on the Constitutionalizing of Labour and Employment Law' (1990) 40 *University of Toronto L. Journal* 117, 135.

[23] Wedderburn, K. W., *Labour Law and Freedom: Further Essays in Labour Law* (London: Lawrence and Wishart, 1995) 188.

[24] Hasselbach, O., and Jacobsen, P., *Labour Law and Industrial Relations in Denmark* (The Hague: Kluwer Law International, 1999) 212; and see above, n. 21.

complex ballot provisions.[25] Similarly, legislation in New Zealand in 1991 transformed the ethos of labour law from that of collective agreements to individual employment contracts, shifted the right to strike from union to individual level, and prohibited secondary action.[26] In Ontario, Canada, a restrictive strike ballot requirement was introduced for the first time in the Labour Relations Act 1995. In Italy, essential service strikes were comprehensively regulated in 1990.[27]

The measures that are most pertinent here are the restrictions on secondary action and the strike ballot requirements. The prohibition of secondary action is particularly disabling for unions in the context of the recent trend towards the decentralization of collective bargaining at both the global and the national level, which reduces the effectiveness of single employer strikes. The strike vote may allow the growing numbers of Weiler's 'gallant dissenters' to impose their will on union leaderships.[28]

Cancellation of trade union supply of social services to members is an unusual, direct deterrent method and is that which the Israeli legislature used in relation to the Histadrut's health fund. Israel's National Health Insurance Law was expressly intended, amongst its other purposes, to sever the funding of Histadrut trade union activity from the membership dues collected as a condition for admission to its General Sick Fund. This policy was a response to complaints about the alleged diversion of funds from health insurance to union activities and the infringement of employees' freedom not to join the Histadrut, or to leave it, on insurance grounds. Although there seems to have been justification for these complaints and, therefore, a definite need for reform, these concerns could have been addressed by a range of measures, for example, requiring publication of the Histadrut's accounting and making provision for the waiver of union membership for persons who could not, for health insurance reasons, leave the General Sick Fund. Such reform, however, was not attempted and, instead, the Law dealt a drastic and immediate blow to the Histadrut's base for attracting members.

Legitimization of an inherently non-unionizable or extra-collective bargaining workforce

In a less direct form of deterrence, legal doctrine may be used to create a

[25] Deakin, S., and Morris, G., *Labour Law* (2nd edn., London: Butterworths, 1998) 870–2.

[26] Anderson, G., 'New Zealand' in Blanpain, R. (ed.), *Strikes and Lockouts in Industrial Market Economies* (The Hague: Kluwer, 1994) 123.

[27] Act 14 June 1990 No. 146. See Treu, T., 'Italy' in Blanpai, R. (ed.), *International Encyclopaedia of Labour Law and Industrial Relations* vol. 7 (The Hague: Kluwer, 1998) 213.

[28] The effectiveness of this measure may be in some doubt, since the English experience shows that the rank and file may be more militant than the union leadership; however, the potential for weakening the power of the leadership to take strike action remains clear.

viable framework for an inherently non-unionizable or extra-collective bargaining workforce. Such a workforce may be composed, for instance, of contingent workers, leased workers, or contract workers. Such workers, by definition, fall outside the jurisdiction of the representative union in the user workplace. Their intrusion into the workplace undermines in-house terms and conditions, which may be undercut by this 'outsider' labour. Although all these forms of contingent employment are the result of employer preferences and labour market developments, it is the labour law system that determines whether the framework of regulation is facilitating or restraining. It is no secret that the concept of the employment is a legal construct with a status element not wholly determinable by agreement between the parties. Hence, the possibility of using workers' services without entering into an employment relationship with them is as much a consequence of law as of economic factors.[29]

A prime example of the way the changing legal construct of the employment relationship serves to undermine collective bargaining potential is the regulation of leased workers. As regards workers leased by labour-only contractors, there has been a progressive liberalization of the laws regulating this triangular mode of employment. Initially, in many countries, there were various forms of prohibition of labour-only contracting. However, the 1990s witnessed a retreat from absolute prohibition in national regulation and a move towards liberalization. This move towards liberalization has been reinforced by the ILO. In 1997, the ILO formulated a policy considerably more facilitative of labour-only contracting than most national regulation, even after its liberalization.[30] ILO Convention 181 does not restrict the use of this mode of employment to temporary work; it does not limit the numerical or percentage extent of recourse to leased workers in order to protect core, in-house employment; it does not equate leased workers' employment conditions to those of in-house employees of the user enterprise; and it does not pre-empt the use of this mode of employment to undermine collective bargaining.[31]

The economic realities of labour-only contracting and the segmentation of the workplace which it produces combine to undermine the bargaining power of unions and ensure that leased labour will be

---

[29] Gonos, G., 'The Contest over "Employee" Status in the Postwar United States: The Case of Temporary Help Firms' (1997) 31 *Law and Society Review* 81, 83.

[30] ILO C181 Private Employment Agencies Convention 1997.

[31] Raday, F., 'The Insider–Outsider Politics of Labour Only Contracting' (1999) 20 *Comparative Labor Law and Policy Journal* 413. The anomalous situation now created is that any call for reform in national jurisdictions based on ILO standards will likely be a call for further liberalization of the labour market and the repeal of national protective measures. See, e.g., the arguments of Blanpain, R., 'Belgian Report I, Reports to the International Conference on the Role of Private Employment Agencies' (unpublished paper, Leuven Belgium, 1998).

employed on relatively low wages and conditions. This, in turn, also weakens union power to represent in-house labour against the undercutting of their terms by leased employees. Studies of the Israeli experience illustrate the impact of the ILO standards on collective bargaining and the strength of the unions. In Israel, regulation of labour-only contracting was formulated in the 1996 Employment through Labour-Only Contractors Law, which was fully in accord with the supervision requirements of the then Draft ILO Convention 181. Under the Law, the employment of leased labour was not limited to temporary work. The ostensible policy of the Law was, instead, to solve the problem of protecting the interests of leased employees through encouraging collective bargaining with the labour-only contractors. Analysis of the collective agreements concluded in Israel under the policy verified the predicted result and showed that such agreements only provided a much inferior level of employee protection;[32] on the basis of these findings, the Histadrut Party (One Israel) succeeded in passing a private member's bill restricting this form of employment to a period of nine months.[33]

Legitimization of atypical employment is a form of indirect rather than direct deterrence of collective bargaining power. In Sweden it seems that unions have succeeded in coping with the shift to the use of atypical employees by organizing them and concluding advantageous collective agreements on their behalf. The implication of the Swedish unions' success in dealing with the 'temp business' is not, however, an indicator that labour-only contracting does not deter unions. On the contrary, it is an indicator of the innate strength of the Swedish union movement and its deep-rooted place in social tradition and values that it managed, as Fahlbeck comments, to accomplish a 'seemingly impossible feat'.[34] This ethos, when combined with union flexibility in devising new solutions to new problems, appears to have won the day. Furthermore, there was popular support for the unions' action on this issue.[35] Even in Sweden, moreover, legal regulation may still be regarded as an important factor in maintaining a high level of union power as, on all counts other than labour leasing and privatization (as discussed below) which both constitute only indirect deterrence, the Swedish legal system is supportive of unionism and not deterrent.

Facilitating employer exit from the collective bargaining framework

Privatization and transfers of undertakings indirectly undermine collective

---

[32] See Raday, above, n. 31.

[33] Amendment to the Law of Employment by Labour-Only Contractors, 2000.

[34] Fahlbeck, R., *Nothing Succeeds Like Success*, Acta Societatis Juridicae Lundensis No. 136, (Lund: Akademibokhandelni, 1999) 37–41.

[35] Ibid.

bargaining power. In modern labour relations there is a greatly increased incidence of identity change of employer, whether through privatization and/or transfers of undertakings in their various forms; this often brings with it, by design or otherwise, the termination of collective labour relations. Although there are exceptions, much of the legal regulation of these transformations seems to have been facilitative of the demise of the collective bargaining framework.

Privatization has been one of the major policies undermining union power. There is a clear correlation between privatization and a fall in union membership.[36] This result follows naturally where there is a higher level of unionization in the public than in the private sector, as seems to be the case in most European states, the USA, and Japan. Moreover, since privatization is usually advocated as a way of increasing efficiency, typically by workforce reduction, it will obviously be deleterious to union image and power.

Furthermore, in the process of privatization, unions will often be deprived of a voice. In EC law, for instance, the classification of privatization as a transfer of an undertaking is considered problematic because of difficulties associated with the identification of privatization as the transfer of an 'economic entity'.[37] In so far as this precludes the application of the EC Acquired Rights Directive (ARD) to some privatization initiatives, it also deprives the union (or employee representatives) of a right to be consulted. The union is then left with no opportunity to protect its standing after privatization, and no leverage in bargaining.

Similarly, where a change of control can be achieved by the transfer of shares, with no formal legal change of ownership, employees are, in legal terms, in a situation of unchanged labour relations with the *same employer*. The protections conferred by the ARD do not, in these circumstances apply.[38]

Even a legally protected transfer of undertaking involving a change of the employer's legal identity may undermine union power. Where a firm is an organized workplace and has a tradition of bargaining with a certain union or unions, the likelihood of continued recognition and bargaining is greater with the old than with a new owner. Indeed, recognizing the threat to the collective regulation of labour relations, the ARD expressly provides that 'the transferee shall continue to observe the terms and conditions agreed in any collective agreement . . . until the date of termination or expiry of the collective agreement,' and 'Member States may

[36] See above, n. 11, 44–5.

[37] See, e.g., the ECJ decision in Case C–13/95, *Süzen* v. *Zehnacker Gebäudereinigung GmbH Krankenhausservice* [1997] IRLR 255 considering the scope of the Acquired Rights Directive (Council Directive 77/187 [1977] OJ L61/26), and generally Deakin and Morris, above, n. 25, 221–5.   [38] Ibid., 226.

limit the period for observing such terms and conditions, with the provision that it shall not be less than one year' (Article 3(3)). The Directive also imposes an obligation on employers to consult employee representatives in good time prior to transfer (Article 6). Addressing the individual insecurity of employees, the Directive guarantees that the 'transferor's rights and obligations arising from a contract of employment or from an employment relationship existing on the date of a transfer . . . shall, by reason of such transfer, be transferred to the transferee', effecting thereby the transfer of individual contracts of employment (Article 3(1)). None of this, however, amounts to a guarantee of continuity of *recognition of the union* for the purposes of collective bargaining after the transfer.

Indeed the protection EC law confers on individual employees may actually herald the swansong of the union. If individual employees have only one right, the right to be transferred, then a transfer of undertakings, too, becomes a seamless web in which the union has no leverage with which to bargain for individual employee benefits or the continuation of a collective bargaining relationship. The right of employees to refuse to be transferred is a right that might have given the union some additional say in the process. Indeed, such a right existed under general principles of contract and assignment[39] but has been eroded in the modern labour law of some, though not all, European countries. This erosion has taken place under the auspices of the ARD, as interpreted by the ECJ. The Court in *Katsikas*,[40] although endorsing the freedom of employees to refuse to work for the new owner, as provided by the German legislation under review, refrained from interfering with Member States' regulation of the impact such a refusal has on an employee's relationship with the previous employer. This residual freedom leaves unchallengeable legislation in Member States which voids the employee's contractual rights *vis-à-vis* the prior employer, leaving him or her with the option of transferring or resigning. As a consequence, the employee's autonomy to refuse transfer has been systematically eroded in some EC Member States, specifically, England and France.[41] Both countries' legislation has been severely criticized from within.[42] Further, it should be noted that not all European

---

[39] *Nokes* v. *Doncaster Collieries* [1940] All ER 549, 556.

[40] Case C–132/91, *Katsikas* v. *Konstantinidis* [1992] ECR I–6577, [1993] 1 CMLR 845 involved an unsuccessful challenge to the contractual autonomy of employees to refuse to be transferred, which had been recognized by a German Federal Court as required by freedom of association and principles of human dignity.

[41] See Transfer of Undertakings (Protection of Employment) Regulations 1981; SI 1981, No. 1794, reg. 5(4B) (UK) and Art. 23, 70, book 1 of the Code du Travail, Etude JCP (1963) 37 *La Semaine Juridique* 1753 (France).

[42] See *Hay* v. *George Hanson (Building Constructors)* [1996] IRLR 427 (UK); Schaeffer, E., 'L'envers de L'article 23, 7° livre I du Code du Travail', Etude JCP (1963) 37 *La Semaine Juridique* 1753.

systems have followed suit: legislation in Italy[43] and Sweden[44] follows the German model (vindicated in *Katsikas*). Furthermore, in France and Denmark, although the individual employee does not have a right of refusal, the union's rights to bargain and strike against privatization or a transfer of the undertaking are fully protected and effectively used.

In Israel, in the absence of any legislation regulating the issue, the English model has been adopted by the National Labour Court in the case of an attempt by the Israel Aircraft Industries to transfer and separate a plant of 300 employees from the main body of the Industry, a government company with 15,000 employees.[45] The long-term strategy behind the transfer is preparation of the company for privatization. The *status quo ante* is presently being preserved by special collective agreement provisions, while the issue is on review in petition to the Supreme Court.

A way of facilitating the unilateral termination of a collective bargaining tradition by the employer was illustrated in the UK in *Associated Newspapers Ltd*. v. *Wilson* and *Associated British Ports* v. *Palmer and others*.[46] In these cases (heard together), the employers had adopted a policy of change from collective agreement governance of employment conditions to individual employment contracts. In this context, they had offered a pay increase to employees willing to sign individual employment contracts. This pay increase was withheld from employees who, as union members, refused to sign individual employment contracts and chose to retain the conditions fixed in the pre-existing collective agreement. The House of Lords held that the employers' 'omission' to give the pay increase to employees who refused to sign individual contracts did not amount to 'action' short of dismissal for purposes of deterring union membership under the freedom of association provisions in the Trade Union and Labour Relations (Consolidation) Act 1992 (section 146). This judicial decision served to reinforce a legislative policy originating in the Thatcher era, which promoted individualism and the restriction of trade union freedoms.[47] Bob Hepple and Sandra Fredman describe the legislative policy of Thatcherism in the following terms:

The policy of encouragement of trade union membership changed radically when Mrs Thatcher's Conservative government came to power in 1979. A central tenet of Thatcherism has been the view that trade unions impede the operation of the free market and threaten individual freedoms. Legislation has been introduced

---

[43] See Arts. 410 and 411 of the Code of Civil Procedure (1996) 14 International Labour Law Reports 231, 232.

[44] See (1997) 15 International Labour Law Reports 302, 303.

[45] *The Histadrut* v. *Israel Aircraft Industries* (1996) 29 PDA 601.

[46] [1995] 2 WLR 354.

[47] Simpson, B., 'Freedom to Associate and the Right to Organise: the Failure of an Individual Rights Strategy' (1995) 24 *ILJ* 235, 251.

placing increasing restrictions on trade union freedom and the government no longer aims by its own practices to encourage employers in the private sector to permit and recognise trade union organisation.[48]

There is convincing evidence of a correlation between direct deterrent policy and decline in union power. In England, where the drop in union density was, at 27 per cent, amongst the highest in post-industrial democracies over the 1985–95 period, there is a clear correlation with deterrent policy towards unions. Legislative restrictions on the ability to take strike action, combined with a liberal policy regarding contingent labour, and judicial endorsement of employer techniques to discourage collective bargaining are all legacies of the Thatcher era and took their toll on union membership and power. It should be pointed out that since the fall of the Conservative government in 1997, the new Labour government has introduced some auxiliary legislation to support unions, including the right of unions to recognition for collective bargaining purposes, some amendment of the procedures governing strike ballots, and greater protection against dismissal for striking employees.[49]

In Sweden, where union membership density was maintained, and in Italy, where the drop in density was a mere 7 per cent, direct deterrent policies were not in evidence. Germany is an apparent exception: although direct deterrent policies were not adopted, there was nevertheless a considerable drop in membership density, about 17 per cent, in both the former GDR and GFR; however, there may be extrinsic explanations for this apparent antithetical case in view of the 'shock of unification'.[50]

In Israel, the drop in union membership density was, as we have noted, the highest to be found anywhere. There is no doubt that this took place in the context of a direct deterrent policy introduced by the National Health Law, and the more indirect deterrence of a changing political-legal environment, with growing pressures for privatization and liberalization of the use of contingent employment and foreign workers. Both legislative and judicial policy combined in the decade from 1985 to 1995 to move Israeli society away from socialist collectivism towards an individualistic and capitalist free market ideology, with the rapid introduction of wage and income inequality. As a postscript on Israel, it must be added that,

---

[48] Hepple, B. A., and Fredman, S., *Labour Law and Industrial Relations in Great Britain* (Deventer: Kluwer, 1986). The Labour government has since changed the law so that omissions now fall within the notion of 'detriment' for purposes of the 1992 Act. However, the ideological message of *Associated Newspapers* has not been categorically overturned. See Deakin and Morris, above, n. 25, 724.

[49] Employment Relations Act 1999. See Lord Wedderburn, 'Collective Bargaining or Legal Enactment: the 1999 Act and Union Recognition' (2000) 29 *ILJ* 1.

[50] Streeck, W., 'German Capitalism: Does It Exist? Can It Survive?' in Crouch, C., and Streeck, W. (eds.), *Political Economy of Modern Capitalism: Mapping Convergence and Diversity* (London: Sage, 1997) 33.

since 1997–9, the Israeli courts have backtracked somewhat from the
earlier shift towards individualism,[51] and the Knesset has recently
promulgated legislation restricting labour-only contracting.[52] However,
these moves came only after the Histadrut had been reduced from a giant
to a dwarf union.

Neutral policy

The initial moves of legal systems, in the late nineteenth and early twentieth centuries, to repeal the various liabilities accompanying trade union
activity were grounded in neutralist policies and, indeed, for much of the
twentieth century, neutralism was considered an appropriate stance. The
abrogation of repressive measures could obviously be defined as a shift
towards neutralism, taking the form of an assertion of basic liberty and,
hence, a solely facilitative measure.

However, beyond such abrogation of prohibitions, neutralism is, of
course, hard to define. Which, for instance, is more truly neutral, the
enforcement of collective agreements (ubiquitous) or the non-enforce-
ment of collective agreements (English common law)? The traditional
English system (pre-Thatcher), with its lack of legislation on collective
bargaining and strikes, is often paraded as the prime example of neutrality (tolerance).[53] It is not clear that the non-enforceability of what is, in
essence, a contractual obligation can be considered neutral in all circumstances. It may be intervention in favour of the employees, where it is the
binding effect of peace obligations that is being denied, or intervention on
behalf of employers, where substantive terms cannot be enforced. What
kind of recognition of union representative status is the more neutral:
bargaining unit elections (the North American model) or membership
competition (the Israeli model)? Whether or not a policy is neutral in
effect depends on complex factors, such as the methods of collective
bargaining and the attitudes of the collective bargaining parties in the
specific political and social context.[54]

The Canadian constitutional experience is considered by Paul Weiler to
be a prime example of neutrality. In a fascinating inquiry into the way the
Charter has affected the quality of life in the workplace, Paul Weiler
concludes that it has not affected it at all.[55] The reason for this appears to
be that the courts have, for the most part, 'rejected the use of the new

---

[51] See Raday, F., 'The Trials and Tribulations of *Associated Newspapers* in Foreign Forums'
(1997) 26 *ILJ* 235.
[52] See above, n. 33.   [53] See above, n. 10, 322.
[54] On the need for caution in comparing the impact of legally binding and not legally
binding collective agreements see above, n. 23, 214.
[55] Above, n. 22, 152, 162.

Charter to overturn established labour and employment law principles'.[56] This pattern of non-constitutionalization in the Canadian labour courts has developed, as Weiler himself notes, in the context of an asymmetrical attempt to resort to the Charter by labour and management. Almost all the cases in court were brought by employees or unions; only a scattered handful by employers. This might have been taken to justify a sociological interpretation of the non-intervention by the courts as revealing a judicial bias in favour of management. However, Weiler concludes otherwise, arguing that the restraint was not based on a pro-employer bias but rather on 'an explicit posture of judicial self-restraint towards workplace policies fashioned by our legislatures'.[57] Weiler's view is not beyond controversy.[58]

Neutralism was relevant in the historical phase of cancelling prohibitions. However, in the current era of freedom to organize and bargain collectively, where the basic liberties are taken as given, neutrality, it seems, lies in the eye of the beholder. Rather than seeking out truly neutral policies, which can, in any case, neither deter nor promote unionism, I shall concentrate on the deterrent and supportive poles of the policy spectrum.

Supportive intervention

In countries that have retained their prior levels of union membership into the twenty-first century, a variety of supportive policies promoting continued union organization may be found. These policies are policies that enhance or maintain union power: the power to participate in state institutions; to canvass members and collect membership fees; monopoly rights to the distribution of public goods; and rights to recognition or measures which secure the financial viability of the union. Under some of these policies, there may be a direct incentive to union growth or power while, under others, the impact may be only indirectly beneficial.

Corporatism and union representation in state institutions

In the Nordic countries and in Germany,[59] a right to represent employee interests in the social institutions of the welfare state is bestowed on unions. In 1992, Nordic experts summarized the situation of Nordic unions as follows:

---

[56] Ibid., 167.   [57] Ibid., 167.

[58] Beatty, D., *Putting the Charter to Work: Designing a Constitutional Labour Code* (Kingston, Ont.: McGill-Queen's University Press, 1987).

[59] Weiss, M., 'Labour Law and Industrial Relations in the Federal Republic of Germany' in Blanpain, R. (ed.), *International Encyclopaedia of Labour Law and Industrial Relations* (The Hague: Kluwer, 1994) v, 132.

The present day Nordic trade union movement is not only a pressure organisation in relation to the Government and the employers; it is also an integral part of the state structure. With the support of legislation and the corporative system, trade unions are represented in a number of state committees and organs, ranging from the Labor Court (in all Nordic countries) to various official decision-making bodies (including Universities in Sweden). Corporatism is well established in Sweden, Norway and Finland.[60]

Fahlbeck, in his book on Swedish unions, listing some twenty-three factors influencing union density, includes among them the degree of union involvement in the administration of public labour market policies.[61]

In Israel, the Histadrut, along with the government and the Chamber of Economic Associations (the major employers' association), has been part of a corporatist model. As such, the Histadrut was designated by statute to represent employee interests in matters such as the implementation and adaptation of protective labour laws, consultation on the exercise of power to extend collective agreements by the Minister of Labour, and the appointment of public representatives to the labour courts. These powers remain in place today, in spite of the drastic decline in membership of the Histadrut, and it remains to be seen whether the corporatist model can survive this *de facto* decline.

The official recognition of trade unions as representatives of employee interests in state institutions lends power and legitimacy to the union movement. In the Nordic context, the connection between recognition and power as mutually reinforcing has been noted:

In an international comparison, the level of unionization in the Nordic trade union movement is unique, as is shown by the membership figures. . . . The movement also has a unique social legitimacy, which is partly an explanation and partly a condition for this mobilization. . . .[62]

Employee (non-union) representation in state institutions or in the workplace

Legal systems may confer corporatist power on non-union employee representatives. This is the case in Austria where legislation confers power on statutory representative bodies, including a labour chamber, to supervise the enforcement of statutes and delegate representatives to the management organs of the social insurance services.[63] It is also a feature of German and Swedish co-determination legislation, which confers

[60] Brunn, N., Flodgren, B., Halvorsen, M., Hyden, H., and Nielsen, R., *The Nordic Labour Relations Model* (Aldershot: Dartmouth, 1992) 18.

[61] See above, n. 34, 28.

[62] See above n. 60, 18.

[63] Strasser, R., *Labour Law and Industrial Relations in Austria* (Deventer: Kluwer, 1992) 186–7.

power within the workplace on workers' councils.[64] It is often thought that workers' council legislation is supportive of trade union growth. While it is certainly true that the concept of co-determination is a model conferring legitimacy on employees' voice in workplace management, it is not necessarily a technique that gives power to unions. It is often observed that, in order for workers' councils to be effective, strong union support is essential. Hence, it seems probable that strong unions are a prerequisite for workers' councils rather than workers' councils being a prerequisite for strong unions.

These statutory measures—delegating statutory power to employee bodies other than unions—may not directly enhance the status of the unions. However, unions will as a rule be involved in their implementation and, hence, indirectly gain in influence as a result.[65]

Monopoly over the distribution of a public good

Bestowal upon the union of a monopolistic right to distribute a public good to employees seems to be one of the most effective supportive policies towards unions. Thus, for instance, in Finland,[66] Sweden,[67] and Belgium,[68] the unions administer the payment of social security rights such as unemployment insurance. This monopoly is not a direct incentive to union membership, as the right to benefit from unemployment insurance arrangements is not restricted to union members. Nevertheless, it must certainly create an image of the union as having central importance from the perspective of insured employees and, in more prosaic terms, create a forced point of contact that may induce a commitment to union membership.

In some cases, the monopoly over a public good may create a direct incentive to membership. This seems to be the case as regards bankruptcy payments in Sweden, where the unions have the right to advance payment of employees' claims against their employers in bankruptcy and take over employees' preferential creditor status.[69] This constitutes a statutory monopoly for unions over a public good that may be distributed to members only. The effectiveness of such a monopoly in increasing union power can be demonstrated by the example of Italy's legislative recognition of a quasi-monopoly of the unions over public employment

---

[64] See above, n. 59. [65] Ibid.

[66] Suviranta, A. J., *Labour Law and Industrial Relations in Finland* (2nd edn., The Hague: Kluwer, 1997), 36.

[67] Adlecreutz, A., 'Sweden' in Blanpain, R. (ed.), *International Encyclopaedia of Labour Law and Industrial Relations* (The Hague: Kluwer, 1998) xii, 27.

[68] Loi du 28 decembre 1944 concernant la sécurité sociale des travailleurs; Ârreté royal du 25 novembre 1991 portant regulation du chômage.

[69] See above, n. 67, 89–90.

and unemployment lists in the local labour markets in agriculture in the 1970s, which resulted in 99.8 per cent unionization.[70] These policies can be regarded as a legislative mirror image of the Israeli case. In Israel, the Histadrut had itself established a public good to distribute to members— health care insurance—and government intervened to divest the union movement of its quasi-monopoly over distribution.[71] This measure was taken in the name of freedom of association. The removal of the Histadrut's power to distribute health insurance had, as shown above, an immediate and drastic impact on the reduction of union membership.

The public good that the unions distribute may also be the fruits of collective bargaining. The unions have a monopoly over the distribution of this public good where they are entitled to determine to whom the fruits of collective bargaining will be awarded. This kind of monopoly or quasi-monopoly can be assisted or obstructed by legal techniques. There is assistance in Germany, for instance, where collective agreements have a legally binding and normative effect only if the employee is organized in the contracting union.[72] In contrast, collective bargaining rights become a non-monopolistic public good where employees who are not union members become entitled to collective bargaining achievements as a consequence of legal principles which preclude derogation.[73] By this technique, all employees in the categories covered by a collective agreement benefit from the union's bargaining achievements. Where the collective agreement benefits are freely available to non-members and the union is not allowed to condition eligibility for those benefits on union membership, the power of the union to attract members will not be directly enhanced by their bargaining achievements.

Collective bargaining achievements may also be removed from the purview of union monopoly by governmental extension orders.[74] France, Germany,[75] and Israel[76] are examples of legal systems which have well-

---

[70] Treu, above, n. 27, 143.

[71] This was only a quasi-monopoly since there were other health funds available to the public; the element of a quasi-monopoly was to be found in the fact that for many years the Histadrut's health fund was the one which dominated health insurance, with about 90% of the population being insured through it.

[72] See above, n. 59, 139; in practice, however, non-union employees normally receive the same conditions as union members. It is arguable that the theoretical power of the union to restrict collective agreement rights to union members remains an indirect incentive to membership.

[73] See ibid., 138. See also Suviranta, above, n. 66, 55; Brunn *et al.*, above, n. 60, 94.

[74] Treu, above, n. 27, 184.

[75] See above n. 59, 128–9.

[76] I have discussed the impact of extension orders on collective bargaining freedom elsewhere; see Raday, F., *Adjudication of Interest Disputes—the Compulsory Arbitration Model* (Jerusalem, Institute for Legislative Research and Comparative Law, Hebrew University, 1983).

established systems of governmental extension orders that apply certain collective terms and conditions to wide sectors of the non-unionized labour force. It is clear that the social benefits of extension orders may be at the cost of union marketability. It is notable that, in the Nordic countries, there are no governmental extension orders, which would extend the benefits of collective bargaining to non-unionized employees.[77]

Right to recognition

As Paul Weiler, in his comparison of Canadian and US legislation, has exhaustively shown, legally required procedures for recognition of a union as the representative union may either encourage or discourage union power. His analysis resulted in the clear conclusion that the relative stability of unionism in Canada compared with its drastic decline in the USA could be attributed to differences in the fine-tuning of their ostensibly similar systems for recognition and union elections. He demonstrated that the American legislation allows more opportunity for employers to frustrate union organization and facilitate its demise. Weiler thus argued that, in the absence of material differences in the socio-economic context of labour relations in the two countries, it was these statutory variations which explained the difference.

Not only at the stage of initial organization but also in their ongoing activities, recognition rights for unions may help them weather rough times. This support is pronounced in systems where union bargaining representativity is recognized on the basis of the union's traditional role as bargaining partner, or of other flexible tests that do not rest on the ability of the union to canvass majoritarian support in the bargaining unit at any given time. Such is the case, for instance, in Denmark,[78] Italy, Belgium, Sweden, and France.[79] Wedderburn comments that this system may appear strange in the context of American notions of democracy, according to which union representativity is based on a fully-fledged voting system. He concludes, however:

The adjustment of union 'equality' and promotion of the representative union on a non-elective basis have been required by the need to fashion a mechanism of

---

[77] The Israeli case demonstrates how the system of extension orders may undermine the union's ability to use the power to distribute collective agreement achievements as an incentive to membership. When the Histadrut lost its quasi-monopoly over health insurance, it sought other ways to strengthen its position; one such way was to repeal the extension order system. The Secretary-General of the Histadrut, Amir Peretz, argued that the system would make union membership irrelevant for the working population. The government rejected the suggestion, ostensibly for social policy reasons; the Histadrut then suggested taking agency fees from employees covered by extension orders but this suggestion too was rejected.

[78] See above, n. 24, 242: the union represents a loose, informal collectivity of wage-earners.

[79] See above, n. 23, 189.

democracy that serves both workers' interests and the stability of the system, not abstract precepts of democracy.[80]

The problem of majoritarian requirements for union representativity is demonstrated in Israel. Union representativity is based on membership numbers; the union to which the greatest number of organized employees belong is the representative union and, in the case of plant-level agreements, at least a third of employees in a bargaining unit must be members of the union for it to gain representativity status.[81] Although the membership requirements are not even majoritarian, in current times, with the drastic fall in Histadrut membership, the validity of plant-level collective agreements is in question, even in plants where the Histadrut has been the recognized bargaining partner for the entire life of the enterprise. It is perhaps appropriate, at this juncture, to point out that the decline in Histadrut membership has not been a point of departure for organization for collective bargaining in alternative unions and this means that the effect is not a change of representative union but the threat of elimination of representative unions altogether.

Financing arrangements

Systems which provide by law ways for unions to secure the financing of their activities, for example, legal measures allowing unions to finance their activities through 'check-off' of union dues or the collection of agency fees are systems with a measure of supportive intervention. This provides a source of income and secures some financial stability for unions. The arrangements for check-off and agency fees are usually the product of collective bargaining but the legal system has a role to play. The legality of the arrangements is, of course, a *sine qua non* for their viability. This legality has been challenged in many systems.[82] The legality of various forms of union security has survived the challenge in some legal systems, whether in legislative or judicial provisions. In Canada, the Rand Formula of the 1980 Ontario Colleges Collective Bargaining Act, which legalized agency fees, was upheld in the Supreme Court decision in *Lavigne*,[83] and, in Italy, the right of representative unions to collect dues was expressly sanctioned in the Statute of Workers' Rights 1970, and upheld by the Italian Constitutional Court.[84] In Finland, there is additional support for this source of union financing through the recognition of union dues as tax deductible.[85] In Sweden, union dues, like church fees,

---

[80] See above, n. 23, 189
[81] Collective Agreements Law 1957, s. 3.
[82] See above text at n. 20 ff.
[83] *Lavigne* v. *Ontario Public Service Employees Union et al.* (1991) 81 DLR (4th) 545.
[84] Treu, above, n. 27, 162–3.
[85] Suviranta, above, n. 66, 288.

are recognized as a necessary element in the cost of living basket used for calculating income maintenance levels.

Subsidies

In France, the government has directly subsidized unions. In contrast, when a legislative proposal was touted in Israel to subsidize the Histadrut after the National Health Insurance Law was passed, it was defeated, at least temporarily. The reason the government offered for its refusal to promote the Bill was that it would be contrary to the principles of freedom of organization. The Histadrut itself decided not to promote a private member's Bill since it assessed that no proposal to subsidize unions could muster support in the Knesset.

II CORRELATION BETWEEN UNION POWER AND STATE POLICY

This survey has verified the existence of measures of deterrence of collective labour power, both direct and indirect, as well as supportive intervention on the part of different states and sometimes within the same state. This, of itself, disposes of the prevailing thesis that labour law and relations are currently in a general phase of supportive intervention. Indeed, the more prevalent norm seems to be that of deterrence and not of support. Most unions in the democratic world at the start of the twenty-first century are functioning in a (neo-)liberal economy, and this entails the creation of a deterrent environment for union development. Policies of privatization, transfers of undertakings, and official encouragement of non-traditional and contingent labour arrangements all combine to undermine union power in the workplace.

It seems clear that the strength of neo-liberal forces in a global economy is such that unions are going to have a difficult time surviving into the next millennium. Streeck writes that the German model—as 'a capitalist economy, governed by nationally specific social institutions that made for high international competitiveness at high wages and, at the same time, low inequality of incomes and living standards'—cannot be sustained in the global economy because:

beyond the nation-state, there are no organized social groups with the capacity to maintain and build a floor under international markets, or correct international market outcomes by negotiated redistribution. Other than states, the only major actors in the international arena are large firms, increasingly institutional in character, with ample resources to pursue their interests individually, unconstrained by union or government pressure forcing them into class solidarity, and indeed with a growing capacity to extricate themselves.[86]

[86] Streck, above, nn. 50, 52.

The question whether the collapse of the welfare state is, indeed, an inevitable prospect of globalization is beyond the scope of this chapter, but it should be noted that such inevitability has been questioned by others at the economic and political levels.[87] The state may not be the only actor but it does remain an important actor in the international arena. The fate of unions is not written in the stars, and the decline of unions is not a mere market inevitability. Political-legal policies may be crucial in tipping the balance between survival and disappearance.

In some countries, directly deterrent policies have been adopted towards unions: the invalidation of union security arrangements, restrictive strike policies, the cancellation of union monopolies on social services, and the facilitation of employer exit from collective bargaining. Although directly deterrent policies towards trade unions are not confined to those countries in which there has been a steep decline in union power, they seem to be more prevalent in those systems. Deterrent policies have been typical of the USA, as well as the UK during the Conservative era of 1979–97. Moreover, they directly correlate with the near collapse of Israeli unionism in the post-1995 era.

In countries in which union membership or union power has been maintained at a high level, measures of supportive intervention are to be found: representation in state institutions, employee corporatist power in the workplace, monopolies over the distribution of a public good, rights to recognition, and the facilitation of union financing from dues or agency fees and state subsidies. This has been the route taken by the Nordic countries, Germany, France, and Belgium.

There is an apparent correlation between the balance of deterrence and supportive intervention in a state and the thriving of unions within it. This cannot be taken as evidence of cause and effect, but it can indicate that legal regulation is a relevant factor in the decline of unionism. A comparison between states shows how, even within global capitalism, variations in the legal environment coincide with variations in union strength, indicating the possibility of some correlation between union weakness and deterrent policy, on the one hand, and union strength and supportive policy, on the other. That being so, it seems that strong unions frequently seek support from the state, and the state frequently uses deterrent policies to undermine weak unions. The claim that legal regulation is a correlative factor in union strength or weakness is only that. It is not intended to exclude or diminish the importance of other factors. For example, the traditional strength of unions as a social institution, and the

---

[87] See, for instance: Mishra, R., *Globalization and the Welfare State* (Cheltenham: Edward Elgar, 1999); Fligstein, N., 'Is Globalization the Cause of the Crises of Welfare States?' *EUI Working Paper*, SPS No. 98/5 (Florence: EUI, 1998).

way in which unions and workers respond to measures of deterrence or support will also be significant in determining the fate of the union movement.

In a postmodern world, it may be contended that the shoring up of union power by the state on the ground that unions are an important social institution is an undesirable interference with employee freedom. 'If employees do not vote with their feet for unions, what business does the state have supporting them?' This objection would be based on an anti-parentalistic (traditionally known as 'anti-paternalistic') critique. As such, the appropriate responses are those which may be offered to justify any parentalistic policy. Individual choice is not always made under adequate 'free market' conditions. Where an individual lacks information or patently lacks autonomy, there may be a need for intervention; the absence of an individual's demand may reflect free-riding enjoyment of a public good.[88] Furthermore, as a matter of logic, whatever the fate of liberal claims against supportive policies, it must be shared as regards deterrent policies. If support is illegitimate intervention, then clearly deterrence must be so. Post-modernist arguments should not be allowed to defeat the legitimacy of supportive policies for unions. The importance of unions—politically, economically, and socially—justifies a transnational agenda of supportive policies that will help unions to survive neoliberalism.[89]

[88] Zamir, E., 'The Efficiency of Paternalism' (1998) 84 *Virginia L. Review* 229–86.
[89] See above, n. 16.

19

The Voyage of the Neptune Jade: Transnational Labour Solidarity and the Obstacles of Domestic Law

JAMES ATLESON

'An injury to one is an injury to all.'[1]

> Sympathy strikes ... are becoming increasingly frequent because of the move towards the concentration of enterprises, the globalization of the economy and the delocalization of work centres. While pointing out that a number of distinctions need to be drawn here ... the [ILO Freedom of Association] Committee considers that a general prohibition on sympathy strikes could lead to abuse and that workers should be able to take such action, provided the initial strike they are supporting is itself lawful.[2]

Recent analyses addressing labour concerns have advocated a return to notions of workplace equity and industrial democracy. In the global economy, many have begun to consider whether labour rights could be deemed international human rights. The idea that all citizens of the world possess basic rights has gained currency, and it is certainly reasonable to argue that the workplace, the location in which people spend most of their lives, should be the locus not just of labour rights, traditionally conceived, but also transnational human rights. Various international conventions and documents do indeed set forth workplace rights, and unions may be able to expand or enforce those rights by their own efforts. Nevertheless, national legal rules often create serious obstacles to expressions of transnational labour solidarity. Labour unions will have to consider how they can take part in the world market and engage in actions that aid fellow workers elsewhere.

Labour lawyers and unions, at least in the USA, have thus far not stressed international labour rights, and international human rights groups have not focused on labour rights, at least collective rights.[3]

---

[1] A common variation of the Preamble to the Constitution of the Industrial Workers of the World, 1908.

[2] Freedom of Association and Collective Bargaining (Geneva: ILO, 1994) 74.

[3] Leary, V., 'The Paradox of Workers' Rights as Human Rights' in Compa, L., and Diamond, S. (eds.), *Human Rights, Labour Rights, and International Trade* (Philadelphia, Penn.: University of Pennsylvania Press, 1996) 22.

Recently, however, a sense of the internationalism unions talked about in the late nineteenth and early twentieth centuries has returned, although most of it has focused on attaching some recognition of minimum standards to trade pacts. In this context, the subject of international trade has tended to dominate any assertion or discussion of international labour rights. The creation of new trading blocks and especially the WTO has moved the issue to the front page. Is there any hope that trade agreements can be an effective vehicle for the promotion of international labour rights? Clearly, worker interests cannot be divorced from trade, and not only because of the 'race to the bottom' argument.[4] The expansion or restriction of workers' rights affects a nation's trade advantage just as do benefits to domestic manufacturers or import duties. The WTO, however, has greatly restricted a nation's ability to implement or enforce provisions for worker protection. Even if a state internally bars the manufacture and transport of goods made, for instance, by children under a specific age, it may not bar such goods made elsewhere despite the effect on its own labour standards. Yet, one could rationally argue that the failure to provide a decent minimum wage or the construction of obstacles to union organization creates a domestic trade advantage, discriminating against those countries that do set minimum wages or accord association rights consistent with ILO standards.[5]

The WTO could consider and adopt some kind of social clause, but this possibility seems remote. Although efforts to use the WTO to establish international labour standards are continuing, the adoption of a 'social clause' in a body dominated by 'free traders' and populated by third-world governments, unions, and employers who perceive such efforts as limitations on their economic success, is unlikely.[6] Although no nation may be an island, labour is deemed localized.

Moreover, although the ILO can be looked to for standards, 'it does not claim to provide, in any true sense, a transnational forum with a mandate to evaluate the conduct of individual companies and unions'.[7] ILO

---

[4] This phrase has two related meanings. The first emphasizes the flight of capital to nations and areas with low labour and welfare standards. The second, more common, perhaps, refers to the incentives that lead nations to compete on the basis of low standards. See Stone, K. V. W., 'Labour and the Global Economy: Four Approaches to Transnational Labour Regulation' (1995) 16 *Michigan Journal of International Law* 987, 992–3.

[5] See Langille, B., 'General Reflections on the Relationship of Trade and Labour (Or: Fair Trade is Free Trade's Destiny)' in Bhagwati, J., and Hudec, R. (eds.), *Fair Trade and Harmonization: Prerequisites for Free Trade?* (Cambridge, Mass.: MIT Press, 1996) ii, 231; Leary, V., 'Workers' Rights and International Trade: The Social Clause', in the same volume, 177.

[6] Arthurs, H., 'The Collective Labour Law of a Global Economy' in Engels, C., and Weiss, M. (eds.), *Labour Law and Industrial Relations at the Turn of the Century* (Deventer-Boston: Kluwer Law International, 1998) 143, 148.

[7] Ibid., 145.

Conventions include powerful statements concerning rights to freedom of assembly, to join unions, and engage in collective bargaining, as well as setting standards dealing with important issues such as child and forced labour and the prohibition of race and sex discrimination.[8] Many, however, believe that the ILO, while useful in setting standards, can be ignored because it has little ability to enforce those standards. Furthermore, the procedures of multi-state arrangements such as the NAFTA labour side agreement, although perhaps useful for publicizing disputes and the lack of enforcement of domestic labour law, are unlikely to 'promote or regulate "normal" ongoing collective relationships in the transnational sphere'.[9] Finally, although private efforts to create, for instance, corporate codes of responsibility show some promise, it seems that, as Harry Arthurs asserts, 'across the global economy, and even within its most advanced regional economic systems, all collective labour relations regimes are essentially local regimes, even when they involve transnational corporations'.[10]

Thus, despite the history of attempts to set international standards for labour, labour law regimes are nevertheless intensely local in character. As Lord Wedderburn noted, 'one is struck by the contrast between the facility of the internationalization of capital and the obstacles that obstruct international trade union action. Capital is not tied, but each trade union movement is tied to the particular social history of the country in which it operates.'[11] Labour law, as well as union structures, is primarily national. Yet, Lord Wedderburn's comments in 1973 remain valid:

> The true correlative to an international agreement securing to capital the right to move and, therefore, organize across the boundaries of national states would be an agreement securing to collective organizations of workpeople the right to take common action in negotiating, bargaining with and, if need be, striking against the multinational enterprises . . . It is not free movement of labour but free international trade union action which is the true counterpart to free movement of capital.[12]

Attempts to forge international relationships among workers or to take action across borders inevitably involve national labour law systems. However, as the following discussion shows, a focus on domestic legal

---

[8] See, e.g., Lee, E., 'Globalization and Labor Standards: A Review of the Issues' (1997) 136 *International Labour Review* 467; Valticos, N., 'International Labour Standards and Human Rights: Approaching the Year 2000' (1998) 137 *International Labour Review* 135.

[9] Arthurs, above, n. 6, 146–7.

[10] Ibid., 151. On the development of corporate codes of responsibility see also Arthurs, in this volume.

[11] Wedderburn, K., 'Industrial Relations' in Hahlo, H. R. , Graham Smith, J. , and Wright, R. W. (eds), *Nationalism and the Multinational Enterprise* (New York: Oceana Publications, 1973) 249.

[12] Ibid, 256.

regimes reveals serious difficulties for unions who wish to promote international standards or the notion that labour rights should be regarded as
human rights.

I TRANSNATIONAL LABOUR SOLIDARITY: THE TROUBLED VOYAGE OF THE
NEPTUNE JADE

If trade agreements or ILO documents provide thin reeds for the advancement of labour's interests, where else may it turn? The very forces of globalization make it unlikely that domestic law can be relied upon to
advance worker rights.[13] This suggests that labour may have to rely on
the possibility of self-help, directed internationally. The idea of international labour solidarity is not new, but, certainly in the USA, it was unfortunately sidetracked by the Cold War. One issue, little researched, is the
extent to which domestic law hinders co-operative efforts across national
boundaries. A good example of the problems posed by domestic labour
law is the action of longshore workers in 1997 and 1998 in many locations
in the world, illustrating just how vulnerable the new global economy
may be to transnational labour pressure.

The Merseyside dockers in Liverpool had been locked out and
replaced for resisting privatization and workforce reductions, and the
shop stewards' organization began a campaign for reinstatement, which
spread from the UK to ports around the world. The Liverpool workers
became an international cause as the symbol of the demise of England's
unionized longshore (stevedoring) industry. They were the last union
workers in the industry, which had been privatized by Britain's then
Prime Minister, Margaret Thatcher.[14]

The dockers held an international conference among rank and file
workers in the summer of 1996 and called for an international effort on
their behalf. According to Kim Moody:

Representatives from twelve ports in eight countries attended and agreed to put
pressure on their own unions and the International Transport Workers'
Federation (ITF) . . . to call a day of action. The first such day, September 28, was
only a partial success. But by 1997 the ITF had called on its members to join in a
week of actions, beginning on January 20, in whatever way they could. An
impressive list of unions around the world signed on.[15]

Dockworkers in Seattle, Tacoma, and other US West Coast ports were

---

[13] Stone, above, n. 4; ead., 'To the Yukon and Beyond: Local Labourers in a Global Labour
Market' (1999) 3 *Journal of Small & Emerging Business Law* 93, 104–26.
[14] *San Francisco Chronicle*, 20 Feb. 1998.
[15] Moody, K., *Workers in a Lean World* (New York: Verso, 1997) 249–50.

asked by the International Longshore and Warehouse Union (ILWU) to stay off the job for one shift on Monday, 20 January 1997, in solidarity with the British dockworkers.[16] Symbolic as well as direct labour actions occurred in over 100 ports, and workers in many locations refused to unload cargo from ships originating in Liverpool. In the USA, the ILWU closed West Coast ports for eight hours on 20 January, while Oregon ports remained closed for twenty-four hours.[17] As Moody perceptively notes, the 'Merseyside dockers had given world labour a lesson in how to counter the power not only of dock, shipping, and the other transportation firms, but of all the TNCs whose vast investments rest on this fragile transportation system'.[18]

The issue can be even more dramatically highlighted by the voyage of the *Neptune Jade*, the Orient Lines' freighter. The ship's cargo had been loaded in Thamesport, England, in 1997 during a dispute which had arisen two years earlier in 1995, when 500 dockers refused to cross a picket line set up by five workers who had been dismissed after reportedly refusing to work additional unpaid overtime. The dispute also involved 329 Liverpool dockers who were sacked by the Mersey Dock and Harbour Company.[19] The refusal to cross a picket line was followed by a lockout under applicable restrictive labour laws (introduced by Thatcher administrations in 1980 and 1990) which, as in the USA, bar secondary activity as well as limiting the scope of a labour dispute.[20]

The *Neptune Jade* proceeded to Oakland, California, where it was met, on 28 September 1997, by a picket line composed of various groups, including the Labour Party's Golden Gate chapter, students from a labour society at Laney College, members of various unions, and members of the Industrial Workers of the World, who had communicated with each other by e-mail.[21] Over a three-day period, longshore workers refused to cross the picket line and unload the ship despite an arbitrator's ruling that this action violated the parties' collective agreement.

---

[16] *Seattle Post-Intelligencer*, 16 Jan. 1997.

[17] *The Journal of Commerce*, 20 Jan. 1997.

[18] Above, n. 15, 251.

[19] *Lloyd's List International*, 25 Feb. 1998. Liverpool seems to have been the only dock in the UK still operating under a collective bargaining agreement. See Cockburn, A., 'The Fate of the Neptune Jade', *The Nation*, 23 Mar. 1998, 9.

[20] For an overview of the changes to collective labour regulation introduced by successive Conservative administrations in the UK during the 1980s and early 1990s, see Hendy, H., *The Conservative Employment Laws: A National and International Assessment* (2nd edn., London: Institute of Employment Rights, 1991). The *Jade* was believed to have been loaded by the unionists' former employer, although the Pacific Maritime Association asserted that the owner of the Thamesport Dock facility was not related to Merseyside (*San Francisco Chronicle*, 20 Feb. 1998). The *Asia Intelligence Wire*, 3 Oct. 1997, reported that 7 of the 160 containers on the *Jade* were loaded at Thamesport.

[21] *San Francisco Chronicle*, 30 Sept. 1997, C2; *Labour Party Press*, 3/3 (May 1998), 4; *Industrial Worker*, 94/11 (Dec. 1997), #1607, 7.

After three days, the ship left the port of Oakland without having been unloaded.[22] The ship then sailed to Vancouver, British Columbia, where a similar scenario unfolded, and, again, the containers were not unloaded.[23] After five hours of picketing by approximately thirty pickets, the *Neptune Jade* left for Yokohama, Japan, where the All-Japan Dockworkers' Union refused to unload the ship.[24] Reportedly, the ship was finally unloaded in Taiwan.[25]

The saga of the *Neptune Jade* is a stimulating example of transnational labour solidarity.[26] Given the international relationship of production and marketing, transportation workers take on a new importance. Non-transportation workers have also been involved in cross-border activity such as providing economic or staff support, for instance, to new independent unions in Mexico, or lending support to strikes or disputes in other countries. The efforts by European workers to protest a Renault plant closing in Belgium and international assistance to aid the US Teamsters strike at United Parcel Service (UPS) are only two of many cases of co-operative efforts.[27] The International Trade Secretariats have recently been active, for instance, in bringing together unions representing workers in subsidiaries of MNCs, and lobbying and public opinion campaigns have been waged by unions and international confederations of unions.[28]

The future role of such action, however, turns on the legality of such pressure under the domestic law of the state in which a union engages in sympathetic action. In the USA and the UK, such pressure directly confronts statutory prohibitions on secondary or sympathetic action. In

---

[22] The business press stressed that Thamesport announced that it was not a subsidiary of the Mersey Docks and Harbour Company and, thus, the 'blacking' of the *Jade* was a mistake (*Lloyd's List International*, 4 Oct. 1997). See also *Oakland Post*, 5 Oct. 1997.

[23] *The Globe and Mail*, 6 Oct. 1997; *Business Times* (Singapore), 7 Oct. 1997, 1.

[24] *Australasian Business Intelligence*, 14 Oct. 1997, 2; *Business Times* (Singapore), 3 Nov. 1997, 1; *Industrial Worker*, above, n. 21, 11.

[25] *San Francisco Chronicle*, 27 Feb. 1998, A21.

[26] In early 1998, the Liverpool dockers decided to end their dispute. According to Jimmy Nolan, chairman of the Shop Stewards' Committee of the Merseyside Dockers, the Labour government refused to intervene or use the power of the 14% holding it possesses in the Mersey Dock and Harbour Company. Since the dockers had been made 'redundant', each docker was entitled to compensation of £28,000 (interview with Suzanne Jones at the European Workers' Conference for the Abrogation of the Maastricht Treaty, Berlin, 31 Jan.–1 Feb. 1998; e-mail from Michael Eisencher, 8 May 1998).

[27] See Russo, J., and Banks, A., 'How Teamsters took the UPS Strike Overseas', *Working USA* (Jan.–Feb. 1999) 75–87; Imig, D., and Tarrow, S., *From Strike to Eurostrike: the Europeanization of Social Movements and the Development of a Euro-Polity* (Cambridge, Mass.: Weatherhead Center for International Affairs, Harvard University, Working Paper Series, Paper No. 97-10).

[28] See ILO, World Labour Report: Industrial Relations, Democracy and Social Stability (Geneva: ILO, 1997–8), 39–44; Greitzer, D., 'Cross-Border Responses to Labor Repression in North America' [1995] *Detroit College of Law at Michigan State University L. Review* 917; La Botz, D., 'Making Links Across the Border', *Labor Notes* (Aug. 1994) 7.

Japan and Canada, as with some other countries, there are no explicit statutory bars to secondary or sympathetic labour action, but there may be statutes which limit the scope of labour activity only to the employers directly involved in the dispute or to narrowly defined collective bargaining purposes. Moreover, many nations explicitly bar political strikes or, as in the USA, treat them within secondary boycott laws.

When national laws restrict sympathetic or secondary actions by workers, whether wholly within one nation or cutting across national borders, they 'deconstruct' class, emptying it of social reality and significance.[29] Indeed, one obvious purpose of secondary boycott restrictions may be precisely to limit the ability of workers to express solidarity *as workers*. The labour laws of many nations treat the very real feeling of solidarity as unworthy of recognition or protection.

II THE PORTS OF CALL: THE LEGAL RESPONSE TO SYMPATHETIC ACTION

Most legal systems prohibit sympathetic or secondary action, no matter what form the legal system takes, whether based upon the common or civil law, and despite differences in history and culture. Indeed, the actions taken by workers in the USA, Canada, and Japan in response to the *Neptune Jade* were probably unlawful in each country. Although the legal result may often be the same in many countries, it is interesting to note that the doctrinal route taken commonly varies.

The United Kingdom—the Americanization of UK labour law

One of the incidents leading to the *Neptune Jade* saga was a picket line in the UK deemed to constitute illegal secondary activity. Striking in Britain has, historically, been considered a freedom and not a right. Throughout most of this century strikes have been regulated by common law doctrines of tort and contract, offset, to some degree, by the conferral of statutory immunities for acts 'in contemplation or furtherance of a trade dispute'.[30] The historical immunities, however, were severely restricted in a series of Acts introduced in the 1980s and 1990s and now consolidated in the Trade Union and Labour Relations (Consolidation) Act 1992 (TULR(C)A). The most relevant restriction is the confinement of protected industrial action to 'disputes between workers and their own employer

[29] Suggested to the author by Howard Kimmeldorf.
[30] Most of the relevant immunities derive originally from the Trade Disputes Act 1906. See generally Hepple, B., 'The United Kingdom' in Blanpain, R., and Ben-Israel, R. (eds) *Strikes and Lockouts in Industrialized Market Economies* (Deventer, The Netherlands: Kluwer, 1994) 183–5.

and at their own place of work'.[31] Secondary action, after these amendments, is no longer protected by a statutory immunity (and, thus, is
subject to tort remedies, including injunctive relief, and a refusal to
handle 'hot goods' (goods produced or supplied by another employer
usually in dispute with his employees) constitutes an actionable breach of
the employment contract by individual employees. Even prior to the
Conservative era, disputes, in order to gain immunity from tort law, had
to be in contemplation or furtherance of a 'trade dispute', excluding, for
example, 'political disputes' from the scope of immunity.

British labour, however, has a long tradition of secondary or sympathetic action, that is, actions by workers not employed by the targeted
employer in aid of workers directly involved. These actions are now
almost wholly excluded from tort immunities after the recent legislation.[32] The message is that workers have no legitimate interest in aiding
other workers, thus limiting the scope of disputes to discrete workplaces.

Canada: the continued vigour of the common law

The Canadian situation is complex because labour regulations derive
from both the federal government and the ten provinces. The federal
government adopted labour legislation similar to the US Wagner Act[33]
during World War II but its jurisdiction is limited to federal civil servants
and, in the private sector, to employees working in what are deemed
'federal undertakings' such as banks, inter-provincial and international
transport, and communication enterprises. Provincial labour laws apply
to 90 per cent of the nation's private sector workforce.[34]

The Charter of Rights and Freedoms, made part of Canada's
Constitution in 1982, protects certain fundamental rights and generally
takes precedence over federal and provincial legislation. The Charter
includes such rights as free speech, freedom of association, equality, and

---

[31] Ibid., 181–3. Previously the definition of a trade dispute was broad enough to encompass disputes between 'workers and employers' and even 'workers and workers'. See generally, Davies, P., and Freedland, M., *Kahn-Freund's Labour and the Law* (3rd edn., London:
Stevens & Sons, 1983), 321–52; Wedderburn, K. W., *Cases and Materials on Labour Law*
(Cambridge: Cambridge University Press, 1967).

[32] TULR(C)A, s. 224. Although the current Labour government has not sought to modify
the Thatcher era statutes restricting collective action, it is possible that the Human Rights
Act of 1998, which incorporates the European Convention on Human Rights into UK
domestic law, may have some impact although, for a number of reasons, the actual effect
may well be slight. See further Ewing, K. D., 'The Human Rights Act and Labour Law' (1998)
27 *ILJ* 275.

[33] For an excellent discussion of the US and Canadian models see Adams, R., *Industrial
Relations under Liberal Democracy: North America in Comparative Perspective* (Columbia, SC:
University of South Carolina Press, 1995), ch. 4.

[34] Carter, D., 'Canada' in Blanpain and Ben-Israel, above, n. 30, 39.

due process. In three major cases in the 1980s, however, the Supreme Court of Canada, contrary to the view of the ILO, held that freedom of association did not include the right to strike or even the right to bargain collectively. 'Freedom of association was viewed as only protecting the right of individuals to associate in activities which are lawful when performed alone', that is, the Charter gave 'no rights to unions over and above those enjoyed by the individual'.[35] Thus, strike actions currently receive no special constitutional protection in Canada, and such activity is properly regulated by legislative action.

One of the most distinctive aspects of Canadian labour legislation is that the legality of strikes is primarily determined by their timing. In short, strikes are banned during the term of a collective bargaining agreement, and disputes are to be resolved via grievance arbitration. In other words, legislation accomplished in Canada what is normally resolved by contractual no-strike clauses in the USA. Moreover, the definition of a strike usually includes any disruption of production if carried out in a concerted manner.[36]

Even if a strike is not related to an underlying collective bargaining purpose, however, as in a political strike situation, the 'prevailing view in all Canadian jurisdictions is that disruption of production and concerted employee activity by themselves are all that is required in order for a work stoppage to constitute a strike and be subject to the statutory restrictions on the timing of such activity'.[37] Thus, the peace obligation is absolute, even if the dispute is not related to the collective agreement or falls outside the grievance process. In US terms, the obligation not to strike during the contract's term is broader that the obligation to arbitrate contractual issues.

Picketing is regulated primarily through the law of torts; it is lawful if the underlying strike is lawful. Yet, even picketing in support of a lawful strike may be deemed illegal if its impact is secondary, that is, it has a 'disproportionate impact upon a third party unconnected to the labour dispute'.[38] Thus, whether secondary or not, any strike during the term of an agreement will be deemed illegal even though the matter may not be resolvable through the grievance process. Indirectly, therefore, the peace

[35] Ibid., 41.

[36] British Columbia expressly exempts from the definition of a strike a refusal to cross legal picket lines, but in other jurisdictions such refusals can be deemed strike action if some aspect of concerted activity is present (ibid., 43).

[37] Ibid. In all Canadian jurisdictions, the labour injunction is the basic, usually the exclusive, civil remedy for illegal strike activity. In some jurisdictions, the agency cease and desist order has replaced the judicial injunction (ibid., 49–50).

[38] Ibid., 51. The Supreme Court of Canada has held that picketing is a form of expression protected by the Charter, but has drastically limited the Charter's scope to actions of the government. Significantly, a judicial injunction is not to be treated as an act of the state.

obligation bars sympathetic strikes, but by a far different route from that in the UK or the USA. Moreover, sympathy strikes or boycotts in support of labour conflicts in other countries 'require no different analysis than such action totally within one Canadian jurisdiction'. Canadian law is 'quite unsympathetic to "secondary" action by employees'.[39] As in the USA, public appeals to boycott products are legal, but such action becomes illegal if it takes the form of striking or refusing to handle hot goods.

Thus, secondary picketing aimed at consumers is of questionable legality. Perhaps the most well known, or infamous, Canadian case is *Hersees of Woodstock* v. *Goldstein*,[40] in which the Ontario Court of Appeals held unlawful secondary picketing aimed at inducing consumers to boycott products made by a sportswear company with which the union had been unable to secure a collective agreement. Hersees, a menswear store, objected to picket signs urging consumers to 'look for the [union] label'. The court held, first, that the purpose of the picket line was to force a breach of contract between Hersees and the primary employer, despite the language of the signs and the doubtful evidence that such a contract existed. Secondly, the court held that the primary purpose of the union was to injure the plaintiff store rather than to advance a union purpose, although the intent to harm the plaintiff was clearly designed to strengthen its collective bargaining demands. But even if, said the court, the picketing was lawful in the sense that it was intended to communicate information, it should still be restrained because it was likely to injure the plaintiff's right to engage in its business. 'Therefore, the right, if there be such right of the respondents to engage in secondary picketing of appellant's premises must give way to appellant's right to trade'.[41] As wonderfully noted by Harry Arthurs, the court made 'a leap of faith from social premise to legal result'; the court's 'therefore,' said Arthurs, 'propels the learned judge across the chasm which yawns between premise and result'.[42]

The vigour of the *Hersees* approach is seen in a more recent case involving secondary consumer picketing by a non-labour group, heard by the Ontario Court of Justice (General Division) in 1995.[43] The court held that secondary picketing is a form of protected speech, but, as in the USA,

---

[39] Langille, B., 'The Canadian Law of Collective Bargaining', 17 (unpublished paper on file with author).

[40] [1963] 2 OR 81 (CA).

[41] Ibid., 86.

[42] Arthurs, H., 'Comments' (1963) 41 *Canadian Bar Review* 573, 580. See also Beatty, D., 'Secondary Boycotts: A Functional Analysis' (1974) 52 *Canadian Bar Review* 388; Bergbusch, P., 'Secondary Picketing in Saskatchewan: A Functional Analysis' (1995) 59 *Saskatchewan. L. Review* 141.

[43] *Daishowa Inc.* v. *Friends of the Lubicon* (1995) 30 CRR (2d) 26.

explicitly excluded secondary *labour* consumer picketing from the protected area. The court referred to a number of decisions, including one from British Columbia, which held that such picketing was unlawful. Indeed, in the BC case, the BC Federation of Labour had instituted a boycott of grapes imported from the USA to aid the efforts of US farm-workers to secure decent working conditions.[44] The difference, according to the *Daishowa* court, was that peaceful picketing could be the exercise of the right of freedom of expression, 'whereas, union picketing can some-times be much more than an exercise of expression and can trigger a work stoppage which effectively closes a business'.[45] This arguable distinction, however, does not distinguish labour from non-labour picketing when consumers are the target.

Thus, as in the USA, labour picketing in Canada, even directed at consumers, is treated differently from non-labour picketing, even if both are 'secondary' in nature. In British Columbia, for instance, where the *Neptune Jade* was boycotted, 'hot cargo' actions have been held to violate the province's statute.[46] If consumer boycotts are sometimes questionable in Canada, then it is clear that efforts to induce 'neutral' employees to strike or not handle hot goods are also unlawful.

Japan: the scope of 'dispute acts'

Japanese workers can take part in 'dispute acts', a concept broader than strikes, as embodied in both post-war legislation and the Constitution. Nevertheless, like a number of other countries, dispute acts 'must be aimed at achieving an objective of collective bargaining'[47] in which context neither political nor sympathy strikes are regarded as proper because they do not involve issues resolvable with the workers' employer. Although Japan has no secondary boycott provision, the absence of such a provision is of doubtful significance, given the defini-tion of a lawful strike. It may be the case that the enterprise structure of unions makes sympathetic and secondary strikes less compelling.

---

[44] *Slade & Steward Ltd.* v. *Retail, Wholesale and Dept. Store Union, Local 580* 69 WWR 374 (1969). The order declaring all grapes imported from California and Arizona to be 'hot' was said to interfere with contracts of service between the employees of the plaintiff and the plaintiff.

[45] Above, n. 43, 88.

[46] See Adams, G. W., *Canadian Labour Law* (2nd edn., Aurora, Ont.: Canada Law Books, 1993) 11–21 to 11–31.

[47] Sugeno, K., 'Japan: Legal Framework and Issues' in Blanpain and Ben-Israel, above n. 30, 101–6. See generally Price, J., *Japan Works: Power and Paradox in Postwar Industrial Relations* (Ithaca, NY: Cornell University Press, 1997).

Secondary and sympathetic labour action in the United States

Secondary labour activity in the USA is treated under the vague, but very restrictive, provisions of the National Labour Relations Act (NLRA). There are two separate aspects of this problem depending on whether the targeted audience is consumers or other workers. First, the potential reach of the First Amendment's protection of free speech has produced a considerable zone of protection for actions directed at consumers: labour *handbilling* directed at consumers, even though at a secondary location, was protected in a 1988 decision,[48] and an earlier decision, *Fruit and Vegetable Packers*,[49] held that unions could picket 'struck' products (that is, the products of an employer in a labour dispute). Both decisions arguably misread the NLRA and the legislative history to arrive at these results. Nevertheless, attempts by picketing to effect boycotts beyond particular products will not be protected. Although non-labour groups are constitutionally entitled to protest, either by secondary picketing or handbilling, the Court has consistently approved the application of the secondary boycott provision of the NLRA (section 8(b)(4)) to certain forms of labour appeals to consumers by means of picketing.[50] The justification for the distinction is the age-old US refrain: picketing involves either coercion or the threat of force, even if there is no evidence of such a threat. Ironically, however, boycott actions by a civil rights organization, the NAACP, in *Claiborne Hardware*[51] were held to be constitutionally protected even though the activity actually involved both threats and actual violence. Moreover, in *Fruit and Vegetable Packers*, the Court recognized the speech aspects of consumer picketing, interpreting the NLRA so as to take consumer picketing of *struck products* out of the statutory prohibition. This accommodation, which has its own First Amendment problems, nevertheless allows some secondary picketing, despite the Court's later expressed view that labour picketing was inherently violent.

Secondly, it is clear that appeals to neutral employees to stop work, or even sympathetic actions by neutral workers themselves, fall within the statutory prohibition. The Court at various times has employed a range of justifications for its approach to union economic pressure tactics. Thus, sometimes, it has treated union picketing as a 'signal', a message to other unionized workers to cease work, presumably enforced by internal union

---

[48] *Edward J. DeBartolo Corp.* v. *Florida Gulf Coast Building & Construction Trades Council*, 485 US 568 (1988).

[49] *NLRB* v. *Fruit & Vegetable Packers & Warehousemen, Local 760*, 377 US 58 (1964).

[50] There is a voluminous literature in the USA, primarily noting the inherent irrationality of US law, but see particularly Minda, G., 'The Law and Metaphor of Boycott' (1993) 41 *Buffalo L. Review* 807; id., *Boycott in America* (Carbondale, Ill.: So. Ill. University Press, 1999).

[51] *NAACP* v. *Claiborne Hardware Co.*, 458 US 886 (1982).

disciplinary procedures. Whether this is factually true in any case is not deemed relevant or, even if true, why the argument makes sense is generally not explained. In any event, the 'signal' rationale has no application when the target of the union's activity is the public rather than other workers.

To begin to complete the circle of logical questions, the Court has explained its ruling protecting the NAACP's boycott in *Claiborne* on the ground that human rights protest has 'elements of majesty' because it is *political*, while labour action is merely *economic*. The argument responds to an earlier judicial formulation of the First Amendment placing political speech higher than other types of speech on the ladder of protection.[52] The distinction is questionable for a number of reasons. First, one goal of the NAACP has included jobs for African-Americans, surely an 'economic' or at least labour-related aim. Secondly, the Court has, in recent years, begun to weaken or eliminate the distinction between political and economic speech. More significantly, the Court has never explained why labour activity may not be deemed political action. As many have argued, labour standards and communication certainly seem to involve public issues and the public is the target group in consumer boycott situations.

But even this argument fades away. The US Supreme Court has permitted the application of the secondary boycott statute to a clearly political act—the International Longshoremen's Association (ILA)'s withholding of labour in protest against the Soviet invasion of Afghanistan, observing:

We have consistently rejected the claim that secondary picketing by labor unions in violation of Section 8(b)(4) is protected activity under the First Amendment. . . . It would seem even clearer that conduct designed not to communicate but to coerce merits still less consideration under the First Amendment.[53]

The withholding of labour was thus treated as conduct 'designed . . . to coerce', and, although the Court was willing to assume that the union's aim might be 'understandable and even commendable' (but not, apparently, containing elements of 'majesty'), its action nevertheless placed a burden on neutral employers. Even a moral aim, or one aimed at 'freeing employees from handling goods from an objectionable source' was insufficient. In addition, it was irrelevant that the action was deemed secondary although there was no primary dispute. Indeed, although the basic dispute was with the Soviet Union, and despite its earlier use of the political/economic rationale, the Court held there was no exception for

---

[52] Pope, J., 'The Three-Systems Ladder of First Amendment Values: Two Rungs and a Black Hole' (1984) 11 *Hastings Constitutional L. Quarterly* 192; id., 'Labour and the Constitution' (1987) 65 *Texas L. Review* 1074.

[53] *ILA v. Allied International, Inc.* 456 US 212, 226 (1982).

political actions, stating that 'the distinction between labour and political objectives would be difficult to draw in many cases'.[54] And this is just the point. With the judicial interring of the 'political/economic' distinction, interested observers in the USA are left with no articulated rationale for the lack of protection for secondary labour picketing (as opposed to secondary non-labour picketing) except for the notion that labour action sometimes, but not always, involves force.

The apparent class-based fear would seem most clear when a union seeks the aid of 'neutral' workers to help them in a primary dispute. This aspect of secondary boycotts involves appeals to 'neutral' workers to cease work in order to aid workers involved in a strike or dispute in another firm or even the unsolicited decision by the neutral workers to aid workers employed elsewhere. Except in very limited circumstances, a union clearly may not appeal to neutral workers to cease work either completely or, at a minimum, not to handle hot goods. Nor may the neutral workers cease work on their own, for this would be a 'strike' with the forbidden object within section 8(b)(4)(B). These workers, it will be said, have no dispute with their own employer—there is no primary dispute justifying their work stoppage. Of course, these workers may feel offended at handling or working on struck goods, and their continued work may well weaken the strike effort. Apart from the inherently political nature of this area, it could fairly be argued that these workers indeed have a dispute with their employer, since they are required—upon pain of discharge—to perform work with products which violates their sense of integrity.[55]

International co-operation may tend to involve either the withholding of labour or inducements to others to withhold their labour rather than appealing to consumers. Without presenting courts with the embarrassment of explaining why appeals to consumers should be treated differently based on the identity of the speaker, appeals to workers seem to face an uphill battle in countries like the USA and Canada. Neither country has approved a distinction between political and economic strikes; indeed, the distinction has generally been rejected. In both Canada and the USA, the primary emphasis is placed upon the protection of neutral employers. It is at this point that law is asked to make a fundamental choice between two views of neutrality. Unions may well believe that firms that continue to work on goods from a struck firm are less than 'neutral'. After all, what unions are generally trying to achieve is a fully effective strike, one that ends production at the struck firm. Should that

---

[54] *ILA v. Allied International, Inc.*, 456 US 212, 225 (1982), 216–25.

[55] Even apart from the secondary boycott provisions, such action is traditionally treated as unprotected action which may lead to discharge or discipline. See generally Atleson, J., *Values and Assumptions in American Labor Law* (Amherst, Mass.: University of Massachusetts Press, 1983) ch. 3.

be achieved, there is obviously no production upon which workers at other firms can work.

In the USA, the most noteworthy recent cases have dealt with the legality of secondary action *outside the USA* in order to benefit unions *in the USA*. Two courts of appeals have reached opposite conclusions on the legality of such action. The dispute in question again involved longshoremen, this time the East Coast ILA. As part of an ongoing dispute between ILA-represented longshoremen and two unorganized Florida shippers, Japanese longshore unions were persuaded to aid the union by refusing to unload ships in Japan that had been loaded by non-union workers in Florida. Prior to a ruling on the merits of the employers' unfair labour practice charge, the National Labor Relations Board (NLRB) sought an injunction under section 10(l) of the NLRA on the ground that the secondary boycott actually occurred in the USA as it was directed at US firms and the economic pain was felt in Florida. The Eleventh Circuit Court of Appeals upheld the injunction on the ground that the application of the statute was not extra-territorial and, moreover, the action of the Japanese unions could be attributed to the ILA based on legal doctrines of agency, ratification or joint venture.

After the NLRB held that the ILA's actions constituted a violation of NLRA section 8(b)(4), however, the Court of Appeals for the District of Columbia held that there was no illegal secondary boycott for a variety of reasons, including the belief that the action was not taken by 'employees' within the Act, since the Japanese were not individuals engaged in 'commerce' as defined by the NLRA. The court also denied the applicability of agency or ratification doctrines, while not clearly focusing on the interesting issue of the possible application of the NLRA beyond US borders.[56]

The Eleventh Circuit's decision, which upheld the injunction, was, it must be said, based upon a quite credible argument. US anti-trust law, for instance, already applies to anti-competitive agreements even though made abroad, if the effects are felt in the USA. The ILA, however, argued that the boycott—the actual refusal to unload the ships—occurred in Japan by Japanese workers who were not covered by the statute, and, clearly, this was factually true. Yet, the application of the statute *would* have been clear if all the activity had occurred in the USA, for the statute would then have applied to the workers either doing the actual boycotting or encouraging them to so act. Does it make sense to separate where the action occurs from where the pain, the injury for which the statute was passed, occurs?

In any case, a strike *in the USA* in aid of striking or locked out workers

[56] *Dowd* v. *ILA*, 975 F. 2d 779 (11th Cir. 1992); *ILA* v. *NLRB*, 56 F. 3d 205 (D.C. Cir. 1995).

in another country is likely to be treated as an illegal secondary boycott, leading initially to an injunction by the NLRB via section 10(l) of the NLRA and, subsequently, to a cease and desist order after a ruling on the merits. In addition, the NLRA permits employers to seek damages directly in federal court. The secondary boycott provision in the NLRA covers strikes to induce a 'person' (generally an employer) to cease dealing with another 'person'. Given the Court's ruling in the Soviet Union boycott, the moral basis of the workers' actions is less important than the economic effects.

The saga of the *Neptune Jade* may raise special issues, but there is little reason to believe the boycott would have been deemed lawful had the statute been invoked. After all, in the ILA–Soviet Union case, the Court found a secondary boycott even though there did not seem to be any primary dispute. Moreover, the language of the Act clearly was designed to prohibit sympathetic action, and it is not clear why it should matter that the workers being supported are citizens of another country.

III SECONDARY, SYMPATHETIC, AND POLITICAL PRESSURE: THE ISSUES

The discussion thus far involves a number of issues typically arising in labour cases around the world. Although strikes may generally be protected by domestic law, strikes in particular situations may not. Thus, even some types of economic strikes may be prohibited by statute or by contract.[57] Obviously, statutory prohibitions hinder solidarity actions and limit the ability of unions to respond to the new global world.[58] In the USA, at least, this is not surprising. US courts and the NLRB have already made it difficult for unions to deal with multi-unit and multiple-location firms and, especially, conglomerates.[59] In Canada, statutes have not altered the common law's hostility to sympathetic or secondary actions, even directed at consumers. And Japan, like some European countries, confines protected strikes to the specific workplace in which the dispute occurred. Indeed, in all the countries in which the boycott against the *Neptune Jade* occurred, the refusal to unload the ship was unlawful and,

---

[57] Collective agreements in the USA generally bar strikes during the term of the contract, although some unions have negotiated limited exceptions to the contractual prohibition. Even if there is no contractual no-strike clause, strikes may still be barred by judicial interpretation of arbitration provisions. In an important US Supreme Court decision, strikes are barred if they involve matters that could be resolved by the grievance process even in the absence of a no-strike clause: *Local 174, Teamsters v. Lucas Flour*, 369 US 95 (1962).

[58] There may also be specific legislation prohibiting or hampering the ability of national workers' organizations to affiliate with international confederations. See *World Labour Report: Industrial Relations, Democracy and Social Stability* (Geneva: ILO, 1997–8) 37–8.

[59] Atleson, J., 'Reflections on Labour, Power, and Society' (1985) 44 *Maryland L. Review* 841.

perhaps, a breach of the employment contract as well. Thus, domestic legal restrictions provide serious obstacles to transnational labour activity, although unlawful action will, nevertheless, occur. The practical effect of such legislation, in Lord Wedderburn's words, 'is to fragment and inhibit trade union action while the power of internationalized capital is constitutionally guaranteed the maximum flexibility'.[60]

Can primary and secondary strikes be distinguished?

A strike is merely a labour boycott: the workers stop working for the employer with whom they have a dispute. This action may have secondary effects, disrupting production and, thereby, disturbing the normal interactions between the primary employer and other firms with which it does business. Indeed, one of the purposes of a picket line at the primary site is to urge workers employed by other firms to respect the line and so induce their employer to 'cease dealing with' the 'struck' employer. Thus, all primary picket lines have secondary effects and the real task of the law is to distinguish between types of secondary *effects* and not between primary and secondary activity.

In most nations, picketing at 'neutral' firms which do business with a firm in a labour dispute is not legally protected even though the effect on the alleged neutral would be the same if the primary strike forced the employer in dispute to close down. Moreover, most attempts to induce workers at other firms to aid strikers will also be treated as improper. Even without a secondary picket line, workers at other firms may not legally strike in aid of workers in the primary dispute even though the work they do helps the primary employer to continue production during the strike. The normal justification for this state of affairs is that the workers engaged in sympathetic action have no real dispute with their own employer and, thus, are unfairly causing a neutral employer to suffer economic harm. However, a contrary argument exists: if an employer insists that workers handle or work on goods (usually called 'hot cargo') in circumstances which they find are inconsistent with their principles, either because they wish to aid workers elsewhere or express political revulsion about the source of the hot goods, why is this not deemed a lawful or primary and not a secondary strike? The workers' boycott may well be based on deeply held beliefs. In other words, when workers refuse to work on 'hot goods' in order to aid workers elsewhere, can it be said that they have no real dispute with their employer? Why is this type of action less important than a strike to obtain higher wages or, as in the

---

[60] Wedderburn, above, n. 11, 256.

USA, the right to handbill consumers?[61] One could certainly argue that the right to dispose of your labour, especially to defend or assist others, is a more keenly felt and significant interest than the right to persuade consumers how to spend their money.

On the ground that sympathy or secondary strikes affect those employers not in a position to satisfy the worker's demands, a number of countries bar such solidarity efforts. Japan, as noted, limits the legality of strike action to the collective bargaining process. On the other hand, this is not a uniform position. Sweden has recognized the right of unions to engage in solidarity actions[62] and Morgenstern, writing in 1984, suggests that some western nations may permit local boycotts intended to aid workers in other countries.[63] The legality of sympathetic action, like strikes, is usually determined by the law of the place in which the sympathy action occurs, and the usual requirements are that the strike being supported must itself be lawful and that the sympathy action must have a 'direct connection with it'.[64] There may, however, be special rules dealing with the support of foreign strikes and the manner in which the general restrictions are applied to foreign situations. As Morgenstern notes, however, European decisions on 'support of foreign strikes are isolated and relatively old'.[65]

Is there a distinction between economic and political strikes?

Generally, the law of many states begins with the assumption that the objectives of the strike must be legitimate, and most assume that the aims must relate to work demands or the process of collective bargaining. German law reflects the approach of many states. Since strikes are legal only if their purpose is to arrive at a collective agreement, it follows that political as well as secondary and sympathy strikes in Germany are illegal, although narrow exceptions may exist.[66] Yet, given that democratic nations protect political speech, it seems relevant to note that strike demands often have wider social or economic objectives. First, and

---

[61] The answer, no doubt, lies in the limited status courts assign to workers, a status revealed in cases in which workers seek to control some aspect of their work. Decisions have long held that workers may not stay at work and decide which parts of their labour they will perform. Similarly, slowdowns are not protected. See Atleson, above n. 55.

[62] Ben-Israel, R., 'Strikes, Lockouts and Other Kinds of Hostile Actions' in Hepple, B. (chief ed.), *International Encyclopedia of Comparative Law* (Deventer: Kluwer, 1988) xv, *Labour Law* 15–16.

[63] Morgenstern, F., *International Conflicts of Labour Law* (Geneva: ILO, 1984) 114.

[64] Ibid.

[65] Ibid., 115.

[66] See Westfall, D., and Thusing, G., 'Strikes and Lockouts in Germany and Under Federal Legislation in the United States: A Comparative Analysis' (1999) 22 *Boston College International and Comparative L. Review* 29, 45–8.

excluding strikes by government workers whose pressure is obviously political in nature, the pressure in a political strike is 'not directed against the employer but rather against the state. Acceptance of the strikers' demands by the state will result in changing government policy or amending legislation, and will not be expressed in signing a collective agreement'.[67] The pressure is felt by the targeted employer although it is not in a position to grant the demands. Yet, it is certainly possible to argue that all strikes are political as they often challenge existing distributions of income, the validity of existing law, and often involve appeals to the public. Such a notion, of course, would threaten the protected nature of many strikes.

The most central, internationally recognized, right of workers is freedom of association. The ILO has stressed the fundamental nature of this right in numerous conventions and, indeed, in its constitution of 1919.[68] Although the ILO's Freedom of Association Committee considers the right to strike to be 'a basic right', it is not explicitly expressed in the body's constitution or in important Labour Conventions such as 87 and 98. The Committee, however, has noted that the right 'seemed to have been taken for granted' in the discussions which led to Convention 87 and has been mentioned in a number of ILO reports. Nevertheless, the Committee recognized that the right to strike cannot be considered an absolute right. For example, the Committee 'has always considered that strikes that are purely political in character do not fall within the scope of freedom of association'.[69] The Committee has noted the, often difficult, problem of distinguishing the political aspects of a strike from those that impact directly upon the working conditions of the strikers and has recognized workers' right to criticize government policy:

In the view of the Committee, organizations responsible for defending workers' socio-economic and occupational interests should, in principle, be able to use strike action to support their position in the search for solutions to problems posed by major social and economic policy trends which have a direct impact on their members and on workers in general, in particular as regards employment, social protection and the standard of living.[70]

Unsurprisingly, this has proved to be a controversial position, and 'in all countries strikes which are purely *political* in nature are in principle considered as unlawful'.[71] Many countries believe that such strikes may 'affect the system of representative democracy or the competence of the

---

[67] Ben-Israel, above, n. 62.   [68] See above, n. 2, 2–5.
[69] Ibid., 72.   [70] Ibid., 57.
[71] Jacobs, A. T. J. M., 'The Law of Strikes and Lockouts' in Blanpain, B., and Engels, C. (eds.), *Comparative Labour Law and Industrial Relations in Industrialized Market Economies* (Deventer: Kluwer, 1993) 431.

constitutional bodies, especially where their mode of expression endangers the sovereignty of public institutions and prevents them from freely evaluating the requests advanced by other groups'.[72] Yet, some countries have permitted political strikes for short durations, and many have wrestled with the fact that political and occupational aspects may be intertwined in a specific dispute. Japan and the UK have pronounced such strikes as illegitimate, although Italy, Spain, France, Israel, and the Netherlands have generally recognized political strikes as least so long as they involve the defence of worker' interests.[73]

On the other hand, one may distinguish domestic and internationally focused disputes on the ground that other channels of influence are not available. Thus, the very argument used to bar political strikes can be reversed to argue for their protection, at least in a transnational situation. 'A greater international solidarity of workers should be developed and this could be a good argument for allowing political industrial action when ordinary channels are not available.'[74] The same, of course, may be said for the foreign control of a local firm over which local entities, state or union, may have few channels to exert political or social pressure. Trade unions have few avenues to influence international capital, yet it is clear that capital can influence national labour law.[75] This argument can obviously be broadened to encompass all transnational efforts at co-operation, whether 'political' or not.

IV CONCLUSION

Why should strikes aimed at supporting workers elsewhere not be deemed to involve basic rights? If a nation privileges political speech, why are expressions of views, voiced by withholding labour, not considered worthy of protection? The poignant absurdity to which this issue gives rise is illustrated by US law's protection of the right of unions to handbill consumers even though action is secondary, on the ground that it is protected by the First Amendment. The question is why is the withholding of labour not deemed as basic a human right as the right to persuade consumers not to purchase products? Why can workers who cease work on, for instance, certain 'hot goods' not be said to have a dispute with their own employer, expressing, as they may be, deeply held views about the solidarity of labour.

In analysing whether (and what) labour rights should be considered

---

[72] Ibid.
[73] Ibid., 432.
[74] Edlund, S., *TCO-Tidningen* (1968), cited in Wedderburn, above n. 11, 253.
[75] Ibid., 253–4.

human rights, what accounts for the assumptions in legal systems which permit strikes over wages or working conditions, but bar the withholding of labour for other reasons, for example, to protest working conditions elsewhere, or to assist workers embroiled in a dispute in another company or nation? Secondary or sympathetic actions have often been restricted on the grounds that they unduly widen a labour dispute, involve others without an interest in the dispute, or unfairly pressure neutral employers and employees. (I suspect, in addition, they are grounded in a judicial fear of class-based action.) All of these explanations have serious problems. Yet, as Bob Hepple has noted, by making workers' rights fundamental and constitutionally enforceable 'we shift the resolution of disputes from the political and industrial spheres to the sphere of public lawyers and the judiciary'.[76] The concern, however, is that judges will interpret the law, whether legislative or constitutional, according to their own values, informed by a concern for property and individualistic notions embedded in the common law, or simply by opposition to union action.[77] In so far as the state participates in the setting of ground-rules for labour regulation, however, no resolution of this problem has yet been discovered. In any event, it seems rational to argue that the right to withhold one's labour should be entitled to great respect, and the traditional labour opposition to working on 'hot goods' should be as worthy of protection as striking to improve wages or distributing leaflets or even picketing consumers.

Finally, the apparent necessity for transnational union co-operation should not disguise the difficulty of seeking and obtaining this goal, even apart from the legal difficulties described above. Differences of culture, language, and history provide serious obstacles to co-operation. The argument for greater co-ordination does not mean that the unions—or companies or governments—necessarily favour transnational co-operation, let alone bargaining, not least because workers, suppliers, communities, states, and provinces and countries are all in competition for production facilities and for the jobs and taxes which they generate. Moreover, workers in different countries may well see foreign workers as competitors, as part of 'the problem'. Nevertheless, without vibrant, militant unions, and, perhaps, a new vocabulary that considers workers as a valuable, organic part of the enterprise, as long-term participants with a valuable citizenship stake, there may be little hope for ameliorating the problems of a domestically-focused labour movement.

---

[76] Hepple, B., 'The Future of Labour Law' (1995) 24 *ILJ* 303, 319–20.
[77] See Atleson, J., 'Confronting Judicial Values: Rewriting the Law of Work in a Common Law System' (1997) 45 *Buffalo L. Review* 435.

20

Mexican Trade Unionism in a Time of Transition

CARLOS DE BUEN UNNA*

Wide authority vested in the president, centralism, corruption, and lack of democracy have long been characteristics both of the Mexican political system and of one of its fundamental structures, Mexican labour unions. The political system and the industrial relations system long had a symbiotic relationship. As Maria Amparo Casar says, 'the history of the constitution of the political regime and the history of the constitution of modern union organization and practice run in parallel'.[1] The stability of each was entwined with the stability of the other. Thus, the maturing of Mexico's political crisis destabilized union organizations and the entire system of unionism. The on-going political upheaval in Mexico, accompanied by the enormous economic changes of recent decades, is forcing a revision of Mexico's decadent form of trade unionism, which thus far has proved unable to adapt.

After seven decades of monopolistic power, the Institutional Revolutionary Party (PRI) suffered a momentous defeat in the presidential elections of 3 July 2000. When he took office the following December, Vicente Fox became the first non-PRI president since the PRI was founded. While Fox's election is the most salient event of the political transition to date, the collapse of the PRI's political hegemony and unravelling of the political system have been in progress for some time.

A major source of the crisis was the inefficiency of the economic strategies and industrial relations patterns promoted by successive PRI administrations. Mexican industry was born and developed in a closed and highly protected economy encapsulated in a corporatist, paternalist, and authoritarian order. Business competition was very limited and restricted in scope to national companies sharing similar legal privileges. There was little incentive for productivity growth or economic innovation, and the system's inefficiency imposed heavy economic costs. In years past, employers were content to bear those costs in exchange for protectionist trade policies. But these policies are no longer viable in today's world of

---

* With thanks to Joanne Conaghan, Paddy Ireland, and Karl Klare for editorial assistance.
[1] Casar, M. A., 'Movimiento obrero, estabilidad y democracia' in Rodriguez Araujo, O. (ed.), *México: estabilidad y luchas por la democracia 1900–1982* (Mexico City, Centro de Investigación y Docencia Económicas and Ediciones el Caballito, 1988) 277.

increasing international economic integration. With the opening of the Mexican economy and the fall of trade barriers, employers became unwilling to tolerate the economic burden of the traditional industrial relations system. This prompted a restructuring of the basic rules of the game, embroiling unions in the transition process.

Political transition implies democratization not only of the government itself but also of Mexican unionism. It implies unions breaking free from the ties of corporatism and becoming internally democratic. It means genuine union autonomy from government. Unions can continue their involvement in politics, but can no longer depend on a single party which is itself in crisis and losing effectiveness.

This chapter explores the challenges Mexican unions face in this period and also the opportunities transition holds out to build a stronger and more representative labour movement. It first recounts the origins and development of the current political crisis, and then steps backward in time to sketch the history of Mexican unions and the development of Mexico's particular system of industrial relations and unionism. The concluding portion discusses the current crisis of the corporatist model and the prospects for Mexican unionism that lie ahead.

I ORIGINS OF THE POLITICAL CRISIS

Which of several different moments when one might date the beginning of the period of transition depends on the relative importance the analyst accords to various aspects of the PRI regime. From the perspective of party politics, one might identify the pivotal moment as occurring with the 1994 assassinations of Luis Donaldo Colosio, the Party's Presidential candidate, and José Francisco Ruiz Massieu, its General Secretary (especially since the available evidence points to the conclusion that these crimes were carried out by PRI members). This period also saw more frequent electoral defeats of PRI state-governor candidates and fierce intra-party battles during the run-up to the 2000 presidential election.

Viewing the crisis in economic terms, one would choose an earlier date. By the early 1980s, Mexico was engulfed in an economic crisis that directly affected the great majority of people, with profound political ramifications. The government was compelled to re-examine the protectionist model constructed by President Miguel Alemán in the 1940s which, as Crespo argues, 'had reached its limits'.[2] Under Miguel de la Madrid and his predecessor, José López Portillo, an emerging 'techno-

[2] See Crespo, J. A., 'La evolución del sistema de partidos en México', 124 *Foro Internacional* (Apr.–June, 1991) 604–5.

cratic' elite, many trained in foreign universities, replaced traditional politicians in key appointments to government posts, and soon the new 'technocrats' were given the opportunity to test their economic models and theories.[3] The economic opening was carried out through a series of abrupt actions taken by the de la Madrid government. The vast majority of the import-permit requirements were unilaterally eliminated in 1985, and the government commenced negotiations to join the General Agreement on Tariffs and Trade (GATT), leading to formal membership in 1986. In this period, enormous problems of foreign debt, inflation, and exchange rates led the country to accept conditions imposed by the International Monetary Fund (IMF). Once an unruly child who wanted to skip school, Mexico suddenly became the best-behaved and the most diligent pupil in the international finance class.

In the broadest historical perspective, 2 October 1968 is probably the decisive date when the transition process was set in motion. The massacre in Tlateloco by soldiers and the police of over 300 students who were protesting against the government of Gustavo Díaz Ordaz shocked the nation. The president of the Republic, until then a quasi-divine figure, fell into widespread disrespect. As Soledad Loaeza tells us, these events marked a 'rupture with the past' and saw the 'full entrance into independent political life of the middle classes', who had previously played a passive role. The emergence of these groups as authentic political participants 'signalled the gradual, but increasingly accelerated' dismantling of a regime which acted with impunity and a state that enjoyed a monopoly over political organization.[4]

However, the state structures were then still solid enough to contain the problem and to isolate the students from the workers and peasantry. Respected leaders openly supported the repressive measures with which the Díaz Ordaz government responded to the demands of the students, who were portrayed as enemies of the working class. On the other hand, the economic crisis, the effects of which were directly felt by the great masses of people, fuelled the crisis of political legitimacy.

Subsequent events provided further evidence of systemic decay. The López Portillo administration undertook political reforms in the late 1970s. In 1982, the new President, de la Madrid, started a campaign for 'the moral renovation of society', a slogan that implicitly recognized the corruption and lawlessness that had proliferated under the PRI. Prior to the 1988 elections, a schism occurred in the PRI. Cuauhtémoc Cárdenas, son of Lázaro Cárdenas, one of the most renowned symbols of 'PRI-ism', left the ranks of the party after a fruitless attempt to democratize it from

---

[3] Ibid.
[4] Loaeza, S., *El llamado de las Urnas* (Mexico City: Cal y Arena, 1989) 25.

within and formed the National Democratic Front (FDN), a leftist coalition that challenged the PRI candidate, Carlos Salinas de Gortari. The opposition's strong showing forced the PRI to resort to 'post-electoral methods' to preserve its hegemony, a new tool in the arsenal of instruments it used for that purpose throughout its history. Ironically, since this was the first election employing the marvels of modern technology, the cover for the party to use these techniques was a supposed computer failure.

As Héctor Aguilar Camín and Lorenzo Meyer have said, 'the slowness of the count of election results, the apparent manipulation of the process by the authorities and the lack of credibility in the public eye cast a dark shadow of doubt and accusations of fraud over the July 1988 elections'.[5] Officially, Salinas was declared the winner with a little more than 50 per cent of the votes, the lowest number of votes the PRI had ever received in a presidential election. Thirty per cent of the votes went to Cárdenas, and 20 per cent went to the conservative National Action Party (PAN). However, many observers and international media sources doubted the accuracy of the official figures, and the election left in its aftermath a climate of confrontation and dispute.[6]

The lack of credibility of the PRI's 1988 electoral victory permitted Cárdenas not only to maintain his position as the leading opposition figure during Salinas' term, but also to consolidate the organization. The FDN became the Party of Democratic Revolution (PRD) and emerged as a real electoral alternative to the PRI. People disaffected with the regime were no longer limited to a 'protest vote' in favour of the PAN, which was identified with conservative forces and whose most important role as an opposition organization until then was to legitimate the triumphs of the PRI. The 1988 elections represented the PRI's worst results ever, not only in the presidential tally, but also for its legislative candidates, both for senator and deputy. For the first time in its history, a PRI government was obliged to confront substantial opposition representation in the Chamber of Deputies, although the opposition presence was divided between the PAN and the PRD. The PRI had only a little more than 50 per cent of deputies. It also lost its monopoly of power in the Upper House.

Significantly, among the PRI's losing candidates were a considerable number promoted by the workers' sector of the party. Their defeat called into question the political effectiveness of the PRI-dominated unions and their established leadership. In exchange for a share of power, the unions traditionally delivered large numbers of votes to the PRI. The 1988 elec-

---

[5] Camín, H. A., and Meyer, L., *A la sombra de la Revolución Mexicana* (Mexico City: Cal y Arena, 1989) 284.
[6] See ibid.

tion indicated a loss of their control over their members' votes. Instead, working class votes went predominantly to the coalition headed by Cárdenas. This illustrates the close link between the crisis of the Mexican political system and the crisis of its unions. Corporatistic unionism was simply not credible enough with workers to maintain its power and their allegiance along the neoliberal road of painful 'adjustment measures' imposed by the IMF.

Salinas took some actions that produced favourable economic results, such as renegotiation of the foreign debt and reduction of the rate of inflation. These were seen as positive steps, despite the overall burdens imposed by the adjustment measures. It seemed Salinas might be able to restore the image of the presidency, and, to a lesser extent, that of the official party. At the beginning of his term, he took spectacular action against certain very unpopular union leaders, such as Carlos Jonguitud Barrios, leader of the teachers, and Joaquin Hernandez Galicia (known as 'La Quina'), leader of the oil workers. This, too, rekindled hope that the government might set the country on the right track.

But the crisis of the unions was so deep that structural changes were demanded, not merely changes in personnel. Salinas's actions had not really changed the way industrial relations in Mexico were conducted. As Arturo Anguiano said at the beginning of the Salinas administration:

the longer the government and the privileged classes take to reshape the domination of their class and the political regime in order to adapt to the new social and productive reality, the more they will face internal difficulties, particularly among the subordinated classes, who might work out an alternative to their power, that is, a profound reorganization of society and the state.[7]

The presidential term came to an end without this reshaping. However, with impressive use of the media and with electoral goals clearly in mind, Salinas created the National Solidarity Programme (PRONASOL) in order to sell his version of neo-liberalism (which he renamed 'social liberalism') and to attempt to recapture the working class votes which the unions seemed increasingly unable to deliver to the PRI.

Although some important macroeconomic successes were achieved in the Salinas era, mainly in controlling inflation, and Mexico's international image was improved, the recovery forgot about social justice. The gap between rich and poor widened still further, revealing the ineffectiveness of the 'social' aspects of Salinas' social liberalism and of PRONASOL. On 1 January 1994, violence born of misery, which the

---

[7] Anguiano, A., 'El desenlace del corporativismo' in Bensusán, G., and García, C. (eds.), *Estado y sindicatos, crisis de una relación* (Mexico City: Universidad Autónoma Metropolitana Xochimilco and Fundación Friedrich Ebert, 1989) 37.

regime had been able to suppress until then, broke out in Chiapas. Once again in Mexican history, it was the peasants who impelled change—previously in the era of Venustiano Carranza, eighty years later under Carlos Salinas. And once again, union leaders sought to counterpose the interests of urban and rural workers, as they recounted stories of the Carranza era 'Red Battalions', pro-regime workers who fought against peasants. Then the platform was the *Casa del Obrero Mundial* (House of the World Worker); this time their views were voiced by Fidel Velázquez, the main leader of the Confederation of Workers of Mexico (CTM). But apparently contemporary Mexican workers had sufficient reasons to avoid the mistakes of their predecessors.

The 1994 elections followed important reforms to the federal electoral law and were much more carefully monitored both domestically and internationally. Despite the regime's problems and the outbreak of the insurgency in Chiapas, the PRI did very well. It maintained the same 50 per cent of the vote it had officially obtained in 1988. The PRI largely concentrated on attacking Cárdenas. Fomenting what became known as 'the vote of fear', the PRI predicted that, should the PRD win the elections, economic catastrophe would follow in the form of the return of inflation, devaluation of the peso, and capital flight. The PRI was also able to turn to advantage the atmosphere of insecurity produced by the events in Chiapas. Some union leaders who were PRI candidates for deputy or senator regained positions lost in 1988, indicating some return by working class voters to traditional political loyalties and possibly a partial reinforcement of the corporatist framework.

The 1994 elections also prompted a reconfiguration of the opposition forces. The conservative PAN recovered the second place position it had traditionally held. The PAN argued that the economic successes attributed to Salinism had actually been achieved through measures previously advocated by PAN itself. Cárdenas had taken second place in 1988 under the FDN banner, but this time, running as the candidate of the PRD, he fell to third place.

The new government of Ernesto Zedillo inherited the legacy and therefore all of the problems of Salinist neo-liberalism. Within a year of taking office, the government confronted precisely the economic catastrophes that the PRI had predicted would be triggered by a PRD victory. The regime was forced to devalue the currency and to seek foreign aid (primarily from the United States). But the economic crisis deepened, and new devaluations, heightened inflation, growing external debt, capital flight, rising unemployment, and a decline in the real value of wages followed. The stage was set for the momentous political events of 2000.

II THE HISTORY AND DEVELOPMENT OF MEXICAN UNIONISM

Although the number of workers involved in the Mexican Revolution was small, this limited participation nevertheless had great and lasting social significance. The organized workers supported Carranza, the revolutionary commander who was destined to become president. As Héctor Aguilar Camín has argued, the so-called *Casa del Obrero Mundial* pact of 1914 in many ways determined the relationship of workers not only with the Revolution but with the post-revolutionary governments of the twentieth century. In their pact with Carranza, the first organized workers abandoned the commitment to direct union action and independence from any government, which they held until then, and offered their military contribution and political support to the Constitutionalist troops. In exchange they asked for the first monopoly privilege: the right to unionize all the workers in the territories conquered by Constitutionalist troops.[8]

Carranza was a conservative, but due to pressure from deputies attending the drafting convention, the Constitution of 1917 consecrated the right to professional association and collective bargaining, and the right to strike. In 1918, the Mexican Regional Confederation of Workers (CROM) emerged out of a national congress summoned by Carranza himself. The CROM leader, Luis N. Morones, had a personal alliance with President Álvaro Obregón (who had replaced Carranza), and CROM soon became the most important organization in the country. 'Prototype of the new union leader, Morones made a secret pact with Álvaro Obregón, who allowed him to form his own political party, the *Laborista Mexicano* party. This marked the beginning of a strategic change toward so-called "multiple action", usually deemed an open concession to the government. In this way, Morones became Secretary of Industry, Commerce, and Work in Obregón's cabinet, assuming the responsibility to manipulate the workers' movement so it would proceed in convenient directions'.[9]

Today, we identify official unionism with PRI structures. However, the corporatist pattern came into place earlier, during the 1920s, when the rule of the *caciques* (chiefs) matured into a system of political institutions. The personal alliance between Obregón and Morones became an institutional alliance between the government and CROM under the administration of Plutarco Elías Calles. Calles had replaced Obregón after the latter's failed bid for re-election. The ever undisciplined Morones fell

---

[8] Aguilar Camín, H., *Después del milagro* (Mexico City: Cal y Arena, 1991) 62–3.
[9] Santos Azuela, H., 'El sindicalismo en México' (1992) 7 *Ars Iuris, Revista de la Facultad de Derecho de la Universidad Panamericana* 201.

from power after he flouted Calles' wishes by trying to reach the presidency himself and after alleged responsibility in the 1928 assassination of Obregón. Calles remained the most powerful political figure even after retiring from the presidency. In 1929, he created the PNR (National Revolutionary Party), forerunner of the PRI, to channel and direct negotiations within the ruling classes. According to Lorenzo Meyer, the PNR 'was founded not to contest with other parties for the right to govern, but as an instrument for institutionalizing the internal negotiations of the political elite . . . [This led] almost inevitably to a formal democracy and to real authoritarianism. A benevolent authoritarianism with ample social corporatist foundations dating from the late 1930s, but an authoritarianism nevertheless.'[10]

In 1933, Vicente Lombardo Toledano, a former member of CROM, founded the General Confederation of Workers and Peasants of Mexico (CGOCM) which promptly became the second strongest workers' organization in the country. The CTM, the dominant labour federation today, eventually arose from the CGOCM. The corporatist union model was perfected during the presidency of Lázaro Cárdenas. The CTM was incorporated into the regime and into the structures of the dominant party, now renamed by Cárdenas the Party of the Mexican Revolution (PRM). Cárdenas turned the PRM (which became the PRI in 1946) into a modern party of mass mobilization, with sectors representing workers, peasants, and popular organizations. Aziz Nassif defined the system established by Cárdenas as corporatist with a mass base, as in Italy; however it was not fascist, but instead had 'a formally democratic character and [with aspects borrowed from the US] New Deal such as state participation in the economy and the provision of social welfare'.[11]

Some other labour confederations arose following the CTM model. While not directly participating in the PRI as one of its sectors, they acted as if, and were commonly considered to be, part of the party. Some important labour unions, such as those representing railway employees, telephone operators, and the electrical workers, preferred to remain autonomous from the CTM, but not from the PRI. However, whether joined in the CTM or not, all these organizations observed the rules of the game imposed by the system. Despite this, they were attacked by the government when they tried to assert and defend their rights. For example, the 1959 strike of railway workers was repressed by a President, Adolfo López Mateos, who styled himself a leftist. CTM leader Fidel Velázquez sided with the government on that occasion. No party other

---

[10] Meyer, L., 'El límite neoliberal', 163 *Nexos* (July 1993) 25.
[11] Nassif, A., 'Las confederaciones obreras y el Estado en México: el caso de la Confederación de Trabajadores de México', *Colección Documentos de Trabajo*, No. 34 (Mexico City: Fundación Friedrich Ebert, 1990) 24.

than the PRI established significant alliances with union organizations, and independent unions have never been numerically significant in Mexico (although in the most recent years some signs have appeared of an opening to new, independent forms of union organization).

The perfection of corporatism should be placed in the context of the country's economic development. In the Cárdenas era, the Mexican population consisted primarily of peasants. A semi-urban working class was beginning to form, made up of workers coming from rural areas who worked in enterprises that had existed before the Revolution, primarily in mining, and the textile, electric, and railway industries. Some new private enterprises appeared during World War II, taking advantage of gaps left in the market as the industrialized countries converted to war footing. At the conclusion of the war, these new enterprises could not compete against foreign firms that reconverted to their normal peacetime operations, so they appealed to the government for protection. After World War II, the Mexican government, like most in Latin America, adopted an economic policy of 'inward development' or import substitution. The goal of these policies was to protect domestic industry by means of high tariffs and import permits, overvalued currency, and exchange rate controls. As we have seen, these policies in due course led to the economic and political crisis.

In terms of the legal grounding of labour relations, it is important to note that, although Article 123 of the 1917 Constitution entrenched basic workers' rights (the right to professional association, to bargain collectively, and to strike), labour relations was not regulated at national level until 1931, when the first Federal Labour Law was promulgated. Prior to this, labour regulation was left to state legislatures. Collective rights were inhibited due to confusing local regulations. Notwithstanding the broad terms of Article 123, the Federal Labour Law established important limits to the rights it protects and granted government considerable control over unions. For example, requirements for forming and registering a union, the requirement that the authorities recognize its representatives, and restrictions on the right to strike seriously limit union autonomy and freedom of action. In addition, so-called 'exclusion clauses' allow unions to require that all workers in a company join the union and therefore to procure the discharge of dissident workers who challenge the union by the technique of expelling them from membership.[12] Quite apart from these legal restrictions, the authorities frequently leave the collective rights of workers unenforced. A very wide gap separates legal doctrine from the realities of enforcement by organs of the state. In Mexican labour

---

[12] Editors' note: while this book was in production, a landmark decision found such clauses in violation of the 1917 constitution.

law, the realities of state policy have 'divorced' the rules of law. And it is all too common for union leaders to put their own interests and those of the PRI government ahead of the interests of their own members, let alone the interests of employers.

III FUNDAMENTAL CHARACTERISTICS OF THE MEXICAN CORPORATIST MODEL

We can identify several fundamental characteristics of Mexican unionism.

First, Mexican unionism is (or was) a mechanism for the PRI to mobilize and capture large numbers of workers' votes. Unions served as recruitment agencies for the PRI and promoted party candidates. Indeed, in the case of the CTM, union members automatically belonged to the PRI.

Secondly, it is (was) a mechanism for legitimating governmental policy and decisions. Generally, the first mass support for controversial government decisions comes from the 'official' unions.

Thirdly, Mexican unionism is (was) a channel of social mobility and access to the elites. For workers, becoming a union leader has represented a viable path to improve one's economic and social position.

Fourthly, the system gives (gave) government monopolistic control over workers' organizations, exerted through the PRI with the assistance of the labour authorities. Even among independent unions, the vast majority have either belonged to or been linked with the PRI and (at least until now) invariably gave propagandistic and economic support to the party's candidates. The process of union registration plays a fundamental role in this respect. Under the applicable regulations, labour authorities have the power to grant or withhold recognition of the legal existence of a union and therefore its corporate capacity to exercise the collective rights of workers, including the rights to bargain collectively and strike. Labour authorities can also influence representation on unions' governing boards.

Fifthly, the system of unionism is (was) a mechanism through which government pressured and controlled industralists, through its power either to encourage strikes or threats of strikes or to repress direct action by workers. A very effective way that PRI governments elicited political support from initially reluctant employers was to aid a strike or simply to remain temporarily passive in the face of labour conflict. Government always had the power, at the appropriate time, to step in and mediate a solution, or declare the strike illegal, or even repress it, as suited the PRI's interests in a particular case.

Sixthly, the system was essentially despotic and exhibited none of the features of democratic unionism. The great majority of unions have never been democratic, particularly those linked to the CTM and to other large federations such as the Revolutionary Confederation of Workers and Peasants (CROC) and the CROM. Apparent changes in union governing boards often left power in the same hands. According to Lorenzo Meyer, 'the majority of the Mexican union organizations are part of the PRI, their managements constituting one of the strongest elements preventing national policy from adhering to the rules of a legal democracy'.[13] Meyer believes that there would be large repercussions if the unions proceeded in democratic fashion, producing changes in the rules of the political game and significantly affecting vested interests.

Seventhly, the corporatist system of labour relations has also been highly inefficient. In the policy environment in which Mexican unionism developed—protectionism for companies and paternalism for workers—no one placed priority on improving productivity, certainly not the unions. Since the opening of the Mexican economy, it has often been said that Mexican labour law is too rigid and is responsible for preventing productivity growth. The system is rigid, but the fault is not in labour law as such, but in the privileges historically granted to unions by the employers, with government encouragement. For example, it is quite common for employers to assume in collective contracts an obligation to retain a fixed number of employees on the payroll, regardless of the enterprise's actual demand for labour. For union leaders, these clauses guaranteed a certain number of jobs for members, which is a source of considerable political power. The government was content to use this device both to raise job levels and fight unemployment (even at the cost of inefficiency) and also to secure votes.

Eighthly, and somewhat paradoxically, the Mexican industrial relations system is (or was) basically adversarial and assumes conflict and confrontation between the respective interests of employers and workers. In the culture of Mexican unions, anything considered good for employers was automatically thought to be bad for employees. The obligatory union rhetoric encouraged confrontation with and hatred towards employers and permitted union leaders to present themselves as working class heroes. Although it is easy for workers to feel spontaneous aversion to employers, the truth is that, in Mexico, union leaders have often been responsible for creating this feeling. At present, workers have become much more concerned about improving productivity and quality, but this change in consciousness is driven more by a sense of the perceived necessities of modernization than conviction.

[13] Meyer, L., 'La debilidad histórica de la democracia mexicana' in Cordera, R., Trejod, R., and Vega, J. E. (eds.), *México el reclamo democrático* (Mexico City: Siglo XXI, 1988) 80.

Ninthly, Mexican unionism is totally corrupt. Huge amounts of money flow into union leaders' pockets from sweetheart alliances with owners and employers at the expense of the workers' interests; from underground deals to get contracts and concessions from government agencies; from the sale of jobs in governmental institutions; from participation in corrupt practices involving public officials; and, more generally, from threats, blackmail, and illegal pressure placed on employers. In addition to all this, union fiscal immunity has allowed them to charge many expenses, real or fictional, to the national treasury, generating a huge 'tax-free' income for them.

<h2 style="text-align:center">IV THE CRISIS OF CORPORATISM AND THE
TRADITIONAL UNION MODEL</h2>

The old corporatist model of unionism remained viable as long as Mexico grew economically. All parties to the arrangement enjoyed benefits from the labour relations model: union leaders obtained a share of power from the PRI and profited at the expense of employers and workers; employers gained control over their workers and support from the government; PRI governments obtained votes, controlled the unions, and appeared to create jobs.

But during the 1970s, the economic system went into deep and lasting crisis. Rising inflation, imbalance in public finance, and growing public debt were the most visible problems. The public did not appreciate the full extent of the crisis until 1976, when, shortly before passing his office to López Portillo, President Luis Echeverría was forced to devalue the peso, thereby reducing the purchasing power of wages, an extraordinary and hitherto inconceivable event for the vast majority of Mexicans. The unions were unable to offer any solution; indeed, they were unable to launch a fight. The traditional model of unionism was not designed for circumstances of this sort, and union officials were not trained to provide workers with the leadership in times of economic crisis.

During the mid-1980s, the government of Miguel de la Madrid saw changing the traditional pattern of negotiating with unions as a necessary component of restructuring the economy in order to cope with the crisis. Terms such as 'modernization', 'flexibility', 'industrial conversion', and 'social agreement' entered labour discourse. As Lorenzo Meyer observed:

[n]aturally, the social cost was huge because during the de la Madrid period social expenditures were reduced, wages lost half of their buying power—they went from thirty-six per cent of NIP [Net Internal Product] to twenty-nine per cent, NIP stagnated, inflation remained unchecked (it was eighty per cent in 1983 and 159

per cent in 1987), and the unconventional economy grew due to lack of employment in the conventional sector.[14]

According to José Antonio Crespo, 'the lack of resources which caused the crisis had repercussions on the relations between the state and the corporate bodies affiliated with the official party, because the smooth functioning of the corporatist pact demanded not only restrictions on, but monetary tributes from union leaders, union headquarters, and affiliated organizations'.[15]

The crisis of the corporatist unionism model was clearly evidenced by the defeat, in 1988 elections, of so many PRI candidates drawn from the working class:

The system based on the hegemonic party was torn apart by pincers in 1988: from the bottom, the processes of social change and long-lasting economic crisis undermined [the PRI's] electoral base; and from the top, [it was torn] by the collapse of consensus among the elites. The paralysis of some of [the PRI's political] arrangements, the split of the cardenistas, and the radicalism of opposition leadership weakened [PRI's] political support.[16]

Salinas de Gortari (who was president from 1988 to 1994) made a show of supporting the unions, but his rhetoric conflicted with his neo-liberal beliefs. His labour policies were rent by contradiction as a result of his attempt to combine two essentially incompatible objectives, modernization and preservation of the corporatist model. To quote Meyer:

The strong social foundation of support for the Presidency [and] the corporatist apparatus of the PRI . . . was shocked and weakened because [PRI's] members were forced to bear a considerable part of the social costs resulting from the economic crisis, and also because in the [emerging] neoliberal economic model, workers are supposed to negotiate their wages and benefits with an eye toward productivity, not their political participation inside the party. . . . In short, corporatism weakened with the economic changes, although it did not disappear but kept [trying to] enact the same role as before vis-à-vis presidential power: subordinated support.[17]

The government repressed attempts to build more combative and representative unionism in big enterprises such as Ford, Volkswagen, the Modelo Brewery, and the Cananea mining company.

---

[14] Meyer, above, n. 10, 31.
[15] Crespo, J. A., 'Crisis económica: crisis de legitimidad' in Bazdresch, C. *et al.*, *México: auge, crisis y ajuste* (Mexico City: FCE (Fondo de Cultura Económica), 1992) 11, 28.
[16] Aziz Nassif, A., and Molinar Horcasitas, J., 'Los resultados electorales' in González Casanova, P. (ed.), *Segundo informe sobre la democracia: México el 6 de julio de 1988* (Mexico City: Siglo XXI, 1990) 145–6.
[17] Meyer, above, n. 10, 32–3.

Mexican unionism had long served the government's purposes effectively, but only because the workers had faith that unions could achieve gains through manipulation and tricks, because union membership was a condition for obtaining certain jobs, because the workers feared that militancy would lead to repression and job loss, and because union leadership was recruited from workers whose ambition was to rise to elite positions within the traditional structures. Moreover, the average wage of union workers was consistently higher than that of workers without a collective contract. Unionization brought enhanced, if still very low, wages, and this was a price employers willingly paid in exchange for control over the workforce.

The model gradually decayed under the pressure of political and economic crisis, and we can say with confidence that it is no longer effective today. Formerly, unionized Mexican workers believed in their leaders or at least accepted their control and direction. The PRI could once count on the automatic vote of unionized workers. But these bases of support for the system have eroded through years of decline in the purchasing power of wages and growth of the gap between rich and poor, growing awareness by workers of the injustice of the system, and fatigue resulting from unfulfilled promises. The ineffectiveness of union leaders in these new circumstances further debilitates them and reduces their share of power. That union leaders still retain some power is due to the Federal Labour Law and the collaboration of the authorities in the union registration process, enforcement of exclusion clauses, and other legal tools for controlling worker independence. But these are thin reeds which may snap at any time.

President Zedillo did not fully appreciate that his projects of democratization and modernization were incompatible with preserving corporatist unionism and its corrupt leaders. Nevertheless, the nation experimented with changes during the 1990s. This allowed Mexicans to cherish hopes for a break-through by the democratization process in the union field that would finally allow workers to exercise the rights of professional association and collective bargaining, and the right to strike consecrated by the Constitution more than eighty years ago. Some opening by the authorities to more democratic forms of union organization, such as the UNT (National Union of Workers), occurred even before the 2000 elections. The new government is expected to make major changes in labour law that will open the door wide for democratic organizations to fill the vacuum that the increasingly weak, traditional unions—which have barely managed to survive the death of Fidel Velázquez—are leaving behind.

Moreover, some independent unions, notably the FAT (Workers Authentic Front), have been exploring new strategies. For example, they have converted the North American Agreement on Labour Cooperation (NAALC) into a forum to expose and denounce violations of workers' rights and the inefficiency and complicity of Mexican labour authorities. They have worked collaboratively with unions in the USA and Canada to provide mutual support in processing complaints to the National Administrative Office (NAO) for each of NAFTA's three signatories. As Lance Compa has observed, '[b]efore NAFTA and the NAALC, cross-border solidarity took place at a thin, high level of bureacratic meetings among top union officials and occasional letters of support to workers in struggle. Now trade union leaders and activists up and down the line are working together in concrete projects dealing with the effects of economic integration in their continent.'[18]

The recent election results are certainly good news for democracy; however not everything looks rosy. At the moment, differences between the right and left are diminished on the Mexican political landscape, and honesty and progress are more important for most Mexicans at this juncture than political ideology. On the other hand, the ascendancy of PAN advances the interests of the right, not so much in contrast to the ideology of PRI, if any, but against the thwarted the hopes of the left to show itself as the alternative.

The left still believes that Cárdenas was denied victory in 1988 only by government fraud. Having said that, Cuauhtémoc Cárdenas and the PRD had a chance to prove themselves when Cárdenas became the first elected governor of Mexico City in 1997 (previously, city governors were appointed by the president). Many supporters who expected big changes were disappointed by Cárdenas. No major changes have occurred thus far concerning unionism in Mexico City. The PRD lost a good deal of ground in the 2000 elections, particularly at the national level, even though they retained control of the Mexico City government. Many PRD supporters cast their votes for PAN candidates in the belief that a PAN victory was the only real possibility to defeat the PRI candidate for President. Even some high-profile personalities who had supported Cárdenas and the PRD in the previous election joined the Fox campaign, seeing him as representing the interests, not of the right, but of democracy.

Obviously, the recent presidential elections will profoundly influence the unions' destiny. Traditional union leaders will have to change their modes of operation. No doubt some will offer their services to the new

---

[18] Compa, L., 'The North American Agreement on Labor Cooperation and International Labor Solidarity' in Bouzas Ortiz, J. A. *et al.*, *Encuentro Trinacional de Laboralistas Democráticos* (Mexico City: Universidad Nacional de México, 1999), 210. This collection was sponsored by UNAM (Universidad Nacional Autónoma de México), UAM (Universidad Autónoma Metropolitana), FAT (Frente Auténtico del Trabajo), and AFL-CIO.

president despite the fact that he comes from the PAN, not PRI. Within days of the election, Víctor Flores, general secretary of the railway workers' union and known as one of the most corrupt union leaders, approached Fox to say that he was willing to work together with him. Other leaders have been more deliberate and have made a point of saying that they expect labour rights to be honoured by the new government. Nevertheless, these leaders have recognized the significance of Fox's triumph.

As of this writing (July 2000), it is difficult to know whether union leaders will be sufficiently clever, persuasive, and strong to make the changes necessary for the traditional unions to survive in a democratic country. It is even harder to predict whether the PRI will be able to transform itself into a true political party; whether, if so, it will be able to sustain its alliances with the biggest unions; and, more importantly, whether it will someday genuinely advance the interests of workers. The Mexican labour relations system has come to a crossroads, and it is very hard to see what lies ahead. One thing is clear enough, however, and that is that only a truly representative and independent unionism will be able to meet the challenges of economic opening and political transition.

21

A New Course for Labour Unions: Identity-Based Organizing as a Response to Globalization

MARIA L. ONTIVEROS

In the United States, labour unions have traditionally focused their organizing efforts on the workplace, an approach US law encourages by limiting the protections and privileges accorded to union activity to workplace issues. This chapter makes the case for a shift to identity-based organizing. It begins by briefly describing identity-based organizing and explains why it may provide a promising strategy for labour in an era of globalization. The chapter then describes the limited view of labour union issues found in US law and discusses the particular impediments that US labour law poses to identity-based organizing and some strategies for overcoming them.

I IDENTITY-BASED ORGANIZING

Defining identity-based organizing

Identity-based organizing is a way of organizing the whole identity of a human being, not just his or her workplace identity. It involves recognizing those aspects of a person which are integral to his or her identity. One set of important identity factors includes a person's race, gender, ethnicity, national origin, citizenship status, community, sexual orientation, and religion. We can call these personal identity factors. Another important set of identity factors includes a person's job, social class, career, income, and wealth. We can call these class identity factors. Identity-based organizing means taking into account all these factors when discussing labour organization and labour issues. It means recognizing the personal as well as the class identity of all workers, including workers of colour; and recognizing also that these two different types of identity are interrelated, both in defining the oppression faced by workers and in finding solutions to it. Identity-based organizing, as used in this chapter, is not limited to the 'organizing phase' of a campaign; it relates also to organizing in a broader sense—bringing workers together and empowering them through the labour movement.[1]

The principles of identity-based organizing are exemplified in several union efforts aimed at empowering Latino immigrant workers in California. For example, the Service Employees International Union (SEIU), in its Justice for Janitors campaign, successfully organized high-rise building janitors in Los Angeles and other cities. The campaign recognized the class and personal identity of the janitors in planning its strategy for empowerment in the workplace, union, and community. The first decision made was to focus the theme or message of the campaign as one of dignity and justice, rather than higher wages or other workplace demands. Such a call reflects the personal and class identities of the janitors because it recognizes the specific affronts to human dignity encountered by immigrant workers, as immigrants and as workers. To take one example, some workers carried oversized toothbrushes to protest the requirement that janitors scrub the floor with toothbrushes—a form of manual, on-your-knees labour that demeans all workers and that many felt would not be required of white or non-immigrant workers.

Next, the union decided to avoid the traditional administrative process used by unions in the USA. The administrative process envisages an organizing phase that results in workers signing cards expressing an interest in union representation, a campaign phase where the union and employer vie for the votes of the workforce, a board-certified election phase, and (if a majority of workers vote for the union) a negotiation phase where union and management negotiate the 'terms and conditions of employment'. In contrast, in the Justice for Janitors campaign the workers took to the streets in large, loud, visible processional protests demanding a contract with terms and conditions that would show respect for them as human beings and as workers. Their strategy was to force employers to offer such contracts through public pressure, rather than election and negotiation.

This strategy of circumventing the traditional, administrative process recognized that the latter would not work. Most accounts of the campaign view this strategy as a response to the complex structure of employment in this industry, where janitors frequently work for maintenance contractors who, in turn, work for management firms hired by the owners of the buildings, who, in turn, lease space to the commercial tenants whose

---

[1] For a vivid illustration of an effort to collapse the 'organizing' and 'representation' stages of unionization—and to bridge the gap between personal and workplace identity factors in the service of worker empowerment—see the 'one-on-one' model of organizing pursued by Kris Rondeau and her colleagues in the ultimately successful campaign among the clerical and staff workers at Harvard University, a story retold in, among other places, Hoerr, J., *We Can't Eat Prestige: The Women Who Organized Harvard* (Philadelphia, Penn.: Temple University Press, 1997).

offices the janitors clean and maintain. The campaign virtually ignored the contractors who were the janitors' technical 'employers' and instead chose targets such as building owners and commercial tenants. This was undoubtedly one of the keys to its eventual success. But of equal importance was a recognition of the limited utility, given the identity of the janitors, of the traditional administrative process. Many were undocumented immigrants, who would be vulnerable to discharge and/or deportation if their identity were disclosed and scrutinized, as would happen during the traditional process. And while US labour law prohibits discharge in retaliation for union activities—and that prohibition has been held to apply to undocumented immigrants—the principal remedy is reinstatement, which is of little value to such workers since its availability is conditioned on lawful presence in this country.[2] The best way for immigrant janitors to achieve better workplace conditions and dignity was thus through direct action.

The forms of direct action chosen by the janitors also utilized identity-based organizing. Drawing on the religious festivals and political militancy many of the Salvadoran immigrants had experienced in their country of origin, the protests resembled processions from home. The workers carried banners and oversized props, wore red bandannas tied high upon their faces, and blew whistles and horns. Other union organizing efforts have used religious identity more explicitly by holding Catholic masses at key times, organizing prayer vigils, and displaying religious signs such as the cross and images of the Virgin of Guadalupe.

In the janitors' campaign, the union also communicated in ways that took into account identity issues that went beyond the presence of bilingual and bicultural organizers. For example, they communicated their message through a *fotonovella*—a mystery/romance story, illustrated with photographs—about the disappearance of a janitor. Fotonovellas are a very popular type of publication in Mexico, and it helped the janitors to see and understand the issues in a way that was familiar to them. The union also used home visits to become part of the extended family and community that is so important to Latino immigrants. Being bicultural, the organizers understood the gender dynamics of the home and sometimes spoke first with the man of the house, even if the worker was a woman. As one organizer described her conversation with a worker's husband:

Sometimes for women, especially in the Latino culture, if they are married you have to be sensitive enough to start talking to the man . . . You have to go and talk to the husband and organize the husband, convince him so he'll say 'yes, yes, yes, that's right, it's great.' And in some cases that's how you'll get the woman worker

2 See *Sure-Tan* v. *NLRB*, 467 US 883 (1984).

involved. When we're at their home, we just make sure that they know that we're there to help the whole family: the husband, the kids, everybody. You have to ask questions about the whole family.[3]

Finally, non-employees organized workers at the workplace during work time, a practice that is unprotected under US law.[4] This tactic was especially important to the Latina workers who could not attend union meetings outside work for identity-based reasons. The Latinas lacked time for meetings because of their domestic work—raising children and caring for their homes. Further, the man of the household often objected to a woman's attendance at union meetings because this emphasized her role as a worker, which, in turn, reflected negatively on his ability to fill the traditional male role of breadwinner. Finally, some men felt that it was inappropriate for women to go into an unchaperoned context and mix with strange men.

Once the janitors signed contracts for their services, they continued to rely on identity-based organizing to gain power within the union. When the union refused to allow a number of Latino immigrants to hold the positions to which they had been elected on the local's executive committee, they responded with a prayer vigil and hunger strike outside the union office—tactics which once again reflected their complete identity. A new local was eventually formed to allow the janitors to continue the process of creating a union which recognized their personal and class identities.

A final example of identity-based organizing is the recognition of the importance of explicitly addressing immigration issues and understanding how they relate to class issues. Maria Elena Durazo, President of Local 11 of the Hotel Employees and Restaurant Employees, argues that the best way to protect immigrant's rights is by integrating them into the labour movement. She has worked with unions to fight deportations, to challenge Immigration and Naturalization Service raids, and to teach workers their legal rights.[5] Even the national AFL-CIO has recently reversed its traditional nativist approach to immigration. In February 2000, the executive council agreed to lobby for an end to the policy penalizing employers for hiring undocumented workers; for the creation of a new programme to allow undocumented workers to become legally documented; and for an additional programme to educate immigrant

---

[3] Saenz, R., quoted in Milkman, R. L., Rabadan, L., and Wong, K. (eds.), *Voices from the Front Lines* (Los Angeles, Cal.: UCLA, Center for Labour Research and Education, 2000) 26–7.

[4] Although employers may not prohibit their own employees from promoting (or opposing) unionization during work breaks and the like (*Republic Aviation Corp.* v. *NLRB*, 324 US 793 (1945)), they are free to bar non-employee organizers from what is considered trespassing on company property (*Lechmere, Inc.* v. *NLRB*, 502 US 427 (1992)).

[5] Quoted in Milkman, R., *et al.* (eds.), above, n. 3.

workers about their rights. The AFL-CIO began these initiatives under the leadership of current AFL-CIO President John Sweeney, who was, as it happens, President of the SEIU during the Justice for Janitors campaign.

Teamsters Local 890's Citizenship Project in Salinas, California, is currently engaging in some of the most exciting identity-based organizing. Founded in 1995, its concrete focus is to expand citizenship, social, economic, educational, and political participation among the Latino community in which union members and their families live. Its broader aim is to help transform the definition of citizenship from simply meaning naturalization to something based on participation in institutions, including unions.[6] Such a vision encompasses many aspects of identity-based organizing because it seeks to use collective action and participation to empower immigrant workers in their workplace and in their community. It recognizes the way participation and empowerment in the workplace intersect with participation and empowerment in the community. It is working to create a definition of citizenship that encompasses both class identity and personal identity.

Identity-based organizing as a response to globalization

Until recently, at least, organized labour's strategy toward the prospect of global competition was seemingly premised on a simple trade model. The simple model assumed that, as imports increased, the number of domestic jobs decreased; and, as exports increased, the number of domestic jobs increased. Under this model, labour is concerned mainly with fighting management's desire to decrease domestic workplace costs; or with finding other ways to decrease product costs that would enable them to keep their jobs; or with making goods from other countries more expensive through protectionist trade policies. In this model, labour adopts a local, wage-based, limited view of worker interests.

The current global economy works very differently, however, requiring a different labour approach. Globalization is marked by a dramatic increase in cross-border capital mobility and labour mobility. Capital mobility takes the form of cross-border investment by transnational corporations. The corporations have, in effect, established a global assembly line to produce many goods and services, often by moving capital to regions where labour costs are lower. Labour mobility takes the form of migration—internal migration from rural areas to production centres; immigration to countries with higher paid jobs; and emigration out of countries with lower paid jobs. These two phenomena—capital and

---

[6] Johnston, P., 'Citizens of the Future: the Emergence of Transnational Citizenship among Mexican Immigrants in California' <http://www.newcitizen.org> (visited 26 Apr. 1999).

labour mobility—are linked because the establishment of industry disrupts existing social, economic, and familial systems to facilitate the mobility of rural populations, especially women. During the past thirty-five years, international migration has grown markedly. Significantly, those migrating are increasingly women, moving either alone or with families, seeking their own jobs, rather than merely following a male spouse.[7] The dynamics of both cross-border investment and migration highlight some of the advantages of a shift to an identity-based organizing and strategizing.

The current dynamics of exploitation as a problem for identity-based organization

A shift to identity-based organizing can help bring into clearer focus the dynamics of how workers are exploited through cross-border investment. When transnational corporations establish global assembly lines, those most often employed in the lowest paid, least protected jobs are women—especially rural, migrant, and ethnic or racial minority women. Further, the way in which the workers are exploited is often determined by a combination of their personal and class identities. Female workers of colour, for example, are commonly exploited through the collective forces of patriarchy, racism, colonialism, and capitalism. Focusing on personal identity or on class identities alone cannot accurately capture the way in which oppression works for these workers. Thus, their exploitation cannot be understood by looking only through the lens of workplace or class identity. Nor can it be completely understood by looking only at personal identity. All aspects of identity need to taken into account.

All over the globe, for example, women (primarily Asian, although often accompanied by Latinas) are employed in the semiconductor and garment industries. Employers argue that they need nimble fingers to perform the work and that women of colour are 'naturally' suited for these jobs. These women are 'available' because of the dislocations and draws of globalization, as well as government policies that encourage the establishment of enterprise zones and female employment in them. Women are paid less because there is so much available labour in competition for the jobs; because they are viewed as workers whose income is

---

[7] Professor Evely Hu-DeHart, Department of Ethnic Studies, University of Colorado, and Professor Rhonda Williams, Afro-American Studies Program, University of Maryland, developed this analysis and shared it with me during our ongoing Ford Foundation Research Seminar on *Meanings and Representations of Work in the Lives of Women of Color*. For information on migration patterns see Lim, L. L., and Oishi, N., 'International Labor Migration of Asian Women: Distinctive Characteristics and Policy Concerns' (1996) 5 *Asian and Pacific Migration Journal* 85.

merely supplemental to the family (even when it is not); and because they may be undocumented. Often when these women try to assert power in the workplace, management subdues them by convincing the workers that their efforts undermine their femininity or harm their country's advancement.[8]

In the Caribbean, women workers are similarly exploited in the electronics and garment industries, where government policies develop women as auxiliary workers, and labour unions work against female workers because of the ties between the unions and the government. In Colombia, rural women are exploited on coffee plantations, originally developed through colonialism. These practices encourage the class exploitation of certain women and inhibit their efforts to improve their lives. In China and Mexico, the dynamic described above is compounded by sexual exploitation of factory workers. These are all examples of the 'global assembly line'.

In other sectors, such as agriculture, janitorial, and domestic work, the way in which women are exploited because of their race, gender, class, and ethnicity works a little differently. The dislocations caused by globalization still spur their mobility and availability. Employers may again use pre-existing gender and ethnic hierarchies, for example, hiring male supervisors of certain races or ethnicities or by dividing tasks or work-groups along ethnic lines, to control the female workers. In these situations, a *patron* system may be used to assign the best jobs to male workers. In both agriculture and janitorial work, sexual harassment, intimidation, and even rape are also used to pressure women to accept oppressive work conditions. In addition, this work is devalued as the type of work traditionally done by women and people of colour. Finally, these workers are often excluded from those who enjoy the full protection of US labour law or are hired in employment arrangements, such as temporary work or through subcontractors, which make it difficult for them to organize.

Identity-based organizing as a solution to exploitation

Some solutions to these problems may lie in an approach not limited to consideration only of workplace or personal identity. Within the USA, as discussed above, identity-based organizing is essential to successful organization and to the empowerment of immigrant workers. Internationally, attempts to address abuses along the global assembly line, including consumer boycotts and human rights appeals, may work best when the

---

[8] Politically speaking, as this and the other examples show, drawing on hierarchical gender roles—as unions do when approaching male head-of-households in order to organize female Latino workers (see text above)—can cut both ways. For discussion of this and related issues see Rittich, in this volume.

issues are framed in terms of personal and class identity. Cross-border organizing and solidarity are essential to ensure decent standards for all and would work best if responsive to both class and personal identity factors. International laws geared to 'labour issues' could also address the gender, immigrant, and ethnic identity of the workers. Finally, union membership may be more helpful if it is understood as membership of a community committed to the betterment of working people. This approach necessarily goes beyond what are traditionally thought of as narrow workplace issues. Unfortunately, US labour law has a very narrow view of issues affecting workers. It requires revision to facilitate identity-based organizing. The final section of this chapter describes the narrow focus of US law and suggests possible changes.

II THE LIMITED VIEW OF LABOUR ISSUES IN US LAW

US labour law locates labour issues solely and squarely within the walls of the workplace. An individual's labour issues are narrowly defined through the legal system as wage-based and local, rather than political or production-focused. For example, the law defines union 'membership' very narrowly as a financial commitment to pay dues and initiation fees.[9] Further, courts have limited obligatory fees and dues to the amount used to benefit that member directly in his or her collective bargaining relationship. Legal doctrine thus bars unions from the mandatory collection of fees or dues for 'political' purposes or even supporting organizing efforts at other workplaces or attracting new members.[10] The courts have argued that any benefits from organizing other workers and increasing union membership are too distant from the individual employee to require their support or subsidization. Thus, starting with the most basic notions, such as the definition of union membership, US law interprets labour issues narrowly and locally. In order to allow unions to address identity issues, the understanding of union membership must be changed from a narrow, financial transaction to one of community membership, and dues must be available to support broad political and community activities.

The law continues in this narrow vein in a line of cases that circumscribe the topics over which a union may require a company to bargain. The US labour statute requires that employers and unions bargain in good faith over 'wages, hours, and other terms and conditions of employ-

---

[9] *Communications Workers of America* v. *Beck*, 487 US 735 (1988) (citing *NLRB* v. *General Motors Corp.* 373 US 734, 742 (1963)). These cases deal with obligatory union membership, which collective bargaining contracts can require in certain circumstances.
[10] Ibid.

ment'.[11] The US Supreme Court has deemed the term 'wages, hours, and other terms and conditions of employment' to exclude decisions about production, marketing, relocation, plant shut-downs, and other decisions which it considers managerial or entrepreneurial when it believes that labour costs are not a factor in the decision, or that discussion with the union could not change the decision.[12] This limitation prevents employee participation in many of the key issues influencing workers' lives and defines their interests solely in terms of labour costs. A model recognizing the importance of identity-based organizing would not prohibit workers from addressing the full range of issues affecting them and their communities.

A similar limitation is found in the line of cases dealing with 'protected concerted activity'. The statute states that employers may not punish employees for engaging in 'concerted activities for . . . mutual aid or protection'.[13] Although this language appears straightforward, US law has limited its meaning to protecting only activity which benefits 'employees *qua* employees',[14] and not activity which is seen as disloyal or as a challenge to management's authority to run a business.[15] From an identity-based-organizing perspective, concerted activity should be protected if it is found to be in the broad interest of workers' identity, not just their narrow workplace identity.

Further, many issues which impact directly on the workers' community are simply not seen as being a concern of employees. For example, the US Supreme Court has ruled that a company does not have to bargain with a union before changing the benefits it gives to those who have already retired.[16] The Court found that the Act empowers only those currently working and that retirees do not share a community of interest with workers, an approach which fails to recognize that the retirees are the mothers, fathers, aunts, uncles, grandmothers, and grandfathers of current workers. It separates workers from their communities and

---

[11] National Labor Relations Act, 29 USC secs. 158(a) (5) & 158(d).

[12] *NLRB v. Wooster Div. of Borg-Warner Corp.*, 356 US 342 (1958); *Fibreboard Paper Products Corp.* v. *NLRB*, 379 US 203 (1964); *First National Maintenance Corp.* v. *NLRB*, 452 US 666 (1981); *United Food & Commercial Workers, Local 150-A* v. *NLRB (Dubuque Packing Co)*, 1 F. 3d 24 (DC Cir. 1993), cert. dismissed, 511 US 1138 (1994).

[13] 29 USC sec. 157.

[14] *Harrah's Lake Tahoe Resort Casino*, 307 NLRB 182 (1992) (an employee's discharge for advocating an employee stock purchases plan was upheld because the employee was concerned with trying to become an owner or part of management, rather than being concerned with his interest 'as an employee').

[15] *NLRB.* v. *Local 1229, IBEW (Jefferson Broadcasting Co.)*, 346 US 464 (1953) (allowing discharge when employee's act was found to be 'disloyal' because it disparaged the employer's product). This holding places the employer's interest over that of the employee's and limits the employee's role to one of subservience to the employer.

[16] *Allied Chemical and Alkali Workers* v. *Pittsburgh Plate Glass Co.*, 404 US 157 (1971).

prohibits them from using their collective power to help those communities.

The law also limits the ways in which unions may appeal to the community and to other workers, by restricting the availability of boycotts. US law prohibits certain types of boycotts when considered 'economic', while allowing them when considered 'political'. Most union activity is, of course, seen as economic. Further, while all other groups are free to engage in 'secondary boycotts', the law specifically prohibits labour unions from doing so. The 'labor exception' thus prohibits what would be treated as perfectly legitimate protest activity by any other social group. Moreover, when a union is allowed to boycott or engage in strike activity, it may do so only over narrowly defined 'terms and conditions of employment', making it difficult to appeal to the community about broader issues such as enterprise policy or community relations. Clearly, fully to engage in identity-based organizing, unions must be able to engage the community through boycotts and other community campaigns. Somewhat paradoxically, it may be that boycotts undertaken by labour-community coalitions over issues of importance to the community enjoy *more* statutory and constitutional protection than labour law affords traditional union-sponsored boycotts over bread-and-butter ('economic') workplace issues.[17]

Finally, the narrow conception of what labour unionism means in the USA is further illustrated by examining who may organize under the statute without facing discharge or a refusal by the company to negotiate. The law specifically excludes a number of classes of employee from the privilege of protected organization and mandatory good faith bargaining, including agricultural workers, domestic workers, and home workers. It also does not cover independent contractors or supervisors.[18] A disproportionate number of employees who are excluded, as well as a large percentage of those considered 'independent contractors', are women and people of colour who do not occupy the types of jobs traditionally held by white men in the USA or those traditionally found in the US labour movement. Thus, although the exclusion of supervisors may make sense from a class perspective, the US courts have been very aggressive about who is included as a 'supervisor', especially in the largely female field of nursing.[19] As a consequence of their being classified as 'supervisors,' the right of many women to unionize is inadequately protected. The law ought to be expanded to include the many workers, such as temporary workers, student workers, domestic, and agricultural workers, who are not now

---

[17] Pope, J. G., 'Labor-Community Coalitions and Boycotts: The Old Labor Law, the New Unionism, and the Living Constitution' (1991) 60 *Texas L. Review* 889, 896–7.

[18] 29 USC s. 152(3).

[19] *NLRB* v. *Health Care & Retirement Corp. of America*, 511 US 571 (1994).

covered by the Act. Such coverage would allow those workers who are most often exploited by their race, class, gender, and ethnicity to organize and bargain collectively.[20] Other changes also need to be made. In the arena of organizing, for example, union organizers must have access to workers—at home through employer-provided address lists; and at the workplace during working hours—to facilitate identity-based organizing. And the rules governing union democracy need to ensure that immigrants and other new entrants can be fully represented within unions.

Outside the specific labour law statute, reform must start by examining the interplay of the labour, discrimination, and immigration laws. They must be revised to facilitate the empowerment and fair treatment of workers. For example, immigration laws should not be designed to create a surplus of workers who battle over a limited number of jobs. These same laws must encourage empowerment of immigrant workers, by allowing immigrants to bring their families, so they form the type of supportive communities and networks necessary fully to participate in society.[21] Finally, the legality of their immigration status must not be tied to the decision of a single employer to continue their employment; otherwise, the employer simply retains too much control over the worker's life. Employment discrimination and labour laws need to be synchronized so that women and people of colour, including women of colour, are able to battle discrimination both through the collective power of unions and through individual statutes.[22] They also need to be analysed in such a way that women and people of colour are not forced to separate their class interests from their personal identity interests.[23]

At present, however, it may not be wise to put all one's eggs in the basket of a legislative reform agenda that the current Congress and President are unlikely to embrace. Indeed, the failure of modest liberal labour law reform in 1978—with a Democratic House, Senate, and President—may not bode well for ambitious agendas of this sort, even in the medium term. At the moment, therefore, the most effective legal strategies may be those that take advantage of existing labour law, such as the potential 'political' exception in secondary boycott law (above), or

[20] Some recent NLRB decisions, however, suggest a move towards treating the leasing employer as the technical employer of temporary workers, and the Board has recently ordered an election among the teaching assistants at NYU, suggesting a shift in the long standing policy against protecting student workers.

[21] This argument is developed more fully in Ontiveros, M. L., 'Forging our Identity: Transformative Resistance in the Areas of Work, Class and the Law' (2000) 33 *University of California at Davis L. Review* 1057.

[22] Iglesias, E., 'Structures of Subordination: Women of Color at the Intersection of Title VII and the NLRA. Not!' (1993) 28 *Harvard Civil Rights-Civil Liberties L. Review* 395.

[23] Crain, M., 'Between Feminism and Unionism: Working Class Women, Sex Equality and Labor Speech' (1994) 82 *Georgetown L. Journal* 1903; Crain, M., and Matheny, K., 'Labor's Divided Ranks: Privilege and the United Front Ideology' (1999) 84 *Cornell L. Review* 1542.

the legal protection recently approved by the Supreme Court for 'salters' (employees who join a firm for the sole purpose of organizing the workforce, thus taking advantage of the *Republic Aviation* rules for soliciting by incumbent employees).[24] This is in addition to strategies that cross traditional doctrinal borders, such as the use by labour organizations of anti-discrimination suits as well as those that proceed outside existing labour law procedures and structures, such as the Justice for Janitors campaign.[25]

As the world of work changes, both the communities within which workers live and their personal identities are affected. These identities, in turn, affect how they are treated in the workplace and how they respond to that treatment. The changes taking place are not only making identity-based organizing ever more important; they suggest that it may be part of a longer-term political strategy that contributes to wider change. At present, US law is not designed to encourage or, indeed, to allow identity-based organizing. But major changes in this direction are essential to the improvement of the lives of workers, their families, and their communities.

[24] See *NLRB* v. *Town and Country Electric*, 516 US 85, 150 LRRM 2897 (1995) and n. 4 above.
[25] For other examples of similar strategies see Davis *et al.*, in this volume.

22

Difference and Solidarity: Unions in a Postmodern Age

MICHAEL SELMI AND MOLLY S. MCUSIC*

The workplace has always been a place of conflict, and historically that conflict has involved struggle between owners and workers. Today, however, the focus of struggle has shifted as, increasingly, the conflict is seen as involving the diverse interests of workers, a diversity that many believe was previously suppressed in the name of working class solidarity.

In law, this shift in emphasis has gained force through scholars working in the traditions of critical race theory, feminism, and queer theory, all of which have given voice to views and perspectives previously gone unheard. Not surprisingly, these new voices have brought with them a sceptical view of coalition building, and, indeed, of any attempt to find common interests among different groups, based on a fear that the search for commonalities will ultimately result in the weakening, or elimination, of those voices through some version of the 'melting pot' metaphor. Thus, rather than relying on traditional strategies of coalition building, many scholars who stress the importance of identity emphasize the need for separation or isolation from the larger group as a way of preserving one's identity or at least of not subverting one's interests to those of the larger group.

Such calls for separation have recently found their way into the workplace, the traditional location for calls to solidarity among the working class. Much of the recent scholarship concerning labour unions has emphasized the exclusivity of union membership, in particular the way in which unions have often been inattentive to interests that diverged from the traditional union constituency. In light of this growing distrust of unions, several US scholars have suggested that women and minorities should form separate organizations so that each identity group would have its own representation within the workplace.[1] By organizing separately around the

* This chapter is a substantially adapted version of a previous article, 'Postmodern Unions: Identity Politics and the Workplace' (1997) 82 *Iowa L. Review* 1339.
    [1] See, e.g., Crain, M., and Matheny, K., ' "Labor's Divided Ranks": Privilege and the United Front Ideology' (1999) 84 *Cornell L. Review* 1542; Crain, M., 'Images of Power in Labor Law: A Feminist Deconstruction' (1992) 33 *Boston College L. Review* 481, 501; Crain, M., 'Women, Labor Unions and Hostile Work Environment Sexual Harassment: The Untold

concerns of identity, these scholars suggest that each group will be able to express its distinct voice and interests without the silencing effect majority rule can have on non-majoritarian views. For many, then, the workplace is now seen as a battleground among workers and their diverse interests rather than a clash of power between the working class and owners.

It would certainly be a mistake to contest the idea that unions have frequently promoted the interests of their traditional constituency at the expense of women and minorities. Yet, it seems equally clear that the call for separate unions offers faint hope for fundamental structural change because, at bottom, such a strategy targets the wrong enemy. Within the workplace, the goal for employees ought to be restructuring the power relationships that govern economic life. Asserting the importance of identity and emphasizing differences among workers, on the other hand, are unlikely to lead to a restructuring of economic power relationships and present the substantial possibility that all workers will be left worse off than they currently are. Identity unions that do not comprise a majority of workers within a particular workplace are unlikely to secure the power necessary to bargain successfully with employers, and, therefore, are unlikely to hold anything other than symbolic power.

But even symbolic power might be preferred to the existing situation, depending on one's view of the current situation, which brings us to the real question, namely whether any alternative exists between the evils of fragmentation and the sacrificing of one's identity in the pursuit of solidarity. In this chapter, we hope to sketch an alternative vision, one that begins with the important insights of identity politics while seeking to remain focused on the traditional need to restructure power relationships between employees and owners. This project, broadly defined, is intended to forge a community of difference—where difference is celebrated rather than merely tolerated and where differences are used to find commonalities. In so doing we build on the recent re-emergence of scholarship concerning cosmopolitanism, although a cosmopolitanism we hope to demonstrate that offers a distinctly different vision from a strategy of assimilation.

In addition to sketching how a community of difference might look, we will also suggest that labour unions might serve as the source for this

Story' (1995) 4 *Texas Journal of Women and the Law* 1; Iglesias, E. M., 'Structures of Subordination: Women of Color at the Intersection of Title VII and the NLRA. NOT!' (1993) 28 *Harvard Civil Rights-Civil Liberties L. Review* 395, 404–21; and Ontiveros, in this volume. These proposals resemble similar suggestions made during an earlier time. See Lynd, S., 'Government Without Rights: The Labor Law Vision of Archibald Cox' (1981) 4 *Industrial Relations L. Journal* 483; Silverstein, E., 'Union Decisions on Collective Bargaining Goals: A Proposal for Interest Group Participation' (1979) 77 *Michigan L Rev.* 1485; Gould, W. B., 'Labor Arbitration of Grievances Involving Racial Discrimination' (1969) 118 *University of Pennsylvania L. Review* 40.

cosmopolitan renaissance. Unions, we contend, are a place where workers may be able to come together in pursuit of their common interests
without the necessity of either losing their particular identities or subverting their interests to those of a 'universal worker'. In the USA at least,
unions are important to the normative theory we outline in large measure
because they are one of the few institutions that consciously aspire to solidarity. There is also a rich scholarship regarding union ideology and its
effects on identity that closely parallels the broader theoretical work on
what has come to be labelled the 'postmodern society'. For example, by
protecting the group rather than the individual, the US National Labor
Relations Act transforms the operative unit of labour from the individual
to the collective. However, as a price of participation in collective action,
unions have generally required that the individual sacrifice her particular
interests to the greater goals of the working class. As an institution of
community, unions thus pose the critical question whether individuals
can thrive in a communal setting, or whether it is necessary for diverse
groups to go their separate ways in order to advance their particular
interests. We hope to demonstrate that the former ideal remains a possibility.

I THE RISE AND FALL OF THE 'UNIVERSAL WORKER'

For much of their history, US unions, legally and ideologically, have
reflected an image of a universalized worker, one who was generally
thought to be white, married, male, and blue-collar, the kind of employee
who actually constituted the majority of union members. To some extent
it should come as little surprise that unions catered to a model worker,
given that labour law was originally premised on the notion that unions
would operate as mini-legislatures. Under this view, collective bargaining
was seen as a form of democratic self-government by management and
labour complete with general legislative principles, including the principle of majority rule.[2] Just as an individual must accept the political
candidate approved by the majority of voters, the representative selected
by a majority of employees was to provide the exclusive avenue through
which employees would advance their interests against management. As
a result, the interests of individual workers were to be reflected through

---

[2] See, e.g., Cox, A., 'Some Aspects of the Labor Management Relations Act (Part 1)'
(1947) 61 *Harvard L. Review* 1, 1 and 'Part Two' (1947) 61 *Harvard L. Review*. 274, 274–7; Cox,
A., and Dunlop, J., 'Regulation of Collective Bargaining by the National Labor Relations
Board' (1950) 63 *Harvard L. Review* 389; McConnell, G., 'Historical Traits and Union
Democracy' (1958) 81 *Monthly Labor Review* 603; Stone, K. V. W., 'The Post-War Paradigm in
American Labor Law' (1981) 90 *Yale L. Journal* 1509, 1511.

the majority interest, and workers were likewise expected to place the good of the community above whatever individual interests they might have. At various times US law forced workers to join unions and/or to pay dues even when they actually opposed the unions' policies, and in organized workplaces employees are prohibited from negotiating individual contracts, while unions are, at the same time, permitted to enter into agreements that are harmful to some of their members so long as the agreements further the good of the majority.

Because white, married men made up the largest segment of the workforce targeted by unions, it was in their image that the model worker was created. This worker was seen as a full-time industrial production employee in a hierarchically structured, micro-managed workplace with a strict separation of managerial and worker functions. The ideal worker was also the family breadwinner who had a dependent spouse at home responsible for managing the house and children. Indeed, many of the progressive statutory reforms that ultimately shaped the structure of the US labour market—restrictions on female and child labour, compulsory school attendance, the minimum wage, the eight-hour day, restrictions on industrial work at home, and trade unions—were conceived with this ideal in mind. The same construct helps explain the structure of employee benefits, which were largely created around the notion of a full-time male worker engaged in long-term continuous employment with a particular company. Emphasizing sick leave, rather than parental or family leave, was in large part predicated on the notion that the worker had a wife to tend to 'non-work' issues so that the worker would miss work only due to his own illness.

This dominant ideology of the ideal worker also defined what were thought to be the proper interests of labour. The concept embodied by the 'family wage' was that a worker should earn enough money to support a family, with the corresponding assumption that women generally would not contribute to the family income due to their responsibilities in the home. The 'family wage' ideology thus sought to preserve a distinction between the public (the workplace) and the private (family life),[3] and within this paradigm, women who entered the waged labour force were expected to be secondary wage earners with a transient attachment to the workforce. Women were often discouraged from working or joining unions, and any worker demands beyond wage gains and associated benefits—concerns, for example, about childcare or maternity leave—fell outside what were defined as the proper concerns of unions. Unions also frequently failed to seek anti-discrimination

---

[3] See Olsen, F., 'The Family and The Market; A Study of Ideology and Legal Reform' (1983) 96 *Harvard L. Review* 1497.

clauses in their contracts because eliminating discrimination was not in the interests of the majority of members.

By grounding the labour law regime in the interests of the universal worker, the interests of white men were able to predominate in the US workplace well after their majoritarian status began to erode. With the relaxation of explicit discriminatory barriers and changing economic conditions, women and minorities began to enter the primary labour force in substantial numbers in the 1950s and did so in a wide variety of jobs that had previously been closed to them. Despite dramatic inroads, women and minorities generally remained outside the centre of workplace power. A number of reasons contributed to the continued exclusion, ranging from the importance of seniority and the segregated nature of many jobs and workplaces, to the fact that women and minorities often comprised only a minority of workers in any given workplace.[4] As is often the case with a system of democratic governance, their interests went unrepresented in a system that was dependent on majority rule. Unions themselves often contributed to the continued exclusion of minority interests by, in addition to the seniority clauses, restricting membership, and promoting job classifications or shift differentials that often served to separate white men into the highest paying jobs. In some unions, women and minorities were excluded from leadership positions through both formal and informal training programmes, and unions likewise frequently opposed affirmative action plans. Family commitments also limited opportunities for many women to participate in union activities, and these same commitments rendered union seniority agreements of less value to women who often interrupted their careers to have and to care for their children.

Since the early 1970s, a number of forces have helped to loosen this cycle of disempowerment. Certainly an important factor was the decline of union density and influence which, coupled with the changing demographics, challenged workplace orthodoxies in a way that opened opportunities for women and minorities. Relatedly, there was also a distinct shift away from the collective rights model that had long governed the US workplace to an individual rights model built around the new civil rights statutes, a shift that furthered the dissolution of the universal worker prototype.[5] Beginning in the late 1960s, and, increasingly, in the 1970s and

[4] See generally Foner, P. S., *Organized Labor and the Black Worker 1619–1981* (2nd edn., New York: International Publishers 1981); Hill, H., 'Black Workers, Organized Labor, and Title VII of the 1964 Civil Rights Act: Legislative History and Litigation Record' in Hill, H., and Jones, J. E. Jr. (eds.), *Race in America: The Struggle for Equality* (Madison, Wis.: University of Wisconsin Press, 1993) 263, 277, 283–4, 298; Milkman, R., 'New Research in Women's Labor History' (1993) 18 *Signs: Journal of Women in Culture and Society* 376, 385; Romo, R., 'Responses to Mexican Immigration, 1910–1930' in Sedillo, A. (ed.), *Latinos in the United States* (New York: Garland Publishing, 1995) 25, 38–40.

[5] This shift is well-summarized in Weiler, P., and Mundlak, G., 'New Directions for the

1980s, collective rights were viewed with heightened suspicion by the courts and the labour board, as the internal procedures of unions also came under increasing judicial scrutiny. US federal labour policy was thus transformed by the parallel developments of the decline in unionism and the rise in reliance on individualized workplace remedies. This transformation is perhaps most evident in the numerous laws that were passed in the USA to protect individual workers, ranging from health and safety legislation to the civil rights statutes and most recently culminating in the passage of the Americans With Disabilities Act (1990) and the Family and Medical Leave Act (1993).

Not only did workers begin to rely on these new laws for workplace protection, but the legislation also circumscribed the procedures for job allocation, promotion decisions, wage determinations, and employee grievances, all of which had previously been governed primarily by collective bargaining arrangements. Within this individual rights model, identity as defined by racial and gender classifications tended to replace the 'universal' worker as an organizational strategy, and federal law effectively encouraged employees to define their grievances at the workplace with reference to personal or group identity rather than through a union. As one example, under the individual rights model, claims are filed in the USA with the Equal Employment Opportunity Commission rather than with a union representative, and today US federal statutes protect workers from discrimination based on race, gender, national origin, religion, age, and disability—the very categories around which identity groups are often formed.

II IDENTITY ORGANIZING?

A common response to the disintegration of the dominant ideology both in American culture and within the workplace has been to urge a move from integration, or in the context of the workplace a collective identity, to separatism. In the employment context, the poor fit between the collective bargaining regime and the identities of women and people of colour have led some to conclude that American unions have not and cannot represent their interests effectively. As described by one scholar, under the collective bargaining model, women and minorities have 'no home for [themselves] as an integrated whole; to participate in the community [they] had to sacrifice some significant aspect of [themselves]'.[6] For many,

Law of the Workplace' (1993) 102 *Yale L. Journal* 1907, 1913–14; and Stone, K. V. W., 'The Legacy of Industrial Pluralism: The Tension Between Individual Employment Rights and the New Deal Collective Bargaining System' (1992) 59 *University of Chicago L. Review* 575.

[6] Iglesias, above, n. 1, 401.

particularly those who emphasize the primacy of identity, the very notion of a community comprised of diverse groups pursuing joint interests appears inherently coercive and infused with notions of domination and control.

As a result of the failure of unions to represent the interests of non-traditional groups, as well as the larger failure of class-based communities, several scholars have called for multiple representative structures in the workplace to replace a broader unified organizational structure. Rather than having a single union representing the interests of workers, workers would organize at the workplace based on whatever group identity they desired. If women or people of colour found that organizing by gender or race, or race and gender provides a better vehicle for the pursuits of their interests than class identification, they would be encouraged to organize around that identity.[7]

How these identity unions would work would depend on the particular workplace—whether or not it was a union shop, the nature of the work, and the size of the workplace—but the central idea is that women and minorities would be likely to gain more power by organizing around identity than by trying to organize a broader coalition. The proposals vary in their specific details. Within this framework, one might find a number of unions representing different groups even within a traditional bargaining unit, and each union would bargain directly with the employer. To facilitate the development of separate representation, statutory reform designed to eliminate exclusive representation in the workplace would probably be necessary, but it is also possible that identity unions could be formed under existing law to the extent that different groups found themselves in different and distinct jobs.

III THE RISKS OF FRAGMENTATION

Whether a move to separate unions would result in greater power for identity groups is largely an empirical question for which the data are currently unavailable. Nevertheless, it is possible to analyse how these unions might work as a way to understanding whether the proposals would achieve their stated end, or whether traditional unions might still be able to offer greater hope for both increased power and visibility in the

---

[7] See, e.g., Briskin, L., 'Union Women and Separate Organizing' in Briskin, L., and McDermott, P. (eds.), *Women Challenging Unions* (Toronto: University of Toronto Press, 1993), 89; Leah, R., 'Black Women Speak Out: Racism and Unions' in ibid., 157, 163–5. See also Crain, M., 'Untold Story' above, n. 1, 86; and Gould, Iglesias, and Silverstein, also above, n. 1.

workplace. One of the disappointing features of the recent calls for separate unions is that the authors rarely discuss the likely implications of a
multiple-union structure, assuming instead that identity unions would be
a better alternative given the traditional and exclusionary focus of unions.

But this either/or approach ignores the underlying premise for collective bargaining: that employees, organized as a group, would have
greater power than they could obtain individually in dealing with the
employer. Absent some collective entity, employees are left with, at best,
the limited strength of a small group, or, worse, the feeble strength of
one,[8] a strength that can be further diminished when the employer plays
the groups off against each other in a familiar and predictable version of
'divide and conquer'. Historically, employers have used the racial and
gender distribution of jobs and organization tasks as a managerial tactic
to divide the labour force and forestall union organization, and there is
every reason to think employers would try similar tactics if multiple identity unions were to blossom.

Without some collective action, the various identity groups fighting for
recognition within the workplace will be left with little more than
symbolic power, unless a group is large enough, or powerful enough, to
prevail in its demands. Far more likely, individual worker groups will be
unable to effectuate their workplace demands without the various
employee organizations coming together to agree on specific proposals.
This, as should be clear, is largely the condition that the calls for separate
unions complain about today. As chronicled earlier, large and powerful
groups are currently able to dominate unions often at the expense of
minority interests, but an important difference in the multiple-union
structure is that the majority interest would no longer have to concern
itself with minority employee interests at all since those interests would
have been split off into separate unions. To the extent that one group was
able to achieve workplace dominance, then the individual unions would
be likely to negotiate with each other to achieve the most promising
contract, but again, such a condition can and does occur within the
context of existing unions and, indeed, is more likely to occur where the
parties have to come together as a collective entity than when they are
dependent on bargaining with each other to achieve some consensus.

Allowing multiple unions in the workplace would also require determining how conflicts among the various groups would be mediated.
Currently whatever conflicts exist among the union membership are
resolved by the union, and although, as discussed above, this has often
led unions to favour their primary constituency, the alternatives in a

---

[8] Stone, K. V. W., 'The Feeble Strength of One: Why Individual Worker Rights Fail'
(1993) 14 *The American Prospect* 60.

workplace comprised of multiple units are no less problematic. On the one hand, there could be a panel comprised of group representatives designed to resolve conflicts, or alternatively it might be left to the employer to mediate group conflicts. By any measure, the latter prospect ought to be seen as inferior to allowing resolution by the union—otherwise there would be little need for a union in the first place—while the former option offers a solution that is clearly possible within the context of a single union. As such, even under the best scenario, separate unions are likely to offer little more than traditional unions with the substantial possibility that they will, in fact, offer far less.

But the danger from fragmentation includes more than a loss of power for workers through numerical dispersion. More fundamentally, the fragmentation of groups into particularistic notions of identity prevents the forging of larger groups, and prevents the creation of common bonds among workers because, in such a system, employees are left emphasizing their incommensurate differences while ignoring their potential commonalities. Where difference becomes the prism through which the workplace is viewed, it becomes all too easy to lose sight of the economic battle between workers and management. Focusing exclusively on identity will detrimentally affect the ability of employees to join together in order to reconstruct economic relations, and may cause employees to fight for power amongst each other, a situation employers are likely to welcome. Because workplace issues when attached to identity touch upon the core of self-conception, workplace demands can be made as much for symbolic values as for their practical impact upon daily life. Consequently, workers' efforts may become less about control over economic resources and more about the legitimation of the groups' identity.[9] In this way, the demands become important as status goals—as an effort to achieve the principles of equality, respect, freedom, and dignity, independent of tangible economic changes. While these are surely worthy and important goals, they should not be sought in lieu of economic changes, as economic control of the workplace offers the best route to obtaining equality and respect.

Identity politics also adds a divisive dimension to the workplace by concentrating on the absence of a common group—what may be defined as the absence of an 'us' in the workplace. By emphasizing how we are different from one another, we create 'others' in an exclusive and divisive way. The message that flows from an obsession with difference is 'I am not you', a message that serves to multiply differences wherever one looks. In contemporary society, the possibilities for discovering differences never seems to cease: are gay men and lesbians more different from one another

---

[9] See Said, E. W., 'The Politics of Knowledge' (1991) 11 *Raritan* 17, 24 (noting the trend toward the 'affirmation of identity' for its own sake).

or alike and, if different, are they more or less different than heterosexuals or bisexuals? The same is true for women where the focus is so often now on differences among women rather than on their shared experiences, as is, increasingly, true with racial classifications where differences are identified based on class, place of origin, and even colour. Mixed race individuals are also now disrupting the entire multi-ethnic balance as a result of their numerical growth and struggle for inclusion.

By itself this message of difference need not be exclusionary. However, within the framework of identity politics, the message becomes exclusionary because the particular identity group is the holder of a privileged position, of what sometimes borders on truth of the nature of the particular identity. In this perspective, one has to share an identity in order to understand it. Even empathy, where one might expect to ground a basis for understanding someone who is different, is often rejected as a meaningful construct, given that the observer's particular perspective precludes an authentic understanding. Accordingly, the message of identity politics is not only 'I am not you', but 'and you cannot understand me'. The result is the feeling that there is no common shared experience. And without at least some common ground, collective action in the workplace becomes impossible.[10]

Somewhat ironically, perhaps the greatest difficulty with the idea of organizing around identity lies in the decidedly unpostmodern aspects of identity politics—the essentialist thinking and belief in an autonomous self that underlies the emphasis on identity. Organizing around identity implies that individuals arrive at the workplace with a fixed identity—whether women, African Americans, gay men, or lesbians, or some other identifiable group—and that identity is then defined rigidly within closed borders. Otherwise, if there is no fixed or discernible identity, there would be no basis on which to establish a particular identity caucus. Postmodern thought, on the other hand, contests the notion of a coherent identity group—it struggles instead with the notion of an autonomous self; rather, individuals are seen as striving for autonomy against a background of social constraints.[11] Indeed, a defining feature of postmodernism is that the self is created within existing social constraints and created principally through interactions with others.

The difference between these concepts of the postmodern identity and

---

[10] See Stanford Friedman, S., 'Beyond White and Other: Relationality and Narratives of Race in Feminist Discourse' (1995) 21 *Signs* 1, 12.

[11] This theme is central to the work of Michel Foucault. See, in particular, *The History of Sexuality* (New York: Pantheon Books, 1978, i). For additional discussions see Braidotti, R., *Nomadic Subjects* (New York: Columbia University Press, 1994); Lorber, J., *Paradoxes of Gender* (New Haven, Conn.: Yale University Press, 1994) (challenging the coherency of the concept of gender); Frug, J., 'Decentering Decentralization' (1993) 60 *University of Chicago L. Review* 253, 309–11.

those that animate the world of identity politics is a crucial one for the workplace. By assuming a coherent identity for each group, the notion of identity caucuses makes the same mistake that was embraced in the original universal worker model—employees are permanently defined by their birth and home life, and their workplace interests reflect that pre-existing identity. In the understandings of that model, there is little space for change or growth, and through it the discovery of similarity among people located in different identity groups. With so little room to manœuvre, so little room for commonality, there is likewise insubstantial hope for an alliance among workers that will enable them to contest the employer's economic power. Even in the best worlds, this stance leads to what Seyla Benhabib has called 'autonomy without solidarity',[12] a feeling that at least in the workplace produces little tangible reward.

The limits of identity politics can be glimpsed by reviewing the transformation of the legal regime that governs the workplace. The individual rights legal system that has largely displaced the collective bargaining system strikes at an important disparity—disparities among workers—but fails to alter the structure between workers and owners in ways that would address the underlying issues of subordination. Although the laws protecting individual employment rights are critically important, they cannot increase the economic share of all workers, or provide the impetus for employees to participate in corporate decisions that affect their lives. Given the increase in and further diminishing status of low-waged workers, it can hardly be said that the individual rights model has improved their lives, while the individualized basis of the system ensures that, in most cases, whatever remedy is forthcoming will assist only the particular claimant, rather than altering the underlying power structure.

These difficulties have been exacerbated by recent economic and labour market changes in the USA. While the stock market boom of the 1990s provided comfort to many, far more workers were excluded from its benefits and, until recently, real wages had declined over the last decade, and work conditions likewise deteriorated. The impetus to contract out work, and the rise of the contingent labour force have undoubtedly produced great anxiety among workers, and even during a time of historically low unemployment, large numbers of workers still fear they will lose their jobs and, as a result, are unwilling to push workplace demands.[13] The sobering conclusion that flows from the current state of the US workplace is that although unions have neglected many of the concerns of women and minorities, while emphasizing the particular

---

[12] Benhabib, S., *Situating the Self* (New York: Routledge Press, 1992) 198.
[13] See generally Blau, J., *Illusions of Prosperity: America's Working Families in an Age of Economic Insecurity* (New York: Oxford University Press, 1999).

interests of white men, the decline of unions has not improved the labour conditions of women or minorities. To be sure, concerns with identity did not cause the worsening of workers' economic situation but, at the time of an increasingly fragmented workforce, there has been both less wealth for workers and greater inequality overall.

The question, of course, is whether there is a better alternative than the turn toward identity, one that might offer the hope of forging solidarity without suppressing diversity, a question to which we now turn.

IV COSMOPOLITAN UNIONS

We seek to build on the important insights of identity politics, while also emphasizing the necessary role coalitions and allies might play as a means of obtaining greater power for workers, power that, at least in the ideal, will help both to alter material conditions and enable individuals to craft new identities. The underlying question we address is whether it is possible to preserve or celebrate one's identity in the context of a larger community, or whether one's individual identity inevitably becomes lost within the larger group in the name of solidarity. Is it possible to create a community of difference where particular groups or individuals need not relinquish their identities for the common good, but the common good necessarily includes the preservation of identity? We believe the answer is a tentative yes, and hope here to sketch the framework for such a community, although it will be only a sketch—any general blueprint will have to be tailored to specific situations as surely it no longer makes sense to seek a one-size-fits-all solution to gaining greater economic power for workers.

Our notion of relying on difference to create solidarity draws from the theory of cosmopolitanism, a theory with rich roots that is enjoying some current resurgence in political and social thought.[14] Cosmopolitanism is a theory with both universal and particularistic dimensions. As a general framework, cosmopolitanism promotes the universal over the particular but it does so in the name of difference—common humanity unites us, but our vast differences are an equally important unifying theme. Rather than emphasizing national boundaries or the particular rights of citizens,

---

[14] This resurgence has been most pronounced in Europe. For important works see Todorov, T., *On Human Diversity* (Cambridge, Mass.: Harvard University Press, 1993); Kristeva, J., *Nations Without Nationalism* (New York: Columbia University Press, 1993); ead., *Strangers to Ourselves* (New York: Columbia University Press, 1991). For additional helpful discussions see Waldron, J., 'Minority Culture and the Cosmopolitan Alternative' (1992) 25 *University of Michigan Journal of Law Reform* 751; Wolin, R., 'Antihumanism in the Discourse of French Postwar Theory' (1994) 3 *Common Knowledge* 60, 81.

cosmopolitanism asserts the fundamental rights of all against all, as predicated on a common humanity. In this way, cosmopolitanism can be seen as a move away from the self because the move toward the self is seen as exclusive, ultimately creating others who we see and treat as different from ourselves.

Difference remains essential to a cosmopolitan theory. However, in contrast to the focus within identity politics, empathy is a key concept for cosmopolitanism and allows for an intersubjective understanding of those who are different. Gordon Wood has described the influence of cosmopolitanism on the Founders of the American Constitution by noting that, for them, cosmopolitanism meant '[o]ne's humanity was measured by one's ability to relate to strangers, to enter into the hearts of even those who were different',[15]—to enter into the hearts of those who are different without trying to neutralize or eliminate that difference but rather as a way of understanding it.

This emphasis on difference also distinguishes cosmopolitanism from pluralism. Where pluralism often stresses tolerance and assimilation, cosmopolitanism emphasizes the importance of difference or diversity to the larger community—difference is something to build on rather than a subject for compromise or toleration. In a recent work exploring the message of multiculturalism, David Hollinger explains that cosmopolitanism is defined by its 'recognition, acceptance, and eager exploration of diversity' within a universal context and therefore seeks to build broad communities within loose borders.[16] Where pluralism tends to emphasize narrow and rigid borders based on a perceived shared history or culture, cosmopolitanism allows for broader identities and, perhaps more important, stresses the importance of self-identification, what Michel Feher describes as the 'cosmopolitan abhorrence of any measure intended to affix an identity on anyone'.[17]

Although it has deep and ancient roots, cosmopolitanism can also be seen as a quintessentially postmodern theory. As a theory, cosmopolitanism seeks to mediate among the various postmodern selves, whether

[15] Wood, G. S., *The Radicalism of the American Revolution* (New York: A.A. Knopf, 1992) 222.

[16] Hollinger, D., *Postethnic America* (New York: Basic Books, 1995) 84–5.

[17] Feher, M., 'The Schisms of '67: On Certain Restructurings of the American Left, from the Civil Rights Movement to the Multiculturalist Constellation' in Berman, P. (ed.), *Blacks and Jews: Alliances and Arguments* (New York: Delacorte Press, 1994) 263. There are, to be sure, some similarities between pluralism and cosmopolitanism: see, e.g., the discussion in Bohman, J., 'Public Reason and Cultural Pluralism: Political Liberalism and the Problem of Moral Conflict' (1995) 23 *Political Theory* 253, and Torres, G., 'Critical Race Theory: The Decline of the Universalist Ideal and the Hope of Plural Justice—Some Observations and Questions of an Emerging Phenomenon' (1991) 75 *Minnesota L. Review* 993, 1005, both of whom offer ways in which pluralism might be reconstructed to allow for greater differences.

it is the self that is celebrated through identity politics, or the non-autonomous or semi-autonomous self that is shaped and controlled by social forces, or the self that struggles to be within and against existing social constraints. These various strands of the fragmented postmodern self are brought together by preserving differences while stressing commonalities and, in this way, creating a community of difference where difference(s) can flourish. It is this context of loose borders, the absence of expectations, and the presence of ambiguity and contingency that creates the possibility of self-identification free from at least some of our current constraints.

These insights and themes of cosmopolitanism suggest some possibilities for creating a workplace alliance between solidarity and difference. We earlier described various practices and policies that have made many groups, particularly women and minorities, sceptical of the benefits of union solidarity, and explored how that scepticism has yielded a desire for separate representation based on identity. We contend, however, that unions may still offer the best hope for workers to obtain greater power in the workplace and, equally important, that unions may be the place where a community of difference might be created.

In his book, *Beyond Individualism*, Michael Piore explores the potential of unions to foster a cosmopolitan workplace. Piore borrows from the anthropologist, Renato Rosaldo, the notion of creating new identities at the cultural borderland.[18] At the border, Rosaldo explains, new cultures are forged out of the competing and clashing lifestyles that come together. Importantly, these new cultures are not simply a melange of the various cultures existing at the border but instead are transformative, recreating and reassembling the world as it was. Rather than focusing exclusively on the particular groups from which we arose, we find in others an opportunity to share and to learn who we are.

Piore identifies trade unions as constituting a potential transformative border culture. He writes:

The fundamental political problem remains the relative isolation of the new identity groups and the resulting tendency for them to formulate their demands independently of one another and of the underlying economic constraints. . . . But in the relationship between the groups and the economy, the unions would seem to play a unique borderland role, one that introduces an awareness of economic constraints and a vocabulary for discussing them into groups that are constituted in such a way that otherwise would have neither.[19]

Piore notes that in order for unions to regain their power to restructure

---

[18] See Piore, M. J., *Beyond Individualism* (Cambridge, Mass.: Harvard University Press, 1995); Rosaldo, R., *Culture and Truth* (Boston, Mass.: Beacon Press, 1989).
[19] Piore, above, n. 18, 164–5.

the workplace, some changes may be necessary in our labour laws to enable unions to organize more readily. He suggests, for example, that unions be allowed greater flexibility to create employee caucuses and in defining appropriate bargaining units, ideas that meld nicely with the concerns of those who advocate identity unions. At the same time, he argues that unions remain the best vehicle for overcoming experiences of otherness, working toward a truly transformative dialogue where truth emerges through experience and the intersubjective connection of vastly different experiences of the world.

From our perspective, creating an atmosphere for a cosmopolitan perspective out of which transformative dialogue might arise will entail abandoning the concept that unions are mini-legislatures within a pluralist political model. Unlike the pluralist model of legislation where each member votes in his own, exogenous best interest, and the union simply collects each vote and acts on behalf of the majority, in the community of difference model, unions would help develop worker interest in the face of a common opponent. In this way, unions turn from being mini-legislatures to becoming mediating institutions with transformative aspirations much like at the border where changes occur through the clash of cultures. Unions would provide a forum for discussing different group interests, the presence and pervasiveness of difference within the workplace, and possible means for satisfying these various interests and perspectives.

While in any particular workplace, the specific methods of implementation would vary, the steps to creating such a dialogue begin from the common bond among workers—the absence of power in the workplace, power sufficient to gain an adequate piece of the economic pie, to reduce exploitation, and to help structure employee's work lives. At the same time, there has to be a recognition that there will always be conflicts of interests among workers, and, in the specific context of labour unions, there are likely to be conflicts on issues such as part-time work, childcare and family leave, domestic partners, affirmative action, seniority provisions, and the like. Taking cosmopolitanism seriously would require workers to come together in dialogue to derive the best strategy for all members of the group, rather than simply trying to find a position that can obtain majority support. Even on an issue as divisive as affirmative action, workers may find common ground through the realization that it is in their collective interest to play a role in shaping the policy free from outside influence.

Under a cosmopolitan perspective, there would thus be no ideal worker around whom to structure a union strategy. Consequently, there would likewise be no transcendent identity in which a particular identity group might become lost. Abandoning the search for a new 'working class', labour unions would instead accept a 'plurality of subjects' with a variety of common interests and distinct differences, all which would be ultimately transformed through the alliances of those subjects.[20]

In order to foster this perspective, it may be necessary to eschew a majoritarian perspective, focusing instead on what one author has called 'a new form of plural reason', one not steeped in power or domination over other members of the groups, but power in unity and in creating better conditions for all—the very dialogic conditions in which difference can flourish.[21] To create these dialogic conditions, the worker community must simultaneously experience both understanding and conflict. With an emphasis on dialogue, one of the first steps would be to ensure that expressions of individual or group experience and interests are taken seriously by the whole body. For example, when African Americans or women say they feel silenced by others, that they feel excluded or harassed in the workplace, the necessary response is not to contest their experiences but to trust their renditions even when those renditions feel radically different from one's own. At the same time, there must be an agreement to engage in dialogue, one that will require a high tolerance of conflict, critique, and a diversity of opinions among the groups. Indeed, an essential element of any search for solidarity among differences must be the ability to accept the presence of conflict as well as the inevitable need for compromise. Importantly, this means that the barrier to critique that often exists among groups must be removed so that it becomes possible to critique and learn from others without being denounced for being different. Unless there exists an opportunity for critique among groups and outsiders, the end result is unlikely to be dialogue or conversation, but a panoply of monologues, where the all too predictable result is that the loudest voice will prevail.

There remains the question of how a cosmopolitan perspective would alter or influence the workplace, and what might need to be done to bring about such changes. There are a number of particular structural and policy changes that would assist the transformation of unions into mediating institutions infused with a cosmopolitan spirit. Yet, it is important to stress that we do not intend to provide a detailed prescription for change, not only because such a programme would be beyond the scope of this chapter but also because it would be inconsistent with our emphasis on identifying change for the postmodern workplace. What changes or programmes will be necessary to bring constructive change will vary depending on the nature of the workplace and the

---

[20] See Laclau, E., and Mouffe, C., *Hegemony and Socialist Strategy* (London: Verso Press, 1985) 169–82.
[21] Bohman, above, n. 17, 271.

workforce, and what particular issues concern the workers in that locale. Consistently with this spirit, local unions should be afforded broad room for experimentation, realizing that some of those experiments may fail but that there will be value in the efforts nevertheless. That said, certain broad policy changes may help foster an emphasis on local solutions and experimentation.

As a start, unions must not ignore current specific group interests—for example, unions need to provide forums to remedy sexual harassment or hate speech in the workplace, and pay greater attention to the need for childcare or leave policies for child-rearing. Where there is a conflict between speech and working conditions, as often arises in claims of sexual harassment, rather than reflexively protecting the interests of their traditional constituency, unions must look instead for fair and innovative remedies to ensure equal working conditions for all of their members. Depending on the circumstances, unions may also want to create diverse voting structures to ensure that numerical minorities are entitled to an effective voice, which may also include providing limited veto rights to defined groups, as advocated by Elizabeth Iglesias.

Along these same lines, unions may need to reconsider majority rule as the principle decision-making technique within the union, and consider instead ways to increase actual participation of all members. One example of such a proposal might be the equal protection model of the duty of fair representation developed by Michael Harper and Ira Lupu, which requires that all union members be accorded equal respect consistent with the principles developed under constitutional standards.[22] Wider participation by union members in picking leadership and setting the union's agenda and bargaining strategy may also provide minority interests with their first chance to be heard, and may alter the dominant and exclusionary voice that can arise in the union setting. Specific measures to enhance participation may include member representation on the labour negotiating team, member ratification of all contracts, and institutionalized meetings to discuss contract and bargaining agenda. Increasing the information flow to union members may also encourage greater participation, which may be accomplished through mandatory information disclosure rules, as well as providing access to membership lists and funding from the union treasury for all *bona fide* union candidates, with the views of dissident members distributed at union expense. Committees with rotating membership open to all could be formed to deal with various workplace issues and to suggest bargaining strategies. Additionally, direct, rank and file elections of all union

---

[22] *See* Harper, M. C., and Lupu, I. C., 'Fair Representation as Equal Protection' (1985) 98 *Harvard L. Review* 1211, 1261.

446 *Michael Selmi and Molly S. McUsic*

officers and term limits for leadership offer other possibilities for enhancing the voice of the full membership.[23]

All of these changes could generate internal institutional pressure for conversations, enhancing the ability of individuals within the union to place new topics of conversation on the agenda and forcing union leaders to engage in a continuous internal dialogue with members. It is important again to emphasize, however, that the point here is not to detail specific changes that would apply to all workplaces, but to suggest the kind of changes that could create space for a dialogic framework through which consensus and principles would arise, reflecting the broad interests of workers in a particular location. It is equally clear that unions have strong incentives to make these changes in so far as addressing the interests of those they have previously ignored, such as women and minorities, will increase the attractiveness of unions to those groups—groups that are increasingly dominating the workforce. Indeed, it appears that the leadership of the AFL-CIO is now targeting women and minorities as a way to expand and diversify their membership base. While it is still too early to tell whether these strategies will preserve rather than trample differences, there is reason to believe that change may be on the horizon.

V CONCLUSION

Although the shift to identity and away from solidarity has valuably highlighted the exclusionary practices of US unions in the past, at the same time, a model that emphasizes differences and suppresses commonalities is unlikely to lead to greater workplace power or equality. Currently, there is too much emphasis on 'us' and 'them', too much emphasis on difference, and too little focus on potential commonalities among workers. Seeking to preserve those differences within a context of solidarity, and doing so within a cosmopolitan framework may offer a different and better way—a way that would be a move toward the future rather than a return to the past.

[23] Many of these suggestions come from Hyde, A., 'Democracy in Collective Bargaining' (1984) 93 *Yale L. Journal* 793, and Geoghegan, T., *Which Side Are You On?* (New York: Farrar, Straus, Giroux, 1991) 123–36, 182–203.

Part VII

Laying Down the Law: Strategies and Frontiers

23

Is There a Third Way in Labour Law?

HUGH COLLINS*

The Third Way is attractive to politicians. As a slogan to describe a set of political values, it exhibits many desirable properties: it is brief and unspecific, yet it implies that it is at once new, radical, but centrist. The Third Way can be presented as a global movement in politics, yet at the same time it professes a local resonance by claiming to disentangle itself from established party politics and traditional ideological divisions, whatever that politics has been in the past. Above all, the Third Way movement presents itself as a practical political programme, a way to cope with modern problems rather than a fixed set of beliefs. These modern problems that need to be addressed also have a special character: they are new, big, hard to define, and cannot be permanently solved. These problems include the effects of the forces of globalization of the economy, the incalculable risks to the ecology of the planet of continued population and economic growth, the need to provide legitimacy for government in mass societies, and the challenges presented by radical changes in personal and family life.[1] Politics becomes defined by the practical ways in which to tackle these problems, not by grand ideological schemes.

Issues surrounding work have been peripheral, though not absent, in discussions of Third Way politics. Because the Third Way does not propose any change to the basic arrangement of capitalist societies that most people earn their wealth by selling their work through the labour market, the perennial issues presented by this market mechanism still need to be addressed. As ever, work can be hard, stressful, dangerous, denigrating, unrewarding, poorly paid, insecure, and alienating. This chapter describes and analyses how the themes of Third Way politics have been interpreted in relation to legal regulation of employment issues in the UK. Since many aspects of labour law fall within the competence of the EU, I also consider aspects of European legal regulation that fit into a Third Way agenda. But the significance of these developments in the employment law of the UK extends far beyond these borders if they

---

* This chapter is the updated text of a lecture given to the Industrial Law Society in Oxford, 1998.

[1] Giddens, A., *The Third Way: The Renewal of Social Democracy* (Cambridge: Polity Press, 1998).

contain the seeds of a radically new approach to labour law. For the new standards of employment regulation proposed by the Third Way appear to conflict with some aspects of accepted international norms as embodied in the Conventions of the ILO.

It is a characteristic of new political movements that they focus on fresh problems and tend to ignore the old agendas. The Third Way regards the old problems of labour law as those concerning trade unions, collective bargaining, and industrial conflict. A key division in the old politics concerned attitudes towards the legitimacy of trade unions, the desirability of collective bargaining, and restrictions on industrial conflict. But the Third Way no longer regards these issues as especially pertinent. As Tony Blair said in the principal policy statement of his first administration in respect of labour law: 'The White Paper . . . seeks to draw a line under the issue of industrial relations law'.[2] The old solutions to the old problems can be left alone, largely because they are no longer a pressing political problem—there are few strikes these days—and partly because in any case the established solutions more or less accord with Third Way philosophy. The crucial task is rather to address the new problems confronting employment relations.

More controversially, I suggest that the Third Way also diminishes concern about distributive issues in the workplace. Many established political agendas regard the regulation of the workplace for distributive purposes as a key ingredient of labour law. This regulation aims to redistribute power and wealth within the organization by giving workers, either individually or collectively, legal rights to control or influence the decisions of management. Under this agenda, for instance, laws may promote collective bargaining in order to give workers the right to influence management decisions by making collective agreements, or laws may award individual workers rights to be protected against unfair treatment such as discrimination or the provision of unsafe working conditions. Within traditional social democratic political agendas, these redistributive aims were described as achieving industrial democracy and fairness in the workplace.[3] Although the Third Way leaves much of this regulation in place and, indeed, may strengthen some aspects of it, the justifications for this regulation become subtly modified in response to a new agenda.

From the perspective of the Third Way, the number one problem is to improve the competitiveness of businesses. To survive and prosper in the new context of a global economy, businesses constantly have to improve the quality and design of their products, invest in new technologies, and

---

[2] Foreword to the White Paper, *Fairness at Work*, Cm 3968 (London: HMSO, 1998).
[3] Ewing, K. D., 'Democratic Socialism and Labour Law' (1995) 24 *ILJ* 103.

reduce costs. A key ingredient of competitiveness is to use the workforce efficiently and effectively. For this purpose the workforce has to be properly trained and prepared to work flexibly and to co-operate with all innovations. The Third Way believes that labour law, together with other branches of law such as company law, can assist through its regulation of the workplace in the improvement of the competitiveness of businesses. This regulation for the purpose of promoting competitiveness establishes a radically new agenda for labour law. It can justify regulation about old topics such as collective bargaining and individual employment rights, but the objective of this regulation shifts decisively. Instead of regulation of collective bargaining representing either the expression of ideals of industrial democracy, or distributive fairness, or a pragmatic way for resolving fundamental conflicts of interest in an industrial society, the dominant purpose of the regulation becomes the improvement of the competitiveness of the business. Similarly, instead of individual legal rights for employees being justified as representing a fair distributive pattern or recognition of fundamental rights to dignity and respect, the dominant purpose of the regulation is characterized as the promotion of competitiveness of the business. Most of this chapter explores the ramifications of this dominant purpose for employment regulation, but first we need to place this regulation in the context of broader themes of Third Way politics that also have ramifications for the traditional concerns of labour law.

I DISTRIBUTIVE JUSTICE IN THE THIRD WAY

When Tony Blair speaks of the Third Way, he is not seeking a centre ground of the full spectrum of political opinions. He is endeavouring rather to reconstitute left-of-centre policies, to bring together the social democratic tradition and the socialist state tradition.[4] This reconstruction has two strands: a reformulation of the basic values of the moderate left in politics, together with a rejection of any received wisdom about the best way to achieve those ends.

The principal reformulation of values is to drop the traditional socialist commitment to egalitarianism. The goal of achieving greater equality in the distribution of wealth and power is replaced by the goal of creating the conditions for the eradication of social exclusion. These conditions can be described as equality of opportunity, but they go beyond formal conditions of equality in order to tackle the problems of inequality of resources.

---

[4] This paragraph and other aspects of the text are based on: Blair, T., *The Third Way: New Politics for the New Century* (London: Fabian Society Pamphlet 588, 1998).

The objective is to provide every citizen with the necessary resources in terms of education, training, skills, and other financial support, so that they can participate fully in the opportunities afforded by a flourishing market economy. Inequalities of wealth can be tolerated provided that real equality of opportunity is available to all citizens.

The new strand of methods for achieving political objectives lies in the pragmatism about the means to be used. The Third Way rejects any necessary link between the enhancement of state power and the achievement of goals. The presumption seems to be reversed: state power to control the economy and to implement political objectives is to be used only when it can be demonstrated that the market mechanism fails in ways that cannot be remedied by regulatory adjustments. State power is to be used only as a regulatory instrument rather than a replacement of the market mechanism, and regulation must always satisfy the test that it is efficacious and efficient.

When these two strands are combined, they signal a fundamental reluctance to use the mechanisms of the welfare state for the purpose of redistributing wealth to promote egalitarianism. Instead, the political objective is to create real or substantive conditions for equality of opportunity by opening up the market mechanism for the production of wealth to everyone. The implicit ideal is that markets produce a fair distribution of wealth for most people, provided that everyone has a fair opportunity to participate in the market. Those who are denied that opportunity suffer from social exclusion. The Third Way believes that participation in markets will reduce poverty and produce a fair distribution of wealth for most people, but there is no commitment to ensure an acceptable distributive pattern occurs. Individuals have the responsibility to take up the opportunities for achieving a decent standard of living that are facilitated and sometimes provided by the state. If individuals fail to avail themselves of these opportunities without good reason, then under the Third Way philosophy it is not the responsibility of the state to use the social security and welfare systems to provide them with more than the conditions for subsistence. For example, if a single parent chooses not to work but prefers to care for a child at home when affordable child care is available, with the consequence that the family lives in poverty, that is not the responsibility of government. The old agenda of politics that used the welfare state for the systematic and comprehensive reduction of poverty is regarded by the Third Way as impracticable, unaffordable, ineffective, and counter-productive owing to the problem of welfare dependency.

The relevance of these distributive principles for labour law turns on the crucial point that the principal cause of social exclusion is unemployment or the inability to obtain a good job. Labour law must be involved in the task of combating social exclusion. In part, this agenda requires a continuation and expansion of rules against discrimination in the labour market. The value of treating people as equals or of equal worth remains and becomes extended to new groups who suffer from social exclusion such as the disabled and the elderly. But the traditional principle of equal worth is inadequate for the Third Way, because it fails to tackle the structural obstacles that certain groups face in seeking to participate in labour markets. These structural problems are described as the source of social exclusion. In Europe, this ambition of achieving real equality of opportunity is often signalled by the idea of citizenship: the objective of enabling everyone to participate in the benefits of the economy, culture, and society.

The principal cause of exclusion from labour markets is believed to be a lack of education and skills, and an important secondary cause is family and other social responsibilities. The legal regulation that expresses this goal of combating social exclusion extends into many areas that are not traditionally regarded as part of labour law. The ambition is to help people to obtain work and to provide incentives for them to do so. There are three principal strands in the pursuit of this strategy by legal regulation.

Enhancing employability. A main reason for unemployment is perceived to be a defect on the supply side: too many people lack the necessary education and skills to obtain employment. The objective of government policy is to improve 'employability', though not to provide people with jobs. The 'new deals' for young people and the long-term unemployed, policies often described by the slogan 'welfare to work', are aimed at giving them fresh training and work experience, instead of the old policy of subsidizing jobs. The test of the success of this policy is not whether the employer keeps on the worker after the period of six months' subsidized employment, but rather whether the worker has gained skills that enable him or her to obtain a job somewhere else. Access to worthwhile training also becomes a key policy. Financial support is provided through a notional 'learning account' or voucher system to be spent on training. This policy also involves setting standards for the certification of skills, perhaps increasingly at a European level, and removing obstacles for individuals to gain access to training. We will see increasing regulation of access to training, at the outset for youth workers, such the right to time off for study or training in the Teaching and Higher Education Act 1998,[5] but probably in the future for all workers as part of a commitment to lifetime learning.

---

[5] S. 32, which introduces ss. 63A and 63B into the Employment Rights Act 1996, giving a right to paid time off in order to undertake study or training for 16- and 17-year-olds.

Strengthening incentives to work. A second reason for unemployment is perceived to be the problem that work does not improve standards of living for many recipients of welfare benefits, the problem traditionally known as the 'poverty trap'. The principal solution here involves the radical new policy of working family tax credits or negative income tax.[6] If a family earns a low wage through work, its income will be increased through credits in the wage packet via the tax system. Other aspects of the solution to the poverty trap are to remove or reduce taxation from low earnings, to ignore earnings from part-time work for the purpose of calculating welfare entitlements, and to introduce the national minimum wage. The objective of this regulation is to ensure that people will always be better off if they work in comparison to their welfare benefits if unemployed. The incentives can be heightened, of course, by reducing the welfare benefits paid to the unemployed after the period of time judged to be sufficient for the job seeker to adjust to new labour market conditions.

Family-friendly policies. An important criticism of holding individuals to be responsible for their own poverty is that they may face competing and superior obligations towards families and dependants that prevent them from improving their position by participation in the labour market. The radical solution is to develop a comprehensive childcare strategy, including extensive nursery provision, which will enable parents, especially single parents, to participate in the labour market. In addition, more familiar kinds of employment rights can be supplied in order to help parents to reconcile work with family responsibilities. These rights have been developed in the Employment Relations Act 1999, with improvements to maternity leave,[7] the enhancement of parental leave,[8] and the new right to take reasonable time off work for family emergencies.[9] In addition, for parents who choose part-time work, the law requires the employer to observe the principle of strictly proportionate treatment in comparison to full-time workers.[10]

The link between these strands of policy—enhancing employability, strengthening incentives to work, and family-friendly policies—is that they tackle social exclusion. The legal measures regulate the labour

---

[6] Tax Credits Act 1999.

[7] Employment Relations Act 1999, s. 7, Sched. 4, Part I, amending the Employment Rights Act 1996, Part VIII.

[8] Ibid. Maternity and Parental Leave etc Regulations 1999, SI 1999 No. 3312. On the implementation of family-friendly working policies in the UK see further Conaghan, in this volume.

[9] Employment Relations Act 1999, s. 8, Sched. 4, Part II, amending the Employment Rights Act 1996 by inserting ss. 57A and 57B.

[10] Part-time Workers (Prevention of Less Favourable Treatment) Regulations 2000, SI 2000 No. 1551.

market with a view to reducing barriers to access to good jobs. Although this regulation often falls outside the traditional concerns of labour lawyers, we need to recognize that in the new agenda set by the Third Way, these measures represent core policies that have a significant impact on the operation of the labour market. As the central theme of the distributive policy of Third Way politics, these three strands of regulation displace the central role that was formerly attached in social democratic traditions to trade unions and collective bargaining as instruments for achieving greater equality in society.

II REGULATING FOR COMPETITIVENESS

I suggested earlier that the main innovation of the Third Way that affects labour law is the new agenda to use legal regulation to improve the competitiveness of businesses. Notice that this agenda rejects the simplistic view that competitiveness is best achieved through deregulation. At the same time, however, Third Way politics diminishes the importance attached to distributive values and ideals of workers' rights. Regulation seeks to improve the operation of the market, not to replace or impede it. Regulation may protect workers' rights and establish institutional arrangements in the workplace, but the purpose of the regulation is conceived rather differently. The purpose is instrumental: to improve the competitiveness of businesses. The rights are not accorded to workers out of respect for basic values or to ensure compliance with ideal standards of fairness and justice. Instead, the legal rights are justified primarily because it is believed that they will contribute to the enhancement of efficient business methods, innovation, improvements in design, more successful marketing, and so forth.

The implications of regulating for competitiveness extend to all aspects of employment law.[11] I will illustrate some of these implications through two examples. The first explains how the Third Way leads to an endorsement of the style of worker participation known as partnership at work. The second examines how legal regulation that provides individual workers with detailed rights against their employer becomes modified to accord with the goal of regulating for competitiveness.

Partnership

A legal right for workers to participate collectively in management

---

[11] Cf. Collins, H., 'Regulating the Employment Relation for Competitiveness' (2001) 31 *ILJ* 17.

decisions respecting the workplace and the business can be justified on many different grounds. Traditional justifications have tended to emphasize either the need for consultation out of respect for the individual rights of workers to be treated with dignity and respect, or the need for participatory institutions in the workplace as a dimension of democracy in an industrial society. The Third Way agenda has adopted the metaphor of partnership to express its objective in regulating worker participation. The idea of partnership can be viewed cynically as being sufficiently vacuous to appeal to a wide range of political opinion without tying the government to any specific regulatory proposals. I shall argue, however, that once partnership is understood within the context of regulating for competitiveness, its objectives, if not all the details of its institutional arrangements, become sufficiently clear to signal an innovative political agenda. We can grasp the principal elements of the institutional arrangements envisaged by the objective of partnership through a comparison with traditional justifications for worker participation.

The model of partnership

One model of social democracy regards the right of workers to join and participate in trade unions as an aspect of freedom of association, a basic individual right that deserves strong legal protection as part of the constitutional arrangements of society.[12] Legal regulation guards against discrimination and victimization by employers against union members. The right to freedom of association also applies to employers in the form of freedom of contract; employers should not be forced to enter into contracts with individuals or trade unions. The *Wilson* case[13] illustrates this individual rights framework: employees have the right to join a trade union of their choice, but, as part of freedom of association, the employer also has the right to prefer to enter contracts with workers who do not use a trade union as their representative for the purpose of collective bargaining over terms and conditions of employment.

A second model of social democracy views collective bargaining as the best mechanism for achieving simultaneously social justice and the extension of democracy throughout society. It becomes public policy to promote collective bargaining, which can be supported, where necessary, by legal measures. Collective bargaining is perceived as the only realistic way of achieving distributively fairer outcomes in the firm, given the employer's strong bargaining position *vis-à-vis* individual workers.

---

[12] This right to freedom of association as a basic principle of labour law is expressed in, e.g., EC Charter of the Fundamental Social Rights of Workers (1989) Art. 11; ILO Convention (No 87) on Freedom of Association and Protection of the Right to Organize (1948).

[13] *Associated Newspapers Ltd* v. *Wilson; Associated British Ports* v. *Palmer* [1995] IRLR 258 (HL).

Similarly, the collective voice of organized trade unions is perceived to be much more effective than other mechanisms such as individual consultation or consultation with works councils. Under this second model, as well as protection of the right to organize, the law can also force employers to enter into bargaining relations where this represents the democratic wishes of the workforce. Thus under this model the right to freedom of association gives way to more powerful collective values of social justice and democracy. A closed shop can be tolerated as a necessary instrument of public policy (thus interfering with the freedom of association of workers) and union recognition can be imposed upon employers (thus interfering with the freedom of association of employers).

In the Third Way, there is continuing respect for the individual right of freedom of association, but it becomes public policy to promote mechanisms at work that facilitate co-operative work relations on the ground that these are necessary to achieve efficient and more competitive production. These mechanisms for achieving co-operative work relations are described as partnership. The essential elements of partnership institutions comprise the exchange of information between employers and workers together with a commitment to use this information in order co-operatively to improve the efficiency of the relations of production. Collective bargaining might serve this purpose in some instances. As collective bargaining is traditionally conceived, however, in the form of an antagonistic bargaining mechanism to set the price of labour, it is inappropriate and redolent of an old culture that partnership is designed to supersede. Partnership supports consultation about the details and objectives of production, and the business strategy of the firm, but is not particularly interested in collective discussions about the price of labour except in so far as these may be part of productivity-enhancing agreements. This sharing of information and consultation can be achieved by many mechanisms including work groups such as quality circles, works councils, committees of many kinds. It is for each business or each workplace to consider how best to forge effective partnerships.

This Third Way differs from the first model by placing constraints on freedom of association for the sake of promoting partnerships. At the same time it differs from the second model by promoting institutions other than collective bargaining for the purpose of consultation on the ground that partnership arrangements promote competitiveness. These differences set up a tension between the regulatory proposals of the Third Way and international conventions that embody the values of the earlier models. For example, the Third Way can tolerate interference with the employer's freedom of association by imposing models of works councils or other partnership arrangements on businesses. But the Third Way distances itself from the second model, for it has no reason to compel employers to enter into collective bargaining agreements that fix the price of labour, so it rejects any general right of workers to insist upon collective bargaining.

The efficiency of partnership

Why is partnership necessary for improving the competitiveness of firms or, more briefly, for efficiency? One effect of increasing global competition in product markets (and I include services in this as well) is that countries that pay high wages have to compete increasingly on the basis of quality, design, responsiveness to changes in the market, and technological superiority. To meet this need, many major manufacturing companies have altered their relations with their suppliers or subcontractors. Instead of components being purchased according to the manufacturer's design on the basis of competitive tendering from a pool of potential suppliers, manufacturers entered into long-term partnership arrangements with suppliers. These long-term relations involved the introduction of TQM (Total Quality Management) principles into the suppliers, the use of JIT (Just-in-Time) ordering systems, and the sharing of design, technological, and production expertise. Despite increased management costs for the manufacturer and the component supplier, the competitive advantage of these supplier partnerships lies in the potential for permanent innovation in design, continuous improvements in quality, responsiveness to changes in consumer taste, and technological superiority.[14]

The model of supplier partnerships has been translated by Human Resources Management (HRM) into a theory of how to conduct labour-management relations. In order to achieve innovations in design, continuous improvements in quality and efficiency, and technological superiority, it is argued that employers needed to treat their workforce in a similar way, like partners. Employers need to tap into the potential represented by the human capital (the knowledge and expertise) of the workforce. Quality circles were an early sign of this style of personnel management, but HRM theory quickly expanded this practice into a more general theory of the need to establish partnership arrangements with the workforce. The purpose of partnerships is to enhance competitiveness through improvements in quality and efficiency. This purpose requires the exchange of information: management needs to explain its product and marketing plans to the workforce, and the workers need to use their

---

[14] For more detailed explanations see: Sako, M., *Prices, Quality, Trust: Inter-Firm Relations in Britain and Japan* (Cambridge: Cambridge University Press, 1992); Taylor, C. R., and Wiggins, S. N., 'Competition or Compensation: Supplier Incentives Under the American and Japanese Subcontracting Systems' (1997) 87 *American Economic Review* 598; Collins, H., 'Quality Assurance in Subcontracting' in Deakin, S., and Mitchie, J. (eds.), *Contracts, Co-operation, and Competition* (Oxford: Oxford University Press, 1997) 285.

human capital in order to suggest how production and products can be improved. Instead of the old model of an authority relation in which the workers were told by management what to do, the partnership concept insists that the workforce needs to help management to devise methods of production and to create improvements in the product.

This link between partnership and efficiency is supported by theoretical work in institutional economics.[15] Employers can acquire labour power through diverse contractual arrangements ranging from a brief contract to perform a particular job to a contract of indefinite duration with indeterminate obligations. The choice between contractual forms is important, because it can reduce costs (including transaction costs), and it can enable the parties to maximize their wealth derived from the transaction. Most contracts of employment are incomplete by design,[16] because the employer cannot specify in advance what tasks will have to be performed by the worker. The contract obtains specificity by granting the employer the discretion to direct labour to it most profitable use. This transactional model of an incomplete contract with a unilateral governance structure achieves superior outcomes in terms of efficiency whenever the parties to the transaction anticipate that variations in the details of performance will be required and where it is hard to specify in advance adequate measures of work effort. This model provides the conceptual foundation for the traditional (or 'master and servant') legal analysis of the contract of employment of indefinite duration based upon the obligation of obedience to management. This model can also be criticized, however, for having certain inefficient properties. In particular, this traditional model (a) may not encourage active co-operation by employees beyond obedience to orders, and (b) provides little incentive for workers to use human capital to improve the employer's business. To redress these sources of inefficiency, and by analogy with supplier partnerships, another contractual model can be proposed.

In this model, which is sometimes described as a symbiotic contract, the basic framework of incentives is designed as two simultaneous principal and agent relations. We are not using the language of principal/agent in the technical legal sense here; the terms merely describe a type of business relation where one person (the agent) acts according to the instructions and in the interests of another (the principal), and where the principal obtains the residual profits (after costs) of any transaction. Symbiotic contracts have the puzzling feature that both parties act simultaneously not only as principals in their own right but

---

[15] See e.g., Williamson, O. E., *The Economic Institutions of Capitalism* (New York/London: Free Press, 1985), especially ch. 9.

[16] Collins, H., *Regulating Contracts* (Oxford: Oxford University Press, 1999) 161.

also as agents for the other. In order to make this symbiotic model of transactions function efficiently, both parties have to share the profits of the enterprise by having the incentive of being residual owners, and, crucially, the parties have to co-operate by extensive sharing of knowledge and expertise. This analysis has been applied, for instance, to business format franchises.[17] The franchisor is both a principal who uses agents to market the business format and at the same time an agent of the franchisees in the promotion and development of the reputation of the business format.

Applying this principal and agent idea to an employment relation, the symbiotic contract model suggests that at the same time as the employee is the agent for the employer in carrying out the work (as under the master and servant model), the employer is acting in part as the agent of the employee in creating work to be performed and in enhancing the worker's employability.[18] The potential competitive advantage of this model over traditional employment forms is that it creates an incentive for the employees to use their human capital to co-operate by maximizing the joint product in return for the employer undertaking various obligations as their agents. It is important to note that the symbiotic model does not assume that management and workers share a common interest. On the contrary, the idea that both parties are principals in their own right explicitly denies any 'unitary frame of reference'.[19] The interests of management and workers conflict, as in the simple complete contract model, but in order to maximize their self-interest they have to engage in extensive co-operation with each other. The important point about symbiosis is that it is a two-way street: employees have to co-operate, but so too does management. It is this symbiotic quality that the metaphor of partnership tries to express and for which the law must provide an institutional embodiment.

Legal regulation

What remains unclear at this stage in the development of the Third Way agenda is how legal regulation may contribute to the development of partnership arrangements. Partnerships will really work only where both parties want them and decide to make them function successfully. They require the building of confidence and trust, the willingness to share ideas, the acceptance of permanent consultation and change in the work-

---

[17] Schanze, E., 'Symbiotic Contracts: Exploring Long-Term Agency Structures between Contract and Corporation' in Joerges, C. (ed.), *Franchising and the Law* (Baden Baden: Nomos, 1991).

[18] See Collins, above, n. 16, 239.

[19] Fox, A., *Beyond Contract: Work, Power and Trust Relations* (London: Faber, 1974) 248.

place, and adaptation to the particular conditions of the enterprise. It is not possible to impose such partnership relations on unwilling participants; indeed, imposition is likely to be counter-productive, to be a recipe for undermining trust. Nor can the law devise a model for partnership that might apply universally across different firms, for each firm has its own particular needs and priorities. The law therefore cannot be used in any straightforward regulatory manner in the form of 'command and control' to impose partnership arrangements upon business.

In describing the contribution of the law to the programme of promoting partnerships at work, Tony Blair envisages merely a background role: 'the law is there to give shape and support to these new understandings and as a last resort to help resolve differences and disputes if they should arise'.[20] The Employment Relations Act 1999 commences this agenda steering the culture of industrial relations by a number of measures. It provides money to spread knowledge and understanding about partnerships,[21] in order to encourage employers and workers to adopt this best practice. The legislation provides an incentive for employers to adopt mechanisms of partnership by creating the threat, which it is hoped will never have to be realized, of imposing union recognition and collective bargaining upon unwilling employers. Schedule 1 is structured so that every opportunity is given to employers to create their own tailored arrangements for consultation and participation by the workforce. The objective of the legislation is not that of the earlier Employment Protection Act 1975, which was to promote collective bargaining, but is rather to promote institutions of consultation and worker representation. The administrative agency charged with dispute resolution, the Central Arbitration Committee (CAC), has the general legal duty to encourage and promote fair and efficient practices and arrangements in the workplace,[22] not to support collective bargaining. The objective of the new legislation is to induce voluntary arrangements for consultation and sharing of information. Within this objective, it is far more important to expand the range of consultation, as in the case of the new legal duty to consult with a recognized trade union about training,[23] than to compel the employer to bargain seriously about wages. Through further extensive derecognition procedures, the legislation also gives employers a second chance to persuade the workforce that other channels of representation will be more effective and appropriate.[24] The government does not

---

[20] See above, n. 2. [21] Employment Relations Act 1999, s. 30.

[22] Employment Relations Act 1999, Sched. 1, para. 171, inserting a new Sched. A1 into the Trade Union and Labour Relations (Consolidation) Act 1992.

[23] Employment Relations Act 1999, s. 5, inserting new ss. 70B and 70C into the Trade Union and Labour Relations (Consolidation) Act 1992.

[24] Employment Relations Act 1999, s. 1, Sched. 1, Part IV, inserting a new Sched. A1 into the Trade Union and Labour Relations (Consolidation) Act 1992.

want to impose collective bargaining both because it does not believe that imposed relations achieve the desirable form of partnership, and because collective bargaining with its emphasis upon the wage-work bargain is peripheral to the real interest of the Third Way agenda in improving competitiveness.

In my view these measures commence the agenda of promoting part-nership at work, but the law may be needed further to assist in the construction of suitable institutional arrangements. The model of symbi-otic contracts suggests that some degree of profit sharing is required to maximize co-operation, and the law can provide tax efficient models to give the parties incentives to move payment systems in the direction of employee share ownership and performance-related pay.[25] The law can also describe more precise obligations owed between the parties that express the duty of co-operation at the heart of partnership arrangements. Indeed, we may already glimpse such developments in the common law of implied terms in the contract of employment, as in the extension of the implied term of trust and confidence in *Malik* v. *BCCI*.[26] In previous cases, perhaps the best known being the Employment Appeal Tribunal's deci-sion in *The Post Office* v. *Roberts*,[27] the implied term of trust and confidence was used in circumstances where the employer had abused managerial power by treating the employee harshly, arbitrarily, and with disrespect. In such cases the implied term of trust and confidence is used to prevent abuse of power by the employer in the exercise of its discretion to direct labour. In the *Malik* case, however, the implied term was used to describe the duties of the employer as an agent (in the non-legal sense) for the employee as a principal in the way that the business is run: the business should not be run in such a way as to damage the principal's (that is, the employee's) reputation or employability. The *Malik* decision seems to me to rest implicitly on a symbiotic model of employment, the judges reach-ing intuitively towards the idea of the loyalty of the employer to the employee as a quasi-principal. The aim of the decision is the protection of the economic interests of employees in how the business is run by management rather than a method of restraining the misuse of manage-ment's power to direct labour. Management owes a duty of loyalty, because employers are acting (in part) as agents for the employees.

---

[25] Finance Act 2000, Sched. 8, replacing earlier provisions, creates tax incentives for all-employee share schemes. Tax incentives for profit-related payment schemes or bonus payments failed to achieve the correct incentives and were phased out: Finance Act 1997, s. 61.

[26] *Malik* v. *Bank of Credit and Commerce International SA* [1997] 3 WLR 95, HL.

[27] [1980] IRLR 347 (EAT).

Flexibility and security

In pursuing the goal of regulating for competitiveness, the Third Way adopts a particular stance with respect to legal rights granted to individual workers. In traditional social democratic and liberal political agendas, the principal justification for conferring rights upon individuals has been either to accord respect to basic human rights, such as the right to be treated with dignity and respect, or to establish a fair distributive pattern in the workplace. Those justifications usually lead to the establishment of a mandatory minimum set of rights for all workers, and those rights are protected because they are regarded as valuable in themselves. In this vein, for instance, legal regulation may provide standards with respect to maximum hours of work, minimum hourly wage, minimum safety standards, and minimum standards of fairness in discipline and dismissal. In the Third Way agenda of regulating for competitiveness, however, a different approach to employment rights emerges.

The Third Way addresses the following paradox. Fixed legal rights might impede co-operation and flexibility on the part of the workforce, which in turn would harm competitiveness. Yet without some reliable promises of fair treatment, job security, and fair rewards, the workforce is unlikely to co-operate in the flexible way envisaged in the model of symbiotic contracts. Fair treatment is required primarily, not because it is a good in itself, but for instrumental reasons: without fair treatment, employees will not co-operate and will be unwilling to agree to flexible working arrangements, with the consequence of damaging the efficiency and competitiveness of the firm.[28] Thus legal regulation needs to avoid rigid entitlements, whilst at the same time buttressing the confidence of employees that they will be treated fairly in the workplace. Legislation needs to induce employers to make credible commitments about fair treatment at work, to support those commitments, but not to determine the precise content of those commitments in order to avoid the risk that fixed legal rights might obstruct flexibility in work.

How can an employer best make a credible commitment to treat the workforce fairly whilst insisting at the same time upon flexibility in all working practices? Can the law serve a useful purpose here? The most credible promises by employers result from voluntary actions rather than coerced legal obligations. If the employer structures its procedures and rules that comprise the organization around respect for fairness, the bureaucracy is likely to carry out these standing orders. In contrast, reliance upon background legal rights enforceable in an employment tribunal is likely to produce little sense of commitment towards the

---

[28] See *Fairness at Work*, above, n. 2, para. 1.9.

employer. In crude terms, an employee who is concerned about job security is likely to be rather more impressed by an employer's staff handbook that describes fair disciplinary procedures and transparent disciplinary standards than by the employer's legally coerced commitment to pay compensation for unfair dismissal if ordered to do so by a tribunal. In order to enhance the credibility of the employer's commitment, the task of legal regulation is not primarily to grant employees legal entitlements that may be enforced by way of compensation in tribunals, but rather to re-engineer the internal rules of organizations so that they present credible commitments towards fairness. How can such an ambitious agenda be achieved through law?

A crude strategy, but nevertheless sometimes effective, is simply to raise the stakes for employers. If breach of the legal rights of employees leads to sufficiently high levels of compensation, it will be cheaper for employers to introduce fail-safe procedures into the workplace to avoid this potential liability. This is one of the justifications put forward by the government for raising the upper limits on compensation for unfair dismissal: the low limit provided insufficient incentive for employers to adopt fair internal disciplinary procedures.[29] The same effect may be anticipated from the general revision of levels of compensation for breach of legal rights and their future linking to price indexes.

A more subtle strategy for inducing employers to revise the internal rules of their organization is to describe explicitly the kinds of procedures required, though leaving the detail to employers to determine, and to provide incentives to adopt these procedures. For example, the legislation on public interest disclosure is designed to provoke employers to create internal procedures for disclosure, with the incentive that the presence of such procedures prevents employees from 'going public' except as a matter of last resort.[30] The legislation is not about creating a right to blow the whistle, but about giving the employer the right to deter such action by adopting certain procedures. A similar justification was also advanced by the government for supporting the arbitration option in unfair dismissal: disputes are more likely to be settled by voluntary private procedures.[31] In this case, however, I think that the legislation misses the mark, for what is really required is an opt-out procedure. By adopting internal fair disciplinary rules and procedures, the employer could prevent employees disciplined under such rules from bringing any legal claim at all except for an order to enforce observance of such procedures. But the arbitration alternative to employment tribunals does not achieve

---

[29] See *Fairness at Work*, above, n. 2, para. 3.5.
[30] Ibid., para. 3.3 (justifying the Public Interest Disclosure Act 1998).
[31] Ibid., para. 3.4 (justifying the Employment Rights (Dispute Resolution) Act 1998).

that objective at all; it merely provides a cheap alternative forum for adjudication, one which is likely to be stacked against employees and is therefore unlikely to be used. Another example of this method of regulation designed to re-engineer the internal rules of organizations is the European Works Councils Directive.[32] In that Directive, the objective was to induce multi-national corporations to adopt some kind of representative consultation procedure with the entire workforce, and this was achieved by enabling companies to opt out of the legislative model by introducing their own bespoke system earlier.

A third regulatory strategy for achieving the objective of altering the internal rules of organizations has not, I think, been used yet in an employment context in the United Kingdom, but my guess is that it will appear on the agenda. This technique involves the certification of rules in order to enhance their credibility. For example, most employers claim these days to be 'equal opportunity employers'. But this claim has (or should have) no credibility whatsoever, because it is merely an assertion by the employer. It would be very different, however, if such a claim could be advanced only if the employer's internal rules, practices, and procedures had been inspected by a neutral and expert third party and then certified as complying with the requisite standards. This technique is used widely in consumer protection, as in the case of 'kitemarks' and British Standards, with good effect. The same technique of certification is also central to the European Commission's strategy for ensuring quality and safety of consumer goods in the Single Market.[33] In my view this technique is very powerful, and it will not be long before the government perceives that Codes of Practice can be turned into certification standards. For example, in my view a certification procedure for equal opportunities in the workplace would do more than any legal measures to achieve a change in the culture of management practices and a reduction in discrimination, and it has the great attraction that it need not cost the government a penny.

This ambition of enhancing the credibility of employers' commitments to fairness at work by inducing employers to adopt fair internal rules of the organization thus leads to more subtle interventions and less emphasis upon the imposition of legal rights. It is not a policy of abstention from legal intervention, but rather a more sophisticated approach to the issue of what kind of legal intervention is most likely to achieve the objective of credible commitments to fairness at work. I suspect that the policy is informed by recent work in the theory of regulation, which demonstrates

---

[32] Directive 94/45/EC [1994] OJ L254, 64.
[33] European Council Resolution on a Global Approach to Conformity Assessment [1990] OJ C10 1.

how and why simple methods of command and control are less effective in achieving the goals of regulation than more nuanced and indirect approaches. The techniques described above can be fitted into the theoretical prescriptions for 'responsive' and 'reflexive' regulation.[34] The emphasis upon voluntarism or the freedom of business to adapt regulatory standards to local conditions by agreement may also reflect an associated concern about the problems of 'juridification' in the workplace.[35] No doubt the desire to minimize the cost of the employment tribunal system is also a relevant consideration in the government's mind. But the principal ostensible justification for the emphasis on private procedures is firmly linked to the issue of co-operation. The employer needs to make credible commitments that the employees will be treated fairly at work, and such commitments are best made by the employer's introduction of clear rules and procedures that management will follow.

These regulatory strategies do not rule out the possibility of establishing a set of basic legal entitlements for employees. But the concern to promote competitiveness through flexibility discourages the adoption of mandatory and inalienable rights. Fixed rights might either conflict with the optimal arrangement of work from the point of view of efficiency and competitiveness, or they might grant either party the legal right to obstruct alterations to working practices designed to promote co-operation. In many business contexts such as commercial transactions, legal regulation eschews fixed rights in favour of default rules such as implied terms which the parties are free to modify. This style of regulation of commercial contracts is likely to be conducive to efficient outcomes between parties of equal sophistication and bargaining power. But private agreements between employer and employee are likely to be flawed due to asymmetries of information. The crucial problem is that the employee cannot be sure whether the employer's commitments to fairness are credible.[36] In addition, the employee is often like a consumer in being willing to sign written contracts of employment that replace the default rules with terms that heavily favour the employer. These 'market failure' considerations tend to lead to the conclusion that a legal frame-

---

[34] Ayres, I., and Braithwaite, J., *Responsive Regulation: Transcending the Deregulation Debate* (New York: Oxford University Press, 1992); Teubner, G., 'Substantive and Reflexive Elements in Modern Law' (1983) 17 *Law and Society Review* 239; Teubner, G., *Law as an Autopoietic System* (Oxford: Blackwell, 1993); Rogowski, R., and Wilthagen, T. (eds.), *Reflexive Labour Law* (Deventer: Kluwer, 1994).

[35] Teubner, G. (ed.), *Juridification of Social Spheres: A Comparative Analysis in the Areas of Labour, Corporate, Antitrust and Social Welfare Law* (Berlin: Walter de Gruyter, 1987).

[36] Collins, H., 'Justifications and Techniques of Legal Regulation of the Employment Relation' in Collins, H., Davies, P. L., and Rideout, R. (eds.), *Legal Regulation of the Employment Relation* (London: Kluwer, 2000).

work based merely on default rules such as implied terms is unlikely to create the necessary credible commitments to fairness at work.

The objective of regulating for competitiveness in the context of employment points to a more complex strategy that adds to the options of fixed entitlements and default rules. Some employment rights might be alienable or modifiable only as a result of a collective agreement with the workforce. Other legal rights might be alienable only after the event as a result of a settlement that conforms to a fair procedure. The possibilities can be illustrated by the Working Time Regulations 1998,[37] which classify the rights conferred upon employees according to the conditions under which they can be modified or alienated. The maximum hours standard of the forty-eight hour week is alienable by individuals,[38] thus representing a default rule. The rights in relation to night work (limited to eight hours per twenty-four), daily rest (eleven consecutive hours in twenty-four), the weekly day of rest, and short rest breaks are alienable only by contrary collective agreements through collective bargaining or 'workforce agreements'.[39] The right to four weeks of paid holiday is inalienable. The timing of the holiday is, however, subject to individual agreement or managerial direction,[40] which leaves the timing to be fixed by express agreement. My explanation for this varied pattern in the legislation is that in order to support the instrumental goals behind the rights, which in this case include improvements in health and safety as well as wealth maximization, it is believed that alienable rights are more likely to achieve efficient outcomes than fixed entitlements. The differentiation between rights that require collective negotiation for alienation or modification and those that permit individual alienation depends upon an assessment of whether individual employees will have the bargaining strength to achieve the optimal outcome. For example, collective negotiation is required where the employer is likely to be able to use its bargaining power to chip away at the right opportunistically, such as making occasional demands for work without rest breaks or a day off.

The issue of alienability has obviously been considered carefully in relation to the Working Time Regulations, but under the agenda of regulating for competitiveness, it has equal application to other employment rights. For example, the issue applies to legal rights in relation to dismissal. In its legislation, the government eventually favoured the ability of individuals on fixed term contracts to contract out of redundancy payments, but removed this possibility in relation to the right to claim unfair dismissal. The objective here was to facilitate the flexible working arrangement of fixed term contracts, but to keep the legal sanction against

---

[37] SI 1998/1833.   [38] Ibid., reg. 5.
[39] Ibid., reg. 23.   [40] Ibid., reg. 15(2), (5).

unfair dismissal in order to buttress the credibility of the employer's commitment to treat short-term workers fairly. But the Third Way agenda could lead to further developments that permit easier exclusion of legal rights in the event of dismissal, provided that the employer has established alternative, binding commitments, perhaps at a collective level, to comply with high standards of fairness in the workplace.

III CONCLUSIONS

In construing the agenda of a Third Way in labour law, I have no doubt attributed to it a greater coherence than is appropriate for an evolving set of ideas. By stressing the novelty of some of the ideas, I have also downplayed significant continuities, especially the fidelity to civil liberties inherited from traditional strands of social democracy and reinforced by the Human Rights Act 1998. Nor have I sufficiently challenged the assumption of the Third Way that the forces of globalization will permanently reduce some of the previous major sources of industrial conflict. Despite these reservations, I hope that I have offered a persuasive interpretation of some of the key elements in an evolving new agenda for labour law.

The agenda of the Third Way for labour law is set by the political goals of combating the origins of social exclusion and improving the competitiveness of business. These goals lead towards new tasks for legal regulation, such as family-friendly policies to permit equal access to the labour market and to the promotion of credible partnership arrangements. I have also stressed that the achievement of these goals requires more complex and responsive regulatory techniques than the traditional pattern of mandatory employment rights. The regulatory method becomes more subtle and indirect, seeking to provoke the parties themselves to re-engineer their own economic and social relations through partnerships and contractual agreements.

This Third Way agenda presents a wide range of difficult issues that will need to be addressed seriously in the future. The challenge to structural obstacles to equality of opportunity or, if you like, citizenship presents an enormous and shifting agenda for action by government. One can foresee, for instance, that the position of older workers in the labour market will become a crucial concern from the perspective of social exclusion. Government intervention can sometimes itself be part of the problem to be addressed, as in the case of poverty traps, so we must expect a constant process of regulation and re-regulation. At the same time, we are only just beginning the strategy of regulating for competitiveness, and the ways in which the law can promote partnerships and assist employers to make credible commitments to treat the workforce fairly will benefit from the experience of trial and error. Regulatory techniques used in labour law remain relatively crude outside the field of health and safety at work, so we can expect to see much more experimentation. In particular, the possibility of using incentives to induce employers to adopt competitive institutions and fair employment standards has not been explored fully. For example, to promote partnership arrangements in the workplace, the employer could be offered tax incentives or potential exclusion of legal liabilities.

These regulatory techniques may be unfamiliar to labour lawyers. But there is no reason to think that the employment relation will not continue to present a vital area of interest for lawyers, even if the problems to be addressed change radically from those that dominated the twentieth century. Legal regulation of employment and the labour market remains in the Third Way an important dimension of state activity.

24

Private Ordering and Workers' Rights in the Global Economy: Corporate Codes of Conduct as a Regime of Labour Market Regulation

HARRY ARTHURS*

I THE CONTEXT

New technologies, new patterns of consumption and production, new levels of intensity, magnitude, and volatility in the movement of people, information, and capital are transforming the global political economy. Many effects of this transformation become manifest in the domain of public policy, where parties across the political spectrum have embraced the neo-liberal agenda. That agenda has been characterized, perhaps hyperbolically, as the 'hollowing out of the state': facilitation of transnational business activity; reduction of corporate and personal taxes and cuts in public expenditures, especially on social welfare; deregulation of domestic markets. These developments in turn are weakening, perhaps fatally, the labour market strategies and institutions of the prior dispensation, the post-war Keynesian welfare state: counter-cyclical job creation, collective bargaining, protective labour legislation, and equality-enhancing strategies.[1] And most importantly, in the new global political economy, most states have come to feel that they cannot return to their former interventionist approaches to the labour market: either they suffer from a failure of will—they are afraid to alienate transnational corporations (TNCs) and risk losing investment, revenues, and jobs; or they suffer from a failure of imagination—they cannot see how to regulate TNCs more

* I should like to express my appreciation to the Social Science and Humanities Research Council of Canada for its financial support, to Angela Long and Matina Karvellas, my research assistants, for their diligent efforts, and to Carla Lipsig-Mummé and Wes Cragg for their comments on an earlier draft.
    [1] This argument does not address three important claims: (1) that in some respects—immigration, social discipline, and facilitation of corporate activity—the state has become more active, not less; (2) that in the long term, neo-liberal policies will generate a rising tide which will lift all boats (or sink all ships); (3) that in the short term, neo-liberalism has constrained, but not fundamentally damaged, the social welfare state. None of these claims is inconsistent with the point made above—that public policy changes have put at risk familiar labour market strategies and institutions.

aggressively because so many key activities and actors lie beyond their juridical space.[2]

Needless to say, not all consequences of neo-liberalism are felt in the domain of public policy. Some appear in very specific contexts, in communities and workplaces, in the lives of families and individuals. These can be summed up as a shift in power relations in favour of a limited group of corporate actors—TNCs, a privileged group of their business allies and partners, and a cosmopolitan elite of investors, executives, professionals, technical experts, and consultants closely associated with their activities. By contrast, many workers, their unions and families, and local businesses, elites, and communities have suffered a loss of power, and sometimes (not always) of income and well being.

But that is not quite the whole story. Transnational corporations may have promoted, and benefited from, neo-liberal policies; they may have enhanced their power *vis-à-vis* other actors; but they are not totally free to do as they please. States retain residual powers, both in theory and in reality; they can amend treaties, enact regulations, retract concessionary arrangements, and raise taxes if they are prepared to risk the consequences. Thus, neo-liberal policies, though dominant, remain to a degree contestable. After all, even oligarchic governments—even TNCs, even neo-liberal economists—must know that they themselves are at risk in the long term if the promises of globalization remain unfulfilled, if important constituencies become disaffected, if societies are conflicted and disorderly.

Hence the recent calls by some leading figures of world capitalism for more attention to honest and orderly markets, to equitable social and labour policies, to responsible environmental practices and to democratic politics.[3] At least in the view of these leading figures, and of the corporate community they exemplify, citizens do retain some influence—albeit more potential than actual—as moral agents, voters, consumers, strikers, and rioters. If TNCs want workers to work in their factories, consumers to consume their goods, and governments to govern in their interest, they must appear to be 'responsible' in the way they treat workers, consumers, and communities. And by a happy coincidence, a modest body of research seems to suggest that they can be responsible and profitable too. There is money to be made in 'ethical investment' and 'sustainable development';

---

[2] Stone, K. V. W., 'Labor and the Global Economy: Four Approaches to Transnational Labor Regulation' (1995) 16 *Michigan Journal of International Law* 987.

[3] See, e.g., Wolfensohn, J. W., 'The Other Crisis' (Address to the World Bank Group, 6 Oct. 1998) and *A Proposal for a Comprehensive Development Framework* (Discussion Draft, 21 Jan. 1999)—both located at www.worldbank.org/cdf/cdf-text.htm; Schwab, K., and Smadja, C., 'Globalization Backlash is Serious', *The Globe and Mail*, 16 Feb. 1996, B10; Soros, G., *The Crisis of Global Capitalism* (New York: Public Affairs, 1998).

social market policies do not seem to impair the efficiency and adaptability of workers;[4] and economic prosperity may correlate positively with
civic mindedness[5] and progressive labour practices.[6]

However, even if TNCs wish to consolidate their power and profitability by projecting an image of responsible behaviour in labour
markets and elsewhere, they confront a problem of presentation and
persuasion. In the previous dispensation, 'acting responsibly' was fairly
easy to demonstrate—TNCs could say they were meeting their obligations under state labour law in their home country or host countries. No
longer, not with state labour law confined by national boundaries and the
extraterritoriality doctrine, rolled back by aggressive deregulation, enfeebled by the defunding of workplace inspectorates, dependent on the
support of rump unions and workers terrified that their work will be
'outsourced' and their jobs moved 'offshore'. In such a context, state law
is no longer plausible as benchmark for responsible corporate behaviour.

In principle, TNCs, their advisors, and apologists might have solved
the problem of a plausible benchmark by supporting the reinvigoration of
state law, helping to build effective transnational institutions or entering
into a new social contract with workers and communities. However, what
they have chosen to do instead is to promulgate their own benchmark,
their own self-imposed law: 'codes of conduct'. These codes typically
commit TNCs to treating their workers fairly, and some contain compliance procedures designed to give credibility to the project of self-regulation. There is a double irony here. First, by projecting their labour codes
into the transnational economic sphere, TNCs commit themselves to
respecting freedom of association, due process, fair wages, and the
dignity of their workers—norms which were embedded in the very
systems of state law which TNCs themselves were instrumental in undermining. Secondly, by adopting voluntary codes, TNCs have, in effect,
engaged in the 'reproduction' of liberal legality in the transnational
economic field, a strategy which in the field of socio-legal scholarship has
an unlikely provenance—Santos's description of the legal system created
by the poor residents of a Brazilian *favela*.[7]

However, irony should not be confused with coincidence. The proliferation of codes has not only proceeded in tandem with the most recent

---

[4] See, e.g., Blank, R. (ed.), *Social Protection versus Economic Flexibility: Is There a Trade-Off?*
(Chicago, Ill.: University of Chicago Press, 1994). See also OECD, *Employment Outlook* (Paris:
OECD, 1999) ch. 4.
  [5] Putnam, R., *Making Democracy Work: Civic Traditions in Modern Italy* (Princeton, NJ:
Princeton University Press, 1993).
  [6] Sengenberger, W., and Campbell, D., *The Role of Labour Standards in Industrial
Restructuring* (Geneva: Institute for Labour Studies, 1994).
  [7] De Sousa Santos, B., 'The Law of the Oppressed: The Construction and Reproduction
of Legality in Pasagarda' (1977) 12 *Law & Society Review* 5.

wave of globalization; it seems to be causally related. During the 1970s, in response to a wave of third world, trade union, and economic nationalist complaints about rising foreign investment and increasing influence of foreign-based multinationals, various international agencies—as well as the International Chamber of Commerce—adopted model codes designed to promote good corporate citizenship,[8] which in turn triggered a spate of academic writing at the end of the decade and into the 1980s.[9] However, in the 'new world economic order' of the 1980s—with labour in decline, developing countries increasingly dependent on TNC investment, and national political and economic elites reconciled to globalization—the initial international momentum which had produced these codes dissipated. Nonetheless, a new momentum favouring codes developed during the 1980s, as human rights groups—and protest groups with quite varied agendas—sought to curtail TNC investment and business activity in apartheid-era South Africa, Northern Ireland, Soviet Russia, and the People's Republic of China;[10] most of these codes subsided in due course, along with the controversies which provoked them. However, for reasons which will be explored below, codes have come back into fashion. A recent OECD document shows that since the early 1990s, significant numbers of TNCs and their sectoral organizations have adopted codes, some 60 per cent of which deal wholly or partly with employment standards.[11] ILO and UNCTAD reports have also remarked on the recent proliferation of TNC voluntary corporate codes—especially codes of

[8] International Chamber of Commerce, *Guidelines for International Investment* (Paris: ICC, 1972); OECD, *Guidelines for Multinational Enterprises* (Paris: OECD, 1976); International Labour Office, *Tripartite Declaration of Principles concerning Multinational Enterprises and Social Policy* (Geneva: ILO, 1977). A United Nations report recommended adoption of a draft code of conduct for MNEs in as early as 1974; however, it has never been formally ratified.

[9] See, e.g., Baade, H., *The Legal Effects of Codes of Conduct for MNEs* (Bielefeld: Centre for Interdisciplinary Research: University of Bielefeld, International Symposium on Legal Problems of Codes of Conduct for Multinational Enterprises, 1979); Baker, J., and Ryans, J., 'Multinational Corporation Investment in Less Developed Countries: Reducing Risk' (1979) 18 *Nebraska Journal of Econ. & Business* 61; Gunter, H., 'The International Labour Office Declaration of Multinational Enterprises and the International Code of Conduct Movement' (1981) 4 *Loyola of Los Angeles International & Comparative L. Journal* 1; Note, 'Host State Treatment of Transnational Corporations: Formulation of a Standard for the United Nations Code of Conduct on Transnational Corporations' (1983–4) 7 *Fordham International L. Journal* 467; Horn, N. (ed.), *Legal Problems of Codes of Conduct for Multinational Enterprises* (Deventer: Kluwer, 1980).

[10] For a general review see Perez-Lopez, J., 'Promoting International Respect for Worker Rights through Business Codes of Conduct' (1993) 17 *Fordham International L. Journal* 1; Compa, L., and Hinchcliffe-Darricarrère, T., 'Enforcing Labor Rights through Corporate Codes of Conduct' (1995) 33 *Columbia Journal of Transnational Law* 663.

[11] The OECD study identified some 182 codes, promulgated by transnational bodies, by major TNCs, or by influential sectoral and stakeholder associations. Of the codes whose dates of promulgation are given, the great majority came into force after 1995; virtually none was operative before 1990. *Codes of Corporate Conduct*, Working Party of the Trade Committee, Trade Directorate (Paris: OECD TD/TC/WP (98) 74 (Dec. 1998).

employment standards[12]—as have several government, NGO and scholarly studies.[13]

The questions to be addressed in this chapter, then, are why TNCs have 'volunteered' to subject themselves to codes at this particular moment, just when they are becoming increasingly immune from other constraints, whether these codes represent the successful 'reproduction of legality' and how states, workers, unions, and other actors are likely to be affected by them.

I WHY 'VOLUNTARY' EMPLOYMENT CODES?

There is nothing new under the sun, certainly not codes governing employment in transnational enterprises. From the seventeenth to the nineteenth centuries, the Crowley steel works—near Sunderland, in the north of England—was governed by a 'book of laws' (sometimes called the 'ancient constitution') which laid down the rights and obligations of workers in this huge paternalistic proto-global enterprise.[14] The great global trading companies—the Hudson's Bay Company, the East India Company—became quasi-governments and promulgated legal codes which comprehensively regulated the behaviour of their employees (and other people) all over the world. Early Victorian manufacturers and mine owners—a formidable presence in Imperial and international trade—had statutory power to establish their own codes or 'special rules' dealing with safety and work practices.[15] Codes—work rules and employment manuals, adopted unilaterally, and collective agreements, adopted bilaterally—have been a fixture of modern industrial employment. And even

---

[12] ILO, *Overview of Global Developments* (Working Party on the Social Dimensions of the Liberalization of Trade, Report to the International Labour Office, Nov. 1998) GB. 273/WP/SDL/1 found at www.ilo.org.ch/public/english/20gb/docs/gb273/sdl-1.htm. See also United Nations Commission on Trade and Development (UNCTAD), *World Investment Report 1994—Transnational Corporations, Employment and the Workplace* (New York/Geneva: United Nations, 1994) 349 ff.

[13] See Perez-Lopez and Compa and Hinchcliffe-Darricarrère, above, n. 10; Culpepper, R., and Whiteman, G., 'The Corporate Stake in Social Responsibility' in Hibler, H., and Beamish, R. (eds), *Canadian Corporations and Social Responsibility* (Ottawa: The North–South Institute, 1998); and US Department of Labor, Bureau of International Affairs, *The Apparel Industry and Codes of Conduct: A Solution to the International Child Labor Problem?* (Washington, DC: Department of Labor, 1996).

[14] The Crowleys owned the largest steel works in Europe, imported raw materials from Sweden, Spain, and Russia, and exported finished products to India, the colonies, and various European countries: Flinn, M. W., *Men of Iron: The Crowleys in the Early Iron Industry* (Edinburgh: The University Press, 1962).

[15] Arthurs, H. W., *'Without the Law': Administrative Justice and Legal Pluralism in Nineteenth Century England* (Toronto: University of Toronto Press, 1985) ch. 4.

thoroughly globalized, post-modern, post-industrial 'empowered' employees have continued to be ruled by employment codes.[16]

All of these codes share two main characteristics. They operate internally, within the enterprise, to define terms of employment such as wages, working conditions, discipline, and quality standards; to educate workers to adhere to them; and to ensure orderly and consistent enforcement of those terms by supervisors and managers. And they operate externally, by mimicking the rhetoric, forms, and processes of law, to convince conscientious investors, consumers, NGOs, and governments of the legitimacy of what are characteristically unequal, and sometimes exploitative, employment relations.[17] Indeed the ultimate legitimation strategy is to co-opt potential critics by enlisting them as sponsors of a code regime. Finally, some codes are adopted on a sectoral or industry-wide basis. Such codes give each signatory a stake in policing the others, diminish the risk that 'free riders' will benefit from goodwill accruing to the sector as a whole, and make it more difficult for non-complying firms to compete on the basis of their lower labour costs and standards.[18] All of this contributes to the operational efficacy of the code, which in turn makes it a more convincing legitimating device.

The internal functions of codes—their tutelary and disciplinary functions—have been dealt with elsewhere, by authors from E.P. Thompson[19] to Stuart Henry;[20] the appearance of rival, even subversive, normative systems 'in the shadow' of these corporate codes has been documented by Burawoy;[21] the reflexive, rule-generating tendency of large corporations has been addressed by Teubner and others;[22] and I have attempted to situate all of these approaches to workplace codes within a general theory

[16] See, e.g., 'Workplace Ethics' (1986) 31/12 *Management Solutions* 12; Collett, P., 'Codes of Conduct: A Framework for Ethics' (1998) 68/1 *Australian Accountant* 29; Whitehead, M., 'People Don't Seem to Know Right from Wrong' (1999) 5/3 *People Management* 14. See also Sewell, G., and Wilkinson, B., ' "Someone to Watch Over Me": Surveillance, Discipline and the Just-in-Time Labour Process' (1992) 26 *Sociology* 271.

[17] Hepple, B., 'A Race to the Top? International Investment Guidelines and Corporate Codes of Conduct' (paper presented at the W. G. Hart Workshop; London: Institute of Advanced Legal Studies, 1999). Hepple and I both use 'legitimation' in the sense of a calculated attempt to win acceptance for one's actions by appealing to shared values and beliefs. There is considerable controversy surrounding the term. See Hyde, A., 'The Concept of Legitimation in the Sociology of Law' [1983] *Wisconsin L. Review* 379.

[18] See Purchase, B., 'The Political Economy of Voluntary Codes' (Industry Canada, unpublished, 1997).

[19] Thompson, E. P., 'Time, Work-Discipline and Industrial Capitalism' in his *Customs in Common* (New York: The New Press, 1991).

[20] Henry, S., 'Disciplinary Pluralism: Four Models of Private Justice in the Workplace' (1987) 35 *Sociological Review* 279.

[21] Burawoy, M., *Manufacturing Consent* (Chicago, Ill.: University of Chicago Press, 1979).

[22] Teubner, G., *Global Law without the State* (Aldershot/Brookfield: Dartmouth Publishing, 1997).

of legal and industrial pluralism.[23] Their external functions—their legitimating and market regulating functions—are the focus of this chapter.

Of course, there is no clear division between internal and external audiences. For workers and consumers, managers, and government officials to be persuaded to accept voluntary codes as the equivalent of legal protections, all must acquiesce in roughly similar values and assumptions. Hence the importance of the dominant neo-liberal discourse which disparages state regulation and stresses the inevitability of globalization, the positive contributions of TNCs, and the invincible logic of their structures and policies. Moreover, codes must be perceived to achieve results roughly comparable to those achieved through alternative means such as statutory regulation or collective bargaining. If there is excessive dissonance between the reality of workplace life and the rhetoric of an employment code, workers will be disillusioned, the public will be disenchanted, TNCs will be publicly embarrassed, and self-regulation will cease to be regarded as legitimate. Hence the need to create 'legal' procedures that can both bring about and testify to the positive consequences of self-regulation. What is puzzling about the recent proliferation of voluntary employment codes, however, is that their underlying values remain somewhat obscure, their procedures deeply flawed, and their outcomes unverified.

Values first. Traditional hierarchy and reciprocal obligation may have seemed the natural order of things to several generations of Crowleys, their workers, and their latter-day counterparts in developing countries; the inexorable logic of market forces acting upon 'free' contracting parties (backed by occasional state coercion) may have been all that was needed to justify employment practices in the dark satanic mills of nineteenth-century England; and the Wagner Act's promise that workers were to be given democratic voice and vote in their relations with their employer may have been, for a time, persuasive to enlightened employers, militant employees, and an American public concerned about escalating industrial warfare. But none of these seems to have much salience today. Procedures next. Only a minority of codes summarized in the OECD study—and in other studies—actually include any procedural arrangements at all, only a handful involve anything approaching independent monitoring, and virtually none involves third-party enforcement. And, finally, outcomes. To put it plainly, there is little or no evidence about how codes actually affect the behaviour of TNCs. Thus, it is something of a mystery why voluntary codes should have become so numerous in recent years.

[23] Arthurs, H. W., 'The Law of the Shop: The Debate over Industrial Pluralism' (1985) 38 *Current Legal Problems* 83; Arthurs, H. W., 'Landscape and Memory: Labour, Law, Legal Pluralism and Globalization' in Wilthagen, T. (ed.), *Advancing Theory in Labour Law and Industrial Relations in a Global Context* (Amsterdam: Royal Netherlands Academy of Arts and Science, 1998), 21.

Several alternative hypotheses may be advanced. First, transnational corporations are often said to depend upon their 'human capital' for success in a knowledge-based global economy. If they are to attract and retain the workers they need, enlightened self-interest dictates that they should both preach high employment standards—by adopting voluntary codes—and practise them. This hypothesis may indeed hold true for a privileged cadre of peripatetic executives, technical experts, and professionals. However, it does not seem to have much to do with millions of rank-and-file production workers, who—if treated as 'human capital' at all—seem to be regarded as low-yield and essentially disposable assets. Most of these workers are involved in the global economy only in the sense that what they make is ultimately marketed abroad, often under global trade marks; they themselves work in intensely localized labour markets, often in the third world or on the periphery of the advanced economies. Moreover, most of them are not privileged knowledge workers; they generally perform routine manual work, under conditions that are often substandard and sometimes appalling. In any event, they all too seldom enjoy the wages and working conditions that are implicitly promised by corporate employment codes or the many international regimes which mandate them.

A second hypothesis is that globalization has not only benefited investors and other privileged elites, but that it has also strengthened the worldwide acceptance of human rights and worker entitlements. Voluntary codes, on this view, are no less important a source of such rights and entitlements than international treaties and agreements or national legislation; indeed, they are proof that the appropriate norms have percolated into and become operational in actual workplaces, where they count most. Again, there is modest evidence to support this hypothesis; but there is also considerable experience to the contrary. In the *maquiladoras*, the enterprise zones of the People's Republic of China, the carpet factories of Pakistan, or, for that matter, the manufacturing plants of southern Ontario or South Wales, expanded investment, employment opportunities, and markets are premised on government policies designed to establish a 'business friendly' environment. These policies generally involve derogation from established worker rights and entitlements and, in extreme cases, forcible suppression of worker and community organizations. Nonetheless, it is relatively rare for businesses—the intended beneficiaries of these policies—to protest against repressive labour legislation or strategies, or to insist that they would prefer to apply the high standards set out in their voluntary codes, such as protection of the right to organize and bargain collectively. One must ask, therefore, whether a deep attachment to the notion of labour rights and entitlements is in fact what animates the adoption of voluntary codes by transnational business.

The third hypothesis is, to me, the most persuasive. The interconnectedness of the global economy, some note, has made it vulnerable to disruption. Raw materials from one country are processed in another, turned into manufactured parts in a third, integrated into finished products in a fourth, shipped to distributors in a fifth, and marketed around the world. Each stage in the production process, each border crossed, each market served, each part of the larger corporate empire is potentially a site where employment practices can be called into question. Stoppages by production workers, refusals to handle by transport workers, consumer boycotts, and political pressures in any one of a score of countries may have ramifying consequences. This is not to suggest that workers, their unions, or transnational advocacy groups can mobilize support easily, that the legal systems of most countries tolerate such mobilization, or that transnationals lack ample power to defend themselves in most conflictual situations. Nonetheless, it is in the interests of transnational corporations to cosmeticize conflict, if they can, to pacify workers, neutralize unions, and reassure NGOs, governments, and consumers—all objectives that can be facilitated by adopting voluntary codes. This is the most obvious explanation of the recent popularity of 'voluntary codes' which are, in this perspective, not quite so voluntary as all that.

II THE SUCCESSFUL REPRODUCTION OF LEGALITY?

Voluntary codes may cover safe and healthy working conditions, grievance procedures, collective bargaining, measures forbidding discrimination, child labour, or substandard wages. They may establish procedures for inspection, processing complaints, and resolving disputes. Thus, at a superficial glance, voluntary codes of employment may seem capable of reproducing—approximately, if not precisely—many of the substantive and procedural characteristics of state labour legislation.

At a middle distance, however, the differences between state law and voluntary regimes become more apparent. Legislation applies to the generality of enterprises; codes only to those which have chosen to promulgate a code or make themselves subject to one. Unlike the relatively precise and directory language of regulatory statutes, the language of most codes is vague, hortatory, and not well suited to compelling compliance in circumstances which are unclear or controversial. Virtually all statutes are enforced ultimately by the coercive agencies of the state; with rare exceptions, no coercive power is available to enforce voluntary codes. And, in principle, those charged with violating state labour standards are judged by a court or independent regulatory tribunal; those charged with violating codes are generally judged by themselves or their nominees. Codes, then, are at best only a rough approximation of liberal legality, not a strict replication of it.

But, on close examination, the picture is not quite so clear. In effect, we have been comparing an ideal model of legislation and state regulation with the current, flawed reality of self-regulation. If we revisit each of the points just made, we will see that voluntary codes bear a closer resemblance to state regimes than we may care to admit.

Because of constitutional limitations, political influence, and materiality thresholds, the coverage of state regulatory regimes in practice is less than universal,[24] and sometimes no more comprehensive than that of voluntary regimes administering codes adopted by sectoral or stakeholder organizations. Statutory language—especially in labour statutes—may appear clear, but even longstanding interpretations can be frustrated by lengthy challenges or overturned by unsympathetic courts; in both state and self-regulating systems, corporations tend to have the last word. While, in principle, the state's coercive power can be mobilized to secure compliance with labour laws, this seldom takes place in practice. Recently, many states have abandoned aggressive and costly inspection and enforcement programmes in favour of self-reporting and self-discipline by employers, and formal adjudication and punitive action in favour of alternative dispute resolution. State enforcement systems, in practice, have often become no more rigorous than those established under voluntary codes. Even independent adjudication—which supposedly guarantees the integrity of state regulatory practice, and which has no counterpart under voluntary schemes—does not operate as cleanly and decisively as it is supposed to. Even in their golden age, state regulators were susceptible to 'regulatory capture', the outcome of symbiotic association with their 'clientele', of lobbying and patronage, of inadequate resources. Judges, by contrast, remained independent and were never 'captured'; but they did not need to be: they seldom demonstrated much sympathy for workers' interests, or much understanding of their organizations and strategies.

Ironically, then, given that state regulation of the workplace is in disrepair and disrepute, voluntary corporate regimes may not produce such very different outcomes. And now a further irony: intentionally or unintentionally, voluntary regimes sometimes become entangled with state policy-making and state legality instead of merely providing an alternative to the one and a facsimile of the other.

---

[24] E.g., a recent study estimates that 33% of all private-sector workers and 25% of all women workers are excluded from coverage of the US National Labor Relations Act: Cobble, D. S., 'Making Postindustrial Unionism Possible' in Friedman, S. (ed.), *Restoring the Promise of American Labor Law* (Ithica, NY: Cornell ILR Press, 1994) 285.

III VOLUNTARY CODES AND THE STATE

If, as hypothesized, voluntary code regimes are evidence of the immunity of TNCs from state regulation, it must also be said that states themselves actively or passively promote the adoption of such codes and even become directly involved in drafting and administering them.

Governments formulating labour market policies have always conducted an ongoing process of implicit—even explicit—negotiation with advisory bodies, industry representatives, major corporations, unions, NGOs, and other stakeholder groups. In recent times, however, the focus of negotiations has shifted as a result of the desire of neo-liberal governments to win the approval of investors and maintain the confidence of financial markets especially for their macro-economic policies.[25] In the result, public policies affecting the labour market have arguably become even more negotiable than they were during the hey-day of corporatism.[26] However, negotiations now virtually exclude the labour movement, although macro-economic policies shape the labour market and in turn appear to play 'a major role in shaping the trajectory of employer strategies and employment relations'.[27]

How does this new dynamic of policy negotiation lead to the adoption of voluntary codes? Employers in general have been emboldened by their dominant position in the policy process and the labour market, and by widespread acknowledgement of their need to resort to domestic or offshore labour practices which will enable them to respond to global competition. Consequently, some of them may choose—or, from their perspective, be driven—to engage in egregious, irresponsible, and exploitative practices: the use of child labour, brutal repression of a strike, a fatal failure to adhere to safety standards. The consequences of such practices are then publicized by a union or social advocacy group, widely reported by the media, and used as the rallying cry for a boycott of the company's goods or a campaign for legislation designed to suppress the practice and exclude the offending goods from market. Governments, confronted with public demands that they 'do something', often respond by asking the employer in question to promise to behave in the future, a

---

[25] Castles, F., 'The Dynamics of Policy Change: What Happened to the English-speaking Nations in the 1980s' (1990) 18 *European Journal of Political Research* 491.

[26] See Fogleson, R., and Wolfe, J. (eds.), *The Politics of Economic Adjustment: Pluralism, Corporatism and Privatization* (New York/Westport/London: Greenwood Press, 1989); Crouch, C., and Dore, R. (eds.), *Corporatism and Accountability* (Oxford: Clarendon Press, 1990).

[27] Goddard, J., 'Managerial Strategies, Labour and Employment Relations and the State: the Canadian Case and Beyond' (1997) 35 *BJIR* 399.

promise which is likely to be expressed in the form of a voluntary code.[28]

Voluntary codes for employers are obviously attractive for employers: no legal controls or sanctions, lower compliance costs (or none), and good publicity eclipsing bad. And codes are attractive for governments: they permit them to be seen to be concerned and responsive without provoking negative reactions from investors, breaking current ideological taboos against regulation, or incurring the transaction costs associated with inspection, prosecution, and other traditional forms of intervention. Moreover, voluntary codes may actually resolve problems, or at least alleviate them to the point where they cease to be a political issue. And of course, if they do not—if codes fail to produce the desired practical or political outcomes, if, in the end, conventional regulation is unavoidable—governments will at least be able to say to employers, investors, and ideological critics that it was the last resort, not the first. Parenthetically, in some federal states, codes have the additional attraction of offering a way around potential jurisdictional conflicts over who can regulate what.[29]

When legislation is ultimately enacted—with or without the acquiescence of important constituencies—negotiation does not cease. It continues on a daily basis in the context of administration and enforcement. This crucially important element of 'negotiation' results from the fact that the state's resources—its juridical powers, personnel, and political credibility—are seldom sufficient to support inspection of every workplace, prosecution of every offending employer, or proscription of every new hazardous process or practice. Consequently, from the earliest Victorian labour legislation[30] to the present,[31] governments have sought to enhance compliance and lighten the burdens of administration by persuading or compelling employers to take 'ownership' of labour legislation, to inter-

---

[28] As these words are written, publicity is being given to the settlement of a class action against US garment retailers on behalf of 50,000 Asian garment workers on Saipan, a US Pacific territory. The workers, who alleged that they were kept in a form of peonage, contrary to US and international human rights law, agreed to accept the introduction of an employment code, monitored by Verité, an independent monitoring agency with atypically strong complaint and remedial procedures under the joint supervision of the retailers and human rights and labour organizations. See Sweatshop Watch, website at http://www.igc.org/swatch/Marianas/settlement.html.

[29] Canada may be an extreme case, because constitutional interpretations have assigned employee–employer relations to provincial control, despite the fact that, in general, provinces cannot effectively deal with corporations which conduct operations outside their boundaries or abroad. But even in states with more appropriate constitutional arrangements, conflicting local and national interests and values may well make the enactment of national legislation politically awkward.

[30] Arthurs, above, n. 15, chs. 4 and 5.

[31] Levine, D., 'Reinventing Workplace Regulation' (1997) 39 *California Management Review* 98.

nalize its values so that they are routinely translated into workplace norms, without the need for government inspection, admonition, or prosecution. Codes appear to be a promising strategy for enhancing compliance: they are written by employers, administered by employers, and, hopefully, internalized in the operating procedures of employers.

Nowhere is the challenge of securing compliance more difficult than in the case of the offshore operations of domestic employers, investors, or traders. Here, the inspector's writ does not legally run; here, practices are likely to be most egregious; here, workers see confirmation of their worst fears of a 'race to the bottom'.[32] Codes once again may provide the answer. Firms which adopt and adhere to codes in their foreign operations effectively relieve their own governments of the legal, practical, and political challenges of extraterritorial inspection and enforcement. Various privileges—participation in trade missions, export loan guarantees, access to government purchasing programmes—can be extended to firms which are code-compliant, and denied to those which are not. And, finally, if these privileges do not suffice to shield compliant employers from competition by non-compliant firms with lower labour costs, codes can be used as the template for legislation or regulations designed to bar 'rogue' firms from domestic markets. For all of these reasons, states have pursued an active policy of promoting code regimes for locally-based corporations trading abroad through technical initiatives, mediation amongst stakeholders, and public endorsement of specific high profile code initiatives,[33] as well as through direct or symbolic commitment as code signatories.[34]

---

[32] Langille, B., 'General Reflections on the Relationship of Trade and Labour (or Fair Trade is Free Trade's Destiny)' in Bhagwati, J., and Hudec, R. E. (eds.), *Fair Trade and Harmonization* (Cambridge, Mass./London: MIT Press, 1996) 231.

[33] The Canadian government has been particularly active in this regard. It has commissioned a series of research studies which were presented to a major stakeholders' conference on 'Exploring Voluntary Codes in the Marketplace' (Sept. 1996), issued an extensive report—*Standards Systems: A Guide for Canadian Regulators* (Ottawa: Industry Canada, 1998)—and worked with stakeholders to develop a users' guide—*Voluntary Codes: A Guide to their Development and Use* (Ottawa: Industry Canada/Treasury Board, 1998). It has also maintained an ongoing Voluntary Codes Project with an activist Director (Kernaghan Webb, webb.kernaghan@ic.gc.ca) and a website (http://www/strategis.ic.gc.ca/volcodes). Finally, it has helped or is helping to promote the use of voluntary codes, especially by Canadian-based firms doing business abroad. See, e.g., Corporate Social Responsibility Initiative funded by Human Resources Development Canada in co-operation with the Conference Board of Canada, described in Khoury, G., Rostami, J., and Turnbull, P., *Corporate Social Responsibility: Turning Words into Action* (Ottawa: Conference Board of Canada, 1999); International Code of Ethics for Canadian Businesses, described in Culpepper and Whiteman, above, n. 13.

[34] E.g., President Clinton presided over the signing at the White House of the much-heralded Apparel Industry Partnership Code (14 Apr. 1997), *New York Times*, Sec A, 17. The AIP Code has since been denounced by its union and church signatories: see below, text at n. 45.

Finally, voluntary codes of labour standards may, paradoxically, give rise to explicit consequences in domestic and international law.[35] There is little litigation so far involving codes, especially in the labour area, and what follows is largely conjectural. However, in principle it seems possible that codes may, in given circumstances, materially affect the outcome of litigation. For example, codes which originate in agreements within sectoral organizations or amongst stakeholder groups may constitute legally binding contracts. Governments may make compliance with employment codes a formal condition of tendering and performance in procurement contracts, or in order to gain access to markets.[36] And codes may be used by judges to pour substantive content into vague normative standards—'implied' terms on which to ground an unlawful dismissal suit, a standard of 'reasonableness' to define the duty of care owed to injured workers, evidence of what constitutes 'due diligence' by corporate directors who are sued for failing to prevent workplace harassment.

Thus, state regulation and voluntary code regimes are not mutually exclusive alternatives, nor do voluntary code regimes simply reproduce systems of state regulation. To some extent the two systems exist in a state of symbiosis, and are more similar in their strategies and outcomes, more ideologically aligned, more mutually dependent and operationally integrated than is generally believed—but only to some extent. State regulation and self-regulation are neither interchangeable nor—ultimately—compatible systems. Self-regulation represents an assertion by corporations that they should be allowed to decide for themselves to what extent their interests will take priority over the claims of workers, communities, and states—an assertion which has gained both popularity and credibility in a period of globalization and neo-liberal politics. State regulation, by contrast, rests on a more democratic paradigm of governance. It proceeds from the premise that communities and states must be able to respond politically, legally, and practically through enforceable legislation to moral condemnation of the egregious failures of corporate self-regulation. However, moral condemnation tends to be muted in these days of neo-liberalism, and the practical effects of state regulation constrained by globalization and other powerful forces. So self-regulation

---

[35] See generally Webb, K., 'Voluntary Initiatives and the Law' in Gibson, R. (ed.), *Voluntary Initiatives: The New Politics of Corporate Greening* (Peterborough, Ont.: Broadview Press, 1999), 32; Webb, K., and Morrison, A., 'Voluntary Approaches, the Environment and the Law: A Canadian Perspective' in Carraro, C., and Leveque, F. (eds.), *Voluntary Approaches in Environmental Policy* (Dordrecht: Kluwer Academic Publishers, 1999), 229; Horn, N. (ed.), *Legal Problems of Codes of Conduct for Multinational Enterprises* (Deventer: Kluwer, 1980).

[36] However, this form of 'regulation by contract' exposes governments to the risk of being accused of violating international trade rules which ban non-tariff barriers and uncompensated regulatory 'takings', or of exceeding their powers as defined by domestic legislation or constitutional provisions.

and state regulation coexist—with states generally accepting that self-regulation is better than nothing, and corporations acknowledging that they had better at least be seen to regulate their workplaces with some rigour, rather than allow grievances to fester, worker militancy to grow, and pressures to build for the return of the interventionist state.

IV VOLUNTARY CODES AND NON-STATE ACTORS

A new 'discursive community' has grown up in and around the 'code industry'. It includes scholars, consultants, dispute resolvers, ombudspersons, and independent monitors who constitute a kind of civil service for code regimes; norm-setting and monitoring bodies such as the International Standards Organization, the Ethical Trading Initiative, Verité, and the Council on Economic Priorities which promulgate or monitor global labour standards; and—proof positive of the growing market for voluntary regulation—the global accounting and consulting firms which now offer 'independent' auditing services to verify code compliance. By shaping the emerging architecture of codes and code compliance strategies, by defining the interaction between codes and state law and policy, by mediating amongst the parties implicated in specific code regimes, the participants in this discursive community establish the conceptual repertoire and professional discourse of self-regulation. In this sense, they play a central role in determining the success or failure of the project of legitimation which—in my view—lies at the heart of the emergence of voluntary codes at this particular juncture in the globalization process.

   However, legitimation is not simply produced; it must be consumed as well. This may be the source of some difficulty, as corporations, governments, and members of the 'voluntary code community' may see things quite differently from workers who experience the employment practices of TNCs, or the unions, social movements, and advocacy groups which seek to alter those practices. In the former group, there seems to be a degree of optimism about voluntary codes. As a recent Canadian government report suggests:

Voluntary codes represent an innovative approach to addressing the concerns and needs of consumers, workers and citizens while at the same time helping Canadian companies to be more competitive. . . . A supplement and, in some circumstances, an alternative to traditional regulatory approaches, voluntary codes can be inexpensive, effective and flexible market instruments.[37]

---

[37] Introduction by Hon. J. Manley, Minister of Industry, and Hon. M. Massé, President of the Treasury Board, *Voluntary Codes—A Guide for their Development and Use* (Ottawa: Industry Canada/Treasury Board, 1998).

This optimism, also expressed by knowledgeable academic observers,[38] human rights activists,[39] and corporate leaders,[40] is to some extent supported by surveys of corporate practice.[41] However, there is also evidence that some firms are reluctant to adopt codes because of concerns about compliance costs and legal consequences as well as reputational risks stemming from overheated public expectations.[42] And, more importantly, many firms that have adopted codes are not actually implementing them.[43]

For workers and unions, compliance is, of course, the crucial issue. This is true in two senses. They are anxious to ensure that independent, accountable, and effective agents administer codes; and they want to see evidence that codes are actually producing positive outcomes for workers who are supposed to benefit from them. It is precisely on the issue of compliance that one of the most widely heralded transnational code initiatives—the Apparel Industry Partnership[44]—has recently run into difficulty. Labour, church, and human rights groups abandoned the AIP, protesting that corporate members had refused to agree to effective enforcement machinery or to guarantee their employees a 'living wage', and that 'the AIP code could do more harm than good, because it would give corporations a "fig leaf" to cover up their exploitation of workers abroad'.[45]

This judgement may be wrong-headed or simply premature. As some commentators have argued, a second and third generation of codes may overcome the defects of the first,[46] and each partial victory in the struggle against exploitation ultimately contributes to a more effective regime of transnational labour standards.[47] However, that effective regime may be a long time coming. In the global economy, there is no obvious way to

---

[38] Compa and Hinchcliffe-Darricarrère, above, n. 10.

[39] Forcese, C., *Commerce with Conscience? Human Rights and Corporate Codes of Conduct* and *Putting Commerce into Conduct* (Montreal: International Centre for Human Rights and Democratic Development, 1997).

[40] See, e.g., Haas, R. D., CEO of Levi Strauss, quoted in US Labor Department, above, n. 13, 14, n. 19.

[41] Lindsay, R. M., Lindsay, L. M., and Bruce, V., 'Instilling Ethical Behaviour in Organizations: A Survey of Canadian Companies' (1996) 15 *Journal of Business Ethics* 393.

[42] Cottrill, K., 'Global Codes of Conduct' (1996) 17 *Journal of Business Strategy* 55.

[43] Lindsay *et al.*, above, n. 41.

[44] Codes of Conduct in the US Apparel Industry, above, n. 13.

[45] Stephens, M., 'Code Name: Cover-Up' (Winter 1999) *UNITE Magazine*, http://www.uniteunion.org/magazine/win99/pvh.html. It appears that the resignation was actually triggered by the closure of the only unionized plant in Guatemala by one of the AIP corporate members.

[46] Compa and Hinchcliffe-Darricarrère, above, n. 10.

[47] Trubek, D., Mosher, J., and Rothstein, J., *Transnationalism in the Regulation of Labor Relations: International Regimes and Transnational Advocacy Networks* (Madison, Wis.: International Institute, University of Wisconsin-Madison, 1999).

force corporations to adhere to their own voluntary codes. Not through law: there is so far no transnational proxy for the state with a monopoly over coercive action. Not through concerted labour action: unions seldom collaborate across boundaries, and remain divided along fault lines of national origin, interest, ideology, history, and legal norms.[48] Not through consumer boycotts: citizens concerned about labour standards may be persuaded from time to exercise their rights in the 'global market for citizenship'[49] to protest the exploitation of workers at home or abroad, but they lack economic power, legal recourse, and the institutional means to sustain such initiatives.

In such a context, one might argue, half a voluntary code is better than no regulation. But while this argument may have merit, it does not address a further concern of labour, human rights advocates, and social movements: that to acknowledge the potential of corporate good intentions and to accept employer self-regulation even as a transitional measure is to legitimate the existing global economic system and its ultimately unpalatable manifestations in workplaces and communities around the world.

V CONCLUSION

So we return to the issue of legitimacy. Voluntary codes are emerging as the most significant feature of a fragile, inchoate regime of transnational labour market regulation. Employers are supposed to be the object of that regulation, but they are also its primary authors and administrators; they can conjure it up or make it disappear pretty much whenever and for whatever reason they wish. But workers—supposedly the subjects, the beneficiaries, of this regulation—lack the power to create it, significantly to influence its terms, or even to insist that they receive its promised benefits; they can only denounce it and try to rob it of its legitimacy. We must somehow square this circle.

[48] See, e.g., Haworth, N., and Ramsay, H., 'Matching the Multinationals: Obstacles to International Trade Unionism' (1986) 6 *Int'l. Journal of Sociology and Social Policy* 55; Bediner, B., *International Labour Affairs—The World Trade Unions and the Multinational Companies* (Oxford: Clarendon Press, 1987); but for a more optimistic view see Windmuller, J., 'The International Trade Union Movement' in Blanpain, R. (ed.), *Comparative Labour Law and Industrial Relations in Industrialized Market Economies* (4th revd. edn, Deventer: Kluwer, 1990).

[49] Downes, D., and Janda, R., 'Virtual Citizenship' (1998) 13 *Canadian Journal of Law and Society* 27; and see Schneiderman, D., 'Constitutionalizing the Culture-Ideology of Consumerism' (1998) 7 *Social & Legal Studies* 213.

25

Emancipation through Law or the Emasculation of Law? The Nation-State, the EU, and Gender Equality at Work

CLAIRE KILPATRICK*

CLAIRE KILPATRICK*

I GENDER EQUALITY AS AN EU POLICY AREA—THE ROAD TO SUPRA-STARDOM

No star has ever shone or continues to shine so brightly in the EU labour law firmament as that of gender equality at work. To be sure, when the six founding Member States signed the Treaty of Rome (1957) creating the EU's precursor, the European Economic Community (EEC), star labour law status was extremely easy to achieve. The obligation in Article 119 (now Article 141 EC) for Member States to ensure equal pay for equal work was the *only* binding labour law measure which would have any lasting significance.[1] Though placed in a Title of the Treaty entitled 'Social Policy', the remaining labour law content (Articles 117 and 118) consisted merely of exhortatory statements to co-operate in the social field and wishful assertions that realizing the common market would itself lead to improved working conditions and living standards for workers in the EEC. Article 120, which accepted the need to maintain the existing equivalence of paid holiday schemes, was simply a concession to France and played no role whatsoever thereafter.[2]

Nor should it be thought that the inclusion of the obligation to ensure

---

* My thanks go to Karl Klare for very helpful comments on the substance and style of earlier drafts.

[1] At that time it stated: 'Each Member State shall during the first stage ensure and subsequently maintain the application of the principle that men and women should receive equal pay for equal work.

For the purpose of this Article, "pay" means the ordinary basic or minimum wage or salary and any other consideration, whether in cash or in kind, which the worker receives, directly or indirectly, in respect of his employment from his employer.

Equal pay without discrimination based on sex means:

a that pay for the same work at piece rates shall be calculated on the basis of the same unit of measurement;

b that pay for work at time rates shall be the same for the same job.'

[2] See also, again at French insistence, Part Two of the special Protocol concerning France which permitted it to take special measures to safeguard industries penalized by overtime payments. See generally Collins, D., *The European Communities: The Social Policy of the First Phase* (London: Martin Robertson, 1975).

equal pay represented a determined stance on the part of the Treaty's signatories to rout out the evil of gender pay discrimination. This is so for two principal reasons. First, the real motivation for inserting Article 119 (now Article 141 EC) into the Treaty of Rome was French insistence that lower gender wage differentials in key female-dominated French industries, when compared with gender wage differentials in other EEC Member States, would distort competition in the common market.[3] Indeed, the equal pay obligation was originally placed in a title on 'Distortions of Competition' and was moved at the last minute to give some content to the extremely skimpy and late-conceived Title on 'Social Policy'.[4] Secondly, few policy-makers imagined there would be any realistically effective method for enforcing the legal obligation of equal pay against the Member States. The Treaty did not state that its provisions were enforceable by individuals and, in any case, Article 119 was explicitly formulated as a principle addressed to Member States, not as a legally enforceable right for the women of Europe. The only enforcement opportunities clearly set out in the Treaty were either for one Member State to sue another for failure to respect Treaty provisions, or for the European Commission—the Community's watchdog—to take infringement proceedings against Member States for failure to comply with Treaty obligations. At best, this promised sparse and 'thin' enforcement of the equal pay principle. Article 119 sat in the Treaty, unused, no doubt very much as the drafters had assumed.

However, both its presence in the Treaty and its perceived innocuousness proved crucial in the early 1970s. Three new Member States— Denmark, Ireland, and the United Kingdom—joined the original six. This new influx, combined with the entry of a critical mass of informed women into the Commission drafting process, created a policy environment in which further legislative action relating to women at work was seen as an important part of a then broadly perceived need to give 'a human face' to the economic community.[5] Article 119's *presence* was crucial because it provided a textual locus around which arguments that new policy initiatives should focus on gender equality at work could cluster. This is one reason why the EU has a much longer and deeper record of tackling gender inequality rather than discrimination on other invidious grounds, such as race, disability, age, or sexual orientation. The push in the 1970s ultimately resulted in a substantial EC-level legislative output. Two

[3] See Barnard C., 'The Economic Objectives of Article 119' in Hervey, T., and O'Keeffe, D. (eds.), *Sex Equality Law in the European Union* (Chichester: Wiley, 1996) 321.

[4] See Hoskyns C., *Integrating Gender: Women, Law and Politics in the European Union* (London: Verso, 1996) 57.

[5] Shanks, M., 'Introductory Article: The Social Policy of the European Communities' (1977) 14 *Common Market Law Review* 375 and Hoskyns, above, n. 4, chs. 5 and 6.

central directives dealing respectively with equal pay (1975) and equal treatment (1976) at work were passed. Three further directives dealing with statutory social security, occupational social security, and self-employed women workers passed through the EC legislative process in the ensuing decade.

The *perceived innocuousness* of Article 119 was equally critical in prompting this legislative activity. It has been remarked:

> It was important that, on the whole, the officials and politicians who negotiated the women's Directives in the 1970s saw the issues involved as marginal and as ones on which concessions could be made. . . . They clearly had no idea at the time of how far reaching the effects of these Directives would prove to be.[6]

The directives were passed just in time. No sooner had the politicians agreed on the Equal Pay and Equal Treatment Directives than, in 1976, the efforts of a Belgian labour lawyer, Eliane Vogel-Polsky, to see whether the European Court of Justice could breathe some life into Article 119 (now Article 141 EC), finally bore substantial fruit in the *Defrenne* case.[7] This concerned a female Belgian flight attendant working for the SABENA airline who was forced to retire at the age of 40 when male flight attendants were not so required. The Court of Justice's judgment in *Defrenne* kick-started gender equality litigation at supranational level. It is also a crucial staging-post in the history of ECJ 'constitutionalization' of the Treaties.

Several aspects of this case can help us understand and probe more effectively the subsequent trajectories of gender equality as an EU policy area. First, we should consider the genesis of the case. As noted, one reason Member States were sanguine about their 'obligation' to ensure equal pay was that they were convinced that the Treaty afforded no possibilities for individual women to enforce this obligation against them in national courts. True, the drafters had included a preliminary reference mechanism in Article 177 (now Article 234 EC) of the Treaty. This procedure permits national courts to ask the Court of Justice questions ('preliminary references') about the interpretation of Community law, needed to resolve particular cases before them. The Court of Justice answers the national court in a preliminary ruling. The *Defrenne* case came before the Court as a preliminary reference from the Belgian Cour du Travail. As authoritative commentators have remarked, the presence of a 'pre-federal device'[8] such as Article 177 (now Article 234 EC) in the original Treaty

---

[6] Hoskyns, C., 'The European Community's Policy on Women in the Context of 1992' (1992) 15 *Women's Studies International Forum* 22.

[7] Case 43/75 *Defrenne* v. *SABENA (No. 2)* [1976] ECR 455.

[8] Sciarra, S., 'Integration through Courts: Article 177 as a Pre-federal Device' in Sciarra, S. (ed.), *Labour Law in the Courts: National Courts and the ECJ* (Oxford: Hart, 2001) 1.

clearly presaged both assertions of the supremacy of EC law and also, more unusually for treaty obligations, that EC law would be understood to create rights enforceable in national courts ('direct effect').[9]

However, unanticipated and unanticipatable by the Member States were two particular developments relating to the enforcement of Treaty and other substantive obligations and to the Article 177 (now Article 234 EC) preliminary reference mechanism. Although in the earlier seminal case of *Van Gend en Loos*[10] the Court of Justice had ruled that Treaty obligations could in certain circumstances create *directly effective rights* for individuals which required protection in national courts, it had stated that only certain, special types of Treaty obligation would be suitable for operating as directly effective norms. Article 119 (now Article 141 EC) clearly failed to pass the tests making a treaty provision appropriate for direct effect set out in *Van Gend en Loos*. The equal pay obligation in Article 119 (now Article 141 EC) was framed as a general principle, not as a clear legal obligation. Most significantly, the Treaty obligation at issue in *Van Gend en Loos* was negative and unconditional. The Court had expressly adverted to these characteristics as making direct effect appropriate on the basis that the obligation was self-executing and required no further action at Member State level. As Eliane Vogel-Polsky recognized, it was much more difficult, though necessary for a successful outcome, to see Article 119 as self-executing.[11] Because it appeared to establish a positive and open-ended obligation requiring further Member State action, direct effectiveness of Article 119 was apt to provoke non-uniform effects across the Community. Realization of gender pay equality would therefore require ongoing communication between the ECJ and national courts, which would not necessarily be forthcoming and which was highly unlikely to occur evenly across the territory of the Community. Notwithstanding these difficulties, the Court ruled in *Defrenne* that Article 119 was capable of being invoked by individuals before national courts. That Article 119 is expressed as a principle the Court took to mean not that it was vague, but, rather, that it is a fundamental right. That it requires implementation by further action at Member State level could limit but not bar its capacity to be directly effective.[12]

The second unanticipated development was the synergy that emerged between the preliminary reference mechanism (requiring dialogue and

---

[9] Craig, P., 'Once upon a Time in the West: Direct Effect and the Federalization of EEC Law' (1992) 12 *OJLS* 453, 459; Shapiro, M., 'The European Court of Justice' in Craig, P., and de Búrca, G. (eds.), *The Evolution of EU Law* (Oxford: Oxford University Press, 1999), 321, 330–1.   [10] Case 26/62 [1963] ECR 1.
[11] Vogel-Polsky, E., 'L'Article 119 du traité de Rome—peut-il être considéré comme self-executing?' [1967] *Journal des Tribunaux*, cited in Hoskyns, above, n. 4, 68.
[12] See further the analysis of Craig, above, n. 9, 467–9 on which this draws.

co-operation between national courts and the Court of Justice), and the doctrines of direct effect and supremacy. This combination has flourished beyond all expectations. Gender equality became one of the most prominent instances of blossoming communication between courts on EC law sources, with communication not confined merely to preliminary references. These processes of listening and talking about EC gender equality sources have produced some stunning results. The ECJ adopted a helpful position on the relationship between pregnancy and discrimination, particularly when compared with US and Canadian courts. Its jurisprudence holds that pregnancy discrimination is direct and non-comparative discrimination. When a woman is pregnant, it is direct discrimination to dismiss her or subject her to any other disadvantageous treatment, irrespective of whether a sick man would have been treated equally badly.[13] National legislation excluding women from (almost all parts of) the armed forces has been condemned, as has state policy requiring women to leave the armed forces when they become pregnant.[14] The Court also took a strong stand with regard to indirect (disparate impact) gender discrimination against part-time workers.[15] EC law has also made gender discrimination much more costly than it had been under Member State law. Ceilings and limits on the remedies for gender discrimination at work have been found to contravene Community law.[16]

Of course, the results have not always been so favourable. Court of Justice judgments have often been unclear or overly cautious, and they have sometimes demonstrated little understanding of the issues at stake. However, overall it is fair to say that more positive legal developments in the area of gender equality have probably happened because of the existence of the EU than would have happened in its absence. In the legal development of gender equality the 'costs of "non-Europe"' would have been higher in many countries, especially the UK, than the 'costs of Europe' proved to be.

Gender equality has been by far the most active area of preliminary-

---

[13] The central cases being Case C–178/88. *Handels- og Kontorfunktionærernes Forbund i Danmark* v. *Dansk Arbejdsgiverforening (Hertz)* [1990] ECR I–3979 and Case C–177/88 *Dekker* v. *Stichting Vormingscentrum voor Jong Volwassen (VJV-Centrum)* [1990] ECR I–3941.

[14] Case C–273/97 *Sirdar* v. *The Army Board and Secretary of State for Defence* [1999] ECR I–7403; Case C–285/98 *Kreil* v. *Bundesrepublik Deutschland* [2000] ECR I–69. See, in the UK, the Ministry of Defence's admission of liability with regard to the dismissal of pregnant servicewomen and the subsequent significant compensation pay-outs, discussed below.

[15] The seminal case is Case 170/84 *Bilka Kaufhaus GmbH* v. *Karin Weber von Hartz* [1986] ECR 1607.

[16] For detailed analysis of the relevant cases see Kilpatrick, C., 'Turning Remedies Around: A Sectoral Analysis of the Court of Justice' in de Búrca, G., and Weiler, J. H. H. (eds), *The European Court of Justice* (Oxford: Oxford University Press, 2001).

reference making in social policy.[17] Moreover, although employment rights and Treaty bases for making labour law have expanded dramatically, particularly in the wake of the Treaty of Amsterdam, gender equality continues to keep way ahead of the pack. It has now been elevated, by Articles 2 and 3 of the EC Treaties, to the status of a core task and activity of the EC. Gender equality constitutes one of the guiding principles for allocation of monies under the EC's structural funds. It is one of the four pillars of EU employment policy. Gender equality is now a central feature of the *imperium, dominium*[18] and judicial powers of the EU.

Thus to explain the law on gender equality at work today in Italy, the UK, or any Member State requires an appreciation of multi-levelled, polycentric interactions between national and supranational courts and legislatures over a substantial period of time. How does this affect understandings of labour law in Europe? First, it is now clear that this area of labour law, at least, is no longer simply 'national'. Secondly, because of the preliminary reference mechanism and the constitutionalization of the Treaties, courts play a key role in constructing important aspects of labour law. Courts increasingly have the final word over legislatures as well as more discursive freedom to decide what those words should be. Together, these developments accomplished a paradigm-shift in our understanding of what labour law is and where it comes from.

For these reasons, it is vitally important to evaluate what has happened to date and what lessons can be learned for the future evolution of labour law in the EU, especially concerning other discrimination rights. This task is particularly crucial in the light of recent additions to the EU anti-discrimination canon. The Treaty of Amsterdam, which came into force on 1 May 1999, added a new Article 13 to the EC Treaty. Article 13 provides a legal base for the EU legislature to adopt directives outlawing discrimination on a wide number of grounds in addition to sex and gender: racial or ethnic origin, religion or belief, disability, age, and sexual orientation. This legal base has quickly been used to produce two important directives encompassing all these grounds.[19]

Analysis and assessment of the desirability of 'supranationalizing' gender equality can be heuristically presented as two contrasting perspec-

---

[17] In Jan. 2001, 106 references concerning gender equality at work had been made out of an overall total of just under 4,200 references made to the Court on all issues. See Kilpatrick, C., 'Gender Equality: a Fundamental Dialogue' in Sciarra, above, n. 8, 31–130.

[18] See, further, Freedland, M., 'Employment Policy' in Davies, P., Lyon-Caen, A., Sciarra, S., and Simitis, S. (eds.), *European Community Labour Law—Principles and Perspectives. Liber Amicorum Lord Wedderburn* (Oxford: Clarendon Press, 1996), 275.

[19] See Directive 2000/43/EC [2000] OJ L180/22 (implementing the principle of equal treatment between persons irrespective of racial or ethnic origin), and Directive 2000/78/EC [2000] OJ L303/16, establishing a general framework for equal treatment in employment and occupation. This Treaty also renumbered Art. 119 as Art. 141 EC.

tives which I have termed respectively 'the emancipation through law' perspective and 'the emasculation of law' perspective. The first views the 'supranationalizing' of gender equality as an example of the creation of new opportunity structures in legal procedures and texts that can be mobilized in the struggle for emancipation by oppressed groups. EC law provides such opportunities in two ways. On the one hand, by simply going to a local labour court one can shake off the confines of national law and access legal resources beyond the nation-state. On the other, the magnified role of courts allows groups to escape from sole reliance on political or industrial persuasion of sluggish legislatures, employers, and unions to remove discriminatory practices and norms. A judgment from a national or supranational court that a norm does not conform to Community obligations will often suffice to prod legislatures and other norm producers to take remedial action.

Although they can be distinguished, it is clear that the 'public interest' litigation perspective outlined above is, in some respects, related to two other types of perspective. The first encompasses those that are more generally integrationist, that is, those who see the EU project as a positive one and therefore think that the faster and deeper legal integration proceeds the better. From this point of view, integration in the area of gender equality is to be applauded in the same way as progress towards freer movement of capital or a single currency in the EU. The second consists of those who see the EU as forming part of a more general project to harmonize law across national boundaries, to create a single set of legal norms for all of (Western European) humanity. Litigation on extra-national sources is seen as one way of helping to achieve this goal of convergence, as is the making of codes harmonizing different European national systems of private and public law. Proponents of both EU 'integration' and European 'convergence' can point to the supranationalizing of gender equality as an example of the irrational limitations on policy imposed by the national, the need to move beyond the national and the benefits that can be reaped for the peoples of Europe from such moves.

By contrast, the 'emasculation of law' perspective argues, on a number of different grounds, that EU law can have a detrimental effect on national legal integrity, cultural traditions, and political checks and balances. There is both a private law and a public law strain to this argument. Both are largely engaged in challenging the assumptions and exposing the (at times covert) normative agendas of advocates of convergence and integration. These arguments, too, can be associated with other distinct but related perspectives. There is an ever-present danger that arguments within this kind of perspective will lend support to narrow, nationally-bounded, and historically determined visions of law, culture, and democracy.

Both perspectives cast valuable light on the 'supranationalization' project as the following discussion attempts to demonstrate. However, I will also test both perspectives by holding them against a detailed and comparative analysis of the ongoing stories of 'supranationalization' of gender equality. This exercise, it will be seen, challenges empirical and normative assertions of each perspective. Labour law is a key substantive area of Community law (along with environmental and consumer protection law) which provides the toughest challenges for both the emancipation and the emasculation perspectives. Finding an acceptable synthesis of the difficult issues raised by the emancipation and emasculation perspectives is one of the key issues facing labour lawyers (and EU lawyers) in Europe today.

II THE EMASCULATION OF LAW?

I begin with the second of the two perspectives outlined above. Gender equality is a particularly good example with which to examine both the private and public law strains of the emasculation of law arguments, as individual employment rights, in particular those viewed as 'fundamental rights', straddle both private and public law. Because of this, gender equality has been discussed in both sets of emasculation of law arguments.

The private law strain and gender equality

Fortunately, some of the most interesting labour lawyers in Europe have also been active in the private law field. To understand the passion of the emasculation arguments we need to see what private/labour lawyers within the emasculation perspective were arguing against. For this we can turn to the colourful pro-convergence manifesto of Cappelletti:

Twenty-one countries—to count quite artificially, only those in the 'West', from Iceland to Cyprus—each with a distinct legal system, represent an irrational, suicidal division within a modern world which demands larger and larger open areas of personal, cultural, commercial, labor, and other exchanges. Harmonization, coordination, interdependence are absolute needs of our time; and history is there to provide clear evidence that division is not an ineluctable fate, that indeed division is a relatively recent phenomenon in a Continent which, for centuries in past epochs, was characterized by a law common to most of its peoples.[20]

---

[20] 'Introduction' in Cappelletti, M. (ed.), *New Perspectives for a Common Law of Europe* (Leyden-London-Boston: EUI/Sijthoff, 1978) 1.

This neatly summarizes four of the main tenets shared by those favouring convergence. Legal convergence is already happening because of functional societal convergence. However, it is not happening fast enough and urgently needs a helping hand, particularly through the media of legal education and unification of law projects. Failure to converge legally is not only messy but dangerous. Legal convergence is nothing new in Europe; the territorial limits imposed by the nation-state should be seen as an atypical historical blip rather than as an inevitable arrangement.

Cappelletti's vision can be set against the views of Legrand, vehemently unconvinced of the tenets upon which the desirability and possibility of legal convergence are constructed. Legrand contends that legal convergence programmes, such as the project to write a European Civil Code:

effectively represent . . . an attack on pluralism, a desire to suppress antinomy, a blind attempt at the diminution of particularity. Through the ages, there have developed a thousand ways of eliminating 'other' cultures. They all have had in common the desire to institute a unity, that is, a totalitarianism. Culture in the single always represents an act of power . . .[21]

A towering figure in comparative law, private law, and labour law is Kahn-Freund. His vision of when institutional transfers could occur has been expanded upon and recast by both Collins and Teubner, through the application of autopoietic theory. Teubner, drawing extensively on Kahn-Freund, has recently provided a clear and wide-ranging exposition of this specific private law strain of argument against the emasculation of law.[22] He takes issue with three other types of explanation of how law moves between different legal systems. Convergence theorists wrongly assume, first, that global socio-economic convergence is occurring and, secondly, that socio-economic convergence necessarily entails legal convergence. Cultural comparativists, such as Legrand, overcontextualize law so that it cannot be separated out from (national) culture in general. Other comparativists make the opposite mistake when they assume that law is highly autonomous from social, economic, and political factors.

Teubner and Collins use, but recast, Kahn-Freund to escape the impasse of law being either overcontextualized or overautonomous. Law *is* socially embedded but establishes *selective* connectivity of *varying intensity* (from

---

[21] Legrand, P., 'Against a European Civil Code' (1997) 60 *MLR* 44, 53. He also observes '[a] European Civil Code partakes of an ahistoricist reinvention of Europe, for what has long characterised Europe is precisely the cultural heteronomies within the whole [58] . . . [it] is a utopian enterprise, for it suggests that legal cultures which purport to give normative strength to forms of behaviour developed in historically different contexts can be unified [60]'.

[22] Teubner, G., 'Legal Irritants: Good Faith in British Law or How Unifying Law Ends Up in New Divergences' (1998) 61 *MLR* 11.

loosely coupled to tightly coupled) with different social subsystems. This set-up permits the following two propositions to be made with regard to transfers from one legal system to another: First, deep structures of legal culture will be encountered in any type of legal transfer. The 'foreign law' will irritate the system it enters. Unlike a legal 'transplant', it will be neither rejected nor accepted; rather it will unleash perturbations which will transform both it and its surrounding environment. Secondly, in situations of tight coupling between law and a specific social subsystem (such as economics, politics, or science), the additional and highly significant obstacle of resistance to the transfer from outside law will also have to be confronted.

With this in mind we can see why Kahn-Freund in 1978 and, more recently, Hugh Collins, both emphatically concluded that Article 119 (now Article 141 EC), far from being a success story, is a paradigm of an imprudent, intrusive, and undesirable European legal intervention. Kahn-Freund's principal convergence criterion was whether sufficient homogeneity in political and social conditions had been attained between countries with regard to the area where the harmonizing legal intervention was proposed. If it had not, legal convergence measures were highly undesirable. Applying this to Article 119 of the Treaty of Rome (now Article 141 EC), he stated:

Can one impose on a number of old countries with different roles of female labour in the economy, and different traditions, a regime of equal pay without providing a very long period of adjustment? Was it not inevitable that in the practice of the Community, concessions had to be made, and that we have here, as the *Defrenne* case has so clearly shown, that discrepancy between the postulates of the law and the possibilities of society which the prudent lawgiver should shun at almost any cost?[23]

Kahn-Freund's analysis of and reaction to *Defrenne* is therefore principally based on the second proposition outlined above (namely, that local resistance will impede transfers). Hugh Collins, by contrast, bases his conclusions on Article 119 (now Article 141 EC) on arguments derived from both propositions (that is, that transfers will both irritate the recipient legal culture and be resisted by non-legal social systems).[24] Moreover, his conclusions are reached despite the enormous judicial development of

[23] Kahn-Freund, O., 'Common Law and Civil Law—Imaginary and Real Obstacles to Assimilation' in Cappelletti, above, n. 20, 137, 167.

[24] Collins, H., 'European Private Law and the Cultural Identity of States' [1995] *European Review of Private Law* 353. On the second proposition, '[t]he new European . . . encounters similar problems [to those in private law] when dismissing traditional sources of personal differentiation. Consider, for example, the history of Article 119 . . . which insists upon equal pay for women; the new European has no shadow of doubt that this law is fully justified in rejecting the discriminatory culture against women, yet the persistence of differentials in pay between men and women despite the law suggests ideas of women's work and their

EC gender equality guarantees since 1978 when Kahn-Freund made his comments. Collins' arguments with regard to the first proposition—deep legal cultures and legal irritants—are also highly pertinent to considering the supranationalizing of gender equality. He makes two points here. First, common rules can never lead to a uniform approach in different Member States as the conceptual differences between legal systems reflect different 'deep' justifications for the imposition of legal obligations and the creation of legal rights, rather than mere technical contrasts. The implication of this seems to be that common rules are, for this reason, a bad idea. Secondly, separate legal systems are distant environments to each other; autopoietically speaking, one legal system cannot hear 'noise' emitted from other legal systems and will not therefore respond to what it cannot hear.[25]

These arguments offer many positive insights and raise important questions for the emancipationist view. However, first, I note three reservations about these private law/labour law arguments.

The first concerns how to measure the effectiveness of EC gender equality sources and how to use that measurement to evaluate legal intervention. Kahn-Freund and Collins measure effectiveness exclusively in functional terms of whether goal X has been achieved by law Y. In turn, goals are defined in such a way that only macro-level attainment—has Article 119 (now Article 141 EC) narrowed or eliminated gender pay differentials in Europe?—is regarded as valid. This calibration results in a double condemnation of Article 119 (now Article 141 EC). The first, emphasized by Kahn-Freund, is that it is dangerous to use law where it will not work, because of societal resistance, as this dilutes the normative gravity of law in other situations where legal intervention could potentially work. The second, emphasized by Collins, is that it is problematic for European law to impose a certain cultural vision with its associated macro-level goals—gender inequality is wrong and therefore European gender pay-differentials must be closed—on (national) communities that do not share that vision.

Although functional, macro-level goal measurement is clearly one important way of evaluating legal intervention, our understanding of law would be significantly impoverished if it were treated as the most important, or only, method of evaluation. This is particularly true when considering laws to protect diffuse interests, such as environmental protection, or to confer rights on disadvantaged groups, such as women and ethnic minorities, which are often constitutionally protected as fundamental

---

inferior worth run deep in the culture of communities. There is obviously a danger . . . that in drawing a distinction between valuable and invidious aspects of cultural identity, . . . the law will be imposing on the different communities a particular culture belonging to an elitist group' (at 365).

[25] Ibid., 356 and 355.

rights. Here, law becomes a bearer of symbolic messages and, particularly through litigation, a site for struggle by individuals or groups *within* communities. Negatively to evaluate the importance of the UDHR or the new Article 13 EC solely by pointing out the degree of societal discrimination against the disabled, older people, women, gays, or ethnic minorities would surely be to miss the point. This, of course, is not news. Indeed, as we shall see, Collins has provided an elegant exposition of this type of argument elsewhere.[26]

The second reservation concerns the implicit assumption that it is always desirable to avoid irritating a culturally established *status quo* within a social subsystem. Sometimes the aim of law is not merely to tweak or facilitate social ordering but to smash an unjust and unfair *status quo*. From this perspective, the Kahn-Freund and Collins' accounts want law to be too obeisant to existing arrangements in other social sub-systems. Without denying the well-known problems of law as a vehicle for achieving radical social change, the traffic between law and other social sub-systems should not be allowed to go just in one direction.

The third reservation concerns the relationship between EU law and national law. As Collins and Teubner amply demonstrate, writing from the emasculationist perspective tends to appreciate EU norms within the confines of a sensibility that considers them as *foreign* in the same way as, say, US law is foreign to France. But this approach assumes precisely the point at issue, namely whether national law can properly be understood as an autonomous and hermetic legal system. Surely the thick and continuous EU/Member State interactions in the area of gender equality, particularly through preliminary references and other judicial communications, show that this is an inadequate description. To give one example, Spain and Germany have communicated on the meaning of equal value at work for women via the intermediary of the German preliminary reference in *Rummler*, which was picked up and developed extensively by the Spanish Constitutional Court.[27] Does it make sense to reduce these developments to an EU norm 'intruding' into the German and Spanish legal orders? Would not a more authentic characterization also take account of the precipitating role of legal actors within the Member States and the dialogue between them and EU legal actors which perhaps brought

[26] Collins, H., 'Democracy and Adjudication' in MacCormick, N., and Birks, P. (eds.), *The Legal Mind: Essays for Tony Honoré* (Oxford: Clarendon Press, 1986) 67.

[27] See Kilpatrick, above, n. 17, 52, 102–3. Case 237/85 *Rummler* v. *Dato-Druck GmbH* [1986] ECR 2101. The preliminary reference in this case asked whether and how physical strength should be counted in the comparative evaluation of male and female jobs. The ECJ replied that job classification systems must be based on criteria which do not differ according to whether the work is carried out by a man or a woman and must be organized as a whole in such a manner that they do not have the practical effect of discriminating generally against members of one sex.

the three legal environments into a closer relationship? In any event, is it not clear that we need a new vocabulary and new analytic tools to describe the legal space of Europe in which significant bodies of law, such as that concerning gender equality, are neither exclusively produced nor bounded by national legal systems?

The public law strain and gender equality

Harlow provides us with a textbook example of an argument from public law against the Court's extensive rulings in the area of gender equality. In 1993 the Court decided a case brought by a pioneering litigant, Helen Marshall, claiming that a ceiling on compensation in UK law prevented her from obtaining full compensation for the loss she had suffered as a result of gender discrimination with regard to rules concerning retirement age. The Court decided in *Marshall II* that ceilings on compensation contravened the Community law right to an effective remedy. As a result, there is no ceiling on remedies for discrimination under the UK Sex Discrimination Act 1975.[28] At around the same time, the UK Ministry of Defence conceded liability to pay compensation to ex-servicewomen who were dismissed because they were pregnant on the ground that this was gender discrimination contrary to the 1976 Equal Treatment Directive. The *Marshall II* decision meant that substantial numbers of ex-servicewomen could obtain formally unlimited compensation for the losses they had suffered as a result of this policy. The UK government paid out over £55 million in damages. Harlow, surveying this in the context of other related Community-law developments, states that it had the effect of:

Precluding governments from imposing prior restraints on the quantum of compensation (arguably both a legitimate and sensible response from government) . . . £55 million [is] no mean sum even in the perspective of a state welfare budget! It is not wholly irrelevant that the affair attracted a great deal of unfavourable publicity; war veterans' organisations reminded the public that young women who had chosen to rear a family, and many of whom had found new employment, were receiving much greater sums in damages than the pensions awarded to seriously incapacitated war victims or their widows. And since the Treaty covers only gender equality, the decision had the incidental effect of introducing a grave inequality into UK law, as the ruling did not bite in race discrimination cases.[29]

---

[28] Case C-271/91 *Marshall* v. *Southampton and South-West Hampshire Area Health Authority* (*Marshall II*) [1993] ECR I-3313. The ceiling on compensation was removed by the Sex Discrimination and Equal Pay (Remedies) Regulations 1993, SI 1993/2798, made by the Secretary of State for Employment under s. 2(2) of the European Communities Act 1972.

[29] Harlow, C., 'Francovich and the Problem of the Disobedient State' (1996) 2 *European L. Journal* 199, 212.

A number of public law arguments against developments of this nature involve placing courts in context. To begin, courts do not control the desire to litigate which places cases before them. Expansive judicial doctrines can place pressures on courts, with floods of litigation resulting. A second contextualizing move compares the institutional roles of courts with those of the legislature and the executive. Expansive doctrines emanating from courts are arguably problematic in two senses. First, complex polycentric disputes are shoehorned by the nature of the judicial process into bipolar disputes between two 'individuals' (overwhelmingly, in the Community context, bodies corporate). Secondly, the narrow picture produced through judicial resolution allows unplanned, and often less efficient, distribution of limited state resources. Would the £55 million or some part thereof, for example, have been better spent on funding public child-care? Judicial resolution of disputes obscures the issues involved in complex debates about the optimum allocation of finite state resources.

To these general arguments about the roles of courts in democracies, Harlow presents two additional arguments: one concerning culture and one concerning transnational courts such as the European Court of Justice or the European Court of Human Rights. Put together, they provide a three-pronged argument against installing highly contested rights at supranational level. First, in line with the views of Legrand that law is a specific cultural artifact grounded in (national) communities, 'rights have little authority or content in the absence of a common ethical life . . . looking to rights to arbitrate deep conflicts—rather than seeking to moderate them through the compromises of politics—is a recipe for a low intensity civil war'.[30] The error of creating highly contested rights is compounded by the fact that questions about *rights* often end up being decided in courts rather than in other public forums. Where the right concerned is an EU right these problems are deepened as the power of decision is transferred to the Court of Justice. Above nation-state level, courts in Europe have tended to be much stronger players and some have vigorously encouraged rights-based strategies in order to consolidate their position in an emergent European legal space.[31]

Once again there are many valuable points here to which I shall return, but first a reservation. As with the private law arguments discussed above, these arguments, especially those relating to culture, lose considerable nuance by virtue of being directed at a very specific opponent—

---

[30] Harlow, C., 'Voices of Difference in a Polyphonic Community' in Beaumont, P., Lyons, C., and Walker, N. (eds), *Convergence and Divergence in European Public Law* (Oxford: Hart, 2002). See Legrand, above, n. 21.

[31] See also the chapters by Harlow and Kilpatrick in Kilpatrick, C., Novitz, T., and Skidmore, P. (eds.), *The Future of Remedies in Europe* (Oxford: Hart, 2000).

advocates of the convergence of public law in the EU who assume that legal questions are essentially technical matters that are functionally equivalent throughout the EU and reflect common European values.

Neil Walker observes that arguments such as Harlow's, while effective and necessary to combat 'convergence fundamentalists', provide limited assistance in understanding the complex mix of polycentric law production in the EU, as exemplified by gender equality. In other words, the truth lies with the conclusion neither that complete convergence is possible nor that no convergence is possible. The game is elsewhere as gender equality demonstrates: it concerns how to describe, measure, and evaluate the great spectrum of selective convergence developments in Europe.[32]

Walker's reflections provide a convenient bridge between the emasculation perspective and the emancipation perspective:

The demands for cultural recognition from the nation state, and from its defining products, such as its legal system, must be balanced against the alternative demands for cultural recognition from ethnic and linguistic minorities; from national minorities within multi-national states; from 'intercultural' epistemic and functional communities such as refugees, religious movements, business and trading communities and feminist movements; and indeed, from crossnational or supranational movements trying to sustain, develop or defend regional or continental identities.

III EMANCIPATION THROUGH LAW?

The supranationalization of gender equality is more commonly described as an exercise in emancipation. The vision presented is of lone women, their names inscribed in the cases—Gabrielle Defrenne, Helen Marshall, Gisella Rummler, Carole Webb—bravely challenging monstrous discriminatory national laws and practices armed with EU gender equality norms and the assistance of the Herculean Court of Justice. Even the British judiciary has noted this happy conjunction.[33] Progress in gender equality is also a metaphor for the development of the Community legal order by the Court of Justice by reliance on the effective judicial

---

[32] Walker, N., 'Culture, Democracy and the Convergence of Public Law: Some Scepticism about Scepticism' in Beaumont *et al.*, above, n. 30.

[33] 'Appropriately, in the birth of a new legal order, pregnant women have been pioneering litigants'. Lord Justice Mummery, 'The Community Law Impact in Employment Cases' in Andenas, M., and Jacobs, F. (eds.), *European Community Law in the English Courts* (Oxford: Oxford University Press, 1998) 191, 197 (referring to the ex-servicewomen pregnancy awards discussed above).

protection of individuals. This account emanates both from EU-law specialists[34] and, somewhat more cautiously, labour lawyers.[35]

There can be no doubting the excitement and innovation in the sphere of gender equality which this depiction reflects. EU law has permitted litigants to access resources beyond the nation-state which, in a much stronger fashion than international law, are independent of national rules of acceptance for their authority and come backed up by direct effect and supremacy. Moreover, this access does not require preliminary references to be made to the Court of Justice. In particular, as familiarity with EU gender equality sources has evolved, many of the most exciting developments have been realized by national courts utilizing EU sources.[36]

Moreover, the act of litigating can itself be subversive of existing social inequalities. Hugh Collins suggests that the Rule of Law can only be imperfectly realized. For this reason, we should acknowledge and accept that both legislatures and courts in fact operate in part by listening to voices which make themselves heard either by being professionally organized (pressure groups) or being authoritative (scholarly writings). He urges the following agenda:

Although professional and technical elites enjoy considerable advantages in influencing the judicial reasoning, the door is ajar for alternative conceptions of social norms to be presented. . . . The open texture of legal norms makes the legal system a focus of struggle rather than an exclusive implement of the powerful. . . . Critical theory suggests that marginal groups may transform the content of the legal order, and thus of the constitution of society itself, by imitating the professional advocacy of the existing generators of wisdom and norms of behaviour.[37]

These arguments, and the tangible if imperfect victories for gender equality on the legal terrain, also cast new light on how unions, working with

[34] Rasmussen, H., *The European Court of Justice* (Copenhagen: Gad Jura, 1998), 234: '[t]here is something intellectually stimulating in the circumstance that the odd couple of female-dominated anti-sex discrimination activists and organisations and the Court became companions-in arms in a fight for the achievement of quite considerable progress in the cause of gender equality treatment. Together, the two actors succeeded in uprooting many of the vicious phenomena of sex discrimination characterising European job markets while they both at the same time pursued their own agendas.'
[35] Fredman, S., 'Social Law in the European Union: The Impact of the Lawmaking Process' in Craig, P., and Harlow, C., *Lawmaking in the European Union* (The Hague: Kluwer, 1998) 386, 402: '[t]he ECJ, by giving a voice to individual litigants and pressure groups, may well have increased the participative element of democracy in the Union as a whole. Indeed, this is one of the few arenas within the EU in which such individual participation is possible, and in which so direct a response may be elicited'.
[36] See, e.g., the UK *ex parte EOC* litigation discussed in Kilpatrick, C., 'Community or Communities of Courts in European Legal Integration: Sex Equality Dialogues and the UK Courts' (1998) *European L. Journal* 121; see also the use of EU gender equality sources by the Spanish Constitutional Court discussed in Kilpatrick, above, n. 17, 94 ff.
[37] Collins, above, n. 26, extracts from 81–2.

equality agencies and other groups, can realize new types of participation at work by focusing on new constituencies and different goals.[38] The focus shifts from central reliance on collective bargaining and industrial action to multi-layered strategies that include litigation as complementary and, in some circumstances, a more effective tool. Unions in the UK have combined equal pay litigation involving mass participation by 'litigant-members' with negotiation to enhance the position of low-paid women workers in such diverse contexts as the outsourcing of 'dinnerladies' and privatization of the electricity supply industry.[39] Unions in Denmark, in conjunction with the Danish Equal Status Council, have supported important test cases before the Court of Justice on equal pay and the classification of pregnancy-related illnesses.[40]

Hence, the emancipationists (and even their pro-convergence private law bed-fellows) encourage us to maintain a healthy scepticism towards the legal and cultural *status quo* bounded by the nation-state. Their arguments are particularly strong with regard to gender equality, as well as discrimination on other grounds, which have required constant and ongoing struggles against common-sense, tradition-laden ideas of the inferior competences and value of certain human beings. Law and the discourse of rights and equality have been valuable weapons in such struggles. Multi-level governance structures have provided fresh and better opportunities to attack discriminatory practices, particularly those enshrined in national legislation. European Court of Justice jurisprudence becomes a common beacon to which all those involved in such struggles at national level can look. As such, Community instruments and Community-created forums (such as the European Commission Network of Equality Experts and the European Parliament's Women's Group) have created the rudiments of a transnational vocabulary as well as meetingpoints which permit discussions and planning among those fighting for gender equality in different parts of the EU to take place.

However, a number of significant qualifications must be made to this 'win-win' picture of the supranationalization of gender equality.

We can look first of all at the litigants. Those disadvantaged groups which need to litigate are generally those least well-placed to do so. Few of the women depicted as lone individuals in the emancipationist

---

[38] See further Klare, K., 'Countervailing Workers' Power as a Regulatory Strategy', in Collins, H., Davies, P., and Rideout, R. (eds.), *Legal Regulation of the Employment Relation* (The Hague: Kluwer, 2000) 63.

[39] For the 'dinner-ladies' see the House of Lords' decision in *Ratcliffe* v. *North Yorkshire County Council* [1995] IRLR 439 and the Court of Appeal's decision in *Lawrence* v. *Regent Office Care* [2000] IRLR 608. For the electricity privatization see Gilbert, K., and Secker, J., 'Generating Equality? Equal Pay, Decentralization and the Electricity Supply Industry' (1995) 33 *British Journal of Industrial Relations* 191.

[40] See Kilpatrick, above, n. 17, 77 ff.

accounts are, in fact, on their own, for the very good reason that individual women workers only exceptionally have either the financial wherewithal or the expertise to undertake alone what are often very complex cases. This means that where unions are not strongly committed to equality litigation (as in France and Germany), where there is no equality agency (again, in France and Germany) or no highly committed and sympathetic legal personnel (such as judges and practising lawyers), those who make most use of gender equality norms are employers and men attacking positive action measures[41] and female-specific protective legislation.[42]

Secondly, the litigants in these cases have no direct access to the Court of Justice. Access is always mediated through national courts, a point often missing from emancipationist accounts, because of the operation of the preliminary reference mechanism and the institutional structure of the EU. Hence, gender equality litigation is always filtered through local courts.[43] Moreover, when the EU norm is not horizontally directly effective between individuals,[44] gender equality litigation is mediated by local legal doctrinal and interpretative practices. This makes it crucial to look at local legal cultures and the background conditions affecting how excluded groups' voices are heard. Legal cultures are not immutable but they remain extremely important in structuring dialogues on gender equality.

In sum, 'supranationalization' does not imply 'denationalization' of gender equality law. Both emancipationists and proponents of convergence are wrong to claim that judicial activity in the EU is ever liable to

---

[41] See in particular the infamous line of cases from Germany before the Court of Justice: Case C–450/93 *Kalanke* v. *Freie und Hansestadt Bremen* [1995] ECR I–3051, Case C–409/95 *Marschall* v. *Land Nordrhein-Westfalen* [1997] ECR I–6363, Case C-158/97 *Badeck* v. *Hessische Ministerpräsident and Landesanwalt beim Staatsgerichtshof des Landes Hessen* [2000] ECR I–1875. And see also the Swedish reference in Case C–407/98 *Abrahamsson* v. *Fogelqvist* [2000] ECR I–5539. See Küchhold, K., 'Badeck—The Third German Reference on Positive Action' (2001) 30 *ILJ* 116; Numhauser-Henning, 'Swedish Sex Equality Law before the European Court of Justice (2001) 30 *ILJ* 121.

[42] See, e.g., how employers used gender equality in France discussed in Kilpatrick, above, n. 17 at 77 ff.

[43] The situation is different in federal structures, as in the USA, which have a dual court system, including federal courts at local, first-instance level. The US federal courts played an immensely important role in the 1950s and 1960s in dismantling *de jure* racial segregation, which was steadfastly defended by all three branches of government in the southern states.

[44] While Art. 119 EC is directly effective vertically (against the state) and horizontally (between private parties), directives, such as the Equal Treatment Directive, are only vertically directly effective. This results from the ECJ decision in Case 152/84 *Marshall* v. *Southampton and South-West Hampshire Area Health Authority (Teaching)* [1986] ECR 723. Thus, where a woman wants to rely on the Equal Treatment Directive against a private employer, she may do so only indirectly under the doctrine of 'indirect effect' established in Case 14/83 *Von Colson* v. *Land Nordrhein-Westfalen* [1984] ECR 1891 which requires national courts to interpret national law 'as far as possible' in line with the Directive.

produce uniform results for women throughout its territory. This is especially so because it is institutionally imperative for the Court of Justice to maintain a good relationship with its main interlocutors, the national courts.[45] Gender equality and labour law are not the bread and butter of the Court of Justice's work. This lies in interpreting the fundamental market freedoms (of goods, persons, services, establishment, and capital) which, along with competition law, control of national state aids and procurement rules, and agricultural policy make up the core EU market projects. Though the Court of Justice has a genuine attachment to gender equality, it often appears more dependent on national courts and other preliminary reference participants in this area than in its central spheres of competence. This can lead to the Court following suggestions by national courts that are not gender-equality friendly.[46] Emancipationist arguments tend to focus on 'success' stories. The less illustrious judicial decisions are pushed into the background. Yet these disappointing or bad decisions are also applied with at least equal enthusiasm by employers, national courts, and executives to women workers. They must also be fully considered in order to provide a balanced account.

Even successful litigation using EU gender equality sources may involve winning battles but losing wars. Legal constructions must be based upon viable social institutions. The emasculation position—grounded as it is in a functional analysis of law—is right to argue that we must always carefully investigate the effects judicial or supranational legislative decisions have on the ground. Perverse or inefficient effects may be produced for women workers, or workers in general, by what may look, *prima facie*, like historic victories. For example, a significant chunk of the litigation before the Court of Justice—in many instances heavily supported by the British Equal Opportunities Commission—has concerned trying to get the Court of Justice to accept that occupational pensions are 'pay' for the purposes of Article 141 (ex Article 119) EC. Yet the final outcome of this ultimately successful strategy was undoubtedly the impoverishment of women in the EU,[47] not to mention the considerable expenditure incurred on the litigation. Another more ambiguous

---

[45] See further Chalmers, D., 'Judicial Preferences and the Community Legal Order' (1997) 60 *MLR* 165.

[46] See further Kilpatrick, above, n. 17, 89 ff.

[47] See further Fredman, S., 'The Poverty of Equality: Pensions and the ECJ' (1996) 25 *ILJ* 91. Problems with this jurisprudence include the fact that much of the case law is geared towards assisting male litigants achieve the earlier pension ages of women, the very explicit deference to employer and pension fund costs, the acceptance of levelling-down to achieve equality and the decision that women excluded from occupational pension schemes have to pay all the past contributions owed in order to obtain benefits from the scheme. See in particular Case C–109/91 *Ten Oever* v. *Stichting Bedrijfspensioenfonds voor het Glazenwassers-fen Schoonmaakbedrijf* [1993] ECR I–4879 and Case C–408/92 *Smith* v. *Avdel Systems Ltd.* [1994] ECR I–4527.

labour law example, also drawn from the UK, is the decision of the Court of Justice in 1994 that the UK was infringing Community law by failing to provide for some form of worker consultation, as required by two Community directives concerning redundancies and transfers of undertakings, in the absence of union recognition. This has resulted in UK legislation providing opportunities for worker representation which challenge the traditional British model of single-channel representation through recognized trade unions.[48] In my view, the more functionally oriented analyses provide us with potentially richer criteria to evaluate what these developments mean for workers in Europe. However, this will be the case only when the functional criteria adopted are dynamic and imaginative rather than wedded to archaic conceptions of the immutability of legal, cultural, and political practices.

Finally, as part of a bigger picture, we must not look just at what gender equality has done *for women* or *to the nation-state*, but what gender equality has done *for the EU*, in particular the Court of Justice. I have argued elsewhere that labour law cases in general, and gender equality cases in particular, have provided the Court of Justice with a vital supply of real live 'individuals' with understandable stories which have added substance to its claims to be building a European order that must be effective in order to provide effective judicial protection of individuals. The bold case law which is produced then becomes available for use in other areas where the individual's credentials or problems are less immediately compelling.[49]

There are numerous ways of illustrating this important point. Here I take just one. If we examine the public presentation of the Court of Justice through its press releases, we can see how central gender equality has been in giving the EU project a much-needed 'human face' at crucial junctures in its attempts to present itself as a constitutionally legitimate and enlightened governance project. For example, in 1999, the Court of Justice decided 192 preliminary references.[50] Seven of these were gender equality in employment references which constituted 3.6 per cent of its preliminary rulings for 1999. In the same year, it released forty-two press releases with regard to specific preliminary references. Of these, ten concerned gender equality in employment. In other words while gender equality references constituted 3.6 per cent of the Court's preliminary

---

[48] See Davies, P., 'A Challenge to Single-Channel' (1994) 23 *ILJ* 272 discussing the implications of Cases C–382/92 and 383/92 *Commission* v. *UK* [1994] ECR I–2435. See also the new legislative genus of 'workforce agreements' in the Working Time Regulations 1998 SI 1998/1833 and the Maternity and Parental Leave Regulations 1999 SI 1999/3312.

[49] Kilpatrick, above, n. 16.

[50] Table 2, *Statistics of Judicial Activity of the Court of Justice in 1999*, at http://europa.eu.int/cj/en/stat/st99er.pdf.

references work in fact, in the Court's own presentation of itself to the public, it constituted almost a quarter. That is, gender equality at work in 1999 was six times over-represented in the Court's public self-presentation.

Both 'sides' in the emasculation/emancipation debate are concerned with discussing the fate of the nation-state in a transformed European legal space, which creates new 'geo-legal' locations.[51] This analysis has argued that much helpful light can be shed on each of these positions by setting them against each other in the specific context of gender equality. This can in turn assist us in mapping the new terrains of labour law in Europe. Like public lawyers, in an environment in which labour law is increasingly supranationalized though not denationalized, labour lawyers must seek out their own version of the new 'cosmopolitan meta-constitutional'[52] rules governing the production of labour norms.

[51] Harding, C., 'The Identity of European Law: Mapping Out the European Legal Space' (2000) 6 *European L. Journal* 128.

[52] See further the stimulating discussion of Walker, N., 'Flexibility within a Metaconstitutional Frame: Reflections on the Future of Legal Authority in Europe' in de Búrca, G., and Scott, J. (eds.), *Constitutional Change in the EU—From Uniformity to Flexibility* (Oxford: Hart, 2000) 9.

26

Social Rights, Social Citizenship, and Transformative Constitutionalism: A Comparative Assessment

DENNIS M. DAVIS, PATRICK MACKLEM, AND GUY MUNDLAK

I INTRODUCTION

Neo-liberal agendas and processes of globalization in developed countries have produced growing rates of poverty, inequality, and social stratification. Governments increasingly are relying on privatized, market instruments to deliver essential public and social services, and dismantling basic elements of the modern welfare state. Trade union movements and collective bargaining law, which traditionally produced and protected an expansive set of social entitlements, are in decline. To address these trends, critics of neo-liberalism are developing a number of strategies. Trade unions are experimenting with new forms of unionism and employee representation. Socialist political parties, historically devoted to oppositional politics, are pursuing pragmatic policies aimed at winning greater popular support and securing the reins of state power. And legal critics are becoming increasingly aware of the need to develop a transformative constitutional discourse that advances interests associated with social citizenship.

This chapter explores the contours of one such transformative constitutional discourse from a comparative perspective, examining the extent to which constitutional rights, by protecting and promoting social citizenship, can offset some of the corrosive effects of neo-liberalism in Canada, Israel, and South Africa. The relatively undeveloped status of this strategy can be attributed in part to the fact that a primary objective of neo-liberalism is the dismantlement of labour and social welfare entitlements, which typically are not considered to be within the core of constitutionalism.[1] But recognition of their importance was a key aspiration of post-war international human rights law. Social rights—such as rights to work, housing, education, and health—and civil and political

---

[1] Leary, V. A., 'The Paradox of Workers' Rights as Human Rights' in Compa, L., and Diamond, S. (eds.), *Human Rights, Labor Rights and International Trade* (Philadelphia, Penn.: University of Pennsylvania Press, 1996) 22–47.

rights initially were regarded by the drafters of the Universal Declaration of Human Rights as critical to the protection of social citizenship and as interdependent sets of human rights, each necessary for the achievement of the other. As many have noted, however, international law subsequently failed to acknowledge this interdependence, relegating social rights to the margins of enforceability, and few states have seen fit formally to entrench them in domestic constitutional arrangements.

Two developments at the intersection of international law and constitutional law suggest new ways in which to promote social citizenship and vindicate the interdependence of human rights. First, the United Nations Committee on Economic, Social, and Cultural Rights has begun to define and implement social rights at the international level in ways that could vertically aid domestic constitutional efforts to promote social citizenship. Secondly, several states independently provide direct or indirect constitutional protection of interests associated with social rights, creating comparative and transformative opportunities to protect and promote social citizenship in the face of globalization. In an effort to identify and maximize these opportunities, we have chosen to concentrate on Canada, Israel, and South Africa. While each country has accepted the prospect of judicial scrutiny of state action, South Africa's Constitution provides for comprehensive entrenchment of social rights, Israel's Constitution currently provides no formal recognition of social rights, and Canada's Constitution falls between these two extremes. Despite the fact that each of the three countries occupies a different position on the spectrum of formal protection of social rights, their constitutional jurisprudence is remarkably similar in the extent to which it extends substantive protection of interests associated with social citizenship. In all three countries, the judiciary currently appears willing to extend partial constitutional protection to these interests but unwilling to articulate a vision of social citizenship sufficiently robust to judge the constitutionality of neo-liberal agendas.

Two interpretive developments account for this substantive convergence. First, as the South African experience with social rights illustrates, the existence of formal constitutional guarantees does not ensure their implementation. In all three countries, there have been relatively few efforts explicitly to litigate social inequality and, in the few cases that have arisen, the nature of the interests at stake makes for precarious litigation. Secondly, the Israeli and Canadian experiences illustrate that the absence of formal constitutional guarantees of social rights does not preclude constitutional protection of certain interests associated with social citizenship through expansive interpretations of civil and political rights. Freedom of expression, freedom of association, equality, and even the right to property can serve to provide vulnerable social groups with some leverage to improve their position. This chapter seeks to promote constitutional law's transformative potential by defending the need for an integrative approach based on the insight that all rights possess social dimensions. Focusing on the right to health, we argue for a transformative constitutional jurisprudence capable of testing the constitutionality of neo-liberal agendas against the demands of social citizenship.

II THE SUBORDINATION OF SOCIAL RIGHTS

Despite dramatic differences in size and economic and social structures, Israel, Canada, and South Africa share certain similarities. Historically, each has been profoundly influenced by processes of colonization. Socially, each possesses a heterogeneous citizenry, embodying social cleavages based on ethnicity (Canada), race (South Africa), and religion (Israel). Politically, each is a multi-party state operating in accordance with basic principles of parliamentary and social democracy. Legally, each is steeped in similar common law traditions. And constitutionally, each has witnessed the recent entrenchment of a constitutional bill of rights subjecting the exercise of state power to constitutional review. Most importantly for present purposes, each country is actively considering the extent to which interests associated with social citizenship merit constitutional protection. In all three, recent debates concerning the constitutional entrenchment of social rights have been part of a larger social dialogue about the merits of constitutional review.

Israel's constitution is composed of an ongoing legislation of Basic Laws.[2] In 1992 the legislature passed two Basic Laws on human rights.[3] The process of gradually writing a bill of rights subsequently stalled because of political controversies regarding the powers accorded by the 'constitutional revolution' to the Supreme Court of Israel. The Court suggested that this political failure could be remedied by a 'derivative rights' approach, whereby additional rights are derived from the general guarantee of the individual's right to dignity and liberty. Under this approach, the Court has interpreted 'liberty' to include freedom of association, and 'dignity' to include a right to minimum subsistence.[4] In 1997

---

[2] On the constitutional developments in Israel see: Erez, D. B., 'From an Unwritten to a Written Constitution: The Israeli Challenge from an American Perspective' (1995) 26 *Columbia Human Rights L. Review* 309–55; Gross, A., 'The Politics of Rights in Israeli Constitutional Law' (1998) 3 *Israel Studies* 80–118; Hirschel, R., 'The Constitutional Revolution and the Emergence of a New Economic Order In Israel' (1997) 2 *Israel Studies* 136–55.

[3] Basic Law: Freedom of Occupation (1992); Basic Law: Human Dignity and Liberty (1992).

[4] This position has been endorsed most strongly by the Chief Justice of the Israeli Supreme Court, Professor Aharon Barak: see his *Legal Interpretation* (Jerusalem: Nevo Publishers, 1994) iii, 422–5 (Hebrew).

the Department of Justice drafted a Basic Law: Social Rights proposal which holds that 'the State of Israel will make an effort to develop and promote the circumstances necessary for a dignified existence of all its residents, including in the areas of education, health, social welfare and the quality of the environment; progress will be determined according to legislation and executive decisions'. Although formally justiciable, the proposed Basic Law: Social Rights leaves little room for judicial review because the state is obligated only to comply with a general statement of goodwill.

The Constitution of Canada includes the Canadian Charter of Rights and Freedoms, which guarantees a wide range of civil and political rights, as well as linguistic rights and rights pertaining to minority educational institutions. Adopted in 1982, the Charter does not formally guarantee an extensive list of social rights. Federal and provincial governments have since attempted further amendments of the Constitution primarily in an effort to accommodate Quebec's demands for greater autonomy. In 1991, a broad coalition of social activists and anti-poverty organizations proposed a Draft Social Charter as part of any future constitutional reform. It sought to affirm Canada's international obligations to respect, protect, and promote human rights, and guarantee 'an equal right to well-being', which would include an adequate standard of living, universal and public health care, public education, and access to employment opportunities, as well as the right of workers to organize and bargain collectively.[5] In 1992, the federal and all provincial governments agreed to a set of constitutional reform proposals known as the Charlottetown Accord. The Accord proposed a 'social and economic union' clause, setting out a series of non-justiciable policy objectives, including a comprehensive, universal, portable, publicly administered, and accessible health care system, adequate social services, benefits to ensure reasonable access to housing, food, and other basic necessities, high quality primary and secondary education, protection of the right to organize and bargain collectively, and environmental protection.[6] This proposal was roundly criticized for its failure to provide for monitoring or enforcement mechanisms.[7] Its merits quickly became moot as the Accord as a whole was rejected by a majority of voters, and by voters in a majority of the provinces, in a national referendum.

Constitutional developments in Israel and Canada pale in comparison

---

[5] The Draft Social Charter is reproduced in Bakan, J., and Schneiderman, D. (eds.), *Social Justice and the Constitution: Perspectives on a Social Union for Canada* (Ottawa: Carleton University Press, 1992) 155–61 (App. A).

[6] *Consensus Report on the Constitution* (28 Aug. 1992).

[7] See, e.g., Jackman, M., 'Constitutional Rhetoric and Social Justice: Reflections on the Justiciability Debate' in Bakan and Schneiderman, above, n. 5, 17–28.

to the magnitude of South Africa's recent constitutional transformation.[8] The announcement of F. W. De Klerk in February 1990 that all political organizations, including the African National Congress (ANC), were free to engage in political activity marked the commencement of a lengthy and complex process of constitutional negotiation. In negotiations over the interim constitution formally approved by the apartheid Parliament in 1993, the National Party, supported by research undertaken by the South African Law Commission, adopted the approach that social rights were not justiciable.[9] However, during the negotiations at the Constitutional Assembly culminating in the 1996 Constitution, ANC delegates placed social reconstruction and redistribution high on the order of policy priority. The 1996 Constitution bears the mark of these views. Section 26 provides that everyone has the right to have access to housing; section 27 provides that everyone has the right of access to health care services including reproductive health care. Both are qualified by the provision that the state must take reasonable legislative and other measures within its available resources to achieve the progressive realization of these rights. Other social rights enshrined in the Constitution are not subject to such qualifications. Section 29 guarantees everyone the right to basic education. Section 28 stipulates that every child has the right to basic nutrition, shelter, basic health, and social services. And section 23, which owes its entrenchment in no small measure to the influence of the Congress of South African Trade Unions, guarantees everyone the right to fair labour practices, stipulates that every worker has the right to form and join a trade union and to strike, and confers on trade unions the right to bargain collectively.

Despite the dramatic differences in protection that the three constitutional orders formally extend to social rights, they are remarkably similar in terms of the extent to which they provide substantive protection of interests associated with social citizenship. In all three, there are ongoing debates about what rights and interests merit constitutional protection. Compared to veteran constitutional regimes such as the USA, the status of social rights is an ongoing constitutional concern. At the same time, jurisprudence in all three countries manifests uneasiness about the constitutional consequences of social citizenship. This is demonstrated in South Africa by a judicial unwillingness to interpret social rights broadly, and, in Israel and Canada, by a judicial reluctance to interpret civil and

---

[8] For an account of these negotiations and their complexity see Ebrahim, H., *The Soul of a Nation: Constitution-making in South Africa* (Cape Town: Oxford University Press, 1998); and, more specifically, Mureinik, E., 'Beyond a Charter of Luxuries: Economic Rights in the Constitution' (1992) 8 *South African Journal on Human Rights* 464.

[9] The South African Law Commission, *Group and Human Rights* (Interim Report, Pretoria: South African Law Commission, 1991).

political rights in a manner that protects social citizenship. This remarkable convergence no doubt stems in part from the rising ideology of neoliberalism that privileges private property, freedom of contract, and individual liberty. It also stems from views widely held by those who share concerns over the growing rates of poverty, inequality, and social stratification but who resist proposals constitutionally to protect and promote interests associated with social citizenship.

This resistance is brought into sharp relief by the following scenario. Imagine a poor, homeless citizen of a state that extends constitutional protection to social rights, specifically, rights to housing, food, and minimum subsistence. She petitions a domestic court to declare that the state has failed its obligations and requests that the legislature be instructed on the appropriate means to remedy her situation. The judge hearing the petition immediately confronts a number of difficult constitutional issues. What is the nature and scope, say, of a right to food? What obligations does such a right impose on the state? What is the appropriate remedy if the state has failed to live up to its obligations? More generally, is the judiciary overstepping its institutional role when ruling on these questions? This scenario raises concerns regarding the potential breadth of interests underlying social citizenship, the nature and extent of positive state obligations, and the appropriate relationship between the judicial, legislative, and executive branches of government. These concerns have led South African courts to interpret social rights narrowly, and Israeli and Canadian courts to tend to exclude certain interests associated with social citizenship from the ambit of civil and political rights. These concerns, we believe, are misguided.

Positive rights or positive obligations?

Some attribute the inferior status of social rights to the fact that they are positive rights, requiring the state to act in certain ways, unlike negative obligations requiring it to refrain from acting in other ways. But all rights—whether civil, political, or social—give rise to both positive and negative state obligations calibrated to protect certain interests and not others. For example, according to the Israeli Supreme Court, the freedom to protest places an obligation on police to protect demonstrators from hostile bystanders. It further requires police to allow demonstrators to march in streets and public areas, even if a permit to do so would interrupt traffic or the peace of local residents.[10] Similarly, the Supreme Court of Canada has held that the right to life, liberty, and security of the person

---

[10] Cf. HC 153/83 *Levi* v. *The South District High Commissioner of the Police Force*, Piskei Din (Supreme Court Decisions) 38/2, 393.

entitles any illegal immigrant claiming to be a refugee to a formal hearing before an official or tribunal with determinative authority.[11] South African courts have been prepared to impose similar obligations upon the state, insisting that competent legal counsel represent an indigent accused, and have on occasions considered that a similar obligation could be imposed upon the state in civil cases.[12] The right to property, classically conceived as a negative right that requires the state to refrain from interfering with its exercise, requires extensive state action—legislative, judicial, and administrative—for its protection. Zoning legislation, criminal law, the common law of property and tort, and environmental agencies and police forces serve to protect one's property from the actions of others. 'The protection of property', in Neil Komesar's words, 'needs both protection *from* and the protection *of* the government'.[13]

Social rights clearly impose positive obligations on the state. Minority language educational rights contained in the Canadian Charter, for example, compel the government 'to alter or develop major institutional structures'.[14] But social rights also impose negative obligations on the state. Israel's labour court, for example, has held that the National Insurance Institute's refusal to assess an application of a homeless person for welfare benefits because he cannot supply an address violates the right to dignity and minimal subsistence.[15] Thus, a social right can be cast in either positive or negative terms, depending on how one characterizes the state obligations to which it gives rise. For example, state abolition of welfare implicates a negative right to minimal subsistence in that the state cannot deny a person the minimal subsistence to which she is entitled. But it also implicates a positive right to minimal subsistence in that the right obligates the state to secure minimal subsistence to each individual. The key task, then, is not to determine whether a right is positive or negative, but to identify, in specific contexts, the particular configuration of state obligations—positive and negative—to which a right gives rise. This configuration is itself dependent upon the nature of the interests that the right is deemed to protect.

---

[11] *Singh v. Minister of Employment and Immigration* [1895] 1 SCR 177. See also *Schachter* v. *Canada* [1992] 2 SCR 679, 721 ('the right to life, liberty, and security of the person is in one sense a negative right, but the requirement that the government respect the "fundamental principles of justice" may provide a basis for characterizing s. 7 [of the *Charter*] as a positive right in some circumstances').

[12] *S* v. *Vermas; S* v. *DuPlessis* 1995 (3) SA 292 (CC). See also see *Legal Aid Board* v. *Msila* (1997) 2 CLR 229 (E) (state obligations in civil cases).

[13] Komesar, N., *Imperfect Alternatives: Choosing Institutions in Law, Economics, and Public Policy* (Chicago, Ill.: University of Chicago Press, 1994) 245.

[14] See *Mahe* v. *Alberta* [1990] 1 SCR 342.

[15] NLC 04-265/96, *Hasid* v. *National Insurance Institute* (National Labour Court, unpublished 7/97).

The vagueness of social rights

It is often said that the judiciary is an institution that does not possess the capability adequately to engage in the relatively complex task of identifying and enforcing positive state obligations. Social rights are often characterized as vague in terms of the obligations they mandate, progressive in terms of the steps required for their realization, and complex and diffuse in terms of the interests they protect. The hypothetical poor person's petition raises the concern that the right to adequate subsistence does not place an ascertainable obligation on others. It is not immediately clear what may constitute adequate subsistence, why an individual does not have it, and who ought to be held responsible for its lack. Such questions are deeply value-laden, even when presented as answerable by objective quantitative analysis.[16]

It is therefore no easy task to define the nature and extent of obligations that social rights impose on the state in any given circumstance. But vagueness does not inhere in the nature of social rights; it is a result of judicial inaction. Civil and political rights appear more determinate than social rights because they have benefited from repeated invocation, delineation, and evolution in the adjudicative process. The right to privacy, for example, was first identified as a vague residual right that addressed a sense of violation not captured by other rights.[17] Years of judicial and legislative attention have succeeded in defining some of its controversial contours.[18] Similarly, the nature and scope of the right to property are contested and its content differs from one country to another.[19] Unlike civil and political rights, social rights appeared on the western legal horizon only recently, with the enactment of the Universal Declaration of Human Rights in 1948. As the nature and content of all rights develop through a social discourse in which courts, legislatures, and the public take part, the exclusion of social rights from the deliberative agenda

[16] To understand the ideological nature of the debate see, e.g., Sen, A., *Inequality Reexamined* (New York/Oxford: Oxford University Press, 1992), 109–16. As to why individuals do not have adequate subsistence, compare, e.g., Murray, C., *Losing Ground* (New York: Basic Books, 1984) and Handler, J., and Hasenfeld, Y., *We the Poor People: Work, Poverty, and Welfare* (New Haven, Conn.: Yale University Press, 1997). Finally, the issue of responsibility is clearly a political and moral issue rather than a matter for objective scientific inquiry. See, e.g., Blank, R., *It Takes a Nation: A New Agenda for Fighting Poverty* (Princeton, NJ: Princeton University Press, 1997) 191–219.

[17] Warren, S., and Brandeis, L., 'The Right to Privacy' (1890) 4 *Harvard L. Reiew* 193.

[18] DeCew, J. W., *In Pursuit of Privacy* (Ithaca, NY: Cornell University Press, 1997).

[19] Michelman, F., 'Possession vs. Distribution in the Constitutional Idea of Property' (1987) 72 *Iowa L. Review* 1319; Reich, C., 'The New Property' (1964) 73 *Yale L. Journal* 733; Nedelsky, J., *Private Property and the Limits of American Constitutionalism* (Chicago, Ill.: Chicago University Press, 1990); Beerman, J., and Singer, J., 'Baseline Questions in Legal Reasoning: The Example of Property in Jobs' (1989) 23 *Georgia L. Review* 911.

means they are likely to remain vague. But this is a function of, not a reason for, their exclusion.

Moreover, difficulties associated with ascribing determinate content to social rights should not be exaggerated. International human rights law offers a useful analytical framework for identifying and clarifying state obligations. The 1987 Limburg principles,[20] as developed in the Maastricht Guidelines on Violations of Economic, Social, and Cultural Rights (1997),[21] catalogue the state obligations that social rights engender, ranging from a core duty to respect rights to more elaborate and demanding peripheral duties to protect and fulfil rights.[22] The Committee on Economic, Social, and Cultural Rights has proposed that state obligations be understood in terms of obligations of conduct and obligations of result.[23] Robert Robertson argues that state compliance can be measured by indicators that compare state expenditures on realizing social rights to other expenditures, such as military spending, and with other countries roughly equal in economic development.[24] None of these strategies eliminates the uncertainties associated with state duties, but they structure them in a manner that facilitates adjudication, shedding a measure of conceptual clarity on the issues.

Social rights and the separation of power

The homeless person who petitions a court to declare that the state has failed its obligations to fulfil her social rights also appears to require the court to assess the appropriateness of state spending initiatives. It is said that a court lacks the institutional capacity to make the detailed budgetary assessments necessary to determine whether the state has allocated sufficient funds to particular classes of persons. Judicial extension of benefits to one class of persons not contemplated by the legislative scheme implicates the state's overall spending priorities as well as the appropriateness of existing welfare and housing policies. Although true, these problems are not unique to judicial assessment of alleged infringements of social rights.

---

[20] *The Limburg Principles on the Implementation of the International Covenant on Economic, Social and Cultural Rights*, UN Doc. E/CN.4/1987/17; also published at (1979) 9 *Human Rights Quarterly* 122.

[21] The Maastricht Guidelines on Violations of Economic, Social, and Cultural Rights (1997) 15 *Netherlands Quarterly on Human Rights* 244.

[22] See also Van Hoof, G. J. H., 'The Legal Nature of Economic, Social and Cultural Rights: A Rebuttal of Some Traditional Views' in Alston, P., and Tomasevski, K. (eds.), *The Right to Food* (Utrecht: Stiching Studie- en Informatiecentrum Mensenrechten, 1984).

[23] *General Comment No. 3*, UN Doc. E/1991/23, Annex III.

[24] Robertson, R., 'Measuring State Compliance with the Obligation to Devote the "Maximum Available Resources" to Realizing Economic, Social and Cultural Rights' (1994) 16 *Human Rights Quarterly* 693.

Constitutional adjudication invariably plunges the judiciary into the realm of policy. For example, the policy of exemptions for ultra-orthodox people from military service in Israel has recently been determined to be unreasonable, with the Court instructing the state to prescribe a new policy on the issue within twelve months.[25] Constitutional adjudication also invariably implicates budgetary considerations. As the Supreme Court of Canada observes, '[a]ny remedy granted by a court will have some budgetary repercussions, whether it be a saving of money or an expenditure of money'.[26] The key question therefore is 'not whether courts can make decisions that impact on budgetary policy, it is to what degree they can appropriately do so'.[27]

The judiciary possesses extraordinary remedial flexibility in this regard. The Supreme Court of Canada has expressed a willingness to 'read in' statutory language in order to remedy under-inclusive statutory benefit regimes in cases where the addition of the excluded class is consistent with the scheme's objective; where there is little choice about how to cure the constitutional defect; where reading in would not involve a substantial change in the cost or nature of the scheme; and, where the alternative of striking down the under-inclusive provision would be an inferior remedy.[28] In the decision of the Constitutional Court in South Africa declaring unconstitutional a provision of the Electoral Act that prohibited prisoners from voting, the Court addressed the government's claim that it would be extremely costly and administratively complex to implement such a right. The Court acknowledged that it 'does not have the information or expertise to enable it to decide what those arrangements should be or how they should be effected'. Accordingly it ordered the Electoral Commission to table a report indicating how such a right could be implemented.[29]

Remedial flexibility enables the judiciary to adjudicate on matters that possess budgetary implications in a manner sensitive to its institutional role. The fact that the judiciary and the legislature perform different functions in a constitutional democracy ought to inform the extent to which

---

[25] HC 3267/97 *Rubinstein* v. *The Minister of Security*, Piskei Din (Supreme Court Decisions) 52(5) 481 (1998).

[26] *Schachter* v. *Canada*, above, n. 11.

[27] Ibid.

[28] Ibid. For a similar approach in South Africa see *National Coalition for Gay and Lesbian Equality and Others* v. *Minister of Home Affairs* [2000] (1) BCLR 39(CC), where the Court read the words 'or partner in a permanent same sex life partnership' into a statute to save a provision which would otherwise have discriminated in favour of married couples in circumstances where a non-South African partner applied to obtain permanent South African residence. The *Schachter* case was also referred to by the Israeli Supreme Court when adopting a similar approach in the case of HC 721/94 *El-Al Israeli Airlines Ltd.* v. *Yonathan Danilowitz et al.*, Piskei Din (Supreme Court Decisions) 48(5) (1994) 501–42.

[29] *August and Another* v. *Electoral Commission and Others* [1999] (4) BCLR (363), para. 39.

the former can dictate to the latter on budgetary matters, but it should not preclude a court from interpreting constitutional rights in a manner that has budgetary implications.

In sum, it is misguided to resist constitutional protection of interests associated with social citizenship because they impose positive obligations on the state, are vague, or violate the separation of power. All rights give rise to positive state obligations. Any vagueness associated with social rights is a function of judicial inaction. And the judiciary possesses sufficient flexibility when defining the nature and scope of social rights and ascertaining appropriate remedies to minimize their impact on the separation of power. It is therefore necessary to trace the subordinate status of social rights elsewhere.

III THE SUBORDINATION OF THE SOCIAL DIMENSION OF RIGHTS

Although civil and political rights and social rights both give rise to positive as well as negative state obligations, they aim to protect different sets of interests. Civil and political rights typically protect interests associated with individual autonomy and political participation, whereas social rights typically protect interests associated with individual and social wellbeing. But, in one important respect, these two sets of rights overlap. Specifically, with each and every right, whether civil, political, or social, one can identify an *atomistic* dimension that seeks to erect barriers between individuals in society, and a *social* dimension that seeks to connect individuals and protect collective allegiances. These two dimensions rest on opposing views of individual autonomy and choice. The atomistic dimension assumes that each individual has pre-given interests that the judiciary ought to protect by ensuring that others do not interfere with their expression and realization. It thus assumes that preferences are generated by individuals and that, in externalizing and executing preferences, the individual can advance her interests on her own. Collective allegiances are protected only in so far as such allegiances are the outcome of individual choice.

The social dimension of rights, on the other hand, assumes that society provides a shared intelligibility to human existence and shapes the formation of individual preferences. The choosing self celebrated by the atomistic dimension is profoundly affected by the society in which she lives. Her choices are strongly informed by institutional structures, normative baselines, legal entitlements, and social norms. Many individuals cannot externalize and execute their preferences by themselves; exploring new choices and identifying new possibilities require social supports. Drawing boundaries around the individual protects her from social intervention but disconnects her from social life, denying her both the power to affect others and the benefits flowing from the participation of others in the formation of her preferences. On this account, constitutional rights should participate in the construction of a social environment that maximizes opportunities for individuals to construct and live a rich and interactive life.

Together, the atomistic and social dimensions of constitutional rights protect the individual's need to separate from and connect with others, to rely on and remain independent from others, and to associate with and dissociate from others. Identifying the atomistic and the social dimensions of rights enables us to be more precise about the nature of the convergence in the constitutional jurisprudence of the three countries. The interests that social citizenship encompasses relate to individual and social wellbeing. Constitutional jurisprudence in all three countries manifests a willingness to protect these interests in certain circumstances. Israeli and Canadian courts are restricted to protecting these interests in the form of expansive interpretations of civil and political rights, whereas South African courts are free of this formal restriction. Where the three jurisdictions converge is in terms of an unwillingness to protect these interests by interpreting constitutional rights in a manner that emphasizes their social dimensions. What the three jurisdictions share, in other words, is a fear of the social dimension of all rights.

Constitutional jurisprudence on the right to health illustrates this fear. Generally speaking, the right to health is considered a social right in that it protects interests associated with individual and social wellbeing.[30] But it can be seen as possessing both social and atomistic dimensions. Understood atomistically, it is infringed when the state actively prevents an individual from obtaining health care, for example, by passing a law holding that prisoners are not allowed to receive medical service, or when it acts in a manner that risks the health of individuals. Understood socially, the right is infringed when the state fails to provide a level of health-care services to its citizens consonant with the requirements of social citizenship. As will be seen, courts in all three countries emphasize the atomistic over the social dimensions.

South Africa

Article 27 of South Africa's Bill of Rights provides that '[e]veryone has the right to have access to . . . health care services' and obligates the state to 'take reasonable legislative and other measures, within its available resources, to achieve [this right's] progressive realization'. In *Soobramoney*

[30] For an extensive study of the right to health in international law see Toebes, B. C. A., *The Right to Health as a Human Right in International Law* (Antwerp: INTERSENTIA, 1999).

v. *Minister of Health (KwaZulu-Natal)*,[31] the Constitutional Court was presented with its first opportunity to define the nature and scope of social rights contained in the 1996 Constitution. The appellant was a 41-year-old diabetic who suffered from chronic renal disease but whose life could have been prolonged by regular renal dialysis. The public hospital in Durban he attended had only twenty dialysis machines and refused his request, justifying its decision by relying on a policy that allocated available machines to patients awaiting kidney transplants. He appealed to the Constitutional Court and relied on section 11, which provides that everyone has the right to life, and section 27(3), which provides that no one may be refused emergency medical treatment.

Rejecting his claim, the Court found that the right to life entails a duty to protect a right bearer against interference but does not extend to the positive duty to sustain life. With respect to section 27(3), the Court, *per* Chaskalson P, held that '[t]he words "emergency medical treatment" may possibly be open to a broad construction which would include ongoing treatment of chronic illness for the purpose of prolonging life'. In his words, 'this is not their ordinary meaning, and if this had been the purpose which section 27(3) was intended to serve, one would have expected that to have been expressed in positive and specific terms'.[32]

This atomistic interpretation was matched by the Court's interpretation of other social rights in the Constitution, including the right to access to health care. Chalskalson P stated that 'what is apparent from these provisions is that the obligations imposed on the state by s. 26 and s. 27 in regard to access to housing, health care, food, water, and social security are dependent upon the resources available for such purposes, and that the corresponding rights themselves are limited by reason of lack of resources'.[33] This pronouncement is open to the conclusion that the express provision of social rights in the constitution confers no right where it can be shown that there are limited resources. This view was supported by Madala J, who held that:

[s]ome rights in the Constitution are the ideal and something to be strived for. They amount to a promise, in some cases, and an indication of what a democratic society aiming to salvage lost dignity, freedom and equality should embark upon. They are values that the Constitution seeks to provide, nurture and protect for the future South Africa.[34]

---

[31] 1998 (2) SA 958 (CC).   [32] Ibid., para. 13.   [33] Ibid., para. 11.
[34] Ibid., para. 42. See also Michelman, F., 'The Constitution, Social Rights and Reason' (1998) 14 *South African Journal of Human Rights* 500, 502–4. Not all South African decisions interpret social rights by reference to their atomistic dimensions: see *South Africa* v. *Grootboom* (unreported decision of the Constitutional Court of South Africa 4 Oct. 2000) (the right to adequate housing requires the state to devise and implement within its available resources a comprehensive programme progressively to realize the right, aimed initially at those in desperate need).

Coupling a traditional rights analysis with a concern about resources reduces social rights to aspirations to which a society should strive. Thus while *Soobramoney* may well have been correctly decided on the facts, the general approach to social rights adopted by the Court hardly promises a transformation of traditional rights jurisprudence.

Canada

The Supreme Court of Canada has held that the right to security of the person encompasses a right to health that in certain circumstances prevents the state from erecting barriers preventing individuals from obtaining timely medical care. In *R. v. Morgentaler*, the Court held criminal restrictions on abortions, which required a woman to obtain the approval of a therapeutic abortion committee of an approved hospital, to be unconstitutional. A majority of the Court held that they restricted access to the procedure and caused delays in treatment, increasing the risk to the health of the woman.[35] The right to health includes a right to mental health, which in certain circumstances prevents the state from enacting laws that impose serious psychological and emotional stress.[36]

Canada aspires to provide comprehensive and universal health care through a set of interlocking federal and provincial statutory and fiscal instruments. Specifically, the federal government provides financial support for provincial health-care insurance schemes that are publicly administered, comprehensive, universal, portable, and accessible.[37] But whether publicly funded health care is required as a matter of constitutional right has not been definitively determined by the judiciary. While the Court has held the state to account for laws that interfere with the health of an individual or, more broadly, with an individual's bodily integrity, left unsaid has been the extent to which the state is required to legislate for the protection and promotion of health. The judiciary has emphasized the atomistic dimension of the right to health, requiring the state to justify certain laws that pose health threats or restrict an individual's ability to access health care. The judiciary has not ruled that the right to health includes a social dimension obligating the state to ensure an adequate health care system. Indeed, the Court has stated that it would be premature to decide whether 'rights fundamental to human rights or

---

[35] [1988] 1 SCR 30.

[36] *Mills v. The Queen* [1986] 1 SCR 863, at 920, *per* Lamer CJ; *R. v. O'Connor* [1995] 4 SCR 411, *per* L'Heureux-Dubé, J; *Rodriguez v. A.G.B.C.* [1993] 3 SCR 519.

[37] See Canada Health Act, RSC 1985, c. C-6. For commentary see Chouhdry, S., 'The Enforcement of the Canada Health Act' (1996) 41 *McGill L. Journal* 461. For a history of health care insurance in Canada see Taylor, M. G., *Health Insurance and Canadian Public Policy* (2nd edn., Montreal: McGill-Queen's University Press, 1987).

survival' that require state action are protected as a matter of security of the person.[38]

Despite its silence on the social dimension of the right to health, the judiciary has indicated a willingness to protect certain citizenship interests associated with the provision of health care services under the rubric of the right to equal protection and benefit of the law. With funds from the federal government and its own tax base, the Province of British Columbia reimburses hospitals, doctors, and other health-care practitioners for the cost of the medically required services that they provide to the public.[39] A Medical Services Commission, comprised of representatives from government, the medical community, and the public, determines what constitutes a medically required service. Until recently, the Province did not reimburse hospitals, doctors, or other heath-care practitioners for the cost of providing sign-language interpretation for hearing-impaired patients, but the Commission possessed the discretion to deem this a medically required service, and hospitals enjoyed considerable leeway on how to provide for services for which they received funding. In *Eldridge v. British Columbia*, the Supreme Court of Canada held that the failure of the Commission and hospitals to provide sign language interpretation where it was necessary for effective communication violates the equality rights of the hearing-impaired.[40]

Israel

Unlike in South Africa and Canada, the right to health has never entered Israeli constitutional discourse. Until 1995, when the National Health Care Law nationalized the provision of health care, guaranteeing basic coverage for all residents of Israel, Israeli trade unions were the major health-care providers and membership of a health-care service was tied to membership of a union. The new law defines a basic bundle of services and medication that health-care providers must provide to each member. It does not threaten an atomistic understanding of the right to health, which in Israel can be understood, according to the 'derivative rights' approach, as a component of the constitutional right to dignity. On the contrary, it does much to protect the health of citizens. In terms of the right's social dimensions, however, the law raises various concerns. Given that health-care providers are subsidized by the state, the basic bundle of services and provisions is politically vulnerable to budgetary

[38] *Irwin Toy v. Quebec* [1989] 1 SCR 927, 1003–4.
[39] Hospital services are reimbursed through the Hospital Insurance Act, R.S.B.C., 1979, c. 180; services provided by doctors and other health-care practitioners are reimbursed through the Medicare Protection Act, R.S.B.C., 1996, c. 286.
[40] [1997] 3 SCR 624.

cuts. As the basic bundle becomes smaller, national health-care insurance becomes less meaningful and private insurance more significant to most citizens. The downsizing and privatization of the public system threaten the social dimension of the right to health by making effective access to comprehensive health care a purely theoretical issue to those who cannot afford private insurance. It also raises concerns of inequality with respect to those who are seriously ill but are not entitled to public health care because their needs fall outside the basic bundle of benefits.

A number of legal challenges have been brought regarding the exclusion of various services and medication for seriously ill patients, including physiotherapy for patients with multiple sclerosis and new medication for patients with breast cancer. Most of these challenges were grounded in principles of administrative law and did not advance a constitutional claim. In the few cases that asserted a constitutional right to health the Court avoided the constitutional argument altogether.[41] These cases demonstrate a broader pattern whereby social rights or, more precisely, the social dimension of rights, have failed to gain public or judicial attention. This pattern is also apparent in the context of other rights, such as the right to education[42] and the right to adequate subsistence,[43] where the Court has emphasized their atomistic dimensions. At the same time, the recent arguments that drew on substantive claims on the right to health and dignity did have an impact outside the courtroom, and despite the judicial reluctance to assess them, they succeeded in mobilizing social pressure, resulting in the addition of breast cancer medication to the basic bundle.

Comparisons and conclusions

South Africa's explicit constitutional affirmation of the right to health, Canada's guarantee of the right to security of the person, and Israel's derivative approach to the right to human dignity potentially require the state to provide a level of health-care service consonant with the requirements of social citizenship. In all three countries, however, constitutional

[41] Most cases were concluded outside the courtroom and the case law is scant. Cf. NLC 7-5/97 *Yardena Madzini* v. *Kupat Cholim Klalit* (a health care provider) (National Labour Court, unpublished, 7/1997).

[42] HC 7715/95 *Amutat Shocharei Gilat* v. *The Minister of Education*, Piskei Din (Supreme Court Cases) 50(3) 2 (1996).

[43] HC 161/94 *Eliyahu Atari* v. *The State of Israel* (Supreme Court, unpublished, 3/1994). The case law however also reveals a different, albeit a subtle, alternative. This can be demonstrated, e.g., by HC 7081/93 *Botser* v. *The Municipal Government of Maccabim-Reut*, Piskei Din (Supreme Court Cases) 50(1) 19 (1996); NLC 04-265/96 *Hasid* v. *National Insurance Institute* (National Labour Court, unpublished 7/97); NLC 1091/00 *Shitrit* v. *United Health Care Providers* (National Labour Court, unpublished 8/2000); HC 890/99 *Chalamish* v. *The National Insurance Institute* (Supreme Court, unpublished 4/2000).

jurisprudence has stopped short of embracing the social dimension of the right to health, preferring instead to emphasize its atomistic dimension. This dimension bars the state from actively preventing an individual from obtaining health care but says nothing about the nature and extent of state obligations to assist those in need of health care. In contrast, the social dimension requires constitutional scrutiny of the various options that a state may pursue in delivering health care for its citizens. While it does not mandate public provision of health care, the social dimension requires that health care be accessible to all and of a quality consonant with the requirements of social citizenship.

This convergence illustrates the judicial fear of the social dimension embedded in constitutional rights. This fear arises in part because a right's social dimension is thought to require the judiciary to make value-laden choices about appropriate ways of its realization. In contrast, a right's atomistic dimension appears to free the judiciary of this task, because it seeks to shield individuals from outside interference, and enables the individual herself to make choices for herself. The desire to vest in the individual, not the state, the responsibility to make value-laden choices about the good life is perhaps the main reason for the judicial tendency to privilege the atomistic over the social. But what courts fail to realize is that the atomistic dimension is more value-laden than its social counterpart. The atomization of the individual from society is not value-neutral, nor does it authorize a variety of outcomes. It is indicative of a strong preference for market-based, neo-liberal approaches to social and economic organization.

A right's social dimension typically requires the judiciary to define its content in general terms and to leave to the political process the task of identifying the most appropriate means of realization. It does not privilege market solutions over regulatory solutions. It is true that the social dimension of rights does not cherish markets or hold self-reliance to be the only model of relationship between individuals and communities. But nor does it adore the state or other forms of centralized governance. The social dimension treats market and regulatory solutions as strategies and not as ends in themselves, allowing for competition among different ideas, strategies, and ideologies. It is therefore more ideologically disinterested and open-ended than its atomistic counterpart. It does not require the state centrally to fund all health care or mandate centralized health insurance. Individuals denied an agreed level of health care could be granted relief through various means. Some solutions, such as targeted relief to the poor in the context of a private health-care system, are more market-oriented than others, such as mandatory membership in a publicly sponsored health-care system.

It is the atomistic dimension of the right to health that may endanger some of these solutions. It is hostile to the public administration of health care. It does not aid individuals who the public has decided are not entitled to a particular treatment for budgetary considerations but it challenges the inherently coercive features of public health care, such as mandatory participation, as infringements of individual autonomy that prevent individuals from choosing whether to take part in the public system or opt out in favour of private provision.

The atomistic dimension's quest for neutrality masks a quest for simplicity. A constitutional discourse that seeks to erect barriers around individuals is simpler to develop than one that fosters the growth of collective allegiances. Building consensus around the right to health is easier when the right is interpreted as holding that the state should not deny a person from receiving health care or should not directly violate one's health. By contrast, the social dimension involves the judiciary in a much more complex task, as it must struggle with priorities regarding the saving of lives against background conditions of inherent shortage. But in all three jurisdictions studied here, the cost of simplicity is a constitutional jurisprudence that fails to acknowledge, let alone cherish, a crucial aspect of human identity. Limiting constitutional discourse to the atomistic dimension paradoxically secures constitutional protection only to those who have the market power to manage without it.

IV THE FORM AND SUBSTANCE OF SOCIAL CITIZENSHIP

An important difference exists between the extent to which a constitution extends formal protection to social rights and the extent to which the judiciary fears the social dimension of all rights. Table 1 clarifies the difference.

Table 26.1 *The atomistic and social dimensions*

	Atomistic dimension	Social dimension
Civil & Political Rights	**Strong** protection	Some protection
Social Rights	Some protection	**Weak** protection

Formal constitutional protection of social rights is not an analytical truism; it is a function of historically contingent factors associated with the drafting of a constitution to guide the direction and identity of a state. Debates about constitutional transformation in Israel, Canada, and South Africa have been dominated by the question of what rights ought to receive formal constitutional protection. However, the preceding analysis suggests that this focus may be misguided. Constitutional debate should perhaps instead focus on the substance of constitutional rights. Whether this is the case turns on two questions. Can social citizenship be realized without the entrenchment of social rights? And is entrenchment of social rights constitutionally significant?

Developing the social

The purpose of the social dimension of rights is to acknowledge, accommodate, and support community institutions required for a true and practical sense of social citizenship. But where social rights are not formally entrenched in a constitution, social citizenship can be promoted by protecting social interests, elaborating the social dimension of civil and political rights, and grounding its attributes in the right of equal protection.

The rights–interests distinction

Thus far we have spoken of interests in terms of their role in elaborating the content of constitutional rights. But interests also inform when a state is constitutionally justified in interfering in the exercise of constitutional rights. Constitutional rights typically are not absolute and must be weighed against social interests.[44] And although aspects of national security and the public interest are commonly balanced against rights, social interests also are inserted into balancing formulas.[45] For example, in Israel, contract-labour (manpower) companies brought to the Supreme Court a constitutional challenge to a law requiring all such companies to obtain a licence and deposit a considerable sum as a warranty to ensure their employees' wages.[46] The Court held that the law infringed the companies' freedom of occupation and the right of property, adhering in this part of the decision to the atomistic interpretation of rights. But it went on to justify the infringement, holding that it sought to achieve a legitimate end and was not greater than required to attain that end. Although presented as an interest, the court's ruling implicitly acknowledged the social dimension of the rights to work, dignity, and adequate subsistence:

[44] See, e.g., *R.* v. *Oakes* [1986] 1 SCR 103.

[45] See ibid. (in assessing justifications of infringements of constitutional rights, '[t]he Court must be guided by the values and principles essential to a free and democratic society which ... embody ... [a] commitment to social justice and equality'). South Africa was hugely influenced by Canadian jurisprudence in this regard. See in particular *S* v. *Makanyane and others* 1995 (3) SA 391 (CC) as well as s. 36 of the Constitution which in essence follows *Oakes*.

[46] HC 450/97 *Tnufa* v. *The Minister of Labour and Welfare* (Supreme Court, 5/1998).

[t]he law secures the rights of employees and their social security. This is an important social objective that is sensitive to human rights. . . . An end is legitimate if it is aimed at fulfilling social objectives that are necessary to the preservation of a social framework. . . . The protection of workers is a fundamental social interest in our society, and regulating the use of contract labor is of special importance to the protection of a particularly weak group of workers.[47]

In the absence of a formal constitutional acknowledgement of the social dimension of rights, using interests as part of a justification of an infringement of a constitutional right is a feasible strategy for protecting aspects of social citizenship. However, it yields a second-best outcome compared to one that interprets rights by reference to their social dimensions. Construing the social dimension as interests to be included in a justification of an infringement renders it lexically inferior to its atomistic counterpart. The social dimension, constructed defensively as interests, does not achieve the same level of legitimacy as the atomistic dimension, constructed offensively as rights. The needs of those who rely on their relationships with others excuse violations of rights. This strategy produces a constitutional bias against legislation enacted in the name of social citizenship and stigmatizes those who rely on it.

The social dimension of civil and political rights

If a social dimension is embedded in all rights, it is possible to interpret civil and political rights in ways that promote social citizenship. The right of property, for example, understood atomistically, protects private property from state interference. Geared to protecting the existing power of self-reliant individuals, its potential for protecting communal arrangements that foster individual development is limited at best. Yet there are alternative interpretations to the right of property that emphasize its social dimension, including accounts that stress its capacity to protect housing, public assistance, and social welfare entitlements,[48] foster individual identity,[49] promote political participation,[50] and shield individuals from economic oppression. These accounts suggest that an atomistic interpretation does not flow inexorably from the constitutional entrenchment of a right to property.

Unlike the second-best strategy of drawing on social interests as part of a justification of an infringement of a constitutional right, this approach possesses certain advantages over a strategy that seeks the entrenchment

---

[47] Ibid., para. 12. See also *Lavigne* v. *OPSEU* [1991] 2 SCR 211 (emphasizing the atomistic dimension of freedom of association when defining the right but emphasizing the social dimension of freedom of association when assessing a limitation on the right).
[48] Reich, above, n. 19.
[49] Radin, M. J., *Rethinking Property* (Chicago, Ill.: Chicago University Press 1993) 35–71.
[50] Simon, W., 'Social Republican Property' (1991) 38 *UCLA L. Review* 1335.

of social rights. In the absence of an interpretive approach that emphasizes the social dimension of all rights, formal entrenchment of social
rights may see them become the rights of the poor, while civil and political rights remain the rights of the self-sufficient. Emphasizing the social
dimensions of civil and political rights, widely regarded as universal
attributes of citizenship, would not assume the same risk of bifurcation.
In this sense, the quest for universal constitutional rights is similar to the
quest for universal rights in extra-constitutional contexts.[51] The debate on
social citizenship, commonly developed in the context of welfare
schemes, has often pointed to the importance of universal coverage. The
strength of an entitlement is stronger if it is universal, rather than targeted
to a select few, especially if the targeted few are socially weak and politically disenfranchised. A tailor-made constitutional support for the
disabled, wage-earners, or the homeless is likely to become a contested
token of mercy intrinsically inconsistent with its own premises.

Equality

The social dimension of rights seeks to accommodate mutual reliance
with a common standard of citizenship. This requires a basic norm
regarding the entitlements of every citizen. These entitlements, such as
adequate health care, are rarely spelled out explicitly. But the right to
health is not an absolute guarantee but a right to adequate health care for
every member of the community. A person who does not receive care in
accordance with the community standard can raise a claim, arguing that
her right to health has been violated. But she can also cast her claim in
terms of equality. The Canadian decision in *Eldridge* illustrates that rights
to health can also rely on familiar and well-developed principles of equality. Similarly, the South African case of *Soobramoney*, as well as Israeli
litigation over the distribution of limited resources, raises questions of
distribution that cannot be detached from equality concerns. In jurisdictions lacking formal constitutional protection of a right to health, it is
possible to compare the relative lack of health care available to an individual with the care that other similarly situated individuals receive.

The strongest argument against the principle of equality as a substitute for social rights can be made by alluding to the most extreme
example. Consider a state where there is no public health care at all. In
these situations, a formal equality claim will not be feasible for the
simple reason that all citizens are equally denied health care. But cases
where the state eschews its responsibility to provide education, health, or

---

[51] Korpi, W., and Palme, J, 'The Paradox of Redistribution and Strategies of Equality:
Welfare State Institutions, Inequality, and Poverty in the Western Countries' (1998) 63
American Sociological Review 661–87.

welfare altogether are relatively easy for social rights advocates. Either a right to health or a modest judicial commitment to substantive equality, whereby state action is assessed in terms of its impact, will suffice to raise serious questions about the constitutionality of actions that amount to a total abdication of state responsibility. The more difficult cases are those where the state privatizes certain core functions of a public health-care system, for example, by authorizing the establishment of private hospitals or limiting the availability of public insurance for certain prescription drugs. Here, the advantages of relying on equality are evident. Under a substantive version of equality that assesses the justice of outcomes, a challenge to a state decision to abstain from providing an entitlement to individuals can be cast successfullyin terms of equality.[52] Equality guarantees ought to protect those who can claim that the state has denied them certain entitlements linked with social citizenship, disadvantaging them in relation to those who are better off. When the state denies an individual a particular entitlement and leaves her to care for herself, the outcome may constitute inequality.

Like the strategy that seeks to promote social citizenship by expansive interpretations of civil and political rights, reliance on equality is not simply a second-best approach to the use of social rights. As noted, the claim that a social right is too vague to implement is based on the absence of a defined measure of how much health, welfare, or education should be regarded as necessary for compliance. When drawing on an equality argument, the problem becomes less attenuated. In the typical situation, the state determines the appropriate level of benefits, and the equality argument merely seeks to universalize the state-determined level to an individual or a sector of the population.[53]

Promoting the social in the absence of social rights

One might conclude from our comparative assessment that formal entrenchment of social rights bears little relevance to the cause of advancing social citizenship. Social rights rarely receive extensive formal consti-

---

[52] Although this rule may create a problem in regimes such as Canada where state action must be demonstrated to allow for a constitutionally based intervention, it is possible to view the decision to abstain from providing any goods as an affirmative decision. When the state decides to abstain from regulating goods that are commonly regulated, such as education or the labour market, the decision itself implicates the state itself. Social interests underlying civil and political interests can be used as a benchmark for the areas in which the state has some commitment.

[53] The fact that equality may simplify the claim for the fulfilment of a social right is only relative. Equality-based arguments are generally difficult given the 'emptiness' of the equality principle. Because no two individuals are alike, it will not suffice to claim that, if X deserves a certain benefit, so does Y. Equality requires a determination of the relevant features that aid in defining who is equal to whom with regard to particular entitlements.

tutional expression, and even where they are part of the formal constitutional order, as in South Africa, the judiciary appears reluctant to interpret them broadly. Although alternative litigation strategies exist to promote social citizenship that minimize the possibility that victories will be seen as special constitutional treatment, there is still much to be said in favour of constitutional inclusion of social rights. *Ceteris paribus*, a constitution with social rights is better than one without them. A constitution is more than a legal arrangement; it is a cultural artifact that expresses the values of a nation. The preamble to the South African Constitution, for example, states that its purpose is 'to improve the quality of life of all citizens and free the potential of each person'. This purpose does not simply provide judges and lawmakers with a constitutional canon of interpretation; it seeks to articulate a shared meaning of citizenship. A constitution that only entrenches civil and political rights fails to capture what it means to be a citizen in a democratic state. Moreover, a constitution should not force those who seek to litigate social inequality to rely on strategies that emphasize the social dimension of civil and political rights or define social citizenship in terms of justifiable limits on infringements of constitutional rights. A constitution's social message should not depend on complex structures and elaborate balancing acts, important though they are, for they blur the basic commitments that a constitutional order ought to embody.

But one should not overestimate the consequences of entrenching social rights. In part because of their historical subordination, social rights have been under-theorized and under-developed both academically and judicially. Their tenuous status is reflected in the fact that Israel's proposed Basic Law: Social Rights mentions the term 'right' only in its title, requiring the state only to 'make an effort to develop and promote the circumstances necessary for the dignified existence'.[54] Several social rights in the South African constitution are phrased as requiring the state to take 'reasonable legislative and other measures within its available resources, to achieve progressive realization of each of these rights'.[55] If the judiciary continues to apply a lenient standard to their enforcement, social rights may become *de facto* non-justiciable and legally unimportant. And if the judiciary emphasizes their atomistic dimensions, social rights will only guard against worst case scenarios. This is sufficient in itself to justify the inclusion of social rights in a constitutional order. But the problems wrought by neo-liberalism are of a different calibre. If individuals simply cannot afford health care, an atomistic right to health is unlikely to help. If the state does not actively take away from individuals their basic

---

[54] Proposed Basic Law: Social Rights (Ministry of Justice, 1997).
[55] See ss. 26(2) and 27(2) of the South African Constitution.

income but simply takes a passive approach to structural unemployment, atomistic understandings of rights to adequate subsistence, work, and social security present a false utopia to those who cannot take care of themselves. Despite their hortatory value, social rights possess a precarious potential. Their construction and application may undermine the benefits that flow from their formal entrenchment.

Critics of social rights often argue that the debate on social rights is an agenda of the past. According to this line of thought, even if there are no necessary differences between civil and political rights and social rights, the history and evolution of constitutionalism suggest an underlying logic to the subordination of social rights—one that corresponds to the triumph of neo-liberalism. But this critique tends to be a self-fulfilling prophecy. It does not provide any benchmark according to which we can test the quality of current social arrangements. Despite the similarities between the three countries surveyed here, their convergence does not foretell the end of social rights. Their constitutions mark the beginning of a dialogue among citizens, social groups, politicians, and the judiciary about the role and function of constitutional law in an era of neo-liberalism. To be sure, neo-liberal perspectives do not go unrepresented in this dialogue. But they are not exhaustive. The constitutional task is to articulate a rich vision of social citizenship by which to judge the constitutionality of neo-liberal agendas. In this chapter, we have explored a number of strategies that rely on constitutional rights to confront social inequality. In so doing, we hope to contribute to the development of a constitutional jurisprudence that takes seriously the demands of social citizenship.

Index

Index

LABOUR LAW IN AN ERA OF GLOBALIZATION

Transformative practices and possibilities